Challenging and Supporting the First-Year Student

A Handbook for Improving the First Year of College

M. Lee Upcraft, John N. Gardner, Betsy O. Barefoot

JOSSEY-BASS
A Wiley Imprint
www.josseybass.com

Published by Jossey-Bass
A Wiley Imprint
989 Market Street, San Francisco, CA 94103-1741   www.josseybass.com

Jossey-Bass books and products are available through most bookstores. To contact Jossey-Bass directly call our Customer Care Department within the U.S. at 800-956-7739, outside the U.S. at 317-572-3986 or fax 317-572-4002.

Jossey-Bass also publishes its books in a variety of electronic formats. Some content that appears in print may not be available in electronic books.

Library of Congress Cataloging-in-Publication Data

Upcraft, M. Lee.
    Challenging and supporting the first-year student : a handbook for improving the first year of college / M. Lee Upcraft, John N. Gardner, Betsy O. Barefoot.
— 1st ed.
        p. cm. — (Jossey-Bass higher and adult education series)
    Includes bibliographical references and index.
    ISBN 0-7879-5968-5 (alk. paper)
        1. College student orientation—Handbooks, manuals, etc. I. Gardner, John N.
II. Barefoot, Betsy O. (Betsy Overman), 1944-   . III. Title. IV. Series.
    LB2343.3.U63 2004
    378.1'98—dc22   2004014539

Printed in the United States of America
FIRST EDITION
HB Printing   10 9 8 7 6 5 4 3

The Jossey-Bass
Higher and Adult Education Series

CONTENTS

PART ONE:
WHAT WE KNOW ABOUT TODAY'S
FIRST-YEAR STUDENTS AND INSTITUTIONAL
EFFORTS TO HELP THEM SUCCEED

PART FOUR:
CHALLENGING AND SUPPORTING FIRST-YEAR STUDENTS IN THE CLASSROOM

PART FIVE:
CHALLENGING AND SUPPORTING FIRST-YEAR STUDENTS OUTSIDE THE CLASSROOM

PREFACE

Why write another book about the first year of college? The brief answer is that much has changed since 1989 when the first comprehensive text on the first year of college was published. In retrospect, *The Freshman Year Experience: Helping Students Survive and Succeed in College,* written by Lee Upcraft, John Gardner, and Associates, presents a valuable benchmark for where we were at a much earlier stage in what was then called "the freshman year experience movement." Thus, this book seeks to bring into perspective the myriad of programs, services, courses, and other initiatives designed to help first-year students make a successful transition to college and fulfill their educational and personal goals.

Just what has changed since 1989? The answer to this question can be summarized in many ways that are discussed in much greater detail throughout this book. In a nutshell, efforts to help first-year students succeed in college have:

- Expanded rapidly and increased in size and scope
- Become more focused on first-year students' academic success
- Increased faculty involvement inside and outside the classroom
- Been guided by extensive research and scholarship on the first year of college.
- Included expanded efforts to assess the effectiveness of first-year programs, courses, and services
- Been more responsive to the increasing diversity of first-year students
- Reflected the greatly increased presence of technology in the lives of first-year students and the institutions in which they enroll

Moreover, based on the research and scholarship conducted since 1989, our definition of student success has expanded to include civic responsibility, a dimension of the first-year student experience that was largely ignored until recently. Based on our experiences of the past decade, we are also now in a position to suggest principles of good practice for first-year student success.

Also, there is considerable evidence, reviewed in this book, that first-year students are not always challenged to work to their full potential in pursuing their academic goals. College appears to be much less academically challenging than they expected, and first-year students spend much less time studying than the typical faculty expectation. So another look at how to make the first-year student experience more challenging, both inside and outside the classroom, becomes a central focus of this book.

AN OVERRIDING THEME

We present this look within an overriding theme of first-year student education first suggested by Nevitt Sanford over forty years ago. Basically, Sanford (1962, 1967) argued that in order for students to succeed, they must be both challenged (provided with educational experiences that foster learning and personal development) and supported (provided with a campus climate that helps students learn and develop). When a proper balance is maintained between challenge and support, students are positioned to succeed in college. When that balance is not maintained, students are more likely to fail. Likewise, institutions are more likely to succeed in helping first-year students make a successful transition to college if they provide challenging educational experiences accompanied by effective support services and programs. Hence, the theme of this book—challenge and support—applies to both first-year students and the institutions in which they enroll.

OVERVIEW OF CONTENTS

This book begins with an introduction in which we review what has happened in the past decade that dictates revisiting the scholarship and practice of the first year of college, offer a revised definition of first-year student success, and expound principles of good practice for first-year student success. We also suggest a conceptual framework for the first year: challenge and support for both first-year students and the institutions in which they enroll.

Part One provides an overview of what we know about today's first-year students and institutional efforts to help them succeed. The chapters in this part include a description of the demographics and characteristics of today's first-year students, a review of the research on what institutions and students must do to promote persistence into the second year of college, and a review of current practices devoted to helping students make a successful transition to college.

Part Two discusses the important challenge of recruiting and retaining first-year students, the obligation of institutions to help them become engaged and involved in their own education, and the importance of establishing and enforcing high expectations for them.

Part Three is about creating campus cultures for first-year student success, including fostering the success of underrepresented minorities, creating campus climates that reflect the realities of our increasingly diverse colleges and universities, promoting first-year student success in public, urban universities, discussing the importance of first-year student success from a president's perspective, advocating for first-year students, educating first-year students about the impact of technology on their lives, and creating collaborative partnerships between academic and student affairs.

Part Four discusses the many ways in which first-year students must be challenged and supported in the classroom, including suggesting ways in which faculty may structure in-class learning environments to promote student success and how faculty may be supported in their efforts to become more effective in teaching first-year students. Furthermore, other efforts that promote first-year student success are also discussed, including first-year seminars, developmental education, Supplemental Instruction, academic advising, libraries, service-learning, and learning communities.

Part Five discusses the many ways in which first-year students must be challenged and supported outside the classroom by faculty, student affairs professionals, and other staff, including orientation programs, living environments, student support services, and alcohol abuse and other drug use prevention.

Part Six sets out a framework for assessing efforts that promote first-year students' success, provides many practical suggestions for conducting assessment studies, and reviews both quantitative and qualitative instruments for assessing first-year services, programs, and courses.

In the summary and conclusion of this book, we present some principles of good practice to guide efforts to promote first-year student success, summarize the recommendations for the ways in which institutions should organize to promote that success both inside and outside the classroom, and reiterate the importance of making assessment an essential part of improving the first college year. While we strove for continuity among the many topics covered in this handbook, we recognize that because of the length and breadth of this handbook, many readers are more likely to pick and choose among chapters rather than read it from cover to cover.

THE AUDIENCE

This book is intended to provide a blueprint for helping first-year students make a successful transition to college and achieve their educational and personal goals. It is intended for policymakers who develop this blueprint for a campus, such as chief executive officers, chief academic officers, chief student affairs officers, academic deans, and department heads. It is also intended for practitioners who directly provide first-year educational experiences both inside and outside the classroom, such as faculty, student affairs professionals, and anyone else committed to helping students succeed.

CHANGES IN APPROACH IN THIS PUBLICATION

Readers familiar with Upcraft and Gardner's *The Freshman Year Experience* will note several changes in approach from that publication. First, since 1989, the term *freshman* has gradually fallen out of use among first-year student educators. During this time, an ever increasing consensus among higher educators was that this term, because of its sexist connotation, its historical association with traditional-aged students, and its unfamiliarity with international educators, should be discarded in favor of the phrase *first-year student.* We are not alone in making this transition. The two national centers that focus on first-year students are now known as the National Resource Center for The First Year Experience and Students in Transition, located at the University of South Carolina, and the Policy Center on the First Year of College, located in Brevard, North Carolina. To be sure, among the general higher education community, terms such as *freshmen, the freshman-year experience, freshman seminar,* and others are still used, but these terms no longer reflect the realities of the demographics and characteristics of today's entering students.

Second, we did not include chapters on individual student groups by race, gender, age, and other student characteristics. Instead, when appropriate, we sought to infuse issues specific to these groups, as well as other groups, into chapter texts. Including a chapter for each of the many student groups would have made this book prohibitively long and redundant. We have, however, emphasized throughout this book that all efforts to help first-year students make a successful transition to college and meet their educational goals must be inclusive of *all* first-year students.

Third, we asked the chapter authors to summarize their chapters with succinct recommendations for practice, thus providing practitioners and policymakers with easy access to what must be done to help first-year students make a successful transition to college and meet their educational goals.

Finally, since this is a book about first-year students, we have sought, whenever appropriate, to include voices of first-year students to frame the content of our chapters. These are actual quotations from enrolled first-year students that the chapter authors solicited from students they had known; except in the cases where the identity of the student was unknown, they are printed with their permission.

ACKNOWLEDGMENTS

It has been said that when you see a turtle sitting atop a fencepost, you know it had help getting there. We "turtles" could never have put this book together without the help of a considerable number of very important people. First of all, we wish to gratefully acknowledge our program officers from the three philan-thropic organizations whose financial support helped make this work possible (The Pew Charitable Trusts, The Atlantic Philathropies, and Lumina Foundation for Education), who have shared our vision for the importance and need for this book: Russell Edgerton, Theodore Hullar, and Robert Dickeson. Of course, we are extraordinarily indebted to our chapter authors for their exceptional and tire-less efforts to create this contribution to the education of first-year students.

At Penn State University, we are indebted to one of our authors, Jennifer Criss-man Ishler, who was especially helpful in reviewing the manuscript, and to Patrick Terenzini, an excellent resource in framing the research and scholarship on the first-year experience. At the Policy Center on The First Year of College, our colleagues Samantha Landgrover and Angela Whiteside provided an enor-mous amount of cheerful and competent assistance. We are also indebted to our colleagues at the University of South Carolina's National Resource Center for the First-Year Experience and Students in Transition, and the University 101 pro-gram, which helped us lay the experiential and intellectual foundations for this book. Of course, we are especially indebted to our families, friends, and col-leagues for their unqualified support and encouragement throughout the prepa-ration of this book. We also wish to acknowledge nine very special future first-year students: Mary Michael and Sarah Goodykoontz, Samuel Ripley Goodykoontz, James and Wesley Barefoot, Kathleen and Gunnar Kennedy, and Clayton and Cameron Upcraft.

As was the case in 1989, we again acknowledge the significant contribution of the thousands of first-year students we have known, admired, and been chal-lenged by over our careers. They have been, and continue to be, our most impor-tant source of learning inspiration, excitement, challenge, and support.

October 2004
M. Lee Upcraft
University Park, Pennsylvania
John N. Gardner
Brevard, North Carolina
Betsy O. Barefoot
Brevard, North Carolina

THE AUTHORS

M. Lee Upcraft is research associate at the Center for the Study of Higher Education, assistant vice president emeritus for student affairs, and affiliate professor emeritus of higher education at Pennsylvania State University. He received both his B.A. degree in history and his M.A. degree in guidance and counseling from the State University of New York at Albany, and his Ph.D. degree in student personnel administration from Michigan State University. In his forty years in higher education, Upcraft has been responsible for a wide variety of student affairs administrative functional areas, including psychological services, career services, health services, residence halls, orientation, academic advising, student activities, adult learner services, services for women students, services for students with disabilities, judicial affairs, services for veterans, and assessment.

As a faculty member, Upcraft has taught courses and conducted research on topics such as the first-year experience, alcohol and other drug use and abuse, assessment, student persistence, the impact of technology on student learning, residence halls, student development theory, student demographics, orientation, strategic planning, organization and administration of higher education and student affairs, resident assistant selection, training, supervision, evaluation, academic advising, graduate preparation programs in student affairs, professional ethics, and campus activities.

He is the author of eighty-five book chapters and refereed journal articles, and his books include *Assessment Practice in Student Affairs: An Applications Manual* (2001, with J. Schuh and Associates), *Assessment in Student Affairs: A Guide for Practitioners* (1996, with J. Schuh and Associates), *First-Year Academic Advising* (1995, with G. Kramer and Associates), *Designing Successful Transitions: A Guide for Orienting Students to College* (1993, with R. Mullendore,

B. Barefoot, D. Fidler, and Associates), *New Futures for Student Affairs* (1990, with M. Barr and Associates), and the *Freshman Year Experience* (1989, with J. N. Gardner and Associates). He also served as the associate editor of *the New Directions for Student Services* sourcebooks from 1986 to 1996.

Upcraft has received numerous awards and recognition, including the Outstanding Contribution to the Orientation Profession award from the National Orientation Directors Association and the Outstanding Contribution to Literature or Research award from the National Association of Student Personnel Administrators. He is a Senior Scholar Diplomate of the American College Personnel Association and was recognized as a Diamond Honoree by the organization in celebration of its seventy-fifth anniversary in 1998. He also received the Excellence in Education Award from the University at Albany Alumni Association.

John N. Gardner is the senior fellow of the National Resource Center for The First-Year Experience and Students in Transition (which he founded in 1986) and Distinguished Professor Emeritus of Library and Information Science at the University of South Carolina (USC). He is a senior fellow in the National Resource Center and executive director of the Policy Center on the First Year of College, funded by grants from The Pew Charitable Trusts, The Atlantic Philanthropies, and Lumina Foundation for Education. The Policy Center works in partnership to complement the resources and services that the USC Center provides to the higher education community. The basic mission of the new Policy Center is to work with colleges and universities around the nation to develop and share a range of first-year assessment procedures and tools.

Gardner received his B.A. from Marietta College and M.A. from Purdue University, and has seven honorary doctoral degrees.

Gardner is the recipient of numerous local and national professional awards including USC's highest award for teaching excellence, the AMOCO Award for Outstanding Teaching (1975), and the Division of Student Affairs Faculty Award (1976). The University of South Carolina Alumni Association conferred on him its highest award for a non-alumnus in 1997: the Honorary Life Membership "for devoted service in behalf of the University." He was also named the 1998 recipient of the university's Administrative Affirmative Action Award "for an outstanding job in promoting equal opportunities at the University." In 1999, he was the recipient of a university award created and named in his honor, the John N. Gardner Inspirational Faculty Award, to be given henceforth to a member of the university faculty "who has made substantial contributions to the learning environment in campus residence hall life."

In 1986, he was selected by the American Association for Higher Education as one of twenty faculty in the United States who "have made outstanding leadership contributions to their institutions and/or American higher education." In 1996 he was recognized by the Council of Independent Colleges with its Academic Leadership Award "for exemplary contributions to American higher education." In the January 1998 issue of *Change*, Gardner was cited in an article naming approximately eighty people as the "past, present, and future leaders of higher education." The authors of this study drew on the results of eleven thousand questionnaires to name the leaders whom the *Chronicle of Higher Education* dubbed "the movers and shakers." Gardner was included in a special category of eleven "agenda setters."

Also in 1998 Gardner was named one of the "top ten professionals who have most influenced student affairs practitioners." This was based on a random sample of practitioners throughout the country as part of a study, "The Professional Influence Project," sponsored by the National Association of Student Personnel Administrators (NASPA) Foundation and conducted by the University of Georgia. In 1999 Gardner was awarded the Virginia N. Gordon Award for Excellence in the Field of Advising by the National Academic Advising Association (NACADA), to recognize his contributions toward the enhancement of academic advisement in American higher education. In 2002, he was awarded the Lifetime Achievement Award by the American College Personnel Association.

Gardner is best known as the initiator (in 1982) of an international reform movement in higher education to call attention to and improve what he has coined "the freshman year experience" and more recently "the first-year experience." Since 1990 he has developed a special focus on a second critical transition during the college years to improve and champion "the senior year experience." Gardner's special area of expertise in higher education is the creation of programs to enhance the learning, success, retention, and graduation of students in transition, especially first-year students.

Gardner has authored or coauthored numerous articles and books, including *College Is Only the Beginning* (1985, 1989), *Step by Step to College Success* (1987), *Your College Experience* (1992, 1993, 1995, 1996, 1997, 1998, 1999, 2000, 2001, 2002, 2003, 2004, and 2005 with A. Jerome Jewler); *The Freshman Year Experience* (1989, with M. Lee Upcraft); *Ready for the Real World* (1994, with William Hartel and Associates); and The *Senior Year Experience* (1997, with Gretchen Van der Veer).

Betsy O. Barefoot is codirector and senior scholar of the Policy Center on the First Year of College. She is also a fellow with the National Resource Center for The First-Year Experience and Students in Transition at the University of South Carolina. She holds a B.A. degree from Duke University and M.A. and Ph.D. degrees from the College of William and Mary. Currently, Barefoot is directly involved in the development of instruments and strategies to assess the first college year. In addition, she conducts seminars on the first-year experience across the United States and in other countries and assists other colleges and universities in implementing and evaluating first-year programs

Prior to assuming her current position, Barefoot served for eleven years as codirector for research and publications in the National Resource Center for The First-Year Experience and Students in Transition at the University of South Carolina. In this position, she engaged in ongoing research on first-year programming in American higher education and coedited a number of publications, including *Journal of The First-Year Experience, The First-Year Experience Newsletter,* and a series of single-topic monographs. She served as a clinical faculty member in the College of Education and taught graduate courses in higher education, a special topics seminar on the first-year experience, as well as the University 101 first-year seminar. Barefoot was also involved in acquiring grant funds for designing and implementing a campus-wide program to provide training in methods of college teaching for graduate teaching assistants at the University of South Carolina.

Before coming to the University of South Carolina, Dr. Barefoot held the following positions in other college and university settings: assistant to the vice president for admissions at Lambuth College in Jackson, Tennessee; director of the University of LaVerne Residence Center in San Diego, California; assistant to the director of the Virginia Tidewater Consortium for Continuing Higher Education in Norfolk, Virginia; and research assistant in the School of Education at College of William and Mary in Williamsburg, Virginia.

Douglas K. Anderson works in institutional research and policy analysis at Indiana University, Bloomington. He received his B.S. degree in sociology from Brigham Young University. After earning M.S. and Ph.D. degrees in sociology from the University of Wisconsin-Madison, he experienced the first year from the other side of the desk as a faculty member and adviser in the Sociology Department at the University of Southern Maine. His current interests include the roles of financial aid in recruiting and retaining students and access and equity issues in higher education.

Ralph G. Anttonen is the chairman of the Department of Academic and Student Development, professor of educational psychology, and director of the Exploratory Program at Millersville University, a program for undeclared students that won the NACADA 2003 Outstanding Institutional Advising Award. He holds a B.S. degree in mathematics from Tufts University and a Ph.D. degree in educational psychology from the University of Minnesota. In addition, he has been the adviser to the student-run campus radio station since 1975. In 1992 he was selected as an Outstanding First-Year Student Advocate by the National Resource Center for The First-Year Experience at the University of South Carolina, and in 2001 Millersville students selected him as 2001/2002 Person of the Year at Millersville. His current research interests are leadership and change in the academy, methods for bridging the gap between student and academic affairs, and the development of ways to help undecided and undeclared students select a major and graduate.

Leslie A. Banahan is assistant vice president for student affairs at the University of Georgia (UGA). She holds B.A. and M.Ed degrees from the University of Mississippi. Before joining the staff at UGA, she worked at the University of Mississippi, where she designed and implemented orientation programs for international students and later developed and directed a new orientation program for all first-year and transfer students. Banahan has also established and worked with parent-family associations at the universities of Mississippi and Georgia and is a frequent presenter on orientation and parent programs at the regional and national levels. She continues to speak to hundreds of parents each summer during UGA orientation sessions and is the primary parent contact throughout the year for student concerns and problems.

Jay Chaskes is professor of sociology and educational leadership at Rowan University and director of its Center for the Study of Student Life. He holds a B.A. degree from the University of Toledo in sociology and M.A. and Ph.D. degrees in sociology from Temple University. In 1996, he was the recipient of Rowan University's Lindback Distinguished Teaching Award and was named an Outstanding First-Year Student Advocate by the National Resource Center for The First-Year Experience and Students in Transition at the University of South Carolina. He has designed and coordinated both a special seminar and developmental advising programs for first-year students. His major areas of research interest are leadership and change in higher education, the micropolitics of academic organizations, issues of student identity transformation, and the dynamics of the retention process.

Jennifer L. Crissman Ishler is an assistant professor of counselor education at the Pennsylvania State University. She holds a B.S. degree in elementary education from Millersville University, an M.S. degree in counseling and college student personnel from Shippensburg University, and a D.Ed. in higher education from the Pennsylvania State University. Her student affairs experience includes residence life, academic advising, and new student programs. Her teaching experience includes first-year seminars and graduate courses in student affairs and counseling. Her research interests include the first-year experience, assessment in student affairs, and collaboration between academic and student affairs

Bette LaSere Erickson is assistant director of the Instructional Development Program at the University of Rhode Island. She received her B.A. degree in English from St. Olaf College and her Ed.D. degree from the University of Massachusetts, Amherst. She has had extensive contact with faculty from a variety of disciplines and has conducted numerous workshops on issues related to teaching and learning at colleges and universities throughout the country. Her publications include articles on a variety of instructional methods and on faculty development programs; she is coauthor with Diane Strommer of *Teaching College Freshmen*. She was a founding member of the Professional and Organizational Development Network and served as its executive director from 1985 to 1987.

Scott E. Evenbeck is dean of the University College at Indiana University Purdue University at Indianapolis (IUPUI). He joined the faculty at IUPUI in psychology in 1972, after completing his Ph.D. degree in psychology at the University of North Carolina at Chapel Hill. Evenbeck has been a national leader in the design and assessment of general education, including the development, ongoing implementation, and assessment of IUPUI's outcomes for student learning. He has also played a major role in various P–16 initiatives to support student academic achievement and in retention initiatives for Indiana higher education.

Jeanne L. Higbee is professor and senior adviser to the Center for Research on Developmental Education and Urban Literacy (CRDEUL) at the University of Minnesota's General College. She has a B.S. degree from Iowa State University and earned her M.S. and Ph.D. degrees at the University of Wisconsin–Madison. She began her career in developmental education as a graduate student coordinating the Learning Skills Program for the University of Wisconsin Counseling Services. She worked in student affairs at a variety of institutions and then taught in the Division of Academic Assistance at the University of Georgia for fourteen years. She is the recipient of the Henry Young Award for Outstanding Individual Contribution to the National Association for Developmental Education, the award for Outstanding article in the *Journal of Developmental Education* (2000), and the Hunter R. Boylan Outstanding Research/Publication Award (1999). In addition to serving as coeditor for the *Learning Assistance Review* and on the editorial board for the *Journal of College Reading and Learning,* she has edited twelve monographs and published more than seventy-five articles related to developmental education and the first year of college.

Don Hossler is a professor of educational leadership and policy studies and the associate vice president for enrollment services for the Indiana University System and the vice chancellor for enrollment services at Indiana University, Bloomington. He has served as the executive associate dean for the School of Education and chair of the Department of Educational Leadership and Policy Studies. His areas of specialization include college choice, student financial aid policy, enrollment management, and higher education finance. Hossler earned his baccalaureate at California Lutheran University and his Ph.D. degree in higher education from the Claremont Graduate School. Hossler has consulted with more than thirty-five colleges, universities, and related educational organizations and has presented more than one hundred scholarly papers and invited lectures in the United States, Canada, China, and Russia on the topics of student college choice, student financial aid policy, and higher education finance. He is the author or coauthor of eight books and monographs and more than forty-five articles and book chapters. His books include *Mapping the Higher Education Landscape* and *The Strategic Management of College Enrollments.* His most recent book is *Going to College: How Social, Economic, and Educational Factors Influence the Decisions Students Make* (1999).

Freeman A. Hrabowski III is president of the University of Maryland, Baltimore County, a position he has held since May 1992. He holds a B.A. degree in mathematics from Hampton University, an M.A. degree in mathematics, and a Ph.D. degree in higher education administration from the University of Illinois, Urbana-

Champaign. His research focuses on science and mathematics education, emphasizing minority performance. He consults with a variety of federal agencies, universities, and school systems nationwide. He sits on several educational, civic, and corporate boards and is a member of the American Academy of Arts and Sciences and the American Philosophical Society. He is the recipient of the McGraw Prize in Education and the U.S. Presidential Award for Excellence in Science, Mathematics, and Engineering Mentoring. He is coauthor of two books on parenting and high-achieving African American males in science, *Beating the Odds,* and on African American females in science, *Overcoming the Odds.*

Mary Stuart Hunter is director of the National Resource Center for The First-Year Experience and Students in Transition at the University of South Carolina. She holds a B.A. degree in English from Queens College and an M.Ed. degree from the University of South Carolina. Her work centers on providing educators with resources to develop personal and professional skills while creating and refining innovative programs designed to increase student success. In addition to her administrative and teaching responsibilities, she conducts workshops on the first-year experience, first-year seminars, and teaching. Hunter has published on the first-year experience, first-year seminars, and academic advising and edited a monograph on first-year seminar instructor training. She serves on the national advisory boards of the Policy Center on the First Year of College, the National Society of Collegiate Scholars, and the Columbia Pastoral Counseling Center and sits on the Council of Advisers for the Network of Colleges and Universities Committed to the Elimination of Drug and Alcohol Abuse. She was honored in 2001 as the Outstanding Alumnae of the Year by USC's Student Personnel/Higher Education Department.

Maureen Hurley is the associate director of the University of Missouri, Kansas City Center for Academic Development and the International Supplemental Instruction Center. She holds a B.A. degree in English from the University of Saint Mary, an M.S. degree in adult education from Kansas State University, and a Ph.D. degree in urban leadership and policy studies in education from the University of Missouri-Kansas City. Hurley has taught at the middle school, community college, and university levels, and has also served as director of an adult education center. She has coordinated rural Missouri's dual-credit high school video Supplemental Instruction program and, as a certified trainer, conducts Supplemental Instruction workshops throughout the United States and abroad. Hurley's other responsibilities include supervision of Upward Bound, GEAR UP, and Jumpstart programs. She has presented both nationally and internationally at higher education conferences on Supplemental Instruction and video Supplemental Instruction.

Barbara Jackson is associate dean of University College and associate professor of anthropology in the School of Liberal Arts at Indiana University Purdue University at Indianapolis (IUPUI). She holds a bachelor's degree from Hunter

College of the City University of New York and a master's and Ph.D. degree in anthropology from the University of Minnesota. She has provided leadership for the comprehensive development of academic support programs for entering students at Indiana University Purdue University at Indianapolis, including first-year seminars, learning communities, structured learning assistance, and critical inquiry. She has primary responsibility for faculty development and involvement in University College first-year initiatives.

W. Terrell Jones is the vice provost for educational equity at the Pennsylvania State University, where he is responsible for leading the implementation of the university's strategic plan that embraces, supports, and benefits from diversity. He has a B.A. degree in sociology from Lock Haven University of Pennsylvania and M.A. and D.Ed. degrees in counselor education from the Pennsylvania State University. Jones has over thirty years of student development experience and is a highly requested speaker on diversity issues. He is the author or coauthor of several articles on the subject of cultural diversity.

Reynol Junco is an assistant professor and director of disability services in the Department of Academic Development and Counseling at Lock Haven University in Pennsylvania. He received his A.A. degree in psychology from Miami Dade Community College, his B.S. degree in psychology from the University of Florida, and his D.Ed. degree in counselor education from Penn State University. Junco has taught numerous first-year seminars, and his research interests include how technology affects the psychological and academic development of students

Thomas J. Kerr is the president and CEO of Campus Group International Education Services and consultant to Fairleigh Dickinson University in Teaneck, New Jersey. Previously, he has served as the vice president of university partnerships for Fairleigh Dickinson; dean of the College of Evening and Professional Studies and associate professor in the School of Education at Drexel University; associate provost for academic services at Rowan University; and associate dean of academic and student affairs and assistant professor in the College of Engineering at Boston University. Kerr holds B.S. and M.S. degrees in industrial engineering from Northeastern University and a Ph.D. degree in higher education from Boston College. He has gained national recognition for his expertise in curriculum development, recruitment, retention, articulation, faculty advising, and grant writing. Kerr is a charter member of the National Academic Advising Association (NACADA) and served as president of that organization from 1993 to 1995. He is currently serving as journal editor for the *NACADA Journal*. He is a recipient of the NACADA Award for Service to the organization and the Virginia N. Gordon Award for Excellence in the Field of Advising.

Margaret C. (Peggy) King is associate dean for student development at Schenectady County Community College, Schenectady, New York, where she provides leadership for the Division of Student Affairs, directs the Academic

Advisement Center, and supervises counseling and job placement services. She received her B.A. degree in history from Ursinus College and her M.S. and an Ed.D. degrees from the State University of New York at Albany. A founding member of the National Academic Advising Association (NACADA), King was president from 1991 to 1993. She has been a faculty member for the Summer Institute on Academic Advising since its inception in 1987 and serves as a consultant on academic advising for both two- and four-year colleges and universities. King was editor of the New Directions for Community Colleges publication *Academic Advising: Organizing and Delivering Services for Student Success* (1993). In addition, she has authored a number of chapters and articles on academic advising in the two-year college, adviser training, and organizational models and delivery systems. She is a recipient of the State University of New York Chancellor's Award for Excellence in Professional Service, the NACADA Award for Service to the organization, and the NACADA Virginia N. Gordon Award for Excellence in the Field of Advising.

George D. Kuh is Chancellor's Professor of Higher Education at Indiana University Bloomington. He directs the Center for Postsecondary Research, which houses the College Student Experiences Questionnaire Research Program and the National Survey of Student Engagement (NSSE), as well as student engagement surveys for law students and faculty members, and the NSSE Institute for Effective Educational Practice. He holds B.A. degrees from Luther College, an M.S. degree in counseling from St. Cloud State College, and a Ph.D. degree in counselor education and higher education from the University of Iowa. Kuh's contributions in the areas of student engagement, assessment, institutional improvement, and college and university cultures have been recognized with awards from the American College Personnel Association, Association of Institutional Research, Association for the Study of Higher Education, Council of Independent Colleges, and National Association of Student Personnel Administrators.

Jodi Levine Laufgraben is the associate vice provost at Temple University where she is also an instructor in educational leadership and policy studies. She has a B.A. degree in political science and an M.S. degree in higher education from Syracuse University and an Ed.D degree in educational administration from Temple University. She has directed Temple's Learning Communities Program since 1994 and since 2000 has served as a project fellow for the National Learning Communities Project. In January 2004, she was appointed director of periodic program review. She is the author, coauthor, or editor of several publications, chapters, and articles on learning communities, including *Creating Learning Communities* (1999), which she cowrote with Nancy Shapiro. Along with several other colleagues, she and Shapiro are authors of the forthcoming book *Sustaining and Improving Learning Communities* (2004).

Carrie W. Linder is coordinator of research and project development at the National Resource Center for The First-Year Experience and Students in Transition at the

University of South Carolina. She organizes research projects and initiatives, assists educators and visiting scholars with their research efforts and requests, and maintains the center's database on first-year seminar programs across the United States. She also teaches a section of the University 101 first-year seminar or University 101 peer leader seminar each fall. Linder holds a B.A. degree in communication studies from the University of Florida and an M.Ed degree in student personnel services from the University of South Carolina.

Deanna C. Martin is the founding director of Supplemental Instruction and the University of Missouri, Kansas City (UMKC) Center for Academic Development. She holds academic appointments as associate professor in the UMKC School of Education, honorary professor at the University of Port Elizabeth, South Africa, codirector of the Supplemental Instruction research project of the University of Uppsala, Sweden, and special consultant to the Department of Educational Services, St. George's University, Grenada, West Indies. Although retired from full-time service at the University of Missouri, Martin continues to serve as assistant to the vice chancellor for student affairs and director of curriculum development for the Medical Women's International Association. She holds a B.A. degree in English from University of Kansas City and M.A. and Ph.D. degrees in education from the University of Missouri. Martin has an extensive record of publications and international posts. She was awarded the prestigious UMKC Alumnus of the Year award for her contributions to the university and the field of higher education.

Philip W. Meilman is a clinical psychologist at the Office of Counseling and Psychological Services at Cornell University, where he served as director from 1996 to 2003. He also holds appointments as Courtesy Professor of Human Development and associate professor of psychology in clinical psychiatry. Meilman serves as codirector of the Core Institute at Southern Illinois University at Carbondale. He received a B.A. degree from Harvard in 1973 and a Ph.D. degree in clinical psychology from the University of North Carolina at Chapel Hill in 1977. Meilman has authored or coauthored some seventy professional publications, including articles on alcohol and college mental health issues, a book entitled *Beating the College Blues,* and monographs on the aggregated national data sets from the Core Alcohol and Drug Survey.

Richard H. Mullendore is vice president for student affairs, associate provost, and professor of college student affairs administration at the University of Georgia. He is also a fellow of the National Resource Center for The First-Year Experience and Students in Transition at the University of South Carolina. He holds a B.A. degree in speech and hearing sciences from Bradley University, an M.A. degree in higher education from Southern Illinois University at Carbondale, and a Ph.D. degree in higher education administration from Michigan State University. Mullendore is a former president of the National Orientation Directors Association and a frequent presenter on orientation and parent programs at national conferences. He was editor of the 1995 and 1998 editions of the *Orientation Planning Manual,* coeditor of *Designing Successful Transitions: A Guide for Orienting Students to College,* and coauthor of *Helping Your First-Year College Student Succeed: A Guide for Parents.* He has received several awards, including the Bob Leach Award for Outstanding Service to Students, the Outstanding Professional Contribution Award (North Carolina College Personnel Association), and the President's Award and the Outstanding Contributions to the Orientation Profession Award from the National Orientation Directors Association.

Diana S. Natalicio is president of the University of Texas at El Paso (UTEP). Previously she served as UTEP's vice president for academic affairs, dean of the College of Liberal Arts, and chair of the modern languages department. She completed her B.S. degree in Spanish at St. Louis University and a M.A. degree in Portuguese and a Ph.D. degree in linguistics from the University of Texas at Austin. Natalicio was a Fulbright scholar in Rio de Janeiro, Brazil, and held a Gulbenkian fellowship in Lisbon, Portugal. She has written numerous books, monographs, and articles in the field of applied linguistics.

Cheryl Presley is the director of student health programs and assistant to the vice chancellor of student affairs and enrollment management for research at Southern Illinois University Carbondale. She is executive director of the Core Institute and project director on a contract with the U.S. Department of Education conducting a national probability sample measuring drug and related violence on college campuses. She received her B.S. and master's degrees from Southern Illinois University Carbondale and her Ph.D degree in educational psychology/counselor education from Southern Illinois University Carbondale, and is a graduate of the Harvard Management Development Program. As director of the student health programs, she is primarily responsible for management of all administrative and fiscal affairs of the student health programs, which has on average 198,000 student contacts annually. She also directs, coordinates, and analyzes the Research Committee's strategic plan for Southern Illinois University Carbondale.

Karen Maitland Schilling is chair and professor in the Department of Psychology at Miami University, where she has been a faculty member and administrator for the past twenty-nine years. She completed her B.S. degree in psychology at Tufts University and the M.A. and Ph.D. degrees in clinical psychology at the University of Florida. She served as Miami's first University Director of Liberal Education, overseeing implementation of a comprehensive revision of the undergraduate curriculum. Schilling has consulted on curriculum development and assessment at several dozen institutions throughout the United States. She recently directed a FIPSE-supported project on increasing expectations for students' academic effort.

Karl L. Schilling is associate director of the Center for Teaching Excellence at New York University. He received a B.A. degree in English and psychology from

Adrian College and M.A. and Ph.D. degrees in clinical psychology from the University of Florida. He worked as a faculty member and college counselor at Earlham College; as associate dean and associate professor of interdisciplinary studies at the Western College Program of Miami University; as director of the American Association for Higher Education Assessment Forum, and as deputy director of the State Council of Higher Education in Virginia. His primary focus is on student learning and the creation of powerful learning environments.

Charles C. Schroeder is professor of higher education in the Educational Leadership and Policy Analysis Department at the University of Missouri. He received his B.A. and M.A. degrees from Austin College and his Ph.D. degree from Oregon State University. He has served as the chief student affairs officer at Mercer University, Saint Louis University, Georgia Institute of Technology, and University of Missouri-Columbia. He has assumed various leadership roles in the American College Personnel Association, serving as president in 1986 and 1993 and as executive editor of *About Campus: Enriching the Student Learning Experience*. Schroeder has authored over sixty articles and with Phyllis Mable published *Realizing the Educational Potential of Residence Halls* (1994).

John H. Schuh is professor of educational leadership and policy studies at Iowa State University. He holds a B.A. degree from the University of Wisconsin–Oshkosh and a master's of counseling and Ph.D. degrees in philosophy from Arizona State University. Previously he has held administrative and faculty appointments at Wichita State University, Indiana University (Bloomington), and Arizona State University. Schuh is the editor of the *New Directions for Student Services* Sourcebook Series and associate editor of the *Journal of College Student Development*. He received a Fulbright award to study higher education in Germany in 1994.

Betty L. Siegel is president of Kennesaw State University and the first woman to head an institution in the thirty-four-unit University System of Georgia. She has the distinction of being the longest-serving woman president in the nation. Her academic areas of expertise are child psychology and higher education administration. She received her Ph.D. degree from Florida State University, M.Ed. degree from the University of North Carolina at Chapel Hill, B.A. degree in English and history from Wake Forest University, and A.A. degree from Cumberland College. She is cofounder and codirector of the International Alliance for Invitational Education, a nonprofit organization chartered in North Carolina. She is an active member and former chair of the board of directors of the American Association of State Colleges and Universities, as well as a member and former director of the American Council on Education. Currently, she serves on the executive committee of the Business Higher Education Forum.

Maggy Smith is founding dean of the University College at the University of Texas at El Paso (UTEP), a position she has held since the college was created in 2001. Previously, she served as the director of UTEP's Entering Student Program and associate vice president for undergraduate studies. She has also served as director of the first-year composition program in the English Department, where she is professor of English and a member of the graduate faculty. Smith received her B.A. and M.A. degrees in English from the State University of New York at Fredonia and her Ph.D. degree in communication and rhetoric at Rensselaer Polytechnic Institute. She is the author of *Springboard for College Writers* (1996, coauthored with G. Douglas Meyers) and *Teaching College Writing* (1995), in addition to other articles.

Diane W. Strommer currently works in Glion, Switzerland, serving as the accreditation adviser to the administration at the Glion Institute of Higher Education and Les Roches School of Hotel Management. From 1980 to 1998, she was the dean of university college and special academic programs at the University of Rhode Island, where she is now dean emerita. From 1998 to 2000, she was the founding dean of a new national university for women, Zayed University, with campuses in Dubai and Abu Dhabi in the United Arab Emirates. From 2001 to 2003, she served as the special assistant to the president and director of enrollment management at the American University in Bulgaria in Blagoevgrad, Bulgaria. She holds an A.B. degree in English from University of North Carolina, an M.A. degree in American Literature, and a Ph.D. degree in British Renaissance drama from Ohio State University. She has published four books and numerous articles and has consulted widely on advising, general education, and international education. She and coauthor Erickson are currently preparing a second edition of their book, *Teaching College Freshmen*.

Randy L. Swing is codirector and senior scholar of the Policy Center on the First Year of College and a Fellow of the National Resource Center for The First-Year Experience and Students in Transition at the University of South Carolina. He obtained a B.A. degree in psychology from University of North Carolina, Charlotte; an M.A. degree in counseling from Appalachian State University; and a Ph.D. degree in higher education from the University of Georgia. His work focuses on assessment for improving the first college year. He served on the development teams for the national student survey tool, *Your First College Year,* and the *First-Year Initiative* national benchmarking study of first-year seminars; he founded the First-Year Assessment Listserv; and edited *Proving and Improving: Strategies for Assessing the First College Year.* Prior to 1999, Swing held leadership positions at Appalachian State University in assessment, advising, orientation, and the first-year seminar.

Margit Misangyi Watts is the director of Rainbow Advantage and Freshman Seminars at the University of Hawaii at Manoa. She is also the interim director of student housing. She holds a B.S. degree in general studies and an elementary teaching certificate from the University of Michigan; an M.S. degree in social work; and a Ph.D. degree in American studies from the University of Hawaii.

Watts has both published and given keynote addresses on learning communities, the integration of service-learning into the first-year experience, information literacy as key to the understanding of scholarship, and the pedagogy of distance learning. She is a member of the Association of College and Research Libraries Best Practices Team on information literacy. Her most recent book, *College: We Make the Road by Walking,* is a first-year-seminar textbook connecting personal to scholarly narratives and introducing students to the major components of scholarship and the purpose of higher education.

William J. Zeller is the assistant vice chancellor of student housing at the University of California, Irvine. He was formerly the director of university housing at the University of Michigan and has held similar positions at Washington State University and Southeast Missouri State University. He earned his bachelor's degree from Northern Illinois University, his master's degree in college student personnel administration from Western Illinois University, and his Ph.D. degree in higher education administration from Iowa State University. He is the author of numerous articles and book chapters, with particular concentration on the first-year experience and living-learning programs. He has also held several leadership positions in the Association of College and University Housing Officers–International.

Edward Zlotkowski is professor of English at Bentley College, senior faculty fellow at Campus Compact, and senior associate at the Policy Center on the First Year of College. He holds a B.A. degree in English, a master of philosophy degree, and a Ph.D. degree in comparative literature from Yale. Since 1995 he has served as general editor of the American Association for Higher Education's monograph series on service-learning in the academic disciplines. He also served as editor of *Service-Learning and the First-Year Experience: Preparing Students for Personal Success and Civic Responsibility* (2002). Over the past ten years, he has worked with hundreds of colleges and universities on issues related to civic and academic engagement.

Challenging and Supporting
the First-Year Student

INTRODUCTION

The First Year of College Revisited

M. Lee Upcraft
John N. Gardner
Betsy O. Barefoot

Why another look at the first year of college? In their 1989 book, *The Freshman Year Experience: Helping Students Survive and Succeed in College*, Lee Upcraft and John Gardner argued that colleges and universities had to be willing to make major changes in their approach to learning if they were to serve students in the 1990s and beyond. Because of the overwhelming evidence that student success is largely determined by student experiences during the first year, they noted that an important way to do this was for institutions to develop policies, make decisions, and create classrooms, programs, curricula, and services that enhance first-year student success.

In fact, that is precisely what happened. Since 1989, the amount and extent of campuswide, national, and international conversation and then action to change the structure and content of the first-year experience have been extensive. The first-year experience has become a much higher priority for policymakers, resource allocators, and rank-and-file faculty and administrators. With the help of the lay press that has showed a much greater interest in the success of first-year students (examples are *Time* magazine's "Colleges of the Year," *US News and World Report's* reputational rankings, and features in *USA Today* and *The New York Times*), the first-year experience now seems deeply ingrained in the lexicon of higher education. This progress has occurred in spite of fiscal constraints, economic downturns, and in some cases severe reductions in external support.

This progress is even more unusual when viewed in the context of the history of American higher education, which prior to 1960 had an historic sink-or-swim attitude toward student success. Since the 1960s, higher education has engaged in a massive social experiment of providing access to higher education

1

that at its worst included anyone who could fog a mirror and had a demonstrable pulse. We found, however, that as we expanded access, many complaints surfaced about a perceived decline in academic standards. In response to these concerns, we could have raised admissions standards, but that would have reduced access and failed to meet the unfulfilled potential of American democracy and the needs of the American economy for a college-educated workforce.

Instead, we continued to increase accessibility. We recruited older students, economically disadvantaged students, and racial and ethnic minority students. But until the 1980s, we did little or nothing to change how we organized the college experience in ways that adapted to and met the needs of our increasingly diverse student population.

Many factors came together to reform higher education. There was a tough recession in the early 1980s, and federal financial aid policies shifted from an emphasis on grants to loans. Several national reports criticized the status of undergraduate education, including *A Nation at Risk* (National Commission on Excellence in Education, 1984) and *Involvement in Learning* (National Institute of Education, 1984). At the same time, the University of South Carolina established a national center for what was then known as "the freshman year experience," which, through its conferences, publications, and research, has helped the nation focus on the first year of college. Upcraft and Gardner's *The Freshman Year Experience* also stimulated discussion of the first year of college, as well as offering many suggestions for policy and practice.

The result is that as a nation, we are focused more than ever before on reform of undergraduate education, with a particular emphasis on the first year of college.

PROGRESS OVER THE LAST TWENTY YEARS

Over the past twenty years, we have woven a tapestry of proven approaches with newer, more innovative strategies, leading to many accomplishments:

• *Increased campuswide, national, and international conversation and action about the first year of college.* Compared to twenty years ago, the first-year experience is now firmly ingrained in the consciousness of American higher education, and efforts to help first-year students succeed have expanded and diversified. At the same time, first-year-experience and retention specialists' positions have been established to provide better support at the grassroots level.

• *The introduction and revision of initiatives designed to help first-year students succeed.* These include more innovative approaches to classroom teaching and learning, more flexible and varied first-year seminars, more comprehensive developmental education programs, increased use of Supplemental Instruction, newer approaches to academic advising, newer approaches to orientation, learning-centered residential programs, student support services that are more targeted to first-year students, more effective approaches to alcohol and other drug education and prevention, expansion of service-learning opportunities for first-year students, and learning communities.

- *The expansion of research and scholarship on the first year of college.* Our knowledge about first-year students as a unique cohort has been greatly increased by extensive research and scholarship. Thanks to researchers and scholars such as Pascarella and Terenzini (1991), Astin (1993), Tinto (1993), and others, we now know much more about the backgrounds and characteristics of first-year students, the developmental issues that they face in their first year, and the collegiate experiences that contribute to or detract from their transition to college and persistence to graduation. Coupled with more research about students and programs has been an ever-increasing focus on assessment of first-year programs, courses, and services. Although there are institution-specific differences, a body of evidence is building to show a predictable relationship between specific programs such as learning communities and first-year seminars and desired first-year outcomes.

- *The development of closer collaboration between academic affairs and student affairs.* Over the past two decades, there has been a dramatic growth in campus-based partnerships between academic and student affairs, which were previously less inclined to work together to address the needs of first-year students: the faculty, academic administrators, student affairs administrators, academic support personnel, institutional research officers, and others (Cutright, 2002). Increasingly, growing numbers of these personnel are forming partnerships to improve first-year student success through initiatives such as service-learning, learning communities, first-year seminars, and learning-centered residential environments. These collaborations, originally begun by student affairs, are now being driven more often by senior academic administrators.

- *The emergence of credible assessment studies to demonstrate the efficacy of initiatives to help first-year students succeed.* In the past, most studies of the effectiveness of first-year initiatives were institution based, and although they were helpful to individual institutions, they provided little guidance from an overall perspective. However, there are now at least four national centers active in conducting national studies of the first year of college: the National Resource Center for The First-Year Experience and Students in Transition at the University of South Carolina, the Higher Education Research Institute at the University of California at Los Angeles, the National Center for Postsecondary Research at Indiana University, and the Policy Center on the First Year of College in Brevard, North Carolina. Such efforts yield a more comprehensive and representative picture of the first year of college, as well as provide bases of comparisons for comparable institutions.

- *The integration of technology into first-year initiatives.* The influence of technology on the student experience has been phenomenal over the past dozen years, and the first year of college is no exception. From admissions to enrollment to classrooms to residence halls to academic advising to other student support services, technology is fundamentally changing the nature of student learning, both inside and outside the classroom. While many educators view technology as a double-edged sword, on the whole it has improved institutional efforts to help first-year students succeed.

• *The inclusion of diversity in first-year initiatives has become a permanent feature of the first-year student landscape.* First-year initiatives are much more inclusive of the needs of all first-year students, regardless of age, race, ethnicity, sexual orientation, nationality, disability, enrollment status, place of residence, gender, and other distinguishing student characteristics.

• *The classroom has become more central to efforts to promote first-year student success.* The first-year classroom, historically ignored or undervalued, is now center stage. The important work of Barr and Tagg (1995), in addition to a number of national reports and major research initiatives (including Boyer Commission, 1998; Wingspread Group, 1993; and the National Survey of Student Engagement, 2003), have focused the nation's attention on what happens, or does not happen, in undergraduate education, and especially in first-year classes. Furthermore, increasing numbers of institutions are developing, articulating, and measuring the degree to which first-year students achieve desired first-year learning outcomes that include both interdisciplinary cognitive skills and course-specific knowledge (Cutright, 2002; Policy Center on the First Year of College, 2003).

• *External funding in support of the first-year experience has increased.* Major philanthropic foundations such as The Pew Charitable Trusts, The Atlantic Philanthropies, the Hewlett and Teagle Foundations, and Lumina Foundation for Education have designated millions of dollars to support undergraduate education and improvement of the first year. In addition, many campuses have begun first-year initiatives with federal monies, such as the Fund for the Improvement of Postsecondary Education, the National Science Foundation, Title III, TRIO, and Gaining Early Awareness for Undergraduate Programs (GEAR UP).

The conclusion regarding these accomplishments is that attention to the first year of college has become a mature reform movement within the context of American higher education in the late twentieth and early twenty-first centuries. This movement has set aspirational models for other higher education cultures as well. In addition, the manifestations of these models at the campus level are now at varying stages of institutionalization and priority, many at the level of long-term sustainability.

Although there are myriad reasons for higher education to be proud of recent improvements in the first college year, many challenges remain:

• *There is no consensus about a clear sense of purpose in the first year.* No organization that aspires to greatness can ignore the importance of purpose to the achievement potential of its most important objectives. We argue that over the twentieth century, the most obvious purposes of the first year were to make money that could be reallocated to more prestigious functions, deliver instruction in the cheapest way possible, and weed out undesirable or presumed unqualified students. Even if colleges are focused on first-year student success, they are often not intentional about their purposes in relation to first-year students. It happens by tradition, habitual practice, and unexamined assumptions, with no clearly thought out sense of purpose, resulting in a continuation of the status quo. We must ask the question: If we were to create a first-year experience intentionally designed to help students succeed, consistent with the mission of the institution, what would it look like?

• *First-year student academic success rates are still too low.* Although many first-year programs have been shown effective in reducing dropout rates from the first to the second year, institutions on the whole continue to grapple with persistent high rates of attrition from the first to the second year (about one in seven) and to graduation (about one in two), rates that have remained more or less stable for more than twenty years. Furthermore, there is too much failure in historically challenging first-year courses. With only a few exceptions, institutions have increased the level of attention they pay to issues of student retention. In fact, for some institutions, this has become a singular preoccupation. But although there is a great deal of hand-wringing about the issue of student retention, many campuses are reluctant to conceptualize the problem broadly and involve all faculty and staff in its possible solution. Many in the academy continue to believe that retention is a "student problem" and that dropouts are simply nature's way of separating the wheat from the chaff.

• *College is far less challenging than first-year students expect.* There is substantial evidence that today's first-year students are not necessarily challenged to work to their full potential in pursuing their academic goals or fully engaged in the pursuit of their education. When pre- and posttest measures of engagement and involvement are used (for example, comparing results from the College Student Expectations Questionnaire with the National Survey of Student Engagement, or the results from the Annual Survey of College Freshmen with Your First College Year), college appears to be less academically challenging than first-year students expected, and they spend much less time engaged in academic pursuits than the typical faculty expectation. Moreover, high levels of academic disengagement, boredom, absenteeism, and cheating are widely reported among first-year students. First-year students need to become much more engaged in their education, and institutions must shape this engagement by demanding more of them.

• *Building first-year initiatives that are responsive to today's increasingly diverse students is still a challenge.* The academy continues an uneven commitment to access—admitting large numbers of students for whom higher education was never historically inclusive (women, students of color, first-generation students, students with disabilities, adult students, the economically disadvantaged), but often failing to provide the kinds of environments needed for their success. At-risk students are more likely to succeed when institutions provide all students with focused and intentional initiatives, tailored to their individual needs.

• *The link from research and assessment to policy and practice is still weak.* All too often, decisions are made for reasons not linked demonstrably to measures of student success, such as academic achievement, retention and transition to college, and psychosocial and cognitive outcomes. There is substantial assessment-based evidence to show a relationship between selected initiatives and desirable outcomes that often seems to be ignored when developing policies and practices for first-year students. However, sometimes the newest, least politically powerful elements of the first-year design are most subjected to scrutiny, while more established elements, such as the curriculum and teaching and learning in the classroom, become what we think of as "assessment-free zones." We must find ways to put research and assessment findings in the minds of faculty and administrators.

- *Several myths about the first year of college still abound.* For example, too often first-year students are thought of as eighteen and nineteen year olds studying full time, away from home for the first time, and living on campus, when this profile fits only about one in five first-year students. Also, we persist in the myth that if we can only get first-year students through the first six weeks of college, we considerably increase their likelihood of success. Although the beginning of the college experience is clearly important, six weeks is an artificial time limit that promulgates yet another myth: that there is not much we can do after the first six weeks, belying the considerable evidence that first-year initiatives should extend throughout the entire first year of college. Another myth is that first-year initiatives should be targeted exclusively to at-risk students, as if no other students need help in making a successful transition to college.

- *The priority on the first year of college is still not sufficiently high on some campuses.* This is particularly true for two-year public institutions that admit the highest proportion of at-risk students, yet often have the fewest initiatives to help first-year students succeed (Policy Center on the First Year of College, 2000). It is also true that some highly selective institutions believe their first-year students are so academically gifted they do not need special efforts to help them succeed.

- *Institutional efforts to help first-year students succeed are still not sufficiently integrated.* Often such efforts are self-contained, uncoordinated, and even unknown to each other. As a result, what students experience in the first year is an unconnected, unintegrated set of experiences, often artificially separating their academic and out-of-classroom experiences. Even within the curriculum, student classroom experiences are often unrelated to each other. All too often, a campuswide structure for exercising coordination, leadership, and administrative integration of first-year initiatives is lacking. Rarely is anyone in charge.

- *Efforts to help first-year students succeed are too often focused on retention rather than student learning.* Retention as a linchpin for successful first-year initiatives will never be successful in engaging sufficient numbers of educators, particularly faculty. Faculty see themselves as dedicated to student learning in their classrooms, not to keeping students in college, and they are absolutely correct in this belief. Institutions that are serious about what students learn will make the most significant strides toward ensuring student success.

• *There is a continuing struggle for status of first-year initiatives among competing institutional priorities.* Many colleges and universities, both public and private, are faced with significantly dwindling resources, and programs that lack strong political support (including first-year programs) are frequently highly vulnerable for downsizing or elimination. Because the campus is an inherently political environment, struggles for status and power (that is, resources) are legion, and educators who work with and on behalf of first-year students find that the challenge of status within the academy is a never-ending one.

• *First-year students' out-of-class experiences are still a double-edged sword.* Students who manage their lives outside the classroom in ways that are constructive and mentally healthy typically make a successful transition to college and achieve their educational goals. But certain out-of-class behaviors and activities may have a detrimental effect on first-year student success. For example, alcohol abuse among undergraduates on some campuses appears to be out of control; many consider it to be the most serious behavioral issue in American higher education. And hardly a year goes by without national newspaper coverage of a campus tragedy, many involving first-year students—a death by alcohol poisoning, injuries incurred in Greek hazing incidents, or abuse, harassment, or incivility on campus. Those who teach and counsel first-year students are responding to these challenges by using a variety of strategies, but these efforts are met with varying degrees of success. Other out-of-class issues that must be addressed include sexual harassment, campus safety, hate crimes, computer addiction, roommate relationships, nutritional disorders, depression, and anxiety.

• *Many student success initiatives are marginal to first-year students' academic experience.* For example, there are still institutions that focus their orientation programs exclusively on social activities designed to help first-year students get to know one another. Furthermore, some of those involved in the delivery of first-year initiatives may themselves be marginalized and thus less effective. While these initiatives may be necessary, they are not sufficient.

Our lists of accomplishments and challenges are certainly not exhaustive; there are indeed many others. We have attempted to highlight the most salient ones, based on our review of current literature and our own considerable experience over the past two decades. Why another book on the first-year experience? *To update readers on the many accomplishments and improvements in efforts to help first-year students succeed, as well as to offer possible solutions for the many challenges that remain.*

A REVISED DEFINITION OF FIRST-YEAR STUDENT SUCCESS

We have used and will use the term *first-year student success* many times in this book, but what exactly do we mean when we use this term? Of course, there are probably as many definitions of first-year student success as there are institutions of higher education. The narrowest definition of first-year student success is the (1) successful completion of courses taken in the first year and (2) continuing enrollment into the second year. However, most institutions would espouse a broader definition of first-year student success, including one or more of the following:

- *Developing intellectual and academic competence.* First and foremost, first-year students must succeed academically according to the narrow definition described above. It is the issue that first-year students worry most about on entry. It is certainly not a misplaced concern, because if they do not succeed academically, for whatever reasons, they will not succeed at all. But they must also develop the intellectual skills necessary to become an educated person, such as critical thinking, problem solving, and reflective judgment, in addition to reading, writing, technological, and computational skills. Perhaps even more important, they must consider the moral, ethical, and cultural implications of what they learn, and develop an appreciation for the aesthetic side of life. *Thus, successful first-year students must not only get off to a good start academically and learn how to learn, but they must begin to appreciate what it means to become an educated person.*

- *Establishing and maintaining interpersonal relationships.* First-year students express anxiety about finding supportive friends and family to help them in their transition to college. They are right to have such worries, because having supportive friends and family in fact contributes to their academic and interpersonal success. Traditional-aged first-year students who are away from home for the first time must establish new interpersonal support systems and reconsider their family support systems. Older and commuting students must integrate their commitments to existing support systems built around family and friends into collegiate-based relationships with faculty, staff, and other students. Nevertheless, all first-year students must develop the interpersonal skills necessary not only to build supportive relationships, but also to succeed in their many pursuits after college. *Thus, successful first-year students must begin to develop effective interpersonal relationships.*

- *Exploring identity development.* For most first-year students, the question, "Who am I?" gets revisited, sometimes accompanied by great turmoil. According to Erikson (1963), a sense of identity is fully developed when the way we see ourselves is consistent with the ways that others see us. Identity questions based on gender, sexual orientation, race, disability, and other factors may challenge first-year students to think through who they really are, because continuing identity confusion can lead to great personal and academic dysfunction. *Thus, successful first-year students must begin to make some progress in exploring who they are.*

- *Deciding on a career.* Ask first-year students why they are going to college, and many will answer, "To prepare for a career [or find a new career] and get a job." Many come to college with some kind of career goal in mind, and the first year of college is an almost immediate test of that goal. Some career choices withstand that test, but more often, initial career goals are changed because students discover that the career they wanted is not really suited to their interests, or their performance in the major that would prepare them for their initial career choice is inadequate (or both). *Thus, successful first-year students must begin to achieve clarity about their career goals.*

- *Maintaining health and wellness.* The first year of college is often very stressful, and first-year students must be able to cope with this increased stress. They must learn to manage their time to meet their many commitments inside and outside the classroom. Whatever their age or stage in life, they must make decisions about interpersonal relationships, alcohol and other drug use and abuse, sexual activity, nutritional habits, physical activity, and other behaviors. They must begin to think of maintaining health and wellness as an active rather than reactive process. *Thus, successful first-year students must begin to learn to lead healthy lives and deal with stress.*

- *Considering faith and the spiritual dimensions of life.* Most first-year students come to college with some kind of faith, spiritual outlook, or value systems that guide their lives. Until recently, this side of the first-year student experience has been largely ignored or viewed exclusively from a secular perspective. Yet for many first-year students, their faith is very much a part of who they are, what their values are, and how they cope with college life. Even those with little or no faith perspective will likely reconsider or reaffirm their sense of what is right and wrong, their priorities in life, their religious and spiritual beliefs, and how they fit into the larger order of things in the universe. *Thus, successful first-year students must begin to reconsider and internalize what they believe and value.*

- *Developing multicultural awareness.* Many first-year students, perhaps for the first time, will encounter students, faculty, staff, and community members of different cultural backgrounds, ages, religions, sexual orientations, life experiences, physical and mental abilities, races, nationalities, and ethnicities. Some first-year students may be treated differently or discriminated against because of their differences. The diversity of a campus is often, and should be, a positive educational condition, but it can also breed conflicts, tensions, harassment, and even violence. First-year students must make efforts to go beyond their circle of family and friends to learn more about and relate to those who are different from them. *Thus, first-year students must develop an awareness of the multicultural realities of our nation and today's collegiate environment and learn to tolerate and affirm differences among people.*

- *Developing civic responsibility.* First-year students are frequently caught up in their own narrow collegiate worlds, with little awareness of or commitment to their responsibilities as citizens in a democratic society. For example, far too few college students vote in national, state, or local elections. Fortunately, over the past fifteen years, many colleges and universities have a renewed interest in promoting civic responsibility, not only through providing opportunities for community-based volunteer work and charitable fundraising events, but through curriculum and course-based service-learning. *Thus, first-year students must begin to become responsible citizens outside the collegiate environment.*

In summary, first-year student success is more than earning a sufficient grade point average to make a successful transition to college and persist to graduation. It is making progress on becoming a truly educated person in these many ways. Colleges and universities must provide an educational environment that makes this kind of education possible.

AN OVERRIDING THEME

Although it was clear to us and our publisher that the first year of college needed another focused and updated look, organizing this kind of book, particularly an edited tome with multiple authors, presented a daunting challenge. We decided we needed an overriding theme—one that would provide a conceptual basis for our work that was not only descriptive of what we were writing about, but offered a way of looking at the first college year that would provide a basis for understanding and acting on this critical period of the undergraduate experience. After much deliberation, we returned to the writings of the late Nevitt Sanford, a clinical psychologist and professor of psychology at Stanford University, who first postulated the concept of *challenge and support* as the overriding theme of the first year of college.

Sanford's substantive scholarship on first-year college students was published slightly more than forty years ago. Prior to the 1962 publication of his seminal work, *The American College,* very little had been written about first-year students or, for that matter, any other students, except for novels and movie scripts, and virtually no research had been conducted on this important class of citizens and the collegiate environments they inhabit. Sanford was one of the first to ponder how students learn, grow, and develop during the college years; offer some cogent hypotheses about the kinds of collegiate environments that promote first-year student success; and examine why and how students stay in college or leave.

Since that time, the landscape of higher education has been blanketed by a number of important theories and research on college students and the collegiate environment, including seminal efforts such as Astin's involvement theory, Tinto's theory of academic and social integration, Chickering's seven vectors of student development, Kohlberg's theory of moral development, Perry's theory of intellectual development, William Cross's theory of nigrescence, Patricia Cross's concepts of adult student development, Gilligan's notions about gender development, Cass's model of homosexual identity formation, Fowler's model of spiritual development, Kolb's learning styles, Howard Gardner's concept of multiple intelligences, Baxter Magolda's scholarship on cognitive development, King and Kitchener's reflective judgment, and many others.

In addition, researchers such as Ernest Pascarella, Patrick Terenzini, George Kuh, and others have added to our knowledge about how students learn and develop as well as how collegiate environments affect students.

Even with all these complex theories and abundance of research, Sanford's remarkably straightforward notions about how students learn and develop in the collegiate environment are as fresh and relevant as when he first posited them forty years ago. Sanford argued that in order for students to succeed, they must be both challenged (provided with educational experiences that foster learning and personal development) and supported (provided with a campus climate that helps students learn and develop). When a proper balance is maintained between challenge and support, students are positioned to succeed in college. Too much challenge, and students will become overwhelmed and discouraged, and will fail to learn. Too little challenge, and students will become bored, unmotivated, and disinterested in learning. Too little support, and students will feel isolated and lonely, and will be unable to focus academically and socially. Too much support, and students will become apathetic and less focused on their learning and development.

Although Sanford's notion of challenge and support was originally posited as a way of understanding and explaining student success, it can also serve as a framework for institutional efforts to help students succeed. That is, colleges and universities have an obligation to create learning environments that both challenge and support students and avoid creating an imbalance between the two, both inside and outside the classroom. We believe that the concepts of challenge and support provide an overall framework to guide institutions not only in helping first-year students make a successful transition to college and persist into the sophomore year, but helping them achieve success in developing intellectual competence, developing interpersonal relationships, developing identity, deciding on a career, maintaining personal health and wellness, considering faith and the spiritual dimensions of life, dealing with diversity, and developing civic responsibility. When we challenge them to become all they are capable of being and provide them with the support they need to maximize their potential, we have an excellent basis for helping them achieve both academic and personal success.

CONCLUSION

This book brings to the attention of higher education the remarkable progress that has been made over the past fifteen years in developing initiatives that promote first-year student success. Nevertheless, many daunting challenges remain, and we must seek possible solutions to these challenges.

We recognize that some in the academy may disagree with the basic premise of this book: that institutions should be more accountable for student success in the first year. These sink-or-swim advocates believe that any effort to help first-year students succeed, beyond offering them the opportunity to attend class and use the library, is "coddling" those who might otherwise fail, thereby compromising academic standards. Those who subscribe to this point of view will probably find this book a direct challenge to the way they think about first-year student success.

We believe institutions have a responsibility to help students succeed, so long as students fulfill their part of the bargain by investing time and energy in their education and becoming involved in campus life. And we—as educators and as citizens—should expect nothing less from our colleges and universities than a first year focused on entering students, challenged and supported by intentional institutional interventions, both inside and outside the classroom.

PART ONE

WHAT WE KNOW ABOUT TODAY'S FIRST-YEAR STUDENTS AND INSTITUTIONAL EFFORTS TO HELP THEM SUCCEED

Who are today's first-year students? The myth of first-year students as primarily middle class, eighteen years old, single, fresh out of high school, studying full time, living on campus, enrolled in a four-year college, living away from home for the first time, meeting traditional standards of academic preparedness, and completing one-fourth of their courses in one year has been debunked for at least twenty-five years; yet that myth persists. Stereotyped descriptions persist such as the "lost generation" or the "cybergeneration" or "Generation X" or, more recently, "the millennials," even though a critical analysis of today's first-year students' demographics reveals a much more diverse picture, which is almost impossible to stereotype. We begin our look at today's students in Chapter One with Jennifer Crissman Ishler's description of the demographics and characteristics of today's increasingly diverse first-year students.

As we discussed in the Introduction, the scholarship on students in general and first-year students in particular has exploded in the past fifteen years. We now know much more about the first year of college, the first-year student experience, and the personal and environmental factors that affect first-year student success. More specifically, although the myth survives that the persistence of first-year students into the second year of college is exclusively a function of ability and motivation (first-year students who failed were too dumb or did not work hard enough, or both), we now know that keys to student persistence are much more complex and interrelated than was ever imagined even thirty years ago. In Chapter Two, Jennifer Crissman Ishler and M. Lee Upcraft review the research-based evidence of the many factors that contribute to the persistence of first-year students.

We end Part One with a look at what institutions have done and are doing to help first-year students succeed. Over the past fifteen years, institutional efforts to help first-year students make a successful transition to college have exploded. In Chapter Three, Betsy Barefoot takes a systematic look at current institutional practices that are designed to help first-year students succeed, based on the results of several national surveys that describe these practices.

CHAPTER ONE

Today's First-Year Students

Jennifer L. Crissman Ishler

In spite of substantial evidence to the contrary, the myth remains that first-year students are primarily middle class, eighteen years old, single, fresh out of high school, studying full time, enrolled in a four-year college, living away from home for the first time, meeting traditional standards of academic preparedness, and graduating in four years. Consider what Schoch (1980) wrote over twenty years ago:

> Remember Joe College? The young man who, after working hard in high school arrived at Berkeley, where he set out to sample the rich and incredibly varied intellectual feast at the University of California. Joe was independent, strongly self-motivated, and academically well prepared; he was able not only to sample the intellectual wares but also settle down, about his junior year, to a major field of study, which he pursued with diligence and increasing confidence in order to graduate four years after his arrival. Joe doesn't live here anymore. Perhaps, in truth, he never did. But now he can't. Times have changed, things have changed, and Berkeley has changed [p. 1].

Not only has Berkeley changed, but the entire face of students in higher education has changed as well. Young Joe College has been joined by many other students who represent the "new" first-year students in higher education. Consider "Nancy College," who is thirty-five years old and enrolled in the local community college so that she can attend school while raising her two preteenage daughters as a single mother. In addition, Nancy works full time at a department store. After two years, she earned her associate degree at the community college and transferred to the local state university as an elementary education major. Because she was a transfer student, she knew no one in her classes, which made her feel alienated. In addition, she was the oldest student in her education classes.

Working on group assignments was especially challenging for Nancy because the traditional-aged students had very different schedules from her. She was also frustrated with the lack of evening hours for most student services. Nancy did not feel that she connected to the social community of the university because she did not have a peer group and did not get involved in clubs or activities. Nancy struggled to fit in with the academic community as well because she doubted her skills, compared to the younger students in her classes.

Now consider "Michael College." Michael is an eighteen-year-old African American male first-year student who grew up in an urban environment. He was in the top 10 percent of his class and had SAT scores of 1350. He is majoring in sociology at a large university, situated in a rural setting.

He is struggling to adapt to his new environment and is thinking about transferring. The racial climate on campus is volatile, to say the least. African American students are being sent hate mail, and threats are being made on their lives. In addition, he is personally tired of the fact that other students and faculty assume that he is on the basketball team just because he is tall and black (he does not like basketball, let alone play it). He also feels self-conscious in his classes because he is usually only one of the few black students in a class, and often is the only black male. He feels alienated from his peer group because he has decided not to pledge a black fraternity this year. He is thinking about pledging during his sophomore year but not during his first year. In discussing the possibility of transferring with his adviser, the adviser suggested that he visit the multicultural resource center. There, Michael found other students in similar situations, and he also signed up for a mentor, who is an administrator on campus. Michael has decided to stay and finish his first year and give this university another chance.

"Guy College" is another type of student. He is a gay first-year student living in the residence halls. Guy has not yet come out of the closet to his friends or family. He is not completely sure he is gay. He thinks he might be because he never had a serious girlfriend in high school and has never thought of girls in a romantic or sexual way. Guy is afraid to say anything to his new roommate because of a possible homophobic reaction. He remembers the news story about another gay college student who was beaten and killed. During the fall semester, Guy attended all of his classes, but as the semester wore on, he became more distracted by the thought that he might be gay. At midsemester, Guy finally decided to talk to his residence adviser, who referred Guy to the gay-lesbian-bisexual-transgendered resource office. There, he found someone with whom he could explore his sexual orientation issues. By the end of his first year, Guy accepted he was gay, came out to his closest friends and family, and continued to explore his sexual orientation.

Finally, consider "Josey College," an eighteen-year-old first-year female student who is attending college two hours away from her home. She did well academically in high school and had no reason to doubt that she would not continue her academic success in college. She had also attended summer camp growing up, so she did not expect to miss her family or be homesick. All was well with Josey during the first two weeks. College was exciting: there was plenty to do, she had a lot of parties to attend, and no parents were watching over her. But after the second week, she started missing her friends from home, she got sick because she was not eating right or getting enough sleep, and she missed her boyfriend, a senior in high school who was still at home. By the fourth week, she was convinced she did not belong in college: she had done poorly on her first round of tests and quizzes. She begged her parents to come get her, but they told her that she had to stick it out until the semester was over.

Josey decided to cut back on the parties and limited herself to going out only Thursday through Saturday nights, she would study more during the day, she would try to eat better, and she got a part-time job to earn a little spending money. She also joined a club that she had been interested in and that helped her meet friends who shared the same interests. She did not have an outstanding grade point average at the end of her first semester, but she had learned from her mistakes and was looking forward to spring semester.

These fictional yet accurate profiles could go on and on. The student landscape is dotted with almost as many profiles as there are students, and our thinking about first-year students should reflect their diversity. Of course, there are institutions that still educate Joe College, but compared to thirty years ago, many more institutions are busy educating what is now the majority of students in higher education. Yet we still use terms such as *college aged* to refer to college students, in spite of the fact that the average age of college students is now slightly over twenty-five. We still have a negative view of students who take more than four years to graduate. And we still refer to students who enter college for the first time as "freshmen" even though a majority are neither "fresh" nor "men." All of these assumptions fly in the face of who today's students really are.

CHANGING DEMOGRAPHICS

The demographic profile of today's first-year students is constantly changing. This profile is often at odds with conventional wisdom about who they are by age, race or ethnicity, gender, institutions of enrollment, disability, sexual orientation, nationality, and those who are the first in their families to attend college.

Age

There has been a significant shift in the age demographics of college and university students over the past twenty-five years, with the number of older students growing more rapidly than the number of younger students (National Center for Education Statistics, 1999). According to the 2002–2003 annual almanac edition of the *Chronicle of Higher Education,* undergraduate students twenty-five years of age and older now represent approximately 28 percent of all undergraduate students in higher education. Furthermore, Edgerton (1999) reports that fewer than one in six of all current undergraduate students fit the traditional stereotype of the American college student. Although definitions vary, the National Center for Education Statistics (NCES) has come up with seven characteristics that typically define nontraditional students (Flint, 2000, p. 3):

- Have delayed enrollment into postsecondary education
- Attend part time
- Are financially independent of parents
- Work full time while enrolled
- Have dependents other than a spouse
- Are single parents
- Lack a standard high school diploma

Race/Ethnicity

The number of racial and ethnic groups accessing higher education has grown dramatically in the past twenty-five years and reflects the changing nature of our nation's population. For example, according to data from the 2000 census, increases in the Latino and Asian American population are changing the complexion of the nation, and there is no doubt that American campuses will continue to undergo significant changes as well (Roach, 2001). According to these census data, between 2001 and 2015, the nation's population between eighteen and twenty-four years old will increase by 5 million, or about 16 percent. This growth, sometimes referred to as the baby boom echo, will result in a college enrollment increase of 1.6 million by 2015, according to the U.S. Department of Education (Roach, 2001). Perhaps most significant, of that 1.6 million, 80 percent will be nonwhite, and 50 percent will be Hispanic (Roach, 2001).

Currently, the number of minority students enrolling in and graduating from the nation's colleges and universities continues to increase modestly. However, this rate of increase is beginning to slow, according to the 2000–2001 Annual Status Report on Minorities in Higher Education, released by the American Council on Education (Dervaries, 2001). According to this report, postsecondary enrollment of students of color rose by 3.2 percent between 1997 and 1998 (the last year for which data are available), continuing a trend of modest increases that began in the early 1990s (Dervaries, 2001).

The types of institutions that students attend often vary by their race/ethnicity. Minority students made up a greater proportion of the student body at public two-year colleges compared to their Caucasian counterparts. For example, in 2003, 41 percent of African American, 46 percent of American Indian, and 55 percent of Hispanic students attend two-year institutions, compared to 34 percent of white students (Chronicle of Higher Education, 2003). At public four-year institutions, 43 percent of enrolled students were Caucasian compared to 37 percent American Indian, 37 percent African American, and 30 percent Hispanic (Chronicle of Higher Education, 2003).

The Annual Status Report on Minorities in Higher Education (Dervaries, 2001) showed that students of color have experienced gains in academic degree attainment. In 1998, students of color experienced combined increases of 2.5 percent in the number of associate degrees, 5.3 percent at the bachelor's level, 8.8 percent at the master's level, and 4.4 percent at the doctoral level.

Upcraft and Stephens (2000) point out that differences within minority groups may be as great as differences among them. For example, of the four major Hispanic-Latino groups in higher education (Mexican Americans, Puerto Ricans, Cubans, and Central and South Americans), each have different histories, traditions, and cultures. Within-group diversity is also evident with Asians, Native Americans, African Americans, and other groups, which means that reaching conclusions about students based on gross categorizations of race and ethnicity may do more harm than good. Furthermore, there appear to be growing numbers of racially mixed students, although firm data on this trend are incomplete.

One final aspect to consider is the recent court rulings and state actions concerning race-sensitive admissions. Many states have abandoned the use of race in the admissions process, and others have modified their admissions processes that use race as a criteria. Data from the University of Texas at Austin showed that following the 1996 *Texas* v. *Hopwood* decision, African American and Hispanic student enrollment dropped from 4 percent to 3 percent and from 14 percent to 13 percent, respectively (Evans, 2001). In 1999, after two years of the legislated requirement to accept the top 10 percent of each high school class, coupled with increased outreach and recruiting efforts, African American and Hispanic numbers have again reached their pre-*Hopwood* levels (Evans, 2001).

In 2001, the first year of the legislated requirement to accept the top 4 percent of each high school class in California, African American, Hispanic, and American Indian students accounted for 18.6 percent of in-state admitted students in the University of California system. This was up from 17.6 percent the previous year but slightly below the 18.8 percent admitted during 1997, the last year that race was considered in the admissions process (Evans, 2001).

Gender

According to Woodard, Love, and Komives (2000), the number of women students attending college equaled that of men students in 1979 for the first time. Since then, the number of women students has continued to grow. Between 1985 and 1995, the number of college women increased 23 percent, whereas men increased only 9 percent (Hansen, 1998). Today, women represent 56 percent of students in higher education (Chronicle of Higher Education, 2003) and tend to graduate at higher rates than men do (Woodard et al., 2000).

Enrollment Status

In 2001, 29 percent of all undergraduate students were enrolled part time. Part-time students are most likely to be women over twenty-four years of age who are enrolled in two-year institutions. Nearly three of five part-time students are twenty-five or older. Of male undergraduates enrolled part time in two-year colleges, 52 percent are age twenty-five and older, while among females, 65 percent are age twenty-five or older (Chronicle of Higher Education, 2003).

As a consequence of their part-time enrollment, fewer students are completing the bachelor's degree in four years. According to a survey by the National Collegiate Athletic Association, only 56 percent of first-year students graduate within six years. By racial and ethnic group, 74 percent of Asians graduate within six years, followed by 69 percent for whites, 45 percent for Hispanics, 38 percent for African Americans, and 37 percent for American Indians (Wilds & Wilson, 1998).

"Stopping out" (the practice of dropping out and reenrolling at a later date) is also more frequent than it used to be. According to the National Center for Education Statistics (Horn, 1998), nearly one-third of all undergraduates depart institutions of higher education during their first year. Of these, approximately half stopped out rather than dropped out altogether. Students at two-year institutions stop out at nearly twice the rate of those enrolled at four-year institutions (Horn, 1998).

Institutional Type

Today's students enroll at many different types of institutions. Approximately 77 percent of students are enrolled in public institutions, and 23 percent in private institutions. About 76 percent enroll in four-year institutions and 24 percent enroll in two-year institutions (Chronicle of Higher Education, 2003). Not to be overlooked is the incredible rise of for-profit degree-granting institutions. According to the Education Commission for the States (2001), these institutions now enroll roughly 365,000 students, an increase of 59 percent in the past ten years. For-profit institutions include the University of Phoenix, the nation's largest private university, whose enrollment has grown to about 213,000 students in 30 states, including nearly 50,000 on-line students.

Students with Disabilities

The first attempt to provide a postsecondary education for students with disabilities began over 135 years ago when Abraham Lincoln signed legislation to provide funding for Gallaudet, an institution for students who are deaf. Students with other disabilities had little access to higher education until the passage of the 1973 Rehabilitation Act. Section 504 of that act mandated equal opportunity for qualified people in institutions with educational programs receiving federal funds. It was the first national civil rights act that provided equal access to higher education for people with disabilities. Subsequently, the Americans With Disabilities Act (ADA) was signed into law in 1990. The ADA extended disability law from federally funded programs and institutions to those funded by state and local governments as well as private institutions (Hall & Belch, 2000).

Between 1986 and 1994, the percentage of students with disabilities who were attending college or completing a degree rose from 29 to 45 percent (U.S. Department of Education, 1996). A study in 1996 revealed that 6 percent of all undergraduates reported having a disability (National Center for Education Statistics, 1999). In a study conducted in 1998, approximately 9 percent of all entering college students reported having a physical or mental disability (Henderson, 1999).

The types of disabilities students bring to college have changed over the past decade. Ten years ago, being partially sighted or blind was the most common disability among first-year students; it was ranked fourth in 1998 (Henderson, 1999). According to Henderson, the most prevalent disabilities are learning disabilities, health impairments, or poor vision. Of students reporting a disability, 41 percent reported a learning disability, 22 percent said they had other disabilities, 19 percent indicated a health disability, 13 percent indicated they were partially sighted or blind, and 5 percent had speech impairments (Henderson, 1999).

Public two-year institutions enroll more than half of all college students reporting disabilities (National Center for Education Statistics, 1999; Phillippe, 1997). Although enrollment of students with disabilities at four-year institutions has increased in the past decade (Henderson, 1999), most students with disabilities who enter two-year institutions are not transferring to a four-year institution and pursuing a baccalaureate degree (National Center for Education Statistics, 1999).

Sexual Orientation

According to some estimates, as many as 7 percent of today's students are gay, lesbian, bisexual, or transsexual, although most of them choose to remain "in the closet" (Eyermann & Sanlo, 2002). It is likely that these estimates are low because there are some students who would not reveal their sexual orientation under any circumstances. In a review of research on the physical and psychological safety of GLBT students, Sullivan (1998) found continuing evidence of homophobic prejudice, harassment, and violence against GLBT students. In spite of that evidence, some GLBT students are open about their sexual orientation, and committed to creating campus climates that prevent prejudice and tolerate and affirm a diversity of sexual orientations. For example, D'Emilio (2000) found that even on campuses that have proved responsive to gay and lesbian concerns, progress has often come through the work of a handful of people who have chosen to be visible.

International Students

According to the *Chronicle of Higher Education* ("Foreign Student Enrollment Stagnates," 2003), the number of foreign students studying in the United States was 586,323 during the 2002–2003 academic year. However, after a steady growth in this population since 1985, in 2003 there was virtually no growth compared to 2002, primarily due to new security measures adopted by the Immigration and Naturalization Service since the September 11, 2001, terrorist attacks. Asian countries provide the largest number of students in the United States, accounting for 52 percent of all international students. They include India (74,603), China (64,757), South Korea (51,519), Japan (45,960), and Taiwan (28,017). Other countries that provide a substantial number are Canada (26,513), Mexico (12,801), Turkey (11,601), and Indonesia (10,432).

Although the overall number of foreign students has increased, certain segments of higher education have benefited disproportionately. Davis (1999) found that between 1993 and 1998, community college international enrollments had grown by more than 32 percent, while enrollment growth across all types of institutions was 9.2 percent. When examined by Carnegie classification, most international students were enrolled in Research I universities, Master's I institutions, and community colleges. The 323,645 students enrolled in these types of institutions constitute 65.9 percent of all U.S. international enrollments.

Over the past twelve years, the number of U.S. students studying abroad has more than doubled, from 48,483 to the 1997–1998 total of 113,959 (Davis, 1999). The leading destinations for U.S. study-abroad students are the United Kingdom, Spain, Italy, and France. However, in the past ten years, the number of American students studying in Europe has fallen by 15 percent, while the proportion going to Latin America has more than doubled, from 7 percent to 15.3 percent.

First-Generation Students

First-generation students are defined as those whose parents' highest level of education is a high school diploma or less. According to Nunez and Cuccaro-Alamin (1998), first-generation students were more likely to be female, older, have lower incomes, be married, and have dependents compared to their non-first-generation peers, Looking at gender, women comprise 57 percent of first-generation students and men 43 percent. Financially, the families of first-generation students had lower family incomes than those of non-first-generation students. For example, nearly one-quarter (23 percent) of first-generation students had family incomes in the lowest quartile, while 59 percent of non-first-generation students had family incomes in the highest quartile. First-generation students were more likely than their non-first-generation peers to attend public two-year institutions (51 percent versus 37 percent) and private, for-profit institutions (15 percent versus 6 percent). First-generation students were enrolled in different types of degree programs than were non-first-generation students. Noting their greater likelihood of enrolling in two-year colleges, first-generation students were more likely than other students to be in certificate (22 percent versus 12 percent) or associate degree programs (39 percent versus 30 percent), and less likely to be in a bachelor's degree program (23 percent versus 43 percent).

CHANGING CHARACTERISTICS

Family Background

The American family is undergoing a transformation that is having a significant impact on today's students. According to Keller (2001), forty years ago, nearly 90 percent of all children in the United States grew up in homes with a mother and a father; a majority of mothers with children below school age did not work or worked only part time; and only 6 percent of the nation's children were born to unmarried women. Beginning in the 1960s, the nuclear family began to crumble. Between 1960 and 1998, the divorce rate more than doubled, causing the United States to have the highest divorce rate in the industrialized world (Keller, 2001). Furthermore, the percentage of children born to unmarried persons jumped from 6 percent to 32 percent. According to the Stepfamily Association of America (1998), 35 percent of all children born in the 1980s will experience approximately five years of life in a single-parent family before their eighteenth birthday.

The implications of the changing family have an enormous impact on higher education. McLanahan and Sandefur (1994) note that "the basic message is the same: family disruption continues to reduce children's school achievement after high school" (p. 48). Kiernon's (1992) research also found that students who are middle class are less likely to go to a university or to stay when enrolled if they come from divorced or single-parent families.

Physical and Mental Health

Today, more than ever before, students are suffering from serious emotional conditions that run the full spectrum of diagnostic disorders (Heitzmann & Nafziger, 2001). According to Archer and Cooper (1998), "Compared with students in the past, today's students arrive on campus with more problems as a result of dysfunctional family situations, with more worries and anxieties about the future and about the serious problems facing them in modern society, with an increased awareness of their own personal demons, and with a great willingness to seek psychological and psychiatric help" (p. 6). As a result, more students are seeking help, causing an increase in demand for counseling services on college campuses. In fact, waiting lists for treatment in college counseling centers are at an all-time high.

According to a study done by the International Association of Counseling Services, in the 2000–2001 school year, nearly 90 percent of 274 counseling centers in the United States and Canada reported hospitalizing at least one student for psychological problems. Furthermore, 60 percent of the surveyed counseling centers counseled students dealing with stalking incidents. Approximately 30 percent reported at least one enrolled student committing suicide ("R. Sharpe's Parent's Fury," 2002).

Physical health problems are also on the increase, often related to some mental health problems. Eating disorders and substance abuse are two examples of the complex challenges facing counseling services. Both are destructive behavioral problems with social, psychological, and biological components (Archer & Cooper, 1998). Sexual violence on college campuses, which has been called a silent epidemic because it occurs at high rates yet is rarely reported to the authorities, is another issue that counseling centers deal with (Abbey, Zawacki, Buck, Clinton, & McAuslan, 2001). Several reasons contribute to the underreporting of sexual assault cases. Many victims do not tell others about the assault because they fear that they will not be believed or will be derogated (Abbey et al., 2001). Also, sometimes victims do not realize that what happened to them meets the definition of assault. In a study by Abbey, Ross, McDuffie, and

McAuslan (1996), 59 percent of college women surveyed had experienced some form of sexual assault and 23 percent had experienced rape. In a more recent study, Spitzberg (1999) found that approximately 50 percent of college women have been sexually assaulted and 27 percent have experienced rape or attempted rape.

For many students, college is a time of sexual activity. Eighty to ninety percent of college students report being sexually experienced (Douglas et al., 1997). Research has shown that the sexual activity of college students puts them at risk for sexually transmitted infections (STIs) including human immunodeficiency virus (HIV; Lewis, Malow, & Ireland, 1997; Mahoney, Thombs, & Ford, 1995). In 1997, females aged fifteen to nineteen years had the highest reported rates of both chlamydia and gonorrhea among women; males aged twenty to twenty-four years had the highest reported rates of both chlamydia and gonorrhea among men (Centers for Disease Control, 1998). Certain racial and ethnic groups have higher rates of STIs compared with rates for whites. African Americans accounted for about 77 percent of the total number of reported cases of gonorrhea—thirty-one times the rate in whites (Centers for Disease Control, 1998). African American rates were on average about twenty-four times higher than those of white adolescents aged fifteen to nineteen years; and the rate for African Americans aged twenty to twenty-four was almost twenty-eight times greater than that in whites.

Approximately 35 percent of people living with HIV infection were between twenty and twenty-nine years of age at the time of diagnosis. Given the invisibility of infection and the long latency period before diagnosis with AIDS, many of these cases undoubtedly originated in sexual behavior during young adulthood (Eisenberg, 2001).

Academic Preparation

A myth exists that students are scoring lower on standardized admissions tests than they have in the past. For example, while a thirty-year decline in SAT scores between 1957 and 1987 has been well documented (Forrest, 1987), that trend appears to have stopped. In 1989, the total SAT score was 1008, compared to the 2002 score of 1020 (Chronicle of Higher Education, 2003). Furthermore, math scores increased from 502 in 1989 to 516 in 2002. Verbal scores remained unchanged: 504 in 1989 and 2002.

Discrepancies exist in scores by gender, race, and ethnicity, with men scoring higher than women, and majority students generally scoring higher than minorities, with the exception of Asians. In 2002, men scored 39 points higher overall than women and 34 points higher than women on the math SAT (Chronicle of Higher Education, 2003). By race and ethnicity, African Americans scored the lowest overall, with a total SAT score of 857, followed by Mexican Americans with 903, Puerto Ricans with 906, Hispanics and Latinos with 922, American Indians with 962, whites with 1060, and Asians with 1070 (Chronicle of Higher Education, 2003).

More of today's students require remediation in basic reading, writing, and computational skills (Upcraft & Stephens, 2000). According to a recent national report, "Approximately 29 percent of college first-year students enrolled in remedial reading, writing, or math in 1995, about the same percentage that enrolled in 1989. Of those students in remedial classes, 46 percent were 22 years of age or older, and 25 percent over the age of 30" (Chronicle of Higher Education, 1998, p. A72).

Affordability

Before 1955, virtually all students paid for their education with their own or their parents' resources or with limited academic scholarships. Today, only about 30 percent of undergraduates between the ages of eighteen and twenty-two are pursuing an exclusively parent- or student-financed education (Chronicle of Higher Education, 2003). For the past two decades, parents, policymakers, and the public have expressed concerns that skyrocketing tuition threatens to make college unaffordable for all but the wealthy.

According to the National Commission on the Cost of Higher Education (1998), college tuition has increased annually at two to three times the rate of inflation since the early 1980s. Between 1981 and 1995, tuition at four–year public colleges and universities increased 234 percent, while during the same period the median household income rose 82 percent and the consumer price index rose only 74 percent. More recently, according to the College Board's annual survey of tuition and financial aid, tuition at public four-year colleges jumped at the highest rate in three decades. At those institutions, tuition in 2003 was 14 percent higher than in 2002. Tuition at public two-year institutions rose by almost 14 percent as well (Potter, 2003).

Moreover, the problem is not restricted to public universities. In 1976, one Ivy League institution's tuition was $3,790. Two decades later, that tuition was $21,130, nearly a sixfold increase (Larson, 1997). In 2003, tuition at private four-year colleges rose 6.0 percent compared to 2002 (Potter, 2003). Furthermore, the average cost for room and board in 2002 increased 6 percent at public four-year colleges and 4.6 percent at private colleges, compared to 2001 (Hebel, 2002).

As costs have risen, so have the strategies that students and families use for dealing with them. Different methods of paying for higher education include government-sponsored incentives (education IRAs) to encourage families to start saving early for college, institution-based programs (such as prepaid tuition plans which lock in tuition rates at current levels), and federal and state loan programs and other financial aid. According to the College Board, in 1996–1997, $55.7 billion was spent on student aid, of which approximately 54 percent was in federal loans, 19 percent institutional grants, and 15 percent federal or state grants (Cabrera, 1998). Students must cobble together a financial aid package that is complex, difficult to assess, and more dependent on loans and work than ever before to stay enrolled (King, 1998).

Alcohol and Other Drug Use

Drinking alcohol has been part of the college culture since colonial days. However, with the landmark 1993 Harvard study, alcohol consumption has become a national concern. Today's entering students' alcohol-related experiences prior to college may have a direct bearing on their collegiate experience. Entering students are not blank slates on the issue of alcohol when they enroll. In fact, half of students are already drinking before they enroll in college (Chronicle of Higher Education, 2003).

The effects of drinking have become so evident that college presidents rank alcohol abuse as the number one problem on campus (Wechsler, 1996). In an article in *USA Today* ("Drinking Is Biggest Campus Drug Problem," 1999), Graham Spanier, president of Pennsylvania State University, said that although students have been drinking on campuses for a long time, consumption has become even greater today. As a result, universities are devoting more time and energy to dealing with drinking problems. (For a more detailed discussion of student alcohol use and abuse, see Chapter Twenty-Six.)

CONCLUSION

The evidence presented in this chapter suggests that today's entering students are diverse by demographics and characteristics, belying the stereotyped notions of the past. Although it is not entirely incorrect to say that "Joe [College] doesn't live here anymore" because some students still fit this profile, Joe has been joined by a myriad of other students whose lives more closely parallel the demographics and characteristics discussed in this chapter.

Yet national data, while helpful in understanding first-year students in general, are no substitute for an individual institutional profile of entering students. Too often, an institution will assume certain demographics and characteristics of first-year students that are at odds with its actual students. Therefore, it is incumbent on every institution to know who its students are based on information drawn from institutional databases and other sources. These data should be collected yearly so that changes and trends can be identified.

This information should be widely distributed each year to faculty, staff, and policymakers so that decisions, policies, and practices, both inside and outside the classroom, are based on the true demographics and characteristics of entering students. Much of the remainder of this book focuses on how institutions can create learning environments that take the diversity of today's first-year students into account.

CHAPTER TWO

The Keys to First-Year Student Persistence

Jennifer L. Crissman Ishler
M. Lee Upcraft

Ask almost anybody in higher education the question, "What are the keys to first-year student academic persistence?" and most will reply, "preparation, ability, and motivation." That is, if first-year students have the basic academic skills and abilities necessary to succeed and if they are willing to attend class and study hard, they will earn satisfactory grades and persist into the second year and eventually earn a degree. The corollary to this belief is that students who drop out were not adequately prepared, not smart enough, and did not work hard enough to earn the grades necessary to stay in college and graduate. Although it is certainly true that preparation, ability, and motivation are very important factors in first-year student persistence, they are substantially deficient in explaining all the reasons that first-year students persist or drop out.

The purpose of this chapter is to expand readers' conceptions about first-year student persistence, based on the substantial and abundant theory and research dedicated to this issue in the past thirty years. We will discuss some of the most cogent theories about student academic success and review what the research and literature conclude about the variables that influence student persistence.

FIRST-YEAR STUDENT PERSISTENCE

The Introduction to this book offers a comprehensive definition of student success, the first of which was "developing intellectual and academic competence." It then defines intellectual and academic competence in three ways: (1) successful completion of courses with an acceptable grade point average, (2) continued enrollment into the second year, and (3) development of the higher-order intellectual skills necessary to become an educated person, such as critical thinking, problem solving, and reflective judgment.

Although all the other dimensions of student success are important to educating the whole student, most colleges and universities verify directly only two parts of this definition. That is, if students earn the required number of academic credits with a minimally acceptable grade point average, they are awarded a degree. With the exception of gross violations of accepted institutional codes of conduct, most institutions, with the possible exception of those that are church related, restrict their judgments about students' degree worthiness to the academic criteria described above. Furthermore, although most institutions would claim credit for the development of higher-order intellectual skills, these skills are seldom verified independent of course grades. It is assumed that if their students made it through all the course and curricular requirements, they have these skills.

Thus, it becomes important to understand and act on what the research tells us about first-year student persistence into the sophomore year and to graduation. In the ideal world, we would review the research on both grades and persistence. However, because higher education focuses so heavily on persistence (rightly or wrongly) and because earning acceptable grades highly correlates with persistence, we will restrict our research review to persistence only. For readers interested in academic achievement, higher-order intellectual skills, and other definitions of student success, we recommend research reviews such as Pascarella and Terenzini's *How College Affects Students* (1991), Braxton's *Reworking the Student Departure Puzzle* (2000), and *How College Affects Students: A Third Decade of Research* (2005) by Pascarella and Terenzini.

Institutional Motivations for Focusing on First-Year Student Persistence

First-year student persistence has long been a topic of interest and concern in American colleges and universities. Most often, this concern has focused exclusively on retention of first-year students and their persistence to graduation at the institution in which they initially enrolled. For example, Winston and Sandor (1994) noted that ". . . with college enrollment declining and college populations changing, recruitment and retention have become key issues that affect the success of the institutions" (p. 5). According to Bean (1996), this institutional concern with retention is motivated by economical, ethical, and institutional reasons. The economic reason is most straightforward. There is a direct relationship between enrollment and income. When institutions lose students, financial resources decline. However, Bean (1986) also argues that it is unethical to admit students for the "benefit of the institution and not for the good of the student" (p. 47).

Trends in First-Year Student Persistence

The research on student persistence reveals that the largest proportion of institutional leaving occurs during the first year and prior to the second year. According to American College Testing (2002) persistence is very much influenced by institutional type. The 2001 freshman-to-sophomore persistence rate was 73.9 percent at four-year colleges and 54.1 percent at two-year colleges. Persistence rates increased with institutional selectivity. According to American College Testing (2000), which tracked annual data from 1983 through 1999, dropout rates ranged from 16.8 percent at private doctoral-level institutions to 47.7 percent at two-year public colleges, and 8.8 percent at highly selective colleges to 46 percent at open admissions institutions. Most educators would agree that these dropout rates are unacceptable (with the possible exception of highly selective institutions). Institutions cannot afford to admit students and hope that they sink or swim on their own. Many institutions have come to understand the need to both challenge and support the students they admit and make a commitment to help them succeed.

In fact, institutions have changed the ways in which they deal with first-year students. Gardner (1986) has stated numerous reasons that this change has occurred, including a decline of traditional-age students, increased competition for the pool of applicants, poor quality of high school graduates, federal mandates for recruiting and retaining certain types of students, the changing demographics of today's students, and sincere commitments to improve the quality of education that first-year students receive. Gardner also states that attention must be directed to students' needs as they adapt and adjust to their new environments. According to Wilkie and Kuckuck (1989), the first year of college requires a series of profound academic, social, and emotional adaptations. The inability to adapt to the new environment often causes students to withdraw from school during or after the first year or to perform at a lower academic level than expected (Tinto, 1982).

Furthermore, time to degree has increased. According to McCormick and Horn (1996), the typical pattern of entering directly from high school and earning a bachelor's degree four years later is no longer the experience of most undergraduates. Of those who earned degrees in 1993–1994, only 36 percent had completed college within four years of first enrolling. Another 28 percent finished in five years, for a 64 percent five-year graduation rate. These rates are very much influenced by the fact that 37 percent attended more than one institution and took breaks between institutions. When graduates stay at the institution at which they first enrolled, completion rates were 51 percent within four years and 80 percent within five years. Horn and Berktold (1998) found that other reasons for extended time-to-degree rates include students who study part time, including adult learners and others who attend two-year institutions. Students who enter less prepared for college work (as measured by the SAT or ACT scores) and struggle academically in college also take longer to graduate.

MODELS OF STUDENT PERSISTENCE

The reasons that students persist became a major area of inquiry for education scholars beginning in the 1980s. Of the many theories on this topic, we have chosen to focus on two that have become most recognized and used to explain student persistence: Astin's Input-Environment-Output model and Tinto's Theory of Student Departure. (Other viable models of student persistence include Bean & Metzner, 1985; Pascarella & Terenzini, 1991; Stage & Hossler, 2000; and Tierney, 1992. For a more recent critical analysis of retention theory and research, see Braxton, 2000.)

Astin's Input-Environment-Outcomes Model

One of the first attempts to explain student persistence was put forth by Alexander Astin, who created the Input-Environment-Outcome model to serve as a conceptual guide for studying college persistence. He started with the basic commonsense notion that student success is a function of who students were before they entered college and what happened to them after they enrolled. The purpose of his model is "to assess the impact of various environmental experiences by determining whether students grow or change differently under varying environmental conditions" (Astin, 1993, p. 7). Astin's model hypothesizes that students enter college with a preestablished set of characteristics (inputs) that influence their views about college. Astin (1991) identified 146 possible input (precollege) variables, including high school grades and admission test scores, race, ethnicity, age, gender, marital status, religious preference, income, parental level of education, and reasons for attending college. The consideration of input characteristics when assessing student retention helps to understand the influence of students' backgrounds and characteristics on their ability to persist.

Astin (1991) also identified 192 environmental variables that might influence student success, organized into eight classifications: institutional characteristics (such as type and size), students' peer group characteristics (such as socioeconomic status, academic preparation, values, and attitudes), faculty characteristics (such as methods of teaching and values), curriculum, financial aid (Pell grants, Stafford loans), major field of choice, place of residence (residence hall, living at home, apartment living, Greek housing), and student involvement (hours spent studying, number of classes, participation in extracurricular activities, and others).

The final component of Astin's model is outcomes. Outcomes are the effects of college and refer to the student's characteristics after exposure to the environment. He classified his eighty-two outcomes to include satisfaction with the collegiate environment, academic cognition, career development, academic achievement, and retention.

Tinto's Theory of Student Departure

While Astin's model was helpful in explaining the variables that influence student persistence, it was Tinto (1975), building on the work of Spady (1970), who delineated the nature of the interrelationships between and among these variables, ultimately resulting in direct, indirect, and total effects of each factor. Tinto was also the first to address the reasons for, magnitude of, and mediating aspects of persistence that Astin's model did not explore. If a first-year student has the ability to make the initial transition to college, then remaining in college entails the incorporation of the student into the intellectual and social communities of the institution. But Tinto also argues that the institution shares this responsibility for helping first-year students achieve academic and social integration. Although some departures are involuntary (for example, the institution may request that the student withdraw due to academic failure), most departures are initiated because the student perceives an insurmountable problem. Often this problem is the student's perception of not belonging to or not being involved with the institutional community. Tinto argues that both forms of integration, intellectual and social, are essential to student retention.

Consistent with Astin's notion of inputs, Tinto (1993) theorized that students enter a college or university with particular characteristics and skills that affect their initial commitment to their educational goals and their institution. This commitment is increased or decreased depending on the quality and quantity of academic and social experiences. If students experience positive and rewarding academic and social experiences, they will become integrated into the institution. Tinto states that greater integration leads to higher retention rates. Moreover, Pascarella and Terenzini (1991) state that "negative interactions and experiences tend to reduce integration, to distance the individual from the academic and social communities of the institution, promoting the individual's marginality and, ultimately, withdrawal" (p. 53). Tinto (1993) wrote, "The point of retention efforts is not merely that individuals be kept in college. Education, the social and intellectual development of individuals, rather than just their continued presence on campus should be the goal of retention efforts" (p. 145).

While these explanations of student persistence vary in many details, the basic notion is the same: if institutions are to challenge and support first-year students in their academic success, they must focus on both the characteristics and experiences of their students prior to college, as well as their experiences both inside and outside the classroom once they are enrolled and how these variables interrelate. That means more careful attention to who is admitted and to the creation of a collegiate environment that is conducive to student persistence once students are enrolled.

INTERPRETING THE PERSISTENCE RESEARCH: SOME IMPORTANT CAVEATS

The research reported in the remainder of this chapter must be interpreted in the light of the many limitations and contexts of the studies reviewed:

- Many are single-institution studies for which generalizability to other institutions may or may not be appropriate, and those studies will be noted.
- Only studies that controlled for input variables and other appropriate environmental variables will be presented unless otherwise noted.
- There is no such thing as a perfect study. All of the studies cited have limitations, and the reader is encouraged to refer to the original studies to evaluate these limitations.

- Because in many instances the research is not completely in agreement, when conclusions are reached about a particular variable, they will be based on a preponderance of evidence.
- In some instances, it was not possible to draw a conclusion because the research findings were mixed.
- This literature review was not intended to be comprehensive, but the studies cited are generally representative of the genre of studies under review.
- Every effort was made to find more recent studies to support our conclusions, particularly when changes over time were evident.
- Unless otherwise noted, the studies reviewed focus on the influence of particular variables on persistence to graduation.
- Just because a variable has been shown to be related to persistence does not mean that an individual student will necessarily be affected in the same way. For example, although living in residence halls generally is positively related to persistence, there may be students for whom living in residence halls could be a factor in their dropping out.
- It is certainly quite possible that there are variables that affect first-year student persistence that we have overlooked.
- First-year student persistence is very much institution specific; thus, not all strategies will work at every institution. Institutions must develop initiatives consistent with their mission, resources, students, faculty, leadership, and other characteristics.
- Most of the findings reported in this chapter are based on persistence studies of individual institutions, or aggregates of individual institutions. The findings reported, unless otherwise noted, do not reflect those students who start at one institution and may finish at another. In this sense, most studies tend to underestimate overall student persistence because they assess institutional persistence rates, not actual student persistence rates.
- Any effort to generalize about multiple studies is by nature an art rather than a science, and other research reviewers might reach different conclusions based on the same studies.

THE LITERATURE REVIEW ON PERSISTENCE

This literature review is organized around Astin's Input-Environment-Output model, starting with two categories of input variables: student backgrounds and characteristics and institutional characteristics and environments. We then review relevant in-class and out-of-class variables that affect student persistence, both student centered and institutional centered.

Student Input Variables

Yogi Berra was once asked what made for a successful baseball team. He purportedly said, "good players." In that same vein, we might ask what makes for a successful college or university. And the answer, in part, is, "good students." It is no accident that highly selective institutions have much higher persistence rates than other institutions, in part because they select students who are more likely to succeed than students attending other institutions. So the beginning point for looking at first-year student persistence is what the research and literature tell us about which precollege characteristics have been found to influence their success. They include prior academic achievement, socioeconomic status, gender, age, financial aid, race/ethnicity, parent and other family support, and student commitment to a degree. This information is important to first-year students to help them better understand what they must do to persist and to institutions as they consider how to help first-year students persist.

Prior Academic Achievement. There is substantial evidence that the most powerful predictor of persistence into the sophomore year is the first-year student's prior academic achievement, including high school grades (Stage & Hossler, 2000; Allen, 1999; Astin, 1993; Pascarella & Terenzini, 1991) and SAT scores (Astin, 1993; Pascarella & Terenzini, 1991). According to Astin (1993), "Hundreds of studies using various measurements and methodologies have yielded similar results: college grade point averages can be predicted with modest accuracy (multiple correlation around .55) from admissions information. The two most potent predictors are the student's high school grade point average and scores on college admissions tests" (p. 187).

The predictive validity of college admissions tests is less than for high school grades. In a review of this literature, Schwartz and Washington (1999) concluded that although these tests have become essential elements in college admissions, they add little to predictive equations beyond the use of high school grades or rank and do not predict success uniformly across gender and ethnic groups.

Socioeconomic Status. A second input variable that influences the retention puzzle is students' socioeconomic status. According to Astin (1993), those entering first-year students who are most likely to complete a bachelor's degree within four years are from high socioeconomic levels. Moreover, students from families with higher incomes tend to persist more than students from families with lower incomes (Cabrera, Stampen, & Hansen, 1990; St. John, 1989, 1990; St. John, Kirshstein, & Noell, 1991).

Gender. Women students make up more than half of today's college students (Chronicle of Higher Education, 2003) and tend to persist at higher rates than men. Christensen (1990) found that gender was strongly related to retention. Christensen's study identified a substantial difference based on gender, with 30 percent of the persisters being male and 70 percent being female. Astin (1993), Lewallen (1993), and York, Bollar, and Schoob (1993) also reported higher completion rates for women than men when other factors that affect persistence are taken into account. Astin, Tsui, and Avaolos (1996) found that women are more likely than men to attain the bachelor's degree, regardless of the time spent in college. This appears to be true at community colleges as well. In a study of nearly twenty-three thousand students at a three-campus community college over a three-year period, first-to-second-semester persistence was higher for women than for men (Rajasekhara & Hirsch, 2000).

Age. Over the past several decades, the average age of the typical college student has risen. However, little research is available connecting age to persistence. Although numbers of older students have increased, most of the retention research continues to focus on the traditional students ages eighteen to twenty-one years old. Tinto (1987) wrote, "The situation with older students is, in many respects, not unlike that of minority students. In the youthful world of most colleges, they can be equally marginal to the mainstream of institutional life. Older students are much more likely to have significant work or family responsibilities which constrain their involvement in the life of college" (p. 73). Furthermore, according to a literature review conducted by Peltier, Laden, and Matranga (1999), adult learners are more likely to enroll part time, have less skillful study habits, have been out of school for several years, are more likely to have dependent children to care for, live at home, and have more commitments outside college, all factors that contribute to lower persistence rates. But many adult learners tend to have more focused career goals and a stronger motivation to complete their degrees.

Race/Ethnicity. Perhaps no other persistence studies have been more prolific than those researching the relationship between the race/ethnicity of students and their persistence. Such studies are very complicated because variables other than race/ethnicity, such as socioeconomic status, lack of academic preparation, and campus climates that are hostile to minorities, often confound isolating race/ethnicity as a factor in persistence. Furthermore, there are differences within and among various ethnic minorities, which were largely ignored in the early research on minority student persistence, and there is virtually no research on mixed race minorities. Research on minority student persistence is complicated by the assertion of some researchers (Tierney, 1992) that traditional models of student persistence do not necessarily apply to nonwhite students.

Nonetheless, in general, persistence rates of racial/ethnic minorities, with the exception of Asians, are lower than those of majority students, even when these other variables are taken into account. For example, in a review of the relevant literature, Stage and Hossler (2000) concluded that minority students, particularly at predominantly white institutions, are less likely to persist, have differing experiences, and demonstrate more behaviors leading to attrition than their white peers.

Parents and Other Family. Parents appear to be another factor in student persistence, beginning even before their children enroll. For example, Lang and Nora (2001) found that precollege parental encouragement was positively related to persistence. Once students enrolled, parents continue to have a positive influence. For example, in reviewing relevant literature, Stage and Hossler (2000) concluded that parents' higher educational levels and incomes are strongly related to involvement in college and indirectly to persistence. Bean and Vesper (1992) found that parental support and encouragement was a strong predictor of persistence at a small liberal arts college that enrolled high numbers of first-generation students. Although parents may not be a factor for adult learners, family support from significant others such as spouses and children is a critical factor in their persistence.

Student Commitment to a Degree. There is some evidence to support the commonsense notion that a first-year student who is committed to graduating will do so. First-year students who begin college with a commitment to completing a degree are more likely to persist than those with wavering or uncertain commitments. For example, in a study of persistence of students at two-year colleges, Cofer and Summers (2000) found that students who aspired to a college degree were more likely to persist than those not aspiring to any degree. Bell et al. (1999) found that commitment to remain in college predicted retention for first-year, full-time residential students.

Institutional Variables

Ample evidence supports the notion that the institution a first-year student chooses becomes an important factor in his or her persistence because some institutions are more conducive to persistence than others. These institutional variables include selectivity, type (two or four year), size, control (public or private), gender composition, and racial composition. However, Pascarella and Terenzini (2005) note that in general, these persistence variables are less influential than students' experiences once they enroll.

Selectivity. Selectivity appears to be a factor in persistence. Pascarella and Terenzini (1991, 2005) reviewed the literature on institutional selectivity and concluded that institutional selectivity tends to enhance persistence even after variations in the background characteristics (including academic abilities) of students enrolled at different institutions are taken into account.

Institutional Type: Two Year and Four Year. Institutional types (two year or four year) have different persistence rates. Pascarella and Terenzini (1991) reviewed this research and concluded that there was consistent evidence that initial attendance at a two-year rather than a four-year institution lowers the likelihood of a student's attaining a bachelor's degree by fifteen to twenty percentage points. A more recent analysis by Berkner, Cuccaro-Alamin, and McCormick (1996) revealed that the retention rate of students who started at four-year institutions was 56 percent after five years, with 44 percent dropping out entirely and others transferring. For students starting at two-year institutions, the picture is quite different. Of those students seeking a bachelor's degree who enrolled at two-year colleges, only 39 percent transferred to a four-year institution, and only about 8 percent had earned a bachelor's degree within five years.

Moreover, according to Tinto (1993), only a third of all beginning full-time students at community colleges earn associate degrees or certificates. However, according to Pascarella and Terenzini (2005), when students attending a two-year institution transfer to a four-year institution, their chances of earning a bachelor's degree are about the same as those who began at a four-year institution.

Size. According to Pascarella and Terenzini's review of the literature (1991) on the impact of institutional size on retention, the evidence is inconsistent and contradictory. One of the problems in this research is the definition of size. For example definitions of "small" institutions range from those with one thousand students or fewer (Bradford & Farris, 1991) to those with one thousand to five thousand (Kamens, 1971). Thus, the size of institutions may or may not have an impact on persistence, but these institutions may differ on other outcomes, such as social involvement and interpersonal participation (Pascarella & Terenzini, 1991).

Control: Public and Private. After reviewing the literature on institutional control and persistence, Pascarella and Terenzini (1991) concluded that although the evidence is not totally consistent, it does suggest that attending a private rather than a public institution has a positive influence on persistence and appears to be independent of the selectivity of the college attended and other relevant variables. For example, Astin and Oseguera (2002) found that the four-year graduation rates for private institutions were 67.1 percent for private universities, 56.3 percent for nonsectarian colleges, 46.4 percent for Roman Catholic colleges, and 51 percent for other Christian colleges. The four-year graduation rates for public institutions were 28.1 percent for public universities and 24.3 percent for public colleges. It should be noted, however, that the effects of institutional control are confounded by institutional size.

Gender Composition. According to Pascarella and Terenzini's review of the literature (1991) on gender composition and persistence, evidence suggests that attending a single-sex institution is associated with higher levels of persistence, particularly for women. They did, however, point out that the net positive effect is small—slightly less than 1 percent of the variance in persistence.

Racial Composition. According to a review of the literature on racial composition and persistence by Stage and Hossler (2000), persistence rates of minority students at predominantly white institutions are less than those of their white counterparts. For example, Pascarella and Terenzini (1991) concluded after a review of the relevant literature that black students were significantly less likely to drop out if they were enrolled in a predominantly black institution. Research on persistence at institutions that are dominated by other racial and ethnic groups is virtually nonexistent.

There is one caveat to these institutional input variables: although such evidence may be useful to prospective students and their families, it is very unlikely that institutions can substantially change such things as their size and control. However, over some period of time, institutions may be able to affect selectivity, gender composition, racial composition, and other institutional input variables related to student persistence.

Environmental Variables

Many in-class and out-of-class variables influence first-year student persistence. They include first-year grade point average (GPA), major, enrollment status (full or part time), quality of student effort, interactions with faculty, interactions with students, participation in extracurricular activities, work, student satisfaction, alcohol abuse, Greek affiliation, campus climates, financial aid, and participation in intercollegiate athletics.

First-Year Grade Point Average. There is considerable evidence to support the old bromide that nothing succeeds like success. In fact, one of the best predictors of first-year student persistence is the grades students earn during the first year. In their review of relevant research, Pascarella and Terenzini (1991) concluded that undergraduate grades are perhaps the best predictor of obtaining a bachelor's degree. Xiao (1999) found that second-semester academic success was the strongest predictor of retention into the third, fourth, and fifth semesters, as well as persistence to graduation. Belcheir (1997) found that first-semester college GPA "is the most important predictor for retention" (p. 7). In contrast, when Ishitani and DesJardins (2002–2003) reviewed several studies on this issue, they reached the somewhat puzzling conclusion that college grades were negatively related to attrition but positively related to persistence to graduation.

Academic Major Field. The conventional wisdom is that students majoring in the hard or technical sciences are more likely to drop out, but Thomas and Gordon (1983) found the opposite was true, and Pascarella and Terenzini (2005) found that students majoring in the sciences, engineering, business, and health-related professions were more likely to graduate than similar students in other majors.

Enrollment Status: Full Time and Part Time. In general, full-time first-year students are more likely to persist than part-time students. For example, in a study of twenty-three thousand community college students, Rajasekhara and Hirsch (2000) found that the fall-to-spring retention rate was 75 percent for full-time students and 55 percent for part-time students. Somers (1995), in her study of twenty-one hundred university students, also found that full-time students had a first-to-second-semester persistence rate that was higher than part-time students.

Quality of Student Effort. A commonly accepted axiom of first-year student persistence is that the more students invest in their learning, the greater is their likelihood of staying in college. There is some evidence to support this notion.

For example, Tinto (1987) found that hours studied per week were positively associated with persistence. There is also substantial evidence that the quality of student effort affects the extent of student learning (Pace, 1984; Ory & Braskamp, 1988; Kaufman & Creamer, 1991) and thus may have an indirect as well as direct effect on persistence. (In Chapter Five of this book, Kuh presents powerful evidence that quality of first-year student effort is positively related to persistence.)

Interactions with Faculty. In their review of the research on the relationship of faculty-student interactions to student persistence, Pascarella and Terenzini (1991) concluded that "freshman to sophomore persistence was positively and significantly related to total amount of student-faculty nonclassroom contact with faculty and particularly to frequency of interactions with faculty to discuss intellectual matters" (p. 394). More specifically, Lundquist, Spalding, and Landrum (2002–2003) found that specific faculty behaviors contributed to student persistence: faculty members being supportive of student needs, being approachable, and returning telephone calls and e-mails in a timely fashion.

Interpersonal Interactions. One other area that affects first-year students' persistence is their interactions with others, including peers and family. According to Astin (1993), "The student's peer group is the single most potent source of influence on growth and development during the undergraduate years" (p. 398). Peer relations are critical for support, confirmation of one's identity, opportunities for socialization, and persistence (Astin, 1993; Hirsch, 1980). Pascarella and Terenzini (1991) reviewed the relevant evidence on students' interactions with peers and concluded that both the frequency and quality of students' interactions with peers were positively associated with persistence.

Not surprisingly, first-year college students find interpersonal relationships among their highest areas of concern (Paul & White, 1990). Interpersonal relationships between peers not only provide emotional and social support, but also influence one's identity and sense of self (Paul & Brier, 2001). "Much of the college success and retention literature has identified attaching to a significant other or peer group in the university as the factor most predictive of success and coping" (Paul et al., 1998, p. 76). Those who seek social support have shown better adjustment to stressors (Paul & Kelleher, 1995), and the more new friends a student has in his or her social network, the smoother is that person's adjustment to college (Paul & Brier, 2001).

If students do not develop a network of friends at college, they could suffer from "friendsickness," which Paul and Brier (2001) have defined as "the pressing relational challenge for new college students that is induced by moving away from an established network of friends" (p. 77). Friend-sick college students may have an "insecurity both in their ability to have close friends to share with and in their ability to make close, trustworthy friends" (Paul & Brier, 2001, p. 79). If students do not feel connected to a new peer group, their chances of departing from the institution are increased (Paul & Kelleher, 1995). While there have been some studies conducted on "friendsickness" (Paul & Brier, 2001; Paul & Kelleher, 1995; Crissman Ishler & Schreiber, 2002), more research is needed.

In addition to other students, there are other sources of interpersonal support that are important to student persistence. In a comprehensive review of the persistence literature, Nora (2001–2002) concluded that the impact of support and encouragement from significant others is of primary importance to both adjustment of students to their social and academic environments and to persistence as well. Furthermore, the effects of this support and encouragement from significant others are consistent across minority and nonminority populations.

Participation in Extracurricular Activities. Contrary to some conventional wisdom that participation in extracurricular activities is detrimental to first-year student persistence, there is some evidence to support the notion that students' participation in extracurricular activities is positively associated with persistence (Pascarella and Terenzini, 1991).

Work. Many first-year students must work while enrolled in order to pay for their education. According to data from the U.S. Census Bureau (2001), 64 percent of two-year-college first-year students and 38 percent of four-year-college first-year students were employed in the year 2000. Furthermore, by enrollment status, 43 percent of full-time students and 78 percent of part-time students were employed. Thus, the impact of work on persistence is an important issue. Pascarella and Terenzini (1991) reviewed the relevant literature on the relationship of work to persistence and concluded that a part-time job on campus has a net positive impact on year-to-year persistence to bachelor's degree completion and timely graduation. They also concluded that persistence is inhibited by full-time and part-time employment off-campus.

Ishitani and DesJardins (2002–2003) reviewed research on the relationship between hours of employment and dropout behavior and found the persisters tended to engage in part-time employment instead of full-time employment and dropouts tended to work longer hours than persisters. Cuccaro-Alamin and Choy (1998) found that working more than fifteen hours per week reduced the likelihood of persisting, while working one to fifteen hours per week increased the likelihood of persisting. Wilkie and Jones (1994) found that working part-time on campus for an average of eight hours per week throughout the first-year was associated with significantly higher retention rates for traditional-age developmental students than either a lower frequency of employment or no on-campus employment.

Student Satisfaction. Often the notion of student satisfaction is underrated as an outcome of college. There are some who would argue that it does not matter whether first-year students are "satisfied" with their collegiate experience. What really matters is their achievement, what they learned, and if they graduated. However, the research shows that first-year students who are satisfied with their collegiate experience are more likely to persist than those who are dissatisfied (Sanders & Burton, 1996). Thus, institutions that are committed to first-year student persistence must attend to first-year student satisfaction.

Alcohol Abuse. Given the extent to which alcohol is a substantial and detrimental aspect of the first-year experience (see Chapter Twenty-Six), the relationship of alcohol and persistence must be considered. There is substantial evidence that alcohol abuse has a negative impact on nonconsensual sexual experience (Himelein, Vogel, & Washowiak, 1994), dysfunctional interpersonal relationships (Knox, 1997), and campus violence (Barrett & Simmons, 1998). The evidence is also convincing that the consumption of alcohol is negatively related to GPA (Presley, Meilman, & Lyerla, 1993, 1995; Presley, Meilman, & Cashin, 1996). However, there is little evidence that first-year students who abuse alcohol are less likely to persist than those who do not, except for the possible indirect effect: alcohol abuse negatively affects grades, and good grades positively affect persistence. (For a more detailed discussion of the impact of alcohol on the first-year student experience, see Chapter Twenty-Six.)

Participation in Greek Life. Does participation in a fraternity or sorority during the first year of college affect persistence? Astin (1975) found that living in a sorority or fraternity during the first or second year had a statistically significant positive influence on degree completion or continued persistence in college. In a more recent review of the literature on persistence and Greek life, Moore, Lovell, McGann, and Wyrick (1998) concluded that persistence to degree was positively associated with membership in Greek organizations. Tripp (1997) reviewed the relevant literature on this issue and also concluded that Greek membership was associated with higher retention rates than non-Greeks. There may be negative outcomes associated with Greek membership (such as alcohol abuse, lower moral reasoning ability, and lower academic performance), but persistence is not one of them (Peltier, Laden, & Matranga, 1999).

Campus Climates. First-year students' perceptions of campus climate can have an effect on their persistence. For example, perceptions of prejudice and discrimination can account for differences in persistence rates between minorities and nonminorities (Cabrera et al., 1999; Hurtado, Carter, & Spuler, 1996; Smedley, Myers, & Harrell, 1993). First-year perceptions of the climate for women, sexual minorities, students with disabilities, adult learners, and others may also have an impact on persistence, but there is little evidence to support this assumption.

Financial Aid. In a review of research on the relationship between financial aid and persistence, St. John, Cabrera, Nora, and Asker (2000) concluded that finance-related factors (student aid, tuition, and other costs, including living) explained about half of the variance in the persistence process. Furthermore, the type of student aid mattered: students who received a financial aid package made up of grants or with a higher ratio of grants to loans displayed a higher level of persistence (St. John, 1989, 1990; Somers, 1996). There were some single-institution studies, however, that found no relationship between student aid and persistence (Braunstein, McGrath, & Pescatrice, 2000–2001; Somers, 1995).

Participation in Intercollegiate Athletics. Some people believe that students who participate in intercollegiate athletics are more likely to drop out than other students. Contrary to this conventional wisdom, Pascarella and Terenzini (2005) found that such participation had a positive and significant effect on persistence to graduation. This conclusion was true not only for revenue-producing sports such as men's football and baseball, but for all other sports as well, even when controlling for other potentially confounding factors.

Intentional Institutional Interventions. There is substantial evidence that when first-year students participate in the services and programs designed to enhance their success, they are more likely to persist (Kulik, Kulik, & Schwab, 1983). These activities include the classroom, first-year seminars, orientation, residence halls, learning communities, academic advising, service-learning, Supplemental Instruction, developmental education, other support services, and selected combinations of these.

The Classroom. For many first-year students, especially nonresidential students such as commuters and adult learners, the classroom is virtually the only focus of their educational experience. There is some evidence that first-year students' classroom experiences are related to their persistence. For example, Tinto (1987) found that first-year students who were enrolled together in several courses that were tied together by a unifying theme and taught using cooperative learning activities had higher persistence rates than those enrolled in traditional courses. However, most of the research on the classroom focuses on relationships of selected classroom techniques and behaviors to student learning, which may have an indirect relationship to persistence. It is well beyond the scope of this review to cite all of these factors, but they include small classes (Light, 2001), problem-based learning (Polanco, Calderon, & Delgado, 2001), cooperative learning (Johnson, Johnson, & Smith, 1998), study groups (Light, 2001), focused writing assignments (Erickson & Strommer, 1991), and student study groups (Cooper & Mueck, 1990).

First-Year Seminars. One of the most widely researched environmental influences on first-year student persistence is the first-year seminar, which has been in existence for over a hundred years in American higher education. While seminars may vary in structure, content, grading, and credits, they are designed to foster better understanding of the institution, enhance academic interest and integration, and provide opportunities for social integration.

The first-year seminar is one of the most powerful predictors of first-year student persistence into the sophomore year. In general, first-year students who take these first-year seminars are more likely to persist into the third semester than those who do not, even when controlling for other precollege and during-college variables that may influence that outcome (Murtaugh, Burns, & Schuster, 1999; Anselmo, 1997; Barefoot et al., 1999; Ellis & Gardner, 1997; Fidler & Moore, 1996; Hyers & Joslin, 1998, Williford, Cross Chapman, & Kahrig, 2000–2001).

Furthermore, there is some evidence that the grade earned in a first-year seminar is a predictor of first-year student persistence. For example, Raymond and Napoli (1998) found that community college students who completed a first-year seminar with a grade of C or better had higher persistence rates and graduation rates than students who received lower than a C in the course. (For a more extensive discussion of first-year seminars, see Chapter Sixteen.)

Orientation. Virtually every college and university has some kind of orientation program designed to help first-year students make a successful transition to college. There is some limited evidence that these programs are related to persistence. For example, in a review of relevant research, Rode (2000) found an indirect positive effect between orientation and student persistence. Forrest (1985) found that a group of nine institutions with the most comprehensive set of orientation and advising programs for first-year students had a graduation rate 9 percent higher than that of a group of nine institutions with the least comprehensive programs. Pascarella and Terenzini (1991), in a review of relevant literature, concluded that the weight of evidence suggested a statistically significant positive link between exposure to various orientation experiences and persistence, from freshman to sophomore year and through attainment of a bachelor's degree. (For a more extensive discussion of orientation, see Chapter Twenty-Three.)

Living Environments. There is evidence that first-year students who live in residence halls are more likely to persist into the sophomore year than students who live elsewhere. Two landmark studies in the 1970s demonstrated this powerful influence. Astin (1977) conducted a highly controlled study involving more than 225,000 students from 1961 to 1974. He concluded that the most important environmental characteristic associated with finishing college was living in a residence hall during the first year. In fact, residence hall living added 12 percent to a first-year student's chance of finishing college. In a study of nearly 170,000 students, Chickering (1974) reached many of those same conclusions. Since those landmark studies, many other studies have demonstrated the same results (Fidler & Moore, 1996; Herndon, 1984; Kanoy & Bruhn, 1996; Pascarella, 1993; Thompson, 1993; Astin, 1993). (For a more detailed discussion of residence halls, see Chapter Twenty-Four.)

Learning Communities. Learning communities, also known as clusters, linked courses, and freshman interest groups, are another factor that can help improve first-year student persistence rates (Crissman, 2001; Shapiro & Levine, 1999; Tinto & Goodsell Love, 1995; Schroeder, 1994; Tinto & Goodsell, 1993; Gabelnick, MacGregor, Matthews, & Smith, 1990). Learning communities can range from simply scheduling groups of students so that they share two or more courses, to arranging special seminars, study skills workshops, and social events for blocks of students, to housing them together in residences. Tinto and Goodsell Love (1995) note that clustering "groups of students, taking two or more classes together, will provide both social and academic support for each other and in doing so, enhance the classroom experience for all" (p. 15). Tinto and Goodsell (1993) found that cluster benefits for students include retention, decreased withdrawals, better grades, and more positive perceptions about college.

Early attempts at clustering have been effective at improving the retention of students. Gabelnick et al. (1990) found that nationwide for students in clusters, "beginning to end-of-quarter retention rates averaged ten to twenty percentage points higher than typical institution averages" (p. 63). Tinto and Goodsell Love's study (1995) found nearly a 90 percent end-of-quarter retention rate for first-year students in learning communities. And Belcheir (1997) reported that clustered students were more likely to reenroll the following spring semester and again the following fall semester compared to the control group. (For a more extensive discussion of learning communities, see Chapter Twenty-Two.)

Academic Advising. Academic advising is another important environmental component of first-year student persistence, although the evidence of this influence is somewhat mixed. Beal and Noel's research (1980) found that first-year students who use academic advising services persist at higher rates than students who do not use the services. Thomas (1990) also found that the quality of academic advising is a primary retention factor. But in their review of relevant literature on the impact of academic advising on persistence, Pascarella and Terenzini (1991) concluded that the research results have been mixed; they cited a study by Metzner (1989) that showed "that the quality of advising received had only a small and statistically nonsignificant direct effect on persistence. High-quality advising, however, did have a statistically significant positive effect on persistence transmitted through its positive impact on such variables as grades and satisfaction and its negative effect on intent to leave the institution" (pp. 404–405). (For a more extensive discussion of academic advising, see Chapter Nineteen.)

Service-Learning. There is substantial evidence that students who participate in service-learning achieve many desirable outcomes, such as current or expected involvement in civic affairs and improved life skills (Gray, Ondaatje, Fricher, & Geschwind, 2000), enhanced perspectives on service and responsibility to the community (Malone, Jones, & Stallings, 2001), increased performance in selected courses (Strage, 2000), and increased levels of civic responsibility and critical thinking skills (Checkoway, 1997). However, there appears to be little evidence to date that participation in service-learning has a direct impact on persistence. (For a more detailed discussion of service learning, see Chapter Twenty-One.)

Supplemental Instruction. Supplemental Instruction (SI) is a peer-assisted academic support program implemented to reduce high rates of attrition, increase the level of student performance in difficult courses, and increase graduation rates. Many studies have shown the positive influence of Supplemental Instruction on retention (Hills, Gay, & Topping, 1998; Ramirez, 1997; Collins, 1982). Ten percent more students who attend SI sessions persist until graduation when compared to nonparticipants with similar incoming characteristics (Arendale & Martin, 1997; Center for Supplemental Instruction, 1998). According to Congos (2002), "SI is proactive in that students begin attending during the first week of classes and problems in content understanding can be identified early and addressed in SI sessions" (p. 308). (For a more detailed discussion of Supplemental Instruction, see Chapter Eighteen.)

Developmental Education. Developmental education programs that are designed to help first-year students succeed academically appear to have a mixed impact on persistence. For example, in a study of twenty-one public community colleges, Schoenecker, Bollman, and Evens (1998) found that students who completed developmental courses significantly outperformed the course nontakers in persistence rates. But Grunder and Hellmich (1996) found no relationship between persistence and participation in a developmental education program. (For a more detailed discussion of developmental education, see Chapter Seventeen.)

Other Student Support Services. Some evidence suggests that use of selected student support services is related to student persistence. These include counseling services (Wilson, Mason, & Ewing, 1997) and campus recreation programs (Belch, Gebel, & Maas, 2001). (For a more detailed discussion of other student support services, see Chapter Twenty-Five.)

Intervention Combinations. It is not unusual for institutions to combine some intentional interventions in ways that positively affect persistence. Such integrated interventions include learning communities and block scheduling (Soldner, Lee, & Duby, 1999); academic advising, first-year seminar, student mentoring, academic skills, and social support activities (Colton, Connor, Schultz, & Easter, 1999); block registration and mentoring (Mangold, Bean, Adams, Schwab, & Lynch, 2002–2003); first-year seminar, developmental education, and academic advising (Johnson, 2000–2001); first-year seminars and campus residence (Fidler & Moore, 1996); Supplemental Instruction (Yockey & George, 1998); and many others.

PRINCIPLES OF RETENTION

This review of the evidence of student persistence can be very useful, but an overall look at how an institution should approach effective persistence is also important. Tinto (1993) developed principles of effective retention that guide institutional practices to reduce student rates of departure:

- *First Principle: Effective retention programs are committed to the students they serve.* Tinto believes that this very commitment is "at the core of an institution's educational mission" (p. 146) and that it should permeate the character of institutional life. He further believes that the commitment is the responsibility of all members of the institution. Tinto believes that by caring for the students' welfare, the students in turn will care about the institution. He writes, "Commitment to students then generates a commitment on the part of students to the institution" (p. 146).
- *Second Principle: Effective retention programs are first and foremost committed to the education of all, not just some, of their students.* Tinto believes that "effective retention programs do not leave learning to chance" (p. 147). He further argues that it becomes the responsibility of institutions to ensure that new students either enter with or have the opportunity to possess sufficient knowledge and skills to meet the academic demands of the institution.
- *Third Principle: Effective retention programs are committed to the development of supportive social and educational communities in which all students are integrated as competent members.* Tinto encourages institutions to involve students "in the daily life of the institution" and to "provide social and intellectual support for their individual efforts" (p. 147). For his third principle, Tinto emphasizes "frequent and rewarding contract between faculty, staff and students in a variety of settings both inside and outside the formal confines of the classroom" (p. 148).

CONCLUSION

If institutions are to develop an educational environment for first-year student success, they must understand that preparation, ability, and motivation are only part of the persistence puzzle. In this chapter, we have presented a selected review of the theories that seek to explain student persistence and the abundant research that helps us understand that persistence is a result of many interrelated factors. We have also reviewed some of the evidence of the effectiveness of selected institutional interventions that enhance persistence.

However, the conclusions reached in this chapter should not suggest that persistence alone should be the goal of an institution for its first-year students. Lee Noel, one of the early pioneers in bringing persistence to the national awareness, was the first to caution that retention should never be the goal of an institution:

Reenrollment or retention is not then the goal; retention is the result or byproduct of improved programs and services in our classrooms and elsewhere on campus that contribute to student success. If retention alone becomes the goal, institutions will find themselves engaged in trying to hold students at all costs. Pressuring students to stay when it is not in their best interests to do so is not only wrong morally but also counterproductive: it often results in an accelerated attrition rate [Noel, 1985, p. 1].

Instead, Noel argued, "The more students learn, the more they sense they are finding and developing a talent, the more likely they are to persist; and when we get student success, satisfaction, and learning together, persistence is the outcome" (p. 1). The keys to persistence, then, are efforts on the part of institutions to promote the highest-quality education they can. As Noel argues, student persistence will follow.

CHAPTER THREE

Current Institutional Practices in the First College Year

Betsy O. Barefoot

Since Jossey-Bass published *The Freshman Year Experience* (Upcraft, Gardner, and Associates, 1989), American higher education has witnessed, and many of us have participated in, a dramatic increase in intentional institutional initiatives designed to improve the first year of college. This heightened focus on the first year was tracked by two surveys conducted by the American Council on Education (ACE). In 1987, ACE's survey, entitled Campus Trends, found that only 37 percent of American colleges and universities were "taking steps to improve the first year." When the same survey was repeated in 1995, that percentage had swelled to 82 percent and would likely be even higher today (El Khawas, 1987, 1995). But neither the magnitude nor number of these steps to improve the first year is the same for all institutions. Some institutions "improve the first year" by patching on a single course or intervention that at best serves as an antidote to the rest of the experience. Other colleges and universities attempt far more systemic changes that span various points of interface between students and institution.

While the first college year has become part of the national higher education conversation, many questions remain: How is the first year organized and structured in American higher education, and what kinds of policies and practices comprise the curriculum and cocurriculum? How is the first year different in institutions of varying type, size, and mission? Is there evidence that the first year is being designed in ways that are consistent with existing principles of good practice that promote learning and retention? In order to provide answers to these questions, the Policy Center on the First Year of College in the fall of 2000 undertook the first-ever comprehensive national survey of the first year.

This research project was one of several projects of the Policy Center and was supported by a grant from The Pew Charitable Trusts.

This chapter reviews selected results of that national survey and provides observations about the findings as well as implications and recommendations derived from this research. (To see the complete survey report, go to http://www.brevard.edu/fyc and click on "National Survey Findings.")

OVERVIEW OF SURVEYS

The first-year curricular and cocurricular surveys were designed to investigate the way institutions intentionally (or unintentionally) structure and organize the first year. Although some of the initiatives that respondents identified may in fact be exemplary, it is important to note that the surveys did not attempt to validate "best practice" programs, structures, or policies. The surveys found evidence of similarity in some current first-year initiatives but also many differences within and between institutional sectors. Some of the obvious differences relate to two- or four-year status, size, location, and whether students live in campus residence halls. But others are more closely related to mission, how the institution views its primary role in American higher education, and therefore how resources are allocated among competing priorities. Some of the findings supported commonly held views or anecdotal evidence about first-year curricular and cocurricular programs, structures, and policies. But others were in stark contrast to common wisdom or the way the first year is often represented in the media.

Although I, along with other Policy Center staff, analyzed survey data in aggregate, by two-year and four-year status, and by size, we found that the factor that tends to differentiate findings most dramatically was Carnegie classification. This classification system, developed by the Carnegie Foundation for the Improvement of Teaching and revised most recently in 2000, is the leading typology of American colleges and universities and provides a framework by which institutional differences in U.S. higher education are commonly described. Therefore, this chapter references primarily Carnegie-type comparisons, as well as some aggregate findings and differences for which institutional size is the key variable.

In spite of the wealth of information that can be gleaned from survey findings, this research has a number of limitations. The accuracy of responses to each survey instrument relies on the knowledge and perception of a single individual on campus: either the chief academic or chief student affairs officer (or surrogates). It is possible that senior administrators do not always have a completely accurate picture of how the first year is being organized and delivered in the trenches, especially on large campuses. Because this is the first national survey initiative of its kind, findings do not identify change from a previous practice or trends over time. Although the surveys review current practices, they do not evaluate best practices. And finally, although findings may serve as a catalyst on some campuses for rethinking the first college year, the survey instruments themselves were not designed to diagnose problems or prescribe ultimate solutions. Rather, findings represent a description of the first year as it exists in American higher education at the beginning of the twenty-first century that offers institutions a way to compare their own approach to the first year, for better or worse, with that of peer institutions.

SURVEY DESIGN, SAMPLES, AND PROCEDURES

The National Survey of First-Year Practices was actually composed of two separate Web-based survey instruments: a survey of first-year curricular practices and a survey of first-year cocurricular practices. Following pilot testing of both instruments, a random sample of 621 institutions, stratified by Carnegie classification, was selected, and names of both chief academic and chief student affairs officers were identified. E-mail messages with an embedded link to the relevant survey instrument were sent to each of these individuals. The e-mail message and link to the first-year curricular survey were successfully received by 586 chief academic officers. Responses were received from 323 chief academic officers or their surrogates for an overall response rate of 54 percent. Precise response rates by Carnegie classification are provided in Table 3.1.

The number of successful transmissions to chief student affairs officers was slightly smaller: 568 received the message with the link to the first-year cocurricular survey, and 291 chief student affairs officers or surrogates responded for a response rate of 51 percent. Precise response rates by Carnegie classification are provided in Table 3.2.

Research findings reference Carnegie institutional types as developed by the Carnegie Foundation for the Improvement of Teaching. For readers who are not familiar with changes in the 2000 version of this system, a word of explanation may be helpful. The 2000 version is a significant revision of the earlier system, which designated postsecondary institutions as Associates, Liberal Arts I and II, Comprehensive I and II, Doctoral I and II, and Research I and II (with additional

Table 3.1. National Survey of First-Year Curricular Practices: Responses by Carnegie Classification

Carnegie Classification	Survey Population (n = 586)	Response Population (n = 323)
Associate	237 (40.4%)	120 (37.1%)
Baccalaureate–General	73 (12.4%)	38 (11.7%)
Baccalaureate–Liberal Arts	55 (9.3%)	34 (10.5%)
Master's I and II	154 (26.2%)	90 (27.9%)
Research Intensive	28 (4.6%)	15 (4.6%)
Research Extensive	39 (6.4%)	22 (6.8%)
Unknown	4 (1.0%)	

Table 3.2. National Survey of First-Year Cocurricular Practices: Responses by Carnegie Classification

Carnegie Classification	Survey Population (n = 568)	Response Population (n = 291)
Associate	235 (41.3%)	106 (36.4%)
Baccalaureate–General	70 (12.1%)	34 (11.6%)
Baccalaureate–Liberal Arts	54 (9.4%)	30 (10.3%)
Master's I and II	145 (25.4%)	76 (26.1%)
Research Intensive	26 (4.5%)	13 (4.4%)
Research Extensive	38 (6.6%)	26 (8.9%)
Unknown	6 (2.0%)	

special institutional categories). In 2000, these nine primary categories were consolidated into seven: Associates, Baccalaureate-Liberal Arts (BC-LA) and Baccalaureate-General (BC-GEN), Master's I and II, Research Extensive, and Research Intensive. With reference to the research university category, Research Extensive institutions are universities awarding fifty or more doctorates per year and Research Intensive institutions at least twenty doctorates annually. Master's institutions include many campuses that continue to have a mission grounded primarily in the liberal arts. Therefore, although the new "condensed" system is less cumbersome than the previous one, it creates far more variance within each institutional category. (For a more complete explanation of the new Carnegie classification system and a listing of institutions by category, go to http://www.carnegiefoundation.org/classification/index.htm.)

SURVEY FINDINGS

In this synopsis of findings, I include results for selected questions from both the first-year curricular and cocurricular surveys to provide a more or less chronological view of the first year—what new students encounter from the moment of recruitment and admissions through orientation to their later classroom, advising, and out-of-class interactions. A few questions overlay this chronology, and I address these at various points in the synopsis.

Who's in Charge?

On each survey, an initial question asked which office or individual has primary responsibility for the first-year curriculum or cocurriculum. First-year curricular survey results indicated that across all institutional categories, the first-year curriculum is most frequently the responsibility of the chief academic officer (42.5 percent). However, as institutional size increases, this responsibility is somewhat more likely to be relegated to deans of colleges, department chairs, and faculty. Only eight respondents (one two-year and seven four-year) indicated that a dean of freshmen has responsibility for the first-year curriculum.

Overall, slightly less than one half (48 percent) of institutions designate some-one as being "in charge" of the first-year cocurriculum. The BC-LA colleges were most likely to assign first-year cocurricular activities to one individual or office (70 percent), followed by research-extensive universities (56 percent). Across all Carnegie categories, the unit most often mentioned was the college or university's chief student affairs officer or division of student affairs. Seventeen respondents (6 percent) identified a director of the first year as the person specifically charged with first-year cocurricular initiatives.

Based on our interactions with numbers of first-year educators, my colleagues and I at the Policy Center would argue that the absence of centralized or focused responsibility for the first year, in either the curriculum or cocurriculum, is a cen-tral problem on many campuses. Various departments, divisions, and individuals interact with new students with little or no coordination. And when first-year initiatives are one of multiple responsibilities in a major institutional division or for a senior administrator, they are less likely to command focused attention. Rather, they become just one more in a long list of important responsibilities.

Recruitment and Admissions

The recruitment and admissions function is a critical aspect of an institution's ability to manage its resources and plans for the future. And it is no surprise that the first-year cocurricular survey found a direct correlation between an insti-tution's dependence on tuition as its primary revenue source and the likelihood of a direct reporting line from admissions functions to the institution's presi-dent. Such was the case for 60 percent of BC-LA respondents and 44 percent of BC-GEN. Both institutional sectors comprise predominantly private institutions (75 percent of BC-LA and 80 percent of BC-GEN) in which tuition dollars con-stitute a significant portion of each year's budget. Institutions less dependent on tuition—public research universities and two-year colleges—are more likely to link admissions with other units. The most common reporting line for research university admission offices is to the vice president for academic affairs (44 percent) and for two-year campuses, to the vice president or dean of stu-dent affairs (66 percent).

The cocurricular survey found that continued contact in the first year between admissions representatives and first-year students is rare. Students who attend BC-LA colleges are most likely to experience such contact (47 percent), followed by students who attend two-year community colleges (42 percent). In the community college sector, admissions counseling is often part of a unit that includes follow-up academic and personal counseling. Fewer than one of every ten research universities, however, indicated that admissions counselors have continued contact with first-year students.

While it is easy to understand why opportunities for contact between enrolled students and admissions counselors are infrequent, especially on large campuses, this situation represents a missed opportunity for institutions to con-tinue an important connection between each first-year student and his or her first point of contact with the institution, and for the admissions staff to receive feedback from students about their experience on campus and their level of satisfaction and perception of institutional fit.

For some students, the recruitment and admissions phase also offers the first opportunity for contact with the institution's faculty. The cocurricular survey found that the likelihood of such contact was also a function of both institutional size and type: baccalaureate colleges were most likely to report that over half of first-year students meet faculty during recruitment and admissions (41 percent) and research universities were the least likely (10 percent).

Orientation

New student orientation is one of the core features of the first college year, and the cocurricular survey found that it is offered in one form or another at virtually all American colleges and universities (96 percent). (For more information about current trends and issues in orientation, see Chapter Fourteen.) This survey found also that for 76 percent of institutions, orientation reports to a vice president or dean of student affairs. A similar finding (68 percent) was reported in the 2000 NODA Data Bank of the National Orientation Directors' Association (Strumpf & Wawrzynski, 2000), which is drawn from a survey of NODA member institutions.

Survey responses to a question about the length of orientation yielded few surprises. Two-year campuses are more likely to limit preterm orientation to a half-day (62 percent), research-extensive campuses seem to favor the one and one-half day format (52 percent), and BC-LA colleges are more likely to design orientation that comprises more than two days (73 percent).

Responses indicated that for students entering during any given fall term, orientation may be scheduled in the spring, summer, or just prior to the first day of class; however, spring orientation is rare across all institutions (7 percent). BC-LA institutions are most likely to conduct orientation just prior to the beginning of classes (87 percent), while two-year colleges and research-extensive universities are more likely to conduct orientation sessions during the summer (62.3 percent and 82.6 percent, respectively). Two-year colleges are less likely than other institutional types to require participation of full-time, degree-seeking students in orientation. The survey found that 50 percent of two-year campuses, but up to 80 percent of BC-LA campuses, report that orientation is officially required.

Most four-year institutions (from 85 to 100 percent depending on Carnegie classification) offer some type of orientation sessions for family members; however, family orientation is much less common in the two-year sector (44 percent). Similarly four-year institutions are more likely than two-year institutions to offer special orientation sessions for various student subpopulations. Of special note is the finding that approximately two-thirds of research-extensive university respondents report that their campus offers special orientation sessions for honors students.

A recognized trend in orientation is the inclusion of more academic activities. (See Chapter Twenty-Three.) For all institutions, both two and four year, the academic activities most likely to be included in orientation are small-group sessions with faculty to discuss academic programs (approximately 65 percent).

The institutional type most likely to integrate various kinds of academic activities into orientation is the BC-LA campus. Slightly over 50 percent of these institutions report that orientation includes special reading groups designed to discuss designated books or articles student have read during the preceding summer, and approximately three of every four report that academic convocations are scheduled during the orientation period.

The practice of charging a separate fee for orientation is most common in four-year institutions, with one interesting exception. While over 60 percent of BC-LA, master's, and research institutions charge a separate orientation fee, only one-third of BC-GEN colleges levy such a charge. Only 10 percent of two-year institutions charge a separate orientation fee.

Virtually all institutions (95 percent) report some level of orientation evaluation by some combination of students, faculty, parents, staff, or others. One institution reported, "We conducted a mock orientation for administrators and staff for evaluation purposes."

These findings raise and leave unanswered many questions. There is no empirically validated "one best length" or "one best time" for orientation activities. Rather the timing, length, and composition of orientation are decisions best determined by each campus in consideration of its students and their needs. A somewhat surprising percentage of institutions requires that students participate in orientation, and yet questions still remain about whether such a requirement has teeth or how it is monitored. Although this research finds that most campuses conduct some form of evaluation, the data do not provide more detailed information about the evaluation methods or how findings are or are not used.

The First Year in the Classroom

In this chronological view of the data, we are at a fork in the road: for some first-year students, the next major activity may be involvement in Greek rush or adjusting to campus residence life. But for the majority of American first-year students who neither live in campus residence halls nor join Greek social organizations, it is time for class. The first-year curricular survey asked several questions related to classes and the curriculum, and responses represent some of the most complex and surprising findings of this research initiative. The bottom line is this: Who teaches first-year classes and the size of first-year classes depend on academic discipline, institutional size, and Carnegie classification. The frequent media allegations that all first-year classes are very large and taught by very inexperienced faculty or teaching assistants do not hold up in this particular study. Here is a snapshot of findings across common first-year disciplines:

- Across all institutional sizes and types, first-year English tends to be taught in section sizes of no more than twenty-five students (89 percent).

- Although part-time instructors or teaching assistants teach the majority of first-year English classes at research extensive universities (55 percent), at two-year institutions senior faculty reportedly teach the majority (58 percent) of first-year English sections.

- The majority (from 58 to 74 percent) of first-year math and fine arts courses also are taught by senior faculty at both two-year and baccalaureate institutions (both BA-LA and BA-GEN). In master's and research institutions, the instructor pool is more likely to comprise a mix of senior, junior, nontenured, and part-time faculty.
- At all institutions, the majority (about 60 percent) of first-year psychology, biology, and history classes are taught by senior faculty.
- Large first-year classes (more than one hundred students) are most common at research-extensive universities in the disciplines of psychology and biology.
- At all institutions, first-year seminars use the greatest variety of instructors including nonfaculty (17.3 percent).
- In spite of a body of research evidence attesting to the positive influence of upper-level students on the cognitive development of first-year students (Astin, 1993), the use of upper-level undergraduates in coteaching roles is very infrequent across all first-year classes. When "peer instructors" coteach a class, it is most likely to be the first-year seminar at a four-year college or university (24.5 percent).

Faculty Preparation, Interaction, and the Reward Structure

Related to the first-year classroom are the issues of relevant faculty development, faculty interaction with first-year students—especially out-of-class interaction—and the relationship of first-year teaching or advising to the institution's primary reward structure. Sixty-two percent of respondents overall indicated that within the past five years, their institution has offered a "faculty development initiative focused on teaching first-year students." Only 40 percent of two-year and 57 percent of four-year institutions reported that their institution has attempted to increase the level of out-of-class interaction between first-year students and faculty within the past five years.

Finally, the common myth that teaching or advising first-year students is often negatively correlated with the likelihood of tenure and promotion was not confirmed by this research. The picture is far more complex. The most frequent response was that these activities have no effect one way or the other on tenure and promotion decisions. Twenty-one percent of respondents reported a positive effect, 13 percent an effect that varies by department, and only 0.6 percent (one two-year and one four-year institution) a negative effect.

Developmental Education

The first-year curricular survey posed three questions related to developmental education: whether the institution offers courses that are categorized as developmental/remedial, what percentage of first-year students is enrolled in one or more of these courses, and whether the institution has evaluated success rates in regular introductory courses for students who complete a prerequisite developmental course.

What may be surprising to some readers is the finding that developmental education exists in every sector of American higher education. Not only are 98 percent of two-year campuses reportedly offering developmental course work, 64 percent of research-extensive and 48 percent of BA-LA colleges are doing so as well, albeit to smaller percentages of students. But in spite of the prevalence of developmental education in the four-year sector, it is disappointing that fewer than half of the four-year respondents (42 percent) report assessment to determine whether completion of developmental courses prepares students for the first-year curriculum. In contrast, 67 percent of two-year respondents report such evaluation. (For a more extensive discussion of developmental education, see Chapter Seventeen.)

Institutional Policies: Attendance and Midterm Grade Reporting

Although both attendance patterns and whether students receive midterm feedback on academic performance are issues that affect students beyond the first year, many would argue they have a disproportionate impact on first-year students. Both research and mountains of anecdotal evidence support the importance of class attendance, especially in the first year (Swing, 1998), and yet only 39 percent of institutions report an official attendance policy. Only about 4 percent have an attendance policy for first-year students that "differs in any way from the institution-wide policy."

Over 60 percent of all institutions collect and report midterm grades to first-year students, thereby giving them an important source of feedback on their academic performance. Some educators would argue that midterm feedback is too late: first-year students need some idea within the first few weeks of the semester about their performance, hopefully in time to withdraw from classes that are "hopeless." One interesting finding of this survey is that a few institutions (10 percent overall) report midterm grades to parents, obviously finding some way around federal privacy regulations.

Academic Advising and Major Selection

The first-year curricular survey investigated common structures of advising and found that every advising structure—from centralized advising units staffed by professional advisers to faculty-only advising—is represented within each Carnegie institutional type. Predictably, centralized advising systems are more common at research universities and two-year colleges; 91 percent of research-extensive campuses and 75 percent of two-year institutions indicated that at least some students are advised in centralized units by professional, nonfaculty advisers. In contrast, approximately 60 percent of baccalaureate institutions and 40 percent of master's institutions report that all advising is decentralized and performed by faculty. Although technology will surely continue to have an impact on the way advising is conducted in the future, this survey found that face-to-face adviser-advisee contact is currently mandated by about 75 percent of institutions, whether the adviser is a faculty member or advising professional. (For more information on first-year academic advising, see Chapter Nineteen.)

The first-year curricular survey also found that overall, few institutions (8 percent) require first-year students to declare a major at point of entry. In fact, 36 percent of BA-LA colleges do not permit entering first-year students to select an official major. First-year students at two-year institutions are most likely to be "strongly encouraged" but not required to select a major (45 percent), while at four-year campuses, students are most likely to be permitted to select a major but neither forced nor strongly encouraged to do so (54 percent).

Special Curricular Programs or Structures

The first-year curricular survey investigated the degree to which certain academic programs and curricular structures are used in the first year. These include first-year seminars, learning communities, classes taught in residence halls, service-learning, Supplemental Instruction, "early alert" systems, distance education, and on-line courses.

First-Year Seminars. First-year seminars are offered by 80 percent of all four-year and 62 percent of all two-year institutions. These findings are consistent with research conducted by the National Resource Center for The First-Year Experience and Students in Transition at the University of South Carolina in its 2000 National Survey of First-Year Seminars (http://www.sc.edu/fye/research/surveys/survey00.htm), and indicate that the first-year seminar is the most commonly implemented curricular intervention designed specifically for first-year students. The percentage difference between two- and four-year institutions is noteworthy and begs the question: What factors account for the lower percentage of first-year seminars in the two-year sector, which enrolls the highest percentage of at-risk students? (For a more extensive discussion of first-year seminars, see Chapter Sixteen.)

Learning Communities. Learning communities, defined as two or more linked courses that coenroll a single cohort of students, are now found at 37 percent of four-year and 23 percent of two-year institutions. But within the four-year sector, there are dramatic differences related to Carnegie classification. While 77 percent of research-extensive universities offer these structures, only 15 percent of BA-LA and 22 percent of BA-GEN do so. These findings could indicate that research universities are perhaps seeking ways to make the large environment seem smaller by creating defined, manageable academic structures, while small liberal arts institutions believe this to be an unnecessary expenditure of energy and resources. (For a more extensive discussion of learning communities, see Chapter Twenty-Two.)

First-Year Classes in Residence Halls. Only research-extensive universities report significant use of this structure that is designed to link academic and residential life. Forty-six percent of these institutions report offering one or more first-year classes in a campus residence hall. (For a more extensive discussion of living environments, see Chapter Twenty-Four.)

Service-Learning. Service-learning, described in depth in Chapter Twenty-One, links nonremunerative service with academic courses across the curriculum. Currently, 37 percent of all institutions offer one or more service-learning courses for first-year students, with specific percentages ranging from a high of 46 percent of research-intensive campuses to a low of 29 percent of two-year campuses.

Supplemental Instruction. Supplemental Instruction (SI) is a well-known structure for providing students a weekly supplemental class meeting, attached to high-risk courses, that is facilitated by an outstanding upper-level student. High-risk courses are those with a 30 percent or higher rate of Ds, Fs, or withdrawals. The curricular survey finds that currently 36 percent (39 percent four-year and 30 percent two-year) of colleges and universities offer SI, linked to one or more "killer" courses taken by first-year students. (For more detailed information about SI, see Chapter Eighteen.)

Early Alert Systems. Early alert systems come in many forms but have in common early identification of and intervention with students in first-year classes who are at risk for academic failure. The first-year curricular survey found that 66 percent of four-year and 56 percent of two-year campuses have some sort of early alert system in place within first-year courses.

Distance Education and On-Line First-Year Courses. The curricular survey found these course delivery methods to be far more common in the two-year sector than the four-year sector. Currently, 41 percent of two-year colleges, compared to only 9 percent of four-year institutions, offer first-year courses through distance education. On-line courses are offered for first-year students by 50 percent of two-year colleges but only 15 percent of four-year institutions. Educators interested in alternative methods of course delivery will want to track this particular finding in future national surveys of the first year. (For more information about the implications of technology on the first year, see Chapter Thirteen.)

First-Year Activities, Including Athletics

After first-year students settle into their classes, many begin identifying other out-of-class opportunities that will enrich their academic experience. The first-year cocurricular survey investigated the prevalence of out-of-class activities that are specifically designed for first-year students and the role of athletics in the first year.

Although new students can generally find opportunities for involvement at any campus, they are more likely to encounter special first-year activities, especially leadership and student government activities, at research universities than at other types of institutions. First-year leadership programs are offered by 61 percent of reporting research-extensive universities. Student government opportunities are available for first-year students at 47 percent of research-extensive universities and approximately 42 percent of baccalaureate institutions. Approximately 57 percent of two-year colleges offer no out-of-class programs specifically designed for first-year students.

Involvement in athletics (defined as participating as a team member) is more likely at small, rather than large, campuses. Over one-third of baccalaureate campuses report that 25 to 49 percent of first-year students play an intercollegiate sport, while only 4 percent of research-extensive universities report the same level of athletic involvement. Research-extensive universities are more likely than other institutions to mandate academic support programs for intercollegiate athletes (78 percent), a finding that is not surprising as a larger number of these institutions have NCAA Division I status and are thereby held to stringent NCAA regulations and reporting requirements.

Residence Life

For first-year residential students, the transition from life at home to life in the residence hall carries with it both anticipation and anxiety. The nature of roommate relationships, the condition of the residential facility, and the overall atmosphere of the hall can have a significant impact, for better or worse, on the totality of the first-year experience. Although residence life can be a source of significant culture shock and initial dissatisfaction for first-year students, research finds that residential living is correlated with many positive outcomes of college (Astin, 1993; Pascarella & Terenzini, 1991). (For a detailed discussion of residence life issues, see Chapter Twenty-Four.)

Of the 291 institutional respondents to the first-year cocurricular survey, 192 (66 percent) indicated that they house first-year students on campus. In fact, first-year students are required to live on campus by four of every five residential BA-LA colleges and by three of every four residential BA-GEN colleges. About half of responding residential research universities and master's-level institutions also require first-year students to live on campus. Although two-year colleges are less likely to have residence halls, approximately 20 percent of the two-year respondents (twenty-three institutions) reported that they house some first-year students on campus. Residence halls or wings of residence halls restricted to first-year students are more likely to be found at BA-LA campuses (45 percent) than at other institutional types.

Residence life is linked to other academic programs and structures at 60 percent of residential institutions. The most frequently reported form of faculty involvement is faculty presentations in the residence halls (46 percent). About 24 percent offer residential learning communities for first-year students, 32 percent link residence life with first-year seminars, about 25 percent offer special housing for honors students, and about 33 percent offer tutoring or academic advising in residence halls.

Greek Life

Although Greek organizations involve a small percentage of the nation's first-year students, the impact of Greek life on an institution, for better or worse, is often disproportionate to the actual numbers or percentages of students involved. Many divisions of student affairs have a person or persons charged with monitoring and policing the activities of these organizations, which are all too frequently the subject of troubling national or local media headlines. For students who elect and are selected to be members of Greek social organizations, that experience often overshadows all other social interactions and activities, especially during the first year when students are most impressionable and most anxious to be accepted by other college students.

Of the 291 respondents to the first-year cocurricular survey, 93 (32 percent)—all of them four-year colleges or universities—have Greek organizations that first-year students are permitted to join. But the actual percentages of first-year students who join Greek groups are low: approximately 60 percent of respondents indicated that no more than 10 percent of first-year students on their campus join Greek organizations.

The timing of rush, an issue subject to much debate, is most likely to be during the first term of college (43 percent of all respondents). But over one-third indicated that first-year students must wait until the second term of college to join a fraternity or sorority. About one-third of respondents indicated that hazing involving first-year Greek students occurred on their campus during the past two years. And finally, membership in Greek organizations is reportedly fluctuating. Responding institutions reported an overall increase in female membership but a decrease in male membership in Greek organizations during the past five years.

Assessment of First-Year Initiatives

An overriding interest of the Policy Center on the First Year of College is the issue of assessment. Therefore, both the curricular and cocurricular surveys included several questions aimed at investigating both frequency and types of program assessment. In summary, the majority of institutional respondents indicated that their college or university evaluates orientation (92 percent), residence life (87 percent), Greek life (64 percent), and advising (63 percent), but evaluation is often limited to measures of satisfaction rather than measures of impact. For example, 86 percent of responding institutions that house first-year students reported the assessment of "satisfaction" with the residence hall, but only 37 percent reported evaluating the impact of residence life on retention, 31 percent on academic performance, 18 percent on campus involvement, and 7 percent on social development. One exception to this pattern is that 68 percent of the four-year institutions with Greek organizations evaluate the impact of Greek membership on grade point averages, a measure that is mandated by many of these organizations at the national level. The impact of Greek affiliation on retention, however, was evaluated by only 30 percent of responding institutions. In spite of what seems to be a rather surface-level approach to assessment, 75 percent of respondents to both the first-year curricular and cocurricular surveys judge their institutions to be either "average" or "above average/superior" in their level of assessment as compared to other institutions.

RECOMMENDATIONS

While this national survey was not designed to discriminate between effective and ineffective approaches to the first year, many of the questions were nevertheless developed based on principles derived from research on student success, as well as a set of common values grounded in experience and articulated for many years by John Gardner, other colleagues, and me. A secondary aim of this survey process was to encourage respondents, who were senior campus administrators, to focus on the first year, to consider additional approaches or ways of doing things, and to recognize those areas of the first year that are overlooked, resulting in all-too-frequent "don't know" responses.

Generally, findings from this national survey imply that many institutions are investing in a wide range of programs and structures believed to make a positive difference for first-year students. But the findings also indicate significant room for improvement in a number of specific areas. The following recommendations flow from and respond to survey findings:

- Create an institutional mechanism or structure for oversight of the first year, in both the curriculum and cocurriculum. College and university educators value coherence and seamlessness (Boyer, 1987), but results from the national surveys raised serious questions about the degree to which any meaningful level of first-year coordination exists on most college and university campuses. It is highly unlikely that the first year on any campus will be a coherent, seamless experience unless some person or persons are in charge. There are many ways for this responsibility to be accomplished, from the establishment of a single first-year office or designated individual to the creation of a permanent campuswide committee or task force. Over the past five years, the Policy Center on the First Year of College has worked with over one hundred campuses to design institutionwide first-year task forces to evaluate common practices and both recommend and act on change, whenever and wherever needed. The key is to find an appropriate organizational mechanism for focusing on the first year in order to facilitate cross-functional communication and create a coherent and meaningful first college year.

- Structure numerous opportunities for informal interaction between first-year students and faculty from the point of recruitment and admissions through the first year. This recommendation, reiterated by several chapter authors in this book, is based on the body of research linking out-of-class faculty-student interaction to retention and student engagement (Astin, 1993; Kuh, Schuh, Whitt, et al., 1991; Pascarella & Terenzini, 1991; Tinto, 1993). The survey finds, not surprisingly, that such interaction is easier to accomplish on small, residential campuses than on two-year or large four-year campuses. Admittedly, both large and nonresidential institutions will need to be more intentional and more creative about making this interaction a reality. But the gain is clearly worth the minimal effort involved in recruiting faculty to meet with, eat with, advise, and mentor students while simultaneously encouraging students to take advantage of those opportunities.

- Select first-year faculty carefully (including upper-level student coteachers), and provide faculty development opportunities for them. Decisions about who teaches first-year students are inherently complex and often driven by financial and workforce realities. And there is no hard evidence to indicate that senior faculty "do it better" or part-timers "do it worse." But whoever holds this important responsibility can benefit from focused faculty development activities. Upper-level students also are a powerful source of influence on new students (Astin, 1993) and therefore have a meaningful role to play in coteaching first-year courses across the curriculum. National survey results show that upper-level students are an untapped source of positive impact on the first-year academic experience.

- Understand the impact of class size on the retention and academic performance of first-year students. Although the national survey found that large classes are not as ubiquitous as the media would have us believe, they are a common component of the first year on research university campuses. We need more evidence to determine the impact of large classes on the academic performance and retention of first-year students. Research to date conducted on student learning and its relationship to class size is somewhat inconclusive, although according to McKeachie, Pintrich, Lin, Smith, and Sharma (1990), the weight of the evidence favors small classes. But research does find that large classes are a major source of frustration and dissatisfaction for both faculty who teach them (especially graduate teaching assistants) and first-year students (Carbone & Greenberg, 1998; Wulff, Nyquist, & Abbott, 1987; Ratcliff, 1992; Light, 2001). Although there are always exceptions, many large classes are environments characterized by student boredom, poor attendance patterns, high levels of plagiarism, absence of writing (Stones, 1970), and almost exclusive use of multiple-choice tests (Scouller, 1988). We clearly need more evidence to determine whether the savings generated in instructional costs for large classes are perhaps offset by higher levels of student disengagement and dropout. A recent study conducted by researchers at Iowa State University (Hamrick, Schuh, & Shelley, 2002) does, in fact, provide evidence to support the argument that reducing instructional expenditures may backfire by decreasing institutional graduation rates over six years.

- Investigate the impact of developmental courses on student readiness for the regular curriculum. One of the most troubling findings of this national survey was the percentage of institutions that have no knowledge of whether developmental education actually prepares students to enter nonremedial courses. Campuses within every Carnegie category are teaching some percentage of first-year developmental students and courses, and it is critical that we understand whether, and to what degree, developmental course work is providing students the level playing field they need and deserve.

- Consider the impact of attendance policies (or lack of) on first-year students' patterns of classroom attendance. In brick-and-mortar institutions where classes convene at a fixed place and time, the evidence, both anecdotal and empirical, indicates that attendance matters, especially during the first four weeks of the college experience (Swing, 1998; Friedman, Rodriguez, & McComb, 2001). But each of us can probably recall a class so poorly taught that attendance made little, if any, difference in actual learning. The issue of requiring attendance or punishing absentees for simply being absent represents a major philosophical debate in higher education. But establishing attendance as an institutional expectation, however that is accomplished, gives students the clear message that what happens in class is important. Then it is up to the institution and the student to deliver.

- Two-year institutions should invest more in the first year across the board and not forget the influence of families. It is not my intent to point the finger at two-year institutions for insufficient attention to the first year. This sector of American higher education is bursting at the seams, addressing the needs of students at all levels of academic ability and personal circumstance. But with only a few exceptions, the national survey found that two-year institutions are less likely to report that they offer the kinds of programs and strategies found to correlate with retention and academic success. Two-year campuses are advised to develop a set of intentional intervention strategies to meet the needs not only of developmental students, but also of all students who choose to begin higher education in this sector. These strategies should include some means of involving families (broadly defined) in an orientation to higher education and an introduction to the particular campus in which the student is enrolled.

- Invest in assessment: know what works on your campus. One of the toughest and occasionally most humbling activities in which any of us can engage is evaluating the impact of the programs that we cherish. But if we believe in student learning and overall development as the goals for higher education, our initiatives should contribute to those goals. This national survey found that although assessment of first-year programs (orientation, residence life, academic advising, Greek life) is widely practiced, it tends only to scratch the surface—either taking the form of satisfaction surveys or measuring outcomes that are externally mandated by a particular regulatory body. It is far less common for institutions to report evaluating the impact of various components of the first year on student learning, behaviors, and attitudes.

CONCLUSION: THE ESSENTIAL FIRST-YEAR EXPERIENCE

A central thesis underlying this research is that the first-year experience is the sum of many parts; it is more than a single seminar course, orientation program, or learning community. For some students, it represents total immersion—classes, residence life, student activities, Greek affiliation—and for others, it involves a juggling act between home, work, and a handful of first-year classes. For the impact of the first year to be clearly understood, it is important to view and evaluate it as a whole, comprising many interacting components that may differ according to institutional type and mission, students, and the external environment.

Although there are research-based objectives that can be used to inform the way we structure and deliver the first year (Chickering & Gamson, 1987; Barefoot, 2000; see Chapter Two), much about day-to-day policies and practices and their impact on first-year students is essentially untested. Comparing one institution's approach to another is an important first step. But it is only a first step. As higher education continues to be transformed by market pressures, changing levels of external financial support, and the impact of technology, it is more important than ever before to understand and deliver the essential first-year experience for students. This experience would not be a specific template or a listing of quick fixes but a set of broad constructs that could be used as a yardstick against which to measure current or intended practices. This understanding of what is essential will emerge only as a result of the willingness to engage in continuing evaluation of student outcomes as a function of how colleges and universities organize and deliver the first year and to share those findings broadly within the higher education community.

PART TWO

RECRUITING AND CHALLENGING FIRST-YEAR STUDENTS

Yogi Berra was once asked, "What makes a good manager?" His reply was, "Good players." So the answer to the question, "What makes an institution good at helping its first-year students succeed?" in part, might well be, "Good first-year students!" Taking a look at what is now known as enrollment management makes good sense in piecing together the first-year student success puzzle. In Chapter Four, Don Hossler and Douglas Anderson define and review the enrollment management process and discuss the relationships between enrollment management and functions such as recruitment, admissions, financial aid, and orientation.

Establishing high expectations for academic achievement and engagement in learning of first-year students once they are enrolled also presents an enormous institutional challenge. As suggested in the Introduction to this book, there is substantial evidence that today's first-year students are not necessarily challenged to work to their full potential in pursuing their academic goals or fully engaged in the pursuit of their education. College appears to be much less academically challenging than they expected, and they spend much less time engaged in academic pursuits than the typical faculty expectation.

In Chapter Five, George Kuh presents evidence that suggests that many first-year students have an expectations-experience gap that results in their being far less engaged in their education than they expected. He discusses ways in which first-year students may become more engaged in their education and how this engagement is shaped by different types of institutions. In Chapter Six, Karen Schilling and Karl Shilling discuss the importance of establishing high expectations for first-year students and how institutions can help students meet those expectations.

CHAPTER FOUR

The Enrollment Management Process

Don Hossler
Douglas K. Anderson

I chose this university because of the great personalized attention
they gave me. They made me feel like they really cared.
—First-year student at a large, public university

The importance of first-year students' making a successful transition to college and achieving their educational goals has been noted repeatedly in previous chapters. College and university administrators are now coming to realize that recruiting, admitting, and providing adequate financial assistance prior to enrollment is the first step in this process. In addition, as a result of a more competitive environment for traditional and nontraditional students, an increasing number of two- and four-year institutions have recognized the need to organize an array of student services and classroom/curricular interventions to retain students.

In the mid-1970s, the term enrollment management was first used by Jack Maguire (1976) to describe systematic institutional efforts to exert more control over institutional enrollments. By the mid-1990s, enrollment management divisions were becoming normative at private colleges and universities. By the year 2000, enrollment management units had also become commonplace at public universities.

In this chapter we define the concept of enrollment management and explore its connections with efforts to enhance the first college year. Efforts to manage student enrollments and provide a positive first-year experience rely heavily on institutional research and evaluation. We therefore discuss analytical approaches to several core enrollment management topics. Next, we explore various models of organizing and coordinating enrollment management activities. We then highlight several current issues in enrollment management. Finally, we look to the future of enrollment management, and offer recommendations for practice.

DEFINING ENROLLMENT MANAGEMENT

In 1990, Hossler, Bean, and Associates offered this operational definition of enrollment management:

> Enrollment management is an organizational concept and a systematic set of activities designed to enable educational institutions to exert more influence over their student enrollments. Organized by strategic planning and supported by institutional research, enrollment management activities concern student college choice, transition to college, student attrition and retention, and student outcomes. These processes are studied to guide institutional practices in the areas of new student recruitment and financial aid, student support services, curriculum development and other academic areas, which affect enrollments, student persistence, and student outcomes from college [pp. 5–6].

This definition reveals the key attributes of enrollment management:

- Using institutional research for positioning in the student marketplace and examining the correlates of student persistence
- Using research to develop appropriate marketing and pricing strategies
- Monitoring student interests and academic program demand
- Matching student demand with curricular offerings that are consistent with the institutional mission
- Paying attention to academic, social, and institutional factors that can affect student persistence

The goals of a strong enrollment management organization go well beyond the first year of college. Enrollment managers strive to exert an influence on prospective students from the point of first contact until matriculating students earn their degree and become satisfied alumni. However, the enrollment management process has an important role to play during the first year. A successful enrollment management effort establishes the foundation for a successful transition to college and sets the stage for student success that is likely to exert a positive influence on student persistence and graduation. Hossler (1984) asserted that the goal of every college and university should be to recruit graduates. This captures the goal of successful enrollment management organizations.

There is no single organizational structure for enrollment management units. Typically, however, they include the following offices: admissions, financial aid, orientation, registration and records, and retention programs. Along with these offices, the office of institutional research (IR), or access to staff who can provide analytical skills, are essential to effective enrollment management activities. Increasingly, staff from IR offices are part of enrollment management teams or enrollment management divisions are hiring their own staff members with research skills. In addition, academic advising and academic support services are sometimes part of enrollment management divisions. Enrollment management efforts are closely coordinated with offices such as career planning, international programs, residence life, and initiatives focused on programs for the students' first year. Admissions offices and orientation offices play a critical role, but all offices must work together to provide incoming students a successful first college year. Administrative strategies and practices in all of these offices should be guided by IR efforts.

ANALYTICAL APPROACHES TO ENROLLMENT MANAGEMENT

It is our belief that an IR function should play a major role in successful enrollment management efforts. IR staff can be an invaluable source of information. Offices of IR can carry out analyses to help guide enrollment management strategies as well as conduct assessment and evaluation studies of the effectiveness of various strategies. The science of enrollment management has been continually extended by the development of mathematical models to predict enrollment and academic success; to forecast the impact of federal, state, and campus-based financial aid; and to identify factors that influence student persistence. These new tools are discussed in detail in this chapter as well as other chapters in this book. The more that enrollment management professionals know about the characteristics, attitudes, and values of prospective and currently enrolled students, the better able they are to design effective recruitment and orientation programs. Persistence studies conducted by institutional researchers can inform strategies to enhance the success of first-year students. IR professionals can examine the impact of various forms of student financial assistance on matriculation decisions and the academic success of first-year students. A strong IR function is a critical element of a sound enrollment management effort and can illuminate important campus policy issues that improve the experience of first-year students.

Enrollment management offices can be most successful when they take a data-informed approach to constantly examining and improving the first year. This requires a sophisticated database containing an array of prospective and currently enrolled student characteristics and measures of their interests and behaviors to help guide institutional policies and activities. Armed with such data, enrollment managers can monitor the entire scope of enrollment management activities, from first contact to graduation.

To maximize its usefulness, this database should include information that parallels the entire recruitment, enrollment, and matriculation history of the student body. Data should ideally begin at the first contact between the potential student and the school, tracking prospective students through the application process, admission, and matriculation. Since enrollment management continues on through graduation, the database should include information on progress through the institution, retention, and finally graduation and beyond.

Beginning with the first contacts with prospective students, whether by the Web, e-mail, mail, or telephone, data collection should include a running record of contacts and correspondence with the prospective student and basic demographic and geographical variables. Data such as high school attended or postal code can be linked easily to other data sources, which provide rich portraits of groups of potential students.

As prospective students become applicants, the database should grow to include ability measures such as SAT or ACT scores, high school transcript information such as class rank, and financial information. Once students begin school, a complete record should include academic information such as majors and minors, credits attempted and completed, grade point average (GPA), and participation in retention or other academic enrichment programs. Nonacademic information can include housing arrangements, participation in sororities or fraternities, and other campus activities and programs. Finally, a financial history, from application through graduation, should include need, work history including work-study, and all types of financial aid offered and received.

Admissions

Early in the college decision-making process, students select a pool of schools to consider. The first order of business for enrollment managers is to ensure that their institution has broad marketing efforts in place to make the institution visible and sufficiently attractive to ensure that desirable prospective students are motivated to consider them seriously.

By studying the characteristics of past applicants and enrollees, enrollment managers can create a profile of desirable students to whom their college or university is likely to appeal, then target their marketing efforts based on relevant student characteristics. These marketing efforts can be segmented to enhance racial and ethnic diversity of an enrolled student body. They can help increase the geographical or socioeconomic diversity among undergraduate students as well as increase the academic quality of the class or even develop specific strategies to increase the number of students who are interested in specific academic majors.

Once prospective students have expressed interest, campuses need to provide the right information at the right time in order to be perceived as a good match and thereby attract applications. Parental income and education, racial and ethnic background, the academic success of students while in high school, their willingness to travel farther away from home, plans for commuting to school or attending a residential campus, and their major and eventual career plans interact in complex ways to influence the college choice process of individual students. It is incumbent on enrollment managers to understand how these factors influence the number and type of students who are potentially interested in attending their institutions.

For students planning to commute from home to attend a college or university, distance from home, cost, and availability of specific majors are key factors in their application decisions (Hossler, Braxton, & Coppersmith, 1989; Paulsen, 1990). For students who plan to attend a residential campus and are willing to travel greater distances to attend an institution of their choice, the enrollment decision is more complex. These students are typically willing to consider a wider array of institutions and are therefore appropriate subjects of more extensive recruitment efforts.

While most admissions offices have well-developed criteria and strategies for admitting applicants, many could benefit from research-based refinements. If the task is to admit satisfied graduates, then it is sensible to give weight to the factors that predict persistence through to graduation and to those factors that predict academic success. While SAT and ACT scores are meant to do just that, institutions have additional data at their disposal that have the potential to make better predictions. For example the number of high school courses taken in subjects such as math, science, and foreign languages can often be good indicators of success and persistence (Adelman, 1999; Breland et al., 1995). In the light of court cases and state policy developments in California, Florida, Texas, and Michigan that have raised questions about the criteria used to make decisions about which students are admitted to public universities, there is increased interest in validity studies that are used to determine the effectiveness of admissions policies to select applicants who will be successful once enrolled. For example, both the American College Testing Program and the College Board conduct admissions validity studies for institutions using data submitted by campus administrators about the academic performance of enrolled students who took either the ACT or SAT exams. Similarly, some colleges and universities have developed formulas for rating the quality of high schools that are based on the success of these students once they have matriculated to a specific institution.

During the past ten years, enrollment managers have come to rely on institutional databases and market research techniques to understand their market position in order to position their institutions in what has become an increasingly competitive marketplace for traditional-age residential students. It would be easy to be critical about such efforts and cynical about the sophisticated marketing approaches that colleges and universities have started to use. However, in some ways, these new approaches to enrollment management are operationalizing the concept of student-institution fit (Litten, 1984; Hossler & Litten, 1993). It would be naive and would greatly overstate the influence of marketing to suggest that campus marketing and recruitment efforts can manipulate students to the point that most of them will choose schools that would be poor choices for them. This can happen, but in most instances, these analytical approaches to marketing help students to find colleges that will be a good match for their interests and backgrounds. It does not serve the long-term interests of students or institutions to attract students who will not succeed academically. All are served best when schools recruit graduates, not just students.

Financial aid has been used as a recruitment tool for many years. Scholarships based on merit have been used to make schools more attractive to the best students, while assistance based on need has been used to provide access to students of modest means. However, the past few years have seen a dramatic increase in the use of merit scholarships for students without demonstrated financial need. For some schools, an effective use of targeted campus-based financial aid dollars (often referred to as tuition discounting) can increase the quality of the incoming class and generate tuition revenue that more than pays for the program. This requires an assessment of admissions trends, including application and enrollment yields, estimation of the effects of scholarship dollars on enrollment, and careful targeting of discounts. For many schools, the discounts required to produce substantial effects on enrollment and the composition of the incoming class would be prohibitively large. We discuss other aspects of tuition discounting later in this chapter.

Using a data-informed approach to admissions recruitment has turned college admissions into both an art and a science. Once the appropriate student markets have been identified, it is still incumbent on admissions professionals to provide timely and accurate information about the institutions they represent. Providing timely and personalized information to prospective students is critical for effective student recruitment. Recruitment literature, Web sites, and admissions presentations, however, not only help prospective students make sound choices, but also help them to get ready for their college experience if these materials provide information not only about the academic programs and social life on the campus, but also about the academic expectations that faculty place on students and what it takes to be a successful student. Marketing experts often exhort colleges and universities to use less text in their print and Web-based recruitment material because students do not read text-heavy promotional materials.

Marketing experts also advise organizations to keep the print material they want audiences to remember short and simple so that they will remember what is being communicated (Beckwith, 1997). Similarly, they encourage admissions offices to make sure Web sites open quickly and that they are easy to navigate. Admissions officers are wise to keep this advice in mind. By focusing on the things prospective students need to do after they enroll, admissions professionals can help new students become successful in the classroom. By providing repeated academic messages about topics such as the importance of attending class regularly, keeping up with assignments, and seeking help from faculty and academic support centers when it is needed, admissions offices can help ensure a successful first year for students.

Orientation Programs

Orientation programs can be the last part of the recruitment process and the first among many formal retention initiatives undertaken by institutions. Attanasi (1989) and Braxton, Vesper, and Hossler (1995) provide additional empirical links between enrollment management efforts and the transition to college. Braxton and his colleagues found that prospective students who reported having more information about the colleges they were considering were more likely to be satisfied. Attanasi, in his qualitative study of Latino students, concluded that prospective students who were "getting ready" to matriculate— that is, students who were visiting colleges, talking to others about going to college, and in general, psychologically getting ready to go to college—were more successful after they enrolled. Emphasizing the importance of first-year experience programs, House and Kuchynka (1997) found that participation in a first-year seminar had a statistically significant positive impact on student persistence. Professionals in both admissions and orientation offices can aid prospective students in preparing to negotiate the academic, social, and physical environments successfully after they arrive. (Orientation programs are discussed in greater detail in Chapter Twenty-Three.)

Enrollment Forecasting

In indirect but important ways, early and accurate enrollment forecasts support success in the first year. Early and accurate prediction of the number of new students who will matriculate each fall can help academic and nonacademic administrators prepare for the incoming class. Forecasts are usually based on historical ratios of applicants, admitted students, or students who have paid their enrollment deposits to the number of students who eventually matriculate. For many campuses, these patterns tend to be similar over time, so it is possible to devise statistical models that predict future new student enrollments based on past enrollment trends. These forecasts allow academic units to provide sufficient space in courses. Enrollment forecasts also enable student affairs units such as student housing, academic advising, and orientation programs to assemble appropriate resources, averting student dissatisfaction and preventing costly excess capacity.

Successful enrollment forecasts can be based primarily on the flow of applications and acceptances and can be updated frequently as data become available. Accuracy can be improved by using additional data. For example, state schools with significant out-of-state enrollment would almost certainly want to project in-state and out-of-state enrollment separately. Enrollment forecasts can be further enhanced with additional information about students, such as gender, ethnicity, student ability measures, intended major, and financial need. Although more refined data lead to more refined projections, the most sophisticated projection made by extrapolating from past applicant behavior cannot anticipate changes in the higher education market or the effects of external forces such as broader economic conditions, all of which can substantially affect enrollment. Professional judgment and attention to admissions trends remain essential.

Research-Informed Financial Aid Initiatives

Both financial aid and the financial planning that go hand-in-hand with financial aid play a role in the first year of college. Several studies conducted by St. John and his colleagues (St. John, 2003; St. John, Kirshstein, & Noell, 1991; St. John, Paulsen, & Starkey, 1996) and Choy (2002) have amply demonstrated that the type and amount of financial aid that students receive can exert a positive, or negative, impact on the likelihood that they will persist. Students with inadequate aid, or who attend schools they cannot afford, are more likely to drop out. This may be because they simply cannot afford the tuition or because they work too many hours, which takes important time away from their course work. There is ample evidence that first-year students who work too many hours are more likely to have academic difficulty and to leave (Astin, 1975; Nora & Cabrera, 1996; St. John, 1991).

It is also worth noting that recent changes in federal financial aid policy require that students make good academic progress toward their diploma or lose their federal aid. Increasingly, financial aid planning, financial planning, and academic planning can no longer be separated. Financial aid professionals help first-year students negotiate the complex world of federal, state, and institutional financial aid policies and in doing so help students and their families determine how they will pay for a college degree. In this way, financial aid offices play an important role in enrollment management efforts and help facilitate the success of first-year students.

Because adequate financial aid can enhance success and persistence during the first year, it is incumbent on enrollment management staff to regularly explore the relationships between student financial aid and student success during the first year (Nora & Cabrera, 1996; St. John, 2003). Although a large body of research using national databases has examined the relationships between financial aid and student success, IR efforts on each campus remain an important part of enrollment management efforts because broad general trends can mask the effects of financial aid and loans on specific populations on individual campuses. Institutional studies should focus on the relationship between students' academic status and progress (course load, GPA, persistence) and financial factors such as the amount of unmet financial need, the number of hours students work during the week, their use of college work-study funds, and their loan debt. Associations between these factors may reveal the need for more financial support for some students in order for them to be successful. Financial stress, including having need not met by aid, taking out large loans, or working too many hours, may be particularly problematic for certain students, such as first-generation, minority, and nontraditional students. Analysis of local institutional data can reveal problems and vulnerable groups of students in need of additional financial aid or other support.

Student Retention

Few colleges or universities have formal retention offices. Instead, they have retention programs that can be organized by a range of academic and student life offices. The chief academic officer, the chief student affairs officer, or an enrollment management division can sponsor academic support programs. A number of institutional interventions are known to exert a positive influence on student success and persistence during the first year of college. These include enhanced in-class and out-of-class interaction between first-year students and faculty, staff, and other students; working on campus; living on campus; engaging in student activities and events; forming clear career and academic goals; establishing good study habits; attending classes regularly; developing strong orientation programs; special support programs for international students and students of color; and facilitating family and spousal or partner support for degree completion (Braxton, 2000; Morelon, Patton, Whitehead, & Hossler, 2003; Tinto, 1993).

The factors that actually influence persistence on individual campuses vary by institution. Some of the most common retention interventions focus on efforts to enhance student-faculty interaction, academic advising, and academic support programs. Programs such as theme-oriented residence halls, learning communities, first-year student interest groups (at residential and nonresidential campuses), and enhanced faculty advising are frequent interventions for increasing contact between students and faculty. For campuses with professional advisers, initiatives such as intrusive academic advising programs can also contribute to student success. Academic support programs can take a variety of forms. Study skills and tutoring centers, computerized tutorial programs, specialized instructional approaches for courses where students face high risk of failure, and even the use of on-campus cable television networks can be used to deliver remedial assistance and improve the academic success of first-year students.

Early warning programs can be another retention strategy. The office of the registrar often manages early warning programs. One of the best examples of such a program is the Pathfinders Program at Mississippi State University, where first-year students who miss more than two classes in the first six weeks of college can expect a friendly phone call, e-mail, or personal visit to remind them of how important attendance is to academic success. Since the initiation of the program in 1997, first-to-second-year persistence rates rose from 76 percent of students to 81 percent in 2003. Furthermore, first-year average GPAs increased from 2.52 to 2.67, and in 2002, first-year students without absence problems earned a first-year GPA of 2.82, compared with 2.00 for those with attendance problems.

Beyond this foundation for enrollment management efforts during the first year is an array of offices and programs that can positively influence the transition and the first year in college. The specific set of programs, how they are organized, and how they are funded vary from campus to campus depending on the mission and location of the institution. There are also a variety of structures and reporting relationships found among enrollment management organizations. These also exert an influence on the nature of the campus initiatives focused on the first college year.

PUTTING THE PIECES TOGETHER: ORGANIZATIONAL MODELS FOR ENROLLMENT MANAGEMENT

Kemerer, Baldridge, and Green (1992) delineated four basic organizational approaches for enrollment management. Although organizational structures and practices related to enrollment management continue to evolve, the four archetypal models continue to form the foundation of enrollment management organizations: the enrollment management committee, the enrollment management coordinator, the enrollment management matrix, and the enrollment management division.

Enrollment Management Committee

An enrollment management committee is usually charged with looking at institutional efforts in the areas of marketing and student retention. Sometimes two separate committees are established: one for marketing and one for student retention. Like most other committees, the membership of an enrollment management committee includes faculty, administrators, and students. Usually the director of admissions, an academic administrator, an advancement professional, a student affairs administrator, or a faculty member is asked to chair the committee. This can be an effective vehicle for educating large numbers of faculty and administrators about recruitment, retention, and the importance of the first year. It can be a good way to build campus support for enrollment management activities, and it is less likely to raise issues of administrative turf because no administrative restructuring is required. In addition, this model does not require a large investment of institutional money.

There are, however, disadvantages to the committee model. Committees have little influence over institutional policymaking, and feedback mechanisms to senior-level administrators are slow. It is also hard for committees to engage in sustained efforts. Since this approach does not require high levels of administrative support to implement, it may also lack sufficient support to bring about any needed changes. Although there are several advantages to establishing an enrollment management committee, this approach is seldom a long-term organizational solution. It can be a good place to start, but enrollment management systems usually need to evolve into more centralized organizations.

Enrollment Management Coordinator

The enrollment management coordinator is a more centralized approach. The coordinator is charged with organizing recruitment and retention activities and is usually a midlevel administrator, such as the director or dean of admissions or financial aid. Like the committee model, the coordinator model requires little organizational restructuring and less administrative support than more centralized models.

An important disadvantage is that the coordinator model provides no formal mechanism for linking enrollment concerns into the decision-making agenda of senior-level administrators. The lack of administrative support required to implement this approach might exacerbate this problem. Enrollment concerns remain problems for midlevel administrators. In addition, the success of this model is highly dependent on the administrator who is appointed to the position.

Enrollment Management Matrix

The enrollment management matrix moves toward an even more centralized organizational approach. In this model, an existing senior-level administrator such as the chief academic officer, the chief student affairs officer, or institutional advancement directs the activities of the enrollment management matrix. In the matrix model, administrative units such as financial aid or student retention are not formally reassigned to a new vice president. Instead, the administrative heads of these units continue their existing reporting relationships, but they also become part of the enrollment management matrix. One of the important advantages of the matrix model is that enrollment management becomes the direct concern of a senior administrator. In addition, a vice president is more likely to have the resources and the authority to make decisions in a more timely fashion. Although this approach is a more centralized model, it does not require administrative restructuring, which can be costly and antagonize administrators and faculty who do not wish to see major changes take place. The primary disadvantage of the matrix model is that the vice president who is assigned to direct the activities of the matrix may not have the time to devote to enrollment management concerns.

Enrollment Management Division

The most centralized, and therefore the most systematic and structured, of the models is the enrollment management division. In the division model, a vice president or associate vice president is assigned the responsibilities for most or all of the administrative areas that influence student enrollments housed within one large functional unit. This model requires high levels of administrative support; usually the president or a senior vice president has to become a strong advocate of this model. There are several advantages to this model. Enrollment management strategies are easier to identify and implement. A senior-level administrator is given full responsibility to direct administrative activities that affect the recruitment and retention of students. An enrollment management vice president can carry enrollment-related concerns directly to the president and the governing board.

This centralized approach, however, is not without its drawbacks. Unless a campus is in the midst of an enrollment crisis, it is difficult to create a new administrative division. Existing vice presidents do not like administrative units removed from their divisions. Professional and support staffs of most organizations do not deal well with rapid organizational change. At campuses where an enrollment management division has been put into place quickly, staff turnover has been high, and there can be extended periods of low morale among new and remaining staff members.

Choosing the Organizational Model

It is worth noting that campuses often move through these models in an evolutionary manner. As a college or university that starts with a committee approach becomes more focused on enrollment management goals, it moves from a committee to a coordinator or matrix approach and eventually to an enrollment management division. As important as the organizational model is the reporting structure and the orientation of the senior enrollment officer. Senior enrollment managers can come from a variety of backgrounds. Most often they come from offices such as admissions, financial aid, institutional research, and other student affairs offices. However, senior enrollment managers can also come from the faculty, the ranks of professional academic administrators, and institutional advancement. Indeed, with the emergence of integrated marketing, there is a modest trend toward merging of enrollment management with other areas of institutional advancement.

It is more likely that enrollment managers who come from academic affairs or student affairs will have an experiential base that brings a strong focus on the first year of college. However, this does not necessarily need to be the case. As long as the senior administrator of an enrollment management unit makes it a priority for the unit to focus on the transition to college and the first year, any organizational structure or reporting relationship can work.

Regardless of the organizational model employed, enrollment management efforts should be strongly connected with the first-year college experience. Students are more likely to withdraw from a college or university during the first year than at any other time in their collegiate experience (Tinto, 1993). As a result, enrollment managers have strong incentives to focus on the transition to college and the first year as a means of enhancing student success and as a result improving persistence rates from the first to the second year.

CURRENT ISSUES IN ENROLLMENT MANAGEMENT

A number of public policy and institutional concerns have a direct impact on enrollment management efforts at the campus level. The most pressing topics are the changing role of standardized tests in the admissions process, the increasing use of merit-based campus financial aid, the growing impact of college rankings publications, the use of technology, and recruitment ethics.

Role of Standardized Tests in Admissions

Standardized tests such as the SAT and ACT have long been commonly used as admissions requirements. By playing an important role in the admissions process at most institutions, they help to determine the composition of the student body, thereby exerting a profound influence on the first year. There are several important concerns around the SAT. First, there is considerable question about what the SAT measures and the extent to which it should be emphasized in college admissions decisions. Second, there are competing interpretations of the correlation between SAT scores and grades and other measures of collegiate success. Third, there are profound concerns about the persistent race/ethnic differences in test scores and the effects of SAT use in admissions on campus diversity.

For much of its long history, the SAT was the Scholastic Aptitude Test. It purported to measure aptitude, or an innate ability or capacity to learn. Since 1996, the letters have been just a name, standing for nothing more than SAT. The College Board now says that the SAT "assesses verbal and math reasoning skills," which remain somewhat independent of schooling (College Board, 2001). Thus, the SAT purports to be one mechanism by which promising students with inadequate schooling can overcome their disadvantages and be noticed by colleges. However, University of California president Richard Atkinson (2001) suggests that far from serving the needs of disadvantaged students, a focus on the SAT serves to perpetuate the advantages of the already advantaged, who can afford expensive tutoring, and creates an unhealthy focus on test taking, distracting from learning. In his view, admissions decisions would be more appropriately based on mastery of secondary school curriculum as measured by high school grades and standardized achievement tests. He suggests the SAT II tests, with their focus on achievement, are a step in the right direction.

Business leaders have joined the chorus in calling for less emphasis on the SAT, with more attention given to other factors more important for business success, such as integrity, communication, and leadership skills (Gehring, 2001a). There is a wide consensus that admissions and scholarship decisions should never be based on SAT or ACT alone, yet Hossler (2001) indicates that the use of standardized tests increased during most of the 1990s at the expense of high school rank or grades. It is too soon to see if this trend has been reversed as a result of the recent criticisms of standardized testing.

While it is not clear to everyone what the SAT measures, SAT scores are consistently correlated with first-semester college GPA (Gehring, 2001b). Although the correlation is statistically significant across many populations, there is much debate about the substantive significance of the relationship. Some charge that the correlation is so modest as to make the SAT practically worthless (Fairtest, 2001). Others point out that the SAT is second only to high school rank in predictive strength (College Board, 2001). Judging strictly by the statistical correlation between SAT and first-semester success, a rational admissions officer seeking to admit students who will succeed could hardly ignore SAT scores. Of course, this does not mean that other assessments could not provide additional or better information. However, it seems likely that new holistic assessments of student applications will be both expensive and filled with unknown biases that are different but not necessarily more benign than any biases in the SAT.

Another concern about the SAT centers on campus diversity and the effect of standardized tests on the admission of African American and other racial/ethnic minorities to selective institutions. This concern sometimes includes gender and socioeconomic status as well. It is clear that racial diversity can be enhanced by admissions policies that deemphasize the SAT. Florida, Texas, and California have implemented policies of admission to students in the top percentages of their high school graduating classes. This can increase the number of minority students admitted compared to a strict SAT formula.

It is also possible to use SAT and ACT scores in new ways that account for differing opportunities and circumstances. Goggin (1999) has suggested a "merit-aware" approach that would focus not on absolute scores but on students' scores relative to peers in their own high schools. St. John and colleagues (St. John, Simmons, & Musoba, 1999) have simulated admissions decisions and found it possible to use a merit-aware model to increase diversity without having race as an explicit criterion in the admissions decision. This approach is conceptually similar to the "strivers" approach suggested by the Educational Testing Service (Dockser, 1999). Strivers are students who have been more successful in high school with respect to grade point average, class rank, and general student involvement than would be predicted on the basis of their family background and standardized test scores.

The role of the SAT and other standardized tests in admissions is a contentious topic with no ready resolution in sight. Recent rulings by the U.S. Supreme Court on the University of Michigan affirmative action cases (*Grutter* v. *Bollinger* and *Gratz* v. *Bollinger*) have helped to clarify but not settle the appropriate role of standardized tests and other criteria used in admitting students. The Court ruled in favor of holistic admissions reviews but did not establish a well-defined role for standardized tests.

It is clear that no standardized test should be the sole basis for high-stakes decisions such as admission or scholarships. Measures of class rank and the rigor of the courses taken in high school are strong indicators of the ability of students to be successful in college (Adelman, 1999) and should be part of the criteria for the admissions decisions of selective colleges and universities. Enrollment managers will need to stay abreast of judicial cases and state policies as they craft institutional policies that will be legally and morally defensible and serve the needs of students and institutions.

Merit-Based Campus Financial Aid

Financial aid can be a powerful tool for addressing a variety of often competing institutional goals such as excellence, access, diversity, and revenue enhancement. The 1990s saw a sharp increase in the use of merit-based scholarship across all institution types. Between 1988 and 1996, the number of non-need-based scholarship recipients at public four-year schools increased over 160 percent, and the average award amount nearly tripled. This large increase in institutional aid disproportionately went to funding middle- and upper-income students rather than those with demonstrated need (Redd, 2000a). This use of financial aid to attract the best and the brightest without regard to need has come to be called tuition discounting (Loomis-Hubble, 1991). Redd (2000b) defines tuition discounting as a form of institutionally funded grants designed to attract specific groups of undergraduates to help them pay all or a portion of their tuition and fee charges in order to increase the probability that these students will attend the institution offering the grant.

While conceptually similar to the academic merit and athletic scholarships that have been used for decades, the widespread use of discounting has added a new element of expensive competition to the admissions landscape. This strategic use of discounting to leverage enrollments has been supported by the emergence of a number of sophisticated analytical tools including econometric modeling (see, for example, Brooks, 1996).

Discounting has caught on precisely because it has been effective. However, as bidding wars escalate among schools competing for the same small pool of the "best and the brightest," there is a danger of further concentration of resources on those who need them least, squeezing the neediest students out of the market entirely. However, Baum (1998) notes that equity does not necessarily suffer from discounting. At least conceptually, it is possible to use revenue generated from discounting to fund need-based aid.

Although discounting may be rational and efficient for each school acting alone, the sum of the actions can perversely lead to a market of discounts so steep that discounting ceases to enhance revenue, fails to increase diversity or class quality, and ultimately diverts resources from other critical areas. Redd (2000b) calls this scenario "discounting toward disaster."

In the short term, tuition discounting can help to recruit the more desirable students from the existing applicant pool, providing a marginal boost to measures of incoming student quality, or enhancing diversity, or increasing revenue. However, no institution has enough money to entice large numbers of excellent students to a mediocre school. Any long-run strategy must include steps to improve quality, and the perception of that quality, thereby expanding the applicant pool and increasing the strength of the institution in the marketplace.

College Rankings

In the past decade, the number of publications that offer advice on choosing a college has increased dramatically. During the same time, a number of publishers have developed reports that purport to rank the quality of colleges and universities. Increasingly, prospective students and their parents, college trustees, alumni, faculty, and even some public policymakers are interested in how different colleges and universities fare in the world of rankings (Hossler & Foley, 1996). A number of higher education scholars have argued that rankings publications primarily measure input variables such as SAT scores, institutional selectivity, or faculty characteristics rather than what students gain during their college experience (outcome measures) (Hossler, 2001; Pascarella, 2001). Nevertheless, rankings appear to be gaining in visibility and influence. As a result, despite their flaws, enrollment managers, especially those employed at residential campuses, cannot afford to ignore them or their influence on which students consider attending their institutions.

The pressures of rankings are forcing more and more campuses to seek ways to improve their rankings. It is difficult for institutions to increase their number of faculty, lower their student-faculty ratio, or increase alumni giving. As a result, campus administrators tend to focus on admissions selectivity. This focus is not healthy. There are a finite number of students who have high GPAs and high standardized scores. This leads to spiraling levels of competition for top students that are reflected in ever-larger merit-based scholarship programs. It can also lead institutions into dubious strategies of distortion in order to make themselves look more selective than they really are. Hossler (2001) has delineated a number of these efforts, which include encouraging students who are not admissible to apply so that they can be rejected, early decision programs that increase yields, and misreporting admissions statistics.

Instead of rankings, many scholars and observers of higher education in the United States have suggested that the kinds of data collected by the National Survey of Student Engagement (NSSE) represent much more useful information about the quality of a college experience (Hossler, 2001; Pascarella, 2001;

Confessore, 2003). NSSE asks students how they spend their time in academic and out-of-class activities while attending college. It measures the extent to which students are engaged in their college experiences. Students are also asked to estimate their cognitive and noncognitive growth as a result of their college experiences. Efforts like NSSE provide data on the actual experiences of students rather than indirect measures of institutional quality. (For further information on the NSSE, see Chapter Five.)

Enrollment managers need to tread a fine line when dealing with rankings. They are well advised to educate key campus constituents about the problems with rankings. Nevertheless, senior enrollment officers cannot simply ignore rankings and their impact on their applicant pools.

The Role of Electronic Technology

Technology is becoming an increasingly important part of enrollment management. The uses of the World Wide Web, streamed video, and e-mail communication have become key tools for offices ranging from admissions to financial aid and registration and records. E-mail can enable prospective and current students to communicate with colleges and universities in a timely and direct manner. E-mail also makes it possible for admissions professionals to communicate with prospective students without the costs associated with direct mail. The Web can provide information about academic programs, students' bursar bills, and how to seek academic assistance. Some futurists have suggested that traditional direct mail will disappear and all admissions recruitment will be done electronically. Similarly futurists suggest that all student services will be delivered twenty-four hours a day, seven days a week. Recent research published in *Student Poll* (Internet is now . . . ," 2000) reveals that the use of the Internet, the Web, and e-mail are rapidly becoming universal among traditional-age high school students who are college bound. Whether traditional forms of recruitment disappear over the next decade remains to be seen.

The use of electronic enrollment management tools also raises a host of privacy issues that are gaining more and more attention. Offices such as financial aid and registration and records now have large databases stored electronically with personal information that is protected by privacy laws. Regularly, however, electronic hackers find ways to get through electronic security measures and access institutional databases. The same databases can also be accessible to other kinds of hacking. The well-publicized event where an admissions professional from one Ivy League school hacked into the electronic admissions files of a competitor Ivy League school ("Princeton Official Ousted for Snooping," 2002) reveals the fragility and legal issues associated with the new uses of electronic tools in enrollment management.

Recruitment Ethics

There are other ethical issues associated with the efforts of colleges and universities to manage their enrollments. During the recruitment process, institutions should be careful to portray the campus accurately. Written publications should accurately describe the location of the campus, the academic offerings, and the composition of the student body. Admissions folklore is replete with stories of admissions representatives who have told prospective students that they could earn a degree in a major that the campus did not even offer, or the campus that used aerial photographs to make a campus that was thirty minutes from the ocean appear as if it was almost on the beach. One major public university fell under heavy criticism for electronically inserting pictures of students of color in existing photographs in order to make the campus appear to be more diverse. These kinds of recruitment practices are unfair to students and harm both the institution as well as the entire higher education system. The general public, students, and their families can lose confidence in the mission and purpose of American higher education.

THE FUTURE OF ENROLLMENT MANAGEMENT

Administrative fads come and go in American higher education. The concept of enrollment management emerged in the mid-1970s and early 1980s, a result of the declining number of traditional-age high school students and the resulting growing competition for students. Increased competition for students explains the emergence of this new enrollment-oriented organizational construct. In many parts of the United States, we are entering a period of growth in the traditional-age student population.

In this context, it is possible that like many other fads, interest in enrollment management will fade. However, this seems unlikely for a number of reasons. Student tuition dollars have always been the largest and most predictable source of revenue for most private colleges and universities. Increasingly, this is becoming true for public institutions. Federal and state appropriations for higher education have been stable or declining in most states (Heller, 2001). As a result, student tuition dollars have become a more important source of revenue for public universities. Administrative structures in all organizations, including colleges and universities, reflect the need to protect important institutional priorities. Garnering revenue is an important priority in nearly all organizations. This suggests that managing enrollments will continue to be an important institutional priority.

In addition, pressures around institutional rankings are likely to maintain a focus on rankings and the need for a senior campus office to focus campus energies on efforts to sustain or enhance rankings. Finally, there tend to be normative factors at work in the way all colleges and universities organize themselves. The establishment of enrollment management organizations has become common at both public and private institutions (Noel-Levitz, 2000). College presidents now look to senior enrollment professionals to manage the complex world of recruitment, financial aid, and rankings and to focus campus efforts on student success and persistence. Much as the professional development officer emerged during the 1950s and 1960s and has remained, the professional enrollment officer is probably here to stay.

One of the problems most campuses face is the dearth of qualified enrollment managers. Many campuses experience failed searches for senior enrollment professionals. Many smaller or less affluent campuses cannot afford to hire qualified senior enrollment administrators. Often they have to appoint internal candidates, administrators or faculty, and then train them to assume the role of senior enrollment officer. At the moment, there are few graduate programs in universities that focus on the education of enrollment managers. The University of Miami has recently launched a master's degree program and a certificate program. The American Association of Collegiate Registrars and Admissions Officers, the College Board, the American College Testing Program, the Noel-Levitz consulting organization, and the National Resource Center for The First-Year Experience and Students in Transition are attempting to provide professional development programs to help train and develop enrollment managers. Over time, these efforts may increase the supply of qualified enrollment managers.

RECOMMENDATIONS

Effective enrollment management efforts can be an important part of successful first-year programs. Equally important, first-year-experience programs can play a major role in the success of enrollment management efforts. Administrators responsible for the first-year experience and those who work in the area of enrollment management have the same goal: a successful and growth-producing experience for students during the transition to college and during their first year. In order to achieve these goals, enrollment management divisions must:

• Select enrollment management professionals who are experts on the college student. They need to know why students choose colleges, why some students persist, and why others leave, and they need to be knowledgeable about the college student experience.

• Select enrollment management professionals who have an analytical orientation in order to study and understand the unique enrollment and persistence decisions of students attending their campuses.

• Coordinate and influence the array of offices dedicated to first-year student success, including academic support, admissions, advising, financial aid, institutional research, orientation, and relevant student life units.

• Have an awareness of the norms, the values, and the organizational culture of the institution at which they work in order to work effectively with a myriad of student affairs and academic units.

• Be guided by reflective practice. Without reflective practice, enrollment managers run the risk of believing they exert more influence and control over student enrollment and student persistence than they really do. Without reflective practice, enrollment managers may lose sight of the ethical issues they confront daily in their work.

- Focus on enrollment and retention figures, financial aid modeling, and other easily measured indicators while at the same time remembering that the ultimate goal is to enroll students who will find the educational experience at any college or university to be both challenging and supportive.

CONCLUSION

Enrollment management is a comprehensive approach to student success that starts with an institution's recruiting and admissions processes; continues with support including registration, financial aid, admissions, and orientation; and finally focuses on helping students persist to graduation and fulfill their educational goals. Such an approach indicates that an institution has a serious and continuous commitment to student success.

CHAPTER FIVE

Student Engagement in the First Year of College

George D. Kuh

I want to use and abuse this school to the fullest. I want to experience everything this institution has to offer. I do not believe my college experience would be the same if I don't. I want to make this the best four years of my life and getting a hand in everything I possibly can is the only way I know how to.
—Emily, first-semester student

For many new students, especially first-generation students and those living away from home for the first time, the initial weeks of the first academic term are like being in a foreign land. With only intermittent feedback and classes meeting but two or three times a week, students who think they are doing well are sometimes surprised to discover after their first midterm exam reports that their academic performance is subpar. After six or eight weeks, some have dug a hole so deep that getting back to ground level seems almost impossible. It does not have to be this way. Colleges and universities committed to student success intentionally organize the first weeks and months of college to reduce the prospects that their students will find themselves in such straits.

In this chapter, I offer some suggestions for what schools can do to increase the odds that more of their students will survive and thrive in the critical first year of college. I base these observations on more than a quarter-century studying undergraduate students, scores of campus consultations, and two national databases of student reports about their college experiences. I also draw on examples from institutions making headway in this regard, including my own campus, Indiana University, which received national recognition for creating a challenging and supportive campus environment for first-year students (Barovick, 2001). Because student engagement is a key factor in student success, broadly defined, I first summarize some of the more important findings about student engagement in the first year of college. Then, I provide some suggestions for what institutions should focus on to promote student engagement and success in the first college year.

STUDENT SUCCESS IS EVERYBODY'S BUSINESS

There are many definitions of student success. Some would argue that student success is simply a matter of earning grades good enough to be awarded a college degree. Others would assert that successful students should have achieved desired learning outcomes and personal objectives. The book editors in their Introduction offer a comprehensive eight-part definition of first-year student success that is broad, holistic, and inclusive. While we in higher education may not know all the variables that contribute to this broad definition of student success, we do know that the best single predictor of student academic success is the individual student's academic preparation and motivation. Thus, some would conclude that the surest way for an institution to increase the number of its students who succeed academically is to admit only well-prepared, academically talented students. Such an approach has been fueled in recent years by collegiate rankings that reward institutions with improved positions in the hierarchy if they are able to raise their entering students' average SAT scores.

From a human capital and public policy perspective, enhancing student success by focusing on well-prepared, high-ability students is indefensible. Colleges and universities must educate more people than ever before from a much wider, deeper, and more diverse pool of undergraduates. Both the proportion and number of people with a postsecondary education are at unprecedented levels, far exceeding that of any other country. And for a host of reasons, the number must grow as more students today than ever before need to go to college. One recent estimate is that as many as 85 percent of high school graduates in the coming decade will need some form of postsecondary education to acquire the knowledge, skills, and competencies to be able to manage effectively the increasingly complex social, economic, and political issues the future will bring (McCabe, 2000).

This is a daunting challenge. Since admitting only the most talented and well-prepared students is not the solution, are there other promising approaches to enhancing student success? The answer is yes. After controlling for student background characteristics (such as ability and academic preparation), the student development research indicates that a key factor in student success is student engagement (Kuh, 2001).

Student engagement represents two critical features. The first is student driven: the amount of time and effort students put into their studies and other educationally purposeful activities. The second is institution driven: how a school deploys its resources and organizes the curriculum, other learning opportunities, and support services to induce students to participate in activities that lead to the experiences and outcomes that constitute student success (persistence, satisfaction, learning, and graduation). Higher education has recognized the importance of student engagement for years (Astin, 1977, 1985; Chickering, 1969, 1974; Feldman & Newcomb, 1969; Pace, 1979;

Kuh, 1981; Sanford, 1962). Even so, many colleges and universities have not yet created the conditions that research studies show to be effective educational practice.

ENGAGING STUDENTS IN THEIR FIRST COLLEGE YEAR

Before an institution can take steps to enhance student success, it must first understand who its students are, what they are prepared to do academically, and what they expect of the institution and themselves. Expectations are especially important today because so many students appear to start college already disengaged from the learning process, having acquired a cumulative deficit in terms of attitudes, study habits, and academic skills (Levine & Cureton, 1998a; Marchese, 1996, 1998). For example, in the mid-1990s, high school seniors reported studying only about six hours per week on average, well below the amount that is traditionally assumed necessary to do well in college. Compared with their counterparts of a decade earlier, they were also more frequently bored in class and missed more classes due to oversleeping or other obligations (Sax, Astin, Korn, & Mahoney, 1997). Even so, record numbers reported B + or better high school grades and expected to earn at least a B average in college and to attend graduate school. Because behavioral patterns established in elementary and secondary school tend to persist through the college years (Astin, Parrott, Korn, & Sax, 1997; Schilling & Schilling, 1999), we should not be surprised that this generation of students expects to get reasonably good grades for less academic effort compared with previous cohorts.

Assuming students today come to campus with an entitlement mentality, what they expect to do in college and what faculty members and institutions of higher education are providing could result in a problematic mismatch of sizable proportion, advantaging neither party. This is because expectations serve as a filter through which students compare what is unfolding with what they think should happen and decide whether certain activities are appropriate, meaningful, relevant, and worth their time, and what opportunities or activities to ignore (Bandura, 1982; Cantor & Mischel, 1977; Dweck & Leggett, 1988; Feldman, 1981). Thus, what students expect shapes their behavior, which in turn affects their academic performance and social adjustment to college life (Kuh, 1999).

To find out more about the relationships between student expectations and experiences we developed the College Student Expectations Questionnaire (CSXQ) for a Fund for the Improvement of Postsecondary Education (FIPSE) project (Schilling & Schilling, 1999) in the mid-1990s (Kuh & Pace, 1998). It is typically administered to first-year students during orientation and asks students what they expect to do during the first year of college in selected areas, such as study time, course-learning activities, interaction with faculty members and peers, cocurricular activities, and other educationally purposeful college activities. The CSXQ is adapted from its parent survey, the College Student Experiences Questionnaire (CSEQ). Now in its fourth edition, the CSEQ was introduced in 1979 by C. Robert Pace and has about double the number of questions as the CSXQ, covering more college experiences in greater detail. The CSEQ is usually administered near the end of the academic year. This allows us to compare what students expected to do when they entered college (CSXQ results) with what they subsequently experienced (CSEQ results). Where appropriate, I corroborate trends from the CSEQ data with information from the National Survey of Student Engagement (NSSE), an annual survey of first-year and senior students established in 1999 with a grant from The Pew Charitable Trusts. Conceptually similar to the CSEQ, NSSE includes some of the same items as the CSEQ and is also administered near the end of the academic year. Additional information about the CSEQ and NSSE projects including the survey instruments can be found at their respective Web sites (www.iub.edu/~cseq and www.iub.edu/~nsse).

THE EXPECTATIONS-EXPERIENCE GAP: THE EVIDENCE

In many respects, what students actually do in the first year of college falls short of what they expected to do (Gonyea, Kish, & Kuh, 2001; Kuh, 1999; Olsen et al., 1998). That is, when starting out, most first-year students say they will engage in more academic and other educationally purposeful activities more frequently than they actually reported doing near the end of the first year. Although students may be somewhat idealistic in terms of what they can accomplish during college, their expectations are generally unrealistic in terms of the amount of reading and writing that faculty members assert is appropriate. At the same time, it is possible that the gap is even wider than the data suggest, as some fraction of students who answered the CSXQ at the beginning of college were no longer in school the following spring. It is quite likely that among those students who left school early is a disproportionate number who were less motivated and had lower aspirations and expectations compared with their peers who persisted through at least the first year.[1]

Women expect to engage in more activities compared with men. And they do, except for recreational sports and science-related activities. Older first-year students (twenty-four years of age or older) are much less likely to use electronic technology to complete assignments or discuss course topics with peers and instructors (Kuh et al., 2001). Older students also are disproportionately attending part time, taking fewer classes compared with their younger counterparts (more of whom are full time), and spending more time working and caring for dependents. Younger students (twenty-three years of age or younger) interact more frequently with peers from diverse backgrounds because they are more likely to live on campus and thus spend more time in the company of diverse peers. With these unsurprising differences in mind, certain student and institutional behaviors need to be better understood to promote student success.

The expected and reported levels of engagement vary in predictable ways by institutional type (Astin, 1993; Pace, 1990). For example, students at smaller, selective colleges have greater expectations across the board, and they subsequently report being involved to a greater extent in more activities. They also, on average, expect and find their campus environments to be more supportive. However, some large schools outperform some small schools on these dimensions (National Survey of Student Engagement, 2001; Kuh, 2003).

Preparing for Class

First-year students fall into four groups in terms of the number of hours they expect to study in college. About a quarter think they can get by with ten or fewer hours per week, another quarter between eleven and fifteen hours, the third quarter between sixteen and twenty hours, and the remaining group expect to study more than twenty hours per week. Of the last group, only 9 percent say they will study at least twenty-six hours per week, which is what most faculty members declare is necessary to do well in college—at least two hours preparing for every class hour (Table 5.1). So one area where student expectations are much lower than institutions espouse is in the amount of time they think they will need to study.

Table 5.1. First-Year Student Responses to Selected CSXQ and CSEQ Items: Participation in Course-Related Learning Activities

Item	Response Options	Percentage of CSXQ Respondents	Percentage of CSEQ First-Year Respondents
During the time school is in session this coming year, about how many hours a week do you expect to spend outside of class on activities related to your academic program, such as studying, writing, reading, lab work, rehearsing, etc.?	5 or fewer hours weekly	4	13
	6–10 hours weekly	22	28
	11–15 hours weekly	25	22
	16–20 hours weekly	25	18
	21–25 hours weekly	14	10
	26–30 hours weekly	6	5
	More than 30 hours	3	4
During the coming school year, about how many textbooks or assigned books do you expect to read?	None	0	2
	Fewer than 5	7	24
	Between 5 and 10	38	40
	Between 10 and 20	39	26
	More than 20	16	9

Item	Response Options	Percentage of CSXQ Respondents	Percentage of CSEQ First-Year Respondents
During the coming school year, about how many term papers and other written reports do you expect to write?	None	0	3
	Fewer than 5	8	23
	Between 5 and 10	31	31
	Between 10 and 20	39	29
	More than 20	21	13
During the coming school year, about how many essay exams in your courses do you expect to write?	None	1	7
	Fewer than 5	11	29
	Between 5 and 10	33	31
	Between 10 and 20	36	23
	More than 20	20	10
Take detailed notes during class	Never	1	1
	Occasionally	10	10
	Often	39	29
	Very often	49	60
Contribute to class discussions	Never	1	3
	Occasionally	24	32
	Often	44	36
	Very often	31	29
Try to see how different facts and ideas fit together	Never	1	5
	Occasionally	18	30
	Often	47	36
	Very often	34	28
Prepare a paper or project where you had to integrate ideas from various sources	Never	1	3
	Occasionally	22	26
	Often	49	38
	Very often	28	33
Write a major report for a class (20 pages or more)	Never	22	78
	Occasionally	55	13
	Often	18	5
	Very often	5	4

Note: The items listed are from the CSXQ; CSEQ items differ slightly. CSEQ items are worded in the past tense to reflect activities in which students engaged over the course of the academic year.

The biggest drop in number of study hours per week in the first year of college is in the eleven- to fifteen-hour range. Although about two-thirds (64 percent) of students start college expecting to spend at least that much time studying, by the end of the first year, only half actually do (Table 5.1). By the end of the first year, more than two-fifths spend ten or fewer hours per week studying. NSSE data show that somehow, 9 percent of full-time first-year students get by with no more than five hours, ranging from a low of 5 percent of students at baccalaureate liberal arts colleges to more than a tenth (11 percent) at master's-level colleges and universities. In addition, more than a fifth of students say they "frequently" come to class unprepared. That is, they have not done the assigned reading or completed written and other assignments (National Survey of Student Engagement, 2001, 2002).

Course Learning, Advising, and Academic Support

In a few areas related to classroom activities, students do a bit more than they expected to do, such as taking detailed notes during class. But in other areas, they fall short, such as contributing to class discussions, summarizing major points, and applying class material to other areas of their lives (Table 5.1).

Academic Advising. One of the more important things educationally effective institutions do to help promote student success in the first year of college is provide high-quality academic advising. The National Survey of Student Engagement (2001) shows that students who rate their advising as good or excellent are more likely to interact with faculty in various ways, perceive the institution's environment to be more supportive overall, are more satisfied with their overall college experience, and report they gain more from college in most areas. Moreover, the quality of academic advising is the single most powerful predictor of satisfaction with the campus environment.

Fortunately, students are reasonably satisfied with the quality of their academic advising. Only 7 percent of first-year students describe it as "poor." At Carnegie classification liberal arts colleges and general colleges, advising is "very good" for first-year students and even better for seniors. A smaller percentage (65 percent) of part-time first-year students say advising is good or excellent; more say advising is poor (11 percent). Why? Possibly because part-time students spend less time on campus and have less time to meet with an adviser, which may translate into less favorable ratings because student needs are not being met. They are also twice as likely to be undecided in terms of major, which may require different types of advising skills (less information dispensing and more career exploration).

Academic Support. When starting college the vast majority of students (87 percent) say they will at least "occasionally" use campus academic support services such as writing skills centers. Yet by the end of the first year, almost half (46 percent) have not done so. For a point of contrast, only 15 percent never used campus recreational facilities (Table 5.2).

Table 5.2. First-Year Student Responses to Selected CSXQ and CSEQ Items:
Out-of-Class Learning Activities

Item	Response Options	Percentage of CSXQ Respondents	Percentage of CSEQ First-Year Respondents
Use the library as a quiet place to study or read	Never	7	26
	Occasionally	48	48
	Often	33	16
	Very often	12	10
Read assigned materials other than textbooks in the library (reserve readings, etc.)	Never	8	38
	Occasionally	48	42
	Often	33	15
	Very often	11	5
Use email to communicate with an instructor or classmates	Never	6	4
	Occasionally	21	10
	Often	29	15
	Very often	44	70
Participate in class discussions using an electronic medium (e-mail, list-serv, chat group, etc.)	Never	28	55
	Occasionally	46	22
	Often	18	11
	Very often	8	12
Search the World Wide Web or Internet for information related to a course	Never	2	4
	Occasionally	14	18
	Often	32	26
	Very often	52	52
Attend a lecture or panel discussion	Never	14	35
	Occasionally	55	41
	Often	24	15
	Very often	7	9
Use a learning lab or center to improve study or academic skills (reading, writing, etc.)	Never	13	46
	Occasionally	48	33
	Often	29	14
	Very often	10	7

Note: The items listed are from the CSXQ; CSEQ items differ slightly. CSEQ items are worded in the past tense to reflect activities in which students engaged over the course of the academic year.

Information Sources: Libraries and Electronic Technology

Almost everyone starting college today expects to have access to a computer to do academic work—if not their own machine, then one available somewhere on campus or at their place of employment. This is true for older students as well, although they use the technology much less frequently. It is a good thing computers are ubiquitous because it is clearly the medium of choice for acquiring information. In fact, searching the Web for course material is as popular an activity as using campus recreational facilities, with 78 percent of all first-year students doing both "frequently" (combination of "often" and "very often"). That said, fewer students use electronic technology to discuss course topics (56 percent say they "never" did it). And it is mildly surprising that students use e-mail more than they expected and the library less. Indeed, the library is no longer a popular study venue: only about a quarter of first-year students go there "frequently" for this purpose, and another quarter "never" study there. Faculty members may be contributing to this trend, as 38 percent of students never read assigned materials there, although 92 percent of incoming students thought they might at least "occasionally" do so when they started college.

Grades

Although on average students spend far less time studying than faculty members assert is necessary, most do surprisingly well. For example, no one starting college expects to get a C or lower average, although about 6 percent report such grades at the end of the first year. Two-thirds think they will earn at least B+ or better grades, and 44 percent actually do. About 28 percent have B– or lower grades, more than three times the number who expected these grades. Interestingly, the same fraction—14 percent—who began college expecting to achieve an A average did so during the first year, at least by their own report.

Contacts with Faculty

Virtually everyone agrees that student-faculty interaction is an important factor in student success (Astin, 1993; Kuh et al., 1991; Pascarella & Terenzini, 1991; Tinto, 1993). Students starting college seem to agree. For example, 94 percent say they will at least occasionally ask their instructor about their performance. However, less than two-thirds actually do so. The majority (69 percent) expect to socialize at least "occasionally" with faculty members outside the classroom, but only about two-fifths (41 percent) report doing so. More than three-quarters (77 percent) expect that they will "frequently" ask their teachers for information about the course (assignments and such), but only about half (54 percent) do so. Perhaps the difference is that students are not certain how often they will need to ask faculty members for information, and so they err on the high side (Table 5.3). The discrepancy between what students expect and experience in terms of interacting with faculty is also partly due to reward systems and large first-year classes that discourage such contacts.

Table 5.3. First-Year Student Responses to Selected CSXQ and CSEQ Items: Faculty Interaction

Item	Response Options	Percentage of CSXQ Respondents	Percentage of CSEQ First-Year Respondents
Ask your instructor for information related to a course you are taking (grades, make-up work, assignments, etc.)	Never	1	5
	Occasionally	22	41
	Often	44	34
	Very often	33	19
Discuss ideas for a term paper or other class project with a faculty member	Never	4	21
	Occasionally	43	46
	Often	40	23
	Very often	13	10
Socialize with a faculty member outside the classroom (have a snack or soft drink, etc.)	Never	31	59
	Occasionally	56	27
	Often	10	9
	Very often	3	5
Ask your instructor for comments and criticisms about your academic performance	Never	7	34
	Occasionally	43	40
	Often	37	18
	Very often	13	8

Note: The items listed are from the CSXQ; CSEQ items differ slightly. CSEQ items are worded in the past tense to reflect activities in which students engaged over the course of the academic year.

For some topics and forms of interactions, "occasional" or infrequent contact between students and faculty members may be quite acceptable. For example, it is sufficient for most students to talk once or twice a term with a faculty member about matters such as career plans, to clarify assignments, or to ask for elaboration on course requirements. Faculty members could require such meetings, but apparently not many do so.

But we should be concerned about the relatively little interaction related to such areas as discussing term papers. More than a fifth (22 percent) of students say they "never" did so through the entire first year. This is in large part because faculty members do not require students to write many such papers. For example, more than three-quarters (78 percent) of students say they did not prepare any major reports (twenty pages or more) during the first year. Thus, we should not be surprised that there is a substantial gap (20 percent) between the number of students who expected to "frequently" put together different facts and ideas (81 percent) and students at the end of the year who say they did so (61 percent).

Cocurricular Activities

There is still a core group—the "collegiate tenth," I call them—that expects to participate actively in the formal cocurriculum such as student government, clubs, and other social organizations ("very often" worked on a campus club or organization). And about this same fraction does (Table 5.4). However, close to two-fifths (38 percent) of all first-year students never went to an organizational meeting of any kind, and only about half as many students who expected to work on a campus committee (78 percent) actually did (40 percent).

This is consistent with a growing body of evidence that today's students (especially men) prefer more spontaneous, informal peer group-initiated activities (Kuh, 1999; Levine & Cureton, 1998a; Marchese, 1996, 1998). Of course, more students are working while going to school and may find it difficult to fit

Table 5.4. First-Year Student Responses to Selected CSXQ and CSEQ Items: Extracurricular Activities

Item	Response Options	Percentage of CSXQ Respondents	Percentage of CSEQ First-Year Respondents
Use recreational facilities	Never	4	15
(pool, fitness equipment,	Occasionally	21	27
courts, etc.)	Often	34	26
	Very often	40	32
Attend a meeting of a campus	Never	13	38
club, organization, or student	Occasionally	40	27
government group	Often	30	15
	Very often	17	20
Work on a campus committee,	Never	22	61
student organization, or service	Occasionally	44	18
project (publications, student	Often	23	10
government, special event, etc.)	Very often	11	11
Manage or provide leadership	Never	29	68
for an organization or service	Occasionally	46	16
project, on or off the campus	Often	18	9
	Very often	7	8

Note: The items listed are from the CSXQ; CSEQ items differ slightly. CSEQ items are worded in the past tense to reflect activities in which students engaged over the course of the academic year.

traditional campus organization meetings into their schedules. Also, television, computers, and other visual media have had a pervasive influence on how this generation of students spends their time and prefers to learn.

Diversity Experiences

Experiences with diversity have substantial and positive effects for virtually all students and on a wide range of desirable college outcomes (Chang, 1999, 2001; Gurin, 1999; Hurtado, Milem, Clayton-Pedersen, & Allen, 1999). For example, Gurin (1999) argued that a diverse student body creates a learning environment that increases the probability that students will interact with peers from different backgrounds. Such interactions positively affect critical thinking (Pascarella et al., 2001) and also make students more open to subsequent diversity experiences (Pascarella et al., 1996; Whitt, Edison, Pascarella, Terenzini, & Nora, 2001).

If behavior is a window into what people value, first-year students seem to think diversity is important. However, they expect to have more interactions with students from different backgrounds than they subsequently experience. Their expectations in this respect are fairly high, with two-thirds thinking they will become acquainted with students from racial and ethnic backgrounds different from their own. But substantially fewer have "frequent" substantive discussions during the first year (42 percent) than they anticipated (60 percent) (Table 5.5). A fifth "never" had such discussions, about four times the number (5 percent) who thought this starting college.

First-year students were more likely than sophomores, juniors, and seniors to interact with students from different racial and ethnic backgrounds (Hu & Kuh, 2001b; Umbach & Kuh, 2003); this difference is likely a function of the fact that more first-year students live on campus in close proximity to people who are different. Students at doctoral and research-extensive universities are slightly more likely to interact with students from different backgrounds, perhaps because there are proportionately more students from diverse backgrounds attending such institutions. It might also be a result of concerted efforts to provide diversity-related programming.

THE EXPECTATION-EXPERIENCE GAP: IDEALISM OR SYMPTOMS OF SYSTEMIC PROBLEMS?

One explanation for the gap between students' expectations and their subsequent behavior during the first year is the "freshman myth." This view holds that matriculating traditional-age students see the college experience as interesting and exciting and wish to take advantage of everything that is within reach (Berdie, 1966; King & Walsh, 1972; Pace, 1970). As a result, they overstate what they can and will do, not to impress or be disingenuous but rather to express enthusiasm for what is before them (not unlike the broken New Year's resolution

Table 5.5. First-Year Student Responses to Selected CSXQ and CSEQ Items:
Interactions with Diverse Students

Item	Response Options	Percentage of CSXQ Respondents	Percentage of CSEQ First-Year Respondents
Make friends with students whose interests are different from yours [a]	Never	1	2
	Occasionally	22	30
	Often	46	41
	Very often	32	27
Make friends with students whose family background (economic, social) is different from yours [a]	Never	1	2
	Occasionally	17	25
	Often	47	41
	Very often	35	33
Make friends with students whose race or ethnic background is different from yours [a]	Never	1	3
	Occasionally	18	32
	Often	46	34
	Very often	36	31
Have serious discussions with students whose philosophy of life or personal values are very different from yours	Never	4	13
	Occasionally	32	36
	Often	38	29
	Very often	26	22
Have serious discussions with students whose religious beliefs are very different from yours	Never	7	16
	Occasionally	35	35
	Often	33	26
	Very often	24	22
Have serious discussions with students whose political opinions are very different from yours	Never	10	23
	Occasionally	39	36
	Often	32	23
	Very often	20	18
Have serious discussions with students whose race or ethnic background is very different from yours	Never	5	20
	Occasionally	34	36
	Often	36	23
	Very often	24	20

Note: The items listed are from the CSXQ; CSEQ items differ slightly. CSEQ items are worded in the past tense to reflect activities in which students engaged over the course of the academic year.

[a]CSEQ items begin, "Became acquainted with. . . ."

that quickly fades into memory). This is evident in almost every category of activity represented on the CSXQ and CSEQ and especially in the "enriching educational experiences" cluster of items on the NSSE, where larger proportions of first-year students than seniors indicate they plan to do them (for example, study abroad, study foreign language, do community service). This pattern also is evident in the responses to the "extracurricular organizational involvement" items where substantial proportions of students say they will "occasionally" do almost everything. It turns out that most do not do any of these.

In addition, students at the beginning of college expect the campus environment to be friendlier and more supportive than they experience by the end of the first year. The largest drop in favorable perceptions is with the college administration, where 76 percent of students starting college expect administrators to be responsive and helpful; by the end of the first year, only 54 percent see it that way. This is to be expected, perhaps, as the more experience one has with an organization, the more likely one will encounter some difficulty with the bureaucracy.

At the same time, students' expectations for academic and intellectual activities do not seem highly inflated or unrealistic. In fact, they are generally consistent with what faculty members assert is a reasonable level of academic effort in terms of amount of reading and writing. What is troubling, then, is that student experiences in most of these areas fall well short of what they and their teachers say they expect. Recall that while students apparently think they will need to study more in college than they did in high school, the majority still does not expect to come close to the ratio of two hours of preparation for each class hour. In addition, a significant fraction frequently comes to class unprepared. Even so, most earn B or better grades. This level of academic commitment does not comport with a definition of student success that will serve either students or the nation well in the long term. All this suggests a troubling mismatch between what students do and what they need to do to benefit from college.

CONSIDERATIONS IN CLOSING THE FIRST-YEAR STUDENT EXPECTATIONS-EXPERIENCE GAP

Colleges and universities have two primary obligations to first-year students. The first is to establish appropriately high performance expectations, inside and outside the classroom, that are appropriate to students' abilities and aspirations. The second obligation is to consistently use throughout the institution what the research shows to be educationally effective policies, programs, and practices:

- Get to students early. Students who have a more realistic understanding of what college life is like are more likely to make wise college enrollment decisions (Hossler, Schmit, & Vesper, 1998), devote higher levels of effort to educationally purposeful activities (Kuh et al., 1991; Olsen et al., 1998; Pace, 1990), be satisfied (Astin, 1993; Pascarella & Terenzini, 1991), and earn a baccalaureate degree (Astin, 1993; Pascarella & Terenzini, 1991; Tinto, 1993). This suggests we need to tell students early and often about what it takes to succeed. Although parents, siblings, and friends have considerable influence on the expectations and behavior patterns that students bring with them to college, the institution can make a difference by sending clear, consistent messages about what they can expect academically and socially (Kuh et al., 1991; Pascarella & Terenzini, 1991).

Teaching newcomers what is expected and how to behave is everyone's responsibility and must be well planned and conscientiously coordinated and implemented. Converting expectations into behavior must begin long before students arrive on campus. Indeed, the months prior to matriculation and the first six to eight weeks of the first semester are critical because it is during this period that students form impressions about the university environment and whether they "belong" in college (Pascarella & Terenzini, 1991; Tinto, 1993; Upcraft & Gardner, 1989).

With this in mind, staff members in the Indiana University Bloomington Offices of Admissions and Student Financial Assistance undertook a systematic review of their activities and the messages they were sending to prospective and matriculating students about academic and social norms, expectations for campus life, and the behaviors associated with academic success. To increase student-institution fit, special efforts were made to communicate to students and their families the institution's values and expectations, especially the importance of balancing the time and energy students devote to in-class and out-of-class activities.

Concomitantly, orientation program staff redesigned their print materials and programs in order to reinforce the academic messages the admissions office was sending to new students. Currently enrolled students created a video for matriculating students that focused on what to expect in the first year. Incoming students and their family members were strongly encouraged to watch it together. About two-thirds of those who saw it viewed it together as a family, and about three-quarters found it helpful in preparing for the transition to the university.

Some campuses (Miami University, University of North Carolina-Chapel Hill, University of Washington) use common readings to help set academic expectations prior to and immediately after students arrive on campus. One particularly creative twist, now institutionalized at Appalachian State University, is to have the book's author come to campus to meet with students and faculty members. Among the books recently used are *Who Wrote the Bible* by Richard Friedman (Augustana College in Illinois) and *Henry Ford* by Italo Calvino (Rider University) (Fidler, 1997). (For more information about summer and orientation readings, contact the National Resource Center for The First-Year Student Experience and Students in Transition at the University of South Carolina.)

Fall welcome week sets the tone and must reinforce the messages sent by admissions personnel and others. My university completely redesigned its welcome week to focus on inculcating academic values. The campus increased the amount of academic and intellectual content in programs and events, and reduced by half (from six to nine days to four on average) the amount of time students would be on campus prior to the first day of classes. The shorter, more compact schedule substantially cut into the amount of unstructured free time students had and resulted in record attendance (more than seven thousand) at the annual freshman induction ceremony and the president's picnic (more than five thousand). Residence life staff report that first-year student participation in campus cultural events is on the rise.

Faculty members must reinforce these same messages when meeting their classes in the early weeks of the semester, and design assignments that challenge and engage students for longer periods of time consistent with the learning goals of the course. They must hold students accountable for the quality of their academic efforts and perhaps even occasionally cajole them to go beyond what they think they can do academically (Chickering & Gamson, 1987; *Faculty Inventory: Principles for Good Practice in Undergraduate Education,* 1989). New students typically rely on previously learned ways of coping when they encounter novel circumstances, including preparing for class. A substantial fraction may not fully understand and appreciate their role as learners. To address these possibilities, faculty members and student affairs professionals must clearly and consistently communicate to students what is expected and provide periodic feedback as to the quality of students' performance. To paraphrase English professor Richard Turner (1998, p. 4), student success in college may require that professors explain more things to students today that were once taken for granted: "You must buy the book. You must read it and come to class. You must observe deadlines or make special arrangements when you miss one."

• Be smart in building programs and services that encourage student engagement in their own education. Interventions for promoting student success must be aligned with the institution's educational mission, students' characteristics, and effective educational practices. The NSSE assesses effective educational practices in five clusters of student and institutional performance: academic challenge, active and collaborative learning, student-faculty interaction, enriching educational experiences, and supportive campus environment (Kuh, 2001, 2003).

At big, organizationally complex campuses, it is not possible to immediately adopt and use good practices on a large scale. Thus, the scope and focus of improvement efforts must be manageable. It is wise to design an intervention that addresses a student behavior that can make an immediate difference in performance. Recall that far fewer students use campus learning and support services than expect to. At my campus, institutional research shows that students in high-risk courses were almost twice as likely to seek tutoring when it was available in their own residence hall as when the same service was provided in other campus locations. Student use of academic skills centers jumped when the centers were moved closer to where students lived, thereby increasing access. Now, three such centers have been placed in residence halls in different parts of the campus. Students who use these skill centers for mathematics and writing skill improvement are much more likely to persist to the second year and get higher grades than peers who do not, even though they are similar in most background characteristics, including academic ability (Hossler, Kuh, & Olsen, 2001).

• Do not assume first-year students will use the programs and services offered to encourage their involvement. In the movie *Field of Dreams,* hordes of baseball aficionados trekked to see the manicured baseball diamond in the middle of a cornfield. But simply having performing arts centers or libraries on a college campus does not guarantee that students will use them. Success-oriented colleges and universities find ways to get students to participate in activities and use venues that add educational value. If an institution espouses the importance of its students' cultivating aesthetic qualities, then students must be exposed to the cultural arts. Some institutions, such as Berea College, know that their students—because of their backgrounds—are not likely to attend cultural and performing arts events on their own, so they require them to take part in a certain number each semester. These experiences are more likely to have the desired impact if they are linked in a meaningful way to one or more classes the student is taking, such as tying trips to the theater to humanities or social science class assignments and asking students to connect what they observed to readings (Kuh, 1996). If we believe something is important, the curriculum should feature it and we should require students to experience it.

For example, faculty members can promote higher levels of student engagement by asking students to write papers that require synthesizing information from different fields, using e-mail to discuss course topics, and discussing feedback on assignments. Faculty members can influence the degree to which students contribute to class discussions or apply class material to other areas of their lives. The latter can be encouraged by designing assignments that feature and assign weight to the activity, such as placing materials on reserve in the library so students become familiar with the venue. Other powerful institution-driven learning experiences are consistent with the approach outlined here, such as service-learning courses and faculty-student research projects. Of course, all this depends on whether faculty members see these as valuable pedagogical techniques. In some instances, such as using electronic technology, the evidence is promising but not yet conclusive.

• Adapt services and programs to first-year students' backgrounds and characteristics. John N. Gardner reminds us that we are obliged always, without exception, to the students we have, not those we wish came to our college. Many colleges have responsibly responded to the call to educate a larger fraction of society. Too few have redesigned their learning environments to embrace these additional new students and promote their success.

Among the more successful efforts to prepare students from educationally disadvantaged backgrounds to meet the academic challenge they will face is the summer bridge program. Variable in name and format, some of these are geared to talented students, others to students who need academic enrichment, and others are open to anyone who is interested in getting a head start on college.

Programs with a strong residential component are among the more effective, allowing students to become familiar with the physical environment of the campus where they will matriculate, such as the Intensive Freshman Seminar and Groups Program at Indiana University Bloomington (Barovick, 2001). It is imperative that students in these special summer programs also fully participate in regular fall orientation activities alongside the rest of their classmates. Otherwise some unintended negative consequences might accrue, such as peers' perceiving certain groups of students as "special," a status that is difficult to shed and can have debilitating consequences for self-worth and academic achievement.

Early-warning systems and early feedback can be critical to student success. It is too late to wait until midterm exam time to give students an idea of how well they are performing. At large institutions, the system simply cannot respond quickly enough to help students salvage a poor semester if they need to wait until well beyond the midpoint of the semester before someone contacts them to formally suggest they need immediate attention to their academic work. Here, advisers and academic support program personnel can do some of their most important work. Some institutions, such as Truman State, are using the CSEQ to help students see how their in-class and out-of-class activities compare with those of their peers in terms of study time, talking with faculty members about various matters, and participation in cocurricular activities, to name a few.

Finally, institutions should fashion a success-oriented campus culture. Policy and programmatic interventions are necessary but insufficient to shift a campus to a student success paradigm. The cultural aspects of college life must also be addressed head-on in order to teach newcomers what the institution values and to imbue in them a sense of ownership and belonging. Toward this end, success-oriented colleges use rituals and traditions to introduce newcomers to the academic ethos and institutional norms, with a special sensitivity to welcoming and affirming members of historically underrepresented groups (Kuh, 1993; Magolda, 2001; Young, 1999).

Elon University has developed a powerful induction ceremony where students are introduced to the institution's values and its expectations for student performance are made plain. Under a stand of tall oak trees during the opening fall convocation, the Elon president personally hands each incoming student an acorn. He describes what the acorn represents, a seed such as themselves, that when placed in a nurturing environment can grow to be a tall, sturdy oak. Elon's spring commencement takes place in this same setting. Thus, four years later, the circle is completed when the president reminds them of the acorn they received during orientation their first year. Then each graduating senior receives an oak sapling, symbolizing his or her growth during the previous four years at Elon. Seniors are charged with planting their sapling in a place where they can nurture it to grow into a tall, mature oak, implying that intellectual and personal development does not end with college graduation but continues long after.

An equally powerful and compelling example is Amherst College, where faculty in full academic regalia lead students into the chapel to start the new academic year. Similar events occur at Macalester College and elsewhere around the country. Macalester goes one step further to demonstrate its value and commitment to community service by having all new students do some form of community work within the first few weeks of class as part of a first-year seminar course.

Some large universities such as Texas A&M and Western Washington University (Carey & Fabiano, 1997) stage first-year student induction ceremonies that can be powerful unifying events. At Indiana University Bloomington, parents are invited to participate to symbolize the breaking away from the family of origin to the academic community.

RECOMMENDATIONS

If an institution is serious about student engagement in the first college year, it should:

- Structure ways for first-year students to spend time in the company of peers. The best way to do this is to require students to live on campus. Students who live on campus are more engaged and gain more from their college experience. They are more likely to use the cultural and artistic venues the institution provides as well as have access to faculty and serious-minded peers. They also have more experiences with diversity.

Not all students can live on campus, of course. Because peers are so influential to student learning and values development, institutions must create ways to harness this influence in the context of educationally purposeful activities. One such approach with considerable appeal is some form of learning community where students take two or more courses together (Matthews, 1994; Tinto, 1996, Tinto, Goodsell Love, & Russo, 1993b).

- Limit who is allowed to come to campus before welcome week begins. Some institutions, in the spirit of being flexible and accommodating, allow new students to move into campus housing days, and in some instances more than a week, before formal welcome week activities commence. Of course, some students must be on campus before fall orientation or welcome week activities begin for auditions, athletics, and the like. Generally, these students will be kept busy enough in productive activities and not have large amounts of discretionary time to develop undesirable habits. However, other students can acquire anti-intellectual habits during this period without the institution's being able to counter with more appropriate socialization experiences. It is essential that to the extent possible, students' time be structured with meaningful, educationally sound, and socially cohesive activities that are consistent with the academic ethos from the moment they arrive on campus. We abdicate our responsibilities as educators if we leave students to their own devices to create alternative socialization patterns. Institutions must take a hard, firm line and allow few, if any, exceptions, for such exceptions serve no one's best interests.

• Balance academics and social activities during orientation and welcome week. Many colleges give too little emphasis to academic socialization, erring toward activities that are designed to help new students "become comfortable" in their new surroundings and "have fun" with their new acquaintances. As a result, welcome week has become the sole province of student affairs professionals with little involvement by the faculty, sending the wrong messages to everyone about what college is for and what the institution values. If there is one thing students do not need much help with, it is finding ways to have fun. Schools should minimize the amount of time new students are on campus before classes start to a maximum of three days. Any orientation activities that cannot be accomplished are either not important enough or can be accommodated in the first few weeks of the semester.

• Stitch together academic and social experiences. Whatever special academic programs are planned for first-year students, efforts must be made to intentionally connect the in-class and out-of-class spheres of students' lives. In general, efforts that tie the academic program to students' out-of-class experiences are likely to be the most successful. Examples of these are service-learning, freshman interest groups, and other forms of learning communities. During the mid-1990s, Portland State University developed a fall orientation program, the centerpiece of which was a scavenger hunt organized around substantive topics covered in the required Freshman Inquiry course. Thus, instead of simply putting students in small groups to get to know one another through the traditional scavenger hunt on campus, this one was based on the curriculum with activities that introduced students to both the academic program and resources of the campus and the City of Portland.

• Require a first-year seminar. First-year seminars are becoming more popular and take different forms. Particularly popular is the University 101 seminar developed at the University of South Carolina, which is primarily focused on an orientation to college and teaching students survival and academic success skills. Another variation is to organize academic offerings in the first year so that all first-year students have at least one discipline-based course with twenty-five or fewer students taught by a faculty member. Such seminars will be more fulfilling for students as well as instructors (faculty members, undergraduate mentors) if the latter are provided a structured opportunity to prepare and reflect periodically on their experiences in the company of colleagues.

• Reclaim and reward academic advising as a valued form of teaching. Although student perceptions are generally favorable in terms of the quality of their advising, much more can be accomplished through these important interactions between students and the institution. Advising need not be the exclusive responsibility of faculty members, though that arrangement is highly desirable. Professional advisers, student affairs staff, and librarians can be exceptional resources in this regard.

• Feature diversity throughout the first year. Student diversity is a significant educational resource. Institutions of higher education are expected to play a major role in preparing students from different backgrounds to live and work in a diverse society. Any attempts to improve undergraduate education inside and outside the classroom should include ways to encourage students to have multiple forms of interactions with students from different racial and ethnic backgrounds, as these experiences appear to have salutary effects on enhancing learning and personal development (Hurtado, Milem, Clayton-Pedersen, & Allen, 1999; Orfield, 2001; Umbach & Kuh, 2003). One reason it is important to establish patterns of interacting with people from different backgrounds in the first year is that the frequency of interactions with people different from oneself diminishes somewhat as one moves through college (Hu & Kuh, 2001a; Kuh et al., 2001), in part because students are more likely to live off campus after the first year. Because student and institutional characteristics explain only a small portion of the variance in diversity experiences (Hu & Kuh, 2001b), promoting informal interactions between students from diverse backgrounds will likely have desirable positive effects across the board. Thus, more programs and activities are needed that intentionally bring together people with different political views and religious traditions and from different countries of origin. These types of opportunities not only appear to have positive effects for all students, but also are more important than ever before in the light of recent world events.

CONCLUSION

Students' expectations for college often surpass the academic demands they are presented. That is, students typically study less, write less, and read less than they come to college expecting to do. The gap between expectations and experiences also extends to life beyond the classroom.

Low expectations almost always produce low levels of engagement. Both students and institutions bear their share of the responsibility for students' failing to realize the relatively high expectations students have when they start college. "Expect more and you will get more," Chickering and Gamson (1987, p. 5) opine. We must heed their advice. Students need to work harder and take advantage of more of the learning opportunities colleges and universities offer. Institutions need to hold students accountable for meeting mutually espoused standards of performance. We simply must do better at converting good intentions into educationally purposeful action.

We can do so by offering a challenging curriculum appropriate to our students' educational goals and aspirations. We can build and sustain a supportive campus environment. We can make available a variety of opportunities inside and outside the classroom that enrich the academic program and students' overall educational experience. And above all, we can teach newcomers how to use these resources and opportunities to educational benefit and make students feel as though they matter. All of these things can and have been done on many different types of campuses (Barefoot, 2000). All campuses must muster the will to do so as well.

Note

1. The CSXQ (expectations) data reported here are from thirty-two thousand students at three dozen four-year colleges and universities who filled out the survey when they were beginning college between 1998 and 2001. The CSEQ information is from about thirty-five thousand students at 121 four-year colleges and universities who filled out the survey near the end of their first year of college between 1998 and 2001. The NSSE database includes more than sixty thousand first-year students from 470 different four-year colleges and universities who completed the NSSE survey in 2000 and 2001. Although students from different institutions are represented, the student respondents in each data set are fairly similar in terms of background characteristics.

    For example, 95 percent of both CSXQ and CSEQ first-year respondents were nineteen years or younger, and most (83 percent) lived on campus, with almost everyone else living at home with parents when they started college. About a third were first-generation college students; 80 to 82 percent were white and 7 to 8 percent were African American, with the remainder distributed among other racial and ethnic backgrounds. Almost all started college at the school they were then attending (understandable in that the CSXQ is typically admitted to first-time first-year students). In addition, the proportions declaring various major fields line up quite well with other sources of major field distributions (Sax et al., 1999), with 18 percent indicating business, 9 percent education, 5 percent communications, and so on. The only difference in characteristics between the two groups—those completing the CSXQ and CSEQ—was related to gender, with about 53 percent of those completing the CSXQ and 62 percent of the CSEQ respondents being women.

    The demographic information aligns well with the larger NSSE database and the Cooperative Institutional Research Program (CIRP), although NSSE first-year respondents are somewhat older and more diverse in terms of race and ethnicity than CSXQ and CSEQ respondents. In addition, the key trends reported in this chapter essentially mirror those found in single-institution studies of the same students at the beginning and end of the first year of college (Olsen et al., 1998).

CHAPTER SIX

Expectations and Performance

Karen Maitland Schilling
Karl L. Schilling

*Well, before I came, I had tons of images of what college would be like. I was
scared because I didn't know if I could handle all of the work I'd be given.*
—Susie, first-year student

*I expect to not only grow intellectually, but also emotionally. I expect
to develop myself so I am well rounded and completely
ready when it is time to enter the real world. . . .*
—Annette, first-year student

*I thought in college . . . the classes would be extremely hard, with
students being happy to pass courses. I thought everyone would be
open-minded and much more liberal. I thought I would learn
many things and be able to take any course I wanted to.*
—Jim, first-year student

Imagine for a moment that these first-year students are seated in the front row
of the auditorium on your campus with several hundred other first-year students. It is the first day of a new school year. You have been asked, as an
administrator, to welcome incoming students and to set the tone for the work
that they will be facing at your institution. Or perhaps you, as a faculty member,
are sitting with a group of these students, reflecting somewhat anxiously on the
design of the new syllabus for the course you will be offering to a number of
these entering first-year students in the weeks ahead. Or maybe you are an
adviser. You look out on the sea of new faces and reflect for a moment on the
thousands of questions you anticipate trying to answer in the next few weeks.

But why should you care about what your first-year students' expectations
are when they come to your institution? These student expectations may or may
not seem particularly interesting to you. Even if you find them fascinating, you
might ask, "Shouldn't our focus as faculty, staff, or administrators be on sharing
our expectations for student engagement with our institutions?" Isn't this what
we mean when we talk about "raising the bar"? Isn't it our expectations, not
the students', that really matter? Why is awareness of students' expectations
important for my work? As faculty and staff, isn't it our job to create expecta-

tions for students through our syllabi, lectures, institutional policies, and grading standards, not the other way around? Clearly, this is not an either-or question. Both students and faculty have expectations of themselves and for each other. We think it is important to focus on both student expectations about what college will be like as well as faculty and institutional expectations for students and then examine the gaps between these sets of expectations. It is in these gaps that we find the greatest sources of student dissatisfactions as well as the greatest faculty disappointments with students. Narrowing these gaps can help facilitate successful transitions for students to college.

In this chapter, we will briefly review discussions of expectations in the higher education community and present a quick overview of the perspectives offered by psychologists on the importance of expectations in shaping human performance in a broad range of domains. We will suggest some strategies for learning about expectations on your campus. We will lay out what is currently known about expectations of students and the expectations of institutions for students. In this chapter, we present results from some of our research conducted at Miami University. Because this institution enrolls traditional-age, predominantly white college students from middle- and upper-middle-class backgrounds, this research cannot be generalized to institutions with more diverse first-year students. However, we do believe that the techniques used in this research can be adapted effectively to other institutions, regardless of the makeup of the student body.

We will also present several approaches to getting information about the expectations of students. We will argue for the critical importance of the first year in providing an intentional socialization of students to their appropriate role, suggesting the important functions that experiences in the first year play in putting in place patterns of behavior that will endure over the students' years at our institutions. We will identify other gaps, in addition to the gap between student expectations and faculty or institutional expectations that may limit the educational effectiveness of our colleges and universities. We will end with a discussion of implications of this research for practice and policy development on campus, including offering a list of some suggested actions.

WHY CARE ABOUT FIRST-YEAR STUDENT EXPECTATIONS?

By the time first-year students arrive on campus, they have a myriad of expectations swirling around in their heads about what college will be like. For some students, these expectations have been building for a long time; college has been a family goal for them almost from birth. For others, the idea of college is more recent, and their expectations may be less specific and differentiated than those of students who have parents or siblings who have been orienting them to college long before they set foot on a college campus. However, it is safe to bet that most students arrive with fantasies and nightmares about what will happen to them at college. No first-year student arrives with a truly blank slate.

It is important for faculty and staff to realize this when they try to write their expectations on a student's slate: these new expectations will be interpreted in the context of what has already been written on that slate.

From the literature in psychology (Bandura, 1982; Dweck & Leggett, 1988; Feather, 1966; Zajonc & Brickman, 1969), we know that expectations are very important in shaping human behavior. Researchers have found that merely stating an expectation results in better performance, and the higher the expectations are, the higher the level of performance given is. Expectations can influence students' willingness to take on, actively engage in, and persist in responding to intellectual challenges.

Higher education policy leaders have also sought to bring a focus on expectations. A report by the National Institute of Education (1984) called for institutions to heighten their expectations for student learning. This report acknowledged that students come to college with widely varying educational backgrounds and skill levels. The report's authors urged faculty and institutions to challenge students to perform at a higher level, with the understanding that faculty would provide the necessary support to allow students to attain these higher levels of performance. More recent influential works, including Involving Colleges (Kuh et al., 1991) and An American Imperative: Higher Expectations for Higher Education (Wingspread Group, 1993), have echoed this call for heightening expectations for student performance.

But what is the strategy that is most likely to achieve the goals identified in these reports? Even within the homogeneous Miami University sample cited at the beginning of this chapter, the range of student responses to our question about expectations is remarkable and presents a challenge to anyone wishing to deliver a message about higher expectations. If I am eighteen years old and pumped up with new feelings of independence, how am I going to hear a presentation on the exciting new general education requirements? If I am already scared to death about how hard classes will be, how am I going to react to the amplification of that theme in the emphasis on the demanding nature of college work? If I am scared to death that I will not even be able to find the rooms where my classes are meeting, how will I hear the invitation to undertake new and exciting risks? If I am looking around for women to date, I may not fully share the presenters' excitement over this new first-year seminar. Or if I am really excited about all of the new things I am going to learn in new and challenging ways, how am I going to react to courses and modes of instruction that sound and feel a lot like the boring high school classes I thought I had left behind?

Much of the recent discussion of the importance of shifting attention on campuses from an emphasis on teaching to an emphasis on learning (Barr & Tagg, 1995) recognizes the difficulties in assuming that even the best-delivered message to students will be received intact and suggests that we may be using the wrong metaphors to shape thinking about interactions with students. If faculty continue to think of their role as one focused on delivery, they may find that no one is home to receive their "packages." In discussing our work with students in the teaching and learning process, we might more productively employ the metaphor of taking a journey together. In this chapter, as we think about our expectations for students, their expectations of themselves, their expectations for their collegiate experience, and of their professors, we try to envision all of us—students, faculty, and staff—together in the same boat. Having a shared understanding of expectations of where we are trying to go and how we are going to get there—paddling in the same direction—is more likely to foster a successful journey through college.

The current national preoccupation with standards may seem to parallel this focus on high expectations. There are important differences, though, between the discussions about standards and those around expectations that relate to our investments in facilitating successful transitions for students. The discussion about standards is about raising the bar—focusing on the competence that should be there at the end of students' educational journey. This powerful rhetorical stance for higher standards—achieving better "end products" from the educational systems—does nothing, however, to illuminate for students the steps that they must take to reach these new levels of performance. Setting high expectations involves sharing with students what we know about the steps that they need to take in order to meet these new, higher standards. However, currently many students are seemingly on the job without a job description. As educators, we have a choice: help provide this job description (Schilling, 2001) or continue to let students write their own job descriptions as they go along, based on their evolving and very partial sense of what it takes to succeed on campus, while we sit back smugly observing their struggles or choosing to look the other way when they fail.

UNDERSTANDING STUDENT EXPECTATIONS

If we agree that understanding expectations is important, how do we go about learning more about student expectations and also clarifying faculty and institutional expectations for students? There are basically two choices: an institution may proceed on its own by asking its students about their expectations of their collegiate experience or participate in national studies such as those suggested in Chapter Five. Or some combination of both might fit best.

The more local and personal approach begins with asking first-year students before they enroll to respond to selected prompts. In other words, if we are interested in learning about students' expectations, why not ask them? The student quotations that opened this chapter were produced in free-writing exercises. At either summer orientation or the end of the first semester in college, first-year students were asked to respond to prompts. At summer orientation, the prompt was: "Write for five minutes about your hopes, dreams, fears, and expectations for the fall semester." At the end of the fall semester, it was this prompt: "Before you came to Miami, what did you think college would be like?" Students were instructed to write for a few minutes, not removing their pens from the paper.

The results, as the illustrative quotations suggest, provide insights into students' lives without requiring a significant time investment. We have sometimes conducted systematic content analysis of collections of such free-writes in order to make some generalizations about students. We have also often found it helpful to share an unedited collection of student responses to such questions with faculty for their consideration and discussion. For several years, in the School of Interdisciplinary Studies at Miami University, first-year students and their parents were asked each year during summer orientation to write briefly about their "hopes, dreams, and aspirations for the coming year." These responses were collected, duplicated, bound, and then distributed to the entering class and faculty at the beginning of the fall semester as an introduction to the new class. The responses of each class and their parents had a distinctive character that seemed to follow entering classes across their college years.

Another approach is to use a more standardized approach to understanding expectations through use of available questionnaires that focus on students' expectations. Perceptions, Expectations, Emotions, and Knowledge About College (PEEK) developed by Weinstein, Palmer, and Hanson (1995) samples student expectations in three major domains: personal, social, and academic. With help from Deborah Olsen and George Kuh and their support staffs at Indiana University, we developed a modification of the College Student Experiences Questionnaire (Kuh, Vesper, Connolly, & Pace, 1997), called the College Student Expectations Questionnaire (CSXQ), which focuses on student expectations as they enter college. The CSXQ, discussed by Kuh in Chapter Five, uses modified versions of many of the questions from the CSEQ survey about student experiences to gather data on student expectations about the same areas that are explored on the CSEQ: library and information technology, student interactions with faculty members, course learning activities, writing experience, campus programs and facilities, clubs and organizations, student acquaintances, scientific and quantitative experiences, topics of conversation, information in conversation, and amount of reading and writing. The parallelism between the two forms allows ready comparison of students' experiences after a year or more in college with their initial expectations.

WHAT WAS LEARNED ABOUT STUDENTS' EXPECTATIONS?

When we have asked students to respond in an open-ended fashion about their expectations for their college or university experience, we have found, consistent with Weinstein et al. (1995), that these responses most often fall into three domains: academic, personal, and social. As reflected in the quotations at the beginning of this chapter, entering first-year students most often compare and contrast the expected difficulty of college classes to their high school classes. They talk of fears of hard, intimidating, and aloof professors and large classes with intense competition. They express excitement about learning new things and maturing intellectually. Not surprisingly, personal issues are also on students' minds. Particularly in this group of eighteen year olds, students emphasize freedom and independence, missing family and friends, increased responsibility, maturation and self-development, and having their values tested. Expectations also center on social engagement or campus life: fitting in to new groups, being exposed to diverse peoples and perspectives, making commitments to new activities, and partying.

Faculty, staff, and administrators may despair in reading comments like these from incoming students about their personal and social expectations for college, wishing to see students place greater emphasis on the purely academic. However, it is important to note the similarity of these domains, identified by students in stating their expectations for college life, to the domains identified by faculty committees in their attempts to formulate statements of general education goals and objectives for students. There is a convergence here that is almost never identified. General education programs typically emphasize new learning in traditional academic areas, but they also emphasize development of personal values and sense of self and social engagement—those tasks most often associated with responsible citizenship—which are the same personal and social domains identified in student expectations.

On most campuses, though, faculty and staff bemoan student "resistance" to general education and puzzle over how to overcome the student view of general education as "something to get out of the way." How is it that understandings of student expectations in the personal and social domains do not provide the foundation for these broader general education goals? Perhaps if we had a bit more insight into students and their expectations for college—expectations very similar to those that faculty and staff hold for them in the personal, social, and academic domains—we would not have to work so hard at convincing them of the things we think would be good for them.

It is interesting to imagine what a general education program would look like if it were to begin with this set of assumptions about goals already shared by students and faculty. It might begin in student statements like those at the beginning of this chapter, with discussion of reasonable expectations for academic engagement, and move on to discussions of social and personal engagement. Today on most campuses, we struggle to get students on board. We then paddle in different directions, all the while bemoaning the fact that we are getting nowhere fast. If we take the time to listen, we may find that students are on board already. Recognizing and acknowledging publicly our shared concerns and goals can change the tone of the conversation. Think of how far we could go if we all paddled in the same direction.

MAKING THE LEAP FROM HIGH SCHOOL TO COLLEGE-LEVEL INVESTMENTS

When entering first-year students describe their expectations for college-level work, most identify the need to work harder than they did when they were in high school. Many recall a specific interaction with a high school teacher who chided them, "Just wait until you get to college!" as instrumental in this change. But even if they get this message, students rarely recognize the differences in scale that are involved. Working twice as hard may seem to be a real stretch. But if the student's daily total investment in out-of-class work during high school has been about an hour a day, as the data collected annually from the Cooperative Institutional Research Program would suggest is accurate for the average high school student in the last year of high school, then the change that would represent the needed investment identified by most faculty in their "two to three hours outside of class for every hour in class," would mean working ten times as hard as they did in high school—a stretch that may seem nearly impossible to imagine even for the most committed student.

But perhaps this imagining is not really necessary. We have compared student expectations, indexed by the CSXQ at the start of the first year, and these same students' reported actual experiences in their first year, indexed by the CSEQ at the end of the first year. Following students longitudinally is always a challenge, but the insights that come from these repeated assessments can be very powerful. Consistent with the findings presented in Chapter Five, not only do students report working less than they expected, but also they do fewer additional readings outside class than they expected, they read less about scientific theories and concepts, go to art exhibits and varied cultural events less than expected, and so on. The overall pattern of results suggests that although students' initial expectations for their academic involvement may be less than faculty might wish, their actual engagement is even less than those initial expectations.

Students' grades, however, do not suffer proportionally. Earlier researchers (Berdie, 1966, 1968; Stern, 1970; Whiteley, 1982; Baker, McNeil, & Siryk, 1985), observing a similar discrepancy between students' reality and their expectations, described this gap as the "freshman myth." However, such a formulation placed the blame on students for the disappointing reality of their engagement—asserting that they had unrealistic expectations for their own engagement—rather than crediting students for being good economists and accurately reading the environmental cues in their new surroundings about how much they needed to work in order to achieve the grades they desired. Imagine the impact if curricula and course expectations lived up to this freshman myth. What if colleges fully engaged those initial expectations of entering first-year students? The curricular challenges offered would have to go far beyond current levels.

Based on our longitudinal studies of student time use, we have written elsewhere (Schilling & Schilling, 1999) of the importance of the first year in establishing durable economies of time investment for students. Using the well-established methodology of event sampling (Larson & Csikszentmihalyi, 1983), we have been able to profile students' allocation of time during a typical week in a semester. Using programmable watches, we periodically signaled students in preset random patterns over a week's time. Each time a student is signaled, they record in two to three words the activity they are engaged in at that moment. This sampling has allowed us to specify economies of time for individual students—to identify categories of behavior such as academic work and socializing and to catalogue students' relative apportionment of time to these various activities in the course of a typical week.

This approach to understanding time on task can graphically and powerfully represent for students the choices they make about investment of time in academic work as well as in other activities. Students often initially express surprise at their time investment profiles, but on reflection, they have typically expressed considerable enthusiasm for the accuracy of the method for capturing their time investments. First-year students often have commented on how different their pattern of time investment was from what they recalled of their typical time investments during their last year of high school. In trying to summarize these data for faculty to talk about typical first-year students, we observed considerable variability across students in patterns of time investment.

However, in contrast to this variability across students in patterns of time allocation, we observed remarkable consistency across years for students in their individual patterns of time allocation. We were able to enlist the participation of students across several years in these event-sampling tasks. These longitudinal profiles are particularly illuminating. Students appear to set in place in their first semester the pattern of time allocation that will serve them across their years at college. The patterns of allocation of time observed in a student's last year of college mirror the patterns of time allocation in the first year. Time apportioned for academic work is remarkably stable over students' four years. So if little time investment is required to master the demands of the first-year curriculum, that minimal time investment will likely characterize students' academic engagement in their senior year. Students are busy making up that job description for "college student" in their day-to-day activities in their first year. This is not the typical justification offered for putting in place a challenging general education curriculum, but perhaps we should be giving less attention to the content of general education and more attention to general education as intellectual basic training or boot camp: demanding introductions to college or university life that are designed to exercise the mind and produce a fitness for later college-level work—work designed to live up to the freshman myth and narrow another troubling gap between expectations and experience.

UNDERSTANDING FACULTY EXPECTATIONS

Faculty and staff also come to each year with a set of expectations about what the year will be like and who their students will be. Through their syllabi, faculty communicate a set of expectations for students' performance in the design of their assignments and their grading criteria. We have asked faculty time and again during visits to campuses across this country how they communicate their expectations to students. There is remarkable convergence about a statement made on the first day of class—in community colleges, liberal arts institutions, and comprehensive and research universities: "I expect you to put in two [or three] hours outside of class for every hour in class." This statement has made it into student guidebooks, deans' or presidents' welcoming speeches for new students, and faculty course syllabus overview sessions with students at the beginning of thousands of courses each term. When asked the origin of this bit of advice to students, faculty, time and again, have reacted with surprise. "Isn't that what everybody says?" "That's what I was always told." "Seems about right." Occasionally a professor will say, "That's how long it will take to do the work well enough to really understand it." Rarely do professors detail the nature of student assignments and the kinds and amounts of work that will be necessary to complete the course to the specified level of proficiency. Many first-year students sit puzzled, trying to figure out what they should be doing in those two hours dedicated to each class when they have completed the assigned tasks in less than an hour.

Our work suggests that it is important for faculty to realize the important role that they play in the design of their first-year classes and the significant impact that this course design can have on the socialization of students. By detailing the specific activities that will lead to success in their courses, professors will define college-level work for their first-year students. Can faculty do a better job of clueing students in on what they believe it takes to succeed? Most faculty have a clear sense of what they view as college-level work. They know the kinds of papers they would like to receive in their senior seminars. Can they share with first-year students the steps it will take to get from here to there?

We have developed an interview protocol to help faculty to enhance the clarity of their expectations for students. Some sample questions from this interview are included in Exhibit 6.1. Most faculty in their own educational background have had the experience of being the "good students" in their classes. Many of the steps for gaining understanding that were obscure to other students were obvious, almost automatic, for these faculty when they were students. Then as faculty members, these "former good students" tend to be less conscious of teaching the steps that may be necessary for their students to follow in order to achieve identified class objectives. If faculty are able to clarify their expectations for students, they too will be more satisfied with the level of student accomplishment in their classes.

CULTURAL AUDIT: THE CUES WE GIVE ABOUT WHAT WE EXPECT

We have discussed how faculty expectations may not be communicated to students with sufficient clarity or detail. It is also the case that as students scan the campus environment, they may encounter a broad variety of cues related to expectations that may either support or contradict the messages of the faculty and staff about expectations. What messages do typical campus viewbooks communicate to prospective students about their role as a student, for exam-

Exhibit 6.1. Sample Questions from a Faculty Interview About Expectations

1. What do you expect a student to bring to this class, i.e., what kinds of knowledge, skills such as reading and writing, ability to ask questions, etc., do you expect from a student who will likely earn the equivalent of a B grade in this course?
2. How much time devoted to this class would you expect that a student enrolled in this course who wishes to earn the equivalent of a B grade would spend outside of class each week?
3. How is this expectation communicated to students?
4. What kinds of activities would you expect a student in your course to engage in, for what amounts of time?
5. What kinds of expectations do you have for attendance?
6. What would be your expectations for in-class hours? What kinds of activities would students engage in?
7. What kinds of assignments do you typically require in this course?
8. Do students typically need to use the library or a laboratory to complete these assignments? How about a computer? To do what?
9. Do you expect that they [students] will use other resources on or off campus to complete the work for this course? If yes, what are they?
10. Do you expect that they [students] will meet with other students, need to attend campus lectures or other events, travel to another site, etc., to complete these assignments?
11. How often do you expect that students will get together outside of the classroom around the focus of your course?

ple? What do the all-too-common outdoor campus scenes of tanned students sitting under leafy trees on sunny days communicate about expectations for intellectual engagement? Or do they contribute to the confusing mixed messages that students receive about college life? The intersections of policies on grading, minimum hours of registration, and financial aid are problematic for faculty who are committed to setting high expectations on many campuses. Students may confront faculty on the "$10,000 C" they just received in their class that will make the difference in their continued eligibility for financial aid.

We have developed a cultural audit to guide exploration of cues about expectations on campus. Sample questions from this audit are included in Exhibit 6.2. The logic behind this assessment strategy and the others identified thus far is simple and straightforward: if faculty and staff understand the expectations that entering first-year students bring to campus, if they work consistently to support and heighten these expectations, and if they clearly and consistently state their own expectations for students, then student performance likely will be enhanced. By getting all the parties paddling in the same direction, we will likely get somewhere that is different and better from the place where we started, and our shared journey will be much more interesting and rewarding.

Exhibit 6.2. Sample Questions from a Cultural Audit Focused on Expectations

1. What are the best features of academic life at _____ How are these promoted?
2. What is attendance like at special campus lectures, arts events, etc.?
3. What do your promotional materials sent to prospective applicants convey about the academic focus at _____?
4. What are your library hours? How many students are in the library on a weekday night? On the weekend?
5. When does the weekend begin? How do you know? When does it end?
6. What newspapers and magazines are readily available on your campus? Are they well used?
7. Does your campus newspaper give prominent coverage to academic life on campus? Do academic achievements get equal billing with social or athletic achievement?
8. Are there visible and prominent ways to recognize the academic achievements of students on your campus?
9. How prominent are student literary magazines, student productions, student poster sessions, etc.?
10. Are there vehicles for students to play an active role in curriculum and pedagogical development?
11. On a stroll through campus residence halls, what percentage of students is reading or studying? What percentage is watching television? Other prominent activities?
12. What are the strongest academic traditions on your campus?
13. If a student is really excited about an idea, what does it take for that student to get support to do focused independent work in that area?
14. What does your admissions staff communicate to prospective students about the academic experiences of students on your campus?
15. What messages about campus policies on financial aid eligibility, dismissal, suspension, etc., communicate academic expectations to students?
16. How readily can you distinguish a first-year student from a graduating senior on your campus? What are the differences you identify?

RECOMMENDATIONS

If an institution is serious about establishing high expectations for first-year students, it should:

• Encourage faculty and staff efforts to shape student expectations with their initial engagements with first-year students, because the chances of success will be greater than at any other time during their college careers.
• Work to collect, understand, and respond to the expectations of first-year students. They arrive on campus with expectations about what their college

experience will be like based on their experiences in high school and what they have heard about college from their older siblings, friends, movies, and other sources. There is already writing all over what we have presumed to be a blank slate. What we write anew will be interpreted in the context of what has been written previously. If we work to collect, understand, and respond to expectations of entering students about college, we can play a more productive role in helping students make a successful transition from high school to college.

• Intentionally socialize first-year students to a rigorous, demanding college life. First-year students come to campus expecting to work harder than they actually do during the first year. In referring to this gap as the freshman myth, previous researchers have wrongly suggested that this is a student problem—a loss of motivation or inaccurate perceptions about college. A more compelling explanation for this gap comes from examination of the actual level of academic demands presented to students in the first year.

• Integrate students' expectations with general education goals. Students' expectations for college usually focus on academic, personal, and social domains. These are the same domains of focus for general education programs on many campuses. Greater student buy-in to the goals of general education can come from identification of this convergence and enhanced faculty understanding of student expectations as a starting point for general education.

• Design the first-year curricula to create the kinds of students we wish to have in senior seminars. The initial experience in college sets patterns of time usage for students that will remain durable throughout their collegiate experience. For example, students who devote 15 percent of their waking time to academic efforts in their first year are very likely to devote about 15 percent of their waking time to academic activity in their senior year. Those entering our institutions learn how to be college students in their first months on campus. Faculty should be more reflective about their own pedagogical practice and more willing to share with their students realistic information based on data about the kinds and amounts of effort that students must engage in to be successful in their classes.

• Encourage faculty to share with their students realistic information based on data about the kinds and amounts of effort that students must engage in to be successful in their classes. They need to incorporate this message into their pedagogical practice.

• Use first-year seminars to reorient students to the college experience. Provide a description based on evidence about what it takes to be a successful college student at the institution.

• Conduct campus culture audits that collect data and information on student as well as faculty, staff, and administrators' expectations. Institutional policies, procedures, and day-to-day practices often send conflicting messages to students about what they must do in order to succeed on campus. It is rare for students to receive consistent messages about expectations for their behavior. Audits of campus culture can identify these conflicting messages and guide institutional actions to communicate more clearly and consistently about expectations for students. Institutional cultures are different based on the kinds of students served, the nature of the faculty, and the history and traditions of the institution. Thus, each institution should gather its own data and information on students as well as on faculty, staff, and administrators' expectations.

• Share data about student time use, cultural audits, student interviews, and portfolios of actual student work with faculty, so that they can engage students in meaningful conversations about expectations. These conversations can be used to help clarify institutional goals related to student learning. Orientation and admissions and recruitment programs that are rooted in such clarified goals are likely to be much more successful.

CONCLUSION

In order for the expectations-experience gap to be narrowed or eliminated, institutions must develop very intentional strategies to create and sustain high and clear expectations for first-year students. That includes knowing what first-year students' expectations are and transforming them by challenging them with experiences that result in a rigorous academic and collegiate experience. Creating a challenging educational environment can happen only if faculty, administrators, and staff make an intentional and concerted effort to do so.

PART THREE

CREATING CAMPUS CULTURES FOR FIRST-YEAR STUDENT SUCCESS

There are some misguided institutions of higher education that believe that all they have to do is string together a series of unrelated courses, services, and programs to promote first-year student success. To be sure, these efforts are very important and will be described and discussed throughout the remainder of this book. However, a more subtle yet equally important effort in promoting first-year student success is to create a challenging and supportive campus environment that enables these students to succeed. According to Upcraft and Schuh (1996), a campus environment is defined as the elements and conditions of the college campus milieu that affect student learning and growth. Creating this kind of campus environment is not an easy task, because it involves a whole array of interrelated and integrated efforts on the part of all the various constituents of the institution: the leadership, the faculty, student affairs professionals, administrative staff, and, perhaps most important, first-year students themselves.

The late Ernest L. Boyer Sr. (1990) offered a useful framework within which to view campus environments. He identified five principles on which to build a challenging and supportive campus community. First, it should be a *purposeful* community, that is, a place where the intellectual life is central and where faculty and students work together to strengthen teaching and learning. Second, it should be a *just* community, where the dignity of all individuals is affirmed and where equality of opportunity is vigorously pursued. Third, it should be an *open* community, where freedom of expression is uncompromisingly protected and civility is powerfully confirmed. Fourth, it should be a *disciplined* community, where individuals accept their obligations to the group and well-defined governance procedures guide behavior for the common good. Finally, it should be a *caring* community, where the well-being of each member is sensitively supported and service to others is encouraged.

Boyer (1997) held that students' educational experiences should not be compartmentalized by time, space, or curriculum, but rather should be connected in a highly integrated fashion. Nowhere is that more true than with institutional efforts to create challenging and supportive campus climates for first-year student success. Most colleges and universities organize themselves as if the first-year experience were neatly compartmentalized into business, academic, and student affairs instead of organizing it in ways that Boyer envisioned—an institution that is connected in a highly integrated and coherent fashion, unrestricted by artificial organizational boundaries.

The chapter authors of this part of the book have written about ways that institutions can create campus environments consistent with Boyer's assertions. First, consistent with Boyer's principle of a just campus, institutions must create campus environments that provide an equal opportunity for all first-year students to succeed. In Chapter Seven, Freeman Hrabowski III argues for creating institutions that establish high expectations for and avoid negative stereotyping of first-year students, particularly those historically underrepresented in higher education. He suggests several ways of meeting this challenge. In Chapter Eight, W. Terrell Jones explores the realities of the diversity of today's first-year students and how to create campus environments that are both tolerant and affirming of all students, regardless of their backgrounds and characteristics. In Chapter Nine, Diana Natalicio and Maggy Smith present a case study of an urban, public university's efforts to build a campus climate that fosters first-year student success, which is consistent with Boyer's notions of purposeful, disciplined, and caring campus communities.

Committed and effective campus leadership is essential to building challenging and supportive campus environments, consistent with Boyer's notion that an institution should be connected in a highly integrated and coherent fashion, unrestricted by artificial organizational boundaries. In Chapter Ten, Betty Siegel discusses the important role of the president in organizing for first-year student success and building support among the entire collegiate community to accomplish that goal. But a president alone cannot create a challenging and supportive campus environment. Just as important is faculty and staff support of campus environments that promote first-year student success. In Chapter Eleven, Jay Chaskes and Ralph Anttonen make the case for the important role of first-year student advocates in building and sustaining first-year courses, programs, and services that create such environments. Yet all of these efforts to create challenging and supportive environments are weakened if there is not close collaboration among all parts of the institution, but especially academic and student affairs. In Chapter Twelve, Charles Schroeder examines why collaborative partnerships between academic and student affairs are important to creating campus environments that promote first-year student success and discusses several strategies to attain this goal.

Another important aspect of creating challenging and supportive campus environments is the enormous impact of technology not only on the first-year student experience but the overall campus environment as well. Undoubtedly, the massive infusion of technology into the lives of first-year students, both before and during their enrollment, is a significant influence in their collegiate experience, an influence that in turn has affected most other aspects of the campus environment. Technology has an especially powerful influence on Boyer's notion of an open community. So we explore the challenges technology presents to both students and the institutions in which they enroll. In Chapter Thirteen, Reynol Junco reviews the many ways in which technology touches the lives of first-year students, for good and for ill, and discusses ways in which technology can be used to contribute to first-year student success as well as improve campus environments.

CHAPTER SEVEN

Fostering First-Year Success
of Underrepresented Minorities

Freeman A. Hrabowski III

George Kuh (in Chapter Five) and Karen Maitland Schilling and Karl Schilling (in Chapter Six) highlighted the importance of establishing and maintaining high standards and expectations for first-year students. These efforts certainly are important for all first-year students, but they are especially critical for first-year underrepresented minority students. This chapter focuses on critical factors and best practices related to the academic performance of these students, with an emphasis on African American, Hispanic, and Native American students. That emphasis in no way implies that other minorities are less important, but typically efforts to foster first-year success among underrepresented minorities have focused on these three groups. Moreover, much of what is known about student success is relevant to other minorities as well.

It is important to examine the experiences of these minority students because they represent an increasingly large portion of American college students and trail significantly behind their white and Asian American counterparts in terms of high school completion, college participation, and college graduation rates. This chapter discusses the importance of establishing high expectations for minority students and avoiding their being stereotyped. It also addresses such potentially positive factors as institutional commitment, focused efforts to recruit these students, faculty and staff commitment, the out-of-class environment, and campus leadership. Throughout this chapter, I will offer a variety of examples involving the academic performance of minorities in the sciences, because these groups do least well in these disciplines.

Now, more than ever before, it is important to examine issues related to the first-year success of underrepresented minority students. There are now slightly over 4 million racial and ethnic minority students in higher education, or 27 percent of all students (Chronicle of Higher Education, 2002). For the foreseeable future, enrollments of these students will continue to grow at a modest rate (Dervaries, 2001). In 1999–2000, they also accounted for nearly 22 percent of bachelor's degrees awarded and nearly 26 percent of associate degrees (Chronicle of Higher Education, 2002).

ESTABLISHING HIGH EXPECTATIONS AND AVOIDING NEGATIVE STEREOTYPING

School systems across America, working to elevate the achievement level of all students, are focusing special attention on initiatives to close the achievement gap between minority and other students. Colleges and universities, often supported by federal agencies, corporations, and foundations, are implementing multidimensional programs to recruit and educate minority students. Such heightened interest in minority achievement has also produced growing research in this area, often focusing on model programs and best practices. What stands out is that many underrepresented minority students are ill prepared for college work, and even those with relatively high SAT scores and strong high school grade point averages (GPAs) often fail to persist, for example, in the science pipeline (Seymour & Hewitt, 1997). Moreover, many minority students, even those with strong academic backgrounds, offer evidence that variables other than K–12 preparation and innate ability account for low minority achievement and persistence. Such variables may include motivational and performance vulnerability in the face of negative stereotypes and low expectations for performance, academic and cultural isolation, peers who are not supportive of academic success, and perceived and actual discrimination (Garrison, 1987; Nettles, 1988; Allen, 1992; Steele & Aronson, 1995; Seymour & Hewitt, 1997; Maton, Hrabowski, & Schmitt, 2000; Gandara & Maxwell-Jolly, 1999).

Particularly perplexing among these variables are negative stereotypes and low expectations. For many underrepresented minority students, the threat of being negatively stereotyped is a self-confirming concern. In such instances, students find themselves in situations (such as testing) where they perceive an external expectation that they will fail or perform poorly based on their minority status; this perception generates anxiety, which can lead to poor performance, thereby confirming the students' concern. In a revealing study conducted by psychologist Claude Steele (1997), first-year mostly minority students at the University of Michigan who were judged to have remedial needs were recruited to live in a dormitory to participate in a remedial program promoted as challenging and having high expectations. The black students in the program performed substantially better in first-semester courses than black students who had participated in other remedial programs. These same students also demonstrated almost no underachievement compared to white first-year students. (Follow-ups revealed that these black students did well throughout their sophomore year and dropped out far less often than black students who participated in other remedial programs.) In another study, Steele and Aronson (1995) also found that when black students were given difficult verbal-ability tests, they did not perform as well as whites when they took the tests under the condition of stereotype threat (students believe that no matter what they accomplish, they will be perceived through the generalized stereotypes of the majority group and a negative campus climate), but they did perform equally as well as whites when the conditions of stereotype threat were absent.

Expectations, both those that students have for their own performance and those frequently held and projected by teachers and professors, also have a significant influence on the academic performance of underrepresented minorities. Regarding self-expectations, it has been shown that many African American and Hispanic students have poor estimates of their abilities to perform well academically, especially in comparison to white students, while Asian students have expectations of performance equal to those of whites (Mayo & Christenfeld, 1999). There also is evidence of the long-term effects of both low and high teacher expectations on student performance based on the students' intelligence, demographics, and personality (Alvidrez & Weinstein, 1999). Researchers verified the value of establishing high expectations when they found that in cases where teachers overestimated children's intelligence relative to IQ at an early age, the degree of overestimation actually predicted the students' high school GPA and SAT scores. In other words, positive discrepancies in teachers' judgment predicted more positive student performance in the long term. Unfortunately, however, teacher expectations have been found to be lower for African American students than for white students (Weinstein & McKown, 1998), and concerted efforts by school systems and colleges and universities must be made to elevate expectations of minority student performance and articulate those expectations to the students.

INSTITUTIONAL COMMITMENT AND BEST PRACTICES

To foster success among first-year minority students, institutions need first to ask themselves to what extent first-year student academic performance is considered an institutional priority. The question is fairly easy to answer. We know when something is a priority based on the level of resources applied to the effort, and in the case of first-year student academic performance, we need to look at the quality of faculty teaching the courses, the extent to which faculty are regularly examining instructional practices and developing and revising innovative teaching materials, and the extent to which the institution has developed an understanding of those factors most critical to students' success. Such factors for both majority and minority students include the rigor of students' high school preparation, including test scores, grades, and the difficulty of the course work, as well as the students' attitudes about college work, their willingness to take advice and to be involved in supplemental support work, and the level of the students' motivation to succeed.

Other important questions to consider include the following: Has the college or university analyzed pertinent data on first-year student grades and course loads to determine who actually succeeds in the first year, who does not, and what differences exist between the two groups? To what extent is the institution using data on first-year performance and attitudes in shaping and reshaping policies and practices related to admissions, orientation, advising, tutoring, and curriculum? Are faculty and administrators assessing levels of effectiveness of different initiatives and strategies designed to help first-year students succeed? In general, we find that institutions where minorities are succeeding in their first year are usually institutions that have thought about the first year for all students. In other words, many of the strategies helpful to students in general will also be helpful to minority students.

Focused, Anticipatory Recruitment of Underrepresented Minority Students

Institutions with the strongest first-year intervention programs for first-year students understand the importance of not waiting until students reach college to begin addressing the importance of building academic skills. In fact, colleges, universities, and community colleges can begin working with elementary, middle, and high school students both in this regard and to motivate them to want to attend college. One of the most effective college–high school partnerships has been the federally funded Upward Bound program in which first-generation college students, including large numbers of minority students, receive supplemental education in reading, math, and writing during summers in high school.

In some cases, these programs help high school students with their academic work and in preparing for standardized tests, include tours of the campuses, and devote time to working with students on college financial aid materials. An important reason for the success of this program and others like it is that their approach is holistic, taking into account not only the students' academic needs but also the obstacles they will face gaining admission to and succeeding in college. One very effective component of the Upward Bound program is a summer bridge program for students during the summer following high school graduation. The program is designed to prepare students for college-level courses and the expectations of faculty and to provide them with opportunities for interacting with peers and college faculty and staff. A number of institutions have implemented similar pre-first-year student programs in an effort to support students' transition to the college.

Successful intervention programs also work with feeder schools to evaluate how well high school course work prepares students for first-year college courses and include giving the high schools feedback on how different groups— minority students and others—have done at the college. These programs provide opportunities for teachers from the feeder schools to have substantive interaction with faculty from the university. The benefits of this interaction include developing more trust between the institution and feeder high schools, learning more about the challenges that minority and other students face prior to coming to college, and, in some cases, providing teachers and counselors of minority students with opportunities to shed light on students' strengths and weaknesses, their family backgrounds, and ways of motivating the students. What we find with such programs is that the more personalized the support system is, the more effective it will be. Most important, these practices can be effective at any college or university, regardless of the racial composition of the student body or institutional type. Minority students, like other students, are more likely to succeed on a campus where professionals know as much as possible about their backgrounds, both academic and personal.

In addition, there are some very practical, strategic steps that colleges and universities can take to recruit minority students who will be successful academically. It is important that institutions keep the following points in mind:

- One size does not fit all; neither does one recruitment plan. Institutions need to be specific about their minority student recruitment goals and tailor their plans in ways that are sensitive to the interests and needs of different minority groups.
- Early identification is critical. Academically well-prepared students have options, and some well-prepared minority students have even more options. Clearly, the pool of eligible candidates is far too small, and consequently, colleges and universities often are competing for the same candidates. An effective recruitment plan will begin identifying and communicating with minority students early in high school—in the students' sophomore year or even earlier. This "grow-your-own" strategy (like those at SUNY–Stony Brook and the University of California, Riverside) involves identifying high-achieving students who might be recruited to the campus and succeed academically.
- Recruit the family, not simply the student. Understanding the important role of the family in recruiting minority students is critical. Minority families often have a strong sense of family commitment and obligation that may influence a prospective student's interest in attending college away from home. In addition, extended family members often play a major role in students' decisions about college applications. Institutions are well advised to make families feel included in the recruitment process and to engage them along the way.
- Understand the role of the community. Through their families, many minority students have strong ties to community churches, clubs, and civic and social organizations, which should be the focus of recruitment efforts. In many African American communities, for example, large churches often include college and career planning as part of their educational and spiritual mission. Many host well-attended college fairs or college nights with guest speakers from area colleges. Church leaders can be some of the most influential leaders in students' lives.
- Quality is even more important than quantity. One of the benefits of having a strong minority presence on campus is that prospective minority students and their families see an environment in which students are comfortable and

successful academically. It also is important for minority students already enrolled to be having a positive experience and to be willing to discuss their experiences with prospective minority students and their families.

Faculty Commitment

A good sense of the institution's commitment to the success of first-year students can be obtained by looking at who teaches the courses that these new students typically take. Are full-time, tenure-track faculty (in addition to part-time faculty, instructors, or graduate students) involved in this work? (And if graduate students are used extensively, to what extent do they receive special training and support during the process?) And to what extent are these faculty involved in professional development aimed at improving their instructional effectiveness in general and especially in regard to minority students?

Some of the most successful strategies are to engage faculty and administrators in discussions about student performance (for example, grades and retention in first-year courses) and to have discussions among faculty in and across departments. These discussions are designed not to point fingers at students or faculty but rather to understand the level of student performance by course, and even by section and faculty member. (Understandably, the faculty need to be assured that the purpose is to improve performance, not to embarrass anyone.)

In one institution's chemistry department, for example, where almost half the students were performing below a C in the first-semester course, the initial reaction of some faculty during these conversations was that students were either poorly prepared, working too many hours on the outside, or not sufficiently serious about their course work. After discussion with students, however, faculty found that students clearly needed more feedback earlier in the semester (for example, graded homework and quizzes); that students did not always understand the connection between lectures and graded exams; that most of the students were not accustomed to studying in groups but rather were relying exclusively on themselves individually to prepare for tests; that few students took advantage of the department's tutorial center because they mistakenly viewed it as a place for poor students only; and that no one had discussed with them the critical relationship between numbers of hours of outside part-time employment and amount of time devoted to studying in the course to ensure success in it. As a result, many students in general—not just minority students—were not succeeding.

Since that time, this department has revised its first-semester chemistry course, making it more interesting to students by using a team-teaching approach and by having some of the department's most productive faculty discuss their research in relationship to concepts introduced in the course so that students can see connections to real-life science. In the process, students also sense the faculty members' enthusiasm for their work. In addition, the department encourages students to work in groups. In fact, some assignments require group work as a means to encourage collaborative work and to teach students how to collaborate. The chemistry tutorial center has become a place where students go when they want to earn A's, not simply passing grades. Considerable time also is devoted at the beginning of the semester through orientation and in classes to discussing the relationship between external commitments and study hours required for success in first-year courses and subsequent courses.

The lesson here is that when first-year students do not do well, the reasons often are more complicated than simply assuming that one group—faculty or students—is not doing what it should be doing. Rather, certain themes are very clear: when student performance has improved, faculty have taken ownership of the problem by looking at the data on student performance in great specificity; by discussing with faculty, students, and support staff (possibly through focus groups) the attitudes and perceptions of each group; and then, based on those discussions, proposing and implementing initiatives designed to strengthen teaching and learning.

Providing feedback to first-year students through more homework assignments and quizzes is especially effective. Often first-year students receive much less feedback, particularly later on in the semester, than they were accustomed to receiving in high school. In one case, when the college department chair suggested giving much more feedback to students, the response she received from one of her faculty was, "We don't want to spoon-feed the students," to which the chair responded, "If spoon-feeding leads to more students having a strong foundation in their first-year courses, then let's spoon-feed them."

In another instance involving a first-year biology course, one faculty member worked with a science education faculty member who observed and evaluated the biology instructor's teaching and helped to devise strategies for him to have more interaction with his students, to use technology more effectively to enhance learning, and to give more students added time and opportunities to digest materials and ask questions.

These two examples focus on students in general, not simply on minority students. To the extent that we improve the learning environment for all students, we are increasing the likelihood that minority students also will profit. In fact, some of the same themes hold for improving the first-year performance of minority students, who do best when faculty have taken the time to look specifically at the students' performance, in specific courses and overall, and when the faculty talk both about what works well with minority students and about the problems and challenges they may be facing working with these students.

These discussions can root out inaccurate assumptions that both faculty and students sometimes make about students' performance in the classroom. In one case, faculty and students began the semester with the assumptions that if a minority student earned a C in organic chemistry, the student was doing well. In this instance and others, frank discussions about previous performance of minority students in particular courses and the expectations of both faculty and students can lead to surprising and useful findings. Minority students also tend to do best when departments identify faculty who have been most effective in motivating and working with minority students, including when faculty have selected minority students to work with them on research projects.

Since faculty-student interaction is vital, one of the challenges first-year students often face, including minorities, is that of adjusting to the speech patterns and accents of faculty members and graduate students teaching first-year classes. If first-year students have had little or no exposure to people from different cultures, they often have difficulty both understanding and being able to relate to the instructor. It is incumbent on institutions to address this issue head on by helping students develop more tolerance for speech and behaviors related to different cultures and by working with the instructors they place in the classroom to ensure that they are speaking standard English clearly (providing opportunities for training as needed). This is especially important in science and technical areas, where there are disproportionately large numbers of faculty and graduate students from other countries. In these disciplines, it is virtually impossible for students simply to read the textbook and understand difficult concepts; they need instructors who can explain the concepts with clarity.

Another critical challenge is that many minority programs are directed by dedicated minority staff members but enjoy little involvement on the part of faculty members, who bring a different perspective and also need to understand the perspective of minority students. Whether minority students are studying in community colleges, four-year liberal arts colleges, or research universities, they are more likely to succeed if they receive support from faculty. We observe this when faculty interact with minority students beyond the classroom, as in campus residential life activities; when they are encouraging minority students to be involved in initiatives related to their majors; when they invite the students to work with them in their research; and when they know not only the students' achievements and successes but also the special challenges and problems they may be facing. The success of minority students should be viewed as an institutional priority, not simply a minority issue.

Staff Commitment

Staff also play a vital in fostering the first-year success of underrepresented minority students. It is important that staff have professional development opportunities that focus on learning how to help first-year students set high expectations and become comfortable with their differences and on becoming adept at handling conflicts that inevitably arise among human beings in general, and particularly among people from different ethnic, cultural, and racial backgrounds. Staff members can support first-year students, and especially minority students, in their professional capacities as admissions counselors, academic advisers, tutors, health professionals, librarians, security staff, and student activities coordinators. Perhaps equally important, staff members have regular opportunities to be supportive of these students on a personal level, expressing their interest in the students' academic progress, cocurricular and career interests, and general well-being.

Orientation

Staff can be particularly supportive in the orientation process as minority students adjust to their new environment. This means helping students become academically focused as well as socially and emotionally secure. This objective is crucial because the most important factors affecting minority first-year students are those that adversely influence their academic confidence and ability to connect to the institution (Smedley, Myers, & Harrell, 1993). Orientation and intervention programs that are most effective in improving minority student retention are those that help these students understand the relationship between the social and academic challenges they will face as a result of interacting with students and faculty of other races. Equally true, and without regard to racial differences, students' personal development is a critical factor in their adjustment to the first year of college (Ting & Robinson, 1998). Effective orientation programs can help students learn how to take responsibility for their own behavior, cope with change and handle stress, exercise self-discipline, manage time, and develop leadership skills—qualities useful to students in adjusting to college life.

During the initial orientation period, it is important that staff spend time with first-year students talking about expectations regarding behavior and ways in which institutions celebrate differences among students. In this process, it is helpful for staff to be sensitive to a variety of social, personal, and academic variables. We know, for example, that among African American first-year students, those attending historically black institutions adjust most smoothly to college life when they have had substantial immersion in the African American community; those attending predominantly white universities tend to adjust best when they have had considerable prior interracial experience (Adan & Felner, 1995).

Under the direction of staff, both general programming and orientation activities in campus residence halls should focus on multicultural issues and race relations, giving students opportunities to talk about their own backgrounds, personal experiences, and what they bring to the campus community as a result of their cultural heritage. Some institutions have special orientation sessions specifically for minority students and their families so that these new students can hear from upperclass minority students on the campus about their experiences. Campuses can reinforce these efforts through posters and written messages that place multicultural issues in a positive context and welcome students from different backgrounds. Also, whether students are living on campus or commuting, they are more inclined to remain at the institution and interact with student peers, faculty, and staff if they become involved in activities beyond the classroom. These cocurricular activities help students develop a sense of belonging, bond with groups of students, and view themselves as valuable members of the campus community.

Advising, Counseling, and Developmental Education

Successful first-year programs use staff or faculty, or both, as academic advisers who work with students on course selection and setting academic goals. In some cases, institutions have rethought the number and type of courses first-year students might take during their first semester in order to heighten the students' chances for success. One such practice for science majors limits the number of mathematics, science, and engineering courses they may take during their first semester or two. This practice is somewhat controversial because most colleges encourage or require students interested in majoring in science or engineering to take three courses in these disciplines in their first semester, in addition to other courses.

The rationale for limiting the number of courses is, first, that students need time to adjust to college-level teaching and testing, and second, that focusing on a smaller number of science or technical courses, in combination with other courses being taken, can build a stronger foundation and contribute to higher grades the first semester, which helps to increase the new student's self-confidence. In short, whether focusing on performance in the sciences or other disciplines, we find that the most effective programs for first-year students help them understand that academic success may require them to be in college more than four years (especially if they are working substantial hours off campus). Moreover, they should be careful at least in their first-year course selection. It is far better to develop a strong foundation and confidence gradually than to rush through without developing either.

Another key to a strong advising system is to encourage faculty and staff to monitor carefully the level of courses students take in relationship to their prior course work and level of performance. This is especially important in the case of first-year students because studies show that high school GPA is the most significant first-year predictor (Ting & Robinson, 1998). Also, it is not unusual for first-year students to be unrealistic in signing up for courses simply because the courses sound interesting, though they may not have taken the appropriate prerequisites. Indeed, unless there is a technology system or person in place to monitor the situation, students will find themselves in courses that are over their heads and for which they are not well prepared.

I find a similar situation among first-year students who earn poor grades in one course yet attempt to move on to the next-higher-level course because they fail to understand the strong relationship between first- and second-level courses. One of the most effective recent practices for minorities in science is to encourage students who are earning C's in first-year courses (in physics, engineering, and chemistry, for example) to retake those courses in order to develop a stronger background and foundation. Also, when degree programs are built on a sequence of courses, it is very helpful when faculty and staff look to see whether students' performance reflects sufficient preparation for the next course in the sequence. It also is important for institutions to be willing to revise policies and practices depending on what they learn.

Developmental education (described in greater detail in Chapter Seventeen) continues to be an important factor in the first-year experience of many minority students. In fact, one study of minority first-year students in California's public colleges and universities (Roach, 2000) determined that nearly three-quarters of all black first-year students and almost two-thirds of all Hispanic first-year students needed developmental mathematics courses, and over 60 percent of both black and Hispanic first-year students required developmental English. With such large numbers of minority students in need of developmental work, it is crucial that campus tutorial and learning resource centers be able to respond effectively. Their work should reflect a strong institutional commitment and cultural sensitivity. The work should also provide accurate entry-level assessments, skilled tutors and mentors, current computer technology, and a system of accountability to ensure heightened student competencies (McClenney, 2000). Such a system should include monitoring the performance of first-year students who advance from developmental to regular college courses (Arenson, 2000).

OUT-OF-CLASS ENVIRONMENT

The out-of-class environment has a powerful influence on first-year student success (see Chapter Two). Among the many out-of-class interventions designed to improve this success are initiating student study groups and building a sense of community and program values.

Student Study Groups

More than ever before, colleges and universities are coming to understand that encouraging students to participate in study groups outside the class or laboratory leads not only to better academic performance but also to helpful social support and constructive interaction. Unfortunately, first-year college students tend to frown on the notion of group study; typically they have had little experience with it prior to coming to college and often are accustomed to thinking of collaborating with others as either a hindrance or a form of cheating. What one often hears from students is that the group that begins studying ends up talking about other matters and not getting the work done.

Successful first-year programs focus on teaching students how to set up and work effectively in groups. Students need to follow certain basic rules. For example, all of the students need to prepare for group sessions by studying the work in advance, determining what they do and do not understand about the topics so they can be helpful to one another, and present well-formulated questions on aspects of the topics that may be troubling them. Other basic rules include ensuring that only the task at hand is introduced during the group study time and setting time limits for discussing the chosen topics, with clear understandings about break periods.

Building a Sense of Community and Program Values

The most effective programs for first-year students, particularly for minority students, provide a family-like social and academic support system. This system includes opportunities for older students to be supportive of first-year students and for each first-year student to have a designated mentor, who may be a faculty or staff member (in some cases minority) and may or may not be different from the student's academic adviser.

Successful programs also begin to develop a set of implicit expectations among first-year students that take hold fully over time—for example, that peers will support each other both academically and personally; that it is useful and wise to seek support from a variety of sources; that it is important to set clear and attainable academic goals; and that it is important to explore possible careers related to one's intended major. In some cases, these programs are so effective that graduates of the universities sometimes return to campus and visit the programs in order to see how they can help to inspire and support first-year students.

The most effective programs also emphasize to first-year students the value of service and giving back to one's community. A number of campuses encourage students to work with those in need—from children in inner cities to the disabled and senior citizens—engaging the students in tutoring and mentoring, serving as role models, or focusing on special projects such as Habitat for Humanity, that help students put in perspective both their studies and their potential for contributing to the larger world. On one campus, for example, the following statement is often heard among students: "From those to whom much is given, much is expected."

Harvard education professor Richard Light (2001) emphasizes the importance of encouraging students to be involved in the arts and cocurricular activities as a way of strengthening their connection to the campus. For minority students in particular, participating in choirs, ethnically oriented student clubs, and other cultural initiatives can strengthen their sense of belonging, helping to ensure an appropriate fit between the students and the campus environment.

The general climate on a campus, so important to the success of first-year students, and particularly minority students, is heavily influenced by the level and quality of interaction among students from different racial and ethnic groups (see Chapter Eight). Sometimes these groups stay to themselves the entire time. It therefore is a special responsibility of staff and faculty to create opportunities for all students to interact with people from different backgrounds. It is not enough simply to see diverse groups on a campus: the critical question is whether these students are having substantive interactions with people from other groups. Indeed, it would be a real tragedy if, despite the growing diversification of student bodies throughout our country, these groups learned little about living and working together.

One inspiring example from my own campus comes to mind. A young first-year African American woman from an inner-city high school asked the student housing administrator to change her room assignment because she thought her roommate, who was from another country, had looked at her strangely and did not like her. The administrator talked with the African American student and convinced her to spend at least one semester in the room, trying to work through the situation. At the beginning of the next semester, when the administrator was holding a focus group for some of the first-year students to see how their first term had gone, the African American student spoke up and thanked the administrator for asking her to remain in the room with her roommate. In fact, she said, she had learned several important lessons: first, that her roommate was just as uncomfortable as she was; second, that both women were initially suspicious of how each regarded the other; and finally, that she was amazed by the number of hours her roommate studied each night. In fact, she said that for the first half of the semester, she never saw her roommate sleeping because she was always at her desk studying—both when she went to bed and when she arose in the morning. And finally, feeling frustrated, she simply decided she would not go to bed and would continue studying until her roommate retired also. With great pride, she also sometimes awoke earlier than her roommate to study. In the focus group discussion, the young woman concluded by saying that she had no idea that human beings could work so hard, and she was amazed that her extra hours of study really did improve her grades substantially.

CRITICAL ROLES OF THE CAMPUS LEADERSHIP

As persuasively argued later in this book by Betty Siegel in Chapter Ten, presidents, provosts, and other senior campus leaders have an instrumental role to play in creating a healthy multicultural institutional environment and elevating minority first-year student performance (see Chapter Ten). Through speeches, focus groups, and everyday actions, the president, provost, deans, department chairs, and others can set the tone for the campus climate and demonstrate their commitment in visible ways—for example:

- Allocating sufficient resources to support the first year and multicultural activities

- Talking about the fact that more and more students on campuses will be from different ethnic and minority groups, both in the United States (chiefly Hispanic, African American, Asian American, and American Indian) and from abroad

- Emphasizing the importance of helping first-year minority students (and students in general) to feel welcome on the campus and become engaged

- Promoting and encouraging practices that help to build successful minority enrollments (including K–16 initiatives)

- Providing incentives for faculty to focus on their teaching effectiveness in relation to minority students and to engage minority students in substantive research experiences and cocurricular initiatives

- Encouraging faculty and staff, minority and majority, to talk about issues involving minority students and to engage in focus group discussions

In addition, the institutional leadership has a responsibility to recruit and support faculty and administrators of color to reflect the diversity of the student population. All students can learn from faculty and professionals with racial and cultural perspectives different from their own, and in the process, come to appreciate and value the talents of every group.

At one recent opening-year orientation session for faculty and staff at a community college, the president and provost had arranged for a group of students, many of whom were minorities, to talk with the entire faculty, staff, and administration about their first-semester experiences on that campus. Some students talked about how isolated they had felt at the beginning of their first semester and how close they had come to leaving because they did not think they could fit in or succeed. However, what was especially encouraging about the students' experiences was that many of them could point to an individual faculty or staff member who had been critical to their success because the individual had established a personal relationship with them to help them feel welcome. The significance of this session was that the students, ranging in age from eighteen to their forties, were given the opportunity to talk about their first-semester experiences, and they made suggestions about how to help other students during their first semester on the campus. Most important, faculty and administrators heard new perspectives on this critical topic. The important point is that the campus's senior leadership understood that everyone—faculty, staff, and students—needed to hear these students firsthand. Ideally, we also need to hear from those students who are not successful, including their perspectives and suggestions for improving the first year.

Presidents and other campus leaders are well advised to take the time to learn more not only about how new students are reacting to the campus environment, but also about the language they can use to welcome new students to the campus. Too frequently, those of us who have been on a campus for many years forget (or perhaps have never experienced) what it feels like to be new in an environment where most people are different from us. Some institutions have worked to sensitize white faculty and administrators, including having them spend time on a minority campus so that they have the experience of being different from the majority group. Moreover, because the majority of college and university presidents and faculty are white, it is important for leaders regardless of race to speak out on issues involving support for students of color, giving special attention to those minority groups having difficulty.

Both during times of crisis—possibly involving international terrorism or racial strife on the campus—and, equally important, during periods of relative calm, it is important for presidents and other leaders to be vocal about encouraging faculty and staff to work with students, especially first-year minority students, to ensure that they receive the academic, personal, and emotional support and encouragement they need in order to be comfortable and academically successful.

RECOMMENDATIONS

Based on the literature and experience of my own and other campuses, there are several recommendations I can offer to institutions to foster first-year success of underrepresented minority students. These suggestions focus on minority student recruitment, faculty and staff development, minority students' experiences outside the classroom, and campus leadership.

- Develop and implement recruitment plans that are sensitive to the interests and needs of different minority groups. Develop early identification plans for minority students; recruit the family as well as the student; understand the role of the community; and involve current minority faculty, staff, and students in the recruitment process.

- Provide faculty and staff development programs designed to created a commitment to the success of first-year minority students. Involve and train faculty who teach courses typically taken by first-year students; create opportunities for faculty to discuss strategies for enhancing first-year student success; make sure faculty have accurate information about the academic skills of their students to offset possible negative stereotypes; and encourage faculty-minority student contact outside the classroom.

- Develop staff commitment to the success of first-year minority students. Programs designed to help students make a successful transition to college, such as orientation, academic advising, personal and career counseling, developmental education, and other support services and programs, must emphasize the unique needs of minority students.

- Create an out-of-class environment that supports minority student success. This means creating out-of-class student study groups, building a sense of community and program values, and creating a climate of acceptance and affirmation by majority students for minority students.

- Focus on the critical role of campus leadership. Recognize that a strong commitment is needed from presidents, provosts, and other senior campus leaders to create a healthy multicultural institutional environment that will contribute to an elevated performance of first-year minority students.

CONCLUSION

When institutions are truly committed to ensuring the academic success of first-year students, particularly minorities, they can take advantage of growing numbers of models and best practices developed by institutions that are experiencing success. The special challenge in this regard is that large numbers of underrepresented minority students are not as well prepared academically for college-level work as their white and Asian American counterparts (partially because of negative stereotyping and low expectations, their own and others'), and these students may not feel comfortable in a new setting, whether the student body is predominantly white or minority. The challenge is especially difficult when we consider that over 85 percent of all African American undergraduates and the majority of other minority students are enrolled at predominantly white colleges and universities, where few minorities are in key leadership or faculty positions.

Even before institutions welcome new first-year students to their campuses, they can be working with K–12 school systems to help build the academic skills of young students, ensure the appropriateness of school curricula, and increase the pool of well-prepared college-bound students. Once these students matriculate, campuses can use institutional data about first-year students' performance and attitudes and engage in institutional conversations involving faculty, staff, and students about effective instructional techniques and initiatives. In this way, they can develop and implement multicomponent programs to strengthen the performance of first-year students. Such programs geared specifically to the needs of minority students must effectively address the students' academic and social integration, their development of specific knowledge and skills, their need for various forms of support and motivation, and their need for monitoring and advising.

In all of these areas, faculty and staff have a central role to play. It is especially important that they be open to evaluating their interaction with students—including teaching, advising, and informal conversations—and be willing to modify their approach as needed, finding ways to be supportive and to engage first-year minority students in classrooms, laboratories, and other settings on campus. It is important that faculty set high expectations for the students, provide helpful and early feedback on courses and other work, encourage the students to study in groups and take advantage of tutoring services, and clearly communicate the importance of spending sufficient time mastering course work that will be a building block for success in future courses (particularly in the sciences and engineering). It has become increasingly clear that students should be encouraged to engage in cocurricular activities. Perhaps the greatest gifts the institution can give these and all other students are enthusiasm for learning—helping them to see connections between their studies, their experiences on campus, and their future in society—and a commitment to high academic achievement and service to others.

CHAPTER EIGHT

The Realities of Diversity and the Campus Climate for First-Year Students

W. Terrell Jones

I never realized the importance of diversity until I started college. In all my years of school at home I never had a lesson on diversity and I don't recall any teachers stressing it in the classroom. I also never understood why colleges would speak highly about their diversity when I would visit them. Now that I've finished my first year, I've come to realize how important diversity is. It gives students the opportunity to understand and accept people's differences.
—Ashley, first-year Caucasian student

I recently viewed the movie *Remember the Titans* based on a true story set in Virginia in 1971. Herman Boone had just become the first African American high school football coach of a federally ordered desegregated school district. His goal was to have a winning football team. To achieve that goal, he had to get white and African American football players to learn to trust each other and play as a team, no easy task. They would have to overcome their prejudices, stereotypes, and old ways of relating to each other. In accomplishing these tasks, the team members learned more about themselves and character than about football. The players and coaches discovered what it takes to be a winner both on and off the field. The team's triumph changed not only the members of the team but also the whole community.

In many ways, the challenges the team faced in the movie are metaphors for the challenges we are facing in higher education by attempting to develop a campus climate that is supportive of diversity in the first year. For the team to be successful, the players and coaches had to do more than just learn to tolerate each other: they had to come together and create a new paradigm that reflects the values, beliefs, and customs of all the groups involved in the team.

In 1971, public schools throughout the South had not been integrated yet. It was not goodwill or changes in attitudes that brought down segregation and gave the team this opportunity and challenge; it was a change in the law. More important to this discussion, the national racial segregation of our past that was abated only through the courts has returned. While future student characteristics forecast a significant growth in the percentage of minority students in the potential K–12 college-going cohorts, it is also instructive to describe some of the demographic factors that shape the worldviews and attitudes of students toward diversity.

At a time when many Americans believe that segregation has been consigned to our past, the facts do not support that conclusion. Orfield and Yun (1999) found that K–12 desegregation efforts reached their zenith in 1980. Since then, K–12 desegregation has retreated to levels found in the pre–civil rights legislation of the 1960s. At present, the average white new college student comes from a K–12 experience that is 81.2 percent white, while the average African American and Latino new college students are from K–12 experiences where they make up the majority of students in their schools. Consider these data in the light of the reality that minority students are also more likely to attend schools where nearly half the students are economically poor (Orfield & Yun, 1999).

These data suggest that reported first-year student encounters such as "You're the first . . . I have ever talked to" are more likely to be heard today than in the 1970s. In reality, many students do not get along because they have never learned how or had a chance to get along. It is also ironic that while we are sending our students the message to embrace diversity, many patterns in the larger society give them the opposite directive.

This new generation of college students differs from previous generations of college students in significant ways, a situation that has an impact on their ability to understand diversity. New college students do not come to campus with a clean slate. Long before these students became college students, they were actively and passively taught attitudes and behaviors related to racial, gender, and cultural differences. Cortés (2000) and Tatum (1997) both assert that through many different sources, students have been educated about diversity long before college. As the Rodgers and Hammerstein song from South Pacific instructs, "You have to be carefully taught to hate." New students should be provided with a campus climate that provides them with safe spaces and unlimited opportunities where they can engage each other about cultural differences and diversity.

Not long ago, I was involved in a discussion with a group of higher education administrators. We were lamenting the increasing incidents of racial intolerance and acts of hate. While it was clear that many of us could identify with these concerns and were perplexed with the increasing level of campus incivility, there were those among us who assessed these incidents as aberrations and longed for a return to times when the campus climate was not so volatile. As I processed the discussion, it appeared to me that a significant factor in our inability to create a campus climate for diversity might be a function of how we defined the issue.

On more than one occasion, administrators have asked me, "When are we going to get back to normal?" It is important to recognize that this is normal and the solutions to our problems just might be in understanding who these new students are, accurately assessing their attitudes toward diversity, and planning for a positive campus climate. I am advocating a realistic appraisal of the components that make up a positive campus climate for diversity, restructuring policies and curricula to promote diversity, and institutional leadership to address the needs and concerns of first-year students, our institutions, and our society. In this chapter, I will discuss first-year students, faculty, administrators and institutional attitudes toward diversity, the impact of poverty and social class on student access and success, larger public attitudes toward diversity, and implications for higher education restructuring.

GENERAL FIRST-YEAR STUDENT ATTITUDES TOWARD DIVERSITY AND CAMPUS CLIMATE

Levine and Cureton (1998c) paint a portrait of today's college students that sharply contrasts with accepted myths about student attitudes, beliefs, and values. According to these two researchers, today's first-year students are much more likely to:

- Come to college less academically prepared than in the past
- Have higher career and professional aspirations
- Be more culturally diverse and nontraditionally aged
- Spend much more of their out-of-class time working in jobs that are not related to their career goals
- Come from economically disadvantaged backgrounds

These first-time students are likely to perceive the campus climate for discussions of diversity and multiculturalism as painful and many times heated. Levine and Cureton (1998c) assert that students also differ in how they view the campus climate for diversity. Tensions arise from a preoccupation with difference, a phenomenon called mitosis of student groups (differences among student groups are getting larger and more focused), a perceived segregation on campus, and a growing sense of victimization. Today's college students appear to live in a world where they perceive little common ground, environments where traditional student organizations, clubs, and activities do not meet their needs for affiliation and identity. Students, rightly or wrongly, perceive that they have little in common with students from other cultures or ethnic groups, and they see themselves, regardless of affiliation groups, as victims of some other group's perceived advantages. This plays out as the students' recognition of being in a campus environment with very few people who are like themselves.

Left to interact on their own, first-year students appear to be repeating old social patterns and support systems that are single gender, ethnic, and cultural. This is not a new occurrence. Many in higher education fail to assess traditional student organizations, such as fraternities, sororities, and student government, as monocultural and gender groups. We must also assess these groups in the light of their historical exclusionary customs and their impact on diversity. This is not to say that these student organizations are intentionally restrictive. However, in practice, these monotyped group organizations are often referenced in the media as the locations for activities where diversity, civility, and inclusion are low in priority. Successful first-year student campus climate initiatives must stress the importance of inclusion in all organized student associations.

FIRST-YEAR STUDENTS OF COLOR

Many minority students find campus environments to be dramatically different from what they had expected. Institutional brochures and recruitment propaganda may paint a picture of a happy campus where everyone gets along. However, first-year minority students are more likely to find themselves in surroundings similar to those reported by new international students where customs, values, and the culture are foreign and it is they, the first-year minority students, who make most of the adjustments.

To one degree or another, most new college students of color at predominantly white institutions of higher education have in common complaints about the campus climate for diversity. While the campus climate can have a different impact on ethnic groups, all new groups comprising students of color evaluate the climate at best as insensitive to cultural differences and at worst as intentionally biased. Students of color are not alone in their negative assessment of the campus climate. Women, sexual minorities, nontraditional-age, international students, and marginalized religious minority groups have also found themselves to be the targets of hate crimes, incivility, and a negative campus climate for diversity. There is some validity to their complaints. Almost weekly, new reports of hate crimes on college campuses become national stories. On the Tolerance.org Web site, a news report dated February 19, 2002, cited 2,067 hate crime incidents in 1999. However, because many of these crimes go unreported, experts suggest that this number is only the tip of the iceberg.

Students cite examples of incivility both on and off campus, including in the classroom, institutional policies, and local community interactions with businesses and police, where their cultural ethnicity, gender, or sexual orientation has made them the victims of cultural insensitivity or outright bias and hate. These incidents range from irritating and naive questions about cultural differences and negative classroom environments to outright acts of hate that broadcast the message that they and their concerns are not welcome. Students of color at my own campus emphasize that the little everyday insults are sometimes more fatiguing than any blatant acts of hate.

Many of these targeted first-year student groups identify with more than one unwelcome group (for example, African American and socioeconomically disadvantaged), thereby exacerbating and complicating the development of both effective resolutions and a positive campus climate. Many of these students of color have had previous positive interactions with majority students in their home communities. However, given what we know about increasing segregation in grade levels K–12, cultural understanding and cross-cultural communication skills vary greatly from one student or community to another. Often students of color find that majority students and faculty they encounter at the institution have little knowledge of other cultures and are uncomfortable discussing cultural differences. One first-year student put it bluntly: "I never had any problem getting along with white people from my home community, but here white students and teachers are very different. They don't want to acknowledge that you are even here."

The negative campus climate for these first-year students can also have an impact on the institutional effort for access and success. Steele (2000) asserts that when academically capable students of color fail to perform as well as their white counterparts, the explanation often has less to do with their ability than what he calls "stereotype threat," whereas students believe that no matter what they accomplish, they will be perceived through the generalized stereotypes of the majority group and the negative campus climate. Steele says that a chilly campus climate that does not value diversity creates an environment where competent students of color choose not to perform at reasonably attainable levels of academic success.

NEW MAJORITY COLLEGE STUDENTS

Many first-year majority students come to campus with limited understandings of diversity. Their K–12 school environments and host communities may be racially segregated, providing limited opportunities for cross-cultural understanding, and so these students lack the cross-cultural competencies to engage in meaningful dialogues. Majority students' attitudes about diversity and multiculturalism appear to fall into two major divisions: one group that is characterized by outright rejection of diversity as a serious concern and a second group that recognizes the problem but feels powerless to do anything about it. No matter which side of the argument these students are on, discussions with students of color are viewed as mine fields where it is safer not to tread.

Levine and Cureton (1998c) describe this inability to engage in dialogue about diversity as a perceived no-win situation for students. They argue that for white students, the new pejorative terms and phrases on campus are racist, sexist, and homophobic. Those who reject that there are real issues view discussions about diversity and discrimination as relics from the past. Although almost all these students believe that racism is morally unacceptable, they appear to perceive acts of hate and prejudice as individual events perpetrated by the few, and they are likely to reject notions of institutionalized discrimination and privilege.

The few students for whom diversity issues do not seem relevant appear to cope by wanting to surrender their majority status and are prone to feelings of shame and regret. When they compare their attitudes toward diversity to those of the average white students, their family, and home community, they view themselves as atypical. However, given the institutional policies and culture of higher education, they feel powerless to effect any real change.

ISSUES OF SOCIAL CLASS

Social class can be more debilitating than race, ethnicity, gender, disability, or sexual orientation. Often definitions of diversity fail to include socioeconomic variables into the discussion of campus climate. The effects of poverty cannot be measured just by low student retention and graduation rates. For many of these first-year students, poverty has been the defining issue of their lives (Kozol, 1991, 1995). Many times, a student's academic deficiencies are by-products of poor and underfunded primary school systems and a pervasive culture of poverty. Campus climate efforts that fail to acknowledge the culture of our nation's poor are doomed to failure. Gladieux and Swail (1998) found that disadvantaged students were six times less likely to complete college than economically advantaged students. These disadvantaged students and their families, who are not a success, are many times less well off financially.

On campuses, the gap between the haves and have-nots seems to grow. To provide student aid, remedial courses, and tutors for academically deficient poor first-year students is simply not sufficient. Primary school preparation has never been equal. For poor students to succeed, institutions of higher education may need to revamp student services and curricula completely. In order to get to the root causes of the problems of these economically disadvantaged students' poor retention and graduation rates, higher education must also play a more participatory role in assisting these students long before they get to college. Some of the strategies that have proven track records of success are institution and government funded collaborations such as TRIO programs. TRIO programs are five initiatives administered by the U.S. Department of Education, dating to 1965, designed to increase college access, success, and degree attainment for economically and educationally disadvantaged youth. More recent initiatives that show promise are early recognition of talented students; college, community, and school partnerships; and college academic student service learning projects.

FACULTY AND ADMINISTRATION

Unfortunately, many higher education prognosticators both inside and outside academia explain campus climate problems by blaming the victims. For A. Bloom (1987), H. Bloom (1994), Steele (1990), D'Souza (1991), Schlesinger (1991), and Herrnstein and Murray (1994), it is the new students of color, affirmative action, and multiculturalism that create incivility and a negative campus climate. D'Souza (1991) asserts that white students are for the most part non-racist and open to interactions with minority students. According to many conservatives, it is the students of color and faculty who support these attitudes that have made them indigestible in the campus climate. It is interesting that D'Souza uses the term indigestible to describe the "melting pot" myth where it is incumbent on the newcomers to fit into the existing culture by changing who they are.

Many other faculty members characterize campus climate problems as out-of-classroom issues to be addressed by student affairs professionals and the central administration. These faculty members are prone to make no connection between the lack of multicultural focus in the curriculum and a negative campus climate for diversity. If the campus climate does not affirm diversity, perhaps it is the students themselves who cause these problems. It is rare to find an instructor who is fully comfortable discussing diversity issues in the classroom. Most faculty and staff, academic curricula, and services are not prepared to address the many new college student issues that accompany human diversity and multiculturalism (Jones, 1987).

Higher education has a reputation for being slow to change. Nowhere else is that reputation more deserved than with the curriculum. This suggests curricula are more than just what we teach, but are also our culture with a shared sense of customs, values, beliefs, and worldview. For many faculty members, the curriculum is who we are and what we believe and hold dear. Those who would propose changes are not just disbelievers but heretics. Curriculum transformation and multiculturalism or even a three-credit diversity requirement are many times viewed as a threat to the very foundation on which we rely for meaning and reality.

For many faculty, the suggestion of curriculum changes and multiculturalism is more than just rethinking what is to be taught. It is an assault on who they are. Bloom (1994) maintains that those who lobby for multiculturalism and curriculum inclusion are part of the school of resentment, and their goal is to overthrow the academic canons in order to advance supposed nonrigorous programs designed to promote social change.

Many administrators appear to be caught between a rock and a hard place, where the demands for change are juxtaposed against an institutional culture designed to withstand modifications. In the face of ever-rising budget costs and limited external financial support for higher education, administrators find themselves in a precarious balancing act between competing forces of change and those who view change as a violation of institutional bedrock values.

One possible helpful resource for campuses to address the daunting challenge of adapting their curricula to the challenges of diversity is the Association of American Colleges and Universities. For many years, this organization has been at the forefront of helping its member institutions redesign their curricula and pedagogy in this regard by offering alternative models.

LARGER PUBLIC ATTITUDES ABOUT DIVERSITY

A positive or negative campus climate for diversity does not happen in a vacuum. To understand fully the events that occur on campuses, we must also observe how diversity is addressed in the larger societal context. Highly publicized events such as the Rodney King videotapes, the associated Los Angeles riots, and the terrorist attacks on September 11, 2001, can affect the national climate for diversity. Economics, politics, social, and international issues also affect the national discourse on diversity.

About five years ago, I spent a month in Bangladesh. It was a great experience and a wonderful opportunity to compare and contrast our two educational systems. Bangladesh is halfway around the world and by our standards a poor country. It has a landmass about the size of Nebraska and the world's eighth largest population. The area has a rich historical and cultural past.

After a bloody conflict with Pakistan, modern Bangladesh was established in 1972. The college students attending Dacha University then were at the heart of the movement for Bangladesh's independence, and many of them paid for that independence with their lives. In discussions with my host from Bangladesh I learned that students were still politically active, so much so that most national issues were debated and acted out on campus before anywhere else. My Bangladeshi host lamented the intense levels of campus violence, segregation, and incivility caused by these conflicts. Those outside the university seemed to tolerate these conflicts and evaluated this student unrest as part of what young adults are sometimes likely to do. Many did not make the connection between intolerance on campus and larger societal concerns.

I returned home thinking that we here in the United States operated differently. I no longer believe that we are different. What I have observed recently on campuses disturbs me a great deal and is surprisingly similar to what I observed in Bangladesh. I call it the politics of the extremes: liberals and conservatives from both inside and outside the institution indoctrinate and use young people and campuses in much the same way that politicians do in Bangladesh. Those from the extreme propagandize new college student attitudes; they attempt to replace legitimate inquiry with an authoritarian-style rigidity that leaves little space for compassion or common ground.

In higher education, we place a high value on the freedom of speech and academic inquiry. However, the politics of the extremes are generally not those of most first-year students. The dictionary defines *teaching* as the process of imparting knowledge and preaching as giving a sermon. Too often, many of us in higher education are guilty of the latter and not the former. When first-year students are told what to believe, we deprive them of their common ground for discussions and exchange of ideas and severely damage the campus climate for diversity. This is not a new phenomenon. Dan Carter (1995) in his book *The Politics of Rage: George Wallace, the Origins of the New Conservatism, and the Transformation of American Politics* links the Reagan revolution to its real progenitor, George Wallace. Wallace, like many of those who use divisive "shock jock" dialogue methods, was not interested in a discussion of the facts. Many who employ the politics of the extremes also use the moral compass of ambition where the means always justifies the end. As Ron Robinson asserts in *Protecting Your Constitutional Rights: The Conservative Guide to Campus Activism* (1993), "Conservatives should stop pretending that college and university officials are neutral observers; they are often our mortal enemies" (p. 94).

PREJUDICE REDUCTION

A friend is fond of saying, "If you don't know where you are going, then any road will get you there." Too often in higher education, we have been guilty of not thinking holistically about the creation of a positive new student campus climate. In the case of campus climate, the sum is greater than its parts. More important, these parts are interrelated and dependent on each other.

The study of prejudice has been a topic of inquiry throughout most of the social sciences. Oskamp (2000) writes that while the goals of most of the investigations of prejudice have been reduction, most of the studies have focused on the nature, causes, and consequences. Relatively little research has been done on how to reduce prejudice. Given the increasing rates of incivility on campus, the development of models of prejudice reduction is essential to the improvement of the campus climate for diversity.

Attempts to reduce prejudice need to be grounded in an understanding of the causes of prejudice. Duckitt (1992) suggests four levels of prejudice-reduction factors:

Level 1: Genetic and evolutionary predispositions

Level 2: Societal, organizational, and intergroup patterns of contact and norms of segregation for intergroup relations, that is, laws, regulation, and norms of segregation or unequal access, which maintain the power of the dominant groups over subordinate ones

Level 3: Mechanisms of societal influence that operate in group and interpersonal interactions, that is, influences from the mass media, the educational system, and the structure and functioning of work organizations

Level 4: Personal difference in susceptibility to prejudiced attitudes and behaviors and in acceptance of the specific intergroup attitudes

At Duckitt's (1992) level 1, the genetic and evolutionary predisposition factors appear not to be susceptible to short- or intermediate-term alterations of patterns of behaviors and attitudes. This almost biological inclination is alterable only through long-term efforts designed to reduce prejudice. It is possible that interventions directed at the subsequent factors will assist in changing these long-term patterns of prejudice. To reduce prejudice at this level, institutions of higher education may want to consider providing prospective students with accurate information about the institutional rationale and commitment to diversity and educational expectations for first-year student involvement.

At Duckitt's (1992) level 2, societal, organizational, and intergroup patterns of contact and norms are subject to change because of changes in laws, policies, and widespread norms. In fact, it is at this level that societal and organizational change has its greatest opportunity to reduce prejudice. The civil rights legislation of 1954 and 1964 and the actions of the Greensboro Four's integration of the lunch counter at Woolworth's in downtown Greensboro, North Carolina, set in motion profound changes in society. For example, the story about the Titans would never have happened without the civil rights movement and the subsequent changes in the laws that precipitated those events. So too can institutional leadership and changes in accepted norms make a difference in prejudice reduction. Social scientists and educators tend to focus more on efforts at levels 3 and 4; however, we should not minimize the profound impact that laws have on our ability to create a campus climate supportive of diversity. Higher education institutions should consider the negative diversity impact of long-standing existing academic and social policies and procedures on historically underrepresented populations.

At level 3, the mechanisms of societal influence operate in group and interpersonal interactions. Duckitt suggests two subgroupings of this level: those with mass influence and those that target a specific population. Examples of mass influence are mass media systemwide interventions designed to reduce prejudice. Although the impact of these interventions is not as measurable as controlled studies, they have the ability to change institutional and organizational norms, and their value to change widespread norms and beliefs should not be underestimated. The second subgroup of prejudice reduction programs at level 3 falls into generally smaller-scale interventions and focuses specific goals on a target group of participants who usually have a set period of contacts. In this intervention, role modeling and setting standards for interaction appear to make a difference in the ability to relate to members of a perceived different group. Activities with cooperative common goals, equal status between groups, and support for contact by authorities have registered some promising results (Allport, 1954; Rokeach, 1979; Parker, Archer, & Scott, 1992; Pedersen, 1994; Cheatham & Associates, 1991; Banks, 1997a). It is clear that this is the level where educational interventions are most effective. Institutions should offer a variety of curriculum-focused interventions such as first-year seminars and academic service-learning opportunities that aid first-year students in understanding the first-year experience.

Duckitt's (1992) level 4 concentrates on individual personality factors that cause individuals to be receptive to messages that are both prejudiced and nonprejudiced. Duckitt speculates that prejudice reduction at this level is best addressed through significant group or individual counseling or psychological interventions. All of these interventions speculate that carefully planned efforts to address prejudice need to be developed for all four levels; however, interventions at level 1 or 2 have greater potential for prejudice reduction at an institutional level than do those at level 3 or 4. Institutional efforts targeted at this level should focus on preventing prejudice. Ponterotto and Pedersen (1993) suggest the following emphasis: primary prevention where programs are intentionally designed for groups currently unaffected by bias with the purpose of assisting new students to continue functioning in ways that facilitate cultural awareness and tolerance; secondary prevention, which refers to early recognition of problems and appropriate intrusive follow-up interventions; and finally tertiary preventions, after a serious incident where significant conflicts are clear and acknowledged by the majority of the campus.

ASSESSING DIVERSITY

Smith (1999) suggests that an assessment of diversity efforts in higher education should encompass a multidimensional assessment. She argues that in order to understand the potential impact of diversity and its added value to the campus climate, one must appreciate the necessary dimensions of a successful diversity initiative. She emphasizes that an assessment of the components of diversity initiatives is essential to understanding and developing a holistic approach to progress in improving the campus climate for diversity. According to Smith, the four dimensions are (1) access and success, (2) climate and intergroup relations, (3) educating all students for a pluralistic society, and (4) institutional viability and vitality. In the case of campus climate, the whole is greater than the sum of the parts. They are interrelated and dependent on each other, and attention to how they correlate also highlights the uniqueness of each component.

Access and success refer to the inclusion of historically underrepresented populations and social justice issues. The focus is largely on numbers and specific target populations who have not had the same opportunities for participation in higher education as majority group populations. Their historical underrepresentation is not by chance. Societal and institutional barriers have made their opportunities for participation less likely and success more difficult. In this dimension, progress is measured through initiatives and statistics that indicate increases in access, graduation, and employment of racial, ethnic groups, and women.

Climate and intergroup relations expand the discussion of diversity to include groups not considered in dimension 1. Here the focus is on the interactions between the total communities that make up the campus climate. Groups whose customs, cultures, and issues have traditionally not been recognized (for example, sexual orientation, marginalized religious groups, students with disabilities, returning adults, veterans, economically disadvantaged students, and the climate for women) become part of the dialogue. This dimension also focuses on creating civility among all aspects of campus community. How new populations are treated in the campus community is a function of traditional patterns of interactions.

Educating all students for a pluralistic society involves the rethinking and restructuring of the curriculum to meet the needs of a pluralistic society, which must also consider its links to a shared and connected global community. While some view curriculum transformation and multiculturalism as fads, those with an eye for the future of students, society, and world must understand the necessity of these issues. Our society has always looked to higher education for solutions. Issues of poverty, world hunger, racism, discrimination, terrorism, and world health must be central to any curriculum that prepares students. We must also practice what we value. Diversity in the curriculum is hollow without the inclusion of faculty, administration, minorities, and women that reflects a commitment to these goals. The interrelation of the four dimensions is very clear. Institutions that cannot make a significant effort in educating people for a pluralistic society will not be able to realize their goals for access and success, campus climate, and intergroup relations.

Institutional viability and vitality suggest important questions for the leadership of higher education. An institution's commitment to diversity should be a clear and consistent message from the leadership. This message must be reflected in all four dimensions and permeate the institutional planning and goals. The investment in diversity should be as visible and well defined and multidimensional as the institution's commitment to technology.

RECOMMENDATIONS

Keeping in mind what we know about student attitudes toward diversity, societal patterns, prejudice reduction, and the institutional dimensions of diversity, some suggestions for developing a campus climate supportive of diversity for new students become clear. The task of creating a new student campus climate supportive of diversity is multidimensional and must be addressed with a holistic plan that includes the entire institution and external stakeholders:

• Begin efforts to introduce and assist new students in understanding and embracing the institutional commitment to diversity well before new students enroll at the institution. The institutional commitment to diversity and civility should be clearly articulated and interwoven into all aspects of the institution's recruitment, enrollment, academic college, and department correspondence and information. In the new student recruitment process, the institutional commitment to diversity should be clearly articulated. The institution should consider the direct and indirect signals given by all new student marketing information and staff.

• Develop a common theme for all first-year students at orientation programs and activities that focus on building an inclusive campus climate. Orientation programs for new students should be purposefully designed to enhance new student awareness of diversity. The first few days of the new students' campus experiences have a profound impact on their ability to negotiate cultural and gender differences. Orientation activities that stress interaction and mutual understanding assist in building community.

• Involve faculty and institutional leadership in orientation programs that focus on creating a positive campus climate. Messages about the importance of civility should come from all areas of the institution's leadership. The importance of diversity must be a consistent theme in academic programs for new students. Many times, actions speak louder than words. Institutional administration, faculty, and staffs void of cultural and gender diversity send the signals that diversity is not yet taken seriously in practice.

• Provide institutional financial support for programs designed to create access and success for historically underrepresented and economically disadvantaged groups. New minority and economically disadvantaged student recruitment and retention efforts are linked philosophically. Institutions must develop effective strategies that remove barriers to success for minority and economically disadvantaged new students. In many cases, this will involve institutional talent search–type programs and academic support programs for students at the elementary, junior, and senior high school levels. Institutional development resources should make financial aid available to all economically disadvantaged first-year students.

• Make conscious efforts and commitment to develop student interest in service-learning, community service, and an understanding between formal curriculum learning and social action. New students should be encouraged to get involved in meaningful service projects that flow into and from course objectives that require learning about community problems and some student reflection. Academic service-learning projects require faculty involvement and curricular integration. At many colleges and universities, faculty have traditionally not been recognized or rewarded for involvement with service-learning. If we expect faculty to lead academic service-learning projects for students, rewards must be realigned to encourage faculty participation.

• Assess long-standing first-year student customs, practices, rituals, and organizations that create campus environments that reflect and support an increasingly diverse community. Left on their own, first-year students have a tendency to recreate student programming and activities that support the status quo. Student affairs professionals and higher education institutions must assume responsibility for enhancing the cocurriculum on the college campus. Working with students, administrative leadership should develop purposeful proactive strategies that increase new student opportunities for inclusion.

• Consider the impact of campus and local media on the campus climate for diversity. There is an old saying in the media: "If it bleeds, it reads and it leads." Institutions must hold campus and local media accountable for their impact on the campus climate for diversity. Institutional offices of public information and relations should educate the larger community on the institution's commitment to diversity. Local and campus news sources that have not assessed their reporting of stories for racial and gender bias may be perpetuating old stereotypes and myths. Highlighting criminal activities and tensions found in some minority communities while neglecting to focus accurately on the positive efforts and activities of these communities is unethical. If we agree that diversity has value, then local and campus media providers should make a diverse staff a priority. Training designed to increase the cultural and gender awareness of media staff will also have a positive effect on the sensitivity of reporting.

• Commit institutions to diversify not only their student population but also their faculty, staff, and senior leadership. Institutional goals and plans to recruit new and retain minority students that do not include like-minded short- and long-term efforts to recruit and retain diverse faculty, staff, and leadership will most likely not produce the desired results. Perhaps nowhere else are an institution's values, customs, and history more clearly revealed than in the selection of its personnel. Two excellent resources for increasing the diversity of the faculty are

Building the Faculty We Need (Goff et al., 2000) and *Diversifying the Faculty* (Turner & Sotello, 2002).

• Understand that institutional leadership must stand ready to defend the campus climate from nonstudent external and internal agendas that deprive students of common grounds for diversity engagement and interaction. Institutional leadership for diversity must be visible and consistently champion campus civility. Institutions may also want to consider including statements about the educational importance of respect for differences and campus civility in all new student orientation activities and media presentations. Leadership statements of support for diversity are not effective as a day-after solution to campus conflicts.

• Develop both a short- and long-range diversity plan with measurable outcomes. The plan must have goals for all four of Smith's dimensions of diversity (1999). Diversity plans and evaluations should be open and tied to the institution's Web site. Diversity should be an indispensable part of the institution's planning process.

• Be prepared to explain and defend diversity initiatives to external and internal stakeholders. Leadership must seize every opportunity to affirm institutional support for diversity. The power of the bully pulpit cannot be underutilized: the office of public relations and the alumni association can also play a vital role in actively and intentionally addressing questions and concerns related to institutional diversity goals.

• Develop and implement well-publicized procedures for addressing acts of intolerance and hate. Institutions should establish protocols for addressing hate activity. Students who are victims of hate activities may need counseling and emergency services and should be kept apprised of the investigations and outcomes. Hate activities are also teachable moments; appropriate statements from institutional leaders assist in healing the community. Proactive new student diversity awareness programs also play an important role in addressing hate activities. These programs should begin with new student orientation and be repeated throughout the year. Those involved with new student programs have an infinite variety of educational programming opportunities and options before hate activity events. There are very few that are effective after an event.

CONCLUSION

Developing a first-year student campus climate supportive of diversity must be a total institutional priority. Efforts to promote diversity must be part of a well-planned institutional commitment to new students and the larger society. Given the student attitudes discussed in this chapter, it is reasonable to anticipate conflicts and some difficulty. However, as in the movie *Remember the Titans,* how higher education chooses or does not choose to address campus climate will say much about the future of new students, society, and the world.

CHAPTER NINE

Building the Foundation for First-Year Student Success in Public, Urban Universities

A Case Study

Diana S. Natalicio
Maggy Smith

The success that begins at this university lasts a lifetime.
—Alumni Association President, University of Texas at El Paso

Much of higher education, especially the research university, is struggling to build the foundation for student success in the first year of college, while building a research capacity to sustain the scholar's environment. Because higher education now exists in a highly competitive marketplace where education is more a commodity than an intellectual investment, educational opportunities are literally everywhere in every format imaginable, and institutions are defined by the variety and quantity of options offered (satellite campuses, strategic alliances, for-profit institutions, and distance education, including Web delivery of entire degree programs). For those of us who lead the brick-and-mortar institutions, how we adapt the institution to meet the competitive challenge is critical to our survival; how we adapt the institution to better address the needs of first-year students is critical to their survival in the collegiate environment. The challenges include striving to educate more students for a more intellectually complex world and workplace that demand specialized skills and knowledge beyond secondary school, while sustaining the elements of a traditional college education. This begins with a carefully designed approach to the first year built on institutional mission. If that mission includes a commitment to research and scholarly production, the institution will need to redesign itself as a new breed of research university.

What does an institution do to respond to today's complex and competitive environment? How does a college or university leverage its resources to make it

We thank Diana Guerrero, director of enrollment evaluation and technology at the University of Texas at El Paso, for her assistance in the researching, revision, and editing of the manuscript for this chapter.

possible to attract significant federal resources that bring attention to its research capacity, at the same time that it works to provide access and equity to an under-educated, underserved, and often ignored region? What does this mean for the first year of college? These are the kinds of questions posed in this chapter.

This chapter is a case study of the "new" urban research university, an institution that addresses with equal vigor both the critical need to build a comprehensive approach to the first year of college and the research challenges of a traditional research university. Although the chapter was based on the experiences of a single institution, its messages are broadly applicable to higher education institutions of every type. Specifically, this chapter focuses on the role that the president plays in transforming the first year of college at an urban public research intensive institution; the importance of building the first-year initiative from the institution's strengths and core competencies; the challenges faced in creating a comprehensive program for first-year students, including the planning process, the choices for program components, the development of opportunities for student growth and employment, and the importance of recognition and celebration activities; and the choices for organizational structure that satisfy an efficient and sustainable approach to the first year.

THE URBAN PUBLIC INSTITUTION

The primary mission of most public urban universities is to offer quality higher education programs to residents of a particular geographical region, for whom the institution may represent the only opportunity for professional and personal growth and development. The human and economic development of the region is often closely tied to the success of a postsecondary institution in meeting the needs of the populations it serves.

Such universities are often categorized as access driven, and they are often not recognized for the excellence of their academic or research programs. There are forces both within and outside the institution that have difficulty understanding and accepting the possibility that a college or university committed to creating access for nontraditional students can also offer high-quality programs and research activity. The popular images of traditional higher education—the eighteen- to twenty-one-year-old residential students, football games, and fraternity parties—are strongly embedded in the expectations that many faculty and community members set for the institution. These expectations are the mind-set against which all institutions are measured, and only those that conform are viewed as having the potential to achieve excellence.

Institutions that demonstrate a commitment to creating higher education access for students who differ significantly in age, ethnicity, and socioeconomic level are viewed as having little chance of achieving academic or research distinction. This dichotomy between types of higher education institutions is powerfully reinforced by such publications as *US News and World Report,* whose use of traditional measures of academic success (average SAT scores of entering students, endowment size, and graduation rates, for example) leads to rankings that place traditional universities at the top and access-focused urban institutions at the bottom. "What's more, rankings are almost always about popularity, prestige, and perceived quality of education, but they say virtually nothing about what happens after a student enrolls—they say nothing about the educational experience itself" (Nelson, 2002, p. 56). The experience of the University of Texas at El Paso (UTEP) shows that test scores and four-year graduation rates are not accurate measures of performance for the majority of first-generation minority students. UTEP students' entering test scores are below the national average, its six-year graduation rate is 25 percent, and yet we find that our graduates are able to compete with graduates from all over the country and with people from all backgrounds.

The experience offered to first-year students at all colleges and universities is where the commitment to student success really begins. This experience is particularly critical at the public, urban university. Here begins the process of transforming the individual lives of often highly vulnerable students and promoting the socioeconomic development of the region. A commitment to access is meaningless if students are not provided institutional support to ensure that they have every opportunity to succeed, and such support must be strongest and most visible during the first year of enrollment. As Frank Borkowski, former chancellor of Appalachian State University, observes, "Our campus efforts to enhance the total commitment to our learning environment all start with freshmen" (Gardner, 2001, p. 3).

THE PRESIDENT'S ROLE

The responsibilities of the president of a public, urban university are increasingly complex, particularly when students must be better educated to enable them to participate productively in the global economy and colleges and universities are challenged to provide educational opportunities and options to an increasingly heterogeneous set of constituents. The president must believe strongly and be able to defend passionately the important mission that such institutions play in ensuring a sustainable future for our society. The president must embody the mission and be able to articulate clearly and convincingly both the opportunities that such institutions offer and the challenges that they face. Often the president of such an institution must be tenacious and thick-skinned, resisting the many pressures to abandon the commitment to access in favor of a more elitist approach to higher education—pressures from faculty on campus, as well as from elected officials, media, and community members.

If a college or university expects to serve as an agent of its region's human and socioeconomic development, it must have a clearly defined institutional strategy to attract area students, build their confidence that the institution believes in them and is committed to their success, and engender a solid institutional fit between the student and the institution by providing support mechanisms that have demonstrated capacity to foster that success.

The investment of human and financial resources in the design and implementation of the first year is the single best indicator of the institution's true commitment to student success and retention. The fundamental value that under-lies that investment is a belief that talent is everywhere, extending across socio-economic, ethnic, gender, and geographical boundaries, and that what is lacking is the level playing field that enables that talent to be discovered and developed.

INSTITUTIONAL VISION AND MISSION

The campus's mission statement sends a clear signal about what is to be done and for whom it is to be done. The mission must be authentic within the institution's setting and closely tied to the population that is to be served. Once the mission statement is shaped and accepted by the major stakeholders of the institution, it must be widely and regularly articulated. Lack of clarity in defining, or ambivalence in articulating, the institutional mission can seriously under-mine an institution's credibility and, ultimately, its effectiveness. The president's role is critical in ensuring that the mission permeates the institution, from the top down to its lowest levels.

Between 1970 and 1987, the demographics of the El Paso region and of UTEP shifted dramatically. Hispanics were growing significantly in numbers in El Paso County and, to a lesser extent, on the campus. Hispanics had become the fastest-growing and least-well-educated segment of the national and El Paso population. As the only public university within more than three hundred miles in Texas, UTEP had a responsibility to try to create higher education opportunities for all residents of this area, especially Hispanics, whose numbers on the campus did not mirror the demographics of the county from which more than 80 percent of the student body was drawn.

For an institution of higher education whose student population comes primarily from its surrounding region, drawing community members into the planning process offers them the opportunity to participate in the new direction of their college or university. Forming a community-based advisory group was UTEP's answer to community voice. The 2001 Commission was established in 1988 to work with the university to identify the issues that were of importance to constituents in the community and to create a vision for what the university should look like and seek to accomplish by the year 2001. Focusing on such topics as educational opportunities, leadership, and economic development, the commission presented a report in 1990 that created a context for a revised and more authentically grounded mission statement. It was clear that UTEP's vision and mission had to address the needs of the surrounding region, which meant addressing access and the needs of first-year students, including their transition to the university environment:

UTEP Vision Statement
The University of Texas at El Paso commits itself to providing quality higher education to a diverse student population. The University aims to extend the greatest possible educational access to a region, which has been geographically isolated with limited economic and educational opportunities for many of its

people. UTEP will ensure that all of its graduates obtain the best education possible, one which is equal, and, in some respects, superior to that of other institutions so that UTEP's graduates will be competitive in the global market place. UTEP also envisions using its binational location to create and maintain multicultural, inter-American educational and research collaborations among students, faculty, institutions, and industries, especially in northern Mexico. Through the accomplishment of its mission and goals via continuous improvement, UTEP aspires to be a model of educational leadership in a changing economic, technological, and social environment.

The UTEP community—faculty, students, staff, and administrators—commits itself to the two ideals of excellence and access. In addition, it accepts a strict standard of accountability for UTEP's institutional effectiveness as the University educates students who will be the leaders of the 21st Century.

UTEP Mission Statement

The University of Texas at El Paso is dedicated to teaching and to the creation, interpretation, application, and dissemination of knowledge. UTEP prepares its students to meet lifelong intellectual, ethical, and career challenges through quality educational programs, excellence in research and in scholarly and artistic production, and innovative student programs and services, which are created by responsive faculty, students, staff, and administrators. As a component of The University of Texas System, UTEP accepts as its mandate the provision of higher education to the residents of El Paso and the surrounding region. Because of the international and multicultural characteristics of this region, the University provides its students and faculty with distinctive opportunities for learning, teaching, research, artistic endeavors, cultural experiences, and service.

Once revised, UTEP's vision and mission statements were widely disseminated across the campus. They appear in most official publications and are framed and posted on walls in all buildings. They convey to students, faculty, and staff who we are as an institution and what we seek to become. They remind us all why what we do is important and why participating in higher education is a privilege for both students and the faculty and staff who serve them. They guide institutional practices and policies, from hiring and tenure decisions, to the development of academic programs from the first year to the doctoral degree. They keep us grounded in who we are and ensure our authenticity. The process of developing vision and mission statements also helped us define our institutional strengths, those academic areas of which we could be proud and on which we should focus, and the place from which our students' first year should begin.

INSTITUTIONAL STRENGTH: THE PLACE TO BEGIN THE FIRST-YEAR EXPERIENCE

A number of considerations play a critical role as the institution thinks about and commits to developing a first-year experience for its incoming students. If bold, new initiatives are not integrated with departments and programs that are already strong and recognized, no matter how exciting and important the initiative, leveraging human, fiscal, and physical resources will always be an uphill struggle. The criterion is whether the institution's strongest and most visible programs will benefit. Once first-year programs are institutionalized in these academic areas of strength, the initiatives can migrate to other areas naturally and more easily. For UTEP, a former mining and engineering school, that point of strength has always been in science and engineering. As a result, the inaugural program for first-year students at UTEP began in science and engineering. Funded through a National Science Foundation Model Institutions for Excellence award, this program was created in 1997 to serve first-year students intending to major in math, science, or engineering. The heartbeat of this program, a learning-community model called Circles of Learning for Engineering and Science, had an immediate impact on student success and retention in science and engineering, so the institution began to ask, "What if . . . ?" for the rest of the student body.

To begin the development of a first-year experience for the general student body three years later, the institution looked closely at the overall retention and success measures. This exercise revealed disappointing first-year outcomes: barely 62 percent returned for the second year, too many students failed to continue beyond the second year (45 percent), and the six-year graduation rate dropped to 24 percent. UTEP might not have recognized the transition needs of first-year students as quickly if we had not made aggressive changes three years earlier at the point of academic strength in science and engineering. This was the academic area where retention had been recognized as a challenge long before the institution as a whole focused on the issue. Although the universitywide program bore little resemblance to that in science and engineering, the fact that it built on the first-year experience concept is what really mattered.

BUILDING QUALITY IN THE FIRST-YEAR PROGRAM

Creating access is one important dimension of the role of a public, urban college or university. Flexible admissions requirements are critical because standardized tests often mask the potential of first-generation, low-income, and minority students, who are often in the majority at these regional universities. With that flexibility, however, comes a responsibility to ensure that all students, whatever their level of precollege preparation, have the tools they need to be successful at the institution and after. There can be no compromise when it comes to the quality of graduates' educational experience. This includes the urban public campus's responsibility to continually improve the quality of its programs so that all graduates have the capacity to compete with their peers from any other institution in the world as they move on to graduate programs, professional schools, or professional careers.

Once access becomes part of an institution's mission, care must be taken to avoid creating a revolving door through which the dreams and aspirations of generations of underrepresented students become illusions and they fail to return because they were never fully engaged within the campus community. The complement of access is retention, which Spicuzza (1992) characterizes as a by-product of student satisfaction. One way of promoting student satisfaction and retaining students who might otherwise leave is by adding value from the time the student enters the institution until graduation, a responsibility that begins with new student orientation, continues through the first year, and culminates with the senior year.

Key to developing a student-centered and "value-added" approach to education is the commitment of the faculty and staff, whose interactions and implementation of policies and procedures facilitate student success. Faculty must be not only highly capable participants in their own disciplines, but they must also embrace the institution's mission and commitment to first-year students and to making them feel that the university experience is relevant to their lives. They must not only secure grant funding to enhance their research achievements, but also seek to provide learning experiences and on-campus jobs for undergraduates. They must not only be supportive of students' efforts to achieve undergraduate degrees, but also encourage them to pursue graduate or professional school opportunities.

Like other urban, public, regional institutions, a successful merger of equity and excellence will ultimately determine whether UTEP fulfills its mission. We are committed to changing the stereotype of urban and minority institutions, which have seldom been recognized for academic and research excellence. UTEP intends to demonstrate that excellence can be built within an equity context, without sacrificing the values on which the institution's commitment to access rests, from first-year excellence to doctoral distinction. We know that underrepresented minorities, as individuals and collectively, can compete successfully if they are provided the level playing field of enriched undergraduate and graduate education opportunities. We know too that investing in research and graduate programs will contribute to opportunities that we offer incoming students.

Research and graduate programs are critical to the model of this new kind of research university. Instead of considering them to be incompatible with the goals of a public, urban institution, they become sources of strength. Faculty recruitment and retention depend on creating a context in which faculty can achieve their aspirations in research and scholarship. Most faculty members want to know that the institution is committed to providing a context conducive to their success, as well as to that of their students. Laboratory space and instrumentation, library materials, technology, and graduate students are all a part of creating a context for excellence in scholarly productivity. Institutional resources must be committed, and ongoing assessments must be conducted to ensure that student and faculty needs are being met and appropriately balanced. The key is keeping our collective eyes on two critical targets—first-year student success and excellence—and constantly assessing our progress in balancing the demands of both while seeking to foster their convergence.

BUILDING PARTNERSHIPS

Enriched opportunities for students at public, urban institutions are enhanced by collaborative partnerships both off- and on-campus that are designed to facilitate the seamless path of education up to and through secondary education and in the transition into and through the first year of college. Developing strategic partnerships become a priority as the institution focuses on building both its research capacity and its first-year programs.

Many regional universities operate in a somewhat closed loop, with most of their students coming and often commuting from the surrounding area. The interdependency—the reciprocity of interests and benefits—is obvious: the university depends on the K–12 sector to prepare students for success in higher education, and the K–12 sector depends on the university to prepare highly qualified teachers. Building these relationships with the schools in the area is one of the most critical components in shaping the characteristics and quality of future first-year students.

UTEP has invested heavily in building a partnership with school districts in El Paso County, from which 82 percent of its students come. An estimated 60 percent of the teachers in area schools are graduates of the university. To be successful, we must work together. One way to build partnerships that foster education across the K–16 boundaries is to create a university-led coalition among higher education, public school districts, and the community. This type of collaboration is committed to increasing the academic achievement of a region's children and to help ensure that all students who graduate from area high schools are prepared to enter and succeed in college, reversing, in some cases, the historic patterns of underrepresentation of poor and minority students in higher education.

In UTEP's case, the El Paso Collaborative for Academic Excellence has been successful in bringing together the university, the community college, and the school districts to raise the K–12 educational attainment and aspirations of all young people in the region, eliminating the achievement disparities seen between socioeconomic groups, and graduating better-prepared teachers. Through its participation in the work of the collaborative, the university has learned a great deal about the first-year student population it serves, and it has greatly expanded its efforts to share expertise with the school districts that prepare those students.

LESSONS FROM THE UTEP EXPERIENCE

The first step in meeting the challenge of creating true access for those who have been underrepresented in higher education is to focus sharply on the point of clearest interface between the precollege experience and the college or university: the first year of college. Many students come to campuses as nonresidential, nontraditional in many ways, first-generation college students; some are from low socioeconomic backgrounds; many are academically underprepared; and many fit all of these categories that disadvantage them beyond the average college transition challenge. A critical question must then be asked: How does the institution mobilize its resources to create a nurturing and supportive, yet challenging, environment for first-year student success? Because many of these students never dreamed that they would or could become college students, the campus environment must be welcoming and supportive personally as well as intellectually and must comprise a set of structured academic and social opportunities from which students' learning is enhanced and their sense of community is defined.

Understanding First-Year Students

Success in creating access for those historically underrepresented in higher education requires a clear understanding of the context from which these students come. Data collection and analysis of K–12 education in the region are essential for an urban public institution. Analyses of such variables as family education and income, language spoken in the home, dropout rates by school and year, and number of graduates from each high school who continue on to postsecondary education will help shape the design of outreach strategies to encourage more young people to continue their education and more of their parents to believe that it is affordable. Ultimately, these data shape the programs created for the first year of college.

In addition to learning more about future students and preparing for their transition to the campus, it is critical to study closely and continuously those who are already enrolled. Surveys of entering students, graduating seniors, and alumni all help ensure that we know whom we are serving and what special challenges and opportunities they present. Where do students come from, and where do they go when they have completed their education? Do they reside on or near the campus, or do they commute long distances in unreliable vehicles or across difficult roadways? Do they live with parents who cover all living costs, or do they help support younger siblings or disabled parents? Do they have their own families to support? How many hours do they work each week? Do they work on or off campus? Is a degree their goal, or are they enrolled in selected courses for professional development? How was the university helpful in encouraging students to continue pursuing their education despite family or financial challenges? What impediments, if any, did the university present to students as they moved toward graduation? Do graduating seniors and recent alumni think that the university effectively prepared them for graduate or professional schools or careers? The important next step is to use the information gathered from such surveys in the design or redesign of programs and strategies. Using the information requires making it widely available to faculty and staff who are responsible for program design and implementation.

A majority of faculty and staff have probably come from backgrounds quite different from those of the students they are attempting to serve, and their personal experiences often act as obstacles to understanding the special challenges faced by first-generation, low-income students. Helping faculty and staff develop an awareness of the values, attitudes, perceptions, and expectations that students bring with them to campus is critical to their understanding and response to student behavior, because when personal and institutional values conflict, students may become at risk. Developing sensitivity to cultural values, such as the importance of family, response to authority, competition, and goal setting, is also invaluable to campus administrators. In a culture that has a strong sense of family, if a student has to make a choice between family and school, family may very well win out. "A female student may miss class to take care of a sick brother or sister because there may be no money for day care, it is unthinkable for the father (if present) to miss work, and if the mother misses work she may have no vacation or sick leave and the wages lost may be the week's grocery money. This means not that school is unimportant, but rather that overriding family pressures take precedence within her value system" (Guerrero, 1998, p. 176).

One person or one office cannot identify the myriad factors that affect new students or all the information that needs to be considered to develop a real understanding of a particular student body. People with a variety of experiences in dealing with first-year students at different entry points into the system are essential in developing an understanding of the different facets of an institution's character.

Task Force to Study First-Year Issues

Most of us have used the committee system for a variety of purposes to solve any number of problems. Using a project team or task force to study a problem and initiate change or to look into the first college year is both effective and efficient because the nature of the first year should involve representatives from all areas of campus. "The well run *ad hoc* team has several attributes that make it the ideal organization for change . . . This model of change presents a diametric contrast to our bureaucratic heritage—the pyramid style of management" (Waterman, 1990, pp. 19–20). This type of task force or project team has a starting point, a charge, and an ending point. If the task force chair is empowered by an authority figure such as the president, the provost, or the vice president, the chair will get cooperation, interest in the project, and ultimately hard work from committee members.

At UTEP, a task force was formed to examine first-year and retention issues: What was happening to our students? Why were they not returning? Where were they going? What were we not doing? What could be done to facilitate the transition of first-year students to college in a way that would encourage them to continue and to succeed?

To address this retention challenge in the way described above, the first step is to identify the institutional departments and positions that must be represented on a task force addressing this kind of institutional thinking and reform. In our view, several criteria for individual membership were salient:

Decision makers: Participants from key areas on campus with decision-making capacity. Often these are the high-ranking campus administrators from academic affairs and student affairs or their representatives.

First-year leaders: People who play key roles in first-year policy and program areas on campus. Depending on how broad a look at the first year the committee is conducting, this group may include several faculty members (English, mathematics, and so on), new student orientation staff, and academic advising staff.

First-year enthusiasts: Faculty and staff on campus who want to be involved because they care deeply about first-year transition.

Naysayers: Those on campus who will offer substantially differing opinions or who might oppose outright the first-year initiative idea (after all, they succeeded in college without all this fuss!). Those in this group who are visible campus leaders or voices are especially important to include in the discussions.

Students: UTEP's task force included students but not community members. The student representatives were self-selected from a group of student leaders who had worked as orientation leaders and who knew the student culture and demographics.

This diverse representation will create a large task force, which provides the resources to divide the group into subcommittees for specific assignments but still permits a wide variety of voices overall. The UTEP task force included about twenty members appointed by the provost from across all major campus divisions: academic affairs, student affairs, business and finance, and research. The chair of the task force never refused membership to anyone who expressed interest. It was always understood that the president and the provost were interested in the work of the group and eager for reports and results. The task force was charged with identifying the issues that were of importance to students' successful transition to UTEP and with creating a plan for an entering student program that would provide an integrated experience for UTEP's first-year students. The program would introduce students to the university environment, help cultivate their academic potential, and provide insight into the long-term value of a college education and its impact on their futures. The task force was asked to address, but not be limited by, the following questions:

- What should the components of the UTEP entering student experience be?
- How does UTEP move in the direction of offering students a coherent program?
- How do the administrative and organizational functions collaborate to promote a unified, student-centered program for first-year students?
- What role does academic advising play?
- What curriculum changes would the university strive to implement?
- Is there a role for a first-year seminar?
- What academic support services will play an integral role?

In a nutshell, the task force was asked to identify the needs of first-year students and then to address what the university should be doing for its entering students to ensure their continuing participation and timely graduation. This process was framed by two questions.

The first question was, "Who is being served?" Defining the student to be served by whatever initiatives are created is an important decision for the task force. For UTEP, the students to be studied and served by any new programs were "entering students," that is, any student entering UTEP for the first time, transferring to UTEP, or returning after an absence from the university. In addition, all transfer students, returning students, or new students who had not completed the core curriculum or were not yet accepted into a major were to be flagged as entering students for the purposes of this task force. Subcommittees focused on such topics as academic advising, curriculum, and instruction issues related to student transition to college and the institution's organizational structure. When the task force work was completed approximately nine months later, a report to the president, the vice presidents, and other key administrators made recommendations about how the university could better serve its students, improve its retention and graduation rates, and have more successful and satisfied students.

The second question was, "What do students need?" The task force wanted to depart from traditional models of student participation. As a result, they looked at the student from a holistic perspective because they believed that the interaction among student needs was what would enable a student to grasp the University culture and become successful. Figure 9.1 shows how UTEP looked at the student experience holistically. By placing the student in the center of our thinking, we were able to envision what services could collaborate to facilitate students' successful participation on our campus. Student needs were broadly defined as individual, social; academic, intellectual; transitional; and future. While some would argue that in this context, all student needs were

Figure 9.1. Model for Delivery: Moving Students from Participation to Success

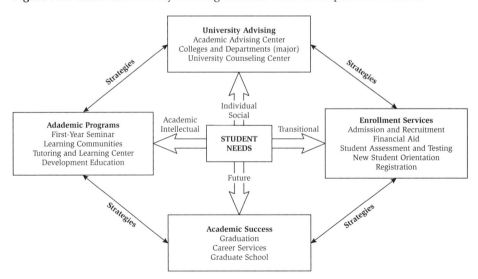

subsumed by the "transitional" category, others took a firm stand for transition as a separate category. With the student always in the middle of the picture, the student was always visually guiding our discussions. We were able to ask, "What services do we have? What services do we need to develop to address these sets of needs for first-year students?" The results of those discussions are displayed in the boxes surrounding the center "Student Needs" box in Figure 9.1. Each of these services is a strategy that answers those needs and that, given a unified mission to enhance the first year, delivers an interactive developmental model to move students from participation to success. This approach was designed as a matrix management model, without regard for institutional reporting lines.

UTEP's Entering Student Program

As an outcome of the task force deliberations and the recommendations made to the senior administration of the university, the president announced in an institutionwide memo the formation of UTEP's Entering Student Program (ESP), designed as a partnership between academic affairs and student affairs, as displayed in Figure 9.2. The organizational partnership worked well for UTEP because of the cordial and collegial relations among departments across those

Figure 9.2. University of Texas at El Paso Entering Student Program

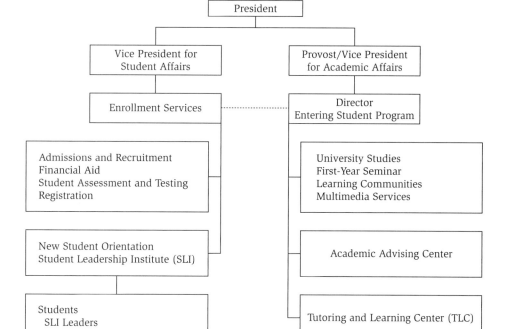

divisions. This was also a cost-effective first step in trying out this new program, and it allowed the institution the flexibility to invest the available resources in those activities that would benefit the students without investing institutional funds in additional organizational structure.

Situating the leadership for the new program in academic affairs was important for a number of reasons. The primary reason was that the president wanted the ESP to be seen as an initiative that would ultimately enhance students' academic performance. A second critical reason was that we were developing the first-year seminar as a credit-bearing course that would be part of the institution's inventory of academic courses. Leadership for the First-Year program is yet another place to ask the questions "Where is our point of strength? Where do we have the leverage?" For UTEP, it was academic affairs. Initially, the program was composed of those major areas whose synergy would deliver the Entering Student Program as displayed in Figure 9.2. A faculty member holding an administrative position in academic affairs was appointed to be the ESP director.

When the president announced the ESP to the campus, she also established its mission:

> The Entering Student Program (ESP) promotes the academic, social, and personal success of all entering students at UTEP, including all first-time students, transfer students, and returning students. The ESP ties together five major services that accompany a student from the time his/her name is first brought to UTEP's attention until that student is linked to an academic department and/or major: Undergraduate Recruitment, New Student Orientation, Undergraduate Academic Advising, University Studies (the first-year seminar including learning communities), and the Tutoring and Learning Center. Broadening the scope of these services and integrating them into a coherent program enables us to foster greater student participation in academic and extracurricular programs and activities on campus and increase opportunities for student-faculty interaction.

It was important that the president make this announcement. This message had to come from the institution's leader in order for everyone to take it seriously. The president's imprimatur provided credibility for the leadership team and especially for the director. It would not have been enough for one vice president to make such an announcement. Emphasis on working within the matrix could come only from the top. Vice presidents, faculty, and staff had to work across reporting lines to resolve issues such as resource utilization, money, space, and curriculum development. Presidential involvement demonstrated institutional investment in this program and in these students.

BECOMING A UNIVERSITY COLLEGE

Two years later, the partnership between student affairs and academic affairs for administering the ESP had proven that we were doing the right thing: retention was up; students were more satisfied; overall grade point averages (GPAs) were up. Because the ESP had been so successful, we wanted to ensure its sustainability, as well as to promote continued institutional effectiveness and efficient use of resources. As the next step in serving the first year of college, nine departments were brought together into a university college, an administrative unit that integrated the ESP with several additional departments critical to entering student transition and success. All departments focused on the first year now had a single reporting line (see Figure 9.3).

Because UTEP wanted to make the bold academic statement that we were investing substantial resources in students' entry, transition, and continuation at the institution, we chose the university college model among other various options such as an enrollment management division, a college of general studies, or a first-year college. The university college fit with our needs, our values, and our mission. As we worked through this structural change, we consulted with others who have made similar structural change. On-line organizational charts from a number of colleges and universities were invaluable. Telephone calls to colleagues around the country provided us with stories and cautions. One of the most useful exercises for us was visiting other campuses. North Carolina State University at Raleigh, for example, has a first-year college. Although it is a residential campus with an advising- and residence hall–based first-year college, its experiences and challenges were invaluable.

The University of Houston-Downtown has a student demographic profile much like UTEP's. In conversation with institutional representatives, we learned that this campus delivers first-year programming through its university college. Indiana University Purdue University-Indianapolis also has a student body demographic profile much like UTEP's. This university delivers first-year programming in much the same way we were considering: learning communities,

Figure 9.3. University of Texas at El Paso University College

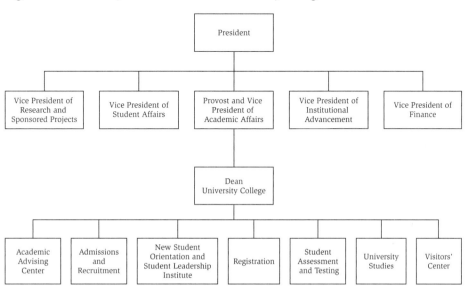

interdisciplinary seminar, and developmental advising. Its initiatives were just a few years ahead of ours. In each case, when we communicated with other institutions, their enthusiasm for offering help was not unlike what we are doing for our first-year students: changing the way we do business, moving to new roles, taking on new responsibilities that are somewhat intimidating, but in all cases knowing that what we are doing is making a difference in students' first year and overall success in college.

As the administrative structure evolved, the components central to a comprehensive first year at UTEP continued to develop based on the needs of the first-year student as identified by our years of experience in dealing with this group:

- Academic programs (a first-year seminar, learning communities, tutoring and learning center activities, and multimedia course enhancement)

- University advising (academic advising, department and college major advising, counseling, and career services)

- Academic support services (recruitment and admissions, new student orientation, student leadership training, registration, student assessment and testing, financial aid)

- Academic success (graduation, career services, and graduate school)

First-Year Seminar: Seminar in Critical Inquiry

First-year seminars give an institution the greatest opportunity to begin to shape and educate first-year students from the very outset of their college or university education (Gordon, 1989). For institutions such as UTEP, the first-year seminar provides an opportunity to teach students what it means to be a college student and how to make the most of the resources that are available on campus in the context of an academically rigorous class. (For a more detailed discussion of first-year seminars, see Chapter Sixteen.)

A team of faculty and staff from across campus initially designed UTEP's first-year seminar; a steering committee continues to provide administrative oversight. University staff and faculty from each of the academic colleges serve two-year rotations on the committee. Because of UTEP's student demographics, the seminar was designed to be a core curriculum credit-bearing course. The advantages of this course design are that it combines academic content, introduces students to the university and its resources, and engages students in the university community. Course instructors design the academic content based on their own interests. Through such varied themes as the American dream, "Reel Business" (business as presented in movies), mathematical discoveries, environmental issues, and memoirs of place, students learn college success and transition skills as these skills are applied to and integrated with the academic content of the course.

Intertwining the academic content with the student success topics is probably one of the greatest challenges of teaching the seminar with an academic emphasis. Each section of the seminar includes activities or assignments created to meet a set of common goals:

- Strengthening students' academic performance and facilitate their transition to college
- Enhancing students' essential academic skills in critical thinking, communication (oral, written, and electronic), research, and study skills
- Increasing student-student and student-faculty interaction
- Encouraging students' self-assessment and goal clarification
- Increasing students' involvement with UTEP activities and resources

A small financial supplement is provided for instructors because they are required to attend workshops, use innovative pedagogy, and follow up with students for an additional semester.

In addition to the seminar, we encourage students to participate in learning communities: clusters of two or three courses that students attend as a cohort. This arrangement facilitates students' transition to college while helping them develop relationships that serve as a basis for study groups and sources of encouragement.

Professional Academic Advisers

Prior to the establishment of the Entering Student Program, UTEP had not employed a full-time professional advising director, relying instead on the part-time assignment of a faculty member to manage these duties. Student peer advisers and an occasional part-time faculty member advised students. However, our experience suggests that for students who need direction, who have never dreamed of going to college, and who have few, if any, role models to give them direction, professionally trained advisers and comprehensive advising can be an important link to campus and one of the best investments an institution can make. In *Making the Most of College: Students Speak Their Minds* (2001), Richard Light says, "Good advising may be the single most underestimated characteristic of a successful college experience. Graduating seniors report that certain kinds of advising, often described as asking unexpected questions, were critical for their success" (p. 81).

The ESP invested in the development of a fully staffed academic advising center, with a full-time professional director, full-time professional advisers, and several positions divided between advising and teaching the first-year seminar. The center serves all students who are not eligible for department-based advising, including provisionally admitted students, students who have not declared a major, and students whose potential majors do not offer premajor advising. Additional factors that influenced the organization and delivery of the advising center were our commuter student population and their need for more centralized and intrusive advising, the nature of the programs we offer, faculty interest, budget, facilities, and university organizational structure (Upcraft, 1995).

Students in the center are assigned to professional advisers on a caseload basis. Career exploration software and other resources are available for them, as well as regular and consistent advising. A developmental, rather than prescriptive, advising approach is taken, where the adviser's role is to facilitate student growth and responsibility.

Student Leadership Institute

There is little doubt within higher education that students new to campus are more likely to succeed if they can make emotional and intellectual connections to their course of study. This includes significant interactions between faculty and students, involvement in out-of-class activities, and assistance and support from peer leaders. In an effort to promote the use of upper-level peer leaders in first-year seminars, UTEP created the Student Leadership Institute (SLI). Now in its third year, the SLI provides a comprehensive leadership curriculum that centralizes basic student leadership development training activities into a single area to maximize efforts and minimize duplication. Training includes topics such as leadership theory, interpersonal communication skills, working within groups, time management, diversity, study skills, and classroom teaching techniques. After completing a six-month, 120-hour selective training program, these students are prepared for positions of leadership throughout campus.

Rewarding students for their participation in the SLI allows UTEP to keep its very best students on campus in positions where they can help others succeed. Therefore, participating students receive an hourly wage during their training period. The access new students have had to these experienced and trained peer leaders has yielded extraordinary results. After interacting with a peer leader for a semester, one first-year student stated, "I had someone to talk to that knew what I was going through. Not someone that experienced college thirty years ago—but someone who was going through college at the same time I was."

This significant interaction spills beyond the classroom door and onto the sidewalks of campus where peer leaders are often stopped to field questions on campus services or for guidance on personal matters. A recent peer leader reflected, "I never realized the impact I had on others until one of my students stopped me at a basketball game so that she could introduce me to her parents. From conversations they had had around the dinner table, the parents knew my name and all the activities we had done in class. The student had told her parents over and over that I was the only thing keeping their daughter from going crazy with the stresses of college." These stresses and the confusion associated with attending college for the first time are key areas of concern that all entering student programs must address.

An unexpected benefit of the SLI has been an increase in the number of peer leaders who are considering teaching as a career. A key component of the training experience is a focus on classroom management and student learning styles. "I never ever considered becoming a teacher. But over the past year, my professor has worked with me on developing lessons on time management, study skills, and using campus resources. I get stressed out talking in front of twenty-five students, but when it's all over I have this tremendous sense of achievement." Many peer leaders credit the SLI with providing them a comprehensive foundation from which to begin their work. "I was planning to be a businessman, but now I want to be a college professor. I will remember the lessons and activities we did in SLI and use them in my own classroom. Collaborative learning is the best way to encourage students to learn."

Increased Student Employment Opportunities

On-campus employment can be a significant factor in retaining students who must work to finance their education. The focus is to keep the students on campus beyond class hours, to encourage their engagement with campus activities, so that they will begin to feel at home on campus. As part of the ESP, we have created many new opportunities for student employment. These include becoming a peer leader in a first-year seminar or working as a peer adviser in the Academic Advising Center or as a peer tutor providing free walk-in tutoring to UTEP students in the Tutoring and Learning Center.

Celebrations and Recognitions

Celebrations are an integral part of any successful program; they both recognize the accomplishments of people and serve as vehicles to showcase and publicize the new program. Each year the president and the ESP host an ESP recognition event to honor student, faculty, and staff achievements during the past year. The president favors hosting the event at the university's presidential residence so that students have a chance to see where the president lives, where faculty, community leaders, and other dignitaries often meet, and where high-level university functions are held. Following the example of the National Resource Center for The First-Year Experience and Students in Transition, UTEP presents the prestigious Advocate for Entering Students Award to one faculty and one staff person each spring at the university's honors convocation. These awards attest to the importance of the first year of college at UTEP.

Celebrating with the same enthusiasm with which you work can be richly rewarding and can continue to promote a message of institutional commitment. A recent ESP recognition event was a joyful occasion filled with music, anecdotes, thank-yous, and great food. It culminated with the president, the ESP director-dean of the University College, and the assistant director of university relations being very reluctantly coaxed on stage where, as the Supremes, they karaoked their way through "Stop! In the Name of Love," demonstrating an exuberance and generosity of spirit that spoke volumes to the crowd as it said again, "There are very few things we will not do for our students."

RECOMMENDATIONS

As we step back to reflect on the UTEP story, several broadly applicable principles guided the process for institutional change. We offer the following recommendations for managing the change process and building the foundation for first-year students.

- *Model change management from the top.* Having presidential support and interest in change is essential. Then begin any first-year program initiative at the point of institutional strength. This may be the most visible academic program or college on campus. Build the initiative from the institution's vision and mission statements. Form a project team (or task force) that is broadly representative of campus, strategic, and inclusive. Get the highest-level administrative support that you can, and use that position to your advantage.

• *Make the first college year a priority on campus.* Be vigilant about taking and seeking opportunities to increase awareness about what you are doing and why. Offer awards, recognition, and events on a regular basis. Use every opportunity possible to talk about first-year students in a positive way.

• *Establish the right organizational structure.* Look closely at the organizational delivery system to make sure you have the right organizational structure to sustain the efforts when the personnel change. Organizational structure not only makes a statement about what and whom you value; it also makes effectiveness, efficiency, and sustainability possible.

• *Build a comprehensive first-year program in stages.* Review other institutions' efforts, and modify those programs to accommodate your own particular demographics—student body, institutional mission, and type. Once again, build from the point of strength. Someone must be in charge of the program.

• *Partner educational success at all levels.* Think K–16. This focuses on the changes needed across the board in both higher education and in the K–12 sector—in standards, assessments, curriculum, and graduation (Haycock, 1999). Focus on the talents that students bring with them and what you can offer them in transition—not on their deficits. This means developing functional working partnerships with strategic players in your educational context—your K–12 community, the community colleges that may send students to the college or university, the local community, and federal programs.

• *Foster first-year seminar growth and development.* The first-year seminar course can be the anchor for the overall approach to the first year. Select the design that complements your campus profile. Consult with campuses where courses have developed and that have similar transition issues and comparable demographics. If the seminar is a credit-bearing academic course, make it an intellectual experience that integrates transition skills; include the librarians in the course design; and whatever the delivery structure, have an advisory or steering committee composed of institution-wide representation that rotates on a two- to three-year cycle. Keep class size small. Most important of all, include students as members of the instructional team.

• *Include students in all aspects of the first-year program.* Not enough emphasis can be placed on how important and influential other students are. Include them broadly.

• *Continually assess the program based on critical feedback.* First-year efforts are predictably dynamic; therefore, data collection, assessment, review, and revision are constants. Trend data on first-year retention and grade point average are obvious indicators of student progress. Other important information can be gleaned from student experience surveys in the seminar, orientation, and learning communities; national instruments such as the National Survey of Student Engagement; faculty, adviser, and peer leader surveys; and review of course completion rate and grading and withdrawal patterns of faculty. First-year programming is always a work in progress, requiring constant and positive change that is always responsive to the changing environment in which students live and work and study.

CONCLUSION

As the model for the new research university unfolds, institutions such as UTEP struggle to balance institutional priorities, investing in first-year student success and in the research enterprise to remain relevant within their social context in the new century. The new research university must redefine its mission to embrace a commitment to a successful first year for its students, while maintaining its focus on research and scholarly production.

In the early 1970s, there were bumper stickers and T-shirts depicting the University of Texas at El Paso as "Harvard on the Border." Humorous on one level, and indicative of the institution's image problem in the community on another, this notion that UTEP would aspire to become an elitist island in the Chihuahuan Desert also revealed considerable pathos. Why would an institution want to be something that it is not and should not ever want to be? Once UTEP's mission was defined and articulated, we became proud of what we are, where we are, and whom we serve. We began to celebrate our uniqueness, our strengths, and our cultural heritage and knew that our success as an institution was measured by the quality of our graduates rather than by the stringency of our admission requirements. In terms of the university's responsibility to the publics it serves, that meant granting access to higher education to the people of this region, providing them with the academic, enrollment, and student support services necessary for a successful first year, continually telegraphing a message of inclusion, and maintaining quality programs that will challenge and sustain them through graduation. Supporting students as they enter their first year of college and investing in their future and that of the institution is simply the right thing to do.

CHAPTER TEN

Inviting First-Year Student Success

A President's Perspective

Betty L. Siegel

*First-year programs at their best can inspire us to shift our attention
toward the more deeply satisfying rewards of our work, and to
remember that teaching and learning are part of a lifelong process
of joy, personal discovery, and collaborative service. Isn't it joyous,
after all, to see our students respond to the invitations we send them?*

In his still influential book *College: The Undergraduate Experience in America,* Ernest Boyer (1987) defines a successful first-year program as one that invites students into "an intellectually vital, caring community" (p. 57). He envisioned a campus climate where personal relationships, integrity, and free expression are highly valued. This is the ideal version of campus life, one that has survived intact into an era of higher education marked by rapid and unprecedented change. Advances in technology have been responsible for much of this change, but increasing diversity on campuses has caused a more fundamental shift in higher education. What we often refer to as the nontraditional student—the working mother dedicated to pursuing her undergraduate degree, for instance—is looking more and more like the norm on many campuses, and "traditional" or popular notions of the college experience no longer match the reality as it is lived day to day by students.

More than ever before, it seems, we need to foster the kind of colleges and universities that will inspire first-year students to dedicate themselves to campus life and follow through on their educational goals. We need to create intellectually vital, caring campus communities that will capture the minds and hearts of students as well as challenge and support them during the crucial early days of their first year of college. Even Boyer's language, though, betrays a slight uncertainty about how this vision of a successful first-year program will be made real. "The spirit of community will be sustained," he writes, using the passive voice, not specifying who will be creating "a climate on the campus" necessary for the program's success. The question of where to assign responsibility for a first-year experience program must be the first one asked by any campus wishing to begin or improve its own program. Unless the answer centers on the president and other top administrative leaders, however, those involved in the program will be working against the odds to gain truly campuswide support.

In reflecting on the twentieth anniversary of the national first-year movement in 2001, John N. Gardner outlined several areas for much-needed improvement:

> The first-year reform movement is still not one primarily of faculty, even though it is more than twenty years old. The first year is still not linked intentionally enough to the institutional mission statement and to the desired outcomes of the senior year. . . . We still do not have enough senior institutional leaders, let alone presidents and chief academic officers, who can empathize with the problems of contemporary college students [p. 4].

In listing three separate areas for improvement, Gardner is really listing but one, for it is the role of senior institutional leaders, especially presidents, to build communities that nurture first-year students. Presidents must be responsible for making this goal part of their institutional missions and for rallying their faculty to the cause. If, to use Gardner's language, a president begins to "empathize with the problems of contemporary college students," then he or she will have taken the first step in changing the campus culture so that first-year efforts will thrive.

The chapter explores the steps campus leaders should take to bring the first-year philosophy to fruition in a successful and wide-ranging program. This process requires not only that they take concrete actions—appointing a task force, recruiting faculty, hiring staff, and apportioning budgetary support—but also that they encourage more abstract reflection on the priorities of higher education. Indeed, the first year should be the subject of a campuswide dialogue including all major campus constituencies, with each discussion centering finally on the welfare and development of students. The ultimate goal of creating this early dialogue is to enroll others in a shared vision of the significance of the first year to the overall institutional mission. As the dialogue continues, even smaller programs may develop into campuswide initiatives, bringing seemingly unrelated parts of the community together into productive partnerships.

The chapter outlines a few components of the first college year common to many institutions and concludes with a discussion of invitational leadership as a way of building faculty and administrative support for first-year programs. Learning to lead by inviting others to follow their own interests and passions has been the most meaningful and significant lesson I have absorbed during twenty-three years as president of Kennesaw State University. My belief in the efficacy of invitational leadership is inextricably tied to my investment in the first-year experience program. As the first-year program is founded on the notion that all students are able, valuable, and capable, so invitational leadership begins with the act of asking colleagues to realize their full potential as teachers, learners, and leaders. I have seen firsthand that a campus can be transformed by its commitment to the first college year. A president can be changed by the program as well, discovering a new style of leadership in the first-year philosophy and, more important, embarking on a far-reaching collaborative enterprise with the entire campus community.

DIALOGUE AND COLLABORATION: BUILDING THE PROGRAM

In her essay "The First-Year Experience: Are We Making It Any Better," Barefoot (2000) offers a series of thought-provoking questions to promote a dialogue on college campuses about "reshaping the academy and its critical first year for new generations of students":

> If we were to start from scratch to create a system of higher education focused on student learning in the first year, how would it look? Who among us would we choose to deliver knowledge, however it is defined, to the newest members of the academy? What structures or techniques would we use in the transmission of knowledge? And how would learning be measured? [p. 18]

Her questions give a sense of the seriousness of the task for any institution wishing to develop its own first-year program, as well as the exciting collaborative possibilities opened by that decision. She also points to the larger issues involved in the first college year, particularly those about defining and delivering knowledge and measuring student learning. The ideal first step for a president wishing to transform the idea of a first-year experience program into reality is to form a task force charged with the responsibility of answering questions like those posed by Barefoot. This task force's members should represent all major groups of stakeholders in the institution: faculty, staff, students, administrators, and even trustees.

Although different institutions will by necessity focus on different goals for the program, the one goal held in common by all first-year programs is student success. The president's message to institutional stakeholders, then, must inevitably revisit the fundamental purposes of higher education, and especially the question of what it is our students are learning in our colleges and universities. This is the question Barefoot singles out for our attention—"And how would learning be measured?"—and it is one that Lee Shulman, Ernest Boyer's successor as president of the Carnegie Foundation for the Advancement of Teaching, has dedicated much of his work to answering. In promoting a new approach to institutional research, Shulman (1999) suggests that we rethink existing models of assessment and accountability, where student success is measured largely in relation to such categories as credit hours or retention and graduation rates. Instead, he insists, "The questions we should be concerning ourselves with are questions about quality—and particularly about the quality of what our students come to understand, believe, and do on our watch" (p. 7). Questions about retention and graduation rates, then, should always be asked in the context of larger questions about purpose and mission. This is not to say that administrators should cease doing research in these areas—far from it.

Rather, administrators must approach institutional research from a much wider, more considered perspective.

In an essay (1999), Hutchings and Shulman posit the following questions as central to a more meaningful kind of institutional research: "What are our students really learning? What do they understand deeply? What kinds of human beings are they becoming—intellectually, morally, in terms of civic responsibility? How does our teaching affect that learning, and how might it do so more effectively?" (p. 6). These questions presuppose institutional stakeholders who share basic assumptions about the purposes of higher education—that it has more to do with educating dedicated, engaged citizen-leaders than with merely providing a ticket to the world of work, that it places moral reasoning high among the critical thinking skills, and that it encourages students to give serious consideration to their obligations to the larger polity or community. This is the kind of vision for higher education the president must present to the first year task force, highlighting the connection between the day-to-day work of institutional stakeholders and these larger questions of purpose.

Recruiting Faculty

Without the enthusiasm of the faculty, no approach to the first-year experience can succeed. Even if it is prompted by a presidential initiative, first-year programs must be based on collaboration and collegiality among the faculty and between the faculty and administration. For a remarkable number of faculty, the first-year experience program provides a kind of professional renewal that becomes its own success, and this should be communicated clearly during early task force meetings, perhaps directly by faculty from other institutions with proven programs. Much has been written about the importance of faculty-student interaction to the students in the first-year program, but less has been documented on the importance of such interaction to the faculty. Ideally, these programs should allow faculty to reconnect with their students on a deeper level as they are driven to consider what it is their first-year students need most to hear from them on entering college.

Discussing this issue in task force meetings—or in workshops held once the program has been established—is one way to debunk the myth that first-year programs are composed of remedial courses that hold little or no interest for tenured faculty. While first-year seminars should include some introduction to the basic requirements of the college experience—that is, study skills, test-taking skills, library use, and course scheduling, for example—they should also involve far more significant issues: how to be part of a community, how to develop positive relationships with peers and faculty members, how to make the first-year experience the first step toward the rest of your life and career. These issues will also emerge from other aspects of successful first-year programs—learning communities or service-learning projects, for instance. Treating these more complicated, even deeply psychological and philosophical, subjects, the first-year program asks participating faculty to consider their role in each student's larger life experience. This is no small task, and it can reconnect faculty members with the impulse or inspiration that brought them to college teaching in the first place.

Furthermore, because the program at its best involves faculty from many different disciplines, participating faculty will have the opportunity to think more carefully about the college experience as a whole rather than only from the point of view of the English department, say, or the chemistry department. In other words, they will become more conscious of their roles in a much larger enterprise, especially if they collaborate with faculty members from other disciplines in a particular course. Although faculty are always aware in some sense of their place in the campus community, the first-year experience program highlights the fact that educating students is collaborative work. This may seem to be an obvious point, but it is often too easy for college teachers to become cut off from one another, so that they remain largely unaware of what happens outside their classrooms. As Palmer (1998) reminds us in *The Courage to Teach,* all teachers "need the guidance that a community of collegial discourse provides— to say nothing of the support such a community can offer . . . and the cumulative and collective wisdom about this craft that can be found in every faculty worth its salt" (p. 142). Working together with colleagues from across campus, faculty members may come to feel more than ever before that they are part of a vibrant, connected community of educators and scholars.

At every stage of the program's development, then, a president must convince faculty members of the many possibilities for professional renewal in the first-year experience. Still, no president should forget the importance to faculty of professional success. Indeed, there must be a clear message to faculty that teaching first-year courses and participating in related programs will be rewarded in concrete ways, especially in relation to tenure and promotion. This is not to say that the only way to raise the status of the first-year experience program within the academy is to dangle the carrot of career advancement before uncommitted faculty. Rather, it is to say that campus leaders have a responsibility to signal forcefully the importance of the program to the institution as a whole. In order to create a culture that places the experience of first-year students at the center of the institutional mission, a president must be willing to pledge support in action as well as words.

Involving Administrators

If first-year programs never find a proper home—both a literal space and wide-ranging support—within a university, the failure is most likely not one of community interest but of institutional—that is, administrative—priorities. In addition to signaling to faculty the benefits of their involvement in the first-year program, a president must also signal to appropriate staff members that they will be rewarded for their part in making a positive difference in the experience of first-year students. Certain staff members, such as student affairs personnel or counselors and advisers, will have obvious roles to play in welcoming and nurturing first-year students, and these colleagues should be included during the very first task force meetings about the first-year program. Their intensive day-to-day interaction with students at all stages of the college experience will make their voices indispensable in the campus dialogue.

Other staff members may not have a direct role to play in building the first-year program, but they should be made aware of its existence and purpose through campus announcements and in both campuswide and departmental meetings. The first-year ethos—treating each student as a valuable and able person and capable of realizing his or her full potential—should be reinforced at every opportunity, particularly when administrative leaders speak to campus groups. There are very few staff members who have no contact at all with students, and some—in offices such as registration and financial aid or in facilities like the library and bookstore—have daily contact with a great number of students. The briefest exchange between a staff member and a first-year student can improve that student's experience. It is imperative that staff members, like faculty, be reminded that treating students respectfully and courteously is a vital measure of professional success.

The strongest message a president can send about the first-year program is to give the program itself the facilities and staff support necessary for its success. This means not only hiring full-time administrative assistants to offer clerical and logistical support to a full-time first-year coordinator, but also appointing interested staff members from other departments and divisions—student affairs, development, marketing and university relations, admissions—to lend their expertise to the first-year enterprise. From the earliest task force meeting, the ultimate goal is to make this enterprise a collaborative project among stakeholders, so that everyone, from those who screen student applications to those who raise money for the institution, will take some responsibility for the program's future. Only with this kind of broad-based staff support can the first-year experience become a sustainable program, though the question of how long that support continues depends in large part on campus leadership.

Maintaining Creative Leadership

In many ways, the first-year experience program is the perfect vehicle to bring a college or university's administrative team together philosophically. So many issues related to first-year students really involve the entire student population: What do we want to teach our students? What kind of citizens do we want them to become? What kind of community are they joining? How should they participate in our community? How can we most effectively help them along toward their futures? Here is how the issue is framed by John Gardner and his colleagues in their suggested questions for campus administrators evaluating first-year programs: "Has your campus defined what is meant by 'new student success'? Relative to this definition, what should new students on your campus experience, and how can this be assured? What kinds of resources are necessary to facilitate these experiences, and are those resources available and allocated to support new students?" (Gardner, Barefoot, & Swing, 2001, p. 12).

These questions clarify the connection between institutional mission—how to define student success—and more concrete, detailed decisions about policies and procedures. Once a first-year experience program has been established, the campus leadership should revisit these questions regularly and evaluate the program in relation to their answers. Above all, the president and his or her cabinet must be prepared to respond to changing student needs and to approach the campus culture with flexible and innovative thinking.

Such thinking can lead to fundamental organizational changes in campus administration, especially when a productive dialogue develops on the question of how seriously the institution takes its responsibility for students entrusted to its care. At Kennesaw State University, for instance, we drew on our experience of the first-year program in order to develop the new Division of Student Success and Enrollment Services, headed by a vice president serving on the president's cabinet. Clearly we needed an entire division responsible for more than just student affairs—admissions, registration, and student organizations, for instance. We needed to give an official institutional structure to our overriding wish to ensure student success, with all that might mean for our students academically and personally. The lessons we learned from students and faculty about our first-year program were directly translated into the structure of this new division. At the same time, the University System of Georgia began to place greater emphasis on student retention, a goal we ourselves had adopted in planning for our original first-year experience course. With the Division of Student Success and Enrollment Services, we began to combine the goal of higher retention rates with the less easily measured goal of making students feel welcome, part of a caring and concerned community, and dedicated like all of us to the overall success of the institution.

Similarly, a president can give greater institutional support to the first-year experience program by connecting it with a larger organizational division. Think, for example, of the benefits of housing the first-year program within the division responsible for general education. From this decision, it is only a small step to the development of learning communities and sophomore- or senior-year experience programs. Again, presidents and their cabinets must be willing to experiment creatively with structure and organization if they are to act on the lessons learned from the first-year experience. Whether the change is small (approving a request to hire new office support for the first-year program) or fundamental (appointing a new cabinet-level position), the goal must be to uphold the institutional mission of nurturing student success.

ASPECTS OF THE FIRST-YEAR EXPERIENCE: FROM SUCCESS TO SIGNIFICANCE

Research on the effects of first-year programs points overwhelmingly to their positive impact on students. Here are a few key areas in which students involved in first-year programs noticed the most significant positive change (from the 2000 Your First College Year Survey, www. gseis.ucla.edu/heri/yfcy/index.htm):

- Academic skills and abilities

- Comfort level and quality of interaction with professors

- Adjustment to the college experience

- Self-discipline and motivation

- Spiritual lives

- Moral and social values

- Multicultural understanding

This list covers a wide range of topics, from the practical to the spiritual, and clearly different programs emphasize different skills and values. Even a stand-alone, one-credit first-year seminar, however, can influence students in nearly all of these areas. In their study of students who had taken the one-credit first-year seminar at Bloomsburg University, a state university in Pennsylvania, program administrators found the following to be true: "Students enrolled in the course had greater levels of peer group interactions, interactions with faculty outside of the classroom, perception of faculty concern for student development, academic and intellectual development, and institutional and goal commitment" ("Bloomsburg University," 2000, p. 4). First-year programs, regardless of the host institution's particular characteristics or the program's range, seem especially effective in improving these particular areas of the overall student experience.

The reason for this positive impact is easy to locate. Beginning with orientation, best practices among first-year programs point to the care and concern with which the institution has prepared for its first-year students. For instance, in Appalachian State's Summer Reading Program for its incoming first-year students, students read the same novel, along with study guide materials, in preparation for a discussion session during orientation and for assignments in various first-year classes. As the Appalachian State orientation handbook explains, "This will provide a way to have . . . orientation move beyond . . . questions about such things as attendance policies, to actively engaging you in . . . one type of intellectual activity in which you will be engaged in your university career. . . . The process will serve to remind you about how strongly Appalachian values your intellectual and academic development" (p. 11). From before the beginning of fall semester, first-year Appalachian students are encouraged to think of themselves as intellectually engaged contributors to a campuswide dialogue. The program is successful because it has a straightforward and compellingly simple goal: to make first-year students feel welcome, valued, and connected.

The following aspects of proven first-year programs should give campus leaders some guidance as they work with colleagues toward this goal. They chart a progression many colleges and universities have followed, from the establishment of stand-alone first-year seminars, to the development of learning communities, to the incorporation of service-learning requirements into the first-year experience.

The First-Year Seminar

A staple of the first-year experience program is typically a stand-alone course giving students the necessary skills with which to succeed in higher education. Subjects covered include study skills, time management, campus resources, career decisions, critical thinking, student life, and the larger campus community. In most cases, this kind of first-year seminar includes more thought-provoking, philosophical discussions about the place of the college experience within an engaged and successful life and career. Other topics and approaches are specific to particular institutions. DePaul University, for example, includes a required Chicago-themed course in its first-year program curriculum. Frank Conte, program coordinator for DePaul's First-Year Program, explains, "What we're trying to do is acclimate students to their surroundings so they aren't overwhelmed by the experience" of living in a major city that is in many cases unfamiliar ("Immersion Key to DePaul FYE Program," 2000, p. 2). Appalachian State, located in the much more rural setting of Boone, North Carolina, seeks to introduce first-year students to the culture of Appalachia, requiring attendance at cultural events and local activities and lectures as part of the first-year seminar. First-year seminars should encourage students to define themselves in relation not only to the campus community but also to the larger polity or culture beyond the campus borders.

Other first-year seminars focus on more strictly academic topics in order to welcome new students into their intellectual community. The College of the Holy Cross, a Jesuit liberal arts institution in Worcester, Massachusetts, invites a new group of faculty each year to design first-year seminars and activities around a question framed by Tolstoy: "How, then, shall we live?" As Holy Cross makes clear on its Web site, this approach to the first-year seminar is productive for both personal and academic reasons, for students and faculty alike: "Whether one is a student making college-course and life choices, or a faculty member grappling with the demands of family and professional life, this is the question everyone in the first-year program asks and works to answer." Holy Cross explicitly links the college experience with fundamental moral issues, taking the first-year seminar far beyond topics of student acclimation and preparation. In this, the Holy Cross program truly embodies the best of the first-year philosophy. (For a more extensive discussion of first-year seminars, see Chapter Sixteen.)

Communities for Learning Success

The positive momentum from a popular, influential first-year seminar can lead directly into programs that expand on the first-year ethos. As the research proves, students in first-year seminars benefit greatly from the opportunity to forge meaningful relationships with both their instructors and their peers. At Kennesaw State University, this result of the course owes to two significant factors. First, limiting enrollment to twenty-five students for any given section of the course encourages students to establish close relationships with one another through classroom discussions and out-of-class projects. Second, we continue to stress the faculty's responsibility to serve as mentors to their students—that is, to take each student seriously as an individual, to offer considered guidance and advice, and above all to listen carefully to students to gauge responses to the often overwhelming first-year experience.

The next logical step for our first-year program was to create more opportunities for this kind of meaningful interaction among students and between students and faculty members. Using the first-year seminar as a foundation course, we planned a series of Communities for Learning Success, with each community comprising twenty-five students taking the same three courses during their first semester. In addition to the first-year seminar, students are required to take a composition course in the English department and one other general education course (in communication, math, philosophy, science, or computer science). Like the Holy Cross first-year seminar, these learning communities serve to introduce students to a vibrant intellectual community, where the pursuit of knowledge is in significant ways a collaborative journey. One student comment sums up the benefits of learning communities for Kennesaw State: "This semester has given me the encouragement I needed to keep going. I actually feel my professors are real, like I could connect with them. As far as peer relationships go, I have made some wonderful friends in my classes. I'm never alone between classes anymore, and they actually give me incentive to come to school."

Because Kennesaw State is a commuter college, it is often difficult for students to connect in any significant way with their peers, especially when the vast majority of students must work part or full time to pay for their education. The pressures facing these students are enormous, and if they discover no sense of community on campus, then surely the temptation to drop out must always be close at hand. As the student quoted above makes clear, the Communities for Learning Success help students feel connected to faculty and peers, even providing them with an "incentive to come to school." Once a student understands that the college experience is in many ways a collaborative enterprise, and that he or she has an indispensable role to play in that collaboration, then he or she becomes inspired both academically and personally.

We are working hard to encourage the same kind of student response in the new living and learning residence halls that opened recently on campus. Although only a few hundred of our sixteen thousand students are living on campus, this development signals a significant shift in how we will define our institution. We already have plans in place to give our residential students a full living and learning experience—a way of thinking about university life as an education for the whole person. As with students in Communities for Learning Success, students in the new residence halls will be invited to succeed along with others rather than being left alone to struggle towards a seemingly distant graduation date. (The topic of learning communities is discussed in greater detail in Chapter Twenty-Two.)

Service-Learning

There has been increased emphasis in the past decade or so on the role of service to community in higher education, as public and private institutions alike have sought to define their social obligations in much more specific and practical terms. Judith Ramaley (2001), former president of the University of Vermont, helps to define what "civic responsibility" can mean for higher education:

> The most fundamental means by which any educational institution can enhance civic responsibility is (1) to find a means to link learning and community life through the design of the curriculum, and (2) to serve as a center and resource for community building on the community's terms. Beyond these fundamental means, each institution can use its distinctive strengths based on its traditions, institutional history, and resource base to contribute through scholarship and outreach or engagement to the strengthening of community life and community capacity to identify and solve problems [p. 15].

In this conception of service in higher education, colleges and universities must define their institutional mission directly in relation to the needs of the larger community, and, importantly, they must connect student learning with civic engagement. Students in this model, like faculty and staff, will be evaluated at least in part by their contributions to the strengthening of community life.

If campus leaders are to be successful in promoting service as an institutional goal, then clearly they need to create specific, workable programs to transform administrative rhetoric into action. As many campuses have discovered, the first-year-experience program is ready-made to absorb an added emphasis on service-learning. First, asking students to consider their place in the larger community should already be tied to first-year efforts to prepare them for the invigorating challenges of the future. Second, campuses with established learning communities have prompted students from the beginning to work together toward common objectives. There is a natural progression for students from understanding academic life as a shared experience to comprehending their responsibilities as citizens. Third, the first-year program should ideally combine the best of practical-minded studies—test-taking skills and career planning, for example—with more philosophical reflection: how to form lasting relationships, how to interpret the impact of your education on your life generally. Service projects combine these two learning styles; building a house with Habitat for Humanity, for instance, raises questions about class distinctions, economic policies, ethical commitments, and a whole range of other thought-provoking issues.

If these projects are to be incorporated into a first-year seminar, faculty and administrators must work diligently to make service requirements an integral part of the class and the final evaluation of student performance. They must also schedule class time for reflection and dialogue on what students are learning from these service projects. By explicitly linking academic success with civic involvement, first-year programs can inspire students with the understanding that their studies have a direct bearing on the most pressing issues facing their communities. Administrators, faculty, and staff can learn profound lessons as well about the personal and professional rewards of service. Together with students, they can reflect more deeply on their individual and collective responsibilities, developing a much more vivid sense of their institution's potential impact on community life.

Thomas (2000) refers to the role of the "university as citizen," whereby the entire campus community works to "generate good will and respect, internal excitement and high morale, meaningful social change, and positive role models and learning opportunities for students" (p. 94). To incorporate service-learning into a first-year program is to take a significant step toward creating the kind of university she describes. At the very least, service-learning asks students to think beyond the borders of the campus and the limits of their own experience. This result alone is reason enough for making service a vital component of any first-year program. While success—raising one's grade point average, preparing for the Graduate Record Exam, loading the résumé with memberships in student organizations—may be the immediate goal of the academic regimen, true significance—learning one's obligations to community, realizing one's personal and professional potential, defining an ethically motivated life—must be the goal of the educational experience as a whole. (For a more extensive discussion of service-learning, see Chapter Twenty-One.)

SIGNIFICANT LEADERSHIP FOR THE FIRST YEAR OF COLLEGE: THE INVITATIONAL MODEL

Much has been made in this chapter of the importance of getting first-year students to see beyond their immediate situation, whether this means considering their future career choices, the stages of their moral development, or their place in the larger community. For campus leaders, too, becoming involved in the first-year experience program should be a call to what really matters in higher education. Martin (1982) reminds us that a great deal can be lost if "the style of presidential leadership [changes] from charismatic to bureaucratic, from ideational to managerial, from seat-of-the-pants to the computer-style professional" (p. 91). Twenty years later, Martin's warning has a new immediacy, as in many respects we are living in the golden age of the bureaucratic, managerial, computer-style college president. It should be clear by now that this style of leadership is at odds with the spirit and ethos of successful first-year programs. Based on a philosophy of education that all students should be treated with respect and dignity, the first-year experience program can teach presidents crucial lessons about their obligations as campus leaders, as well as their place in the collective enterprise of higher education. The program places a great responsibility on the shoulders of campus personnel, entrusting them with the care of the hearts and minds of our most vulnerable students. In sum, the program is a call for caring leadership from all involved faculty, staff, and administrators. We might call this style of leadership *invitational.*

"Invitational leadership" means precisely that: leadership as a means of inviting others to succeed. Many of us tend to think of leadership as something that is exerted by one individual *onto* others—that is, the leader, having earned a position of dominance and power, begins to issue orders and direct subordinates. No matter how kind and generous they might be toward their associates, such leaders are of the command-and-control variety. By contrast, invitational leadership is a generous and genuine turning toward others in empathy and respect, with the ultimate goal of collaborating with them on projects of mutual benefit. The emphasis shifts from command and control to cooperation and communication, from manipulation to cordial summons, from exclusiveness to inclusiveness, from subordinates to associates.

The invitational leader is unique in asking others to meet their personal and professional goals as a condition of his or her own success. This is not merely a by-product of this particular leadership style. On the contrary, encouraging others in their quest for self-fulfillment is embedded in the principles of invitational leadership—as it is part and parcel of the first-year philosophy. Leadership of this kind becomes a mutual commitment between colleagues rather than a series of orders issued from the top down. In addition to treating students with dignity and respect, the invitational campus leader will invite his or her colleagues to succeed on their own terms, explore innovative ideas about the first-year program, reflect on their individual styles and philosophies of teaching, and become invitational leaders themselves.

LEADERSHIP AS SERVICE

In "Essentials of Servant Leadership," Greenleaf (1970) makes an eloquent case for the necessity of leaders to be concerned above all else with serving others: "The servant-leader is servant first. It begins with the natural feeling that one wants to serve. Then conscious choice brings one to aspire to lead. The best test is: do those served grow as persons; do they, while being served, become healthier, wiser, freer, more autonomous, more likely to be become servants?" (pp. 23–24). There are two important implications for our purposes in Greenleaf's definition of the servant-leader. First, by positing service as the prerequisite for inspired leadership, Greenleaf implies that leadership without service is something far less substantial: ego driven rather than altruistic, selfish rather than empathetic. The first-year experience program teaches a style of leadership based on service to others—one that is rooted in a philosophy of altruism and respect, collaboration, and cooperation.

Second, Greenleaf believes that leadership involves teaching and mentoring and that one of the major requirements of leaders is that they move others toward service. It is not enough that leaders concern themselves with organization and management; rather, they must inspire and instruct by example. This is a challenge for everyone involved in the first-year experience program. At all levels of a college or university, leaders must create an atmosphere in which students and colleagues are invited to realize their full potential as leaders themselves and, more generally, as human beings. As it is in the first-year classroom, so should it be in administrative and faculty meetings. Furthermore, by stressing that campus leaders should emerge from every area of the institution, invitational presidents can create a collaborative culture of innovation, giving secretaries and academic deans alike a sense of their pivotal role in shaping the program's collective future.

Finally, if we are asking students to consider their obligations to the larger community by incorporating service-learning into the first-year program, then campus leaders must take their responsibilities as citizens more seriously. Service is a natural part of an institutional mission—service toward students on one level and service on behalf of the future on a more abstract level. It is this second level of obligation that Colby and Ehrlich (2000) discuss in *Civic Responsibility and Higher Education*. Here is their first suggestion for campuses seeking to have a more direct and concentrated role in preparing our communities for a better future:

> A high degree of institutional intentionality in fostering moral and civic responsibility is the hallmark of those colleges and universities that lead in this arena. The campuses not only have mission statements that include this goal, but the statements are well known and understood by most students, faculty members, and staff. The administrative leadership speaks and acts in ways that promote the goal, as does faculty leadership [p. xl].

If, to cite Boyer (1987) once again, we are to create "an intellectually vital, caring community" on our college and university campuses, then we must do so with a "high degree of intentionality." Campus leaders must themselves serve as inspiring examples, both speaking and acting in accordance with institutional goals. As we have learned, this mixture of clear-sighted speech and intentional— and invitational—action is central to the success of any first-year experience program. Faculty and administrators must convince the campus community that they have both a personal and professional stake in the program's success.

RECOMMENDATIONS

First-year experience efforts involve all segments of the campus—faculty, staff, and administrators—and therefore the work of bringing these forces into alignment is crucial to its success. The following recommendations highlight the necessary steps in communicating the importance of the first year to the entire campus community.

- *Develop a task force comprising major institutional stakeholders*—administrators, faculty, staff, students, and trustees—to begin a focused dialogue on what the first year means for your students now and what it should mean ideally.
- *Recruit faculty* by convincing them of the professional rewards, both tangible and intangible, of participating. Connect the importance of first-year teaching with overall institutional goals.
- *Involve key staff members*—from student affairs, development, marketing and university relations, admissions—from the earliest stages of the program's development to ensure broad-based support.

- *Give the program the facilities and staff support necessary for its success*, yet another way the administration can signal in concrete terms the importance of the program to the institution's overall mission.

- *Maintain flexibility in administrative decision making* and be willing to change to accommodate the first-year program as it develops. Consider linking the first-year program to a larger administrative division with access to the president's cabinet.

- *Continue task force meetings* to discuss the possible evolution of the first-year program beyond a stand-alone seminar to include learning communities, service-learning projects, and other possibilities.

- *Extend the first-year experience ethos* into an invitational style of leadership, summoning both students and colleagues toward their full potential as leaders themselves.

CONCLUSION

What can be learned from the first-year program largely transcends traditional distinctions among institutional types, even though these distinctions will dictate certain choices in the evolution of any given program. What remains consistent from college to college is how it can transform the campus constituency. At Kennesaw State, for instance, we have seen our first-year program transform our students by giving them new-found confidence and security. We have seen it transform faculty, allowing them to collaborate across disciplines on projects of mutual benefit and recapture something of their original love for teaching. We have seen it transform campus leaders, helping us connect the goals of the program with the larger objectives of the institution. Finally, the program has transformed our university's approach to education generally, teaching all of us that what happens in our classrooms has implications far beyond the borders of our campus.

Still, it is in the hallowed space of the first-year classroom that the invitational model of leadership is put to the ultimate test. All campus leaders should return to that space periodically in order to understand their students more fully—their likes and dislikes, their fears and desires, their priorities and goals, their wishes and dreams. It is there, in the classroom, as Levine wrote in 1989, that we discover "the challenge, and the promise" and "the best chance we have to touch the hearts and minds of our students" (p. 24). It is there, in other words, that we may begin to invite our students into lives of true significance.

CHAPTER ELEVEN

Advocating for First-Year students

Jay Chaskes
Ralph G. Anttonen

Thank you for making me love college.
—First-year student after completing a first-year seminar course

It is our bias that there is a common knowledge base, set of strategies, and skill set shared by those who successfully advocate on behalf of first-year students. This chapter discusses the nature of each of these three elements in a nuts-and-bolts fashion and concludes by suggesting how they are integrated to produce advocacy as a process. Those seeking to initiate change on behalf of first-year students, to advocate for them, are assuming a leadership role by virtue of that advocacy. Advocates are likely to encounter various obstacles and impediments to change, and we offer a variety of suggestions for managing these obstacles and impediments.

We have recently examined the skill set, strategies, and tactics used by individuals who have been successful in building first-year ventures on their campuses (Anttonen & Chaskes, 2002). This research was based on a survey of sixty-four award-winning first-year advocates. The University of South Carolina and Houghton Mifflin Publishers give this award annually to approximately ten individuals from among hundreds nominated by college and university presidents. The research findings and our own extensive experience (we are both award-winning advocates ourselves) are woven into the fabric of this chapter.

ADVOCATING FOR CHANGE AS ACADEMIC LEADERSHIP

The quotation at the beginning of this chapter was a comment made to one of us by a first-year student at the beginning of spring semester after the completion of her first-year seminar in 1995. The student's words uniquely capture, we believe, the essence of why higher education professionals become advocates. One study (Anttonen & Chaskes, 2002) suggests that for most advocates, their role as change agents was very much a calling for them. Even among those advocates for whom the role was part of their normal administrative duty, most reported that it was simply the right thing to do. They speak for those first-year students who are without a voice. The reward is both intangible and intrinsic.

The role of advocate requires the individual to be a change agent to the extent that policies and procedures have to be changed in order to programmatically meet the needs of first-year college students. Change agents assume a leadership role, one usually shared with others, as well as understand and work within the governance structure of their college and university.

The structure and charter of America's postsecondary institutions vary from small two- and four-year colleges to large "multiversities" with multiple campuses, hundreds of undergraduate and graduate programs, and thousands of students. In addition, postsecondary institutions range from privately owned, to private-public partnerships, to almost wholly supported public institutions. Thus, we believe that no one leadership style is appropriate for all postsecondary institutional settings. Having made this assertion, it is also our bias that there is a common knowledge base, set of strategies, and skill set shared by those who successfully advocate on behalf of first-year students.

LEADERSHIP IN COLLEGES AND UNIVERSITIES

Many personnel in colleges and universities eschew "academic politics" as something outside their range of competence or as something that distracts them from their professional obligations. To do nothing in the face of programs one finds ineffective or even injurious to students is to give approval, albeit tacit, to those programs. Thus, we argue that doing nothing is in fact being political. Those who overtly seek change on behalf of first-year students are playing a leadership role by virtue of their advocacy. If we can mentally expunge the "strong leader" Hollywood stereotype (John Wayne, George C. Scott, or Russell Crowe), it is much easier to imagine ourselves and our colleagues as advocates for first-year students.

The particular leadership style of those committed to programmatic change on behalf of first-year students must be compatible with both the governance structure at their institution and their own personality traits. Also, these change agents must possess the requisite micropolitical skills to navigate the political milieu of governance that is challenging for the neophyte and veteran alike. Clark Kerr (1991) observed:

> Governance within higher education is, by all odds, the most complicated I have known, and I have substantial experience with corporations, unions, government agencies, and foundations. More than any other, it is better understood as a strung-along series of independent or quasi-independent entities; and it is less

well understood as a unified institution with one dominant form of governance. The intricate dynamics of the governance of academic institutions is founded on the fluctuations of the interactions of the several entities and on the changes in the inherent nature of the entities themselves [p. 201].

Unlike management, leadership as advocacy does not emphasize control, coordination, or supervision by those in authority or those who value the status quo. We concur with Rost (1993, p. 102) that "leadership is an influence relationship among leaders and followers who intend real changes that reflect their mutual purposes."

Most important, leadership is about process—one that allows those who advocate on behalf of first-year students to navigate the "organized anarchy" of the academy in order to effect programmatic change (Baldridge & Riley, 1977). When Rost (1993) asserts that the leadership process "intends real change," he refers to changes that are "substantive and transforming" in nature. These advocates for change have a sense of mission that gives them the patience and the determination that the change process requires (Anttonen & Chaskes, 2002). Professionals with considerable experience in higher education, who understand the intricacies of the governance process, have honed their micropolitical skills in service to their institution and, most important, have garnered the respect and trust of many of their colleagues throughout the institution.

Our own research on award-winning first-year advocates suggests that regardless of institutional type, certain skills and characteristics made us successful as change agents at our respective institutions (Anttonen & Chaskes, 2002). These skills and characteristics explored in detail in this chapter are congruent with the distinctive characteristics of the governance environment of postsecondary institutions and at the same time manifest themselves in a variety of leadership styles.

A KNOWLEDGE BASE FOR ADVOCATES

In order to be successful, advocates for first-year students must understand the distinctive governance environment of colleges and universities, when to initiate change, organizational clocks and time lines, and the truth and myths about resources.

The Distinctive Governance Environment of Colleges and Universities

Many students of organizations recognize that organizations present a challenge to overcoming the inertia of their stability. Postsecondary institutions possess a unique array of organizational features (Baldridge, Curtis, Eckert, & Riley, 1978; Hasenfeld, 1992) that present an obstacle to advocates wishing to effect change. These organizational features also help us appreciate the leadership skills required for effecting organizational change on behalf of first-year students. The requisite leadership skills, discussed later in this chapter, are partially a function of the organizational features that produce a distinctive governance environment. The character of governance in these organizations adds an additional layer of uncertainty and ambiguity to the already uncertain and ambiguous change process.

Colleges and universities are "people-changing organizations," and thus the organization's "raw material" is people (Hasenfeld, 1992, pp. 4–5). Unlike inanimate raw material, students may respond to programmatic change in an unanticipated fashion because they respond to change within the framework of their own experience, values, and beliefs. They may resist the efforts of others who attempt some alteration of student life as a response to an institutionally defined problem. For example, in some instances, Greek letter social organizations have continued to rush first-year students, albeit underground, when college officials have banned the practice.

Goal ambiguity is often a feature of colleges and universities because these are organizations where goals rest heavily on social, economic, and political values. Unlike profit-driven business organizations, "colleges and universities have vague, ambiguous goals, and they must build decision structures that grapple with uncertainty and conflict over those goals" (Baldridge et al., 1978, p. 20). Thus, the notion of goal consensus becomes problematic. Not only do various interest groups compete among the constituents that a given college or university serves, but goal consensus among faculty, professional staff, administration, and students within the same institution may well be problematic. For example, some faculty may believe that advising undeclared first-year students is primarily the role of professional advising staff, while the administration may view that as a vital aspect of retention best served by the faculty. Indeed, faculty may view retention efforts as undermining their role as guardians of the institution's academic standards.

The goals of students may conflict with the goals of the faculty. While students seek more vocationally oriented aspects of their major program, faculty may wish to emphasize its more traditional liberal learning aspects (Levine & Cureton, 1998c). Baldridge and his associates (1978, p. 21) note that "not only are academic goals unclear, they are also highly *contested*. As long as goals are left ambiguous and highly abstract, people agree; as soon as they are concretely specified and put into operation, disagreement arises."

Establishing a cause-and-effect relationship between the technology used and the desired outcomes may be challenging because the latter are not tangible or easily defined (Hasenfeld, 1992). Baldridge (1978) and his associates note:

> Because they serve clients with disparate, complicated needs, client-serving organizations often have problematic technologies. Serving clients is difficult to accomplish, to evaluate, and to show short-term success. Considering the entire person is a holistic task that cannot be easily separated into small, routine technical segments. If, at times, colleges and universities do not know *what* they are doing, they furthermore do not often know *how* to do it [pp. 21–22].

In assessing the effectiveness of a first-year seminar, if we define "making a good adjustment to college" as graduating in four years, "effectiveness" appears rather straightforward. However, suppose a portion of those students who persisted changed their major program more than twice in their first two years or were placed on academic warning for their second year. Can we claim them as having made a "good adjustment" to college?

When the goals are ambiguous and when the technology is nonroutine, the organization places the core tasks under the aegis of professionals. This is certainly true for colleges and universities where academic and academic support tasks are given over to professional personnel. Professional employees cherish their decision-making autonomy with respect to their expertise and eschew supervision. A tension frequently exists between the professional's adherence to the canons of the profession and the bureaucratic demands of the organization. This tension can be observed in the turf issues that arise between administrators and faculty. So, for example, the suggestion by a university provost that the faculty consider creating a first-year seminar may be greeted with some hostility on the part of the faculty, who see such a suggestion as encroaching on their curricular prerogatives.

Unlike more bureaucratic organizations, colleges and universities have overlapping and shared decision-making responsibilities. The notion of turf is not always as sharply drawn as with curricular issues. Accordingly, the desire of a college or university to redesign its first-year orientation involves the faculty, various offices of the division of student affairs, and several administrative personnel. All of them have some modicum of decision-making responsibility with respect to orientation.

While each group brings its own expertise to the project, groups also bring a set of values that reflect their professional commitments. Thus, the faculty values learning, discovery, the unique, the esoteric, and the importance of analytical thought and action. Student affairs personnel value learning, personal growth, the power of the peer group, and the centrality of the person as a multidimensional entity. The administration values predictability, efficiency, control, and coordination. Shared or overlapping responsibility provides a nexus for differing, and potentially conflicting, professional subcultures.

Those who manage organizations attempt to reduce the level of uncertainty (or increase the level of predictability) to a degree that is tolerable, if not comfortable. Uncertainty is particularly crucial with respect to the day-to-day operation of the organization's activities. Colleges and universities, as "people-changing" or "client-serving" organizations, have an added measure of uncertainty in the normal operation of the organization. It is hardly surprising to find that some investigators have characterized colleges and universities as organized anarchy (Baldridge et al., 1978; Birnbaum, 1988) given the character and structure of their governance system.

Timing: When to Initiate Change

Although there is no single catalyst for the creation of a first-year program, increasing student retention remains the primary catalyzing issue. A single factor or a confluence of factors may serve as a program impetus. Program creation might be the response to a crisis or a single traumatic event. A widely replicated first-year seminar was developed at the University of South Carolina almost three decades ago partially as a response to student riots and unrest on its campus (Gardner, 1986). A program initiative can originate with the wish to ameliorate potentially injurious student behavior such as binge drinking.

A general sense of "needing to do something to fix this mess" is an invitation to act. Other common situations that invite advocates to act are a self-study in preparation for the visit of an accrediting agency; interest in program development emerging from a strategic planning initiative; the arrival of a new dean, provost, or president with experience and an interest in first-year programs; and some combination of these factors. Although no invitation to act is necessary in order to advocate for change on behalf of first-year students, timing does have some bearing on how well this call for action will be received.

Organizational Clocks and Time Lines

As part of the planning and implementation of first-year programs, those doing the actual work will construct time lines for the completion of various stages of the process. Often neophyte advocates misjudge the time required for their program to become operational. Although the actual time required varies by the size and complexity of the project, each institution seems to have its own organizational clock that stubbornly runs at its own pace, in spite of the advocate's best efforts. Creating first-year programs requires patience and a good sense of humor to get beyond the stress of numerous and unforeseen delays. We not only believe in Murphy's law with respect to time lines but subscribe to O'Malley's corollary, which cautions, "Murphy was an optimist!"

Institutions of higher education essentially employ two calendars and two clocks. Which calendar and clock one selects to measure time is typically a function of one's position. Most administrators have a "business day" clock in their head, while faculty use an "academic clock" (the number of class periods in a day) to divide up the day. While administrators use the faculty's ten-month, two-semester calendar for some purposes, they also use the twelve-month fiscal cycle calendar that may not be congruent with the January through December twelve-month calendar. Also, administrative planning often starts sooner and plans for longer periods than do faculty and professional staff. Be mindful of the administrative day clock and planning calendar when scheduling and planning.

Myths and Truths About Resources

Our own experiences and research on advocates suggest that you can overestimate the importance of some types of resources while underestimating the salience of others. At the top of the list of resource myths is the one that gives primary importance to money:

• Myth 1: "We can't afford the program." Some financial resources are almost always necessary, but not to the extent aspiring advocates might think. Two-thirds of the advocates in our study never mentioned money as an obstacle to success (Anttonen & Chaskes, 2002). The reason is that many programs do not require substantial dollars to operate. Academic work is labor intensive. By far the largest share of the academic dollar is spent on salaries and benefits. When faculty and staff conduct first-year programs, it is most often done with minimal financial compensation or as part of their regular teaching responsibilities (Barefoot & Fidler, 1996).

The retention benefits of programs and services designed to help first-year students succeed show that these efforts are a very good investment. We are not, however, asserting that these programs are cost free. There is some cost incurred in the administration of a program—for example, the wise investment in the training of faculty and staff and program assessment. These costs are quite minimal and can be shared by more than one office, department, or division, which serves to minimize the budgetary impact on any one office.

• Myth 2: "First-year programs should be launched with grant money." When someone proposes a new or innovative program of some type, there is always some individual who says, "We'll apply for a grant!" That may not be good advice for several reasons. The program's development is solely contingent on the institution's ability to secure a grant, one that requires funding over several years. Often, there is a rather attenuated period between the first application for the grant and the arrival of the funds on campus. In that time, the enthusiasm of several key people may have waned because they have committed their time to other projects. Finally, the institution's willingness to fund a first-year program speaks volumes about the administration's commitment to the project, particularly to the faculty.

• Truth 1: At many institutions, physical space is a truly scarce resource. Physical space does not initially become an issue when developing a first-year program, but it can have a major impact on the shape and extent of the program itself, particularly if the program will operate concurrently with classes. If an institution is introducing a first-year seminar as an additional course to the curriculum, for example, it needs to have classroom space for it that is available at a convenient time for both students and instructors. Those new to advocacy may assume the necessary space will simply appear when needed. The registrar becomes a key resource manager. Early consultation with the registrar or others who control space utilization is essential.

An additional space issue becomes apparent once the program is in operation. You might find yourself looking around your office and asking, "Where am I going to put all this stuff?" The rapid accretion of administrative paper, syllabi, posters, pamphlets, training materials, and assessment questionnaires is surprising. It is the ability to foresee these needs that keeps program development from becoming overwhelming.

• Truth 2: The most essential resource is trust. The most important resource that advocates have is the trust and confidence they engender at all levels of their institution, and above all at the top. More than half of the advocates surveyed indicated that the principal reason for their success was the support they received from the president or other chief operating officer of their institution

(Anttonen & Chaskes, 2002). The advocate is going to ask administrators, professional staff, faculty, and often students to act on the veracity of his or her "story" about the need to bring about change on behalf of first-year students. These individuals must be capable of motivating and rallying support throughout key decision-making centers on campus.

While many individuals in a given institution would support the creation of a first-year program, such support remains nascent until one or more respected and trusted members of the institution, usually from among the ranks of administration and faculty, promote the need for the undertaking. The legitimacy of the programmatic need being advocated is very much a function of the trust the administration, professional staff, and faculty are willing to impart to the advocate. The perceived integrity of the advocate to speak for students is the most important resource the advocate must possess.

THE MICROPOLITICS OF ADVOCACY: STRATEGIES AND TACTICS

In their role as advocates, change agents use a variety of styles when "being political." Advocates can stay within the comfort zone that their personality dictates and still play micropolitics effectively. The award-winning advocates we studied even remotely failed to fit the stereotype of the Machiavellian professor or administrator who manipulates colleagues through stealth and guile in the "name of appropriate goals justifying unsavory means." Our respondents were politically effective because they were overwhelmingly senior and trusted members of their institution. What follows is a description of four key strategies and some tactics associated with successful advocates.

Doing Necessary Homework: Researching and Benchmarking

This is a crucial aspect for gaining support for any proposed first-year program. Not only is it vital to understand the types of first-year programs and their benefits, it is very useful to benchmark these programs by comparing them to comparable institutions.

Perhaps the most valuable source of information about first-year programs rests with the National Resource Center for The First-Year Experience and Students in Transition. Its annual conferences, preconference workshops, training workshops, publications, staff, and teleconferences are an invaluable source of vital information. In addition, the Policy Center on The First Year of College, located in Brevard, North Carolina, and established in 1999, is an influential and valuable source of information about assessment of the first college year. In addition, a growing number of books present both theory and practice on the subject of retention and related issues (for example, see Braxton, 2000; Moxley, Dumbrigue, & Najor-Durack, 2001; Tinto, 1993; Astin, 1993; Pascarella & Terenzini, 1991). Attending conferences and networking with those who have already been successful in becoming advocates for first-year programs is also an excellent source for information gathering.

What Naysayers Say and How to Answer Them

There will always be some individuals—administrators, faculty, or professional staff—who will speak against, and perhaps resist, any proposed changes on behalf of first-year students. Although their reasons for opposing first-year programs may vary, it is important to answer their objections, particularly when they are people in positions that command respect among their colleagues.

A cautionary note is in order at this juncture. Considerable support for first-year programs has been growing as the word of their success spreads, especially among administrators and student affairs professionals. The respondents in our study found substantial support among administration and faculty for first-year initiatives, almost half of administrators, and almost a third of faculty (Anttonen & Chaskes, 2002). Respondents also indicated that the single most common source of resistance was the lack of knowledge concerning the first-year experience movement and its efficacy.

Answering objections requires having done some research about first-year programs before beginning to build support and face the naysayers. Not only is it beneficial to understand the benefits that accrue to institutions that have first-year programs, but it is also crucial to locate comparable institutions that have viable and effective first-year programs in place. We have discovered the persuasive power of pointing to institutions similar to ours (especially sister institutions in our state and region, our direct competitors, or institutions we aspire to emulate) that have a well-established first-year program. Those offering resistance to first-year programs often espouse one or more of the ideas in opposition to change discussed below along with some suggested responses.

Academic Darwinism. Those subscribing to this notion argue that academic standards will suffer if a sink-or-swim approach is not taken. The undergraduate program, especially the first year, is where the faculty should sift out those not suited for the college academic experience. If we "coddle" and "spoon-feed" students, then we have de facto lowered the standards established for successful completion of our degree program.

While an ever-greater proportion of high school students are entering college with the intellectual capability to succeed, they lack the skills and understanding to make a smooth transition to college life. First-year students are very much like immigrants to a new country. They are "strangers in a strange land" who are very capable but lack knowledge of the new culture of higher education they have adopted (Chaskes, 1996). Many first-year students meet the institution's admissions criteria but lack the skill set and appropriate understanding of the performance expectations of higher education. This lack of preparedness on the part of otherwise qualified first-year students is so pervasive that first-year programs can be found at respected institutions around the world. In fact, the reputations for academic excellence among many postsecondary institutions no longer rest simply on the rigor of their programs and the quality of their faculty. An added criterion now gaining acceptance is the proportion of qualified students who successfully complete their course of study, and do so in a timely fashion.

Not the Role of the Faculty. Some faculty members maintain a restricted view of their role as educators. This view appears with some variation on the general theme that first-year issues are beyond the scope of faculty matters. One variation on this theme is that retention issues are the purview of administration and student affairs personnel. Another variation holds that developmental education, remediation, and cocurricular matters "are not part of the job description." At institutions with a strong commitment to graduate education, some maintain that undergraduate teaching is not important to them.

The best response to faculty with this attitude is to point out that often first-year students are not prepared for the academic expectations of college-level work. Who but the faculty best understand the increased workload, importance of writing and critical thinking, the faster pace of instruction, the fewer opportunities for student evaluation, the vanishing extra credit assignments, and the like? They are the institution's professional educators. This is very much their issue. The relevant research suggests that faculty-student relationships have a profound effect on student retention as well as student development (Pascarella & Terenzini, 1991; Astin, 1993). The more research-oriented the faculty are, the more difficult it will be to persuade them that first-year programs should be very much their concern. Nevertheless, there will usually be sufficient student-oriented faculty, even among those with an active research agenda, to garner the support needed.

Resistance to Change. For some members of the academy, the thought of programmatic change is disquieting. There is a saying among the Islamic mystics that "all change brings loss." Some people have a low threshold for change, and when that is complemented by the level of organizational uncertainty found among institutions of higher education, some members of the academy will offer resistance to the implementation of first-year programs. We believe that active resistance is less of an issue than is a more passive form of resistance best thought of as militant apathy. This "I could not care less" attitude is more of a challenge because those possessing it will nevertheless continue to debate the issue.

The best response to those resistant to change is to remind them that the cost to the institution is significant when retention is at issue, particularly in private institutions. As the cost of a college education continues to increase at a rate beyond inflation, parents and students (who are increasingly assuming debt in order to pay for their education) want to know that their money will not be wasted and that the student will receive the necessary support to complete his or her education. The issue is not simply retention. First-year programs improve the quality of academic life, student services, the campus climate, and certainly student satisfaction. Answering the naysayers is but one strategy in developing a first-year program.

Coalition Building

Advocates recognize the importance of finding partners in the change process who are also committed to improving the lives of first-year students. The desired goal here is to garner support from a wide range of persons and offices across campus. The more trusted and respected these individuals are, the more effective the coalition will be in moving a proposed program from planning to implementation. Advocates typically know some or all of these individuals on campus either personally or by reputation. People you know will lead you to like-minded people.

In addition to being student centered, members of the coalition should, when possible, represent varying segments of campus decision making. Especially important are coalition members from major academic divisions and relevant student affairs staff. A coalition does not constitute a committee, although some coalition members might be part of one or more committees responsible for aspects of program development and decision making.

Perhaps the most crucial members of a coalition are those who are directly responsible to manage the institution. The support of the president or chief executive office, the chief academic officer, and other executive officers is crucial for developing a first-year program. Fortunately, their support is often easy to enlist because they are more likely than others to already have some knowledge of first year programs. In our study of award-winning candidates (Anttonen & Chaskes, 2002), we found that the most often cited reason respondents offered for their success was that they had the support of their president or other chief administrator (55 percent). Often campus skeptics in positions of influence can be made allies by making them part of the planning process. By co-opting them, skeptics get an insider's understanding of the issues and an appreciation of the benefits of first-year programs.

Many respondents in the study noted the importance of reaching out across the boundaries of their organizational division to create a network of support that represents many segments of the campus culture. First-year programs have benefits for many sectors of the campus. Having done the homework, the advocate is in the position to answer the question, "What's in it for me?" Other allies, whom advocates may want to enlist for their support depending on the nature of the institution's governance structure, include an executive officer of the faculty senate, influential student affairs personnel, key student leaders, and respected members of the bargaining agents if the campus is unionized.

Planning with Alternatives and Modifications in Mind

This step comes after researching, benchmarking, and networking with others. The commonly cited wisdom with regard to having a plan B and C is good advice.

As coalition building proceeds, the art of the possible in the planning process becomes clearer. The availability of resources, particularly funds and space, comes into sharper focus. Advocates also begin to gain a more accurate estimate of how much change the campus culture will support. Planners begin to assess how much they are willing to compromise, and perhaps give up, in order to implement a program.

The planning process must include preparation for training any personnel in the new program and establishing appropriate mechanisms for assessing the program. Training and assessment is one of the few ways those who will over-see a first-year program can exert any direct control over the quality of the program. Plan to have a pilot project with the appropriate training and assessment. Aside from its obvious benefits, it gives some assurance to those who have made critical resources available. Ongoing assessment not only offers continued quality control but also permits those supervising the program to accrue a record of accomplishment that gives added legitimacy to the program's future. In this regard, seeking assistance from the campus office of institutional research is highly recommended.

Planners need to have a strong commitment to their primary plan while recognizing what will be lost and gained if an alternative plan must be considered. How much can you modify the original plan before it is no longer viable, and plan B must be considered? It is during this process that the research, resources, and timing become vitally important. In addition, remember that organizations move at their own unique speed. Advocates develop, through experience, a realistic sense of how much time to allot for program development and what aspects of the development process cannot be hurried.

We have described the knowledge base and the strategies and tactics that successful advocates use in creating change on behalf of first-year students. However, becoming an effective change agent requires a particular skill set that permits advocates to use their knowledge base and put the necessary strategies and tactics into operation.

THE MICROPOLITICS OF ADVOCACY

Successful advocates will say "play politics" or "be political" when offering advice to others. This should not connote anything conspiratorial or Machiavellian. Rather, they are suggesting that one work within the existing governance structure to effect change. Once again, we note that successful advocates are mostly senior personnel with substantial understanding of and experience with the decision-making processes on their campus. The award-winning advocates we studied had accrued a median of 17.5 years of service at their college or university where they conduct their award-winning work (Anttonen & Chaskes, 2002). This, along with other data, suggests that these advocates had years of experience in the governance process and were trusted members of their institution. This is the political background that advocates typically bring to their role when engaging in micropolitics.

These advocates show leadership by combining their knowledge with effective strategies that are enacted through a series of personal traits we call a skill set, which they use when exercising their leadership on behalf of first-year students:

- Having a passion and caring for first-year students and programs
- Being an active listener
- Being creative and flexible
- Being a risk taker

- Having a good sense of humor
- Being patient but persistent

This skill set provides advocates with the tools needed in order to make it all happen, that is, to use their knowledge base and strategies effectively. This is how the three elements of first year advocacy—knowledge, strategies, and skills—are integrated to produce effective leadership. These combinations dictate no particular school of leadership. Also, we do not believe that any one advocate can excel in the use of all four strategies or demonstrate equally effective use of each of the traits in the skill set. However, we do subscribe to the notion that a coalition of individuals, all with a high level of passion, caring, and experience, can successfully advocate and demonstrate effective leadership for building first-year programs.

RECOMMENDATIONS

Based on our experience and that of other first-year advocates, we offer the following recommendations:

- *Recognize that there are common knowledge bases, sets of strategies, and skill sets* that are shared by first-year student advocates that should be considered in shaping their involvement in first-year student success.
- *Understand that first-year advocates have an important leadership role* in challenging and supporting first-year students to succeed.
- *Recognize that timing is important in initiating change.* Organizations have clocks and time lines that first-year student advocates must take into account.
- *Understand that advocating for first-year resources is an important aspect of developing resources for first-year students.* The legitimacy of this advocacy depends on trust between the administration, professional staff, faculty, and first-year advocates.
- *Develop strategies for dealing with those who resist changes* to challenge and support first-year students, and work to overcome academic Darwinism and resistance to change.
- *Build coalitions with those committed to change.* Garner support from trusted and respected individuals who may be in a position to make change happen.

CONCLUSION

Those who successfully advocate on behalf of first-year students share a common knowledge base, set of strategies, and skills. These advocates will encounter many obstacles as they seek to initiate change on behalf of first-year students and advocate for them. Their challenge is to overcome these obstacles and build support from administrators, faculty, and professional staff in helping first-year students succeed.

CHAPTER TWELVE

Collaborative Partnerships Between Academic and Student Affairs

Charles C. Schroeder

During the past two decades, institutions have made great strides in creating innovative first-year programs. Although a variety of initiatives have been sponsored by units in both academic and student affairs divisions, these programs and services are usually implemented in isolation from one another. Despite these innovations, some higher education leaders argue that we are not even close to achieving the full educational potential of the first year (Barefoot, 2000). Perhaps the problem resides not with the individual initiatives but rather with the absence of linking and aligning the parts with the whole. What appears to be missing is a bold, unified vision of a highly integrated and coherent first-year experience . . . that intentionally aligns curricular and cocurricular components in a seamless fashion. Collaboration is the principal strategy for creating such a vision; in fact, it is the only way to bridge the great divide between the curriculum and the cocurriculum—between academic affairs and student affairs—that has existed for decades. Indeed, building partnerships between the two groups on campus most committed to students is the best way to create a truly integrated and coherent experience and, in the process, realize the full educational potential of the first college year.

From the plethora of reform reports to less-than-flattering articles in the popular press, colleges and universities are being challenged to provide first-year students with a more cohesive, less fragmented, and more effective educational

I acknowledge the assistance of the following individuals for their contributions to the section on student success centers: Nancy McDaniel, Auburn University; Pat Long, Johnson County Community College (currently at the University of Missouri-Kansas City); Edie Sample and Michael Miller, Rockford College; and Joe Johnston and Bonnie Zelenak, the University of Missouri-Columbia.

experience—an experience that enhances learning, challenges students to achieve higher levels of success, and provides support for them to do so. The late Ernest L. Boyer Sr. argued that the best way to achieve these objectives was to create new forms of collaboration and partnerships that would unite faculty, students, and administrators in a common mission to transform campus environments into a seamless web of learning within and beyond the classroom (Boyer, 1987, 1990, 1997). Boyer championed educational experiences that were not compartmentalized by time, space, or curriculum, but rather were connected in a highly integrated and coherent fashion. Accomplishing his vision requires the creation of effective partnerships, particularly between academic affairs and student affairs, for improving the undergraduate experience.

This chapter focuses on why collaborative partnerships between academic and student affairs are important for challenging and supporting first-year student learning and success. Essential characteristics of collaborative partnerships are described, as well as barriers that must be overcome if partnerships are to succeed. Strategies for nurturing and sustaining successful partnership are illustrated along with examples of highly effective collaborative initiatives that foster learning and success for first-year students. The struggles and lessons learned from forming and sustaining partnerships through the design of four student success centers are then delineated. The chapter concludes with a discussion of implications for the future of academic and student affairs partnerships.

THE IMPORTANCE OF COLLABORATIVE PARTNERSHIPS

Higher education is in the midst of a major transformation. Changing economic agendas, shifting demographics, eroding public confidence, demands for accountability, and increasingly diverse student populations are changing the character of most institutions. In recent reports on the status of higher education (Wingspread Group on Higher Education, 1993; Boyer Commission on Educating Undergraduates in the Research University, 1998; Kellogg Commission on the Future of State and Land Grant Universities, 1998), researchers have stressed the need to connect all undergraduate experiences with student learning and development. The common theme for all of these reports is putting student learning first.

Countless studies have focused not only on classroom learning but on the influence of out-of-class experiences on learning and student success (Kuh, 1996; Pascarella & Terenzini, 1991; Terenzini, Pascarella, & Blimling, 1996; Whitt, 1999). According to the research, the two most important influences on student learning and development are (1) interacting in educationally purposeful ways with an institution's "agents of socialization" such as faculty, staff, and peers, and (2) directing a high degree of effort to academic tasks. These studies also reveal that academic and cognitive domains are positively shaped by a variety of out-of-class experiences, and the most powerful source of influence on student learning appears to be students' interpersonal interactions, whether with peers, faculty, or staff. Finally, the learning impacts of students' out-of-class experiences are much more cumulative than catalytic: that is, "a majority of important changes that occurred during college are probably the cumulative result of a set of inter-related experiences sustained over an extended period of time" (Pascarella & Terenzini, 1991, p. 610). There are a number of implications of this suggestion; however, none is more important than realizing that the cumulative impact is likely to be much stronger when learning experiences are part of coordinated, mutually supportive, and reinforcing sets of programmatic and policy interventions that blur the functional (if not the structural) boundary between academic and student affairs divisions (Terenzini et al., 1996).

Recommendations from various reform reports plus the findings from empirical research on the impact of out-of-class experiences on student learning have led student affairs educators to view fostering student learning as their mission and primary purpose. Three recent documents—*The Student Learning Imperative: Implications for Student Affairs* (*SLI*; American College Personnel Association, 1994); *Principles of Good Practice for Student Affairs* (American College Personnel Association & National Association of Student Personnel Administrators, 1997); and *Powerful Partnerships: A Shared Responsibility for Learning* (American Association for Higher Education, American College Personnel Association, & National Association of Student Personnel Administrators, 1998)—all draw attention to the centrality of student learning and the need to foster effective educational partnerships between academic affairs and student affairs to promote it. As emphasized by the SLI, "Student affairs professionals attempt to make seamless what are often perceived by students to be disjointed, unconnected experiences by bridging organizational boundaries and forging collaborative partnerships with faculty and others to enhance student learning" (American College Personnel Association, 1994, p. 3).

Bridging boundaries to create seamless learning environments is vitally important to addressing the highly fragmented nature of the undergraduate experience, which is akin to expecting first-year students to assemble the pieces of a jigsaw puzzle without showing them a picture of the finished product. The ambiguity and complexity associated with such a task would undoubtedly result in frustration, disappointment, and rapid disengagement—responses that are all too common among students who encounter highly differentiated and fragmented academic and cocurricular experiences during their first year on campus. It is precisely because of these and other challenges that partnerships have such a special role to play in developing a solid first-year experience. No one division or unit, acting autonomously, can create an integrated, coherent, powerful, and seamless experience for first-year students. This can be achieved only through building alliances and partnerships between academic and student affairs.

According to Kuh (1996, 1997), creating seamless learning environments—environments where in-class and out-of-class experiences are mutually supporting, students devote more time and energy to educationally purposeful activities, institutional resources are marshaled and channeled to achieve complementary learning outcomes, and students take full advantage of all institutional resources for learning—provides the integration and coherence that enables first-year students to make appropriate and necessary intellectual connections, thereby fostering their learning and development. The creation of seamless learning environments requires cross-functional collaborative partnerships so that organizational arrangements and processes can be linked and aligned appropriately (Bloland, Stamatakos, & Rogers, 1996; Garvin, 1993).

Although *collaboration* and *partnerships* are now frequently used and fashionable terms in higher education, effective collaborative partnerships are difficult to create and often harder to sustain. Collaboration, for example, is a very time-consuming, difficult, and complex process that requires an in-depth knowledge of essential characteristics and components.

ESSENTIAL CHARACTERISTICS OF COLLABORATIVE PARTNERSHIPS

Transactions between various institutional agents, such as faculty, students, student affairs educators, and academic administrators, can be conceptualized on a relationship continuum ranging from no interaction to highly collaborative encounters. Between these end points, transactions can be viewed as undesirable but necessary, complacent, cordial and courteous, cooperative, and, occasionally, collaborative. Historically, transactions between academic affairs and student affairs have usually occurred at the lower end of the continuum. Recent research (Kolins, 2000), however, is more promising, at least in community colleges, where some twenty forms of collaboration, ranging from consultation to program development and delivery, were identified by 327 chief academic affairs and chief student affairs officers.

Although there is significant interest in forging collaborative partnerships, particularly among student affairs educators, a major challenge concerns defining the nature of partnerships, particularly with regard to distinguishing between the role of cooperation and collaboration in the partnership formation process. Too frequently, *cooperation* and *collaboration* are used interchangeably when, in reality, there are subtle and not so subtle differences between the terms, even though both are absolutely essential attributes of partnerships. Cooperative ventures, for example, are often short term with limited objectives, shorter time agreements, and less commitment and investment among participants. Because they often involve going along with an established direction, less risk taking is usually encountered. Furthermore, cooperation is often driven by expediency—something needs immediate attention and must be resolved quickly.

In contrast, collaborative ventures are often long term in nature, involve considerable amounts of shared decision making and risk taking, require substantial commitments and investment on the part of collaborators, and are more likely to require common philosophical ground as participants work to design agreed-on goals and objectives (Stein & Short, 2001). In collaborative partnerships, as opposed to cooperative ventures, participants often see themselves as highly invested cocreators, generating something new and innovative.

It is common for collaborative partnerships to be confused with a variety of traditional working groups—committees, councils, task forces, and others—that are quite common in higher education. At their best, these structures help members share information and insight, make informed recommendations or decisions, and provide participants with useful feedback (Wergin, 1993). Collaborative partnerships are quite different in that they are fundamentally team-centered, goal-oriented structures. According to Katzenbach and Smith (1993), "A team is a small number of people with complementary skills who are committed to a common purpose, set of performance goals, and approach for which they hold themselves mutually accountable" (p. 112). Ideally, collaborative partners have a strong, ongoing, and enduring relationship: they are comfortable working together and have an appreciation for one another.

Communication in collaborative partnerships is excellent, and relationships are open and honest. Partners trust each other, and differences of opinion are negotiated within the context of respect, comfort, and honesty (Schroeder, 1999a). The behavior of individuals in collaborative partnerships is similar to that of members of Division I athletic teams; that is, team members share a common goal; they engage in intense, frequent interaction; they share adversity; they recognize that each individual has something important to contribute; and they have a common enemy (Wolf-Wendel, Toma, & Morphew, 2000). Like collegiate athletes, collaborative partners share work, planning, goal setting, decision making, and problem solving, as well as vision, philosophy, values, and ideas.

Although a number of practical strategies and tips for forging effective collaborative partnerships are set out later in this chapter, the following essential principles can be very useful in guiding the development of partnerships between academic and student affairs (Schroeder, Minor, & Tarkow, 1999):

- Partnerships are successful when they are developed from a common reference point or common purpose: a shared vision of undergraduate education, an institutional problem (such as lack of engagement for first-year students or poor retention and graduation rates), or a major triggering event (such as an accreditation review, externally imposed undergraduate education mandates, or budget crisis).

- Successful partnerships involve cross-functional teams, joint planning and implementation, and assessment of mutually agreed-on outcomes.

- Effective partnerships require thinking and acting systemically by linking, aligning, and integrating a variety of resources—human, fiscal, and so on—to achieve desired results.

- Partnerships require senior administrators in academic and student affairs to be strong champions and advocates for innovation and change, and they must make visible their commitment to developing, nurturing, and sustaining partnerships.

- Effective partnerships occasionally require participants to step out of their comfort zones, challenge prevailing assumptions, and take reasonable risks.

Although these principles are central to partnership formation, there are a number of very significant, and often overwhelming, barriers that must be acknowledged and addressed if partnerships are to succeed.

BARRIERS TO COLLABORATIVE PARTNERSHIPS

There are numerous longstanding and deeply embedded institutional barriers that must be overcome in order to forge effective collaborative partnerships. One of the most significant barriers is a fundamental difference in the core assumptions characteristic of academic affairs and student affairs cultures. The powerful role that assumptions play in defining reality is illustrated by the following story (Parker, 1982; compare Turnbull, 1962):

> A noted British anthropologist, Colin Turnbull, spent almost twenty years studying a tribe of pygmies that lived in a totally isolated rainforest in South Africa. The rainforest was so dense that over time, members of the tribe had become functionally nearsighted—they simply had no need to see long distances.
>
> After weeks of coaxing, Turnbull persuaded the old chief to leave the comfort and security of the rainforest and return with him to England. Since the chief had never left the rainforest, this was a most formidable challenge. The chief eventually consented, and he and Turnbull spent weeks hacking their way through the thick vegetation. On the nineteenth day, they finally stepped out of the rainforest on to a plain or savannah. Off in the distance, perhaps 200–300 yards were some water buffaloes. Turnbull asked the chief to identify the objects. The chief, without hesitation, said they were bees. As they walked closer and closer to the herd, Turnbull again asked the chief to identify the creatures. After some deliberation, the chief stated they were buffaloes. Turnbull said, "But chief, I thought you said they were bees." The chief responded, "They were bees, but magic has changed them into buffaloes."

This story illustrates phenomenological absolutism—the assumption that the world is as we see it. Although we often subscribe to a notion that seeing is believing, in reality, believing is seeing. Our fundamental assumptions and beliefs ensure that our established truths and traditional practices provide security, stability, and continuity as the rain forest did for the chief. And like the chief, we may find it disquieting to journey beyond our familiar boundaries to explore realities in other rain forests. Even when change is viewed as desirable, we often long for the safety of the known. Thus, we create systems to maintain balance and continuity, and in such a process, custom tends to become a tyrant. The tyranny of custom prevents us from challenging prevailing assumptions and, like the chief, we become functionally nearsighted—so focused on the traditions, norms, and customs within our organizational boundaries that we fail to recognize distant opportunities for enhancing first-year student learning and success through bridging boundaries to create partnerships with individuals in other rain forests. Initiating an organizational bridge-building journey is as risky for potential partners as it was for the chief because it requires partners to step out of their comfort zone, challenge prevailing assumptions, and take reasonable risks.

The rain forest story illustrates a constellation of barriers to collaboration that can best be described as *cultural and historical.* The core assumptions of academic affairs and student affairs are often different, deeply rooted, and thus very difficult to change. Although there are many instances in which faculty and student affairs educators might agree, what matters to faculty is sometimes opposite, and even antagonistic, to what student affairs educators value. For example, some faculty and student affairs educators would undoubtedly respond in very different ways to the question, "What does it mean to educate students?" Some faculty responses would probably focus on the primacy of students' intellectual domains: cognitive development, content mastery in the discipline, and the acquisition of important intellectual skills. In contrast, most student affairs educators would focus on students' affective domains including interpersonal and intrapersonal as well as practical competence, leadership skills, and humanitarian values. Not surprisingly, these differences in core assumptions result in very different views about the relative merits of in-class and out-of-class activities between faculty and student affairs educators.

In addition to fundamental cultural differences, a variety of other factors can be barriers to collaboration, including the historical separation of the formal curriculum from the informal cocurriculum; a prevailing view that the role of student affairs is ancillary, supplementary, or complementary to the academic mission of the institution; competing assumptions about what constitutes effective undergraduate learning; and different expectations and rewards for academic faculty and student affairs educators (Blake, 1979, 1996; Kuh, 1997; Love, Jacobs, Poschini, Hardy, & Kuh, 1993; Schroeder, 1999b; Whitt, 1996). These differences, along with the differential status afforded the two groups in higher education, have often resulted in perceptions of lack of respect and serious misunderstandings. At the extreme, people in student affairs often believe that faculty do not care about students, do not work hard, and are unresponsive to students' problems (Creeden, 1998). In contrast, some faculty view student affairs educators as anti-intellectuals who create inappropriate cocurricular activities that distract students from the rigors of academic life.

Not only do the preceding differences exist between student affairs and academic affairs, they also manifest themselves within student and academic affairs divisions. For example, there are multiple communities of practice in student affairs that exhibit different values, beliefs, roles, and responsibilities. Some believe the primary purpose of student affairs is to advance the academic mission of the institution through focusing on student learning, while others stress the centrality of administering and coordinating various support services (Blimling, 2001). Furthermore, while most student affairs staff view themselves as educators, many faculty embrace the label of "academic," not "educator," since, in their minds, educators are elementary and secondary teachers.

Another constellation of factors, perhaps best labeled *bureaucratic-structural,* can also create substantial barriers to collaborative partnerships. During the past thirty-five years, college and university enrollments have more than quadrupled. As institutions have become more complex, complexities have been addressed through specialization, and in this process, organizations have become increasingly fragmented. Today many campuses—especially large public universities— are characterized by loosely coupled independent principalities and fiefdoms, each disconnected from the other and from any common institutional purpose or transcending value. It is not uncommon for student affairs divisions, as well as colleges and schools, to be quite autonomous, with different foci, priorities, and expectations for staff, faculty, and students. These highly specialized, hierarchical organizations have become increasingly compartmentalized, often resulting in what has been popularly described as functional silos or mineshafts (Schroeder, 1999a).

Vertical structures, while often modestly effective at promoting interaction within units, create obstacles to interaction, coordination, and collaboration between units. And as Coate (1990) and Cotter (1996) suggested, tightly bounded organizational entities that provide predictability, stability, and security often unintentionally limit risk taking, innovation, collaboration across boundaries, and organizational effectiveness. They can also foster insular and self-referencing orientations, as the rain forest did for the chief. Even within student affairs divisions, staff are often geographically separated and isolated, focusing on their specialty areas while unaware of the efforts and contributions of their divisional colleagues. Furthermore, in most institutions, student affairs educators and academic faculty report to different administrative officers, who, not surprisingly, often have different philosophies, beliefs, and priorities.

A final set of factors that can be barriers to forming collaborative partnerships are best described as *attitudinal-leadership* barriers. Senior administrators in academic and student affairs must be strong champions and advocates for innovation and change. They must articulate the rationale and benefits of collaboration and consistently expect, encourage, and reward collaboration (Kuh & Banta, 2000). Often leaders do not encourage collaboration because they fear that they will be giving up rather than gaining something—that they will lose power, relinquish some of their autonomy, and lose individual and institutional decision-making authority. Similarly, some leaders are simply unwilling to challenge the status quo for fear that a collaborative initiative will not succeed and they will look bad.

Although daunting, the preceding barriers can be overcome to create effective, collaborative partnerships. A key to accomplishing this is to identify important issues that lend themselves to a collaborative effort.

INSTITUTIONAL ISSUES THAT LEND THEMSELVES TO A COLLABORATIVE RESPONSE

Interest in collaboration in higher education is gaining in popularity. As Magolda (2001) suggests, it is fashionable to be a proponent of collaboration in higher education for a number of reasons but primarily because collaboration sounds intuitively right. Before allowing collaboration to become the strategy de jure, Magolda suggests asking a fundamental question: Is collaboration a good idea? Perhaps one should be reminded of the three year old who, when given a hammer, suddenly feels that everything needs hammering. Obviously, some institutional opportunities and challenges of significance to first-year students lend themselves to a collaborative response, and others do not. The key is to identify issues that people really care about—issues that often respond to the self-interest of institutional stakeholders. Although critical issues differ between and among institutions, the following opportunities often lend themselves to a collaborative response on the part of individuals in academic and student affairs (Schroeder, 1999a, 1999b):

- Improving retention and graduation rates by enhancing students' success; increasing success rates in high-risk courses, particularly for first-year students

- Enhancing multicultural awareness, understanding, and respect; fostering civic engagement and leadership through service-learning; establishing and articulating institutional expectations that assist first-year students in becoming integrated with the institution

- Extending the definition of general education outcomes to include knowledge and skills gained through cocurricular experiences; fostering higher levels of educational attainment for students in historically underrepresented groups

- Improving the effectiveness of advising, especially for undecided first-year students

- Developing learning communities that foster faculty and first-year student interaction and provide integration and coherence among various disciplines and cocurricular experiences

- Increasing the utilization of technology to enhance teaching and learning in multiple campus settings

- Improving performance in general education courses for first-year students

- Expanding institutional assessment initiatives to include learning outcomes that reflect more than content mastery—outcomes such as humanitarian values, character development, communication skills, and inter- and intrapersonal competence

- Making academic support services more geographically accessible for first-year students, such as creating academic learning centers in residence halls

- Creating comprehensive early-warning systems to identify first-year student problems before they become unmanageable

In addition to the preceding issues, Fried (1999) suggests that collaboration between faculty and student affairs educators can improve student learning in the following areas: extended orientation courses over the entire semester where first-year students learn a variety of academic and educational skills; coordinated programs that involve the major components of a general education curriculum and the creation of an experiential education paracurriculum that is organized and presented by student affairs staff; multicultural learning where faculty and student affairs educators collaborate in creating "communities of truth" in classrooms where conflict or apathy has frozen learning; and distance learning, which presents a multitude of challenges for faculty and student affairs alike.

Addressing issues such as these is impossible if individuals in student affairs and academic affairs are unaware of the significance of the issues to their institutions and the success of first-year students. Identifying problems and challenges that lend themselves to a collaborative response requires leaving the comfort, security, and the predictability of our organizational "rain forest," and it involves understanding synergies between parts and wholes. For example, the major issues previously listed are, of course, not discrete (Pascarella & Terenzini, 1991). Increasing success rates in high-risk courses, for example, generally improves retention and graduation rates. Enhancing multicultural awareness and understanding strengthens campus community and fosters higher levels of educational attainment for students of color. Learning communities not only provide integration and coherence among various disciplines and cocurricular experiences, they also enhance academic achievement, social and academic integration, and retention for first-year students. To be sure, creating seamless learning environments through collaborative partnerships addresses the interdependent nature of these institutional issues. By linking, aligning, and integrating resources, partnerships can create synergies for student learning and success.

PARTNERSHIPS THAT RESPOND TO THE NEEDS OF FIRST-YEAR STUDENTS

The following collaborative partnership examples respond to many of the institutional issues, challenges, and problems outlined here. Although the institutions highlighted differ in size, complexity, and mission, the triggering events for launching the partnerships are quite similar across institutions.

Improving Success Rates in High-Risk Courses

A major self-assessment initiative at Indiana University-Bloomington revealed declining enrollments and poor performance in required high-risk courses. Through systematic assessment, Hossler, Kuh, and Olsen (2001) determined that almost 40 percent of students who enrolled annually in gateway mathematics courses, such as M118 (finite math), received a D– or F grade or withdrew from the class. Because the class is required for business and other majors, it became the catalyst for developing a partnership between enrollment services and the math department to improve student performance and educational attainment. The finite math interventions were designed to produce the best curricular arrangement that meets first-year students' learning needs and performance demands. The primary initiative was the development of a two-semester reduced-pace equivalent to M118. Students were advised to register for reduced-pace sections both before the semester and after it started. This allowed students whose performance was predicting a D or an F final grade to fall back to the reduced-pace course and master the complicated concepts of finite mathematics at a more manageable pace.

In addition, a cross-functional team developed an extremely innovative, interactive television supplement, the Finite Show, which was produced to appeal to media-oriented undergraduates, many of whom have nocturnal study habits. The show, which airs Monday through Thursday evenings over the campus cable system, is hosted by an accomplished M118 instructor and guest lecturers, uses a combination of problem solving and live calls from students, and is available in all residence hall rooms as well as off-campus living arrangements. These innovative interventions have substantially enhanced first-year student performance: 90 percent of the students in the two-semester reduced-pace sequence achieved a grade of C or better, and similar results have been recorded for students who view the Finite Show on a regular basis.

Engaging Alumni in the Life of First-Year Students

At DePaul University, an urban, Catholic institution in the center of Chicago, a number of successful collaborative partnerships were forged with core academic units as well as city agencies and corporations. One of the most successful initiatives was a partnership created between enrollment services, alumni relations, the career center, and the College of Liberal Arts. Through this partnership, an innovative program, Alumni Sharing Knowledge (ASK), was developed to engage alumni in the life of the institution while simultaneously promoting new student success. At DePaul, each first-year student is assigned an ASK alumni mentor. The students are expected to conduct informational interviews with their ASK mentors on topics related to the relevance of their academic field of study to their eventual career, their undergraduate learning outcomes, and their overall career evolution. Through a journal kept by the first-year students, it is clear that the partnership created a meaningful learning opportunity for these students by helping them reflect on the career relatedness of the liberal studies curriculum.

Fostering Student Success Through Freshman Interest Groups

With the arrival of a new chancellor in 1992, the University of Missouri-Columbia established a goal to "recapture the public's trust" by focusing more attention on promoting student success through enhancing undergraduate experiences. Not only was new leadership a triggering event, but more important, enrollment had declined precipitously and the Coordinating Board for Higher Education had established new retention and graduate rate performance criteria associated with legislative funding. To respond to these challenges, the new vice chancellor for student affairs facilitated an educational partnership among the College of Arts and Sciences, residential life, the campus writing program, the English department, and the office of the provost to design residential learning communities that would substantially improve student success and help the institution achieve a variety of enrollment goals. By using cross-functional teams, a number of freshman interest groups (FIGs) were created. Students who participate in FIGs are coenrolled in three general education courses, live on the same floor of a residence hall, and participate in a one-credit-hour "pro-seminar" cofacilitated by their peer adviser, who also lives with them, as well as a faculty member who teaches in one of the FIGs courses.

Longitudinal research conducted by the Office of Student Life Studies indicate that students participating in FIGs make much higher grades, have higher retention and graduation rates, are more satisfied with their residence hall and collegiate experiences, and demonstrate much greater gains in general education outcomes. In fact, freshman and sophomore retention rates increased 8 to 10 percent annually over the past six years. As a result of the success of the FIGs program, the University of Missouri-Columbia is now sponsoring 125 learning communities for thirty-six hundred resident students—70 percent of all students living on campus (Schroeder, 2000). (For a more detailed discussion of FIGs and other learning communities, see Chapter Twenty-Two.)

Enhancing Diversity

In addition to enhancing student success through the development of a variety of learning communities, the University of Missouri-Columbia launched a bold and aggressive program in 1992 to significantly improve the recruitment and retention of students of color. A key triggering event, among others, was the new chancellor's revelation that the 1992 class included only ninety-two African Americans—less than 3 percent of the class even though 12 percent of the population in Missouri is African American. In response to this crisis, the chancellor, vice chancellor for student affairs, and the provost became institutional champions for developing innovative institutional strategies for recruiting and retaining much higher numbers of African Americans.

By using a variety of systematic assessments, factors associated with success rates for African Americans, not only for the institution at large but within each of the colleges, were identified. Other areas assessed were the relationship between financial aid and enrollment patterns as well as institutional image problems affecting African American recruitment in major markets. After the data were analyzed, a number of cross-functional teams were created to develop a comprehensive institutional strategy for addressing the problem.

By implementing a massive outreach effort, the cross-functional teams developed partnerships with African American clergy in the university's major market; sponsored an educational speakers series at the annual St. Louis Black Expo; developed a partnership with parents of prospective and admitted students through the I-70 Connections program designed to help parents understand the nature of the first year for their sons and daughters; created financial aid–leveraging strategies—such as diversity awards and residential leadership grants; launched learning community initiatives that featured coenrollment of minority students in general education courses; and built partnership with other important external stakeholders such as INROADS, an organization that has proven to be a major pipeline for high-ability minority students. The net effect of these collaborative partnerships has been to increase African American enrollment by 85 percent in five years. Perhaps more important, African American first-year-to-sophomore retention rates have increased from 76 to 87 percent during the same time.

BEST PRACTICES LEARNED FROM DESIGNING AND IMPLEMENTING FOUR STUDENT SUCCESS CENTERS

The success of the collaborative partnerships at Indiana University-Bloomington, DePaul University, and the University of Missouri-Columbia was the result of a number of factors and best practices that can be useful to others as they consider responding to important institutional issues for first-year students by forming cross-functional partnerships. Here, we highlight these best practices along with the significant struggles that are often encountered by different stakeholders as they engage in the collaborative partnership process.

Promoting student success, especially for first-year students, has been an espoused goal of colleges and universities for decades. First-year students, however, often have difficulty connecting to their institution and their studies while developing appropriate academic and social skills necessary to their success. To address this problem, many institutions have designed and implemented comprehensive, integrated, and service-oriented student success centers.

Recently, four very different institutions—Auburn University; Johnson County Community College; Rockford College; and the University of Missouri-Columbia—created student success centers. Each institution engaged in a collaborative planning process that lasted from one to six years and involved a range of stakeholders from student affairs and academic affairs. Auburn University, for example, used twenty cross-functional teams of faculty, staff, and students who studied every aspect of the services and activities available to students on their campus. Similarly, Johnson County Community College involved over 150 individuals in thirteen teams to address critical questions essential to the collaborative planning process. The catalyst for these collaborations ranged from institutional self-studies that highlighted the need to improve retention and graduation rates substantially to senior institutional leaders who championed a vision for integrating, in a coherent fashion, experiences and services that would enhance first-year student learning and success. Regardless of the triggering event or the structures used to foster collaboration, each of the four institutions embraced a fundamental, transcendent goal: to link, align, and integrate existing services in a new configuration to promote higher levels of student success and student learning. Although this vision was exciting, and quite admirable, leaders on each campus described a number of major, almost overwhelming, challenges, they encountered throughout the change process.

The most immediate set of challenges concerned institutional hurdles common to each campus—basic gaps in processes that limited the effectiveness of serving first-year students and in assisting them in their growth and development:

- *Major processes were segregated.* Academic and student support services were in different buildings and reported to different administrators. Staff were often unaware of the roles and responsibilities of colleagues in different functional areas even though these units had similar educational purposes and goals.
- *Systems were not integrated.* Not only were technological systems not integrated, thereby preventing the sharing of important data on students, most programs continued to be stand-alone initiatives that often duplicated programs and services in other areas. Similarly, staff focused on their functional responsibilities while often neglecting dysfunctional processes that inhibited first-year students from making informed decisions related to their success.
- *Communication was extremely limited.* Due to segregated processes and different reporting structures, communication within and between academic and student support services was limited and ineffective. Although many staff had worked on the same campus for years, they had limited knowledge of one another and rarely worked cooperatively across boundaries.
- *Administrative and academic functions were not linked and aligned.* First-year students often encountered a variety of discrete, independent, and disconnected services. On one campus, for example, the primary goal of academic advising was to match first-year students with five courses in less than ten minutes. If students were unclear about their academic and career goals or apprehensive about performance in high-risk courses, they were encouraged to seek assistance in the career center or learning center, both of which were located in different areas of the campus. What was missing on each campus was a vision of a performance support system that linked, aligned, and integrated these functional units into a seamless whole committed to first-year student success.

In addition to the rather obvious institutional hurdles encountered by key stakeholders on the four campuses, there were a number of more subtle, and hence more challenging, issues that threatened the collaborative partnership process. These institutions, for example, were not characterized as collaborative

cultures, and in the words of one team leader, "It has been a challenge to initiate collaboration within a system that does not seem to trust or value the practice." Furthermore, overcoming the tyranny of custom was a major hurdle that
collaborators on each of the four campuses faced. According to leaders at
Auburn University, "the method of service delivery has required a paradigm
shift. Units historically responsible for delivering focused services are now
required to address the 'whole' student, taking into consideration transitional,
academic, personal, and career needs" (McDaniel, James, & Davis, 2000, p. 28).

Shifting paradigms is a challenging, threatening, and even dangerous process
because it forces individuals to challenge deeply rooted assumptions and fundamentally change their behavior. Collaborative partners on each of the four campuses emphasize the difficulties associated with helping individuals shift their
focus from their functional authority and responsibilities to a systems perspective, moving beyond what is to what could be and understanding the relationship
of the parts to the whole. A colleague at Johnson County Community College put
this challenge in perspective by using the analogy of designing and sewing a quilt
to describe the development and implementation of the college's integrated student services model. The staff member commented, "Individual pieces of a quilt
are unique in size, color, and design and without real beauty or function until
they are sewn together to make a beautiful, intricate, and strong covering."

Related to challenges associated with paradigm shifts were issues that
focused on individuals' basic survival, safety, and security needs—all illustrated
by Abraham Maslow's hierarchy of needs model. The substantial amount of
change needed to create and implement effective student success centers
required overcoming initial resistance through a process that built trust, openness, and appreciation for diverse viewpoints. On two campuses, key stakeholders felt that collaboration was being forced on them, and one colleague
commented, "It became quite clear that as staff were told about their reassign-
ment, concerns about their physical space needs became paramount. They were
reluctant to participate in conceptual planning until these needs were addressed.
There was also a significant amount of grieving over lost offices, separation from
colleagues, and fear that their roles and expectations were changing into something unrecognizable and 'not part of their job descriptions.' Indeed . . . they
initially focused on what was to be lost, not gained." A colleague on another
campus commented, "It was clear that our respective supervisors couldn't
'make us' understand one another—we had to do that together. We also had to
go through a period of doubt before we got to this point." Clearly, these leaders realized that collaboration cannot be forced, but it can be facilitated.

RECOMMENDATIONS

The challenges and struggles faced by institutional leaders at Auburn, Rockford, the
University of Missouri-Columbia, and Johnson County Community College
as they designed and implemented comprehensive, integrated student success

centers have yielded some important lessons about the collaborative partnership formation process. Indeed, there are a number of best practices that should be considered as key principles and guidelines in the creation of collaborative partnerships. Chief among these are the following recommendations:

- *Realize that the potential of collaborative partnerships is achieved when it is built around important issues of consequence for participants.* Individuals are motivated by opportunities that respond to their self-interests. Hence, a critical issue is identifying an important issue or problem that concerns or affects all members of the potential partnership.
- *Determine the primary, as well as ancillary, stakeholders central to the partnership.* Identify individuals who have the authority and influence to make things happen and bring them into the partnership to share their expertise and insights.
- *Building collaborative partnerships is not a discrete event but rather an ongoing journey.* Work to create a sense of team identity, identify common goals and values, and use these as a foundation on which to plan and implement the team's vision. Take a long-term perspective and create processes that build trust, respect, and openness. Create opportunities early on for partners to learn about each other's roles, responsibilities, values, and philosophy, and promote discussion of how these affect the planning process as well as desired outcomes for the project.
- *Remember that change can be threatening.* Resistance to change should be anticipated, and strategies for dealing with it should be developed.
- *Seek opportunities that are most likely to result in early success.* Identify and pursue easy wins and accomplishments early in the collaborative process. Save the bigger issues for later, after trust has been established among key stakeholders.
- *Communicate constantly, and share all relevant information in a timely, comprehensive fashion.* Be sure to communicate with those who are not directly involved in the partnership but may be affected later in the process.
- *Involve in a very meaningful way all stakeholders in the design and implementation of the collaborative project.* Pay particular attention to the less powerful stakeholders, who may feel marginalized.
- *Accept conflict and difference as natural conditions of authentic collaborative partnerships.* As Magolda (2001) suggests, "Collaborative teams are lightning rods for conflict because they provide space for diverse individuals to interact. Accepting rather than repressing conflict is an important consideration for those who desire healthy collaborative communities" (p. 32).
- *Accept the fact that building collaborative partnerships is hard work that necessitates perseverance and tenacity in pursuit of goals.* Collaborative partnerships require inordinate investments of human capital—time, energy, and expertise. And these investments rarely result in immediate success.

The preceding best practices and recommendations, when combined with the guiding principles listed earlier in this chapter, should be useful tools and perspectives for developing collaborative partnerships that enhance learning and success for first-year students.

CONCLUSION

"Collaborate or die . . .": that was the banner headline in a *Business Week* advertisement sponsored by the J. D. Edwards Company, which stated that collaboration is the key to profitability in the new economy. Although such a mandate would be met with dismay, and perhaps alarm, by members of the academy, many institutions have come to realize that the challenges they face, particularly those related to first-year student success, span many organizational boundaries and thus can best be addressed through a collaborative, cross-functional response. Faculty and student affairs educators must realize that they have a number of common enemies: unacceptable retention and graduation rates; chilly campus climates for students of color; increased incidents of incivility, academic dishonesty, and alcohol abuse; and unimpressive scores on national measures of learning productivity. All of these require a collective, collaborative response if they are to be addressed effectively. Indeed, successful interventions for combating these common enemies are based on the assumption that optimal student learning cannot occur if the central institutional components involved in that learning are separated from one another by structure or commitments or both (Kuh, 1996; Terenzini & Pascarella, 1994). By focusing on improving student learning and success, diverse stakeholders can be brought together to cocreate seamless learning experiences that integrate, in a comprehensive and coherent fashion, activities that foster educational attainment for first-year students and ensure the vitality of their institutions.

CHAPTER THIRTEEN

Technology and Today's First-Year Students

Reynol Junco

Monday, March 1, 7:30 AM: *Beep . . . Beep . . . Beep. . . .* I reluctantly wake up. I search around in the dark for the snooze button, but I realize that my Palm Pilot is clear across my room—oh yes! I put it there last night to make sure that I get out of bed and make it to my 8:00 A.M. composition course. It's 7:30 A.M., just enough time to see who is on-line and to check my e-mail. I stumble over to my computer, which I leave on all night in sleep mode in case I receive any instant messages while I am dreaming of where I will go for spring break. Sure enough, Enrique, my best friend from high school, sent me an instant message last night asking if I had the new Outkast album on mp3. My away message instantly let him know that I was counting sheep. Checking Enrique's away message, I find that he went to sleep at 3:00 A.M. last night and that he is going to skip his 9:00 A.M. math class (not a great idea to announce if his parents check his away message). A quick check of my e-mail and I find five pieces of spam and an e-mail from my father reminding me to check my snail mail today to see if I received the money they sent so I can buy my goggles for biology class. It's now 7:45—I'm going to be late, so I throw on my jeans, a shirt, a sweater, and my shoes and run to class.

Monday, March 1, 8:15 A.M.: My English professor is discussing the intricacies of run-on sentences and I find my attention waning. . . . My professor reminds us that our midterm paper is due this Friday. Oh no! I had forgotten to enter the due date in my Palm Pilot and I made arrangements to go home on Thursday and I haven't even started the paper! After class, I ask the professor if I can send it to her as an e-mail attachment since I will be away because of a family emergency (hey, it works every time!). She said she would accept it as long as she received the e-mail before 8 A.M. on Friday. Excellent! I can type the paper on my laptop

221

while my sister drives home. Since I've got an hour before the next class, I run down to the computer lab to start my paper. I fumble around in my backpack for my JumpDrive—128 Megabytes of memory and where I keep all of my important files. This is the best invention of the last few years—now I don't have to e-mail myself papers and/or worry about my floppy disks being corrupt.

Monday, March 1, 9:25 A.M.: While I am working with my JumpDrive, I open a file to start my paper, and my cell phone rings. I check the Caller ID and discover that it's my mother calling from work. Mom reminds me to look for the check in the mail today—I told her that I would and that I had already heard from dad via e-mail. She also tells me that my sister may have to pick me up a little later than she expected because she is having a makeup exam on Thursday. I send my sister a text-message to her cell phone to see when she can come to get me. I adjust myself in front of the computer again. In addition to opening a file for my English paper, I am checking my e-mail and have logged on to instant messaging. Enrique is still sleeping, but Julian, my roommate, is online along with our friend from down the hall and two of my friends from high school who attend the rival state school. While I'm typing my introductory paragraph, Julian and our other friends plan on meeting at the gym tonight. My friend from high school, Alyssa, IM's me and asks if I saw the music awards show last night. Darn! I completely forgot about it but luckily, Alyssa had already downloaded the whole show from a file-sharing network. She promised she would send it to me later.

Beep, Beep, Beep rings my cell phone—a reminder to call Heather, Sejal, Tim, and Jasmine to arrange a study session for statistics tomorrow. I'll have to snooze this reminder since it's only 9:30 A.M. and I don't think they are awake yet. Better yet, I'll send them a meeting request via e-mail! That way, I can check their calendars to see when they are out of class and schedule our study session at a convenient time for all of us. "Beep" chimes my Palm Pilot. Time to get to my 10 A.M. history class. Instead of reading the 100-page-long chapter on the important battles in World War II, I Googled the terms "important battles world war 2" and found a great summary article written by a History professor at Oxford. Whew! What a time saver! I should e-mail that professor thanking her for making my life easier today. I also found a great Web site on the intricacies of jet engines that included a paper that I could cite for my aerospace class, but I have to be careful since my aerospace professor makes us use turnitin.com to see if we plagiarized.

Monday, March 1, 10:05 A.M.: My history professor starts the class by logging on to the workstation in the classroom and warming up the LCD projector. He also announces that the notes and an audio transcript will be available on our university's portal Web page filed under his class information. Yes! I only wish that I had brought along my laptop so that I could connect wirelessly to the portal, download the notes, and add my own. My handwriting is terrible—I prefer typing any day—it's much easier for me to read. The only problem is that last semester, my physics professor caught me IM'ing my friends who were already on vacation during his lecture. Not good. For our next project, we are supposed to find a picture of a World War II memorial and write a reaction paper. No sweat! I have some pictures saved on my digital camera from my last trip to Washington. I'll download them tonight and add the appropriate text. He'll love it! Time for lunch.

To those of us whose technology skills may be limited to word processing and e-mail, this fictionalized caricature of a half-day in the life of a first-year student may seem incomprehensible. To those of us who are more technologically literate and in tune with the many ways in which first-year students use technology daily, this account may seem a bit over the top but nevertheless close to reality.

Today's first-year students use the Internet and technology in ways that were unknown to previous generations of students. Use of computers and the Internet has increased dramatically across all subgroups of the students, and no other group has seen an increase greater than incoming first-year students. Traditional-age first-year students arrive at college with a comfort and understanding of computers and related technology that seems to be due, at least in part, to their experiences with technology prior to college. Indeed, the State of New Jersey reported in 1997–1998 that while only 36.5 percent of all secondary public school locations had access to the Internet, 100 percent did in 2001–2002 (State of New Jersey, 2003). Furthermore, in a recent study of 276,449 first-year students nationwide, 81.7 percent reported that they used the Internet for research or homework during their senior year in high school (Sax et al., 2003).

Today's first-year students, compared with their counterparts of previous decades, are unique in their use of and familiarity with technology such as surfing the Internet, instant messaging, e-mail, and cellular phones. Many professionals who work with first-year students are unaware of the many ways those students are using technology that may enhance or detract from their academic and psychosocial development. While many first-year students are familiar with technology, there are others who may be at a disadvantage because of their lack of experiences with technology before college, including racial/ethnic minorities, adult learners, women, and individuals from rural and lower socioeconomic status areas. In addition, many faculty and staff members lag in their technological knowledge and skill. These last two factors create difficulties for institutions where policies assume that all first-year students and faculty have equal technological abilities.

Because of the fast pace of technology, some of the terms and specifications of the technologies will change, but the point of this chapter will be the same: it is important to understand that technology plays a major role, more so than ever before, in first-year students' academic and psychosocial development. Even if technological terms and specifications change, there will always be a need for first-year students to use technology for good (to express themselves, communicate, enhance their academic work, and build a sense of community)—and they will sometimes use it for ill (to cheat, harass others, get addicted to computer games, and isolate themselves from others).

This chapter examines the impact of technology on first-year students and the professionals who work with them. The goal is to provide an overview of how first year students use technology, what those technologies are, how those technologies affect their experiences, and what practitioners must do to inform first-year students about the use of technology, and help them use technology in positive ways. In this chapter I will provide definitions of technologies used by students, outline current research on technology and first year students, discuss the impact of technology on first year students, and offer recommendations for practice.

THE TECHNOLOGY

First-year and other college students use a wide variety of technological tools, including instant messaging (IM), electronic mail (e-mail), cellular phones, the World Wide Web, and file sharing.

Instant Messaging

This is a software program that allows individuals to communicate in real time, as messages are sent instantly to the screen of the other user. Using IM to communicate is often referred to as "chatting" because of its interactive and real-time nature, as if two people were talking face-to-face. Some of the more common programs are America Online's Instant Messenger, ICQ's messenger, Yahoo Messenger, Microsoft Network's Messenger, and Internet Relay Chat. All are based on the same principle: users are shown a list of their friends who are on-line and available for chat. Users may then click on the person's name and send him or her an instant message. The person on the receiving end of the message sees the message in the form of a box that pops up on the screen with a space to reply (Webopedia, 2003).

It is possible to run other applications while using IM programs; therefore, students may often work on a class assignment, write an e-mail to a professor, shop, and chat at the same time. Indeed, first-year students are quite adept at carrying on a number of IM chats at the same time. One first-year student reported to me that she chats with over twenty people simultaneously. She believed that this would help faculty members understand her ability to multitask and the fact that she sometimes becomes bored in their classes because they do not move as fast as her virtual world.

The IM conversations in which first-year students engage rarely follow standard English grammatical rules. For instance, it is appropriate to use the letter "u" to mean "you," to leave out articles, and to use acronyms for common phrases such as "brb" for "be right back," "lol" for "laughing out loud," and "ttyl" for "talk to you later." In fact, I spend a great deal of time in my first-year seminar courses discussing how it is important to *not* write papers using grammar as if one is chatting via IM.

E-Mail

This software or Web-based service allows individuals to send asynchronous messages. Messages are typed using a text editor, sent, and routed through Internet servers to reach a recipient's "mailbox." The recipients must check their mail in order to see if they have any new messages. E-mail messages can be received at any time, as servers will save messages until they are checked. First-year students need not be at their computer to receive these messages, and they can also reply to them at any time. One important difference between IM and e-mail is that IM happens in real time while e-mail allows the student to think about a response. E-mail has been used as an effective tool by faculty and staff to communicate with first-year students (Webopedia, 2003).

Cellular Phones

Cellular phones allow students to make phone calls, browse the Web, send e-mails, and send text messages and photographs. With the advent of more afford-able cellular phone handsets and calling plans that make long-distance rates less expensive than ever before, cellular phones have started to replace the traditional telephone land line. Many students use cell phones to stay in touch with each other, and more important, to stay in touch with family and friends. If students are lonely or homesick, they can reach into their backpack, grab their phone, and make a phone call. Some phones have incorporated IM technology so that students never have to log off and can receive real-time messages anywhere.

Cellular technology also allows for the use of wireless hand-held devices such as BlackBerrys and personal digital assistants (PDAs). Although only a few stu-dents are using these technologies at present, more reasonable prices and tech-nological knowledge will likely lead to an increase in use (such as the increase in use witnessed with cellular phones). PDAs are hand-held devices that are used for data storage, scheduling, and some computer applications (such as word processing) that do not require a great deal of memory. They are mainly used to keep a schedule and to keep a list of contacts (like an address book). Some first-year students may use a PDA to store notes for their classes as they can be used as a digital notepad. PDAs can be connected to the Internet via cel-lular connections thereby allowing students to check their e-mail, surf the Web, and chat from anywhere. BlackBerry hand-helds are devices that are connected to the Internet by cellular connections and allow the user to send and receive e-mail anywhere.

World Wide Web

Many first-year students use the Web to perform research for classes, shop, check sports scores, check the weather, obtain stock quotes, play computer games, and do many other things. For example, it has been my experience as a faculty member that first-year students are much more inclined to use the Web to find research instead of using the library. Indeed, librarians are now making greater efforts to help first-year students in doing research in ways that are eth-ical and yield valid information (see Chapter Twenty). The Web also allows col-leges and universities to provide courses and services such as registration, orientation, and fee payment on-line. At most institutions of higher education, first-year students can check their grades, view graduation degree audits, sched-ule classes, and pay fees using the Web.

File-Sharing Software

First-year students use file-sharing software to download music, games, pictures, and so forth. Some of the more popular software programs include Kazaa and WinMx. These programs work by allowing a student to search a network of other users' computers for files. When students find the file they are looking for, it can be downloaded onto their machine with the click of a button. File-sharing software has been in the headlines for several years, with federal courts issuing injunctions against Napster and, more recently, against individual users of file-sharing software for sharing large numbers of music files. Using file-sharing software influences first-year students' view of intellectual property: many of them know that they are sharing copyrighted material but have not thought of the implications of doing so.

RESEARCH ON TECHNOLOGY AND FIRST-YEAR STUDENTS

Some research has been done on students' use of technology and the impact it has on the student experience.

Use of Technology

Current first-year students use technology more than their counterparts from previous generations, and students in general use technology more than the general population. In addition to their experience with technology, research has shown that a large proportion of college students in general and first-year students in particular have used the Internet for communication and school-related activities (Pew Internet and American Life Project, 2002; Sax et al., 2003). Sax et al. (2003) reported that 84.5 percent of first-year students used a computer frequently and that 67.4 percent reported using the Internet for uses other than school research. Furthermore, Sax et al. reported that 64.1 percent communicated via e-mail frequently and 70.2 percent communicated via IM frequently. In a survey of 728 students taking courses that incorporated the use of technology, Shuell and Farber (2001) found that first-year students (as well as graduate students) reported using e-mail more than sophomores, juniors, and seniors did. The most popular use of technology reported was using e-mail to communicate with instructors, with a full 83.4 percent of students reporting doing so.

Researchers have found evidence for differences in technological preparedness based on factors such as gender, race, class, and academic background. For instance, Sax, Ceja, and Teranishi (2001) studied a sample of 272,821 first-year students and found that even after controlling for income levels, Latino and African American first-year students were less likely to communicate via e-mail than were white and Asian American first-year students. They also found that students who had higher academic aspirations (what they termed the "Scholar Types") were more likely to use the Internet and e-mail than other students. Furthermore, students who earned higher grades in high school and took more college preparatory courses are also more likely to use e-mail and the Internet.

Nationwide, more women than men report that use of the Internet has improved their relationships with friends and family (Pew Internet and American Life Project, 2003).

These research findings can be understood by looking at data collected by the National Telecommunications and Information Administration. In a nationwide study and document, *Falling Through the Net: Toward Digital Inclusion* (U.S. Department of Commerce, 2000), the administration reported that:

- Only 23.6 percent of Latino and 23.5 percent of African American households nationwide had Internet access compared to 46.1 percent of white and 56.8 percent of Asian American households.

- In urban areas, almost all groups studied had higher levels of Internet access than in rural areas: 23.9 percent for Latinos, 24.0 percent for African Americans, and 48.3 percent for whites in urban areas versus 19.9 percent for Latinos and African Americans and 40.9 percent for whites in rural areas.

- Internet use is a linear function of income, with those with lower incomes using the Internet at lower rates than those with higher incomes.

- Households earning more than $75,000 per year are highly likely to have Internet access.

- Only 33.7 percent of Latino and 32.6 percent of African American households had a computer as compared to 55.7 percent of white and 65.6 percent of Asian American households.

- Latinos and African Americans are less likely to use the Internet than Asian Americans and whites: 23.7 percent and 29.3 percent compared to 49.4 percent and 44.4 percent, respectively.

Along with the evidence for substantial differences in access to the Internet and computers, there are also differences in how individuals from minority, low-income, and rural backgrounds are encouraged to use computers. Brown, Higgins, and Hartley (2001), Pisapia (1994), and Milone and Salpeter (1996) have summarized research that found that students in public schools in lower-socioeconomic-status (SES) areas are more likely to be using computers for academic practice and quizzing, while students in the higher-SES areas were more than three times as likely to be learning how to program them. In other words, those in lower-SES areas are being controlled by the computer while those in higher-SES areas are learning how to control the computer. Furthermore, schools attended by students from minority or lower-SES backgrounds tend to provide less access to computers and related technologies, and when they do have computers, they are often located in areas inaccessible by students.

Differences in how women use the Internet have also been reported. The most recent data, provided in Cyberatlas (2002), showed that men logged on to the Internet more, spent more time on-line, and accessed more content than women, even though women's Internet presence (numbers of individuals using the Internet) equaled that of men in the United States. Worldwide, Nielsen and

Cyberatlas reported that the Internet population is predominantly male and historically has been male dominated. Research has also suggested that men may be more comfortable using technology for expressing emotional issues (Junco & Salter, 2004).

It is clear that there are differences along ethnic, gender, income, and geographical lines when it comes to familiarity with and use of computers and technology. Students with disadvantaged technological backgrounds attend institutions of higher education that place similar technological demands on all students. First-year students who are less prepared are also more likely to struggle figuring out how to do some things that other students may take for granted, such as e-mailing an assignment to a professor, registering for classes, setting up their computer accounts, and figuring out how to use a computer to complete assignments.

In addition to ethnic, gender, income, and geographical issues, there are also striking differences in how first-year students as a whole use the Internet and technology compared to other individuals. Studies show that students use the Internet much more than the general population. The ongoing Pew Internet and American Life Project investigates the impact of the Internet on various sectors of society. One project study, *The Internet Goes to College: How Students Are Living in the Future with Today's Technology* (2002), focuses on college students and the time they spend on-line. The study found that:

- 72 percent of all college students check their e-mail daily, while only 52 percent of all Americans with Internet access do so.
- 20 percent of today's college students began using computers between the ages of five and eight.
- By the time they were teenagers, all of today's current students had begun using a computer.
- 85 percent of college students own their own computer.
- 66 percent of college students use at least two e-mail addresses.
- 78 percent of all college Internet users stated that they went on-line to browse for fun compared to 64 percent of all Internet users.
- 60 percent of college Internet users have downloaded files on-line compared to 28 percent of all Internet users.
- 26 percent of college students use IM on an average day compared to 12 percent of all Internet users.

The same Pew survey asked college students questions about the academic benefits of using the Internet. They found that:

- 79 percent of all students reported that the Internet had a positive impact on their academics.
- 46 percent of students reported that e-mail allows them to express ideas to professors that they otherwise would not express in person.

- 19 percent of students reported that they communicate more with their professors via e-mail than in person.

- 73 percent of students reported that they use the Internet more than the library to search for information.

- 68 percent of students reported subscribing to an academic e-mail list (or listserv) related to their academic area.

- 65 percent of students reported absences by e-mail while 58 percent have used e-mail to discuss a grade with an instructor.

Impact of Technology

There are conflicting reports about how the Internet has an impact on students. The Internet may positively affect student interactions with each other and faculty members. For instance, Hu and Kuh (2001a) examined the responses of 18,844 college students at seventy-one institutions on the College Student Experiences Questionnaire (CSEQ). They found that attending a wired campus (that is, one that had more readily available Internet technology, as defined by Yahoo! Internet Life's survey of most wired campuses) was positively related to students' reporting good educational practices (student-faculty contact, cooperation among students, and active learning). Wired campuses did not reduce student engagement in good practices. In fact, students at more wired institutions reported more contact with their teachers and more peer interactions. Of interest was that older, nontraditional students did not seem to benefit as much from technology as their younger counterparts.

In another study using the CSEQ, Kuh and Vesper (2001) found that even when background characteristics and academic ability were taken into account, students who learned more about computers during college ("High Gainers") reported higher gains on skills considered essential for success in college than those who learned less about computers ("Low Gainers"). The improvement in skills included gains in the ability to think analytically, ability to learn on one's own, understanding oneself, and awareness of other philosophies. They also found that High Gainers spent more time studying than the Low Gainers did.

It is possible that the Internet may negatively affect first-year students' academic progress as well as their interactions with each other and faculty members. Kubey, Lavin, and Barrows (2001) conducted a survey of 576 mostly first-year students and found 9 percent of the sample agreed or strongly agreed that they might be a "little psychologically dependent on the Internet." The students in the "dependent" group were significantly more likely to agree or strongly agree that if they had a few more friends, they would probably use the Internet less than those in the "nondependent" group. There was a disproportionate number of first-year students in the Internet-dependent subgroup, and these students felt significantly more alone than other students.

In the Kubey et al. (2001) survey, 14 percent of the overall sample reported that their schoolwork had been hurt occasionally, frequently, or very frequently due to Internet use. Four times as many of the students in the dependent group reported Internet-related academic impairment than did the nondependent group. The group identifying academic impairment reported usage more than double that of the whole sample. Also, a disproportionate number of first-year students in the group reported academic impairment. Those reporting academic impairment due to the Internet were significantly more likely to agree or strongly agree that if they had a few more friends, they would probably use the Internet less than those in the nonimpairment group. First-year students are apparently at greater risk of developing academic difficulties because of Internet use.

While Kubey et al. (2001) reported support for the idea of Internet dependence and its negative psychological and academic effects, other researchers have investigated the nature of this phenomenon and reported positive psychological effects of Internet use. In one study, Morgan and Cotten (2003b), using a sample of 287 first-year college students, found that increased e-mail and IM hours were associated with decreased depressive symptoms (as measured by the Center for Epidemiologic Studies Depression Scale–Iowa Version) while increased Internet hours for shopping, research, or playing games were associated with increased depressive symptoms. In other words, using the Internet for interpersonal connections promotes psychological well-being. Finally, Morgan and Cotten (2003b) found that increased e-mail and IM hours for men yielded a larger decrease in depressive symptoms than for women.

Whether the Internet has a negative or positive impact on first-year students' psychosocial and academic development will be a subject for research and debate for years to come. One thing is certain: today's first-year students are unique in that they use the Internet to communicate and keep a close group of friends through IM, chat, and e-mail. In addition, most first-year students maintain relationships with a group of high school friends by using the Internet, which is markedly different from previous generations of students (Kubey et al., 2001). In addition to keeping high school friends "with them," they can also keep in touch with their family in ways that students might not have done before the advent of the Internet. In one study, the Pew Internet and American Life Project (2000) found that 31 percent and 34 percent of respondents reported that it was easier for them to say frank or unpleasant things over e-mail to family or friends, respectively.

A recent study found that first-year students spent an average of 16.3 hours per week chatting and using IM while spending only an average of 3.9 hours per week using e-mail (Morgan & Cotten, 2003a). The increase in popularity of instant messaging allows first-year students to deal with emotional issues and to be frank or unpleasant without having to deal with someone in person. These sentiments are echoed by comments made by students enrolled in my first-year seminar course:

> As far as on-line disagreements go, I have had one with an ex-girlfriend. She was the shy type, really quiet about personal things. So because of this fact of her being unable to talk about things in person, I wasn't able to find out she liked me and ask her out unless it was on-line. . . . [After a time,] I finally had to end

it since I knew she wanted to but wouldn't. . . . Since I began attendance, I was able to find someone who can actually talk to me in person and on-line!

I told [my boyfriend] it was over. . . . I used e-mail and IM because it was easier. I knew if I did it in person it would be ten times more emotional and I would cry and I didn't want to give him that satisfaction.

I used the e-mail to contact one of my professors, because I missed his class and he saw me the same day. I wanted to e-mail him to let him know why I wasn't in class. The reason for choosing e-mail is because I did not want to explain face to face. Because it is harder to explain yourself in person rather than in writing them a letter, and in a letter to him you don't have to answer questions.

It's easier to say over IM because you can't see their facial reactions that could upset you.

Other first-year students prefer face-to-face interactions, as evidenced by these comments:

I hate fighting or getting mad at people on-line cause when you or they say something you can't tell their tone!

I really hate arguing on the Internet because it is so pointless. I believe it's more respectful to do that kind of stuff in person.

Instant messaging has undeniably become an easy-to-use way of avoiding facing up to emotions and difficult interpersonal situations. But many first-year students reported building and maintaining significant interpersonal relationships using the Internet. First-year students use e-mail and IM to deal with the loneliness that comes with their transition to college. One important research finding is that Internet use driven by social needs positively affects psychological well-being, while Internet use driven by informational needs does not (Morgan & Cotten, 2003b). A student could use IM to build significant interpersonal relationships and deal with otherwise uncomfortable interpersonal situations as part of the trial-and-error learning necessary for developmental growth.

First-year students are able to use IM and e-mail to communicate with faculty and staff members in what is for them a nonthreatening environment. Instead of meeting faculty members in their offices to discuss a grade, a student can e-mail them and meet them "on their own turf." In my experience, many students who otherwise would not have approached me after class or during office hours have used e-mail or IM to communicate ideas. Introverted students are more likely to ask questions about material presented in class over e-mail and IM because it reduces the pressure for a student to self-monitor and become anxious about asking in front of peers. In addition, IM allows first-year students to "check out" a professor to see if she or he is someone whom they can talk to.

TECHNOLOGY AND THE CLASSROOM

In the classroom, students are required to create presentations using presentation software such as PowerPoint. They are also often required to use course shells such as Blackboard to supplement class instruction. Course shells have revolutionized distance and regular course delivery. These systems offer a virtual companion to a regular classroom or can serve as a complete virtual classroom. Many offer testing engines where faculty members may create exams and students may log in, at their convenience, to take the examination. Course shells allow faculty members to hold on-line discussions and grade these discussions in much the same way that class participation might be graded. These shells also allow more introverted students to be more comfortable responding to questions posed by the professor. Furthermore, course shells allow for twenty-four-hour access to assignments, syllabi, news items, and frequently asked questions about the course.

Whereas course shells serve as a supplemental resource to existing courses, on-line courses are completely Web-based courses that have traditionally been geared toward distance education students. More recently, first-year and other non–distance education students are being allowed to take on-line courses that count toward their degree requirements. Both groups of students require support for their on-line tasks. The Western Cooperative for Educational Communications, which publishes a guide to developing on-line student services, gives recommendations, including having financial aid provide on-line loan entrance and exit counseling, providing on-line orientation services, providing advisees access to their own records through a comprehensive on-line advising system, having career services encourage students to build on-line relationships with potential employees, and developing an on-line forum for discussing typical student concerns with the counseling center (Western Cooperative for Educational Telecommunications, 2003).

There are specific technology demands for selected majors to which first-year students must adapt. For example, education majors must learn how to create their portfolios on-line, psychology and social science majors are adapting to collecting survey data on-line, and science majors must learn to use computer models in their laboratories. In addition to these specific demands, first-year students typically use the Internet to perform research for papers instead of going to the library. Most institutions offer on-line full-text journals where students can find all of the research they need from the comfort of their own rooms.

While the Internet makes it easier for first-year students to perform research, it also makes it much easier for them to plagiarize. Students can cut and paste information from thousands of Web sites and articles on the Internet. Because of the vast number of Web sites, it is often quite difficult to trace these instances of plagiarism. For instance, one of my former colleagues prided himself in finding on-line plagiarism. He would spend days performing search engine queries to find those who had cheated and would typically catch an average of eight offenders each semester. Furthermore, students can buy complete term papers from a number of sites that offer "college term paper help." These sites allow students to purchase actual term papers that are often guaranteed to get them an A. The papers can be downloaded and opened in a word processor and edited as needed.

There are few ways to prevent plagiarism through technology, but a small number of companies have produced tools to address Internet plagiarism. Most of these tools come in the form of software programs that check Internet databases for similarities. The most notable company offering an antiplagiarism solution is turnitin.com, which offers an automated method of checking students' work. Students upload their paper to turnitin.com, and the site's software automatically searches the Internet and its database of papers and provides an "originality report" for each paper that is submitted. Each submitted paper is added to the turnitin.com database, thereby reducing the possibility of cross-institution plagiarism. Since the student uploads the paper himself or herself and the results are sent directly to the professor, such a service may be a deterrent for would-be plagiarizers.

Certainly, the ability to communicate effectively through writing should be an essential focus of any institution of higher education. One challenge for those who teach first-year students is the influence that technology has had on writing. Since incoming students more than likely have spent more time using IM than writing term papers, they are prone to write English in the same manner that they use during their IM chats. They are prone to include slang such as "u" for "you," "LOL" for "laughing out loud," and various other slang. Furthermore, with more refined spell check algorithms come new difficulties with spelling. A common mistake that I have encountered is when students use the word *defiantly* instead of *definitely* because spell check replaces misspelled versions of *definitely* with *defiantly*. I make it a point to discuss the difference between the meanings of the two words during my first-year seminar courses and warn students about the fact that spell check makes that and other erroneous changes. I encourage students to proofread their papers carefully.

GAP BETWEEN FACULTY AND STUDENT TECHNOLOGICAL KNOWLEDGE AND SKILL

While technology holds out much promise for enhancing first-year students' academic performance, the gap between faculty and student technological skill and knowledge can limit this promise. For example, while first-year students generally use e-mail and the Internet at high rates, faculty participation lags behind. The National Center for Education Statistics received responses from 882,000 faculty and staff who taught credit-bearing courses at degree-granting institutions (Warburton, Chen, & Bradburn, 2002). They found that:

- 97 percent of faculty had access to the Internet.

- 69.2 percent of full-time and 46.3 percent of part-time faculty used e-mail to communicate with students.

- 40.4 percent of full-time and 34.3 percent of part-time faculty used a course-specific Web site.

- Faculty spent an average of 2.7 hours per week responding to e-mail from students.

- 40 percent of full-time and 34 percent of part-time faculty used course-specific Web sites for their classes.

- 82 percent of those who used course-specific Web sites used them for general class purposes, 70.9 percent for homework information, 25.8 percent for practice exams and exercises, 22.2 percent to post exam results, and 80.6 percent for course-related links.

There are differences in the use of technology, at least in the academic setting, between faculty members and first-year students. For example, according to research by Sax et al. (2003) and Shuell and Farber (2001), first-year students reported using e-mail to communicate with faculty more than faculty reported using e-mail to communicate with students (Warburton et al., 2002). Furthermore, first-year students use the Internet and surf the Web at much greater rates than faculty use the Web in their courses. One reason that faculty are not using the Web in their courses at similar rates to students is that using Web sites for courses and teaching courses on-line requires a different teaching style than the style used in a traditional classroom. Faculty, by virtue of the fact that they have not had the same exposure to technology as their students, generally require more training in adapting to technology (Roach, 2000).

The gap between faculty and students in technological use and comfort affects first-year students directly. Institutions require that students learn about and use a great deal of technology, especially in specific majors. Faculty who work with first-year students must ensure that students are receiving proper education in technological skills. It is also important for faculty to model appropriate and contemporary uses of technology. This way, first-year students have models that communicate the importance of improving their own technological skills.

THE IMPACT OF TECHNOLOGY ON FIRST-YEAR STUDENTS' SENSE OF COMMUNITY

First-year students' sense of community about their institution begins while they are still in high school, when they gather information about colleges and universities. Students form their first impression of an institution by visiting that institution's Web site. The information that is found on an institution's Web pages can significantly influence a student's decision to attend. Furthermore, some admissions offices are using technology to provide prospective students the ability to engage in chats with faculty and other students, thereby allowing prospective students to gain a better sense of the campus environment. Institutions are starting to provide orientation sessions in an on-line format, which may also have an impact on a student's view of the campus environment.

Remember that current first-year students are unique in that they use the Internet and cellular technology to communicate and maintain a close group of friends. This close group of friends includes contacts from high school since the distance between them is shortened through the possibility of IM, chat, e-mail, and low-priced phone service. This ability allows first-year students to build their own sense of community apart from the institution they attend. It could have a negative impact on the connectedness they feel and their involvement in campus activities at their institution.

RECOMMENDATIONS

Over the past fifteen years, technology has had an enormous impact on the first-year student experience, for good or for ill. The issue now is how to direct this pervasive influence so that first-year students will reap the benefits of technology, while minimizing its negative effects. Following are some recommendations in this regard:

- *Level the playing field.* For many institutions, the development of all kinds of uses of technology for first-year students has been and will be helpful to their transition to college. However, not all students have access to or the skills necessary to use available technology. Thus, institutions must first make sure that they provide a level technological playing field for first-year students. For example, not all first-year students have their own computer, so they must have access to campus computer laboratories. They also vary in their computer preparedness, so there must be opportunities to become computer literate through orientation programs, first-year seminars, and other efforts designed to promote their success. Institutions that rely on technology to communicate with and orient first-year students before they enroll must make sure that those without computer access or skills receive the same information as those with such access and skills.

To create a level playing field, institutions should first determine the level of first-year student technological knowledge and skill and use this information to develop strategies to bring all of them to the point where they can use technology to succeed both inside and outside the classroom. This assessment is particularly important for institutions that enroll racial/ethnic minorities, adult students, and others who may not have had the advantages of use of computers prior to their enrollment. Technological knowledge and skill may be just as important to assess as math or English skills.

- *Use technology to enhance the orientation of first-year students before they enroll.* At some institutions, it is possible, through the use of technology, for entering students to inquire about admission, apply for admission, gain acceptance to the institution, pay their tuition and fees, and register for classes without ever having contact with an actual human being. Moreover, there is also great potential for using technology to orient entering students before they enroll by creating opportunities for them to access the Web sites of student and academic services and programs, have e-mail communication with students and faculty, and engage in electronic chats with other entering students, upperclass students, and faculty on transition issues. Focused chatroom discussions with upperclass students on issues such as what a particular major is like, what on-campus residential living is like, opportunities for involvement in campus activities, or how to use technology to be more successful in the classroom can be very helpful to entering students. Furthermore, chatrooms with faculty can be used to initiate discussions about particular majors, how technology is used in conducting classes, and content-focused discussions on topics of interest.

• *Use technology as a major tool in orientation programs and services.* Here again, the use of e-mail, chatrooms, Web sites, and other means of electronic communication can be a valuable tool in orienting first-year students once they are enrolled. For example, accessing Web sites of student and academic services can be a user-friendly and effective way of educating first-year students about the many ways the institution can help them succeed. CD-ROMs on issues such as sexuality, alcohol and drugs, campus safety, diversity, and other important topics can be made available to entering students in addition to face-to-face programs on these issues.

• *Incorporate technology education into orientation programs.* While this education will be especially important for first-year students who lack technological access, knowledge, and skills prior to college, even those with prior technological experience will need to know about how technology is used at their particular campus. For example, all first-year students need to know how to use the Internet to search for information to complete assignments or write papers. They also need to know information about computer laboratories, software, where to obtain technological support, how to access and use e-mail, and other information.

Furthermore, first-year students need to know more about electronic plagiarism and the ways in which institutions try to prevent it. For example, many institutions may have invested in software or Web sites that can detect when a student may have plagiarized assignments or papers. Also, technological copyright issues should be addressed in the light of recent legislation against the widespread practice of downloading copyrighted music. Often first-year students download both music and other software from the Internet and do not think about the consequences.

Finally, first-year students should be made aware that technology is a double-edged sword that can also be used in negative ways. I know of instances where students have become involved in harmful relationships as a result of IM communications. Occasionally students may become addicted to computer use, to the detriment of their academic and social development. And there are also instances where students have illegally hacked into institutional or personal computer files or software. Moreover, students may unknowingly commit plagiarism or violate copyright laws in using their computers.

• *Provide technology education to faculty.* There is a gap between faculty and student technological knowledge and skill, with many faculty lagging behind their students. Of course, every campus has its Luddites who are determined not to let technology interfere with the traditional ways of doing things. I know of a few faculty who refuse to use e-mail, accept Internet Web sites as sources for papers or assignments, or even allow students to submit papers and assignments electronically. No one is suggesting that faculty be forced into the electronic age, but for those who do not use technology because of lack of skill and knowledge, programs that teach faculty how to use technology to enhance student learning should be offered.

More specifically, faculty can use technology for on-line office hours, focused chatroom interactions among students, providing feedback on assignments and papers, providing e-mail addresses for all students in each class, publishing faculty lectures on-line, conducting student research, posting grades so that students can have real-time, confidential access to their grades, and adjust their studying and help-seeking accordingly, to name just a few.

• *Encourage student and academic support units to use technology in the delivery and communication of their services and programs.* On-line student services Web sites often include features ranging from providing information to opportunities for self-guided interactions with these units. Also, first-year students could access on-line tutoring support for math, writing, and other skills by using a chatroom software program with formula and drawing capabilities, such as Yahoo Messenger. Students can log on to a chatroom and discuss math problems with a tutor in a virtual group tutoring session. On-line writing support can take the form of e-mailing papers to writing tutors and using Track Changes and Notes functions to provide feedback.

On-line student and academic support services may also be integrated by centralizing all services on a portal Web page, as illustrated by examples on the Western Cooperative for Educational Telecommunications Web site (http://www.wcet.info/projects/laap/index.asp). From a central Web page, first-year students can, among other things, register for courses; maintain an integrated calendar; set up appointments with faculty, staff, and advisers; and chat with faculty and staff.

Whatever is done with on-line student and academic support services, it is important to assess how each unit is using on-line services to support and communicate with first-year students. Recommendations from the Western Cooperative for Educational Telecommunications (2003) can be useful in considering the best methods for providing on-line student services.

• *Provide help for students who experience academic or psychological difficulties due to technology.* Some students may be academically or psychologically harmed by the use of technology. For example, Morgan and Cotten (2003b) reported that psychosocial difficulties such as depression in first-year students can be a function of how, more so than how much, they use the Internet.

Students involved in using the Internet for noncommunicative activities seem to be more at risk for depressive symptoms than those students who use the Internet for communicative activities. Counseling and advising professionals must be prepared to help first-year students deal with problems associated with technology use and misuse.

CONCLUSION

Today's first-year students are unique in their familiarity with and use of technology. Nevertheless, there are categories of students who may be at a disadvantage because of lack of access to, knowledge about, or skill with using technology. Furthermore, faculty and staff often lag behind students in using technology in the collegiate setting. The challenge for colleges and universities is not only to try to enhance first-year students' educational experiences by providing up-to-date technology, but to make sure that no one is at a disadvantage because of their lack of access to technology prior to college. Creating a level technological playing field should be the first institutional priority. If this goal is not achieved, technology enhancements designed to promote first-year student success may have the unintended consequence of creating unequal educational opportunities.

Technology should not be used in ways that significantly reduce or eliminate human interaction. Personal face-to-face interactions between all members of the collegiate community and first-year students are still powerful and necessary tools in helping them succeed. No amount of technology can or should ever replace this fundamental aspect of the first-year college experience.

PART FOUR

CHALLENGING AND SUPPORTING FIRST-YEAR STUDENTS IN THE CLASSROOM

Although we argued in the Introduction that first-year student success can be defined in many ways in addition to academic success, there is no question that, at least in terms of institutional standards, academic success is a precondition to all other definitions of success. Unless students maintain a C or better grade point average, they will not persist to graduation, regardless of how well they might have succeeded with establishing and maintaining interpersonal relationships, exploring identity development, deciding on a career, maintaining health and wellness, considering the faith and spiritual dimensions of life, dealing with diversity, and developing civic responsibility. To be sure, all of these tasks can be directly or indirectly related to academic success, but from an official institutional standpoint (with the possible exception of church-related institutions) often they are less highly valued than earning acceptable grades and persisting to graduation.

Thus, providing a challenging and supportive classroom environment to all first-year students is critical to their academic success. First and foremost, classroom environments must challenge first-year students to learn and achieve acceptable grades. Of course, student academic success is limited if faculty are not prepared to use instructional strategies that support student learning. In Chapter Fourteen, Bette LaSere Erickson and Diane W. Strommer provide a blueprint for first-year student learning in the curriculum and classroom. Of course, faculty must be properly prepared to teach first-year students, and in Chapter Fifteen, Scott Evenbeck and Barbara Jackson discuss ways in which faculty can be developed to create classroom environments that enable first-year students to maximize their learning.

Student learning in the classroom must be integrated with other efforts to enhance student academic success. In Chapter Sixteen, M. Stuart Hunter and Carrie W. Linder describe the role of first-year seminars in supporting first-year student success. In Chapter Seventeen, Jeanne L. Higbee discusses the importance of developmental education as a way of challenging and supporting the academic success of underprepared first-year students. In Chapter Eighteen, Deanna C. Martin and Maureen Hurley explore Supplemental Instruction as yet another way of helping first-year students achieve academically. In Chapter Nineteen, Margaret C. King and Thomas Kerr review academic advising programs and strategies designed to inform and guide first-year students in the pursuit of their academic goals. In Chapter Twenty, Margit Misangyi Watts explores the critical role of libraries and information literacy on the ability of first-year students to access and use information in pursuit of their academic requirements.

Also important to first-year student academic success is the ability to translate what is learned in the classroom to real-life situations. In Chapter Twenty-One, Edward Zlotkowski discusses the ways in which service-learning can help bridge the gap between classroom learning and practical experience. And in Chapter Twenty-Two, Jodi Levine Laufgraben discusses how learning communities offer an opportunity for first-year students to better integrate their classroom learning with their out-of-class experiences.

CHAPTER FOURTEEN

Inside the First-Year Classroom

Challenges and Constraints

Bette LaSere Erickson
Diane W. Strommer

*In high school, you were led by the hand through every class and told
exactly what had to be completed and what was expected of you. If you
didn't hand in an assignment or take a test, the teacher would approach
you and make an effort to keep you up to date on your studies. College is
a totally different ballpark. You're handed a syllabus and that's your bible.*
—First-year student

Ask veteran faculty what the challenges are in teaching first-year
courses, and they are likely to focus on the students, particularly their
difference from students at some mythical time in the past. Some will
complain students aren't as "good," as well prepared, and as literate as they
once were. Some mention how diverse the students are in backgrounds, interests, and preparation for college work. While they find such diversity exciting
and energizing, it requires attention and responses not demanded by upper-
division students.

Ask students what the challenges are in taking first-year classes, and they
say rather different things. Adult students might say, "Going back to school after
such a long time is really scary. I'm not at all certain I have the skills to make
it in college after all these years away from formal education."

Others mention the distractions of college life. "It's a lot harder to pay attention in college classes. You have so many more things on your mind," one commented. Another student admitted, "I was worried that the material and work
load may be overwhelming. I also thought it might be too much fun, and I might
not be able to concentrate on studies. . . . I am less worried about the workload,
and it hasn't been much fun, so that hasn't been a problem either." Whether
they enter college straight from high school or years after their previous schooling, students generally focus their concerns on managing time, the increased difficulty of courses, and the amount or difficulty of the reading assignments, even
though these concerns may not match their actual collegiate experiences.

A different set of expectations and constraints from other higher education
constituencies is also relevant to the first-year classroom. Students and their

families alike increasingly view college as consumers, expecting a broad range of services, opportunities, assistance, and, sometimes, guaranteed success both in college and after. Prospective employers want graduates with skills, experience, and preparation for lifelong learning, as well as knowledge of a field. While a total shift has by no means occurred yet, it seems clear that defining a college education as mastery of a body of knowledge or as a complete preparation for a lifetime career is outmoded. Instead, we recognize that the needs of graduates—knowledge, understanding, skills, and habits of mind for critical, reflective, and creative thinking, communication, and lifelong learning—change our definition of learning.

The continual rate of information growth, particularly in the sciences, complicates decisions about course content and teaching methodology, challenging faculty to make hard choices about content in those courses that are one student's sole introduction to a field of study and the essential foundation for further work for another. Rising costs, less generous public support, and increasing pressure for research productivity have led some larger institutions to leave some first-year classrooms in the hands of adjuncts, part-time faculty, and teaching assistants and to increase the size of others. These are the constraints and expectations that form the foreground, while in the background is a growing body of research from many fields about what all faculty should do well to ensure that these diverse students actually learn.

A look inside a first-year classroom today reveals a very different scene from that of a generation ago. This chapter first reviews several challenges and constraints that faculty face in teaching first-year college students: students' academic preparation, expectations about and motivations for learning, learning styles, stages of development, as well as new findings from research on basic learning processes. The remainder of the chapter describes five different teaching methods that are especially useful in teaching first-year students and concludes with general suggestions on how to use these methods effectively.

FIRST-YEAR STUDENTS IN THE CLASSROOM

First-year students present a variety of challenges in the classroom, including uneven academic preparation, varying motivations for learning, diverse learning styles, and different stages of intellectual development.

Academic Preparation

Increasing percentages of high school graduates enroll in college, and they have backgrounds very different from those who attended in earlier times. More students attend college immediately after high school—63 percent in fall 2001 compared with 49 percent in 1972 (National Center for Education Statistics, 2001)—and more mature students figure among first-time college goers. This growth in undergraduate enrollments is expected to continue and to be greater for full-time students and at four-year institutions, and women's enrollment is expected to continue increasing faster than men's (National Center for Education Statistics, 2001). Students will remain diverse in age, socioeconomic backgrounds, and academic preparation, all of which affects their readiness for higher education and their first-year classes.

Although national conversations about standards for secondary schools have resulted in more consistency in curricular requirements for graduation, one school's mathematics, English, or science program is not the same as another's. Clifford Adelman, a senior research analyst at the U.S. Department of Education who has conducted years of longitudinal analysis of bachelor's degree attainment, concludes that "the academic intensity and quality of one's high school curriculum (not test scores, and certainly not class rank or grade point average) counts most in preparation for bachelor's degree completion" (Adelman, 1999, p. 16).

Of equal concern are the study habits and skills students bring. Faculty who teach first-year students are often shocked to learn, for example, that more than half reported spending less than four hours per week on homework in high school (National Center for Education Statistics, 2001a, p. 36). At the same time, 77 percent of twelfth graders worked during the school year, and there is "an inverse relationship between hours spent working and hours devoted to homework, with seniors more likely to do no homework or to spend 4 or fewer hours a week on homework as their job hours increased" (p. 36). These data are consistent with those reported in *The American Freshman: National Norms for Fall 2000,* which observed that despite students' spending less time doing homework and studying than any previous class, "high school grades continue to soar" (Sax et al., 2001b).

Students do expect to study more in college. Seventy-nine percent of those surveyed for the National Survey of Student Engagement (NSSE) reported that their institution expects them to study a significant amount. Nonetheless, as Kuh reported in Chapter Five, less than 15 percent of full-time first-year students (or even seniors) spend twenty-six or more hours a week studying. About half said they spend between six and fifteen hours a week, and 10 percent spend five or fewer hours a week preparing for class (National Survey of Student Engagement, 2000). Only 52 percent of the first-year students in that same survey report that they "often" or "very often" "worked harder" than they thought they would in order to meet "an instructor's standards or expectations" (p. 19).

What students do in the name of studying also merits attention. Over the past decade, a number of faculty at the University of Rhode Island have surveyed their students to learn how many hours they studied since their previous class session and which of a dozen or so study activities they engaged in. Students most frequently read the assignment, read over the notes from the previous class, and worked assigned problems in science and math courses. Fewer than 20 percent of students in each class took notes from the readings, wrote summaries of readings in their own words, asked themselves questions to check for understanding, or wrote a summary of their notes from the previous class. If these students are representative, and our work with other, very different campuses leads us to believe they are, the study activities they use least frequently are those most likely to enable them to recall and use information. Our suggested teaching strategies are aimed in part at getting first-year students to study more productively. (Similar study habits are reported by Kuh in Chapter Five and Schilling and Schilling in Chapter Seven.)

Expectations and Motivations for Learning

Given escalating high school grades, it is not surprising that the percentages of first-year students expecting to earn at least a B average in college (58 percent) or to graduate with honors (21 percent) are the highest ever (Sax et al., 2001). That expectation, as noted, often does not translate into increased effort, and many students sink to the levels expected of them. Many will do no more than required, and professors may not require sufficient effort. The NSSE concludes that "the level of academic challenge . . . is uneven across colleges and universities, especially for first-year students." Overall, although there is considerable variation within each institutional classification, "students at liberal arts colleges are challenged more than their counterparts at all other types of schools" (National Survey of Student Engagement, p. 6).

Expectations at many colleges and in many courses may not be sufficiently high. Nonetheless, whether students enter college directly from high school or years later, they are likely to find teaching practices that are common in college unfamiliar and difficult: impersonal lecturing, infrequent testing and feedback on performance, reading that is not explicated in class, stretches of unstructured time, expectation of homework. They may be all too keenly aware of their poor writing or lack of basic math skills; they may secretly believe they are less competent than their peers and do not really belong at college. Many are focused on grades rather than learning (for a fuller discussion, see Erickson & Strommer, 1991; Leamnson, 1999).

Students tend to enter college with extrinsic motivations for learning: to get the grade point average and the credentials they need to reach their goals. According to *The American Freshman: National Norms for Fall 2000*, those goals are, for traditional-aged students, overwhelmingly associated with work: to get better jobs (72 percent), train for specific careers (72 percent), and make more money (70 percent). Many, however, also want to gain a "general education and appreciation of ideas" (65 percent) and "to learn more about things that interest me" (77 percent).

Shifting students away from the extrinsic motivations of rewards and punishment in the form of grades to an intrinsic desire to learn requires student-centered activities and a change in the learning environment (Paulsen & Feldman, 1999). Outlining a framework to motivate diverse students, Wlodkowski (1999) suggests establishing inclusion by helping students make connections and treating them with respect, helping them become favorably disposed toward learning through personal relevance and choice, enhancing meaning by including students' perspectives and values, and engendering competence by creating an understanding that students can be effective learners of things they value.

Establishing a relationship with a caring faculty member, academic adviser, or other mentor can dramatically alter a student's motivation for learning. Richard Light's assessment work has led him to emphasize the importance of academic advising, concluding that "part of a great college education depends upon human relationships" (2001, p. 85). It is particularly as advisers that faculty can force students to "think about the relationship of their academic work to their personal lives," advising that can transform students (p. 88). Light's advice that all new students come to know one professor well and give him or her the opportunity to know them is valuable. Unfortunately, although we know that interactions between students and faculty are important to many goals of higher education, it occurs all too rarely. In the NSSE survey, "across all types of institutions and students this benchmark is the lowest" (2000, p. 8). While it cannot substitute fully for face-to-face encounters, technology can help to increase that interaction. E-mail provides an opportunity for more frequent and personalized contact between faculty and students, and group discussion boards in a course can help to foster a sense of belonging to a class.

Learning Styles

Human diversity extends to how we learn and the differences among us as reflected in research on multiple intelligences and learning styles. Students differ in their preferred learning styles (see, for example, Carskadon, 1994; Claxton & Murrell, 1987; Erickson & Strommer, 1991; Felder, 1996; Svinicki & Dixon, 1987). Some learn best by working in groups; others need quiet reflection before they can comfortably participate in discussions or activities. Some process information better if they look first at the details and move step by step to generalizations; others benefit from looking first at the big picture and then focusing on the concrete. Some are more comfortable engaged in experimenting and acting; others, in observation and reflection.

How does one know of these differences? Typically, faculty come to know the learning styles of their students through direct experience with their classroom activities and assignments. However, there are systematic ways of learning more about student learning styles. For example, Smith and Kolb (1986) have developed an instrument that identifies four basic approaches to learning derived from learning preferences for that which is abstract or concrete, active or reflective:

Converger: Combines the abstract-conceptualization (thinkers) and active-experimentation (doers) learning orientations

Diverger: Combines the concrete-experience (feelers) and reflective observation (watchers) learning orientations

Assimilator: Combines the abstract-conceptualization (thinkers) and the reflective-observation (watchers) learning orientations

Accommodator: Combines the concrete-experience (feelers) and the active-experimentation (doers) learning orientations

Results from this instrument are instructive not only to faculty as they plan learning activities, but to first-year students themselves as they become aware of their own learning strengths and weaknesses.

The challenge to faculty in these differences is not to attempt the impossible task of meeting all of their students' preferences all of the time, but rather to offer a variety of activities and assignments so that students can expand their capacity to respond to different approaches and still have occasional opportunities to learn in the way they prefer.

Stages of Intellectual Development

Students also differ in their stage of intellectual development. Studying primarily male students, Perry (1970) determined that students' perceptions of knowledge, of the role of the teacher, and of themselves as learners changed during the college years and did so in predictable ways. Belenky, Clinchy, Goldberger, and Tarule (1986), whose subjects were mainly women, found predictable stages as well, with some significant differences for women. Because these developmental stages have important implications for learning and teaching, a brief review of the first three positions that these researchers identified follows:

• Dualism/received knowledge. Many students entering college define knowledge as information and facts. They view instructors as authorities, expect them to present information, and give high praise for instructors who "give good notes." They view learning as memorizing what the teacher and the text have said. Although they may find tasks calling for independent thought intriguing, in the end, many concur with the student who said, "Thinking is fine, but learning is what I'm here for" (Erickson & Strommer, 1991, p. 49). Faced with challenges to their views, such as disagreement among authorities or assignments requiring independent thinking, students gradually transform their assumptions.

• Multiplicity/subjective knowledge. Students begin to see that in some areas at least, there seems to be no "factual information" or "right answers." Their initial response is to conclude that one interpretation is as good as another so long as it makes sense to them. That belief does not get students very far with instructors, who ask for reasoned arguments, evidence, and documentation. Students adapt by concluding that college is really an academic game in which the rules emphasize support for interpretations and opinions. Faculty opinions are ultimately no more valid than theirs, but faculty know the rules of the game and students need to play by those rules. Ironically, what starts out as an academic game eventually prompts further transformation and development.

• Relativism/procedural knowledge. Challenged by evaluations of their own and others' thinking, students realize that some conclusions are indeed better than others because the evidence is stronger. They begin to recognize the complexity of the questions and challenges their instructors pose, and they see the need for systematic procedures for thinking through issues and supporting conclusions. They are ready and eager to learn the tools and procedures of the discipline.

Perry's work and subsequent research indicate that most first-year students hold views similar to those described in late-position dualism and multiplicity (see, for example, Baxter Magolda, 2002; Clinchy, 2002; King & Kitchener, 1994; Kurfiss, 1988). Faculty teaching first-year students may face students in each of the developmental stages or positions, however, and their reactions to assignments and activities will be mixed. Assignments that ask students to think independently may be criticized by students who expect instructors to tell them what they need to know, will be welcomed by students who believe their opinions are as good as anyone else's (but only until the assignments are returned with grades), and will be praised by those who are eager to develop skills for dealing with complex situations and problems. Activities such as small group discussions or group projects may bring similar mixed reviews. Students in early stages of intellectual development often view these as a waste of time because the instructor, not other students, knows the information to be learned. Students in later positions welcome opportunities to work with peers, but they often squander them because they assume at the outset that everyone's opinion is equally valid. Eventually students figure out that peers bring different perspectives and that together they can evaluate the soundness of each.

Because students in different developmental stages or positions define learning differently, virtually all of what we do in the name of instruction may garner mixed reviews and very different performances from students depending on their developmental positions. Many of our suggestions about using various teaching methods effectively are efforts to address the predictable responses of students in different developmental positions.

RESEARCH ON LEARNING

The evolving findings about the nature of the human brain and learning from the neurosciences and other disciplines such as cognitive psychology are rich, complex, and tentative. Thus far, however, these findings seem to confirm what we have learned from earlier research, particularly concerning the importance of engagement in learning, adequate time for each phase of information processing with plenty of practice, and a supportive, nonthreatening learning environment. Research-based principles for teaching, such as Chickering and Gamson's "Seven Principles for Good Practice in Undergraduate Education" (1987), and Angelo's "A 'Teacher's Dozen': Fourteen General, Research-Based Principles for Improving Higher Learning in Our Classrooms" (1993), provide useful guidance for the first-year classroom. Also provocative is what researchers have learned about what fosters deep or surface learning.

In 1976, two Swedish researchers, Marton and Säljö, conducted the first of a number of studies on student approaches to learning. They found a continuum of behaviors from deep to surface learning. Like subsequent researchers in Britain, Canada, and Australia, Marton and Säljö found that most of the university students they studied did not get the point of what they were studying "simply because they were not looking for it" (Rhem, 1995, p. 1). What they were doing instead was memorizing facts, concepts, or formulas because they knew that was what they would be tested for. The tests, in fact, signal exactly the level of understanding expected, and they were rewarded for this surface approach to learning. Ironically, those researchers also learned that as students move through education, they increasingly take a surface approach.

Characteristics of courses that prompt a surface approach to learning include (1) an excessive amount of course material, (2) lack of opportunity to pursue the subject in depth, (3) lack of choice over subjects and over the method of study, and (4) threatening and anxiety-provoking assessment (Rhem, 1995). Asking students to reproduce information rather than make sense of it tells them to take a surface approach to learning. One researcher has also found that anxiety, fear of failure, and low self-esteem are also associated with surface approaches to learning and urges faculty to help students take responsibility for their own learning (Marchese, 1997, p. 91).

What we want to foster is deep learning—learning in which students seek to understand the material, incorporating new ideas with existing knowledge and personal experience, to remember it, and to be able to use it. Deep learning is most likely to occur when we (1) help students discover an intrinsic motivation for learning, (2) provide guidance on how to approach the subject and become aware of how they learn, (3) build on students' prior experiences and knowledge (making sure that what they "know" is accurate), (4) connect abstractions to concrete activity, and (5) promote students' interaction with one another.

A CONCEPTUAL MODEL FOR TEACHING FIRST-YEAR STUDENTS

In some ways, teaching first-year students is much the same as teaching all other students. In other ways, they present instructional challenges that are unique to their readiness (or lack thereof) to learn. In 1991, in our book *Teaching College Freshmen,* we developed a way of conceptualizing teaching first-year students (Erickson & Strommer, 1991). We argued that effective instruction demands consistency among course goals, instructional activities, and evaluation procedures, and postulated that the goals for instruction of first-year students should be knowing, understanding, and thinking.

We defined *knowing* as memorizing course content. Unfortunately, for many first-year courses, "knowing" is all that happens, and students are tested almost entirely on their grasp of factual information. That notwithstanding, if first-year students are to think and organize their thoughts, they need something to think about and to think with. If students are to have the information available for thinking and problem solving, they must commit it to memory and be able to recall it when needed. We argued that practice is an important condition for all types of learning, including memorization, and that establishing connections between the information to be memorized and the knowledge students already possess is an important condition for remembering.

We defined *understanding* as the ability to recognize examples. When first-year students understand, they can see the relationships between specific instances and more general ideas. Examples and illustrations are critical because they provide keys to meaning. In addition, students need to practice recognizing or supplying examples and explaining how they represent general ideas. Unfortunately, practice that leads to understanding is all too often neglected in first-year classrooms. Faculty posing examples and students explaining how the examples relate to the concepts under study lead to greater understanding.

Finally, we defined *thinking* as applying what one has learned. It is one thing to be able to define a concept or to summarize a school of thought; it is quite another to recognize how these ideas look in specific situations and use what one has learned to solve problems. First-year students need to learn how to think about well-structured issues and problems as well as ones that are more ambiguous and unstructured. The challenge for faculty is to structure their classrooms in ways that get students to think as well as know and understand. (For suggestions on how to accomplish this task, see Erickson & Strommer, 1991.)

MAKING THE FIRST-YEAR CLASSROOM CONDUCIVE TO LEARNING

What once appeared as the most effective and efficient way to teach and learn—the research university model of faculty who create knowledge and deliver it to students through lectures—falters under today's learning demands and with today's students. While practically it may be too cost-effective an instructional method to abandon totally, the diversity of students in background and learning style, their developmental position, and what we know about human learning all argue for using classroom strategies that actively involve students. The few strategies we discuss here have proven powerful in working with first-year students, are adaptable to any size classroom and in any discipline, and are capable of being incorporated with lectures. (For more detailed guidance and suggestions for further alternatives to the lecture, we suggest Bean, 1996; Brookfield & Preskill, 1999; Davis, 1993; Erickson & Strommer, 1991; McKeachie, 1999; Menges & others, 1996).

Small Group Discussion Techniques

When we think about discussion methods, we often imagine a spirited exchange of ideas involving most, if not all, students in the class. In practice, this rarely happens, even in small classes. More often, the instructor talks most of the time, a few students participate in the discussion, and most others sit quietly, perhaps listening and thinking about what is said, perhaps not. At times, students may benefit from hearing the diversity of views expressed in whole class discussions even if they do not participate, but those benefits will be enhanced to the extent that all students voice their ideas either beforehand or afterward.

Dividing a class into small groups for discussion offers opportunities for more students to participate actively—to voice their ideas, receive feedback from peers, and clarify and refine their thinking. The technique works well as a warm-up for a whole class discussion, as an opportunity for students to react to issues under consideration, or as a follow-up to other class activities. Small group tasks also provide occasions for instructors to encourage deep processing of information and ideas. Instructors may, for example, ask small groups to review, paraphrase, and summarize; connect new information to prior learning; elaborate and extend by thinking of additional examples or contexts; and apply ideas and procedures to new problems.

The base groups recommended by Johnson, Johnson, and Smith (1991) are small groups whose membership is constant throughout the term. Students are assigned to groups at the beginning of the course, they sit together during classes, and they may meet outside class. In addition to the tasks outlined for ad hoc groups, instructors may ask base group members to assume a variety of support tasks—to check on the social and emotional well-being of their group members, make sure group members prepare for class, or contact any members who miss class, for example. Creating base groups is one way to minimize the sense of isolation and anonymity that first-year students often feel in large classes.

Study groups, which some students form spontaneously, also merit systematic attention and direction from faculty who teach first-year students. Research reported by Light (2001) found that students who met in small groups of four to six, even just once a week, to discuss their homework are "far more engaged and far better prepared, and they learn significantly more" (p. 52). The benefits of study groups in the sciences are even more striking: "Whether or not students work together in small study groups outside of class is the single best predictor of how many classes in science they will take. Those who do work in small groups take more science courses" (p. 74). In the light of these findings, faculty might not only encourage but actually help students form study groups, offer suggestions on what groups should do when they meet, design homework assignments with study groups in mind, and meet with study groups during office hours. Davis (1993) offers additional suggestions for setting up study groups.

In project groups, students are assigned to small groups for the purpose of completing one or more projects during the semester. Much of the group work is done outside class, although faculty working with first-year students often schedule periodic group meetings during class to help students get organized and to monitor progress. To work effectively, students in project groups must believe that it is to their advantage to work together rather than independently. Designing assignments that can be better done by groups than by individuals is therefore an important key to the success of project groups. Those who have used project groups also recommend that faculty (1) carefully explain the rationale for project groups, (2) describe how their work will be evaluated, (3) outline the responsibilities of individuals to their groups, (4) alert students to potential problems and ask groups to define ground rules for themselves, (5) provide strategies for groups to deal with uncooperative members, and (6) periodically invite students to evaluate the effectiveness of their own and others' contributions to the group. (For additional ideas about how to support students who, for whatever reasons—cultural background, learning style, previous unpleasant group experiences—have difficulty working in groups, see Bean, 1996; Erickson & Strommer, 1991; Brookfield & Preskill, 1999.)

Such small group activities can be incorporated into very large classes as well as small ones. Base groups or project groups connect students with one another and reduce the isolation of large classes. Stopping a lecture two or three times to have three or four students become an ad hoc group to find an additional example of a point being made, summarize the major theme of what has gone before, or otherwise engage in the material helps to lengthen their span of concentration and focus their attention. Writing-to-learn activities have a similar virtue.

Writing-to-Learn Activities

Traditionally, writing assignments assess what students have learned. Writing-to-learn serves a different purpose. In these exercises, students write to and for themselves in order to collect their thoughts and get them down on paper, where they can be examined and revised. Typically, writing-to-learn exercises are short: a few sentences, perhaps a paragraph or two. Although faculty often collect and skim what students have written in order to see what they are thinking, writing-to-learn exercises are usually not graded.

Writing-to-learn assignments, like small group discussion activities, can serve a variety of purposes. Beginning class, for example, by asking students to write a one-paragraph summary of the previous class helps to connect learning. Pausing periodically during lecture or discussion to ask students to summarize the main points helps avoid overloading working memory and keeps students actively involved. To prompt deeper processing of material, stop from time to time during class and ask students to jot down an example from their own experience, write about another context in which the material might apply, describe the way in which they would go about solving a problem, or react to an interpretation or conclusion. (For additional ideas see Bean, 1996; Sorcinelli & Elbow, 1997.)

Similar writing-to-learn assignments encourage more active and thorough reading of assignments outside class. Because paraphrasing is an important step toward processing information deeply, assignments that ask students to write summaries or explanations as if they were writing to a relative or to a friend are good prompts for deeper study. Depending on the nature of the reading, faculty might ask students to write about an experience they have had related to the reading, provide an example not discussed in the reading, imagine how the author might respond to a current event or issue, think of a possible exception to an author's ideas, or write questions they would like to ask the author. The possibilities are many; the idea is to move students beyond verbatim memorization to deeper processing of their reading. Bean (1996) devotes an entire chapter to using writing to help students read difficult texts.

Small group discussions and writing-to-learn activities provide a good beginning repertoire of instructional methods. Simply by changing the tasks and questions, both methods can involve students in practice for a variety of objectives. They are especially potent for encouraging students to process information more deeply. Even a two- or three-minute discussion or writing-to-learn activity engages students in paraphrasing, summarizing, or thinking of other examples. They work in any size class, even very large ones. By alternating these methods or using them in combination, we accommodate both students who learn by talking things through (extraverts) and students who prefer thinking things through before they engage in activity (introverts).

Other Instructional Techniques

Other dimensions of learning style merit attention and argue for expanding our repertoire of instructional methods. The extent to which students are interested in human or social activities is one such dimension. Research using both the Myers-Briggs Type Inventory (MBTI) and tests of field independence suggest that some people are more attuned to human or social aspects of the environment, more readily remember information about people and social issues, are more interested in learning things that will serve people, and make decisions by considering what's important to people.

Effective instruction addresses both the concrete and the abstract, but students have preferences for which should come first. Research using the MBTI shows that many people—two-thirds to three-quarters of the population, according to some estimates (Carskadon, 1994, p. 73)—prefer inductive approaches that move from the concrete to the abstract. In their study of women's intellectual development, Belenky et al. (1986) found similar concerns about the relationship between the concrete and abstract. They reported that most of their women subjects were adept at using abstractions, but many "balked when the abstractions preceded the experiences or pushed them out entirely" (p. 201).

Much instruction in higher education is conducted at an abstract level, disconnected from practice and experience and stripped of concerns about potential value. If we are to engage students, particularly first-year students, we need different approaches, especially approaches grounded in the concrete that enable students to learn in context. Case studies or scenarios and problem-based learning provide such grounding in a human context.

Case Studies and Scenarios

Case studies tell stories; scenarios present situations. Both have characters and actions, tensions and conflicts, problems and questions. They present relevant background, interactions, and the sequence of events up to the point requiring a decision or action. Good case studies or scenarios promote empathy with the central characters; students can see themselves in the situation or story. They also raise questions or issues that students are likely to care about and for which there is no obvious or clear-cut answer.

While writing cases and scenarios may require some skill in storytelling and dialogue, story outlines abound in newspapers, movies, television, the experiences of practitioners in our fields, and in campus life. Disciplinary journals often include cases. The Electronic Hallway (http://www.hallway.org) offers prepared cases focusing on public policy and public administration appropriate for many beginning social science courses. The National Center for Case Study Teaching in Science at the State University of New York at Buffalo (http://ublib.buffalo.edu/libraries/projects/cases/ubcase.htm) is a rich source for case studies in the sciences.

Two important considerations when using cases or scenarios with first-year students are the complexity of the case and the amount of guidance the instructor provides. Some cases and most scenarios are short—a page or two presenting a fairly structured problem. Others may be quite long, presenting complex stories with all the ambiguity and confusion of real life. Because we do not want to overwhelm students in their first encounters with case methods, it is best to start with shorter, focused cases and scenarios, though even first-year students can handle more complex cases if instructors provide questions and guidance that lead them through the analysis of the case. (For additional suggestions for teaching with cases, see Davis, 1993; Meyers & Jones, 1993; and Weaver, Kowalski, & Pfaller, 1994.)

Problem-Based Learning

Problem-based learning (PBL) uses many features of instruction discussed so far—small groups, learning in context, real and significant problems and issues to contemplate—but it literally turns instruction around. Instead of teaching students what they need to know and then posing problems or cases in which students explore implications and applications, PBL approaches begin with a problem, and the problem drives what students learn and in what order.

The instructor begins by presenting a problem to students. Compared to other problem-oriented approaches to instruction, PBL problems are ambiguous and unstructured. Not all the information needed is given in the problem or in the text; students must do research, discover new material, and make judgments. Most PBL problems contain controversial issues that elicit different opinions from students.

Working in permanently assigned small groups, students discuss the problem with the aim of determining what they already know that might be relevant to the problem and identifying learning issues: questions they need to address, information they need to gather, sources they wish to consult. Groups prioritize learning issues, divide responsibilities, and gather whatever information they believe they need. At an appointed time, often in class, students return to their groups and share what they have learned. Groups discuss what the new information means, identify further learning issues, and assign learning responsibilities for a second phase. Learning groups repeat the cycle, gradually shifting from assignments to acquire information to assignments to propose and defend solutions or courses of action, until the groups are ready (or required) to submit an analysis, proposal, or solution. (Sample PBL problems may be viewed at http://www.udel.edu/pbl/. More detailed discussions are available in Duch, Groh, & Allen, 2001; Wilkerson & Gijselaers, 1996.)

Experiential Learning

Experiential learning approaches—field studies, internships, student-faculty research projects, and service-learning—have been around for a long time. Their increasing appearance in first-year courses is, however, relatively new. Their power to motivate and engage students, integrate theory and practice, develop skills for independent study, and inspire interest in further learning are just as important for first-year students as for others.

Effective experiential learning approaches, like other instruction, should begin with learning goals and experiences identified and structured to serve those goals. Incorporating field experiences in first-year courses requires even more structure and guidance from faculty. We suggest that faculty (1) identify the field experience and make the necessary arrangements, (2) explicitly outline students' responsibilities, (3) require students to keep a journal or log and give specific assignments about what students should record, (4) create assignments that encourage students to reflect on their learning experiences, (5) provide regular opportunities for students to discuss their experiences either in small groups or in class, and (6) develop systematic ways to evaluate student learning from the field experience. (Davis, 1993, and McKeachie, 1999, offer additional suggestions.)

Learning About Content

"What about covering content?" some will ask. "If we incorporate active learning techniques plus try to teach learning strategies, will we be able to cover all the content in our courses?" We do not know the answer to that question. Perhaps if students develop more effective study strategies and discover deeper motivation for learning content, *they* will cover more of it. Then again, perhaps not. We believe, however, that it is folly to try to rush learning in the interest of covering content. Virtually everyone writing about learning research concludes students must be actively involved in all stages of the learning process: setting learning goals, acquiring information, connecting it to what they already know, organizing it in long-term memory, and identifying circumstances for retrieval and application in new situations. Those writing about brain research underscore the need to give learning time. The connections students make between new concepts and those they already know involve biological changes in the brain, changes that stabilize only with experience and repeated practice. (For a good introductory summary of the biological basis of learning and the implications for teaching first-year students especially, see Leamnson, 1999.) In short, for learning to last, the learner must be actively involved—and repeatedly so. That takes time.

RECOMMENDATIONS

While, unfortunately, no magic wand exists for us to induce learning in our students, they will learn more if we follow some basic principles. These recommendations can make a real difference in the classroom.

- *Explain why.* If we wish to help students become independent, lifelong learners, we need to help them understand both their own learning and the reasons that we ask them to learn in certain ways. They need to know, for example, why we ask them to work in small groups. Many are not keen on becoming involved in discussion and would prefer that faculty simply tell them what they need to know, either because they think they can learn best from the "authority" or because their focus is on extrinsic rewards. Whatever the source of students' reluctance to participate actively, it is often powerful. We cannot remind students too often that we believe what we teach in our courses is important, that we know their active involvement is key to their understanding, and that small group discussions or other activities that ask them to be actively involved will help them not only succeed in the course but also become more effective as learners.
- *Provide sufficient structure and practice.* It is almost impossible to give first-year students too much structure, whether it is in the form of a detailed course syllabus with sample exam questions or step-by-step guidance for reading a difficult text or working with a case. The same can be said for practice. Through practice in working with many examples, new applications, and real-world situations, students acquire deep rather than surface learning of new material. Excessive attention to covering content and neglect of sufficient practice are principal reasons that so much of what we learn is surface—quickly gained and more quickly forgotten.
- *Ground learning in the concrete.* Like the rest of us, students are most interested in those matters to which they can relate. Real-life experiences, stories, and concrete examples help to interest students in the material and hence motivate them.
- *Employ variety.* Sufficient variety of instructional strategies helps to maintain interest as well as appeal to the various learning strengths of a diverse class. A class that offers plenty of variety—writing, small group discussion, cases, projects—expands students' approaches to learning and increases their motivation.
- *Evaluate technology.* The same considerations need to apply to the use of technology as they do to any other teaching method. Software and other materials selected should be interactive, relate to real-world issues, foster interaction, and heighten student motivation.
- *Support faculty.* In describing the challenges and changes affecting the first-year classroom, we have implicitly noted both the importance and difficulty of teaching students in the first college year. Instructors—whether they

are full professors or graduate students—need and deserve institutional support in the form of time, resources, and assistance. They need help in knowing their students, in learning about the latest research on human learning and what works in the classroom, and support when they take risks with new ways of fostering student learning.

CONCLUSION

Many of the questions and issues surrounding teaching and learning in the first college year have not been addressed in this chapter. Given the diversity of institutions and college-going students in American higher education, and differences in disciplines and in faculty, many matters of interest have of necessity been omitted. Our focus has been on those challenges and constraints that have had the broadest impact on the first-year classroom and on a small group of teaching strategies of proven effectiveness that work with virtually all students. We urge readers to deepen their understanding of today's first-year classroom by sampling the rich literature on teaching and learning.

CHAPTER FIFTEEN

Faculty Development and the First Year

Scott E. Evenbeck
Barbara Jackson

The greatest single benefit of faculty development is the opportunity it affords for introspection—a chance to look at myself, my teaching practices, and the reasons I do what I do. More than anything else, faculty development interrupted my classroom tendency to autopilot. This is good for me and my students.
—Faculty member

Classroom instructors—whether tenured or tenure-track professors, lecturers, part-time or adjunct faculty, or graduate teaching assistants—are at the center of the collegiate experience for every first-year college student. More than any other group, faculty define the life of the college or university and should therefore be meaningfully involved in working with the newest persons joining the campus. Faculty have a unique role to play in demystifying the campus culture because they control the concepts inherent in higher education and are its central feature, apart from the students. If an institution is to serve first-year students in a way that is sustainable over time, faculty involvement and leadership are critical. As Siegel states in Chapter Ten, without the support and enthusiasm of the faculty, no first-year experience effort can enjoy long-term success.

Although instructors of first-year courses may include senior, junior, and part-time faculty, it is imperative that tenured or tenure-track faculty be in the mix and that they become involved not only in teaching but also in new student recruitment and orientation activities. Furthermore, in order to increase and improve faculty interaction with first-year students, institutions must commit to a higher level of faculty support. This support can come in many forms, including faculty development activities, resources, opportunities to engage in related communities of practice, and the campus reward structure.

Work with first-year students is often the ideal context for transforming faculty culture from what Barr and Tagg (1995) characterize as a culture of "teaching" to an emphasis on "teaching and learning." The pedagogical and curricular "solutions" to increasing the learning and persistence of first-year students are places where this transformation of faculty culture may be addressed. Working with first-year students may not be the primary context for work within a particular discipline, and for some faculty it may be perceived to conflict with their primary interest in research. But a focus on the first year may provide a "safe zone" where faculty are more prone to work together focused on students and their learning.

Boyer (1990) stressed teaching as a public activity. In many first-year initiatives such as learning communities, faculty team-teach or collaborate across disciplines as courses are linked, giving them multidisciplinary contexts within which to work together. Faculty in both learning communities and first-year seminars may often collaborate in instructional teams with librarians, advisers, student affairs professionals, or student mentors, again making teaching more of a public activity. The first year can also be a context for faculty development in terms of Boyer's (1990) articulation of different forms of scholarship, especially the scholarship of teaching.

In Chapter Fourteen, Erickson and Strommer provide information on changing student characteristics, including modes of learning and stages of intellectual development, that will be helpful to faculty working with first-year students, along with some specific teaching tips. But what about the faculty themselves? What about their involvement and development? And given the demonstrated correlation between faculty-student engagement and both student retention and academic engagement (see Chapters Two and Five), how can an institution harness the support and enthusiasm of faculty to become more engaged with first-year students, both in and out of class? This chapter will review the well-documented challenges faced by colleges and universities in providing an effective learning environment for contemporary first-year students. We suggest that the current environment also presents some remarkable opportunities for faculty development in the service of educational reforms for first-year students. From this perspective some general principles of faculty development that serve this work will be articulated. Using Indiana University Purdue University Indianapolis (IUPUI) as a case study example we will demonstrate how these general principles can be translated into effective practices, which intentionally link faculty development with first-year initiatives in a mutually supportive relationship.

CHALLENGES OF WORKING WITH FIRST-YEAR STUDENTS

The challenges of working with today's first-year students have been well documented in specific areas.

Academic Preparation of Students

Increased participation rates in postsecondary education coupled with society's expectations for student success and retention have resulted in significant demands on and challenges to faculty working with first-year students. As an increased proportion of high school graduates attends college, a decreased proportion will have completed the college preparatory curriculum appropriate for success in college (Levine & Cureton, 1998b). First-time adult students may also lack the academic preparation and confidence needed for college-level study (McGrath, 1996). State and national studies (Callan & Finney, 2003) have called attention to the roles of the individual states in preparing an increasingly diverse population of students for postsecondary education. Faculty, who are primarily male and Caucasian (Chronicle of Higher Education, 2003), are faced with the challenges of teaching students who are different from themselves in demographic characteristics, learning styles, attitudes toward the importance of learning, or preparation for academic success. This gap is then heightened by students' reported increase in hours devoted to passive activities such as watching television or hours per week working off campus (Chronicle of Higher Education, 2003).

Disconnect Between Prior Experiences and College

Many students who have completed college preparatory curricula in high school or pass high school graduation examinations (increasingly becoming a mandate by states attempting to raise levels of educational attainment) enter postsecondary education and are placed into remedial courses. The need for remediation also affects adult students, who may have worked for many years and may find that their academic skills have become rusty. Some 28 percent of entering students take at least one remedial course (most often in mathematics) when beginning postsecondary education (Parsad, Lewis, & Greene, 2003).

The disconnect between high school and college learning can be addressed by finding contexts for high school and college instructors to share their expectations for student learning. In central Indiana, Project SEAM, funded by the Lilly Endowment, gives teachers in science, language arts, and mathematics effective structures for such conversations. Among the results was the identification of the common high school practice of moving from writing to literature as the focus for language arts in the senior year. Yet when students enter college, composition is the most common English course. Participants in this project agreed that a better approach would be to continue a strong emphasis on writing in the senior year that would connect with the first year of college. In the same project, high school and college biology teachers rated the importance of what to include in the curriculum and found little connection between high school and college curricula.

While national and state-level conversations and mandates are serving as a catalyst for clearer definitions of student learning and the assessment of that learning, we believe there is no substitute for direct conversations between high school teachers and college faculty, centered on students in particular areas or regions and focused on enhancing the transition from high school to college.

Culture of the Academy

A third challenge for faculty who teach first-year students is the overriding culture of the academy and, in some cases, the institution itself. The *Greater Expectations* report (Association of American Colleges and Universities, 2002) argues that "faculty members feel the strongest attachments to their disciplines, the weakest to the institution as a whole. The departmental structure reinforces the atomization of the curriculum by dividing knowledge into distinct fields, even though scholarship, learning, and life have no such artificial boundaries" (p. 16). On some campuses, especially in the research university sector, teaching first-year students may not be an activity that is valued by academic departments. And on large campuses, limited resources may result in decisions to create introductory classes with hundreds of students and to employ a disproportionately high number of adjuncts or graduate teaching assistants as instructors in introductory courses.

OPPORTUNITIES IN WORKING WITH FIRST-YEAR STUDENTS

These challenges facing faculty and administrators, while daunting, also present some remarkable opportunities for professional development in the service of educational reforms for first-year students. National conversations and multicampus initiatives have resulted in increased institutional awareness of effective strategies for supporting student learning in the first year. Colleges and universities, even in an era of scarce resources, are finding ways to support faculty development and engagement in first-year efforts at both departmental and campuswide levels. While the issues of academic culture can pose barriers to the creation of better learning environments for first-year students, faculty enthusiasm can be marshaled by appealing to fundamental faculty values. For example, the enthusiasm among faculty for learning communities and first-year seminars, cited by Hunter and Linder in Chapter Sixteen, Laufgraben in Chapter Twenty-Two, and Evenbeck, Jackson, and McGrew (1999), relates to the success of faculty in creating new opportunities to enhance student learning, especially around issues of improving academic standards and inculcating a passion for learning.

Some general frameworks for articulating the significance of faculty involvement in first-year initiatives and for engaging faculty creativity and energy include the "fresh slate" perspective, defining and assessing learning outcomes, and foundation for the major.

The "Fresh Slate" Perspective

Complaints about the "declining quality of students" in regard to academic preparation, motivation to learn, and lack of understanding of collegiate-level expectations have become an unfortunate, widely held feature of contemporary faculty worldview. In contrast, recent research, reviewed in Chapter Six by Schilling and Schilling, finds that for some students, college life is less challenging and less engaging than these students expected. While not denying the enormous diversity in academic preparation of today's first-year students, we would like to suggest a paradigm shift: instead of focusing on students' "underpreparation" and "lack of motivation," we invite faculty to see first-year students as "fresh slates" who can be transformed into the kind of learners we want them to be. Through orientation programs and first-year seminars, faculty have the opportunity to set the bar high and establish challenging expectations for all students. Faculty can be engaged, with appropriate support, to see students' academic needs as an opportunity to teach them the strategies of active learning, critical thinking, forming community around academics, integrating knowledge, and valuing diverse perspectives, along with the skills for managing time, difficult reading, and the use of new technologies. Rather than blaming high schools and parents for not doing the job, faculty must be encouraged to accept this challenge and embrace it as a faculty responsibility.

Defining and Assessing Learning Outcomes

Conversations within institutions about general education, while often highly political and contentious, can be effective vehicles for cross-disciplinary interaction around strategies for improving and assessing student learning in the first year. In attempting to build consensus among faculty from diverse disciplines about the desired learning outcomes for all students, faculty are enabled to see first-year students in a more comprehensive way beyond the context of their particular disciplines. Defining learning outcomes is an important step in developing comprehensive assessment of student knowledge and academic abilities. Faculty at many institutions are engaged in developing benchmarks, e-portfolios, and other mechanisms for documenting student accomplishments that extend beyond the content of specific disciplines (Hamilton, 2004). Defining learning outcomes with regard to core communication skills, critical thinking, quantitative literacy, values, and ethics can be an important framework for enhancing faculty engagement with the first year.

Foundation for the Major

Appealing to the interest that departments, as well as individual faculty, have in producing students who complete their major requirements and succeed in postgraduate studies and careers is an effective strategy for gaining faculty support for first-year initiatives. Faculty involvement in first-year seminars, developmental education, improving general education courses, and academic support programs will be viewed as much more meaningful when it is perceived as an opportunity for building connections to and a better foundation for work in the major.

GENERAL PRINCIPLES OF FACULTY DEVELOPMENT

The faculty culture values evidence, and many faculty will demand evidence of effectiveness before committing to any new activity. Therefore, before beginning a faculty development program, it may be helpful to direct faculty to journals, books, and Web sites that address the planning, implementation, and assessment of faculty development activities. Schön (1983) and Brookfield

(1995) have clearly articulated the importance of faculty intentionality and reflection about their work. Angelo and Cross (1993) have provided useful tools for ongoing assessment and feedback, not only for students but also for faculty. Partly driven by the unfolding uses of technology, many campuses now have centers for teaching and learning. The Professional and Organizational Development Network is a national organization with many resources to support faculty development. In terms of preparing faculty to teach and interact with first-year students, we suggest five faculty development principles.

Faculty Direction and Ownership

Faculty must own and direct work with first-year students. In Chapter Ten, Siegel observes that faculty who work with first-year students, particularly in first-year seminar courses, have the opportunity to think more carefully about the college experience as a whole rather than from the point of view of a single department. This hands-on involvement of faculty with entering students is a key principle of faculty development. In involving the faculty, work with first-year students should be developed within the institutional context, within structures that fit the particular campus. Angelo (2003) states, "We might begin by asking how well what we are envisioning fits within the institutional structure and agenda, as well as how it fits into the existing systems of faculty roles and rewards and of students' academic careers" (p. 99). Angelo sees departments "as the most promising units of instructional reform, and heads of departments as the natural leaders in transforming departmental culture" (p. 99). He adds that "experience shows that most successful academic innovations take years to bear fruit. . . . We can begin by sharing examples of successful teaching experiences, definitions of meaningful learning, and examples of exemplary student work. . . . We can work with faculty to develop a shared vision of what students should know and be able to do at the end of a course, a sequence, or the major" (pp. 109–110).

Campuses must not limit faculty development support to full-time or tenured faculty. Rather, institutions must also support part-time faculty and graduate assistants who teach first-year students. Recent data indicate that campuses have expanded the use of part-time faculty (Chronicle of Higher Education, 2003), and that trend is likely to continue. Therefore, institutions that use part-time or untenured lecturers must ensure that these individuals are made true citizens of the campus by including them in ongoing faculty development activities. Laufgraben (2003), for example, reports on the evolution of a faculty development program designed largely for graduate assistants and part-time faculty teaching in learning communities. She describes moving from the "early stage" through a "building stage" to a "community stage" and ultimately to a "sustaining and improving stage" (p. 33), and she outlines the programs and activities helpful in sustaining the program, including workshops, a faculty handbook, and ongoing attention to the curriculum.

If the only faculty working with first-year students are part-timers, untenured lecturers, or graduate students, first-year instruction is marginalized. In our experience, the stigmatization of persons who are themselves marginal in the academy affects not only those persons but also their students. Therefore, we believe that it is imperative that full-time tenure-track faculty be directly engaged in teaching and out-of-class interaction with first-year students.

Strong and Sustained Institutional Support

Sustained leadership is a critical context for faculty work with first-year students. Gardner (2003) has characterized institutions successful in serving entering students as those with sustained leadership and a structural means of bringing together services for first-year students. In Chapter Nine, Natalicio and Smith also state that sustained executive leadership is critical in supporting entering students. On some campuses, senior administrators, eager to move up in the national higher education rankings, chose to focus their attention elsewhere—to developing the institution's research capacity or excellence in graduate and professional education—not the experience of first-year students. But Chapter Nine details the experience at the University of Texas at El Paso, where research excellence and attention to first-year students exist side by side. In Chapter Ten, Siegel argues that a president must convince faculty members of the many possibilities for professional renewal in the first-year experience and that teaching first-year courses and participating in related programs will be rewarded in relation to tenure and promotion.

Addressing All Aspects of Faculty Work

All aspects of faculty life and work should be examined in relation to work with first-year students. Faculty will want to know whether the institution considers research on student success as scholarship, whether involving students in civic engagement activities is considered as service, and whether out-of-class involvement with students counts as teaching or service. Work with first-year students should not be an add-on but, rather, central to faculty life and work for at least a portion of the faculty or a portion of the time of all faculty.

An External Context

A key principle of faculty development is to provide opportunities on campus for those working with first-year students to be engaged with and learn from one another. But institutions should also provide faculty an opportunity to reflect on their work with faculty and staff members from other campuses. Faculty professional life is grounded in the disciplines, and through journals and conferences many faculty find meaning, affirmation, and grounding by communicating with their peers. If work with entering students is to come to life for faculty, these contexts must be available: journals, listservs, professional meetings, networks, and so on. Faculty know they are doing well by the professional affirmation of such participation.

While work with first-year students can happen in a disciplinary gathering, we have found that it is even more powerful when faculty across disciplines can gather to share ideas, publish, and reflect. For years, the conferences sponsored by the National Resource Center for The First-Year Experience and Students in Transition have served as opportunities for faculty and other academic professionals to experience a national and international context for their work with first-year students. In Indiana and other states, statewide gatherings have provided a similar nexus for activity. It is critical that faculty working with first-year students have these contexts for focusing on issues related to teaching and engaging them.

Communities of Practice

In a recent article, Chism, Lees, and Evenbeck (2002) cite the work of Wenger (1998) and Wenger, McDermott, and Snyder (2002) in describing "communities of practice." Communities of practice are defined as "groups of people who share a concern, a set of problems, or a passion about a topic, and who deepen their knowledge and expertise in this area by interacting on an ongoing basis" (Wenger et al., 2002, p. 4). In our experience, such communities are central to faculty development as they provide faculty a campus-based means to work together with others who also serve first-year students.

For example, team teaching with a librarian can provide faculty with new perspectives on student learning. Librarians often have a vast repository of knowledge about how students hear and interpret their research assignments. Often there are few means or contexts for librarians to feed that information back to faculty. But by working in communities of practice with librarians, faculty have the opportunity to alter their assignments as a function of what they learn. Particularly in an era of greatly expanded use of technology, the lessons faculty can learn about both increasing their own technical and information literacy and approaching these topics with students can be invaluable. (Additional suggestions for meaningful integration of the library into the first year can be found in Chapter Twenty.)

Faculty who teach with advisers have the opportunity to gain a more comprehensive view of students' lives and choices. Many faculty still view advising as course selection and do not understand the ongoing debates within the advising community about "prescriptive" versus "developmental" advising (Crookston, 1994) and the importance that students and advisers place on advising (Light, 2001). Advisers have contexts for ongoing relationships with students, advising them over time to make informed choices. A prominent dean on one campus, after coteaching a first-year seminar with an adviser, reflected at the end of the term that he had not known that advisers were also teachers. His gestalt for the work of advisers had been transformed because he saw clearly what advisers do with students. Advisers also benefit from this kind of collaboration. They learn more about life within the classroom and are not reliant only on student reports.

On many campuses, student affairs professionals who work with leadership and diversity programs and other efforts to support student learning outside the classroom are separated from the core classroom experiences. How much more powerful their work would be if these out-of-class activities could be linked with learning inside the classroom. If student affairs professionals are part of instructional teams with faculty, this transformation is more likely to occur.

Most important, perhaps, of the potential "co-teachers" are the students themselves. Research finds that students themselves are the most powerful means of reaching and teaching other students (Martin & Arendale, 1993). When a student is a mentor or a coteacher within a classroom setting or in a setting closely aligned with the classroom, it is possible to foster a peer culture based on learning.

BEST PRACTICES: A CASE STUDY

In this section we present some specific practices that, when taken together, describe a strategy for intentionally linking faculty development and first-year initiatives. These practices were derived from the five faculty development principles we have set out as they have been implemented at Indiana University Purdue University, Indianapolis (IUPUI). IUPUI is a highly diverse research institution with large numbers of both underprepared and commuting students. In fall 2003, 43 percent of IUPUI's entering students began with conditional admission, and 62 percent of the students were first generation.

IUPUI's first-year practices include the following: a first-year seminar, learning communities, a critical inquiry course designed to be a mechanism for academic support, various structures for faculty ownership and direct involvement in the first year, and provision of national platforms for faculty work. While we acknowledge that this case study describes the actions taken by only one urban university, we believe that our experience and lessons learned are broadly applicable to all colleges and universities whether large or small, two-year or four-year, selective or nonselective.

Principle l: Faculty Direction and Ownership

Faculty direction and ownership of programs for first-year students has guided the intentional focus on enhancing student experience in the first year at IUPUI. This began in 1995 with our first efforts at offering a first-year seminar course. Seven core faculty were given the broad charge to develop interventions that would support the transition to college for new students. Their first step was development of a first-year seminar designed to address the transitional needs of IUPUI first-year students. These faculty members were provided with access to national resources (especially literature and activities from the National Resource Center for The First-Year Experience and Students in Transition) and sufficient release time for brainstorming, reflective meetings, and retreats. Their creative energies and experimentation with some pilot initiatives resulted in the development of a unique model, appropriate to IUPUI student needs and institutional context: a learning community formed by linking a first-year seminar with one of several first-semester general education courses.

An innovative feature of this learning community is that instructional responsibility is situated in a team composed of a faculty member, adviser, peer mentor, and librarian. The campus's overwhelming acceptance of this format, with the number of seminar sections increasing from seven to over one hundred in two years, is directly related to faculty direction and involvement in its development. Ongoing faculty engagement in our learning community/first-year seminar format is affirmed through the use of *A Template for First-Year Seminars,* a document that identifies common learning outcomes and required pedagogies and provides a consistent framework for all of the school-specific versions of the seminar. The template is regularly reviewed and modified by a faculty committee. IUPUI first-year seminars have been designed to support student transition to the university environment. They provide students with the opportunity to develop a comprehensive perspective on higher education; establish networks of staff, faculty, and other students; understand their own abilities and goals; practice skills required for academic success; and make full use of IUPUI resources in support of their learning.

The strategy of involving faculty decision making from initial conception through implementation of first-year initiatives was replicated in the development of another recent signature program that addressed the academic development needs of entering students, the Critical Inquiry course. Responding to the campus request that University College, IUPUI's academic point of entry for all first-year students, develop an improved academic support intervention to replace its traditional program of reading and study skills, the dean of University College appointed a transitional education task force in 1999 to examine national best practices and recommend a new program for IUPUI, appropriate to our institutional context. This task force reviewed the literature, employed consultants, and made site visits to selected peer institutions. Task force recommendations resulted in the development of Critical Inquiry, a variable one- to two-credit-hour course "attachment" designed to be compatible with almost any introductory discipline-based course. Open to all, but strongly recommended for first- and second-year students, sections of Critical Inquiry help students learn to read, write, and think critically within a specific discipline and to experience academic growth and success in the linked course. Students are expected to attain and enhance collegiate reading, thinking, and communications skills that are transferable to the rest of their course work.

The mandate to proceed with pilots and subsequent assessment was affirmed by the University College faculty who have grassroots knowledge of both the learning challenges and opportunities inherent in working with first-year students. This success of the Critical Inquiry course may be seen in student academic achievement and the receptivity of departments in offering the general education courses that Critical Inquiry is designed to support. As the course now moves from pilot phase to institutionalization, departments and faculty are enthusiastic about the results and are requesting that Critical Inquiry be added to additional sections of first-year courses.

This principle of establishing faculty as the critical voice in decision making about educational reforms for the first year was also invoked as the campus collectively attempted to deal with the fact that many of our first-year, or gateway, courses were characterized by an unacceptable lack of student success. IUPUI's definition of "unacceptable" is a 30 percent or more rate of D, F, or withdrawal from a particular class. This definition, consistent with Martin and Arendale's (1993) determination of a "high-risk" course, has served as an important benchmark.

While conversations about how to deal with this complex and pervasive problem were encouraged at every administrative level, from departments and programs to the chancellor's cabinet, primary responsibility for leadership in problem solving was given to a new group, the Gateway Group, composed of faculty leaders from departments offering gateway courses. Support for retreats, research, grants, and public meetings is provided jointly by University College and the Office of Professional Development. This group has provided new ideas for all departments, communicating information about effective and transferable practices in particular departments, and stimulating campuswide public conversations about issues of pedagogy, student support, academic policy, and use of resources.

The Gateway Group has implemented changes in pedagogy, course content, use of academic support, and administrative policies that have resulted in substantial improvements in student success in gateway courses. In mathematics, for example, with a large service component and large-enrollment, multisection courses, the Gateway Group has been most beneficial in providing funds for the course coordinators to conduct professional development meetings once every semester. These meetings provide an opportunity for all of the instructors teaching the same course to gather and explore different pedagogical approaches. Coupled with the opening of the Mathematics Assistance Center and other academic support programs, the department has recorded marked improvement in student academic achievement. In 2002, the Gateway Group received national recognition as the recipient of a Theodore M. Hesburgh Certificate of Excellence Award as an outstanding example of faculty development.

Connecting sections of gateway courses to Critical Inquiry has also given faculty a fresh look at student learning in a broader context, thus providing a new perspective on the content of these courses. It has created opportunities to connect content learning to broader learning goals for students, including information literacy, enhanced critical thinking abilities, and other skills that serve and support their majors.

Principle 2: Strong and Sustained Institutional Support

Strong and sustained institutional support, including the creation of a culture that puts the experience of first-year students at the center of the institutional mission, has been a feature of faculty development activities at IUPUI. Undoubtedly, IUPUI's signature action symbolizing its support for first-year students was the establishment of the University College with a distinguished appointed faculty. All appointed faculty agree to provide leadership for the student-centered principles on which University College was founded and to support and promote the unit and its programs.

The appointment of forty senior faculty to University College who represent all the degree-granting schools at IUPUI proclaimed the seriousness of the institution's commitment to first-year students, created a powerful faculty resource for the effort, and paved the way for faculty to learn and develop as teachers and researchers focused on the first year. In addition to these appointments, campus leaders recognized that an adequate resource base for the University College faculty's engagement with first-year initiatives was essential. The university's strategic planning process linked budget allocations with university priorities. Internal funds, coupled with external grant funds, provided an initial base of resources to support the initiatives designed for entering students; later allocations from the university's board of trustees replaced and extended the external resources, thereby confirming the institution's commitment to supporting student academic achievement and persistence.

University College, through its Faculty Fellowship Program, has designed Scholarship of Teaching projects that support both institutional assessment and data collection needs, as well as opportunities for faculty to expand professionally. Projects that have involved faculty in research and the scholarship of teaching about the first year include a review of documents and activities, including *A Template for First-Year Seminars*; assessment of new student orientation; use of mentors in first-year seminars; the role of advisers in University College; support for collegiate-level reading, thinking, and communication; and development of themed learning communities. Generous and continual support for national conference attendance; participation in summer institutes sponsored by the American Association for Higher Education, the Association of American Colleges and Universities, and the Washington Center for Undergraduate Education; and local reflective activities, including retreats and town hall meetings, have sustained faculty involvement.

The faculty fellowship program has resulted in the enhancement of teaching, service, and research accomplishments in annual reviews and promotion and tenure dossiers. Stipends for faculty fellowship research activities have been structured so that there are opportunities for funding course releases or reducing the need for summer session teaching to permit support for discipline-related research.

Departmentally based faculty work related to the first year has been supported by both University College and the Office of Professional Development. This support has been in the form of grants for enhancing school-level learning communities and first-year seminars and improving pedagogy and academic support in large first-year courses, as well as stipends for faculty who wish to link their course with Critical Inquiry. There is now a large IUPUI faculty cohort that has moved from a knowledge base of first-year students that is limited to their departmental activities to one that is actively conversant with issues at a campus and national level.

Principle 3: Addressing All Aspects of Faculty Work

In order to secure full engagement in first-year initiatives from a wide variety of faculty, it has been our experience that professional development related to these initiatives must be couched comprehensively in terms of the third principle, addressing all aspects of faculty work—research and service, as well as teaching. As Angelo (2000) notes, "Most American academic change efforts have not acknowledged or addressed the legitimate reasons faculty have for resisting change" (p. 98). Effective programs that seek to place faculty at the center of first-year initiatives must address the fear that "attempts to increase productivity and promote learning-centered practice will undermine scholarship" and make good on the promise that "attention to teaching and learning will lead to more rewards or recognition" (p. 98).

At IUPUI we have sought to encourage a wide array of professional development activities appropriate to particular faculty, their disciplines, and departmental or program needs. Most often these are task based and reflective, and they may involve mentoring and the conduct of traditional research. Where possible, we have tried to align the products and outcomes of involvement in first-year initiatives with the traditional academic reward structure, and we have attempted to make the work and rewards sufficiently flexible to support the discipline-based expectations for teaching, research, and service.

The charter document, "Defining the Roles, Responsibilities and Recognition for University College Faculty," articulates this perspective. In addition to agreeing to provide campus leadership in support of University College and its programs, appointment to the University College faculty includes the expectation that each member will also assume a set of unique responsibilities reflecting their individual interests and expertise in support of current University College needs and priorities. Some examples of these, organized along the lines of traditional faculty roles, include:

Service—serve on standing and ad hoc committees that set policy, conduct faculty governance, and contribute to the administration and program implementation of University College

Teaching—teach and serve as a resource for University College First-Year Seminars and the Critical Inquiry course

Research—contribute to the development, maintenance, and analysis of information on University College students related to assessment of University College in fulfilling its stated mission; design, conduct, and disseminate research that informs the development of the first-year studies curriculum at IUPUI, promotes the improvement of undergraduate learning, and relates to the assessment of University College programs, faculty, and staff

The definition of what it means to be appointed as University College Faculty is framed with reference to membership in the graduate school: it is conferred in recognition of established accomplishment and commitment to entering students. Annual stipends for University College faculty may be used for any legitimate professional development activity, not solely those related to first-year programs.

Principle 4: Strong National Context

We have tried to adhere to principle 4 by providing a strong national context for faculty involvement with first-year initiatives. This has provided external validation, the opportunity to establish benchmarks for our programs, support for innovators, and familiarity with models found to be effective elsewhere that can be adapted to our institutional context. Strategies for providing national exposure include attendance at major national conferences, participation in multi-institutional-funded projects, site visits to peer institutions, judicious use of consultants and speakers, and access to national resource centers.

Our first-year seminar program has become a model for using multiple national resources to support faculty in programmatic development. We began with a presentation by John Gardner in 1992 at an annual campus teaching symposium. This was followed by attendance at a national First-Year Experience Conference by faculty who had been charged with designing a first-year experience appropriate to IUPUI. Ongoing communication with the staff at the National Resource Center for The First-Year Experience and Students in Transition was an invaluable source of support in the early stages of developing the seminar. Contact, including site visits, with regional peers such as Northern Kentucky University, University of Cincinnati, and Indiana University Kokomo, provided a holistic view of programs in action, as well as access to a broader spectrum of faculty issues and concerns.

Participation in the Re-Structuring for Urban Student Success (RUSS) project, funded by The Pew Charitable Trusts, allowed us to develop a community of practice that extended beyond our own institutional boundaries. This partnership with Temple University and Portland State University provided a close and ongoing view of programs and assessment at two peer institutions. It also provided an ongoing source of peer consultation and national perspective from individuals who had become very familiar with our programs and institution. A key element in the establishment of our model of the first-year seminar (including instructional teams and links to form learning communities) was the RUSS self-study, followed by an external program review by a distinguished panel of national leaders. This year-long enterprise, which brought campus focus and attention to our first-year initiatives, helped us identify the strongest elements of our program as well as make recommendations for change.

As faculty began to develop a more comprehensive plan for supporting students in their first year at IUPUI, it was clear that providing a sense of community with peers, faculty, and others was critical to our commuting, largely first-generation student body. We therefore began to consider ways of incorporating learning communities for first-year students. The Washington Center for Improving the Quality of Undergraduate Education has been a source of ongoing support for this effort, identifying a range of models and pedagogies for linking courses and integrating learning experiences. Through the Washington Center, we were able to establish national and regional peer support networks, in particular institutions involved in the annual Learning Communities and Collaboration Conference. This event provided an important forum for garnering new ideas and best practices from peers, as well as informed feedback on our own faculty's presentations. Our faculty's involvement with this conference has been transformed from simple participation to becoming one of four institutional cosponsors. This role includes annual involvement in program planning as well as rotational hosting of the conference. The American Association for Higher Education's annual Summer Academy is another venue that has provided a national context for faculty development focused on learning communities.

In 2001 the faculty affirmed the need to expand our learning communities (which at that time consisted of two linked courses: the first-year seminar and a general education or "introduction to the major" course) to the next level: the linking and integrating of three or more courses. The challenges of developing and implementing this model at IUPUI have been daunting and have run the gamut from schedule coordination complexities, to inadequate registration technology, to difficulties in facilitating faculty communication, to meeting varying student curriculum requirements. However, with the help of the Washington Center, we have successfully addressed most administrative and curriculum integration issues; seven thematic learning communities, each comprising at least three courses, were piloted in fall 2003.

Faculty development for several of our major programs of academic support has been enhanced by participation in two Fund for the Improvement of Postsecondary Education (FIPSE) dissemination projects. Our Critical Inquiry course and Summer Academy Summer Bridge Program represent an IUPUI adaptation of the "transportable elements" specified by Brooklyn College's Developmental Education Program III: Disseminating "Making the Core Curriculum a Reality for Disadvantaged Students." Structured learning assistance, a variation of Supplemental Instruction that requires students to attend supplemental class sessions, is an award-winning model of academic support developed at Ferris State University. The invitation to participate in these dissemination projects has resulted in an IUPUI program that uses the foundational aspects of structured learning assistance, but has been adapted to use peer mentors in its delivery. Both FIPSE projects have brought national experts to meet and train IUPUI faculty, and have created opportunities for faculty to participate in retreats and training sessions with other grant participants.

Principle 5: Communities of Practice

Collaboration is a learning strategy that is as powerful for faculty as it is for students. A foundational element for any successful faculty development program is building and supporting communities of practice centered on the first year. Administrative support for local communities of practice is essential and should address mechanisms for defining the community's focus, communication, campus identity, appropriate events, reflection, and presentations at the local level and beyond.

At IUPUI our strongest and largest community of practice is related to our most established first-year initiative: the first-year seminar learning community. Connection and dialogue among faculty, advisers, librarians, and student mentors who participate on the instructional teams are maintained through a variety of mechanisms. The "charter" of this community of practice is the *Template for First-Year Seminars,* which articulates all common agreements about the nature, learning outcomes, and appropriate pedagogies for all first-semester learning communities across all schools and departments. Conversations among practitioners about needed changes or enhancements based on assessment data are conducted in the context of the University College Curriculum Committee and the Learning Communities Network, composed of faculty administrators from each unit offering the seminars. An annual Learning Community Colloquium is held each spring, with special sessions for new instructional team members, speakers and workshops on key topics, and poster session opportunities for cross-campus sharing of innovations (such as on-line learning communities) and best practices.

The Gateway Group, from its comprehensive perspective on general education courses taken by first-year students, has encouraged the formation of communities of practice among faculty within and across departments. These communities focus on specific issues of pedagogy and policy affecting first-year curriculum and students. Examples of such communities of practice include those formed around "just-in-time" teaching (Novak, Patterson, Gavrin, & Christian, 1999) and the use of various forms of peer mentoring. Novak and colleagues describe just-in-time teaching as a technique that combines "a collaborative learning environment with extensive use of the World Wide Web. Active learner assignments and enrichment materials are delivered to the students over the Web with electronic responses to these assignments. A subset of these electronic submissions provides immediate feedback to the instructors concerning the state of the class's progress. These assignments, due in the morning a few hours before class, are used to adjust the classroom activities to suit the students' needs" (p. 1). We have found that just-in-time teaching improves both student morale and performance.

RECOMMENDATIONS

In this chapter we argue that because faculty define the central purpose of a college or university, they have a critical role to play in molding the experience of first-year students. And we maintain that faculty need and can benefit from the assistance and support coming from targeted "first-year" faculty development activities. Our experience here at IUPUI and our collaboration with others around the country lead us to offer these recommendations.

  • *Create strong links between campus faculty development resources and first-year programs.* Administrators should support collaboration between units that support professional development and those with first-year program responsibilities. Joint activities may include targeted, specified grants and incentives to involve faculty in research and scholarship-of-teaching projects related to first-year initiatives.

- *Engage faculty in all phases of first-year programs.* The strategy of involving faculty in decision making from initial conception through implementation and assessment ensures that first-year initiatives are central to ensuring faculty ownership and involvement, and to guaranteeing that faculty bring the same creativity and enthusiasm to questions of supporting student learning, especially for first-year students, that they traditionally have brought to research and teaching. Faculty may not be in a position to make structural changes, but they are in a position to study change, recommend change, and become advocates for changing systems, practices, or processes that are not serving students well.

- *Provide links to national peers.* Attendance at national conferences, participation of teams in summer institutes, site visits to peers, use of consultants, and collaboration with peers in multi-institutional-funded projects provide external validation, the opportunity to establish program benchmarks, and support for local innovators.

- *Support the formation of local communities of practice.* Administrative support for collaboration among individuals and units involved in or with common interests in specific first-year program aspects (writing, mathematics, learning communities, first-year seminars) is an important strategy for program development and sustainability.

- *Align products and outcomes with the traditional academic reward structure.* While a long-term goal of educational reform is to change the reward structure of the academy to value contributions to first-year student learning, faculty live with the reality of the current culture. In linking faculty to first-year initiatives, we must, wherever possible, structure the work and rewards to fit discipline-based expectations for teaching, research, and service.

- *Support a wide array of activities for faculty development.* Engagement points with programs for first-year students differ widely among faculty. Opportunities appropriate to particular faculty, disciplines, and program needs must be designed. These should include activities that are task based and reflective, and involve mentoring and the conduct of traditional research.

- *Celebrate positive outcomes of faculty development related to first-year initiatives.* Public recognition for faculty efforts and programmatic success should be vigorously pursued as a significant reward for faculty involvement. Strategies include individual nominations for existing campus teaching and service awards, institutional nominations for regional and national awards, communication of positive assessment outcomes in campus and community media, and the creation of special recognition opportunities and symbols of affiliation with first-year programs.

CONCLUSION

This chapter has sought to connect some established principles of effective faculty development with the challenges and opportunities of supporting the learning of students as they make the transition to college in the first year. Several characteristics of the contemporary landscape of higher education provide new opportunities to energize and engage faculty in innovative approaches to first-year student success. These include faculty interest in defining and assessing learning outcomes and in having academically well-prepared majors.

Several key principles of faculty development have been identified as important in preparing faculty to teach and interact with entering students. Most important of these is firmly securing faculty direction and ownership of first-year programs. We recommend that faculty and administrators find ways to keep faculty "in the middle" with first-year students from orientation through first-year seminars, academic support programs, learning communities, and with the gateway courses in which first-year students enroll. The sooner and more extensively students get engaged with faculty and their commitment to learning, the sooner and more extensively students will capture that excitement and make the transition to successful study.

Finally, based on the success IUPUI has had in connecting faculty development to a strong first-year experience program, we recommend a number of best practices that have the potential for implementation at other institutions. A foundational strategy is for institutions to create strong links between campus faculty development resources and first-year programs. Administrators should also provide access to national peers while supporting the formation of local communities of practice. And while attempting to be agents of change and educational reform, we must be cognizant of the traditional culture of the academy by supporting a wide array of activities for faculty development and aligning the products and outcomes with the existing academic reward structure.

We have presented some general principles and specific practices for creating a symbiotic relationship between first-year programs and faculty development. These principles and recommendations closely parallel Walker's (2002) conditions for faculty well-being. We hope to have demonstrated how the faculty's need for expertise, control of their work, access to reliable sources of support, and feedback on the quality of their work can be supported, rather than diminished, in an environment of positive change in the first college year.

CHAPTER SIXTEEN

First-Year Seminars

Mary Stuart Hunter
Carrie W. Linder

> *My [first-year seminar] experience definitely helped me feel connected.*
> *The students in my class were very diverse and we learned a lot from*
> *each other. I still am in close contact with both my peer leader and*
> *instructor. Their direction, guidance, and advice helped me learn about*
> *the university and how I can be successful as a college student.*
> —College junior

Although far from a recent innovation in higher education, first-year seminars have become a celebrated approach employed by institutions of all types in their efforts to ease the transition to college for new students and systematically address unacceptable rates of student attrition. First-year seminars present an excellent opportunity for colleges and universities to challenge their first-year students to excel academically and socially, as well as support them in that quest.

This chapter will provide a brief overview of the history and development of first-year seminars, present a descriptive definition and a solid rationale for their existence, outline course objectives and content, describe the variety of instructional approaches employed, review recent trends, offer evidence of their effectiveness, and suggest possible future directions for first-year seminar programs that challenge and support first-year student success.

DEFINING FIRST-YEAR SEMINARS

At its core, the first-year seminar is centered on and concerned with the individual needs of entering students, as well as the expectations of the particular institution. While there are many variations among first-year seminars, every seminar aims to assist students in their academic and social development and in their transition to college. A seminar, by definition, is a small discussion-based course in which students and their instructors exchange ideas and information.

In most cases, there is a strong emphasis on creating community within the classroom. As one student said,

> The most beneficial part of [the first-year seminar] for me was the sense of community I felt whenever I was in class. I'm not a shy person, but I was even more open than usual in my class since I was comfortable and had twenty-three friends in class with me. I can still walk around campus today as a junior and see students I had class with and sit down and talk with them as if we were back in time, back to two years ago when I was a freshman.

First-year seminars facilitate learning: learning about a subject or combination of topics, learning about the institution, learning about the diversity within campus communities, but most important, learning about oneself and one's abilities. The very nature of first-year seminars allows faculty to facilitate the growth and development of students while still being flexible enough to accommodate the campus-specific issues that an institution believes are important.

A RATIONALE FOR FIRST-YEAR SEMINARS

The transition to college has been and continues to be the topic of a substantial amount of research, many articles and books for a variety of audiences, conferences, and an abundance of newspaper articles and feature stories in the mass media each fall. Student development and retention theorists (Astin, 1993; Pascarella & Terenzini, 1991; Tinto, 1975, 1993) suggest a positive correlation between student learning and a student's involvement and engagement in the learning process. They also suggest that a student's initial commitment to learning depends not only on the skills and characteristics he or she brings to college but also on elements in the college environment. These theories have prompted college and university faculty, administrators, and staff across the country and around the world to discuss, design, and pilot a number of varied initiatives that encourage and support student development and active participation in learning. The first-year seminar, existing in some form on nearly 74 percent of U.S. campuses (National Resource Center for The First-Year Experience and Students in Transition, 2002), is the most common curricular initiative that addresses these goals.

The popularity of first-year seminars as a programmatic and curricular approach to address student transition and retention issues is based on the fact that an academic course offers a time-honored structure through which orientation efforts can be continued beyond the first week and student development and retention theories can be put into practice. The first-year seminar provides a logical structure for encouraging and intrusively demanding active student involvement in learning and in the life of the institution, for examining and discussing student-institutional fit, and for facilitating social and academic integration (Hunter & Linder, 2003).

First-year seminars as an educational innovation have sustained themselves by meeting institutional and student needs and by becoming an integral element of the first-year curriculum. Like many other educational innovations, however, some first-year seminars are relatively short-lived due perhaps to a lack of broad-based campus support, lack of supporting assessment, or a change in leadership. Others, like the phoenix, die and then reinvent themselves in an adapted form. And still others enjoy a hearty and long life. Successful seminars are defined as those that have been sustained over some period of time and enjoy strong, broad-based campus support. Using this definition, successful seminars are ones that (Barefoot & Fidler, 1996):

- Are offered for academic credit
- Are centered in the first-year curriculum
- Involve both faculty and student affairs professionals in program design and instruction
- Include instructor training and development as an integral part of the program
- Compensate or otherwise reward instructors for teaching the seminar
- Involve upper-level students in seminar delivery
- Include ways of assessing their effectiveness and disseminating these assessments to the campus community

Proving the value and worth of any educational innovation is key to its sustainability, especially in times of budget reductions and curricular reform. Well-developed and well-implemented first-year seminars have the potential to be easily assessed on a variety of levels and from diverse perspectives. Assessment efforts, discussed in detail in Part Six of this book, can be used by program administrators to prove and improve the effectiveness of first-year seminars.

Institutional efforts to examine first-year seminar programs have included a variety of assessment approaches, including achievement as measured by grade point averages, progress toward degree as measured by credit hours attempted and completed, graduation rates, first- to second-year retention, student adjustment and involvement, student satisfaction, and a variety of other outcomes measures (Barefoot, 1993; Barefoot, Warnock, Dickinson, Richardson, & Roberts, 1998).

Professional organizations and national centers focused on undergraduate education and students in transition have been instituted over the years. Several are especially relevant for educators working to design and continually improve first-year seminars and other orientation opportunities. An international professional organization, the National Orientation Directors Association, exists solely to provide professional development opportunities and resources for higher educators charged with new student orientation programs. The National Resource Center for The First-Year Experience and Students in Transition at the University of South Carolina was created in 1986 and continues its work today in providing resources and support for higher education professionals working to enhance the first-year student experience and other significant student transitions. For almost forty years, UCLA's Higher Education Research Institute has been surveying the nation's first-year students to track their attitudes, behaviors, and characteristics. Indiana University's Center for Postsecondary Research conducts the National Survey of Student Engagement, the College Student Experiences Questionnaire, and the College Student Expectations Questionnaire, which together have enriched our collective understanding of the entering student experience. As the newest center focused on the first year, the Policy Center on the First Year of College, founded in 1999, centers its work on assessing the first college year and contributes to the body of research on best practices in first-year initiatives. The work of the Policy Center has been supported by The Pew Charitable Trusts, The Atlantic Philanthropies, and Lumina Foundation for Education.

HISTORY AND DEVELOPMENT OF FIRST-YEAR SEMINARS

Special attention to the first year of college is not new. The creation of the credit-bearing first-year seminar was preceded by the formation of a system of faculty advisers at Johns Hopkins University in 1877 and the existence of a board of freshman advisers at Harvard University in 1889 (Gordon, 1989). This recognition that students arrive on campus with special needs unique in the first year led to a variety of programmatic and organizational efforts to address the needs. A number of noncredit orientation courses evolved over the next two decades at such institutions as Boston University, the University of Michigan, and Oberlin College (Gordon, 1989). Reed College offered the first orientation course for credit in 1911 (Fitts & Swift, 1928). Midway through the twentieth century, a 1948 survey of freshman orientation techniques indicated that 43 percent of institutions offered a required orientation course (Gordon, 1989).

From about 1980 until the present, first-year seminars have proliferated on college and university campuses. In 2000, the National Resource Center for The First-Year Experience and Students in Transition conducted its fifth National Survey of First-Year Seminar Programming. Of the 2,539 institutions surveyed, responses were received from 1,013 institutions, for a 40 percent response rate. Approximately 74 percent of the responding institutions reported the existence of one or more first-year seminars (National Resource Center, 2002). This percentage was validated by a stratified random sample survey including 600 institutions (with a 55 percent response rate) conducted electronically in October 2000 by the Policy Center on the First Year of College, in which 73 percent of the institutions (62 percent of two-year respondents and 79 percent of four-year respondents) reported first-year seminars (Policy Center, 2001).

During the 1990s, there were two subtle but significant semantic shifts related to this topic. The interchangeable use of "freshman orientation course" and "freshman seminar" in the 1989 Upcraft, Gardner, and Associates book, *The Freshman Year Experience,* and in other literature has since been replaced by a more common use of the terms *first-year seminars* or *new student seminars.* The use of *seminar* in place of *course* reflects an increasing academic rigor and acceptance in the academy. In addition, the disappearance of the use of the word *freshman* indicates a shift to a more gender-inclusive and respectful terminology.

TYPES OF FIRST-YEAR SEMINARS

Most first-year seminars fit into one of five categories: extended orientation seminars, academic seminars with generally uniform content across sections, academic seminars on various topics, professional or discipline-linked seminars, or basic study skills seminars. However, these seminars often combine elements from several of these categories. The following information and examples have been taken from responses to the 2000 National Survey of First-Year Seminar Programming and provide a look at the types of seminars offered on campuses today (National Resource Center, 2002).

Extended Orientation Seminars

Extended orientation seminars are the most frequently reported type of first-year seminar. Sixty-two percent of institutions with a first-year seminar offer an extended orientation type. These seminars focus on student survival and success techniques and may be taught by faculty and campus administrators, as well as by student affairs professionals. The extended orientation seminar may be credited as part of the institution's core curriculum, general education, or elective course work, and occasionally it is counted toward students' major requirements.

A number of institutions offering an extended orientation seminar have been innovative in their efforts to acclimate students to the institution. Appalachian State University offers a three-credit seminar that emphasizes building community, introducing institutional history and resources, and strengthening learning skills. In addition to in-class discussion, Appalachian organizes an outdoor low-ropes challenge experience designed to facilitate team building among class members.

Academic Seminars

Two types of academic seminars exist: those with uniform content across all sections and those with topics that vary from section to section. Nearly 17 percent of first-year seminars are academic seminars with common content across sections. These seminars may be either required or offered as an elective, and may sometimes be part of an institution's general education or core curriculum. They focus primarily on an academic theme common to all sections, but may also address critical academic skills such as writing, reasoning, and critical thinking.

Eckerd College offers a two-semester academic seminar with common content to all first-year students. The seminar, Western Heritage in a Global Context, introduces students to the arts and sciences of human civilization. This is accomplished by discussing great works and ideas from Western civilization and comparing them and putting them in context with great works from non-Western civilization. Through the seminar, Eckerd works to develop academic and thinking skills in its first-year students.

Nearly 13 percent of first-year seminars can be classified as academic seminars on various topics. These seminars are fashioned most often on faculty members' individual areas of academic or personal interest and expertise. At a single institution, seminar topics can vary from section to section and most likely cover a wide variety of disciplines and social issues. The University of Michigan offers first-year seminars taught by faculty from various academic disciplines that focus on specialized or interdisciplinary topics. Examples of some past seminar titles are Looking at Traditional China Through Its Most Famous Novel: *The Story of the Stone*; The Poetry of Everyday Life; Colonialism and Its Aftermath; and Inventing Race.

Other Types of Seminars

Professional, discipline-linked, and basic study skills seminars are reported less frequently than other first-year seminar types. Combined, they constitute less than 7 percent of reported first-year seminars. Professional and discipline-linked first-year seminars are designed to prepare students for the demands of a specific profession (such as medicine or law) or academic discipline. Castleton State College offers a variety of discipline-linked seminars such as Introduction to History of Art, Principles of Computer Information Systems, and Basic Musicianship. These and other seminar sections are linked to a common hour, where students meet once a week with student life staff to discuss campus resources and student issues.

Basic study skills seminars are generally offered to students lacking appropriate college-level academic skills. These seminars focus primarily on note taking, test taking, and critical reading skills. Rose State College offers its Educational Planning seminar to all students and requires it for students on academic probation. This course aims to help students identify learning styles, evaluate personal and academic strengths and weaknesses, determine career goals, and develop study skills needed to achieve academic success.

A handful of institutions (2 percent) reported first-year seminars that combine elements from some or all of the above seminar types. Pine Manor College assigns students to a Portfolio Learning Seminar that lasts for two years. The seminar focuses on the development of a learning portfolio that is presented at the end of the sophomore year. Wellesley College offers writing seminars that, while offering instruction in academic writing, also focus on a particular topic related to the instructor's academic interest and expertise. The writing seminars strive to provide a common introductory experience in college-level thinking and writing for all entering students.

RECENT TRENDS IN FIRST-YEAR SEMINARS

First-year seminars have evolved over time. Since 1989 when *The Freshman Year Experience* was published, the look of first-year seminars has changed. There is more variation in the types of seminars and in the amount and type of academic credit offered. Seminars are more frequently recognized by faculty, staff, and administrators as a valid method of developing responsible students and independent thinkers. Although far from universally embraced, seminars on many college and university campuses are esteemed and valued, and they have found their place in the first-year curriculum. The following trends reflect data collected from the five national surveys of first-year seminar programming conducted in 1988, 1991, 1994, 1997, and 2000 by the National Resource Center for The First-Year Experience and Students in Transition (Fidler & Fidler, 1991; Barefoot & Fidler, 1992, 1996; National Resource Center, 1997, 2002).

Shifts in Number and Types of Seminars

Since national data were first collected in 1988, the number of institutions offering first-year seminars has shown a gradual increase (from 68 percent in 1988 to 74 percent in 2000). But while new seminars are created each year, others are dissolved. This is likely to continue as some seminars disappear due to lack of resources or the departure of an influential seminar leader, and others are instituted after a renewed administrative commitment to first-year students.

Recent history of first-year seminars has shown a gradual shift to more traditional academic content. In the early 1990s, almost three-fourths of seminars emphasized extended orientation or college survival material. The most recent national survey saw this percentage decline to approximately 62 percent, while the number of seminars focused on academic topics has increased.

Since 1988, the number of institutions reporting basic study skills or remedial seminars has never exceeded 6 percent and currently is about 4 percent of the total number of first-year seminars. The percentage of reported discipline-linked or professional seminars has remained relatively constant at less than 5 percent, but the movement to include discipline-specific content in already established extended orientation seminars is growing. These hybrid seminars, still classified most accurately as extended orientation seminars, address college success topics as well as introduce students to a particular program of study or career field.

Credit Hours and Course Grading

Findings from the five national surveys indicate that the percentage of institutions offering the first-year seminar for a letter grade has consistently increased. Currently, 80 percent of institutions offer a letter-graded seminar, as compared to 62 percent in 1988. In addition, there have been slight increases in the number of institutions requiring the seminar for all first-year students (from 43 percent in 1988 to 49 percent in 2000) and the number of institutions offering the seminar for academic credit (82 percent in 1988 to 89 percent in 2000).

Since 1988, national surveys have shown that the one-credit seminar is the most frequently reported for both two-year and four-year institutions. In 2000, 47 percent of institutions reported offering first-year seminars for one credit hour. However, results of the First-Year Initiative (FYI) benchmarking survey of first-year seminars, conducted in 2001 by the Policy Center on the First Year of College and Educational Benchmarking, showed that students in courses with only one contact hour per week, compared to two or three contact hours, reported lower gains on all but one of ten outcome factors. The factors included such outcomes as improved study strategies, improved connections with peers, increased out-of-class engagement, satisfaction with college or university, and sense of belonging and acceptance. This indicates that increased contact hours can have a positive impact on learning outcomes and student satisfaction with the first-year seminar (Swing, 2002).

Instruction

Gordon (1989) reported that "many orientation courses are taught by student personnel staff, academic advisers, administrators, or other professional staff" and that "faculty may also be assigned to teach the course" (p. 192). Since 1988, the number of institutions involving faculty members in the instruction of first-year seminars has continued to increase. In fact, on the 2000 National Survey of First-Year Seminar Programming, 89 percent of institutions with first-year seminars reported involving faculty in seminar instruction, by far the most frequently reported group of first-year seminar instructors.

There has also been a slight overall increase in the percentage of institutions indicating that upper-level undergraduate students (second-, third-, or fourth-year students) teach or coteach the first-year seminar. In 2000, this figure was 10 percent. Results from a 2000 National Survey of First-Year Curricular Practices (Policy Center on the First Year of College, 2001) found that the involvement of upper-level undergraduates as first-year seminar coteachers, or peer leaders, is as high as 27 percent for research-extensive universities and baccalaureate colleges. The incorporation of undergraduate peer instructors can have a positive effect on student satisfaction with instructional quality. As reported in the FYI benchmarking study (Swing, 2002), correlations exist between the use of undergraduate teaching assistants and high participant evaluations of seminar pedagogy and overall satisfaction with the seminar.

First-year seminars, more than any other course, also use student affairs professionals and other campus administrators as course instructors. In 2000, 54 percent of respondents reported that student affairs professionals teach one or more seminar sections; 37 percent reported that other campus administrators are involved in seminar instruction (National Resource Center, 2002). These findings indicate that many institutions are committed to involving the entire campus in the education of first-year students.

Seminar Sections for Specific First-Year Student Populations

First-year seminars are highly adaptable and can be altered to meet the needs of particular students. National surveys have consistently found that institutions designate sections of the first-year seminar for specific subpopulations. In 2000, special seminar sections were most likely to be offered for students within a specific major, academically underprepared students, honors students, students in a learning community (see Chapter Twenty-Two), adult students, and others.

Seminar Institutionalization

The level of institutionalization of first-year seminars fluctuates across campuses, depending on myriad factors. One measure of institutionalization is seminar longevity. In 2000, 31 percent of reported first-year seminars had been in existence for more than ten years, but 15 percent for no more than two years. A second measure is self-reported level of overall campus support. In 2000, as compared to previous surveys, levels of overall support for the first-year seminar were more likely to be moderate rather than high or low. Precise percentages were as follows: 40 percent of institutions reported high levels of campus support, 53 percent reported a moderate level of support, and only 7 percent of institutions reported low levels of support (National Resource Center, 2002).

Course Objectives and Topics

Because most first-year seminars are created as institution-specific courses designed to meet the needs and characteristics of the students and the institution, specific goals and content vary from campus to campus. Content also is dynamic in that it changes and evolves to meet the changing needs of the students and the institution. Although formal course objectives and topics listed on syllabi submitted with the 2000 National Survey of First-Year Seminar Programming vary, most first-year seminars aim to help students become better assimilated to and engaged in college-level learning. That mission is accomplished in varying ways and depends greatly on the type and purpose of the first-year seminar on each campus.

Most Frequently Reported Goals

Over half (56 percent) of all institutions with first-year seminars indicated the fostering of academic skills as a top objective of the seminar (National Resource Center, 2002). As one student said, "The main goal of the class was to get us 'thinking.' We had to do in-depth analyses of our reading assignments. We were also required to write papers analyzing ourselves, and how we relate to others in the class, in novels, or in the media. I now see that [the instructor] wanted us to learn how to think broadly."

Also at the top of the list of goals is a commitment to easing the transition to college. These two objectives are broad and cover an array of course topics. More specific course goals ranking near the top of the list include the following: orienting students to campus resources and organizations; fostering personal development in students; developing critical thinking and writing skills; introducing general education requirements and specific disciplines; encouraging career planning; developing a sense of community on campus; increasing student interactions with faculty and staff; and developing support networks and friendships among first-year seminar classmates.

Most Frequently Reported Topics

Reported course topics support the goals set out above. The most frequently listed course topic is academic and study skills, followed by time management, both of which are central to fostering good academic habits. Personal development and self-concept ranked high as well. Additional frequently reported course topics include career exploration, campus resources, transition to college, diversity issues, academic advising and planning, and wellness issues (National Resource Center, 2002). According to one student, "I learned facts about life. I learned how to be responsible, mentally and financially. I found out how to make the most of my time by practicing time management. Alcohol, drug, and sexual awareness were also topics we touched on. I learned how to be more aware of my surroundings. Our class focused on how many hours a week we should study and sleep. We touched on so many things; the list is endless. The class was so enlightening and enriching. It helped me prepare for the next three years."

Instruction in First-Year Seminars

Instruction in first-year seminars must take a different form from what is found in most other courses for first-year students. Unlike many large survey courses in traditional disciplines, most first-year seminars are typically taught in small classes (eighteen to twenty-five students per section) (National Resource Center, 2002). Seminar content also differs from most other first-year courses in that there is no canon, that is, no set common content. Instruction in first-year seminars requires an instructional staff that both understands and champions the distinctive goals, content, and processes of effective first-year seminars.

Staffing

Very few first-year seminar programs have dedicated full-time faculty positions. Usually instructors of first-year seminars are full-time employees of other departments on campus and may include faculty, administrative and student affairs professionals, and undergraduate or graduate students serving as peer instructors. On any given campus, more than one type of educator may be involved in instruction of the first-year seminar. In addition, results from the 2000 National Survey of First-Year Seminar Programming (National Resource Center, 2002) indicate that on 33 percent of the campuses responding, the seminar is taught by teaching teams. Teaching teams can be configured in a variety of ways and may include undergraduate and graduate students, faculty, academic administrators, student affairs professionals, and other campus professionals such as academic advisers, librarians, counselors, and campus clergy.

Preparing Instructors for Teaching First-Year Seminars

Many first-year seminar instructors are exposed to special faculty development or training experiences in preparation for first-year seminar instruction. Data from the 2000 National Survey of First-Year Seminar Programming (National Resource Center, 2002) indicate that 76 percent of institutions offer, and 48 percent require, instructor training prior to teaching the first-year seminar. Content for such faculty development programs includes understanding first-year students, understanding the institution, selecting and sequencing course content, and teaching and learning strategies (Cuseo, 1999). Potential outcomes of effective instructor training efforts include campuswide faculty development, professional and personal development, the development of community, development of faculty–student affairs partnerships, improvements in teaching and learning, quality and consistency across seminar sections, and employee orientation, assimilation, and education (Hunter & Gardner, 1999).

Pedagogical Approaches

Since content for first-year seminars is student centered, effective instruction in first-year seminars usually deviates from the traditional lecture format. The very name *seminar* implies an active learning process, where teaching and learning functions are shared among the instructors and the students. Therefore, instructors must relinquish some of the traditional authority and control associated with teaching. Active learning strategies may include experiential learning techniques, collaborative and cooperative learning, group projects, and oral presentation. One instructor reflected on her first attempt at teaching a first-year seminar and shared the following insights:

> I wonder if those days when assignments or activities blossomed into something special were the result of my teaching or my willingness to allow my students to become personally involved in learning. Students are often overlooked as a classroom resource. They bring a diverse collection of information, experience, and knowledge to every class discussion. The challenge is to properly integrate those contributions and make sure that the focus of a given learning objective is not lost [D. Moore, personal communication, August 20, 2001].

Establishing a community of scholars is a defined goal for many first-year seminars. Engaging in activities that establish and develop friendships within the class contributes to the cultivation of intense communities of learners. Frequent communication between instructor and student is widespread in first-year seminars. Two-way communication is encouraged through the use of formal and informal feedback techniques, formative assessment measures, and significant reflection through journals and other student writing. Student feedback can inform instructional approaches. The same instructor indicated that "student feedback challenged me to question some of my long-held, and perhaps archaic, notions about how teachers inspire learning. Learning can be spontaneous and fun. It doesn't have to be disciplined or structured."

Innovative Strategies

First-year seminars provide fertile ground for the development of innovative teaching strategies. Many institutions reported innovative or "especially successful" instructional activities on the 2000 National Survey of First-Year Seminar Programming (National Resource Center, 2002), including writing assignments; computer, Internet, and e-mail experiences; and activities that explore careers and academic majors. Other especially innovative instructional strategies reported include participation in an etiquette banquet at George-town College, the construction of a diversity quilt at Moorpark College, a simulation on natural selection at Columbia College (South Carolina), and the planting of tulip bulbs to illustrate short- and long-term goals at Marycrest International University.

Impact on Teaching in Other Courses

"Teaching the first-year seminar gave me renewed respect for the responsibility that higher education has to promote intellectual exchange *and to encourage independent thinking*" (D. Moore, personal communication, August 20, 2001).

As this instructor reports, teaching the first-year seminar encourages a rethinking of traditional approaches to teaching and the greater higher education endeavor. As a study conducted by Fidler, Neururer-Rotholz, and Richardson (1999) at the University of South Carolina indicates, many faculty who participate in a first-year seminar faculty development workshop, and then teach a seminar, transfer to their discipline-based courses new teaching techniques that they learned in the workshop. They reported that "attending the faculty development workshop and teaching the seminar boosted faculty morale, helped faculty better meet the academic and non-academic needs of students, and improved teaching in many other courses across campus" (p. 72).

LINKAGES WITH OTHER PROGRAMMATIC INTERVENTIONS

Taking first-year seminars to the next level of institutionalization involves integration with other courses in the curriculum and with other programmatic interventions. Many first-year seminars that during the early years of their existence were freestanding academic units are now linking with other campus programs. As new seminars are established on campuses, they are more likely to be part of a general education reform process.

Learning Communities

When seminars are connected to other campus programs, institutionalization is more likely and more stable. Perhaps the most common linkage is with other discipline-based courses in learning communities. The 1994 National Survey of First-Year Seminar Programming (Barefoot & Fidler, 1996) investigated, for the first time, the linking of the seminar to other courses in a learning community. In that year, 17 percent of respondents reported this linkage. In 1997, the percentage dropped slightly to 14 percent (National Resource Center, 1997). However, the 2000 National Survey (National Resource Center, 2002) found this percentage had increased to 25 percent. A recent national benchmarking study of first-year seminars (Swing & Barefoot, 2002) found that linked seminars produce higher student-reported ratings on learning outcomes and satisfaction measures than stand-alone seminars. (For a more detailed discussion of learning communities, see Chapter Twenty-Two.)

Service-Learning and Community Service

Linkage with service-learning or community service programs is also common and sometimes is a course requirement. Sometimes community service projects are undertaken by the class as a whole; at other times students participate in service activities on an individual basis. Group activities have the added bonus of developing community among class members. In discipline-specific seminars, it is not uncommon to find service-learning embedded in the course content. During the past decade at the University of South Carolina, engineering sections of the first-year seminar participated in a Habitat for Humanity "blitz build" by designing and constructing storage sheds for each of the homes built during the blitz. Other institutions build service-learning into the first-year seminar, sometimes with the help of external grants, as at the University of Rhode Island, where a $1 million grant from the Feinstein Foundation funded a first-year seminar with a service project segment ("Foundation Donates," 1995). (For a more detailed discussion of service-learning, see Chapter Twenty-One.)

Partnerships

First-year seminar programs are likely to facilitate partnerships among and between various campus constituent groups. When both faculty and staff are involved in seminar design and instruction, the traditional gaps between them are frequently ameliorated or, at the very least, lessened. In addition, participating together in a substantial workshop experience in preparation for teaching the first-year seminar facilitates campuswide connections between faculty and staff. The focus on student needs and total student development in first-year seminars serves as a common thread uniting individuals across the campus in a shared area of interest and effort. It is also common for content areas in first-year seminars to be delivered and developed by student development professionals. (For a more detailed discussion of faculty and staff collaboration, see Chapter Twelve.)

Residence Life

A renewed interest on the part of residential life and housing professionals in creating a more academic atmosphere in residence facilities has led residence life divisions and seminar programs to build partnerships. On many campuses, special living-learning sections of the first-year seminar offer one scheduling option for students, and classrooms in residence halls provide a physical setting useful for seminar sections. When students find hallmates in their seminar section, conversations about course content are likely to extend beyond the confines of the class hour. (For a more detailed discussion of living environments, see Chapter Twenty-Four.)

EVIDENCE OF EFFECTIVENESS

It has been argued that first-year seminars are perhaps the most assessed and measured of all undergraduate curricular interventions (Barefoot & Gardner, 1998; Cuseo, 2000). Faced with grumbling from some campus constituents that believe first-year seminars are not "real" courses, seminar proponents continually search for evidence that these courses have a positive impact on both the students enrolled and the institution itself. Administrators, faculty, policymakers, curriculum committees, and even students want proof that first-year seminars work (Barefoot & Gardner, 1998).

Since the late 1980s, the National Resource Center for The First-Year Experience and Students in Transition has collected and published research on first-year seminars in the *Journal of The First-Year Experience and Students in Transition* and in two volumes of *Exploring the Evidence: Reporting Outcomes of First-Year Seminars* (Barefoot et al., 1998). In addition, hundreds of institutions nationwide, of all types and sizes, have conducted formal program evaluations that attribute positive persistence, learning, and socialization outcomes to the first-year seminar (National Resource Center, 2002).

When assessing the effectiveness of the first-year seminar, an institution must ask whether institutional and student needs are being met by the course. Institutions desire to retain and graduate their students. Students, in order to stay enrolled and graduate, need to become acclimated to the campus and its culture. They need information and assistance to help them adjust both academically and socially. Although there have been studies that indicate the first-year seminar has no, or a mixed, effect on first-year students (Davis, 1992; Barefoot, 1993; Barefoot et al., 1998), the overwhelming majority of first-year seminar research has shown that these courses positively affect retention, grade point average, number of credit hours attempted and completed, graduation rates, student involvement in campus activities, and student attitudes and perceptions of higher education, as well as faculty development and methods of instruction (Barefoot, 1993; Barefoot et al., 1998). (For a more detailed discussion of assessing the first-year experience in general, and the first-year seminar in particular, see Chapters Twenty-Two and Twenty-Three.)

FUTURE ISSUES AND DIRECTIONS

Although first-year seminars exist at almost three-quarters of accredited undergraduate degree-granting institutions in the United States and are becoming more institutionalized on individual campuses, problems of full acceptance and appreciation still exist and are likely to persist. Perhaps because the content and process elements of first-year seminars are relatively new to the centuries-old traditions of higher education, those who do not fully understand the goals, objectives, and underlying theory frequently view seminar programs with suspicion. An organizational reality also challenging seminars in times of budgetary concerns is that many seminars are administratively housed in interdisciplinary units, or outside academic departments altogether. That many first-year seminars have been add-ons and loosely coupled to the curriculum also contributes to the fact that many seminars do not survive (Barefoot, 2000). Some would argue that in a perfect world where all first-year instruction included special attention to the individual needs of students, there would be no need for first-year seminars. However, in the absence of institutional and cultural transformation, campuses are likely to continue embracing first-year seminars for years to come.

Several trends in first-year seminar programming seem logical and predictable. The trend that is most likely to shape the future of first-year seminars significantly is assessment. Demanded by campus officials and accrediting bodies alike, assessment of first-year seminars can both verify the worth of a program by proving that program goals and objectives are being met and provide important information about which aspects of a program may need to be improved.

The use of first-year seminars to address important topics, content, and processes that do not fit logically into, or that transcend, existing disciplines has been in practice for some time. Instruction in using campus technology and research resources is likely to grow in complexity and importance. Many seminars already have these important content areas in their syllabus, and other institutions are likely to add them in the future. The use or abuse of alcohol and other illegal substances as well as sexual responsibility are delicate topics that may best be addressed in the small and caring communities developed in first-year seminar sections. Many institutions are already addressing these societal issues in seminars, and even more are likely to do so in the future. The very fact that on many campuses there are no other courses that all students take in common makes the mandatory first-year seminar a logical delivery vehicle for information that institutions want or need to introduce to all new students.

The trends noted earlier in this chapter from the national surveys of first-year seminar programming are likely to continue in the foreseeable future. More linkages with learning communities and other curricular units are expected. An expansion of discipline-specific sections of the extended orientation seminar is also likely. This demonstrates and makes visible the increased ownership of the seminar by academic departments. Upperclass peer mentor and graduate student involvement in team teaching expands the influence a seminar may have on a campus. Connections with other campus programs like summer reading programs will likely increase. Increasing institutionalization of seminars as determined by the amount of credit offered and level of faculty participation is also likely to continue. Finally, the impact of the current budget crisis on first-year seminars and other courses and activities, perceived by some as "nonessential," is unknown at present. But it is likely that in an attempt to tighten the institutional purse strings, some campuses may decide to eliminate these courses. We believe that such an action may be a short-term solution with long-term negative consequences to both students and institutions.

RECOMMENDATIONS

Whether institutions are initiating, improving, or sustaining their first-year seminar, there will probably be some barriers that hinder success. A barrier may come in the form of an academic department's or college's reluctance to make room in the first-year curriculum for an elective first-year seminar. Tenure and promotion committees may not recognize or value first-year seminar instruction as a satisfactory form of teaching or service. Therefore, an institution may have very few faculty willing or able to teach the seminar. The first-year seminar planning committee may propose an increase in the amount of credit offered for the first-year seminar, but not have the institutional support needed to make this change.

Barriers to planning, implementing, and making changes are not uncommon in academe. Conflicting interests and competition for limited resources within an institution sometimes make administering the first-year seminar difficult. Some barriers cannot be predicted or avoided. Others, however, can be minimized when first-year seminar advocates are intuitive and intentional in seminar planning and assessment, are considerate of the institution's mission and curricular structure, work to form campuswide partnerships, and are committed to offering professional development opportunities for staff and instructors. Consider the following recommendations:

- *Involve faculty, students, student affairs staff, and academic administrators in creating new first-year seminars.* When creating a new first-year seminar, institutions should engage in a comprehensive and collaborative process of planning and instructing the seminar.
- *Anticipate possible opposition to seminars* when starting or proposing changes in an existing seminar, and develop strategies to deal with individuals or units with different opinions or viewpoints. Ensure that first-year seminars are not perceived as remedial.
- *Design seminars with specific goals in mind,* including what the seminar is designed to accomplish, given the mission of the institution and its commitment to first-year student success.
- *Incorporate assessment of seminars* from the very beginning. Develop a plan for determining their effectiveness, conduct credible studies, use results to improve seminars and demonstrate their effectiveness, and disseminate results widely.
- *Develop seminars that reflect the needs of a particular campus and its students.* No one model works for every institution, and within an institution, several models may be appropriate. Campuses should determine what their students need, and design a course that meets those needs and is consistent with the institution's mission statement. Avoid developing a seminar for marginal students alone.
- *Design first-year seminars to include elements commensurate with the norm of academic credibility on campus:* academic credit; application of credit toward core, general education requirements or the major; appropriate credentials for instructional staff; and compensation for instructors.
- *Incorporate significant academic content into seminars,* including extensive reading and writing requirements that are relevant to the objectives of the course.
- *Include upperclass students in planning and implementing first-year seminars,* but only with proper training and supervision.

- *Provide preparatory and ongoing training for seminar instructors,* including basic methods of group process, facilitation skills, course content, active learning strategies, and student development and student retention theory. Opportunities should be provided for instructors to share successful ideas and learn from one another.
- *Provide instructors with access to resource materials,* including newsletters, journals, monographs, books, textbooks, and other teaching materials related to first-year seminars.
- *Provide seminar directors with resources,* including participating in discussion forums and listservs, attending conferences, reading publications, visiting other campuses, and engaging in professional development opportunities.
- *Reconsider seminar viability on a systematic basis* by engaging seminar administrators and instructors in continuous improvement through feedback provided by various forms of assessment. Seminars should evolve and adjust to meet the changing needs of students, society, and institutions.

CONCLUSION

First-year seminars provide a proven way of both challenging and supporting first-year students in their quest to make a successful transition to college and fulfill their educational goals. Seminars have shown themselves to be flexible and highly adaptable formats within which to provide students essential information, as well as critical support, in the first year. They represent one of the most dynamic curricular innovations of the twentieth century. What the future holds for first-year seminars, only time will tell. But we believe that first-year seminars have the potential to be one of the most dynamic and enduring curricular initiatives of the future.

CHAPTER SEVENTEEN

Developmental Education

Jeanne L. Higbee

I often think what would have happened to me if I had not had the chance
to enter General College. I was declined entrance to the College of Liberal
Arts or to Agriculture. I was thought to be unworthy, incapable of doing
University work. My work in advancing the "Green Revolution"—
helping developing countries produce more food—as far as I'm concerned,
this work couldn't have happened had I not been given that chance.
—Norman Borlaug, Nobel laureate

This statement was uttered by renowned scientist Norman Borlaug (*Access and Excellence*, 2001, p. 17), recipient of the 1970 Nobel Peace Prize for his agricultural research, as well as the Public Welfare Medal of the National Academy of Sciences in 2002 (Schmickle, 2002), and alumnus of one of the oldest developmental education programs in the United States. He voices the sentiments of millions of alumni of developmental education programs who might otherwise have been denied access to higher education.

In spite of this and many other developmental education success stories, developmental education programs continue to generate controversy in higher education. Developmental education has been a way of providing opportunities to first-year students who, for whatever reasons, are not completely prepared to succeed in college. For some, however, developmental education has come to symbolize decaying admissions and academic standards and almost everything else that is wrong in higher education. The institutional challenge is to provide developmental education programs that maintain academic standards, while providing the support necessary for underprepared first-year students to succeed.

This chapter explores how developmental education programs, courses, and services have provided and continue to provide access to postsecondary education for millions of students, while also enhancing academic achievement and retention. The chapter includes a definition of developmental education, its scope in higher education, theoretical perspectives, significant research, and program models.

DEVELOPMENTAL EDUCATION:
A CONTEMPORARY DEFINITION

At one time a college education was a luxury of the wealthy, but not all students who aspired to and could afford to pursue higher education had attained the necessary level of academic achievement to be successful. Spann and McCrimmon (1998) assert, "Helping underprepared students prepare themselves for college has been a feature of American higher education since Harvard opened its doors in 1636" (p. 39).

Although the scope, mission, and even the name (*remedial education* was a frequently used term) of developmental education have undergone significant transitions over the years to reflect changes in postsecondary education and in society as a whole, institutions throughout the world (Casazza, 2000; Hulme & Barlow, 1998; Lemelin, 1992, 1998; Spriggs & Gandy, 1997) continue to provide developmental education programs, courses, and services to promote access and enhance academic achievement.

For the purposes of this chapter, the definition of developmental education of the National Association for Developmental Education (NADE) will be used: "Developmental education programs and services commonly address academic preparedness, diagnostic assessment and placement, affective barriers to learning, and development of general and discipline-specific learning strategies" (2000, p. 1).

The shift in terminology from *remedial* to *developmental* education reflected a change from centering on deficits to "talent development" (Astin, 1985), recognizing that where students begin is not as important as how much students learn. Remedial education functioned as a medical model, in which a diagnosis led to a treatment and cure. Although the new paradigm for developmental education espoused in the 1970s emphasized both developing skills and changing attitudes, it still focused on the underprepared or "high-risk" student (Boylan, Bonham, & Bliss, 1992; Payne & Lyman, 1996). In 1995, NADE published a new statement that expanded the scope of developmental education to include all postsecondary learners:

> Developmental education is a field of practice and research within higher education with a theoretical foundation in developmental psychology and learning theory. It promotes the cognitive and affective growth of all postsecondary learners, at all levels of the learning continuum. Developmental education is sensitive and responsive to the individual differences and special needs among learners [p. 1].

This statement also included several goals of developmental education, including:

- To preserve and make possible educational opportunity for each postsecondary learner

- To develop in each learner the skills and attitudes necessary for the attainment of academic, career, and life goals
- To ensure proper placement by assessing each learner's level of preparedness for college course work
- To enhance the retention of students
- To promote the continued development and application of cognitive and affective learning theory

This expanded vision of the mission of developmental education, which finds its roots in the theoretical perspectives that guide the profession, has had a profound impact on policy and practice.

For many students, developmental education is a significant part of the first year. Approximately 3 million students in the United States participate in developmental education programs every year (Boylan & Saxon, 1998). Nearly one-third of all students take at least one developmental course (Levine & Cureton, 1998a). More than 75 percent of postsecondary institutions that enroll first-year students provide developmental education courses, and this proportion has remained relatively stable over the past century (Abraham, 1987; Boylan & Saxon, 1998; Moore, 2002).

Furthermore, the majority of deans responding from both two-year (81 percent) and four-year (64 percent) institutions report that the proportion of first-year students who need developmental education has been increasing over the past decade, not decreasing (Levine & Cureton, 1998a). When considering the actual numbers, the majority of students enrolled in developmental education courses are white, just as the majority of all students in colleges and universities are white. However, a smaller proportion of middle- and higher-income, English-speaking Caucasian first-year students are required to take developmental education courses than the proportion of students of color, students from low-income families, students born outside the United States, and students for whom English is not their native language (Burd, 1996). Similarly, students coming from urban school districts and from high schools with higher proportions of low-income and minority students are more likely to score "below basic" in math and reading (Olson, 2001).

THEORETICAL FRAMEWORKS

The shift from remedial to developmental education was shaped by developmental theory, combined with the strong influence of learning, democratic, and multicultural theories.

Student Development Theory

Student development theories developed in the 1960s and beyond have assisted developmental educators in understanding how to address student psychosocial development. According to Upcraft (1995), Sanford (1962) was the first to devise a developmental theory specific to college students when he postulated the overriding theme of this book: support and challenge, which is described in greater detail in the introduction. Sanford's writings were followed by Chickering (1969), who postulated seven "vectors of development" that characterized adolescence and early adulthood. Chickering's work helped put students' academic development into a context of their personal development (Higbee, 1988, 2002; Silverman & Casazza, 2000).

About the same time, Perry (1970) developed a theory of intellectual and ethical development in which students moved through nine stages, from a simplistic, categorical view of the world (dualism) to a more relativistic, committed view. This theory was instrumental in helping educators understand the challenges in facilitating the development of critical thinking skills that enable first-year students to view issues through different lenses and weigh the relative merits of arguments and facts that support them. (For a more detailed discussion of Perry's theory, see Chapter Fourteen.)

Similarly, Kohlberg (1976) developed a cognitive stage theory of the development of moral judgment. In his view, moral judgment is a progression through various stages of development, each stage representing a mode or structure of thought. This structure of moral thought includes many aspects that developmental educators are concerned about, such as decision-making systems, problem-solving strategies, and the logic underlying basic concepts.

With the increased social and cultural diversity of students in the 1980s and 1990s, theories focused on historically underrepresented groups such as women (Gilligan, 1977), racial and ethnic minorities (W. Cross, Parham, & Helms, 1991), adult learners (K. P. Cross, 1981), gay, lesbian, and bisexual students (Cass, 1979), students with disabilities (Fine & Asch, 2000), and many others. Because developmental educators often face great diversity in the first-year students they teach, these theories are especially relevant to creating classroom environments that are sensitive to the unique needs of these student groups. (For a more thorough and timely discussion of student development theories, see Evans, 2003, and McEwen, 2003.)

Theories Related to Motivation

"I didn't mature very early. And when I went to high school, I didn't care about school. It was General College that helped me mature and come to realize there is something important about learning. . . . I started out at the University just interested in playing hockey, but in General College, I got interested in learning. . . . There are a lot of people out there with shortcomings, immaturity, or hard luck who could do very well in our society if given a chance. General College is a portal that gives students that chance" (Hubbard, as quoted in *Access and Excellence,* 2001, p. 15). When exploring affective barriers to academic success, motivation plays an important role, as illustrated in the above sentiments of Stanley S. Hubbard, chair, president, and chief executive officer of Hubbard Broadcasting. Theories that explore locus of control (Rotter, 1966), attributions of success and failure (Weiner, 1986), and self-efficacy (Bandura, 1977) help educators determine what motivates a student and whether the student has confidence in his or her ability to achieve (Silverman & Casazza, 2000). Maslow's (1970) hierarchy of needs also assists developmental educators in understanding the motivation of their students. It is difficult for a student to focus on self-actualization when his or her more basic needs have not been met.

Learning Theory

Developmental educators frequently cite the work of John Dewey (1938), Jean Piaget (1970), and Lev Vygotsky (1962, 1978) as central to understanding how students construct meaning (Caverly & Peterson, 1996; Ghere, 2001; Jehangir, 2001; Shaw, 2002; Silverman & Casazza, 2000; Young, Adams, Davis, Haase, & Shaffer, 1996). Constructivist theory posits that "each individual 'constructs' knowledge instead of receiving it from others" (Scherer, 1999, p. 5). Interaction and collaboration are essential to learning; students compose "communities of learners" (Barr & Tagg, 1995). The recent focus on multiple intelligences (Gardner, 1983) and learning styles (Higbee, Ginter, & Taylor, 1991; Lemire, 1998) has also had a significant impact on practice in developmental education (Arendale, 1997a).

Democratic and Multicultural Education Theories

Any examination of theoretical perspectives for developmental education as a means of access to higher education, and to all the privileges associated with it, would be incomplete without mention of democratic theory (Barber, 1984; Dahl, 1998; Giroux, 1997; Sehr, 1997; Young, 1990) and multicultural education theory (Banks, 1993, 1996, 1997b; Barajas, 2001; Bruch, Higbee, & Lundell, 2003, 2004; Freire, 1985). Barber states, "Democracy means above all equal access to language, and strong democracy means widespread and ongoing participation in talk by the entire citizenry" (p. 197). According to Bruch (2001), democratic theory provides the foundation for "educational enfranchisement" (p. 38). He states, "We need theories of knowledge and power that can help us to ameliorate the gap that currently exists between individualized strategies on one hand and historically, culturally, and institutionally entrenched relations of group privilege and oppression on the other" (p. 38). Banks (1993) proposes five dimensions to his multicultural education theory to address institutionalized bias in education: (1) the integration of multicultural content in all aspects of learning, (2) the recognition of how students construct knowledge in different ways, (3) the implementation of policies and strategies to reduce prejudice and stereotyping, (4) the adoption of equity pedagogy, and (5) the development of school cultures that empower all students.

Developmental educators are well versed in the theories of their individual disciplines, and many have acquainted themselves with the student development and learning theories that are considered basic to practice, but they must also begin to examine the foundations of inequality in higher education if they intend to have a long-term impact on access and retention (Bruch & Higbee,

2002; Higbee, 2001; Higbee, Bruch, Jehangir, Lundell, & Miksch, 2003; Miksch et al., 2003).

Toward a Theory of Developmental Education

Within the past five years, scholars in developmental education have been endeavoring to make the link between theory and practice more explicit and have begun exploring the concept of a unified theory of developmental education (Chung, 2001; Chung & Brothen, 2002; Lundell & Collins, 1999; Wambach, Brothen, & Dikel, 2000). Terence Collins and Patrick Bruch (2000), reporting on a meeting of leaders in the field, pose important questions: "Is the diverse practice of developmental education simply the result of a historical accident and local pragmatics brought to bear on issues of access to higher education? Or can this range of practice be seen to constitute a purposeful and vigorous academic discipline, wrought from the thoughtful interplay of interdisciplinary theories that form our varied practices?" (p. 19). It is difficult for educators representing such diverse academic disciplines to agree on a single theoretical approach. Some are behaviorists (Brothen & Wambach, 2001), and others are constructivists (Caverly & Peterson, 1996). Still others are just beginning to identify their own philosophies of education. What is important is that the national professional organizations for developmental education like the College Reading and Learning Association (CRLA) and NADE and their leaders are taking a more significant role in exploring theoretical perspectives for the field.

WHO ARE DEVELOPMENTAL EDUCATION STUDENTS?

In 1988 Carlette Hardin "identified the characteristics of students needing academic assistance in the hope that if policy makers better understood why students take developmental courses, then those policy makers would be less critical of developmental programs" (p. 15). In her article "Access to Higher Education: Who Belongs?" (1988) and its follow-up, "Who Belongs in College: A Second Look" (1998), Hardin describes "the poor chooser," the adult student, the student with a disability, "the ignored student," and the student with limited English proficiency as students who do belong and can be successful. Hardin describes the "poor chooser" as the student who has made a decision or decisions that have adversely affected his or her future. For example, the student may not have pursued a college preparatory curriculum in high school or may have dropped out of high school and later earned a General Educational Development (GED) diploma. Hardin (1998) notes a U.S. Department of Education (1997) study that reported that only about 20 percent of high school students of low socioeconomic status participated in college preparatory programs.

Hardin's "ignored student" is the student whose academic or physical problems went undetected or were simply ignored in high school. These students may have been shy or withdrawn, or they may have had auditory, visual, or learning disabilities that were never diagnosed. Their lack of academic success may have been attributed to a lack of interest or motivation, or they may have been neither high nor low achieving, and because they did not cause any trouble, they were among the students who are neglected in many educational systems, particularly those that are underfunded and understaffed.

Hardin's final category, "the user," describes the student who is not in college to pursue academic goals. According to Hardin, the user does not belong in college because he or she is taking the place of another student who might be more deserving. When Hardin revisited her typology of developmental students in 1998, she added a seventh category, "the extreme case," whom she defined as the student whose problems are so severe that they prevent the student from succeeding and may also disrupt the education of others.

Although Hardin's typology is helpful in understanding why capable and deserving students may require developmental education courses, it does not begin to encompass the full range of students participating in developmental education programs throughout the United States and the rest of the world (Higbee, 2000b). Today virtually any student enrolled in postsecondary education at any size or type of institution may choose to take advantage of developmental programs such as tutoring or the vast array of services provided in learning centers. Perhaps only one-third of first-year students are enrolled in developmental courses, but many more would meet the expanded definition (National Association for Developmental Education, 1995) of the student participating in developmental education.

PROGRAM MODELS AND BEST PRACTICES

The ongoing debate about the role of developmental education in different types of institutions of higher education may pose a threat to access for traditionally underrepresented populations, particularly to research universities. This debate has also forced developmental educators to reexamine the effectiveness of their programs, rethink assessment and placement policies, and restructure delivery systems (Stratton, 1998b). The traditional "three R" model of developmental education, which has focused on placement of students in mandatory courses in reading, writing, and mathematics, is still in place in many institutions, but is now often complemented by other service delivery models (Commander, Stratton, Callahan, & Smith, 1996; McDade, 2002; Simpson, Hynd, Nist, & Burrell, 1997). Furthermore, many developmental education programs no longer view underprepared learners as their primary target audience. In fact, the programs that have withstood the political debate have often been those that have succeeded in demonstrating that they can play an important role in enhancing achievement and retention among all students at the institution (Higbee & Dwinell, 1998). In an interview with Cheryl Stratton (1998b), David Arendale, past president of NADE, states, "We need to reinvent ourselves as resources for the entire campus, students and faculty alike, in renewing the learning environment. Our institutions need our centers and departments to expand our services to include academic enrichment for all students. We can become comprehensive teaching and learning centers" (p. 30).

The Debate over the Traditional Model

Prior to NADE's (1995) redefinition of the scope and mission of developmental education, the predominant model generally has consisted of what are often considered precollege-level (Bohr, 1996) courses in reading, writing, mathematics, and study skills. Many programs also include an advising component, and some also offer courses taught by professional counselors (Higbee & Dwinell, 1992b). Students may be admitted conditionally to the institution or specifically to its developmental education program based on high school grade point average or class rank and standardized admissions test scores. Or students may be regularly admitted to the institution and then be required to enroll in one or more developmental education courses, which generally do not bear graduation credit, based on the results of placement testing. Critics of the latter approach protest that students do not know they will be placed in noncredit courses until after their college decision is made and they have already attended new student orientation. They are also concerned about an overdependence on standardized testing, which in some programs is the sole factor in determining placement. In other programs, numerous variables may be involved in placement decisions, including essays to examine writing competency or grades in specific areas of high school course work. Some students' admissions test scores may exempt them from placement testing altogether. Standards and practices for placement vary greatly and are sometimes state mandated for an entire system of two-year and four-year colleges, universities, and technical schools (Bader & Hardin, 2002; Crisco, 2002; Hodges, Corkran, & Dochen, 1997).

Usually students must successfully complete their developmental courses prior to enrolling in credit-bearing core curriculum courses in the same subject area. For example, students may not be able to enroll in a first-year composition course until they have met all criteria for "exit" for a developmental writing course. These criteria may include an exit essay that is rated by multiple graders and a standardized measure of basic skills (for example, parts of speech, spelling, and punctuation), as well as a satisfactory grade of C or higher in the developmental writing course. Thus, students may remain enrolled in developmental courses for multiple terms. Retention of these students is a concern for critics and developmental educators alike.

The effectiveness of traditional developmental education courses primarily depends on how they are implemented. Courses that foster the transfer of skills to subsequent core curriculum courses can be highly successful in enhancing achievement and retention (Stahl, Simpson, & Hayes, 1992). Although some students feel stigmatized (Lundell, 2000b; Pedelty, 2001) by placement in mandatory developmental courses, others realize that these courses can give them an advantage over other students. In addition to promoting skill development, participation in developmental education courses usually affords first-year students the opportunity to take classes with smaller enrollments in which they will be able to become better acquainted with both faculty and peers. Although there are notable exceptions, many developmental education faculty are hired specifically to teach and do not have major research obligations. As a result, they are able to give students more individualized attention outside class. They also may have more time to provide extensive feedback on assignments. Teaching, rather than conducting research, is more likely to be what drew them to the profession; developmental educators are generally highly motivated to teach well.

Another facet of traditional developmental education programs is intrusive advising. Many programs have established early warning systems so that interventions are made available before first-year students develop patterns of behavior that will result in academic failure. Although none of these practices is universal, developmental courses are also more likely to have mandatory attendance, regular graded homework assignments, and multiple means of demonstrating the acquisition of knowledge (as opposed to many first-year courses in which final grades are based on several Scantron tests over the course of a term and an objective final examination). Although these policies can assist first-year students in establishing good habits, they can sometimes make students feel as if they are still in high school. However, some of the same students who complain about their sense of stigma while they are in developmental education programs are the first to recognize on completion of mandatory courses that this structure enabled them to be successful.

The three R model of traditional developmental education is still widespread in two-year institutions but has come under attack in public four-year institutions (Stratton, 1998b), where legislators and other policymakers question the appropriateness of paying for what they consider remediation. As a result, some systems of higher education have prohibited the provision of any developmental education programs, courses, or services at four-year institutions (Crisco, 2002; Jehangir, 2002; Moore, 2002). The City University of New York (CUNY), for example, until the mid-1990s operated under a system of open admissions to anyone with a high school diploma or GED, but now denies admission to its four-year institutions to students who fail to pass one or more of its entrance examinations. The California State University (CSU) system's new policy requires that underprepared students enroll in "remedial" classes during their first term, and "demonstrate proficiency" by the end of their first year of college or face possible "disenrollment" (Crisco, 2002). Crisco comments, "It sounds like a sink or swim attitude, as if the policy makers have suggested that a degree from this university simply means pulling oneself up by his or her bootstraps" (p. 47). She goes on to point out that CSU accepts students in the top third of their high school graduating classes, yet half of the accepted students require developmental work; it is clear that the high schools are not adequately preparing students for college. CSU's new policy represents a classic case of blaming the victim.

Although some states continue to support developmental education for all types of public institutions, CUNY and CSU are joined by other public systems of higher education in a growing trend to reduce or eliminate developmental courses in their four-year institutions (Bader & Hardin, 2002; Jehangir, 2002; Moore, 2002). Singer (2002) chronicles how the University System of Georgia's mandate to discontinue precollege-level developmental courses at its universities resulted in the demise of Georgia State University's highly evaluated learning support services for all students. In his interview with Stratton (1998b), Boylan rues this trend and asserts that the very nature of many community colleges and the students who attend them, many of whom are commuters who attend part time, makes it "difficult . . . [for students] to be immersed in the academic culture" (p. 28). Boylan expresses concern regarding the small proportion of community college students who eventually earn a baccalaureate degree. Moore (2002) provides a series of statistically based arguments in support of retaining developmental education courses and programs at four-year institutions, and like Boylan discusses the potential impact on graduation rates of students of color and other traditionally underrepresented groups (including students who are first-generation college students and students with disabilities) if all developmental education is relegated to two-year colleges. Miksch (2002) urges, "As developmental educators, our policy strategies also need to consider . . . how poverty and race are often intertwined . . . and incorporate questions of access into our policy work" (p. 74).

The debate over traditional courses also rages within the profession itself (Maxwell, 1998). In his interview with Stratton (1998b), Arendale argues in favor of programs that offer "concurrent development of learning strategies." He continues, "The professional literature suggests that students need to make direct applications of these skills . . . or they will be unable to transfer them for use in other classes. Offering traditional study skills classes that are isolated from course content is not in step with the research" (p. 31).

Other Course Models

Institutions are exploring alternative methods for assessment, placement, and instruction. Instead of stand-alone courses in reading and study strategies, some developmental educators are implementing Supplemental Instruction (see Chapter Eighteen) or paired, linked, or adjunct courses (Commander & Smith, 1995; Dimon, 1981). These groups of courses function like some forms of learning communities (see Chapter Twenty-Two). First-year students jointly enroll in a course in reading and study strategies, taught by a developmental educator, and a first-year core curriculum course such as biology (Blinn & Sisco, 1996), psychology (Bullock, Madden, & Harter, 1987), or sociology (Resnick, 1993). Developmental educators are also becoming more involved in implementing programs for writing across the curriculum (Wilcox & Jensen, 2000).

At some institutions, first-year students who might elsewhere be placed in noncredit developmental writing programs instead enroll in credit-bearing first-year composition courses taught by developmental educators who embed skill development in regular composition course content (Gess & Klindworth, 2002; Wambach & delMas, 1998). Much less common are programs like those at Kean University that provide expanded developmental course offerings in the sciences

(Best & Lees, 2000). Other examples include an entire core curriculum of credit-bearing developmental education courses such as that offered by the University of Minnesota General College (Higbee, 2003; Wambach & Brothen, 2002). That program includes physical and biological sciences (Jensen & Rush, 2000; Johnson, 2001), social sciences (Brothen & Wambach, 2000, 2001; Pedelty & Jacobs, 2001), history (Ghere, 2000, 2001), the arts (James & Haselbeck, 1998), humanities, statistics, logic, and law (Miksch, 2002), in addition to mathematics and composition. It is critical that these courses maintain the integrity of institutional standards. By using diverse teaching methods such as simulations, mock trial, and other collaborative learning experiences, computer-enhanced instruction, and civic engagement projects, developmental educators promote the development of reading, writing, research, oral communication, technology, and problem solving and critical thinking skills while also covering course content and responding to students' diverse learning styles.

Some institutions continue to offer developmental courses for first-year students, but on an elective rather than mandatory basis. Others have created elective courses, whether for institutional or graduation credit, that promote development of skills such as critical thinking (Chaffee, 1992, 1997; Higbee, Dwinell, & Thomas, 2002) or strategic learning (Hodges, Dochen, & Sellers, 2001; Weinstein, Dierking, Husman, Roska, & Powdrill, 1998). Strategic learning courses focus on four components: (1) skill, such as cognitive learning and reasoning strategies; (2) will, defined as motivation, self-efficacy, and a positive attitude toward learning; (3) self-regulation in areas like time management, comprehension monitoring, and strategic planning; and (4) factors related to the academic environment, such as resources or faculty expectations (Weinstein et al., 1998). Through its Department of Learning Skills, Jacksonville State University offers courses in first-year student adjustment and success, career exploration, multicultural appreciation, and the job search, in addition to traditional developmental courses (McDade, 2002).

At the University of Georgia, as the Division of Developmental Studies underwent its transition to the Division of Academic Assistance (Higbee & Dwinell, 1998), and later to the Division of Academic Enhancement, it shifted its focus from required developmental courses for first-year students to a broad array of elective courses taught by developmental reading, writing, mathematics, and counseling faculty and available to all students at the institution (Higbee, Dwinell, & Thomas, 2002). These courses were originally offered for institutional credit only, but some have now been in existence long enough to establish themselves and are now available for graduation credit. Some of the courses attract predominantly first-year students, while others, like Writing the Research Paper, may be more likely to enroll upperclassmen. One highly successful course that will never be appropriate for graduation credit is Preparation for Precalculus. Students who are failing or simply find themselves in over their heads can switch without penalty from precalculus, the lowest-level mathematics course taught by the Mathematics Department, to the prep course. This is accomplished through a section change rather than the drop-add process. This policy enables students to break the attrition cycle because they are able to build the background they need in math before reenrolling in precalculus rather than signing up again the next term no better prepared to succeed than they were before.

Unfortunately, confounding intervening variables and the many different approaches to developmental education make it difficult to measure quantitatively the relative success of course models. It is also difficult to determine whether elective courses are serving those students who might need them most but may not elect to enroll. On the other hand, it is not uncommon for A and B students to participate in elective developmental education courses to strengthen their skills. One college senior wrote on an anonymous evaluation of a critical thinking course, "I took this course to brush up to be ready for the LSAT [Law School Admissions Test]. But exercises like the one we did on Tiananmen Square [Chaffee, 1997] helped me realize how many different ways there are to look at the world."

LEARNING SUPPORT

Under the expanded umbrella of programs and services that are now defined as developmental education (National Association for Developmental Education, 1995), professionals provide learning support for students at all levels of postsecondary education. The pertinent question is no longer, "Who is the developmental student?" (Boylan, Bonham, & Bliss, 1994; Higbee, 2000b) but, "Who is not?" Campus tutorial services and learning centers (Arendale, 1997b; Chickering & O'Connor, 1996; McDaniel, James, & Davis, 2000; Young et al., 1996) often provide skills assessments, one-on-one and small group tutoring, computer-assisted instruction, videotaped instruction, and other formats to match the preferred learning styles of students. Some developmental education courses are taught on-line (Glover, 2002) or on television (Koehler, 2000) and also are made available to students for the computer or on videotape in the institution's learning center, as well as through public cable access (Thomas & Higbee, 1998). Learning center staff may conduct workshops on topics as broad as active learning techniques or as specific as fractions or exponents to support mathematics courses or comma splices or documenting sources to supplement writing courses. Popular workshop topics include time management, procrastination, and stress management. A series of workshops may also be designed for specific populations, such as students who are attending classes that are not taught in their primary languages (Burrell & Kim, 1998).

COMMUNITY PARTNERSHIPS

Although many developmental educators have been involved for decades with programs like the federally funded Upward Bound, recently they have become increasingly involved in the service missions of their institutions. They are working with high school–to–college transition programs (Spence, Autin, & Clausen, 2000) like summer bridge (Higbee, 2000a; Stratton, 1998a), creating service-learning opportunities for students in conjunction with course work (Borland, Orazem, & Donnelly, 1999; Hutchinson, 2000), and engaging in workplace literacy projects (Longman, Atkinson, Miholic, & Simpson, 1999). Developmental educators are realizing the importance of collaboration on many levels (Bader & Higbee, 2002; Lundell, 2000a).

Of particular interest are myriad recent K–16 initiatives (Bader & Higbee, 2002). In keeping with the expanded mission and definition of developmental education (National Association for Developmental Education, 1995), these collaborations address a multitude of needs and do not necessarily focus on underprepared or at-risk high school and college students. In fact, some programs target intellectually gifted students. Other initiatives, such as the Commanding English (Murie & Thompson, 2001) high school outreach programs sponsored by the University of Minnesota's General College, serve specific populations that are traditionally underrepresented or underserved in American higher education, such as recent immigrant students and first-generation college students.

Meanwhile, recent research projects like the Association of American Universities and The Pew Charitable Trust's *Understanding University Success* (Conley, 2003) assist educators in identifying the specific skills high school students must develop in order to be successful in college. Developmental educators are playing a key role in mobilizing organizations like the Twin Cities (Minnesota) Metropolitan Higher Education Consortium to create regional collaborations that involve secondary and postsecondary institutions. Similar partnerships have also enabled developmental educators to engage in research projects like the Hennepin County African American Men Study (Taylor, Schelske, Hatfield, & Lundell, 2002) and the Multicultural Awareness Project for Institutional Transformation (Miksch, Bruch, Higbee, Jehangir, & Lundell, 2003), which provide important information about the constituencies served by our educational institutions.

ASSESSING DEVELOPMENTAL EDUCATION

Developmental education programs vary so much from institution to institution that it is impossible to make sweeping generalizations about the efficacy of developmental education as a whole or to make relative judgments about different types of programs. A model may be successful at one institution but not be appropriate at another (Lundell, 2000c), or may not be successful at another because of the student population served, the level of administrative support, the experience and training of faculty and staff, or the manner in which the model is implemented.

It is imperative, however, for each institution to use a variety of quantitative and qualitative measures to ensure that its investment in developmental education is cost-effective and meeting institutional goals. It is not fair to expect programs that admit students who would not otherwise gain access to the institution to maintain the same retention and graduation rates as other academic units (O'Hear, 2002), although some do. It is reasonable to expect any developmental education program to be able to provide data that support its continued existence, including evidence that students who have completed traditional developmental education courses such as mathematics and composition are successful in subsequent courses in the same discipline (Bader & Hardin, 2002; McDade, 2002; Thomas & Higbee, 1996).

Too often, assessment in developmental education programs is limited to measures of student aptitude and achievement in reading, writing, and mathematics (Bray, 1987). In order to understand why some students are more successful than others, even when the traditional predictors of high school grade point average or class rank and standardized admissions test scores would seem to indicate to the contrary, it is also imperative to explore affective factors (Dwinell & Higbee, 1990; Higbee & Dwinell, 1990b, 1995). For more than four decades, postsecondary educators have been exploring noncognitive barriers to achievement (Alpert & Haber, 1960; Nisbet, Ruble, & Schurr, 1982; Pervin, 1967). Twenty-five years ago, Sheila Tobias (1978) popularized the notion of math anxiety as a barrier not only to academic achievement among women but to many lucrative careers as well. A number of developmental educators were among the researchers who began studying the effects of test anxiety (Decker & Russell, 1981; Dendato & Diener, 1986; Lent & Russell, 1978), mathematics anxiety (Bitner, Austin, & Waddington, 1994; Fulkerson, Galassi, & Galassi, 1984; Llabre & Suarez, 1985), and other variables (Bassarear, 1991; Dwinell & Higbee, 1991; Fennema & Sherman, 1976; House, 1995; Siegel, Galassi, & Ware, 1985) on mathematics performance and in other subjects as well. In the 1980s, the breadth of research in developmental education expanded to examine the impact of stress more broadly (Archer, 1986; Archer & Lamnin, 1985; Higbee & Dwinell, 1992a; Nowicki, 1978; Roberts, 1989; Williams, Decker, & Libassi, 1983).

Meanwhile, locus of control and attributions of success and failure also have been explored (Allen, Giat, & Cherney, 1974; Arkin, Detchon, & Maruyama, 1982; Arkin & Maruyama, 1979; Deardorff, Kendall, Finch, & Sitarz, 1977; Edwards & Waters, 1981; Hashway, Jackson Hammond, & Hawkins Rogers, 1990; Lao, 1970). Researchers have been looking at how self-esteem and academic self-concept might be related to student achievement (Bradbury, 1991; Full-Lopez, 1991; Higbee & Dwinell, 1996; Mooney, Sherman, & LoPresto, 1991; Morrison & Morrison, 1978; Morrison, Thomas, & Weaver, 1973). Motivation and goal setting are also critical factors that merit further research (Higbee & Dwinell, 1990a; Hill, 1984; Maehr, 1984; Stone, 1994; Weiner, 1984). The theoretical work of Chickering (1969, Chickering & Reisser, 1993), Astin (1985), and others has inspired studies of additional variables such as educational involvement and academic autonomy (Hart & Keller, 1980; Higbee & Dwinell, 1992b; Higbee & Thomas, 1999; Pollard, Benson, & Hinz, 1983; Thomas & Higbee, 2000; Tracey & Sedlacek, 1985; Weinstein, 1987; Wuthrick, 1991). In addition to published instruments, developmental educators can create their own informal classroom assessments (Angelo & Cross, 1993; Higbee, 1996; Higbee &

Thomas, 2000) to measure student learning, determine the effectiveness of teaching strategies, or gain a better understanding of their students.

As suggested in Chapter Twenty-Seven, a comprehensive assessment program should include gathering information about the backgrounds and characteristics of developmental education students, assessing their needs, and measuring their satisfaction with programs offered. Most important, for traditional developmental education programs that include noncredit-bearing course work, there must be evidence that students are increasing their level of academic preparedness, and that must translate into competing successfully in their classes alongside other students. Governments, institutions, and students cannot be expected to provide financial support for courses, programs, and services that cannot demonstrate their own effectiveness. As O'Hear (2002) states, "Our programs tend to be exposed to public scrutiny more often than other departments and programs within our institutions" (p. 50).

Additional research is needed to explore the efficacy of different models of developmental education, but researchers must be careful to avoid overgeneralizing their results. Further attitudinal research is needed to examine affective barriers to achievement, including students' beliefs regarding courses and programs that may stigmatize or segregate underprepared learners. Longitudinal research is necessary to assess the long-term impact of programs. Respondents in a study of former students ten years after their participation in a developmental education program (Higbee & Dwinell, 1997) reported that the program gave them the opportunity to pursue their career goals. Their professions included human resource manager, police officer, broker, mortgage loan officer, teacher, and a marketing manager. One former student who had earned a master's degree in counseling psychology was working with developmental students at another institution in the state. A public relations officer for the Boy Scouts of America wrote, "I honestly do not believe that I would have graduated from Georgia had I not gone through Developmental Studies" (Higbee & Dwinell, p. 59).

RECOMMENDATIONS

The following recommendations for developmental education programs and services are supported by theory and research (Boylan, Bliss, & Bonham, 1997; Boylan & Bonham, 1994; Boylan, Bonham, & Bliss, 1992; Boylan, Bonham, & Rodriguez, 2000; Stahl, Simpson, & Hayes, 1992):

- *Recognize that there are some first-year students who are better prepared and others who are less well prepared in specific academic areas* at every postsecondary institution, regardless of size, type, or location,
- *Value diversity and the assets diverse first-year students bring to the learning process that cannot be measured by standardized tests.* Such widely used tests, although somewhat helpful in measuring student achievement,

should not be the only measure of first-year students' potential for succeeding in college.

- *Focus on building on first-year students' strengths rather than adopting a deficit model.* The deficit model is no longer relevant to today's underprepared students; a more effective approach is to start with the assets students bring to college.
- *Stress the transferability of skills to future tasks and a variety of learning environments.* First-year students must be taught to transfer skills learned in one setting to another.
- *Engage students actively in the learning process.* As Erickson and Strommer suggest in Chapter Fourteen, first-year students learn best when they are actively involved in their own learning.
- *Address both affective and cognitive aspects of learning.* Each of these aspects influences and informs the other and cannot be viewed as separate and distinct categories of learning.
- *Explore alternative models for courses to fit institutional mission and goals.* One size does not fit all; institutions must develop the model that best fits their mission and students.
- *Provide academic support services to enhance achievement among all students on campus,* such as academic advising, Supplemental Instruction, computer facilities, and others.
- *Create partnerships to facilitate the transition from high school to college.* Collaborations may include a variety of types of bridge programs, the dissemination of information about college expectations, and research projects to guide future practice.
- *Implement an ongoing, comprehensive approach to assessment that documents program effectiveness.* It is critical to the viability of developmental education to demonstrate, through systematic assessment, that students who participate show marked improvement in their knowledge and skills, and compete successfully in their academic courses.

CONCLUSION

Developmental education can play a key role in facilitating access, supporting and challenging first-year students, enhancing persistence to graduation, and promoting excellence in all postsecondary institutions, but one of its strengths can also be its greatest weakness. The focus on excellence in teaching, to the exclusion of research activities, can create a dearth of data to demonstrate program effectiveness and ensure long-term support. The relegation of all developmental education courses in public systems of higher education to two-year institutions will only exacerbate this problem. National professional organizations such as NADE and CRLA need to encourage collaborations among institutions to conduct the research that could ultimately guarantee the future of developmental programs to serve first-year students.

CHAPTER EIGHTEEN

Supplemental Instruction

Deanna C. Martin
Maureen Hurley

*The thing I really like about being an SI [Supplemental Instruction]
leader is that I have been there myself. I've attended a lot of SI sessions in
other courses as a student. In a lot of cases there were concepts that I just could not
understand based on the textbook or in the lecture given by the professor. I know
that feeling when you finally understand a difficult concept and how great it feels.*
—SI leader and student

For more than a quarter of a century, Supplemental Instruction (SI) has been a critical and successful student academic support system in several hundred postsecondary institutions in the United States and abroad, largely because of its demonstrable record of effectiveness and efficiency. Supplemental Instruction, a peer-assisted academic support system, is yet another way in which institutions can challenge students to work to their upper limit and provide them the support they need to make a successful transition to college and succeed in the classroom.

This chapter focuses on defining and illustrating Supplemental Instruction (SI) in the context of its development at the University of Missouri-Kansas City (UMKC) Center for Academic Development, its validation by the U.S. Department of Education (USDOE), its dissemination nationally and internationally to colleges and universities, and its applications to first-year courses and programs as well as distance learning. Longitudinal and national data are included along with evidence of its effectiveness for students from two and four-year private and public colleges and universities.

WHAT IS SUPPLEMENTAL INSTRUCTION?

The innovation known in the academic literature as Supplemental Instruction is traditionally characterized as a peer-assisted academic support program that is implemented to reduce high rates of attrition, increase the level of student performance in difficult courses, and increase graduation rates. To accomplish these goals, SI relies on assigning instructor-approved, content-competent student leaders to attend historically difficult courses in which they themselves have achieved high grades. Students in the targeted courses are invited to participate in regularly scheduled, small group, collaborative learning sessions led by the SI leader, who has been trained to integrate course content with effective learning and study practices. Sessions begin the first week of class and continue throughout the term, with an emphasis on helping first-year students discover and practice specific study techniques that translate directly into stronger academic performance.

The SI leader guides students to engage with the material in ways that strengthen their learning. For example, students regularly work through a difficult concept in small groups by demonstrating problem-solving steps; deciphering and making sense of class notes, charts, and graphs; or creating visuals and graphic organizers that help them make a concept easier to capture and remember. In these and other ways, they take away a new or stronger toolbox of strategies and skills that they can directly apply to the content of the target course and similar courses.

SI evolved in the early 1970s shortly after the University of Missouri created a Kansas City campus (UMKC) by integrating the prestigious, urban, private university known as the University of Kansas City. The changeover in student clientele generated a shock wave among faculty and administrators when, for the first time, classes included sizable numbers of ethnic and racial minorities and first-generation students, many of whom were not academically prepared to meet the rigorous expectations of the faculty. The number of D grades and failures skyrocketed among undergraduates, as did attrition rates. Supplemental Instruction, designed by Deanna Martin, was implemented to meet the immediate challenge of reducing student attrition (Martin, Lorton, Blanc, & Evans, 1977; Widmar, 1994).

THE SI PROCESS

Nationally, others defined the attrition problem as rooted in the weaknesses of individual students who were subsequently identified for corrective programs and services (phone survey of thirty-four higher education institutions conducted by Martin at UMKC in 1972; Martin et al., 1977; Maxwell, 1987). In our view, however, the causes of attrition lay in the interaction between the students and their courses, as well as a mismatch between the students' level of preparation and faculty expectations.

Looking for a way to help the most students perform well without singling them out for individual attention, we asked ourselves which courses students were enrolled in when they encountered serious academic difficulty. At this juncture, we had begun to think in terms of high-risk courses instead of high-risk students. The registrar confirmed that on our undergraduate campus, the courses with the highest failure rates were economics, history, biology, physical sciences, math, and chemistry. Serendipitously, our course-specific approach to attrition proved to be particularly advantageous as the Missouri legislature assigned all remedial services, such as developmental education courses, to the community colleges and restricted the state universities from engaging in remedial programs.

Since financial constraints demanded that we be selective in the courses we served, we decided to target large core curriculum courses where we had the opportunity to serve the greatest number of struggling students for the least cost. In the undergraduate College of Arts and Sciences, we targeted American history, macroeconomics, general chemistry, general biology, philosophy, and physical sciences, where low grades, failures, and withdrawals exceeded 30 percent (our arbitrary cutoff point). We always chose classes where we were welcomed by the professor, and it was our good fortune that nearly every professor was a fine lecturer and a dedicated educator.

With the instructor's permission, we assigned a content-competent, trained SI leader to attend each class session and offer assistance to groups of students enrolled in that section of the course. The SI leader, usually an upper-level student, scheduled sessions at times convenient for the majority of students. We supervised the leaders, providing ongoing training as needed. All of us gathered and developed study skill strategies that could be seamlessly incorporated into the SI content discussions.

The SI leader served as facilitator, mentor, coach, and troubleshooter but never as lecturer. Lecturing was the instructor's job. Students came with their notes and texts, and, with the guidance of the SI leader, they all worked together to figure out what they needed to know. When none of them understood, a volunteer from the SI group asked the instructor and reported to the group.

Although SI leaders were never allowed to see examinations in advance or to grade papers, they did provide an immediate and valuable feedback to instructors who wanted to know what kind of questions and concerns their students were identifying. It was not unusual for instructors to respond by reteaching concepts in ways that students found more accessible.

SI sessions were offered three to five times a week depending on the class size and interest. Students attended voluntarily; SI leaders kept scrupulous attendance data; and instructors provided us with student exam grades. Some instructors wanted to give students extra credit for attending SI. We declined, asking that SI attendance remain anonymous so that our data analyses would not be confounded by professorial bias.

DEFINING PRINCIPLES OF SUPPLEMENTAL INSTRUCTION

One of the first things we recognized was the similar pattern among courses students found problematic. The most common elements among these courses were required prerequisite skills. Whether at UMKC or on other campuses, students needed basic math skills prior to college algebra and algebra concepts prior to chemistry. They also needed adequate reading, writing, and note-taking skills for social science courses. Without the appropriate prerequisite skills, introductory courses could turn into "killer" courses for students who lacked appropriate support.

We can extract some generalizations from the behavior of students, particularly from those who struggle to succeed. Here are six principles that have informed our work and are resonant with others in the field (Tinto, 1993; Maxwell, 1987; Upcraft & Gardner, 1989):

• *First-year students need to develop a culture of learning.* In our experience, many first-year college students are not accustomed to taking lecture notes for their high school classes. It is a point of pride for some that they almost never take notes or read their textbooks.

Accommodating to a culture of learning is difficult for those who lack appropriate educational experiences. The greatest obstacle is that students do not know they are missing something they need. They may see the difference between what some students do and what they do, but they do not understand the significance. Acculturation is particularly sensitive because it challenges values and beliefs that are deeply rooted and long standing. Identity issues lurk in the background, and students may interpret encouragement to adopt different behavioral norms as personal criticism or rejection. It may take intense and sustained work from both students and those who support them to develop behaviors that are different from ones those students learned in their home community.

• *First-year students need help in seeking and accessing academic advising.* Undergraduate students, and particularly marginal students, are not likely to show up for SI unless special efforts are made to attract them. The top students willingly come to SI, and data suggest that they profit from the experience. Those who are the most at risk, however, hang back for many reasons, ranging from fear that they will be stigmatized to not realizing that they need assistance. Compared to our early experience with medical, dentistry, and pharmacy students, attendance at SI by first-year arts and sciences students was embarrassingly low (10 to 15 percent as compared to 45 to 55 percent of health science students). It took nearly a year to develop appropriate marketing techniques. Now SI practitioners from our and other campuses offer extended lists of ideas to encourage SI attendance. Their suggestions can be accessed through SInet or the UMKC National SI Center (http://www.umkc.edu/cad/si).

• *First-year students who are marginally prepared in subjects require assistance with lectures.* As we work with students in SI, it is clear to us that many students acquire very little new knowledge during a lecture if they are inadequately prepared for the subject. They often recognize that they heard a brilliant lecture but are quick to acknowledge their inability to recall or discuss major points. Students can be overwhelmed with new vocabulary and ideas if their content background or study skills are marginal, either generally or in a particular discipline. Students need the opportunity to compare notes, ask questions, and discuss what they think they understand. The debate among professionals, then, has been on how much and what kind of support they need.

- *First-year students' study time is often inefficient.* Our work with marginal students in SI has alerted us to some patterns of behavior that handicap the efficiency of study sessions. For instance, if there is a way to get information without reading, marginal students will use it. It is not that they are illiterate; they are nonliterate. They prefer not to read if there is an alternative. They also prefer to get lecture notes from someone else. Furthermore, they do not immediately perceive the relationship between the lecture and the text. They do not know what to do with a syllabus. It may come as some surprise, then, that even with these areas of study skill weaknesses, when marginal students sit down to study, they persist through their frustration. Interviews with students confirm that those experiencing difficulty spend as many or more hours studying than those who are doing well (Boyer Commission, 1998).

Increasing the study efficiency of students is a major goal in SI. Frequently, the SI leader helps students use the syllabus to see where the instructor has been and where she or he is going. Reading assignments can be addressed by helping students preview the chapter. Creating familiarity with the assignment by showing students how to glean a quick overview, or road map, encourages them to finish the reading later with greater willingness and less frustration. The SI leader not only assists students with the day-to-day study tasks but also prepares them to be proactive by helping them recognize, for example, that exam questions are predictable, not random. The informality of the SI session encourages both insights and laughter as the enthusiasm of the SI leader for the subject assures students that even difficult tasks can be fun.

- *First-year students need support and practice to acquire new learning skills.* Skill development, like any other kind of deep learning, takes time and practice. Although students' usual way of approaching learning may not be effective, it has worked for them until now. Unplugging a familiar approach when the stakes are high requires courage and trust. Students need someone in the trenches with them to guide them through their ambivalence while they make the transition from old ways of doing things to new, more effective ones.

- *First-year students need the opportunity to become "apprentice" learners.* Since UMKC has never had the state's sanction to establish a separate, developmental track for underprepared students, our option has always come down to helping students achieve success within the core curriculum itself. As we worked with SI and its newest adaptation, video-based Supplemental Instruction (VSI) (Martin & Blanc, 1994, 2001), we began to appreciate even more how marvelously adaptive our students are. The data on SI and VSI demonstrate repeatedly that institutions do not have to single out large numbers of students for testing and corrective action before they can be successful in regular courses. Instead, students can see for themselves what they need to do and make the necessary adjustments if they have the right opportunities.

Subsequently, researchers and theorists helped us to clarify our thinking in this regard. The research of Vygotsky (1962), Astin (1993), Pascarella and Terenzini (1991), Tinto (1987, 1993), Upcraft, Gardner, and Associates (1989), and others have verified for us the power of the peer group and the importance of making connections. In our application of this wisdom, we thought in terms of masters and apprentices. Apprentices (students) need to be connected with masters (student facilitators), who know how to be successful—not masters of the subject, as professors are, but masters of learning, as the best students are. And students need to be engaged in challenging courses that are part of their degree program or vocational goals. In the SI and VSI programs, then, we employ the master student to work with apprentice students in the context of a difficult academic challenge. Through this apprenticeship process, students equilibrate in response to the demands of the academic culture, relying on the resources of the peer group and their own growing repertoire of skills.

EVIDENCE OF SI EFFECTIVENESS

The early data on first-year students were satisfying. SI participants earned a half letter grade higher than non-SI participants, and the rate of D, F, and W grades was cut in half (Blanc, DeBuhr, & Martin, 1983). In addition, the faculty liked what we were doing. That, however, did not satisfy the dean of arts and sciences, who told us that he believed that we were attracting the most motivated students who would have done well with or without SI.

To control statistically for motivation, we identified students in the class who expressed high interest in SI, both on the first and last days of class, but were precluded from attending because of employment or other scheduled classes. Mean final course grades for this group of students fell midway between the two groups we had reported on previously. These students split the difference in final course grades between those who came to SI and those who did not (Blanc et al., 1983). We observed similar results in a broader study conducted at UMKC in 1996 with 1,593 students enrolled in classes where SI was offered during the winter semester (UMKC Center/National Center, 2000). Similar conclusions emerged from a study at Oxford Brookes University in the United Kingdom (Price & Rust, 1995).

Additional data in support of SI emerged when we noted that there were occasions over the years when we could not find an SI leader for lecturers who regularly used SI. We were therefore unable to provide SI in some courses, some semesters. In those instances, we observed the yo-yo effect of D grades, withdrawals, and failures returning to baseline, only to be reduced significantly when SI was reintroduced.

By far the most comprehensive assessment of SI was undertaken in 1997 in a study conducted by the UMKC National Center for Supplemental Instruction (2000). This study analyzed a national database of information provided by 270 institutions between 1982 and 1996 by examining the impact of SI at different types of institutions: two-year public, two-year private, four-year public, and four-year private. This database contained 4,945 separate courses that offered SI with a combined enrollment of 505,738 students in those courses. The study tracked students with respect to their final course grades in classes in which SI was offered. The fact that data were gathered from a large number of diverse institutions increased our ability to generalize findings that SI was positively correlated with achievement. However, it must be noted that the lack of randomization or matching of student characteristics was a limitation of this national SI research study.

Figure 18.1 indicates the mean final course grades of SI participants versus non-SI participants at two-year public, two-year private, four-year public, and four-year private institutions, respectively. Results of an independent t-test revealed that the mean final grade of SI participants was higher than that of SI nonparticipants. The difference between the means was statistically significant, $p < .01$.

Further study revealed that since 1982, more than a thousand higher educators from 517 postsecondary institutions received SI training. A breakdown of these institutions follows: two-year public, 37.5 percent; two-year private, 1.5 percent; four-year public, 34.0; and four-year private, 27.0 percent (UMKC, 2000).

SUPPLEMENTAL INSTRUCTION ASSESSMENTS FROM THE FIELD

The following two studies show the positive outcomes of SI at a large research university and a private four-year university. The public university study looks at SI's relationship with performance in eight courses, while the private institution's study examines the impact of SI on mean final course grades and the percentage of D, F, and withdrawal grades for students in a science course over three years.

Large Research University

The effectiveness of SI was investigated at a large public research university (Kochenour et al., 1997). Over the 1992–93 and 1993–94 academic years, SI's relationship with performance was examined in eight courses within the disciplines of physical and social science. More than eleven thousand students participated in the study. The researchers examined whether SI participation was

Figure 18.1. Comparison of Final Course Grades for SI and Non-SI Participants, 1982–1996

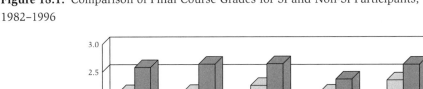

	All Colleges	2 Year Public	2 Year Private	4 Year Public	4 Year Private
☐ Non-SI Participants	2.09	2.09	2.26	2.07	2.31
■ SI Participants	2.42	2.56	2.55	2.36	2.55

related to higher grades, especially when prior achievement (high school GPA and composite ACT score) was included as a covariate.

Including data from 11,390 students, a significant positive correlation existed between SI participation and final grade, $r = .17$, $p < .001$. However, when controlling for prior achievement and course affiliation, it was possible to include data pertaining to SI attendance and final grades for 8,047 students only. This was due to the fact that the measure of precollege achievement was unavailable for some students. Results using the analysis of covariance indicated that the average final grade of students who attended SI sessions three or more times was higher than the average final grade of those who did not attend. The difference between the means, .60, was significant, $p < .001$. The difference could not be explained by the number of hours in which the student was enrolled, worked, or planned to study.

We should add that while most programs offer SI as a voluntary service to students, some institutions require participation from certain students and groups. Others elicit a commitment from students to attend on a regular basis. Ferris State University (Michigan) finds success in requiring participation, and medical students at Uppsala University in Sweden make a commitment to attend a specific SI group.

Private Four-Year University

SI was used to assist nursing students in a private university (Van Lanen & Lockie, 1997). Three hundred eight undergraduates enrolled in chemistry over three years were involved in this study. Except for the math placement test, results on measures of precollege achievement (English placement test, Nelson Denny test, high school GPA, transfer GPA, and admission status) revealed no significant difference between SI participants and nonparticipants in terms of their preparation. Students who attended six or more SI sessions were identified as SI participants ($n = 105$), whereas students who attended fewer than six SI sessions were recognized as non-SI participants ($n = 203$). Compared with nonparticipants, the mean final course grade of participants, 2.52, was higher than that of nonparticipants, 2.21. The difference between the means, .31, was significant, $p < .01$. In addition, a larger percentage of non-SI participants (29.1 percent) than SI participants (14.3 percent) earned D's, F's, or W's. The difference between the groups was significant, $p < .001$, suggesting that SI nonparticipants were less successful in completing the course with average or above-average grades than were SI participants.

COST-EFFECTIVENESS

The bottom line on the cost-effectiveness of SI is that it can return to the campus in terms of reduced attrition more than it costs. That has certainly been the case at UMKC (UMKC Center/National Center, 2000). During 1998–99, SI operated in fifty-two content courses at UMKC. These courses had a total enrollment of 4,110 students. Of these, 48.9 percent (2,010) attended SI sessions during the semester. Students who attended SI reenrolled and graduated at a rate ten percentage points higher than students who never attended SI.

Applying the 10 percent point difference between students who attended SI with students who never attended, one can infer that 201 students reenrolled at UMKC who otherwise might have dropped out. Minimally, the average undergraduate student at UMKC (twelve credit hours) spent $3,300 each year on tuition, fees, bookstore purchases, and other related expenditures. Those students provided approximately $663,300 in revenue to the university. Although the cost-effectiveness data are inferential, administrators at UMKC concluded that the investment in SI was both educationally and financially beneficial.

In a similar analysis, Congos (2002) presented a model for institutions to determine how much money is saved over four years through SI. He also argued that SI not only appears to be cost-effective, but also increases the quality of the educational experience by fostering retention-related affective connections between students.

TECHNOLOGY AND SUPPLEMENTAL INSTRUCTION

The adaptability of SI allowed us to attach SI methodology to videotaped units of medical curricula essential to board examinations and the licensure of physicians. In 1991, charged with teaching biochemistry to foreign-trained physicians whose background in this subject was weak, we used the standard SI model, only to find it ineffective. Because of their poor language skills and inadequate biochemistry background, the students were unable to cope with an hour-long lecture, no matter how well we tried to prepare them. We needed to be able to stop the lecturer at will and allow the students to process the concepts, in English, as they were introduced.

The professor granted us permission to videotape the lectures. We assigned SI-trained facilitators to the student groups and charged them with the task of working on the material until everyone understood it. Typically, the students spent two to three hours on a one-hour lecture. The group leader, as well as students themselves, stopped the tape every few minutes to work through difficult aspects of the material. Provided with this type of support, students not only passed their board examinations but improved their English.

Reflecting on the success of the VSI lecture process, the staff realized that now we had what we previously thought was impossible: control over the pace of delivery. Moreover, unlike SI, we had the continuous opportunity to capture and manage extended periods of the students' learning time. Although we had been successful with highly motivated and sophisticated learners, could we now apply this methodology to underprepared undergraduates? Was it possible to teach both essential skills and prerequisite knowledge within the core curriculum? In 1992 we had a population of students who might be candidates for such instruction: those who had been dismissed from the university for academic reasons, special admit students who lacked either test scores or class rank that would entitle them to regular admission, and student athletes whose competition schedule often took them out of town during key portions of the semester.

In order to try this approach, we found an award-winning professor of Western Civilization who would do anything for his students except water down his course or inflate his grades. Since his course was quite demanding, he agreed to allow us to arrange for his lectures to be videotaped in our campus studio. The professor set up a separate section of Western Civilization for our target population of students. Instead of the usual three lecture hours per week, we scheduled nine hours per week with three hours of additional credit given for Critical Thinking in the Social Sciences (Martin & Blanc, 1994). We tolerated neither tardiness nor absence. These students did the same assignments and took the same exams and met the same timetable as those in the professor's live lecture class. His graduate assistants graded both sets of exams on the same scale, and no special considerations were granted. At the end of the term, our marginal students performed as well as regular students. In fact, they had slightly higher grades, no D's, no failures, and no withdrawals.

Our later experiences with VSI confirmed the strength of the learning model. One student had the following to say about her VSI Western Civilization course: "I feel like I have gotten ahead and that without taking a class in this form I don't think I would be the person I am now. I appreciated my class being a smaller group so I could get more attention. The group work was awesome; that was really great. Not only could you communicate and talk to your friend but at the same time you had more opening up of ideas—you know, a lot of people thinking in group work."

Since that time we have developed VSI courses in Introduction to Chemistry, College Algebra, Physics of Everyday Life, and Math 100 for on- and off-campus use. Our off-campus clientele include rural Missouri high schools that lack the means to provide their students with a college preparatory experience. In 2001–2002, VSI courses were being facilitated in thirty-two rural high schools serving more than four hundred students. In this iteration, VSI has served as a credit-bearing and skills-enhancing program for both teachers and students. The students have the option to receive both high school and university credit for their courses; teachers have the opportunity to hone their skills through participation as facilitators. Administrators and teachers report that teachers gain major insights into the teaching-learning process as a result of spending a year facilitating the six-credit-hour block of curriculum.

Longitudinal data for both the on-campus and high school VSI programs confirm that both VSI populations consistently equal or exceed performance of students in the on-campus program. For the on-campus VSI groups, this fact has some interesting implications since many students who are enrolled in the VSI courses are considered underprepared for college-level work.

UMKC'S ADVANCED PREPARATION PROGRAM

Supplemental Instruction and virtual Supplemental Instruction were two of the core components in the Advanced Preparation Program (APP), under the leadership of the provost of academic affairs, the vice chancellor of student affairs, and enrollment management in fall 2000. The program began with a cohort of more than one hundred first-year students who did not meet UMKC's selective admission criteria. Individuals who are conditionally admitted to the university take part in the APP program. The administration believes that the students can succeed in a structured program using a myriad of support services. The existing program has two primary goals: to widen access to our already diverse campus and ensure the success and retention of the students.

The APP students enroll in twelve hours of course work from a selected list: freshman seminar, VSI math, VSI chemistry, VSI history, an English composition class, or a core curriculum course with SI attached. In addition to math and writing labs, APP students are assigned cohort advisers who meet with their assigned students on a regular basis to discuss their academic progress and to mentor and advise them. In fall 2000, 119 students entered UMKC as APP participants in a pilot project. In winter 2002, more than 200 participated. Data collection and analysis from the first semester revealed that 106 of 111 (95 percent) of APP students reenrolled, and 92 of 106 (88 percent) completed in good academic standing, far exceeding institutional expectations (McCormick, 2001). The results of this program are summarized as follows:

- 111 of 119 (93 percent) APP trial admits completed fall semester 2000
- 106 of 111 (95 percent) completing fall 2000 reenrolled winter 2001
- 45 of 47 (95 percent) APP minority students completed fall semester 2000
- 45 of 47 (95 percent) completing fall 2000 reenrolled winter 2001
- 92 of 106 (88 percent) completing fall 2000 finished in good academic standing
- 50 of 106 (47 percent) completing fall 2000 earned a 3.0 or higher GPA

RECOMMENDATIONS

The collective wisdom gained from our own experience and consistent commentary from the field leads us to offer eight recommendations:

- *Make use of national data on the effectiveness of SI to bring key administrators and faculty on board.* Call or e-mail our center for specific information, including programs in your area that you might visit.

- *Provide training for the campus SI team,* and select an administrator or faculty member to oversee the pilot phase.
- *Start small with two or three course sections* during the pilot phase of SI. Let the program grow as it demonstrates success.
- *Adapt the program to meet specific needs of programs and first-year students* to ensure that all students are served.
- *Train and supervise SI leaders.* Positive program outcomes rely on the SI leader's effectiveness.
- *Collect, analyze, and report data each semester.* Credibility relies on careful and systematic program evaluation.
- *Have the SI program report to a senior-level administrator,* so that access to overall institutional policies and resources is ensured.
- *Make use of available resources,* such as the UMKC National Center if you experience problems or if you decide to contextualize your program. You may also use SInet where you will find colleagues in the field ready to advise you.

CONCLUSION

As we review the past thirty years, we take pride in the continued success and expansion of SI. Aside from the stated reasons practitioners give for implementing SI, we believe that one explanation is that the program strikes a chord of common sense. For more traditional campuses that rely heavily on lecture and text as primary teaching modalities, SI systematically offers students the tools of the informal learning environment. Students can attend weekly sessions that provide the opportunity for open and free-flowing dialogue, spontaneous questions, lively discussions, trial-and-error experimentation, and, most important, the help and support of colleagues. All this is conveniently provided without cost, obligation, or risk to students. Even as new technologies change the landscape of higher education, SI practitioners find innovative ways to keep educational experiences personal and affordable.

If SI and VSI have contributed anything of lasting significance, we think it is the evidence that marginal students need not be sidetracked into developmental curricula; rather, with appropriate assistance, they can master the content of rigorous academic courses as they develop effective skills and prerequisite concepts. In this way, we have avoided the reductionist path that deconstructs areas of fundamental knowledge into a series of finite skills. Instead, we have been the advocates of a more holistic enterprise that treats each individual as capable of adapting to a new environment, given motivation, time on task, and opportunity. In providing a more flexible and informal approach to academic success, we believe that students at all ranges of ability can work together as they learn, and institutions can challenge and support an increasingly diverse population.

Academic Advising

Margaret C. King
Thomas J. Kerr

*Having the Advising Center here in the college is like having an emergency room
in a hospital. There are always knowledgeable staff ready to help resolve the academic emergencies that occur. Whether it's schedule changes, getting on track with
a professor, or midcourse corrections, advisers are right there and ready to help.*
—First-year student

*I returned to campus life after a forty-year absence, full of apprehension about
possible failure and not fitting in. My adviser soon put me at ease, providing order
and substance to my plans and dreams, informing me of the many support services
available, and putting me in contact with the people who would help me get started.*
—First-year adult student

Academic advising is perhaps the most important way that first-year students interact with a representative of the institution. As such, academic
advising can be viewed as the hub of the wheel that establishes links to
all other support services on campus. It can occur through face-to-face interaction, through the mail, by videoconferencing, by telephone, electronically, or
other means. However it happens, academic advising is clearly a key factor in
challenging and supporting students in making a successful transition to college, feeling a part of their institutions, and achieving their educational goals.
As Richard Light states, "Good advising may be the single most underestimated
characteristic of a successful college experience" (2001, p. 81).

Thomas Grites and Virginia Gordon (2000) note that "the academic adviser's
role (whether faculty member or full-time adviser) is to facilitate student learning, hopefully in all three contexts identified by Winston et al. (1984): educational, career and personal" (p. 13). They go on to point out that advising
should focus on student learning within the context of the student's personal
characteristics, such as interests, values, and abilities. Creamer (2000) concurs,
stating that the purpose of academic advising is student learning, and the focus
is the whole person.

Effective academic advising is clearly much more than scheduling and registration. It is a developmental process in which course selection and registration
take place within the broader context of the student's life and career plan. While

many descriptions have been proposed to define developmental advising, the following, by David Crockett (1984), serves as a foundation for this chapter:

> Academic advising is a developmental process, which assists students in the clarification of their life and career goals and in the development of educational plans for the realization of these goals. It is a decision making process by which students realize their maximum educational potential through communication and information exchanges with an adviser; it is continuous, multifaceted, and the responsibility of both student and adviser. The adviser serves as a facilitator of communication, a coordinator of learning experiences through course and career planning and academic progress review, and an agent of referral to other campus agencies as necessary [p. 1].

This chapter will discuss the organization and delivery of academic advising services for first-year students, describing five advising providers and seven organizational models of advising. It will also focus on key components of effective advising programs (including a mission statement, adviser training, evaluation, and recognition/reward), on how first-year advising services can be delivered (either individually or in small groups), on the use of technology in advising, on advising issues as they relate to the diversity of our first-year student populations, and on challenges for the future.

ORGANIZATION AND DELIVERY OF ACADEMIC ADVISING FOR FIRST-YEAR STUDENTS

There is no one right way to organize and deliver academic advising for first-year students. Academic advising approaches are very institution specific and must be based on the mission and organization of an institution and the needs of its students.

Factors Influencing the Organization and Delivery of Advising Services

As institutions review the organization and delivery of advising services for first-year students, with a possible goal of implementing change, it is important to look at factors that will influence how those services can be organized and delivered. The first such factor is institutional mission. This includes the control of the institution (public, private, or proprietary), the level of educational offerings (associate, baccalaureate, graduate), the nature of the program offerings (liberal arts, professional, vocational, and technical), and the selectivity of the institution. Each of these has an effect on the student population, the complexity of degree requirements, and the structure of program requirements, which in turn have an impact on the academic advising system.

The second factor influencing the organization and delivery of academic advising is the student population itself. While effective academic advising is critical to all first-year students, it is especially important that underprepared, undecided, diverse, first-generation, and commuter students be advised by competent advisers with adequate training.

A third factor is the faculty. They also have an impact on the way advising services are organized and delivered. As an institution looks at the role faculty should and will play, it is important to consider faculty interest in advising, their awareness of existing problems, and their willingness to address problems and accept training. Faculty interest and willingness may be affected by other responsibilities, how the administration values advising, and the reward for good advising.

A fourth factor influencing academic advising is the programs and policies of the institution. These determine the sequencing of courses, the complexity of graduation requirements, the scope of the general education requirement, and the degree to which an adviser must approve a variety of transactions. For all of these factors, as the complexity increases, the need for highly skilled advisers working in a well-defined advising organization increases.

Finally, other factors such as budget, facilities, and organizational structure have an impact on the organization and delivery of advising services. There are many ways in which college campuses can provide effective academic advising, and some are more expensive than others. Certain organizational models require space to house an advising center, so the institution's facilities become a factor. The institution's organizational structure determines who ultimately has responsibility for academic advising.

Advising Providers

There are five groups on college campuses that provide effective academic advising for first-year students: faculty, full-time advisers, counselors, paraprofessionals, and peers.

Faculty are the group that most often advises first-year students. Almost 50 percent of the institutions surveyed by the American College Testing Program (ACT) in 1997 report that faculty have the sole responsibility for academic advising (Habley & Morales, 1998). The advantages of using faculty are their program and course knowledge, their knowledge of related career fields, the respect they hold within the institution, the cost to the institution, and the fact that research shows a clear relationship between student interaction with faculty and student retention.

Full-time advisers are the second most frequent group that provides academic advising for first-year students. Full-time advisers are generally more accessible to students as they are typically housed in a central location and have advising as their priority. In addition, they have student development training, are generally skilled in advising exploratory or undecided students, and may have the best skills in interpreting often complex academic requirements to first-year students.

Other groups that can provide very effective academic advising include counselors, who are primarily used in two-year colleges and have strengths similar to those of full-time advisers. Paraprofessionals and peers can also be used very effectively but require careful attention to their selection, training, and supervision.

In determining which delivery system (or systems) for advising first-year students will best meet the needs of an institution, attention should be paid to the importance of each of the following factors: access and availability to students, the priority placed on advising, the knowledge of the academic discipline, knowledge of student development, the need for training, the cost to the institution, and credibility with faculty and staff (Table 19.1). Once an institution identifies the factors that are most important in advising first-year students, it can then determine which delivery system(s) will best meet their needs.

Organizational Models

For many years, little attention was paid to organizational models of academic advising. This was due in part to a belief that institutions were unique and, as a result, similarities would be limited. However, in the early 1980s, research by Habley (1983) and Habley and McCauley (1987) identified seven organizational models of academic advising. Subsequent surveys by ACT expanded that research. Each of the organizational models has strengths and weaknesses, particularly in terms of advising for first-year students.

Faculty Only. The faculty-only model is the only one in which the organizational model and delivery system are the same. In this model, each entering student is assigned a faculty adviser, generally someone from his or her program of study. Undecided first-year students are usually assigned to liberal arts or specially selected faculty. This model may or may not have a campus coordinator, and advisers are accountable to their respective departments.

A key advantage of this model for first-year students is that it promotes the interaction of new students with a faculty member, and much of the retention research on first-year students cites the importance of student-faculty interaction. This can also be particularly valuable if the faculty adviser teaches in the student's program of study, as the adviser would be in a good position to help the student understand the connections between course work and the actual world of work.

A key disadvantage of this model is that many first-year students are not settled in a major and are exploring their career and major options. Faculty advisers are knowledgeable about their specific program area but not necessarily about other areas; consequently, they may not be as helpful to the undecided student. They also may not be as knowledgeable about support services on campus that can assist the exploratory student in making decisions about major and career as well as help with adjustment issues to college. Also, in institutions where all faculty are required to advise, there can be varying levels of commitment, resulting in an inconsistent quality of advising. Finally, the quality of faculty academic advising may be related to the importance of academic advising in the promotion and tenure policies of the institution.

Satellite Model. In the satellite model, advising offices are maintained and controlled within academic subunits (schools, colleges). In these subunits, advising responsibilities may shift from an advising office to specific faculty. There is

Table 19.1. Advising Delivery System Matrix: Strengths and Weaknesses

Delivery system	Access/ availability to students	Priority placed on advising	Knowledge of academic discipline	Knowledge of student development	Need for required training	Cost to institution	Credibility with faculty and staff
Faculty	Low	Low	High	Low	High	Low	High
Professional Adviser	High	High	Average	High	Average	High	Low
Counselor	Average	Average	Average	High	Average	High	Average
Peer	High	Average	Low	Low	High	Low	Average
Para-Professional	High	High	Average	Average	High	Low	Average

Source: King (1988). This material is used by permission of John Wiley & Sons, Inc.

generally a satellite office specifically for undecided students that has campuswide coordinating responsibility. This model is found most often in large colleges and universities, so a key advantage for first-year students is that it helps them make connections in the smaller environment of their school or college. If the institution has a satellite office for undecided students, these students may be better served by advisers specifically trained to assist them.

If advising responsibilities are assigned to faculty in the schools or colleges, advantages and disadvantages would be the same as described in the faculty-only model. If responsibilities are assigned to full-time advisers, students would benefit from having a trained adviser who has advising as his or her primary responsibility, but would be missing the contact with a faculty member and that person's academic expertise. Overall coordination of advising services becomes a special concern in this model because of its decentralized nature, as does consistency in the quality of advising. Close attention must be given to the transition process for students who declare or change majors and to advisement for students with special needs.

Self-Contained Model. In this model, all advising, from orientation to departure, takes place in a centralized unit such as an advising center or counseling center. A dean or director supervises all advising functions. The advantage of this model for first-year students is having trained advisers in a central location with advising as their priority. These advisers are skilled at working with undecided and underprepared students and have a general knowledge of all programs of study in the institution, support services, and student development. Since faculty are often not part of this model, the key disadvantage is that the model does not foster student-faculty interaction.

Supplementary Model. In the supplementary model, faculty serve as advisers for all students, but there is an advising office with a part-time coordinator that assists faculty but has no original jurisdiction for approving academic transactions. That assistance might include maintenance of an advising handbook, being an information clearinghouse and a referral resource, and providing adviser training. In this model, the advising office is small, sometimes headed by part-time faculty or volunteer faculty with trained peer advisers. Supervision of faculty advisers occurs in the academic subunits.

Advantages and disadvantages of this model for first-year students are similar to the faculty-only model. However, this model provides an office to provide coordination and assist faculty; consequently, faculty here are better prepared to assume their advising responsibilities.

Split Model. In the split model, the initial advising of students is split: an advising office handles specific groups such as exploratory, undecided, part-time, or underprepared students, and faculty advisers in the academic subunits advise all others. Once specified conditions are met (for example, a major is declared or developmental courses are completed), the student may be assigned directly to a faculty adviser or to an academic subunit, which may use full-time advisers, faculty, or peer advisers. In this model, a coordinator or director may have campuswide coordinating responsibility and provide training, an advising handbook, and other aspects of advising.

Advantages of this model for first-year students are that it brings together the skills of both key delivery systems, providing trained advisers with the skills to advise special needs students yet also building on the strengths of faculty. The one disadvantage of this model is the need to reassign students from one adviser to another. Often, when first-year students make a connection with an adviser, changing to someone new (once that student meets specified conditions) may not be an easy process, and assisting the student in making connections with the new adviser will be extremely important.

Dual Model. In this model, the student has two types of advisers: faculty advisers who provide advising related to the student's program of study, and staff in an advising office who advise regarding general education requirements, registration procedures, and academic policy. The advising office typically has a coordinator with campuswide coordinating responsibility and also generally advises undecided students.

As with the split model, the strength of this model is that it provides more than one delivery system for first-year students, with the strengths of each. The disadvantage is the potential confusion of which adviser to see for what. The institution must clearly articulate the advising responsibilities of the faculty and the advising office.

Total Intake Model. In this model, all of the initial advising of entering students occurs through one office. Students are assigned to faculty when specified conditions have been met, such as after their initial registration, after their first semester, or after completion of forty-five credits. A director provides campuswide coordination, and an advising office may have additional responsibility for the development and administration of curriculum and instruction and the development and enforcement of policies and procedures.

Strengths of this model for first-year students are that it front-loads the system, providing trained advisers who are prepared to work with all students—exploratory, decided, traditional, nontraditional, developmental, and others. As with the split model, the key disadvantage is having to move to a different adviser after a relationship has been developed and the possible lack of faculty contact initially in the advising process.

Trends in Models. Over the past ten years, research by ACT has shown a decrease in the use of the most decentralized (faculty-only, satellite) and most centralized models (self-contained) and an increase in shared models. Research also shows that academic affairs is the predominant reporting line for all models except the self-contained model, where a greater percentage report through student affairs (Habley & Morales, 1998).

Preferred Organizational Models

Using information on the five groups on college campuses that provide advising services and the seven organizational models, and taking into consideration the typical characteristics of students entering two- and four-year institutions, we have chosen two preferred models for advising first-year students. These models take into consideration the special challenges of advising the first-year population.

For two-year institutions, the preferred advising model is based on the total intake model where there is a centralized advising office with a full-time administrator reporting to the chief academic or student affairs officer. That office, with a core of trained advisers (including full-time advisers or counselors, faculty working part time in the office, and paraprofessionals or peers), would provide all advisement for first-year students and continued advising for students who are exploratory, underprepared, in academic difficulty, or changing majors. Students would eventually be assigned to faculty advisers in their program of study when they are more settled in their major and better able to take advantage of faculty expertise.

The advising office staff would interact regularly with other campus offices, such as admissions, financial aid, registration, placement testing, counseling, academic support services, and the academic departments. It would have responsibility for both preservice and in-service training for all advisers, evaluation of the advising system and advisers, and recognition and reward of exemplary advising. It would also have responsibility for development of adviser and advisee handbooks, coordination of a first-year seminar, the development, maintenance, and distribution of advising files, and provision of on-line advising services.

For four-year institutions, the ideal model for advising first-year students is based on the dual model, where faculty members provide advising related to the student's program of study while full-time advisers or counselors working in an advising office provide advising related to academic policies and registration procedures. Peer advisers could be used to assist faculty in delivery of a first-year student seminar and to help the first-year student with adjustment problems.

In smaller four-year institutions, the advising office would be centralized and would have campuswide coordinating responsibilities. In large institutions, the academic advising office would be college or discipline specific and normally would report to an assistant or associate dean. A committee comprising the college's assistant and associate deans and coordinated by the vice president of academic affairs or assistant or associate provost would provide campuswide coordination. The advising office would also have responsibility for the faculty used to advise first-year students, the seminar courses, and the training, selection, and supervision of the peer advisers. The faculty would rotate as advisers of first-year students. An alternative would be that after two years, the students would be reassigned to another departmental adviser so that advising loads could be balanced.

Peer advisers would be assigned to work with a faculty member as a resource in a first-year student seminar course. The advising office would have responsibility for coordinating all advising for first-year students and would identify specific professionals as first-year student advisers. This office would continue advising students who are exploratory, in academic difficulty, changing majors, or in specialized programs, such as dual-degree or minors. Students could be assigned to non-first-year faculty advisers after completing the sophomore year.

These two preferred advising models have many features in common, the most important of which is the use of full-time faculty as advisers. A great deal of evidence cites the importance of student-faculty interaction outside the classroom, noting that it has a positive influence on student development and decision making, student satisfaction, and student persistence (Tinto, 1975, 1993; Pascarella, Terenzini, & Wolfle, 1986; Kramer & White, 1982; Fuller, 1983). As Astin (1977) states, "Student-faculty interaction has a stronger relationship to student satisfaction with the college experience than any other student or institutional characteristic" (p. 223).

Faculty, however, cannot do it by themselves. There is also a need for an advising center or office staffed by full-time advisers and counselors, peers, and paraprofessionals. The advising office should interact regularly with other offices, services, and departments on campus.

All advising models have advantages and disadvantages. Among the disadvantages of the proposed preferred models would be cost, since the models use full-time advisers, paraprofessionals, and peers, who would be hired specifically to provide advising services. The possible lack of continuity in the adviser-advisee relationship developed in the student's first year is also a concern. On the positive side, some of the costs could be offset by increases in student persistence, as these models use the best advising resources during the times that are most critical to first-year student success and retention. Well-trained advisers with student development backgrounds could be available to assist students during the first term or year when they are most likely to explore various programs and declare or change majors. In addition, students gain the expertise of faculty when they are more settled in their programs and need faculty assistance in making connections among current study, future study, and work. The use of faculty, combined with other delivery systems, contributes to a well-integrated advising system and provides a way of easing heavy faculty advising loads and guarantees that advising services are coordinated and supervised.

KEY COMPONENTS OF SUCCESSFUL FIRST-YEAR ADVISING PROGRAMS

Effective advising programs include the following key components: (1) an advising program mission statement to guide the advising activities, (2) a specific individual designated by the institution to direct or coordinate advising activities, (3) a systematic training program for all advisers, and (4) recognition and reward for exemplary advising.

Mission Statement

A quality advising program needs a clear statement of philosophy to guide advising activities that is built on clearly defined goals and objectives integrally tied to the institution's mission statement. This statement should identify the primary purpose of advising and include a statement of beliefs about students as well as information on the nature of the advising program, the organizational structure, expectations of advisers and advisees, and the goals for advising.

The advising program mission statement at the Pennsylvania State University acknowledges that "advising is part of the teaching and learning continuum and that there is a synergism between classroom instruction and academic advising" (White, 2000, p. 182). A revision to that statement acknowledges "the concept that ultimately academic advising is a relationship between student and adviser, between student and institution, and between adviser and institution" (White, 2000, p. 183). Use of the National Academic Advising Association's (NACADA) Statement of Core Values, and the Council on the Advancement of Standards in Higher Education (CAS) Standards and Guidelines on Academic Advising can be of assistance in creating this statement. Both of these documents can be found in the appendixes of Gordon, Habley, and Associates' *Academic Advising: A Comprehensive Handbook* (2000).

Coordination

Advising programs must have a director or coordinator, who devotes a significant amount of time to that responsibility. Based on responses to the ACT Survey, the most common titles of the person in that role are director or coordinator, director of counseling, vice president or dean of academic affairs, assistant vice president or dean of academic affairs, and vice president or dean of student affairs. Across all institutions, reporting lines through academic affairs outnumber those for student affairs by more than two to one. Most reporting lines through student affairs occur in public two-year colleges.

Of those coordinating advising, 50 percent spent less than a quarter of their time coordinating advising, and only 30 percent spent more than half their time coordinating advising (Habley & Morales, 1998).

Adviser Training

Because academic advising has evolved from a course scheduling activity to a complex process requiring comprehensive knowledge and skills, adviser training is critical to the success of the program. Yet results of the Fifth National Survey on Academic Advising show that training is provided by only 34.8 percent of academic departments, that the most common format is a single workshop of one day or less, and that the most common focus is information and facts (Habley & Morales, 1998).

An effective adviser training program should have realistic, specific, and measurable objectives. The content and format of the program must be designed with the audience in mind. It is important to consider the skills of the advisers to be trained, the experience they have in advising, and their willingness to participate in the training program. A training program for faculty could be quite different from one for full-time advisers or counselors. The format and techniques used for the training should also be designed with the audience in mind. Formats could be a single workshop of one day or less or a series of workshops held throughout the year. Techniques could include an external presenter, panel discussions, brainstorming, role playing, and case studies.

Content of adviser training programs can be broken down into three components: conceptual, informational, and relational. Conceptual components include basic concepts in advising, such as a definition of advising, the relationship between advising and student retention, student expectations of advising, and the rights and responsibilities of advisers and advisees. Informational components include the basic information advisers need to know, such as programs and course offerings, institutional rules and regulations, and referral resources. Relational components include the behaviors that the adviser needs to demonstrate, such as good listening skills, conveying an attitude of warmth and welcome, and asking questions that invite the student's involvement in the discussion. As Habley states, "Without understanding (conceptual elements), there is no context for the delivery of services. Without information, there is no substance to advising. And, without interpersonal skills (relational), the quality of the advisee/adviser interaction is left to chance" (1995, p. 76).

Recognition and Reward

For many advisers, the intrinsic rewards they receive from assisting students and watching them grow and develop are enough reward for their efforts. However, as Habley (1995) states, "The function of advising is too critical to be left solely to those who intrinsically cherish it." Extrinsic rewards for both individual advisers and the institution are important because they demonstrate the value the institution places on advising and can help improve the quality of service provided for first-year students.

Because faculty are the primary providers of academic advising services, research on recognition and reward has primarily focused on them. Kerr (2000) reports that only 31 percent of campuses recognize, reward, or compensate faculty for academic advising and that the ACT surveys have shown a consistent decline in faculty recognition strategies that include consideration in promotion and tenure decisions, as well as release time from instruction, committee work, or research expectations. Whether academic advising is a factor in faculty promotion and tenure decisions is very institution specific, but institutions that do have this factor include Iowa State University, the Altoona College campus of Pennsylvania State University, and the University of Wisconsin College of Letters and Sciences (Kerr, 2000).

Other than consideration in promotion and tenure decisions, the most frequent methods that colleges and universities use to provide recognition and reward for both faculty and professional advisers are release time, stipends, support for travel to conferences, annual campus awards, and external recognition, such as a NACADA Outstanding Adviser Award. Additional recognition for professional advisers could include appointment to a higher-level position in the administration of the advising program.

DELIVERY OF ADVISING TO FIRST-YEAR STUDENTS

Effective academic advising for first-year students can be delivered either individually or in small groups. In either situation, good communication skills, questioning skills, and referral skills are extremely important. In an individual advising session, it is also important that the adviser take time to plan and prepare for the session. Steps in doing so might include the following: (1) developing rapport, (2) reviewing the previous advising session and progress made since then, (3) identifying the purpose for the current session, (4) discussing issues and concerns, and (5) summarizing the discussion and outlining a plan of action. Advisers should also make use of the many assessment instruments and data that are available.

Small group advising can be very effective and can be a good strategy for extending and augmenting advising services. Reasons for using group advising can include a situation where the number of students exceeds the number of advisers, when an efficient and effective way to share information is needed, and where peer groups can be used to reinforce good advising. Small group advising can easily be incorporated into orientation programs, a first-year seminar (where the teacher is also the adviser or where faculty and professional advisers form an instructional team to teach the seminar), learning communities (students enroll in a cluster of courses and participate in meetings facilitated by a peer adviser), and residence halls. It can also be very effective in working with special populations such as students on academic probation, honors students, students in oversubscribed majors, and undecided students.

An alternative to individual and small group advising is self-advising: allowing students to advise themselves. While this may happen more often than we think, and in many ways may be an ideal goal (students become independent learners and active partners in the educational process), it generally is not a good approach to academic advising, particularly for first-year students. It is critical that first-year students have the opportunity to meet with a concerned representative of the institution to discuss their goals, map out their program of study, and develop a relationship with that individual. While we would advocate that this meeting take place in person, it is not out of the question for it to take place on-line. However it occurs, students should not be allowed to register for classes until at least one meeting has occurred. Even with the use of technology such as on-line registration and degree audits, systems can be developed to promote interactions between the adviser and the advisee prior to registration. While one may frequently hear of situations where the student can bypass the system, an institution that is committed to the concepts of developmental academic advising must find ways to prevent any abuses from occurring.

ASSESSING FIRST-YEAR STUDENT ACADEMIC ADVISING

Assessment of academic advising is important for several reasons, the most important of which is to improve the advising programs for first-year students. Assessment can also be used to determine if there is a relationship between academic advising and some intended outcome, such as student satisfaction, career decision making, academic achievement, and persistence. Assessment can be important in maintaining and expanding the resources needed to operate an effective advising program.

Assessment efforts should be planned by a committee that has representation from individuals likely to be affected by the results. That committee should be clear about the mission, goals, and objectives of the advising program; should identify the delivery systems used; and should agree to the purpose of the evaluation and how the results will be used. It will need to identify the questions to be answered by the evaluation, define the focus of the assessment, (individual advisers, the advising program, or something else), determine what data will be collected, and identify the sources that can provide the data and the methods for collecting that data.

Essentially there are three assessment methods: quantitative (the use of standardized methods with statistical outcomes), qualitative (the gathering of detailed descriptions generally done through interviews, focus groups, and direct observation), and a combination of the two. Assessment results of individual advisers can be used in either a formative way (improvement of performance) or a summative way (personnel decisions such as tenure and promotion, although it is sometimes difficult to prevent data collected for formative reasons from being used in summative ways). Overall, evaluation results may enhance advising services, promote increased institutional support, support staffing changes and salaries, and identify areas for increased adviser training.

Assessment of the advising program is critical to providing data that document the impact advising has on student success, satisfaction, and persistence. In a relevant review of the literature, Pascarella and Terenzini (1991) noted that the research results have been mixed. However, they cite research by Metzner (1989) showing "that the quality of advising received had only a small and statistically nonsignificant direct effect on persistence. High-quality advising, however, did have a statistically significant positive effect on persistence transmitted through its positive impact on such variables as grades and satisfaction and its negative effect on intent to leave the institution" (Pascarella & Terenzini 1991, pp. 404–405). Upcraft, Srebnik, and Stevenson (1995) conclude that while the research may demonstrate that advising promotes student success, there is little evidence to determine which methods of advising and which models are most effective in promoting that success. Habley and Morales (1998) concur, stating that the challenge is to provide compelling evidence that academic advising does make a difference in the lives of students and the success of institutions.

A model of academic advising assessment for first-year students developed by Upcraft and Schuh (1996) includes the following elements:

- Assessing first-year student advising needs, so that advising services are designed to meet those needs

- Tracking first-year student use of advising services to ensure that advising is available to, and used by, all students on an equitable basis

- Assessing first-year student satisfaction with academic advising, as it is important that students not only use the service but be satisfied with it

- Assessing first-year student outcomes to determine if advising is having any effect on such outcomes as academic achievement, persistence, career decision making, and the like

- Comparing first-year student academic advising programs with programs at comparable institutions

- Using national standards, such as the CAS Standards, to be sure the advising program is meeting accepted criteria for advising excellence.

For a more detailed discussion of assessing first-year courses, programs, and services, see Part Six.

TECHNOLOGICAL RESOURCES AND DELIVERY SYSTEMS

Although academic advising should be essentially an interpersonal interaction, part of the future of academic advising clearly rests on the degree to which technology can be deployed to increase both the efficiency and effectiveness of advising programs. This is particularly important given the increasing opportunities for distance learning. Retention of distance learners is dependent on their feeling a part of the college community, and that depends greatly on their having access to good academic advising. The technological resources that support advising include the following:

- Degree audits, which match completed course work with degree program requirements, and basically track the student to degree completion

- Computerized transfer course equivalency systems, which are designed to reduce the time expended by transfer credit evaluations and to provide consistent and accurate course equivalency data for all students

- Touch-tone telephone registration systems, which can eliminate registration lines and alleviate adviser involvement in registration

- Computerized appointment calendar systems, which permit students to make their own advising appointments and provide information regarding the nature of the appointment

- Electronic adviser notebooks, which provide a way to collect and report data on adviser contacts
- Automated student profile systems, which are systems where students can enter their own data about high school activities, areas where they need help, activities in which they want to participate, and other information, which is available to the adviser

It is helpful if the registration systems that support advising can allow advisers to "lock" course equivalents for their advisees as well as provide wait-list features for alternative courses if selected courses are not available. The latter relieves the adviser of additional approval processing. Some registration systems block students who do not have appropriate prerequisite or placement scores. While this can be helpful, a good degree audit system that informs students about these circumstances in advance is better. The registration system should not provide advisers with electronic notes; this is a function of the degree audit adviser tool. Confidentiality is maintained through a series of security exercises leading up to the final audit.

Technology delivery systems are ways in which the delivery of advising may be accomplished through the use of technology:

- Synchronous advising: "Same time, same-pace, different place, person-to-person advising" (Sotto, 2000, p. 250), which can include advising over the phone, Internet or video.
- Videoconferencing: Video and audio communication between adviser and advisee.
- Computer chat and computer audioconferencing, by which participants can send text messages simultaneously over the Internet. Audio adds the ability to talk.
- Structural delivery systems, which includes broadcasts over cable TV, radio, and satellite, as well as CD-ROMs, videotapes, audiotapes, and computer disks. These can be good ways to get information to students.
- Asynchronous advising: Anytime, any pace, any place advising, which includes e-mail, video mail, and voice mail.

Advantages to these include convenient access, accuracy of information, and timeliness of feedback. However, such systems do change the person-to-person relationship, and some students may not have access to the technology.

As opportunities for distance learning increase and as institutions struggle to provide effective advising services with limited budgets, effective use of technology becomes even more important. For distance learners, approaches to academic advising must be carefully planned so that students feel connected to the institution and feel that their needs are being met. NACADA, in its "Academic Advising Standards," reaffirms that providers of distance education must offer a minimum set of core services that assist distance learners in identifying and achieving their education goals.

Barbara Krauth (1999) identifies "'Good Practice' Trends" in providing student services for distance learners, noting that they have many of the same qualities as services provided for on-campus students: "(1) Convenience—preferably accessible any time, any place; (2) Easy to understand and access; (3) Integrated into instruction, where appropriate; (4) Equal to—but not necessarily the same as—services provided to on-campus students; (5) Based on an understanding of the types of students the institution is serving at a distance and what their needs are; and (6) Based on redesigned services, not just the introduction of technology" (p. 16). She notes that it is important to provide multiple approaches to meeting student needs.

Brigham Young University has long been known for its innovative approaches to using technology to provide services for students, and its Web Based Student Planning System was recognized by IBM and the Society for College and University Planning as a best practice. This system is "a self-directed, comprehensive, and integrated student administration system that connects students to essential university resources and provides them with a single Web-enabled system to conduct routine transactions with the university. The new student administration system must not only be navigable, accurate, and timely, it must also be personal, allowing the student to 'get off the train' as it were, and to obtain general or specific help from a personal adviser" (Kramer & Peterson, 1999, p. 93).

Other examples of good practice in the use of technology include the Pennsylvania State University Automated Notebook System used in the Division of Undergraduate Studies, the automated calendar system used at Ball State University, the Web-based degree audit systems at Ball State and Brigham Young, and the interactive video advising system at Pima Community College. Additional information on technology in advising can be found in the NACADA monograph, *The "e" Factor in Delivering Advising and Student Services* (Kramer & Childs, 2000).

STUDENT DIVERSITY AND FIRST-YEAR ACADEMIC ADVISING

Academic advising has become a more complex activity in part because of the increasing diversity of the student population and the special needs and issues for each of these groups. Some of the many populations on campuses with special needs and issues are multicultural students, international students, undecided students, underprepared students, gay/lesbian/bisexual students, transfer students, adult learners, athletes, honors students, preprofessional students, first-generation students, and special needs students. In working with these populations, it is important to recognize that there is diversity within diversity; for example, Hispanic students come from many different countries with very different cultures, there are different levels of undecidedness as well as different reasons for it, and there are different levels of underpreparedness.

It is beyond the scope of this chapter to discuss each of these populations. Essentially, the basic advising skills noted earlier need to be used when working with all students. However, students within these populations may bring special needs to the advising relationship that will demand special skills and knowledge on the part of the adviser. This will require creation of an open and trusting relationship, taking time to learn about and understand the student's background, learning about the issues related to that background, becoming knowledgeable about the skills and techniques known to be effective in working with students with those issues, being knowledgeable about the resources on and off the campus to which the student could be referred, and supporting the student as he or she works through those issues.

FIRST-YEAR ACADEMIC ADVISING: CHALLENGES FOR THE FUTURE

Herta Teitelbaum (2000) notes that changes that are reshaping businesses and organizations will influence higher education and academic advising as well. "Resource scarcity, increased competitiveness, downsizing and outsourcing, and a generally more turbulent, less predictable environment are the characteristics of the post-industrial environment in which business enterprises now find themselves. . . . Businesses that successfully take advantage of technological innovations are able to create efficiencies that allow them to recapture and sustain a high level of productivity and competitiveness" (pp. 393–394). She goes on to point out that declining resources combined with expected increases in enrollment will put demands on advisers to serve larger numbers of students with fewer resources. Yet advisers will be called on to maintain high-quality services.

Teitelbaum suggests an exercise that requires evaluation of staffing requirements and identification of alternative, more cost-effective ways of providing service. She has created a matrix that looks at student needs, the level of adviser expertise required to meet those needs, and potential alternatives for satisfying those needs (Table 19.2). Effective use of technology plays a key role. For example, a student's need for information could be addressed through Web-based information rather than an actual adviser. Paraprofessionals and peers could handle such advising situations as degree audits or assistance with scheduling classes. This matrix also suggests that the most efficient and effective advising will be provided by a mix of advising staff, ranging from experienced faculty and professional advisers to paraprofessionals and peers.

RECOMMENDATIONS

Recognizing the importance of a well-organized system for providing developmental academic advising for first-year students, being aware of the increasing complexities of our institutions (including our student populations, our policies

Table 19.2. Types of Student Advising Needs with Corresponding
Adviser Experience Levels and Alternative Advising Modalities

Student Advising Need	Level of Adviser Experience Required	Alternatives for Satisfying Need
Information	Low	Printed information
		Web-based information with FAQs and linked to e-mail
		Group advising
Straightforward advising situations (such as degree progress check, class scheduling)	Medium	Undergraduate advisers (paraprofessionals)
		Graduate student advisers
More complex advising situations (such as probation students, undecided students)	High	Faculty or professional advisers
		Graduate student advisers

Source: Teitelbaum (2000). Reprinted with permission.

and procedures, and our technology), and looking to the future, we offer the following recommendations:

- *Organize and deliver academic advising on the basis of institutional mission, organization, resources, and first-year student needs.* There is no one model that fits all institutions.
- *Advising first-year students is best accomplished through the total intake model for community colleges and the dual model for four-year institutions,* although each institution must decide which model is appropriate based on its needs.
- *Advise first-year students within the framework of the institution's mission,* which should include identifying the primary purpose of advising, a statement of beliefs about students, and expectations of both students and advisers.
- *Develop programs to train advisers.* Regardless of the advising delivery system and who is doing advising, academic advisers should be trained on a continuous basis.
- *Assess academic advising,* using both qualitative and quantitative measures, focusing on first-year student advising needs and satisfaction with advising, determining if academic advising is related to desirable outcomes, comparing advising programs with other comparable institutions, and using national standards.
- *Provide meaningful reward to faculty for academic advising,* preferably within institutional promotion and tenure policies, as well as to professional advisers.

- *Integrate technology into academic advising delivery systems,* but not as a replacement for the interpersonal relationships developed between first-year students and their academic advisers.

- *Ensure that academic advising is sensitive to and meets the needs of the increasingly diverse first-year students.* Bring the needs of underrepresented groups into advising approaches.

CONCLUSION

In *Making the Most of College* (2001), Light points out that first-year students, upon their arrival at college, immediately have to begin making decisions about courses, majors, student activities, how and where to study, and the like. These decisions are often made with little information, yet the consequences of these decisions could be significant. Light states, "Advisers play a critical role. They can ask a broad array of questions, and make a few suggestions, that can affect students in a profound and continuing way" (p. 84).

Institutions need to recognize the importance of advising for first-year students and to organize and deliver advising services in the most effective way by including technological enhancements. Academic advisers and the profession of academic advising must embrace the enhancements that technology can bring to the profession. However, we must issue a word of caution: never let technology enhancements compromise the standards that have been set for the profession as described in the CAS Standards.

If the current literature on academic advising has one theme, it is that of shared responsibility (Frost, 1991). Applying the concept of shared responsibility and having students work with an integrated team of advisers as presented in our preferred models will provide an opportunity for academic advising relationships to develop and will provide learning experiences that prove invaluable to students not only for their first year but throughout college and for their lifetime. By approaching advising as a developmental process and a shared responsibility, having all the critical components for an effective advising program in place, and addressing different levels of advising needs with an appropriate level of adviser experience, institutions will be well prepared to provide comprehensive advising services for first-year students.

CHAPTER TWENTY

The Place of the Library
Versus the Library as Place

Margit Misangyi Watts

Libraries are too quiet. My thought process needs music or noise . . .
so libraries cramp my style. I'm too fidgety for libraries . . . and
they tend to be cold and disrupt my thought processes . . .
and they are full of information that I can never find.
—First-year student

According to the Association of American Colleges and Universities, "Students are flocking to college because the world is complex, turbulent, and more reliant on knowledge than ever before. But educational practices invented when higher education served only the few are increasingly disconnected from the needs of contemporary students" (2002, p. viii). There is no doubt that higher education is in the process of transforming itself; the emphasis is shifting toward learning rather than teaching. And even more important, the academic community is beginning to understand that all students need to be more engaged in their learning, connected to their experiences, and supported in their attempts to understand the world of scholarship. Students, especially first-year undergraduates, need an understanding of standard scholarly approaches to information utilization and evaluation, as well as technology skills and a general conceptualization of the role of higher education in scholarly processes. These issues are not regularly addressed with students in a coherent manner that will ensure the appropriate context for their use of information and ultimate academic success. As one first-year student noted, "Information literacy to me means being able to take something (a thought or an idea) and understand it. This includes both believing it and not believing it. If you are information literate, you will be able to give reasons why or why not an idea is true and defend your position. It's not about memorization, but more about interpretation of an idea. It means being able to explain the information upon request and totally understand what it means, or the purpose behind it."

This chapter addresses the complexity and urgency of the situation and makes a case for shifting away from learning "how to library" to learning how to be information literate. In this chapter, information literacy is defined as the ability to recognize when information is needed and how to locate, evaluate, and finally use the needed information effectively. The library is still at the core, but the interaction of student and place has changed. The trend is to move away from the fifty-minute library orientation model during the first year to a more collaborative (between faculty and librarians) and integrative (across the curriculum) one. The goal is to give first-year students the tools with which to navigate scholarly narratives, understand discourse as a conversation over time, and take part in critically assessing and evaluating information. Students should still be invited to go to the library, ask a librarian, or browse a collection, but this should now be anchored in an overall collaborative approach to helping students understand both how and why they need to be information literate.

THE WAY IT WAS AND THE WAY IT IS

According to a first-year student I encountered, "A library is a place that is cold and kind of scary. It is freezing and rather easy to get lost in, especially the first few times. The library holds a lot of information but none of it will you find because it's hidden and categorized in weird ways. The only ones who truly understand the library are the librarians. They seem to find information so easily. Overall, the library is a vault of information accessed by few. Have a question you need answered? Go to the library. Ask a reference librarian. Anything you want to know or find is at their fingertips, not yours."

This has been the traditional and comfortable paradigm within which we have articulated both the role of the librarian and the structure or place we call the library. In effect, the librarian has been seen as the gatekeeper of this place, a place viewed by most as the storehouse of knowledge. However, the landscape of our world has changed, and we now live in the information age. First-year students today have grown up in a world of beepers, cell phones, instant access, chatrooms, the Internet, interactive television, games, and more. They are not interested in spending much time searching for answers and are not often predisposed to ask a librarian. They want immediate feedback, and they want this feedback at their own fingertips. Pair this notion with the fact that the creation of knowledge has increased exponentially and more and more information is available to everyone, and it becomes clear that learning how to navigate through, as well as knowing how to critically appraise, information will form the cornerstone of being an educated person.

Although students today are very savvy regarding the new technologies, they are not skilled in deciphering what information is relevant, credible, or valuable as they are navigating multiple databases. It is probably not necessary to train students in keyboarding, use of the mouse, Web browsing, presentation software, and the like. What is crucial to their becoming information literate, however, is addressing the astonishing wealth of information at their fingertips, admitting that they are a digital generation, and then teaching them how to take ownership of how they use the new technologies available to them. All of this is not place specific. It does not occur only in the library. This work has to be infused throughout the educational process.

Often the library has been viewed as a neglected resource. One former college president, in response to a budget cut, was overheard saying that shorter hours would not be a problem because the library was just an oversized study hall. Certainly, libraries have always been quiet places to study and contemplate, but what a waste to have ever considered them as merely study halls.

The library used to function as the repository of all that was known, and to peruse the shelves was to encounter the voices of the past. These voices were to both inspire and inform. In his book *College: The Undergraduate Experience in America,* Boyer (1987) embraced the old model and suggested that to "exhort students to use the library is useless if they do not prize a book, and many undergraduates, even when they come to college, have never been introduced to the joy of reading" (p. 164). Today, reading a book is not enough. Boyer further suggested the following as a model for the library:

> For the library to become a central learning resource on the campus, we need, above all, liberally educated librarians, professionals who understand and are interested in undergraduate education, who are involved in educational matters, and who can open the stacks to students, create browsing rooms, reform the reserve book system, help distribute books throughout the campus, and expand holdings in ways that enrich the undergraduate experience [1987, p. 165].

Though he was a seminal thinker, Boyer had not yet been confronted with the explosion of information and technology in our world. Historically, the model was to tell first-year students to go find what has been learned. In other words, go find what you need for your paper, presentation, or group project. Thus, it was convenient to view the library as the place where all things learned were kept, and teaching first-year students "how to library" was the reasonable pedagogy for this approach. First-year students were taught the necessary skills to navigate the various databases and collections, and when asked by a faculty member to "go find some piece of information" they were supposed to use these skills effectively.

The twenty-first-century library can still function in this manner when necessary, but for most students, the virtual library has become the place to "peruse the shelves" and "find that piece of information," especially as a first resort. Why? Because the virtual library is always open. And for most students, especially those in the first year, the Internet has become their library of choice. To quote one first-year student, "In the dawn of the Internet age, my laziness has caused my library-going experience to be less enjoyable over the years. Although I do understand that library sources, if used correctly, in direct correlation to the data you're trying to gather, is perfectly legit, I am much too lazy to go there."

For the past few decades, the model of one or two library instruction sessions has dominated academic library instruction programs. These sessions were usually offered to students during their first year in college. This model has been the mainstay of instruction efforts, yet its effectiveness is ambiguous. As the needs to address critical skills, such as search strategy, database structure, and database manipulation, have increased, the success of the model has been questioned. One or two "how to library" sessions do not provide sufficient time to address the affective, cognitive, and behavior domains for learning. In addition, because of the development of information literacy as an overriding concern and its emphasis on determining an information need and the evaluation of the information resources, greater burdens have been placed on the traditional model, burdens the model has not been able to handle.

THE TWENTY-FIRST-CENTURY LIBRARY

This first-year student seems to have grasped the concept of information literacy and understands how to use the twenty-first-century library:

> Information literacy is knowing how, where, and why to get information. I also think it has something to do with retention of the information as well. When you are information literate you can quickly and easily find information on anything. You can understand the information you've found and apply it if necessary. You have no fear of something you don't know, because you know you can easily find information about it.

The 2000 Boyer Commission report, *Reinventing Undergraduate Education,* suggests that it is time for a change in how the library is viewed. The report suggests that institutions need to move from "the prevailing undergraduate culture of receivers into a culture of inquirers, a culture in which faculty, graduate students, and undergraduates share an adventure of discovery" (p. 16). What, then, has changed? Our world culture has changed, and it is no longer sufficient to just find what is or has already been learned. What is important now is to know how to learn, and information literacy is a conceptual framework for doing this. It is not about retrieving learning products. That old notion of library is dying, especially since the Internet is at one's disposal at all times. The structure of most sources found in a library is in the form of scholarly narrative. Some of these sources might even be available electronically. But not all library holdings will be electronic. And as is the case with on-line shopping, sometimes you will just want to touch the product.

Manuel (2002) is concerned about today's Internet-savvy students and suggests that there might be a problem with this generation's facility with technology. She wonders if their "positive attitudes toward computers can hinder their mastery of information literacy skills." Manuel is concerned that perhaps the comfort with technology leads to their possibly overestimating "their abilities to search for and evaluate computerized information" (p. 198). As one first-year student remarked, "Now in college, I can admit that I hardly use the library. I feel that the Internet is way more convenient and there are so many resources on the Web. But, if I had to choose between the library and the Internet for the most credible and valid information, I would choose the library."

The Internet might have replaced the library as the main source of information. However, the incredible impact of the Internet as an information resource, and the increased incorporation of educational technology into higher education pedagogy, have produced a greater awareness of the library faculty's role in the curriculum. Library faculty are more aware of and skilled with information technology and the cross-disciplinary inquiry it facilitates than many other categories of faculty. The use of the library has taken on a fuller and more process-oriented meaning. Therefore, as the role of library as place has necessarily changed, so will the role of the librarian. Woodard and Hinchliffe (2002) aptly state this need for change:

> The challenge facing librarians in the new millennium is not that new educational technologies are being created, or that the tools used to access information are constantly changing in nature and scope, or that enhanced understandings of how people learn has caused us to change the way we teach. The challenge is that all three areas are converging at once: the ensuing impact has made many of us reel as we attempt to manage the resulting changes in our instruction programs [p. 40].

National trends are moving library faculty to consider many important issues—for example:

- The need for increased course work in information utilization and scholarly processes
- The development of learning communities and other collaborative and integrative approaches to teaching and learning
- The dramatic increase in distance learning alternatives to degree and course work
- The recognition that library faculty have an advanced understanding of information technology, pedagogy, and cross-disciplinary inquiry, including a facilitative, as opposed to authoritative, approach to teaching and learning that is based on their long-established approaches to providing reference assistance

As a result of these national trends, there is a growing recognition that librarians are teachers, and hence faculty, and that a major component of their professional activities should be devoted to teaching in collaborative relationships with other categories of faculty. Their changing role is well stated by Albrecht and Baron: "Librarians are no longer keepers of information, but teachers of information" (2002, p. 72). The teaching role of librarians is being increasingly recognized as coequal to the more traditional roles of reference, collection development, and the various support roles for these functions, such as cataloguing, acquisitions, access services, preservation, and serials management.

Across the nation, academic libraries are experimenting with new models for library instruction, increasingly recognized as "information literacy." Standard elements of these new models are:

- Increased class time with students and new information literacy courses

- Increased development of Internet-based instruction delivery methods

- Increased emphasis on collaborative teaching and learning models that involve partnering with other faculty and academic programs such as first-year seminars and learning communities

- Increased emphasis on assessment in order to determine the effectiveness of teaching content and pedagogy

- Increased involvement of librarians in deliberations and planning for curricular reform

- Increased involvement of librarians in distance learning

The last one hundred years of American academic libraries have seen the development of a philosophy of service where the increasingly important job is to provide support for finding things in a collection. As the universe of information expands, the need for assistance expands as well. For example, it has been my experience at the University of Hawaii at Manoa that students are now reporting that they may go to the Internet for information first, but they trust the information they find from library databases more and seek help from librarians to find information. The library has become a stronger support for these students as part of the learning environment; what is needed is an even further expansion of the role of the librarian as educator. Therefore, the place of the library needs to figure into the overall educational goals of any college or university. A library instruction program for first-year students must be understood in the context of the total activities of the student, the library, and the curriculum. A commitment of resources needs to be made by both, and the core intent needs to be engaging students to become information literate in both formal and informal ways. Collaboration with the faculty teaching these populations will also extend a program's impact.

Not surprisingly, the library profession has recognized the need to enhance the teaching role of librarians. Professional degree programs have increased the course work in user education. A deep and diverse literature exists about teaching in libraries. The second largest section of the Association of College and Research Librarians (ACRL) is the Instruction Section with over four thousand members. ACRL has also established an immersion program, known as the Institute for Information Literacy, which is providing intensive instruction for librarians in information literacy concepts and teaching.

ENGAGING FIRST-YEAR STUDENTS

In considering just what college was all about, this first-year student remarked, "College was not something I regarded as the next step after high school. It was not something I deemed important in order to be really rich later on in life. It was something I considered fundamental to learning about myself and the world around me."

Much of the recent research focused on higher education, such as the 2000 Boyer Report, the National Survey of Student Engagement (NSSE) study, Levine and Cureton (1998c), and Light (2001), suggest that in order to enhance the learning experience of students, there is a need to:

- Increase the level of engagement in learning
- Create the ability to apply knowledge to real-world situations
- Increase the understanding of how knowledge is created
- Foster self-directed learning
- Identify creative exploration as a value
- Offer opportunities for research to undergraduates
- Broaden students' experiences beyond the classroom

In addition, there has been national consensus that the first-year experience needs to be strengthened and that these new students should be at the forefront of efforts to create learning environments that are both challenging and supportive. The 2002 NSSE Report set out several findings that were disturbing. This study offered five benchmarks for excellent education, two of which addressed the "level of academic challenge" and a "supportive campus environment." However, this report suggests that academic institutions are not doing the job as well as they would like. The following are just a few of the disappointing findings from the document:

- About 45 percent of first-year students never discussed ideas from their classes or readings with a faculty member outside of class.
- A fifth of all students "frequently" come to class unprepared.
- About one-fifth of both first-year students and seniors say their institution gives little emphasis to studying and spending time on academic work.
- About 18 percent of all first-year students "never" made a class presentation.
- The cocurriculum, once considered to be a rich reservoir of learning outside the classroom, is undersubscribed. Almost two-thirds of commuting students do not participate, nor do a quarter of all first-year students who live on campus.

Although most institutions would balk at the assertion that they are not challenging or engaging their students academically, these results lead one to believe that students are not necessarily getting what they need, or want, out of their experience in education. The editors of this book suggest that an apt mantra for educating first-year students should be "challenge and support." They outline, in their introduction, an eight-part definition of first-year student success. One of these addresses the need for first-year students to learn how to learn and to become aware of what it means to be educated. Perhaps engaging students in their education and empowering them is more complex than just creating special programs, seminars, and communities of learners. It might require a review of how we do business in higher education. In *The Courage to Teach,* Parker Palmer (1998) suggests that students have been "marginalized in our society" and that they do not feel especially connected to their educational endeavors (p. 45). According to one first-year student, "Being my second day in college, I am still very new to it. I am still trying to get used to how large the campus is and trying to find my way around. Each morning my heart wakes up racing with the morning sun because I really don't know what to expect."

One can see the obvious connection of the concept of "challenge and support" to Levine and Cureton's (1998c) ideas in *When Hope and Fear Collide.* They suggest that students "do not believe a college education provides a money-back guarantee of future success, but they feel it is not possible to obtain a good job without one, much less a lucrative or prestigious job. At the very least, it is a kind of insurance policy to hedge bets against the future" (p. 115). Thus, the challenge is to meet the hopes of the students and prepare them for life after higher education; the support lies in our efforts to do this in a way that not only prepares them but also connects them to what they are learning.

In *Student Learning in the Information* Age, Breivik (1998) asks, "Will they [institutions of higher education] equip their students to move deliberately, wisely, and effectively through today's Information Society or will students be left to coast through life largely at the mercy of the prevailing winds of the popular media and the currents of popular sentiment?" (p. 110). She suggests that academic leaders can no longer be excused for ignoring the effects of the information age and the need to restructure curriculum to help students meet the challenges of this explosion of information. If everyone agrees that higher education should lead to lifelong learning, then learning how to navigate through information is key.

What one finds regularly are programs and workshops for first-year students that primarily focus on the library as a place to tour, ask questions, and find sources. This is the traditional model: finding books, learning about microfiche and government documents, and becoming familiar with new databases. This is not to say that traditional first-year experience models are incorrect in wanting to teach students the skills necessary to navigate library resources; however, what is often missing is the context and the overall premise of going beyond knowing how to find something.

Information literacy has to be an essential ingredient in undergraduate learning. After all, if institutions of higher learning are producers of information and knowledge, then it is necessary to improve the ease of access to this information as well as offer methods for learning how to evaluate and use it effectively. If educators want to give students the tools with which they can eventually contribute to scholarship themselves, a laudable goal, then information literacy skills will need to be integrated into a student's academic life. This may call for new pedagogies, partnerships, and ways of thinking about learning. Boyer (1987) found that most classroom assignments did not ask for the involvement of library resources. Thus, the skills (even if at the time they were more based on "how to library") were not being integrated into the overall learning context of the students. In her article about a process approach to information literacy, Kuhlthau (1993) suggests, "Findings indicate that although students need to develop skills in locating sources and finding information, they also need to develop skill in using information once it has been located" (p. 11). Embracing a constructivist approach, Kuhlthau advocates for library programs that involve students in not only using a variety of sources but actually in problem solving and research.

Nugent and Myers (2000) agree with Kuhlthau and in their study find that purposeful library research is the best way to become information literate. They suggest that infusing information literacy skills into content courses rather than holding on to the traditional separate library course was going to be the best way to build competency skills. Another attempt to review library instruction is highlighted by a study of the Payson Library at Pepperdine University in which Parang, Raine, and Stevenson (2000) highlight what an effective library instruction program should do:

- Use a wide range of information resources in problem-solving strategies
- Make effective use of instructional technologies
- Encompass finding, evaluating, and using information while emphasizing the legal and ethical issues connected to information
- Recognize students as producers as well as consumers of information
- Be diffused throughout the curriculum

What we do not want from first-year students, or any other student, is plagiarism. For most entering students, the notion of using the ideas of others is at best vaguely understood. It is likely that students will be more cognizant of the academic and ethical implications of plagiarism if they have been taught how to engage scholarship in a meaningful way. One aspect of being an information-literate student is a critical understanding of how to evaluate scholarship—both the creator and the content. In this way, students begin to recognize the meaning of intellectual ownership, substantiation of ideas, and so forth. The hope is for these concepts to roll over to their own work and use of sources.

INFORMATION LITERACY

Information literacy is a nexus for the life experiences of the student, the academic world of scholarship, and the postcollege real world of application of learning. An information-literate person has the ability to ask questions and knows the difference between ignorance and understanding (When do I need information?). Information literacy builds a lifelong ability to know where information is kept (Where is the best place to find this?), what forms knowledge is stored in (Which knowledge products will likely have what I need?), and how to get to knowledge. This is a wide range of knowledge. Information literacy relies on the use of a critical mind that can discern credible from not credible, valid from not valid. Information literacy is the laboratory for the creation of the educated student. It is core to the first-year experience. It lasts, while the specifics of particular courses fade over time. After all, the nature of research, the core of higher education, is a learning process: "How do I learn about something?"

This learning process emphasizes the intrinsic, dynamic relationship between information discovery (or perception) and knowledge creation as it constantly evolves and changes. Every course explores what is currently known through the prism of how it became known and how we extend our knowing. Furthermore, students are engaged in the discovery of that dynamic, relating their own experience to it, and finally creating new understanding, perspectives, and knowledge. Faculty, teaching and librarian, work as facilitators alongside students: sharing, guiding, and creating. The library truly becomes less a place and more a way of thinking, and information literacy becomes the learning process.

In January 2000 the ACRL approved standards and published the *Information Literacy Competency Standards for Higher Education.* For purposes of standards, the ACRL used the American Library Association's definition of information literacy. This states that an information-literate individual is able to "recognize when information is needed and have the ability to locate, evaluate, and use effectively the needed information" (p. 2). This ACRL document outlines five standards, each of which has performance indicators and learning outcomes attached:

- The information-literate student determines the nature and extent of the information needed.
- The information-literate student accesses needed information effectively and efficiently.
- The information-literate student evaluates information and its sources critically and incorporates selected information into his or her knowledge base and value system.
- The information-literate student, individually or as a member of a group, uses information effectively to accomplish a specific purpose.
- The information-literate student understands many of the economic, legal, and social issues surrounding the use of information and accesses and uses information ethically and legally.

These standards have become the hallmarks by which institutions across the country are developing programs for first-year students. It is evident from these standards that the movement is away from the traditional "how-to-library" session. To foster the kind of learning necessary for students to begin to meet these standards, instructional librarians are now charged with overhauling their methods of instruction. More important, because these standards are not about the library but about learning, inquiry, and discovery, librarians are increasingly finding themselves in collaborative situations with faculty and information technology experts. In a recent interview, Randy Hensley, public services division head at Hamilton Library at the University of Hawaii at Manoa, focused on the integrity of librarians being dependent on this kind of collaboration:

> The higher education curriculum must be transformed from a static communication experience to a learning process. Similarly, the library must move from a "finding the source process" to an "inquiry process." These new curriculum goals are iterative and dynamic. In order to create a contemporary and meaningful learning context, the new librarian and new faculty must bring together their experiences with how their own environments of library, classroom, and discipline have changed in response to the needs of today's students [personal communication to the author, 2002].

In response to these standards, ACRL supported several initiatives to disseminate the standards and methods for teaching them. One of these was the creation of the Information Literacy Best Practices Project Team. The team consists of seven educators, five of them librarians. The charge to this team of educators was to develop characteristics of best practices in the teaching of information literacy. Nine characteristics were developed for what would be deemed a best practice program in the delivery of information literacy education: a mission statement, goals and objectives, planning, administrative and institutional support, articulation with the curriculum for an information literacy program, collaboration, pedagogy, staffing, and outreach. The document elaborates each of these. Two of these are key to the teaching of first-year students: the concepts of collaboration and pedagogy. A best practices program is a collaboration of librarians, classroom faculty, and other staff and is centered on student learning and the development of skills, leading to lifelong learning. In addition, by engaging in this collaborative effort, there should be a fusion of information literacy concepts and disciplinary content. The pedagogy for a best practices program for information literacy supports multiple approaches to teaching and learning, is strong on active learning, encompasses critical thinking and reflection, and links course work to the real-world experiences of students.

Following the development of these characteristics, a national conference on best practices was held in Atlanta in the summer of 2002. The purpose of this conference was to bring together ten institutions that had already developed a program that met one or more of the characteristics of best practices. These institutional teams were invited to refine the characteristics and to help others when creating programs to meet the needs of students. It is hoped that the work of these institutional teams, the Best Practices Project, and other work by ACRL will ultimately lead to the development of nationwide change in how library skills can be integrated into the larger charge of developing information literate students.

In summary, information literacy is a conceptual framework for learning how to learn. In fact, it integrates neatly with the concept of scholarly narratives, the very foundation of higher education. The following is a simple way of seeing this integration:

Information Literacy Way of Learning	Scholarly Narratives
When is information needed?	Hypothesis, research questions
How can one find the information?	Methodology
Where can one find the information?	Review of the literature
How does one evaluate the information?	Interpretation, significance
What does one think of what one found?	Conclusion

Thus, involving first-year students up front in becoming information literate ensures that they will be more attuned to the nature of research and the rules that apply to the creation of scholarly narratives. In addition, becoming information literate will help students develop an ability to understand scholarship as discourse, begin to understand discourse as a conversation over time, and be able to eventually contribute to scholarship.

ASSESSMENT

There are learning outcomes attached to each of the information literacy competency standards in the document published by the ACRL. These standards focus on the needs of all levels of students; however, the outcomes "serve as guidelines for faculty, librarians, and others in developing local methods for measuring student learning in the context of an institution's unique mission" (2000, p. 6). By looking at the outcomes, one can see the development of lower- to higher-order thinking skills. In addition, the overall context of the outcomes is both general and specific. In other words, for some disciplines, the measure of information literacy will be tightly tied to the content being covered. For others, a general ability to do research will suffice. In this regard, Hensley posits, "Ultimately, it may be more accurate to conceptualize the new learning outcomes as something other than linear (lower to higher), but rather somewhat spiral or iterative, where permutations of the basic information literacy tenets of finding, evaluating, and using elaboration are addressed, as the application of information and learning become more complex" (personal communication, 2002).

If the standards for information literacy are implemented, faculty, librarians, and others can use the outcomes to guide the development of assessment instruments and strategies. Testing the ability of a student to use a database, find materials in the government document section of the library, or illustrate an understanding of various styles of citations will not address the more complex nature of information literacy. Programs will need to develop assessment instruments such as portfolios, research projects, and other integrated learning experiences to evaluate significant student learning. This most likely requires the integration of the teaching of information literacy within the context of content-driven courses.

Although many assessment tools have been developed over the years, most are geared toward testing a variety of skill sets. In other words, they evaluate whether students know how to access microfiche, how to cite in a particular style, or are aware of a certain database. Assessment strategies for first-year students should be developmental in nature. For instance, pretesting students on basic skills and then conducting periodic reviews of these skills is a good first step. Integration of assignments into first-year courses and giving students opportunities to use the skills help define the role of these skills in scholarship. Thus, first-year students might be asked to assemble portfolios of their work over a year to illustrate their understanding of key concepts of information literacy. There should be focus groups during various stages of an undergraduate career and exit and graduation interviews to determine the success of the programs and courses. If information literacy is integrated into general education requirements, then one can assess the impact of these requirements. Finally, offering first-year students forums in which they can demonstrate their ability is a useful assessment strategy. These forums can take the form of oral presentations, contributions to a campus journal, debates, exhibits on and off campus, research studies, miniconferences, electronic publications, and other concrete scholarly works, which might include art, music, and dance. The goal of this kind of assessment plan is to ensure that the students have gained the initial skills and can apply them in a scholarly manner.

There has not been much research on a newer process-oriented approach to evaluating information literacy. However, with the increasing focus on information literacy as integral to becoming an educated person, assessment tools are being developed across the country to look at process and learning outcomes.

THE PLACE OF THE LIBRARY

What has been created in the library of the twenty-first century is an especially dynamic environment for seeking information: challenging, complex, active, and increasingly convenient. Today's library is well suited to this generation of first-year students with their particular learning styles. The new library requires inquiry to produce knowledge. This means that students will need to know how to question, understand how to evaluate, and learn how to determine worth and relevance.

These requirements will lead to success for first-year students and equip them well for their other academic pursuits. The information technology available today makes it possible for the library to be in every classroom, dorm room, or computer lab at any time, to be explored, practiced, and used. In other words, the library as laboratory is now everywhere at any time. But the library and information literacy is also about process. This process of inquiry includes seeking, refining, seeking again, modification of a question, and so forth. All are a part of using databases, navigating Web sites, and checking out a myriad of sources for finding information. Just as higher education has become less about rote and more about a learning process, so too has the library, in the sense that one appreciates the process of asking and seeking and evaluating information.

The nature of research, at the core of higher education, is a learning process. The main question that underlies any kind of research is, "How do I learn about something?" Historically, students were told to "go find what has been learned," and the library to them was by default only a repository of information. Thus, the traditional "how-to-library" training sessions that were popular across the country made sense. Students needed to know how to "go find." Today, it is more important to know "how to learn." It is no longer sufficient to find what others have already learned; students need the skills to know how to learn and keep on learning. The following first-year student understands this concept well: "Facts are completely different from education. Anyone can read or listen and gain knowledge, but education is the process of making oneself smarter. Education is the application of knowledge."

The tradition of library instruction has always focused on helping students find the bibliography of a particular discipline. In other words, a faculty member will ask a student to discover where "are those places where the knowledge of a discipline is managed" and the librarian will help a student find and navigate the various catalogues, on-line databases, and indexes. This helps the student understand where to find the bibliography of what has been known heretofore in a particular discipline. The typical assignments given students across the country are those that ask a student to illuminate the relevant bibliography in response to some query about a topic.

What we should be illuminating for students, however, is the nature of inquiry: what questions need to be asked rather than those that have already been answered. A new approach, and one to which the skills of information literacy are crucial, is a process where we teach students how to question what they know or what is known. How does one determine the best questions to ask, and how do we find questions that have not yet been asked? Students need to learn how to find answers to questions that they are interested in. This parallels Boyer's report on needing to move toward an inquiry-based curriculum rather than the historical knowledge-based curriculum.

RECOMMENDATIONS

An institution must commit to at least a few strategies to make the library central to the educational experience of first-year students. Following are some actions that library faculty, regular teaching faculty, administration, and others involved with initiatives making information literacy a key component of the educational experience could take:

- *Integrate information literacy activities into first-year experience courses and programs.* By focusing on the competencies outlined by the ACRL, a campus could incorporate numerous elements to help students become information literate. One way would be to help develop assignments that are more inquiry based and less a call for the distillation of other people's work. This could be accomplished by developing a Web site with examples of writing assignments or projects addressing the various components of information literacy to be learned and setting up a collaborative team of librarians and first-year faculty to create new curriculum or develop a new course that focuses primarily on the skills of becoming a scholar. (This last suggestion is one that is in place at the University of Hawaii.) Probably the most important action to be taken is to recognize that in order to become an educated individual, a student must have the skills associated with information literacy. Therefore, weaving the teaching of these skills into courses designed to introduce first-year students to higher education would be an important step.
- *Articulate a campuswide commitment to developing these skills for first-year students.* This articulation needs to include the range of educators from administrators to staff. Also, by looking at the ACRL's characteristics for best practices in information literacy, an institution can choose which elements might work best to meet its strategic mission. Most likely, an institution that has special programs aimed at bringing first-year students into academic life will make a public statement about its commitment to these students. Including the standard characteristics of information literacy in this commitment would be a logical step toward integration.
- *Ensure that all first-year students have the technological skills to access information.* First-year students need to understand that the tools used to access information are constantly changing in nature and scope and that their success in the classroom may well depend on their technological skills.
- *Inform faculty about information literacy.* It is not only librarians who are still wedded to the traditional role of libraries; faculty also view the use of a library as part of what is required for their students to complete a research assignment. Librarians and faculty should come together to discuss the various components of information literacy, the learning outcomes that are crucial, and the move toward inquiry-based learning. Librarians report that they offer their services to individual departments, are invited to sit in on faculty meetings, invite faculty to lunch, offer small presentations, find like-minded colleagues and develop small initiatives, and so forth.
- *Tie the library budget to student learning outcomes.* It is probably appropriate to mainstream assessment efforts and make the library accountable for its work with students. This will help strengthen the library's position as central to the educational mission of an institution. It will also help move faculty into understanding the crucial and collaborative role that a librarian has within the institution.

- *Develop an active partnership between first-year experience projects, organizations and programs, and library organizations.* The Policy Center on the First-Year of College and the University of South Carolina's National Resource Center for The First-Year Experience and Students in Transition have partnership projects with ACRL under development, including a monograph on best practices. On a more local level, faculty in charge of first-year programs can invite library staff, instructional technology specialists, and others to coordinate their efforts on behalf of first-year students. Presentations at conferences should cross the traditional barriers separating faculty and librarians so they present at each other's professional organizations.

- *Create an environment where librarians are invited into the conversations about curriculum.* Include librarians in strategic planning, general education review, and program development. Invite librarians to collaborate on the development and teaching of information literacy. View librarians as people with expertise in both curricular development and teaching. Librarians need to view themselves as active members of the academic community with expertise outside the walls of the building they inhabit.

- *Set aside funds to support librarian-faculty partnerships for curricular transformation.* Faculty and librarians are both extremely busy in their own endeavors, and sometimes the incentive of funding might motivate them to work on a project together. Such partnerships could go a long way toward transforming the curriculum into a learning-centered first-year student experience and would be an important investment. Administrative support can help move this kind of initiative forward.

- *Use the learning outcomes included in the information literacy competence standards developed by ACRL as a basis for assessing library efforts to promote first-year student success.* Such use can guide the development of assessment instruments and strategies, test a variety of student skill sets, and help assess general education requirements.

- *Bring first-year programs and libraries together in a physical space.* The traditional model has always been to bring the library into the classroom through assignments, tutorials, and short presentations or, alternatively, to bring students into the library for these same assignments, tutorials, and fifty-minute sessions. One new model might be to bring the classroom into the library by creating physical spaces that are teaching and learning centers for first-year students and bring students and teaching faculty and librarians together. The activities in these centers can range from holding regular classes to involvement in undergraduate research. One such facility exists at the University of South Carolina's Thomas Cooper library, dedicated to first-year seminar instruction and known unofficially as the "classroom of the future." Another example of a new model is at the University of Hawaii, where a foundational class in understanding scholarship is held in the library. Probably even more innovative is the new information literacy research center housed in a residential hall at the University of Hawaii. This center is open to all first-year students and managed by peer mentors, librarians, and faculty alike. Due to the electronic nature of more and more information, using spaces away from the library itself allows the essence of inquiry to be central to learning.

CONCLUSION

If we ask first-year students why they are going to college, they will most often answer in terms of career opportunities, money to be made, better than working for the time being, and family expectations and support. If they ask us why they should go to college, we can no longer pontificate about the benefits of the breadth and depth of knowledge, which comes with a liberal education. They do not buy it. However, they do respond to the concept of becoming educated when they see the connection between what they are learning and how they are living. Furthermore, helping first-year students become information literate and linking their personal narratives to the scholarship they encounter should help them make these connections. Gaining the competence and confidence to contribute to scholarship in some manner will more likely develop students who are engaged in their educational experiences. Perhaps this first-year student said it best:

> Clearly knowledge is having an in-depth understanding of something that you can make useful in your own life. Merely storing information for keepsake is useless. Knowledge that proves to be useful has meaning; it actually benefits us to have obtained useful knowledge. Anyone can memorize random facts of knowledge that may make him or her appear to have an understanding of something. But it is only when someone can apply their knowledge to the outside world that first-year students can be called educated.

What the library has become is what education has become. To be information literate is to be educated. The integration of course content with information-seeking processes is now a necessity for the success of first-year students and their ability to become lifelong learners. The place of the library is at the center of higher education and should be central to challenging and supporting first-year students.

CHAPTER TWENTY-ONE

Service-Learning and the First-Year Student

Edward Zlotkowski

I have never had an English class that taught more than just grammatical issues.
[This class has] not only helped me improve on my English skills but . . .
also taught me a lot about our community. [It] has undoubtedly
made me a more complete and well-rounded person.
—Peter, a first-year student

It is one of the ironies of current attempts to reform higher education that the very fragmentation that reformers lament and seek to correct also informs their own work. The relationship between the first-year-experience movement and service-learning is a case in point. In the same year that Upcraft and Gardner published their groundbreaking *The Freshman Year Experience* (1989), galleys were being readied for Kendall's no less groundbreaking *Combining Service and Learning* (1990). "Service-learning" is not listed in the index to the former; "freshman" is listed once in the indexes to the latter. More significant, *The Freshman Year Experience* reflects almost no awareness of either the potential or the importance of community-based learning, while *Combining Service and Learning* shows no greater awareness of the special needs of first-year students.

Indeed, even as both movements began to mature, achieve momentum, and find national resonance during the past decade, they did so largely in isolation from each other. Despite a small number of programs that recognized the logic of linking the two, it has been only in the past few years that even a significant minority of educators has begun to share this recognition. Most designers and directors of first-year programs can now identify service-learning but still tend to see it as something incidental to their concerns, while designers and directors of service-learning programs still largely fail to appreciate the critical importance of addressing the special needs of first-year students.

What makes this disjuncture especially disconcerting is the rather obvious way in which both the first-year and the service-learning movements model so many features of the same educational gestalt. Bruce Kimball (1995), a historian of education at the University of Rochester, identifies seven concerns that he sees becoming prominent in liberal education today: (1) multiculturalism,

(2) values and service, (3) community and citizenship, (4) general education, (5) commonality and cooperation between college and other levels of the education system, (6) teaching interpreted as learning and inquiry, and (7) assessment. Whether or not one subscribes to Kimball's overall thesis, it would be hard to deny the centrality of most of these concerns to those seeking to develop effective first-year programs as well as to those seeking to establish effective service-learning programs.

One could, in fact, argue that the concerns of these two groups not only overlap but that the better we understand the needs of first-year students and the conditions that make service-learning an effective learning strategy, the more the two concerns would seem to demand cooperation. Consider, for example, the following passage from A. Jerome Jewler's "Elements of an Effective Seminar: The University 101 Program" (1989):

> It occurred to the founder of University 101 that, if faculty could view students more positively, if they could experiment with interactive teaching methods that fostered the development of a community of learners, and if they could meet with other faculty and staff on common ground in this endeavor, the benefits to students, faculty, and the institution would be overwhelming. For freshmen and faculty alike, University 101 subscribes to the belief that development is not a one-dimensional affair but must reach far beyond the intellect and into emotional, spiritual, occupational, physical, and social areas [p. 201].

The importance of developing through interactive teaching a faculty-student collaborative effort, teaching as something shared by an academic community, the necessity of transcending a narrowly intellectual approach to student development: all these positions are also fundamental to service-learning in both theory and in quality practice. Indeed, when just prior to this passage Jewler identifies as two of the "philosophical underpinnings" of University 101— its belief that one of higher education's "most important missions is the development of people who will be the movers and shakers of the next generation" and "the belief that learning should be exciting . . . fun . . . and provide learning for the instructor as well as the students" (p. 200)—he is identifying precisely that social efficacy and academic dynamism that service-learning seeks to bring about by coupling the concepts of community service and academic learning.

In this chapter, I will explore various dimensions of the congruence between service-learning and the first college year. I begin by briefly defining service-learning as that term is used in this chapter. I then explore some of the benefits it can bring to those designing first-year courses and programs. Why the first year deserves special attention from those designing service-learning programs balances that exploration. After a brief review of several programs that have sought to reap the mutual benefits identified here, the chapter concludes with lessons learned and some general recommendations for making the congruence between these two reform movements a matter of strategic advantage.

DEFINING SERVICE-LEARNING

Although there are in print dozens of definitions of service-learning and even more practice-based understandings of this term, it refers here to a very specific kind of undertaking. As defined by Bringle and Hatcher in an influential article (1996), service-learning is

> a credit-bearing educational experience in which students participate in an organized service activity that meets identified community needs and reflect on the service activity in such a way as to gain further understanding of the course content, a broader appreciation of the discipline, and an enhanced sense of civic responsibility. Unlike extracurricular voluntary service, service learning is a course-based service experience that produces the best outcomes when meaningful service activities are related to course material through reflection activities such as directed writings, small group discussions, and class presentations. Unlike practica and internships, the experiential activity in a service learning course is not necessarily skill-based within the context of professional education [p. 222].

For the purposes of this chapter, the important features of this definition are (1) its location of service-learning within the curriculum, (2) its insistence that the service experience reinforce course objectives, (3) its goal of an enhanced sense of civic responsibility, and (4) its understanding of legitimate learning outcomes as going beyond merely technical (that is, "professional") mastery. Through initiatives that result in tangible community benefits, students develop a capacity to effect change, to become the "movers and shakers" Jewler refers to; through reflection on those initiatives, class meetings become "exciting . . . fun . . . and provide learning for the instructor as well as the students."

Because both first-year and service-learning programs challenge traditional academic assumptions about student development, faculty-student relations, and what should be accepted as legitimate learning goals, because both contest the notion that only objective content mastery should be seen as deserving of serious faculty concern, many of the institutional obstacles first-year programs have had to overcome are identical to those that service-learning programs have had to deal with. Principal among these are (1) a supposed lack of academic rigor, (2) the necessity of developing new pedagogical techniques, (3) suspicion regarding the value of partnerships between academic and student affairs, (4) acceptance of the social dimension of learning, (5) interdisciplinarity or cross-disciplinarity, (6) the wisdom of allowing nonfaculty to teach, and, consequently, (7) the tendency of senior faculty to see such work as "beneath them."

Indeed, a failure to distinguish sufficiently between extracurricular first-year orientation programs and academically anchored first-year seminars finds a close equivalent in the still widespread failure to distinguish between extracurricular voluntarism and academically anchored service-learning. It is therefore not at all surprising that the strategy Upcraft and Gardner (1989) lay out for launching a first-year seminar program is by and large indistinguishable from the institutional strategies adopted by most successful service-learning programs (Zlotkowski, 1998).

What tends to make many of these clear and useful parallels confusing is the not uncommon tendency to identify as service-learning any form of community service where there exists reciprocity between the campus and the community and the service activity is informed by some kind of reflection designed to promote student learning and development (Jacoby, 1996). This is not the place to take up the debate as to whether this broader understanding represents an advantage or a disadvantage to adoption and implementation of service-learning as an effective educational strategy. Suffice it to say that an increasing number of high-quality service-learning programs understand the term only in the more restricted academic sense and that the problem of providing opportunities for multilayered reflective activities without the assistance of a for-credit structure should not be minimized. As we will see later in this chapter, even when service-learning is located within the curriculum, the danger of its collapsing back into a form of "good deeds" is considerable. For those designing community experiences for first-year students, failure to identify a service component consistently and clearly as an academic undertaking will weaken many of the educational benefits it can facilitate.

Perhaps the single most important way to avoid this danger is to develop and articulate a multilayered reflection strategy. According to the Bringle and Hatcher (1996) definition cited above, reflective activities seek to help students gain "further understanding of the course content, a broader appreciation of the discipline, and an enhanced sense of civic responsibility." Hence, reflection in a service-learning context involves a variety of concerns: what students reflect on results not just in greater technical mastery ("course content") but also in an expanded appreciation of the contextual and social significance of their work and, most broadly of all, in "an enhanced sense of civic responsibility." Even in a first-year seminar where there is no disciplinary context in the traditional sense, there still exist specific course objectives—relating to both the material to be covered and the development of the student as a learner—to which the service experience must contribute. Ensuring that this does in fact happen, and that the whole results in "an enhanced sense of civic responsibility," is the primary function of reflective activities. For this reason, one can hardly overestimate their importance.

SERVICE-LEARNING AS RESOURCE

If a case can be made that first-year programs and service-learning programs share not only goals and philosophical assumptions but also institutional challenges and strategies, the question nonetheless remains: Why should they join forces? Why would their linkage result in something stronger than their discrete implementation? What is the value that each adds to the other? In this section, these questions will be examined first from the standpoint of first-year programs, then from the standpoint of service-learning. Only if both parties are convinced they have something significant to gain from their alliance will they manage to break out of the silo mentality that affects even higher education reformers.

At the end of his essay on the first-year seminar, Jewler (1989, p. 215) suggested that what distinguishes University 101 from more traditional areas of academic study "is its need to stay abreast of current trends in freshman behavior and to be able to respond to those trends from one year to the next, one decade to the next, one generation to the next." Hence, it is only fitting that in the first chapter of *The Freshman Year Experience* (1989, p. 21), Arthur Levine addresses the question, "Who are today's freshmen?" Referring to traditional-aged students, he describes "a generation lacking in great visions for our collective futures and mired in a parochial and small vision of their own futures" (p. 21). This being the case, what they require by way of an educational agenda is the skills and knowledge needed to live in our world, hope, a sense of responsibility, and a feeling of efficacy.

A little less than a decade later, Levine and Cureton updated this portrait of traditional-aged students in *When Hope and Fear Collide: A Portrait of Today's College Students* (1998c). In an article based on this book, "What We Know About Today's College Students" (1998a), they paint a picture that is, in most respects, quite similar to the earlier one—with one very significant exception:

> Unlike their predecessors of the 1980s, current students have concluded that they do not have the luxury of turning away from [large-scale] problems. . . . Today's undergraduates don't expect government to come to the rescue; instead, they have chosen to become personally involved, but at the local level—in their community, in their neighborhood, and on their block [p. 5].

The shift Levine and Cureton here identify is not unique to students. Since the early 1990s, momentum has been building toward the creation of a far more socially engaged academy. Ernest Boyer, former president of the Carnegie Foundation for the Advancement of Teaching and U.S. commissioner of education under President Carter, was perhaps the most prescient and influential of those who saw the post–Cold War academy as something very different from what prevailed before 1989. In one of his last speeches (1996), he predicted that

> service is going to reemerge with greater vitality than we have seen in the last 100 years, simply because the university must be engaged if it hopes to survive. The social imperative for service has become so urgent that the university cannot ignore it. I must say that I am worried that right now the university is viewed as a private benefit, not as a public good [p. 138].

Reading *The Freshman Year Experience* from the perspective of a post–Cold War academy, one cannot help but be struck by how relentlessly private the book is. Overtly civic considerations are almost completely submerged in developmental concerns that seem to owe little to structured public engagement. Nothing in Upcraft and Gardner's articulation of six indicators of "freshman success" necessarily point to any kind of formative experience, values clarification, or skill set that would require contact, let alone collaboration, with anyone outside the college community. Academic and intellectual competence, interpersonal relationships, a developed identity, career and lifestyle decisions, personal health and fitness, and an integrated philosophy of life: all of these are understood in a way that makes the first year a decidedly on-campus experience and the campus itself an implicitly self-contained social unit. Such a perspective not only conflicts with the fact that many of today's students, first-year or otherwise, are adult and part-time learners for whom the campus is anything but a self-contained experience; it also overlooks the danger of further separating traditional-aged students from larger public concerns. To their credit, Upcraft, Gardner, and Barefoot have addressed this omission by adding "developing civic responsibility" to their revised definition of first-year student success as described in the Introduction to this book.

Wendy Rahn (1998) of the University of Minnesota presented figures that "illustrate in compelling form the steep erosion of support for the American political community among younger generations" (p. 3). Indeed, so disturbing are these and other data that the American Political Science Association's Task Force on Civic Education for the 21st Century has come to the chilling conclusion that "current levels of political knowledge, political engagement, and political enthusiasm are so low *as to threaten the vitality and stability of democratic politics in the United States*" [emphasis added] (1998, p. 636).

Clearly, our understanding of what an effective contemporary education demands and what constitutes a truly inclusive approach to student development has changed over the past ten years. As the faculty advisory committee of the Lowell Bennion Center at the University of Utah (1998) has noted, "Higher education is at a crossroads. At few moments in our country's history have so many questioned the importance and relevance of higher education to contemporary society" (p. J-1). Hence, the committee has recommended that its institution rededicate itself to "the task of educating . . . students to be good citizens" by recognizing that in addition to "foundational" and "professional" knowledge, it must also help create and disseminate "socially responsive" knowledge:

> The many social challenges that now demand our attention force us as academicians to no longer assume that we can perform our teaching role without paying close attention to the impact of that role on the communities that surround us. . . . Simply providing opportunities for volunteer service will not enable universities to meet the social demands of the coming decades [p. J-5].

If one function of substantive first-year programs is to prepare entering students to understand both the challenges and the opportunities of higher education and to appropriate for themselves the identity of truly educated individuals, it is hard to see how such programs can be true to themselves without developing some kind of engaged dimension.

Indeed, one can go even further. Given what we now know about the role of unstructured, real-world experiences in the design of effective pedagogical strategies and the development of lifelong learners, it is hard to see how first-year programs can prepare new students, especially older, more experienced students, to maximize their learning potential unless they abandon the often unexamined assumption that significant academic learning takes place only on campus—in classrooms, libraries, and residence halls.

In a 1996 interview, John Abbott, director of the Education 2000 Trust, discussed what the research now shows about the competencies that will be needed in this new century. After reaffirming the continuing importance of such basics as "skills of numeracy, literacy, and communication," Abbott identifies "a whole series of new competencies" (p. 3)—competencies that cannot simply be added to a classroom curriculum:

> Not to prejudge, but I doubt such abilities can be taught solely in the classroom, or be developed solely by teachers. Higher-order thinking and problem-solving skills grow out of direct experience, not simply teaching; they require more than a classroom activity. They develop through active involvement and real-life experiences in workplaces and in the community [pp. 3–4].

Abbott is not alone in pointing to the critical, formative role of experience as an educational resource. According to Peter Ewell, senior associate at the National Center for Higher Education Management Systems (1997, p. 5), "decades of experimental work in educational psychology and instructional design" suggests several "'big ticket items' [that] are good places to start in remaking instruction." The very first of these is "approaches that emphasize application and experience . . . approaches such as internship and service-learning [that try] to break down artificial barriers between 'academic' and 'real-world' practice (as well as between the curriculum and the co-curriculum)." Along the same lines, the report of the American Association for Higher Education, American College Personnel Association, and National Association of Student Personnel Administrators, Joint Task Force on Student Learning (1998) underscores the fact that "what we know about learning" includes the principle that "learning is enhanced by taking place in the context of a compelling situation." To create such situations, "faculty and staff collaborators . . . establish internships, externships, service learning, study abroad and workplace-based learning experiences" (pp. 3–4).

What makes this research even more compelling is the way in which it dovetails with research on the learning style preferences of new students. According to Schroeder (1993), there exists a serious discrepancy between the preferred learning styles of the majority of new students and the majority of their instructors. Whereas "60 percent of entering students" (and "approximately 75 percent of the general population") feel most comfortable with learning styles "characterized by a preference for direct, concrete experience; moderate to high degrees of structure; linear, sequential learning; and, often, a need to know why before doing something" (p. 22), approximately 75 percent of faculty "prefer the global to the particular, are stimulated by the realm of concepts, ideas, and abstractions, and assume that students, like themselves, need a high degree of autonomy in their work" (p. 25).

Why learning style preferences of new students show the biases they do is not something Schroeder seeks to explain. Nevertheless, another study may provide some clues, at least with regard to traditional-aged students. Hansen (1998) indicates that just 34 percent of freshmen "report having spent six or more hours per week studying during their senior year in high school," that 36 percent of them "report having been frequently 'bored in class' during their last year of high school," and that "the average adolescent . . . views approximately 35 hours of television programming per week" (pp. 4–5).

Studies like these suggest that the interactive teaching styles featured by many first-year programs are not only on the right track, but should be even further developed to help new students overcome the legacy of the passive learning expectations that so many of them associate with formal education. In order to help them become motivated students and lifelong learners, they need to be given a chance to discover how they themselves can better address and solve problems that matter, how they can bridge what Donald Schön (1995) called the "high ground [where] manageable problems lend themselves to solution through the use of research-based theory and technique" and "the swampy lowlands [where] problems are messy and confusing and incapable of technical solution" (p. 28). There may be no more important lessons first-year students can learn.

THE FIRST YEAR AS RESOURCE

Shifting the emphasis in the last sentence from "important lessons" to "first-year students" is all that is needed to refocus our discussion from the benefits of service-learning for first-year programs to the benefits of addressing the needs of first-year students for service-learning programs. At the beginning of this chapter, I noted that in Kendall's groundbreaking *Combining Service and Learning* (1990), "freshman" is referenced only once in the indexes to the three-volume set. That reference is to Georgetown's Freshman Orientation to Community Involvement (FOCI) program, a largely extracurricular community service program with some curricular (for example, fourth-credit) opportunities. Actually, the editors missed one other reference: the Bronx Community College's SHARE program for first- and second-year students. It is interesting, but ultimately not surprising, that only these two of the eighteen programs profiled in Kendall's text explicitly identify first-year students as a focus of their concern. After all, Georgetown is a Jesuit university for which social justice concerns are fundamental, and Bronx Community College, as a largely minority-serving institution, can draw on the same powerful tradition of service as do the historically black colleges and universities (Jones, 1998).

But if civic engagement and public problem solving are now becoming far more central to most other kinds of institutions as well, it will behoove more of them, especially the ever increasing number of those that aspire to become "engaged campuses," to focus their attention carefully on what happens to their students during their first year on campus, on what those students need to become successful not just in the traditional academic sense but also in the light of new social and pedagogical imperatives. In other words, they will have to learn from the research on and experiences of those already designing first-year programs to make sure what they themselves design is not simply an overlay of generic service-learning practice on students with a special set of needs.

The imperative for service-learning proponents to focus careful attention on the needs of first-year students is anchored in a wide range of considerations. As Eyler, Root, and Giles (1998, p. 98) suggest, the fact that "transfer of learning . . . rests on multiple opportunities to apply what has been learned" may well imply that "those planning service-learning programs . . . think about creating a series of community options over the four years of the college program." This is precisely what more and more schools are doing, and it requires them to identify developmentally appropriate activities for students in the first year of their program. For example, the College of Business at Montana State University-Bozeman (Lamb, Lee, Swinth, & Vinton, 2000, pp. 170–171) frames its program with a first-year and a senior-year seminar. The service-learning goals of the school's freshman seminar focus on such foundational issues as "positive team building and introductory exposure to the not-for-profit sector." Its corresponding service activities are also of a nonexpert nature: "[Students] build and repair trails, stock shelves at the local food bank, chaperone junior high dances, visit shut-ins, and participate in a variety of programs in the local schools." By the time they are seniors, these same students are expected to perform on a very different level: "while freshmen engage in short-term, awareness-building experience, seniors engage in long-term, strategic application" (p. 172).

The first college year is of critical importance not just as a foundation for all subsequent engaged learning; it is also the key factor in determining whether the community engagement being required of more and more high school students can be taken to a higher developmental level and whether the off-campus experiences of adult and part-time learners can be transformed into habits of "reflective practice" (Schön, 1995).

According to Kleiner and Chapman (Duckenfield, 2002), the level of community service and volunteer activities of American high school students grew from 27 percent to over 80 percent between 1994 and 1999. Over the same period of time, service-learning programming grew from only 9 percent of all high schools to approximately 46 percent. As one researcher explains (Duckenfield, 2002), "This amazing increase is due to several major efforts over the past decade that have worked in synergy to make service-learning a major educational reform initiative in our public schools" (p. 39).

The challenges this situation presents are multiple. On the one hand, we now have a significant body of traditional-aged students who, thanks in part to well-designed service-learning experiences at the high school level, are already better prepared to learn and lead than many college faculty and staff imagine (Furco, 2002). Will such students be given the kinds of opportunity for intellectual and civic initiative they have come to expect? How can their skills be used to help them help their first-year peers become more motivated, engaged learners?

On the other hand, we have those peers themselves—students whose only service experience in high school was a formal community service requirement. For such students, whose experience of community work is not associated with meaningful learning and recognized leadership, the first college year may turn out to be the death knell of all future civic engagement. Despite a definite increase in the number of first-year students who indicate they expect to be involved in some kind of service activity in college (1990, 14.2 percent, versus 2000, 23.8 percent), the first year remains the time when students with prior service involvement (up to 81 percent in 2000) most frequently turn away from service as a part of their future (Vogelgesang, Ikeda, Gilmartin, & Keup, 2002).

Still a different set of challenges attends those working with adult students. Here one often finds a rich history of service experiences and community involvement unconnected to any educational program. How does one help such students both inventory and harvest the learning in relationships already established? And how does one factor in this experiential base as part of a larger learning plan? (O'Connell, 2002)? How does one design service-learning programs that turn practitioners into "reflective practitioners" (Schön, 1995)?

The challenge for service-learning proponents could not be clearer: they must work with their colleagues responsible for first-year programming not only to see that engagement activities are part of the first year but also to ensure that those experiences are intellectually, personally, and socially significant. This implies a whole new level of collaboration between those whose primary interest is the first year and those whose primary interest is service-learning and civic engagement. Both camps have much to learn from each other. Both have much to offer each other. At this point, it might be useful to look at the ways in which a few institutions have already approached this collaboration.

INSTITUTIONAL MODELS

In 1995, the University of Rhode Island, responding to a presidential challenge to develop "a new culture for learning" (Richmond, 2002), launched a new one-credit first-year seminar, URI 101, Transitions and Transformations. The ground it was to cover is familiar: "academic integrity, values formation, diversity, drugs and alcohol, library skills, career planning, and time management." Less familiar was the decision to include in the course a community service component. This decision, helped along by an outside grant, created for course designers a significant challenge: how to incorporate into a one-credit, six-week course servicing approximately two thousand students in one hundred sections a meaningful introduction to college-level community involvement.

Not surprisingly, this challenge was not met immediately with full success. As part of its comprehensive assessment process, the seminar organizers made some disheartening discoveries after the course's first year. In a series of focus group debriefings, students told them that "the [service] requirement had very little meaning. . . . There was no connection to their course work, or to their career goals. . . . [The] service projects . . . seemed to them trivial or insignificant." Community partners confirmed this response when they commented on the students' "attitude and work ethic." In other words, the URI 101 designers had inadvertently stumbled onto the problem discussed above whereby many traditional first-year students come to higher education with an understanding of community involvement as a formally required set of otherwise meaningless service tasks. What URI was asking of its new students was little more than an extension of their high school community service requirement.

Feedback from course faculty pointed in precisely the same direction: "[They] were unanimous in their assessment that community service had to become a more meaningful part of the curriculum rather than just an 'add-on,' and that they needed [support] to put the service projects into a learning context." In other words, they needed help in transforming URI 101's community service requirement into an effective service-learning experience. And this transformation had to take place in a way that was realistic given the seminar's limited parameters.

URI's solution to this problem can be reduced to two words: greater specificity. First, the course organizers revisited their expectations for the service component and came away with a much clearer sense of priorities. As a result of their community involvement, students would:

- Gain a better understanding of themselves and their involvement in the community
- Become more aware of issues in the community and develop a sense of responsibility for addressing those issues
- Be exposed to diverse communities and dialogue about preconceived notions regarding diversity
- Develop class cohesiveness
- Discuss their own sense of civic responsibility and plan for future involvement

To accomplish these goals, community placements were reorganized around ten thematic areas: Children and Families, Education, the Elderly, the Environment, Domestic Violence, Health Care, Homelessness, Housing, Hunger, and Literacy. Then, on the basis of this reorganization,

> over 100 projects were designed. . . . In each case, students were provided with the materials needed to create a context in which they could understand their service experience. For example, students working at the local food bank would not only learn about the agency's services but more importantly about issues of hunger in Rhode Island, the United States, and throughout the world [p. 69].

In this way, the URI 101 designers were able to make "experiential learning with a focus on service-learning the foundation on which [they] stood" (p. 69). Furthermore, the successful reorganization of the seminar naturally led to other exciting initiatives, such as the development of first-year learning communities:

> These consist of the URI 101 seminar plus a skills course with 25 or fewer students (either writing, communications, or math) and one or two more general education courses. . . . By sharing common courses, students find that they work more in groups, work more on academic issues outside of class (additional time on task) and feel better "known" by their teachers and peers. Now when a community service project is chosen in URI 101, the implications of this project can be reviewed and discussed in the "content" coursers these same students share in common [p. 74].

The development of service-learning as an important part of the first year has followed a different but equally instructive path at Indiana University-Purdue University Indianapolis (IUPUI). Again, it was a top administrator who provided the initial momentum. In 1997, IUPUI's chief academic officer appointed the Service Learning Advisory Committee to advise University College, the campus unit that provides "academic support to entering students prior to their formal admission to a degree-granting school" (Hatcher, Bringle & Muthiah, 2002, p. 80), "to advise faculty and instructional teams on integrating service-learning into the curriculum of first-year courses and to promote co-curricular service opportunities for entering students."

From the beginning, this effort was characterized by a keen awareness that "designing community-based service experiences for first-year students is different than involving upperclassmen who are typically more skilled, more experienced in managing academic responsibilities, and more confident in career direction" (Hatcher et al., 2002, p. 83). Hence, the committee drew up and distributed a list of recommendations for all instructors teaching the required one-credit first-year seminar (at IUPUI called a "learning community" [LC] although it does not involve multiple linked classes). These included an emphasis on group projects, one-time projects, student mentors who are a part of each learning community, and other suggestions regarding project design and implementation.

The chief academic officer's charge did not mandate the incorporation of service-learning into all first-year "learning communities." Instead, this was to be only one of three strategies to introduce new IUPUI students to the importance of community engagement. Another vehicle was the development of Middle School Campus Visits. In this program, the campus's central service-learning office works with instructional teams to support the design and implementation of campus visits hosted by LC students. Learning communities design their campus tours according to the learning objectives of their unit. "For example, a communications class designed a letter exchange program between college students and middle school pen pals and then hosted their pen pals for a campus visit" (p. 83). Through the Middle School Campus Visit program, first-year students not only reach out to children in surrounding communities, helping them begin to see a college education as part of their future, but also bond more deeply with the campus they themselves introduce and represent.

The third and final strategy IUPUI employs in introducing its first-year students to the importance of outreach and community engagement is the incorporation of service-learning into what are called Gateway Courses. Because these discipline-based introductory courses often have large enrollments, the service-learning center staff offer those who teach them several kinds of assistance: consultations on course design and implementation, assistance in obtaining curriculum development funds, and Service Learning Assistant Scholarships that make it possible for these instructors to hire qualified student assistants to help them implement service-learning in their classes.

As these two institutional examples suggest, there is no single right or effective way to introduce service-learning into the first year. The programs reviewed here differ not only in their approach to course design but also in the ways in which they draw on other progressive educational and curricular initiatives. Service-learning as part of the first year often involves utilization of some kind of learning community, whether the latter is understood in a traditional or a more idiosyncratic sense, but it also frequently involves lessons and techniques borrowed from interdisciplinary course design (for example, Portland State University) and collaborative and problem-based learning (for example, Samford University), as well as arrangements that link courses, community, and residence halls (as at California State, Humboldt, and the university of Massachusetts at Amherst) and courses and work histories (Metropolitan State University, St. Paul, Minnesota). However, regardless of the particular design adopted, the key to success in each instance remains a thorough understanding of the special needs of a particular group of first-year students and the significant difference between traditional community service and academic service-learning.

ASSESSING SERVICE-LEARNING

Since service-learning is offered for credit and is graded, the first important indicator of student learning is the grades that first-year students receive in their service-learning courses. Beyond that, service-learning faculty may want to assess periodically first-year student needs with regard to service-learning, measuring student satisfaction with their community experience and determining if their learning is in fact related to one or more desired first-year outcomes, such as academic achievement, retention, and more long-term goals such as an increased awareness of civic responsibility and an interest in seeking out other community-based experiences. Those individuals who are responsible for providing service-learning opportunities should also have an opportunity to assess service-learning from a program perspective. (For a more detailed discussion of assessment, see Gelmon, Holland, Driscoll, Spring, & Kerrigan, 2001, as well as Chapters Twenty-Seven, Twenty-Eight, and Twenty-Nine in this volume.)

RECOMMENDATIONS

The most important lesson we can learn from those who have pioneered the powerful combination of service-learning and first-year programming is that without a thorough understanding of first-year student needs and the ways in which service-learning differs from traditional community service, one starts at a perhaps fatal disadvantage. Without an understanding of the former, one can easily overtax students at a time of great personal vulnerability, distressing rather than empowering their sense of self—or one can fail to take into account the experiential background they bring to their first college year. Without an understanding of the latter, one may well find oneself surrounded by students, faculty, and even community partners frustrated by what seems to be an ill-conceived, academically inappropriate exercise in do-goodism.

Most other lessons flow from this first one. Faculty development and faculty support are critical until instructors have acquired some reliable experience and expertise. This is especially true with regard to reflection—perhaps the single most important means of turning raw experience into usable learning. Furthermore, to satisfy both faculty and student demands for academic—and preprofessional—relevance, one may want to consider thematically organized placements and explicit disciplinary connections. Regardless of the strategy employed, comprehensive assessment of all stakeholder experiences can help identify problems before they become intractable. Frequently seen red flags include failure to identify specific service goals, failure to integrate the service experience with other aspects of the class, insufficient student preparation, lack of sufficiently early or substantive faculty contact with the community partner, failure to match service task with course parameters and student abilities, and lack of adequate on-site supervision.

These lessons yield a few key recommendations for those who choose to move down this path:

- *Carefully and consistently differentiate service-learning from traditional community service.* It is an academic undertaking that demands academic rigor.
- *Design service-learning projects to match and to stretch, but not strain, the capabilities of first-year students,* whether they are young or adult. Ideally, such projects should build on participants' prior levels of experience.
- *Remember that faculty need logistical support to do service-learning well.* Most quality programs operate in conjunction with a center that facilitates campus-community connections and makes available both orientation and assessment resources.
- *Provide faculty professional development opportunities,* especially with regard to designing student reflection opportunities. Most faculty were never taught to do inductive, experience-based work.
- *View evaluation and assessment as powerful diagnostic tools* that can ensure that the community's as well as the students' and the faculty's needs are adequately met.

CONCLUSION

All of this amounts to a significant challenge—so great a challenge one may well be tempted not even to try. This would indeed be unfortunate. Both those working to improve the first year and those developing service-learning know equally well that our dominant educational assumptions and practices are not delivering what either students or society needs. At bottom, both groups share a set of developmental beliefs and academic concerns that is far more important than the differences in emphasis that distinguish them. I began this chapter by identifying some of those commonalities. It would be unfortunate if in the end it turned out that the one that mattered most was their inability to transcend the academy's culture of fragmentation and make common cause together.

CHAPTER TWENTY-TWO

Learning Communities

Jodi Levine Laufgraben

I am really glad I registered for a learning community (despite having to get up early). I wish I could do it again. It really helped my transition into my freshman year. The group really did become a community. If you don't already, you should make learning communities available throughout one's collegiate career.
—First-year student

Learning communities—clusters of courses organized around a curricular theme that students take as a group—strengthen and enrich students' connections to each other, their teachers, and the subject matter they are studying. They also challenge first-year students to redefine their educational goals in broader terms and provide the support for doing so. More and more campuses across a variety of institutional types are exploring or implementing curricular learning communities to create a more coherent and connected curriculum, promote student success, and create community, particularly for first-year students.

A National Survey of First-Year Curricular Practices conducted by the Policy Center on the First Year of College (2001) showed the pervasiveness of learning communities in higher education, particularly among research institutions. According to the survey, about 75 percent of the research-extensive institutions that responded reported offering learning communities. Carnegie-classified master's institutions reported use of learning communities to be nearly 40 percent, and research-intensive institutions reported use of learning communities at just under 40 percent. Associate degree–granting institutions that participated in the survey reported use of learning communities to be over 20 percent, and baccalaureate colleges reported use of learning communities to be approximately 18 percent.

For the first-year student, learning communities offer an introduction to the academic and social life of an institution. Programs such as learning communities that organize students into smaller communities have a positive impact on student learning, satisfaction, persistence, and graduation rates. From within smaller communities, students are more likely to develop personal connections to the larger campus community.

After a brief review of the literature that highlights the benefits of organizing students, teachers, and courses in this way, this chapter provides an overview of definitions, characteristics, and models of learning communities, illustrated by examples of successful programs, including those designed for unique populations of first-year students. Practical advice for implementing and assessing learning communities is also provided.

WHAT IS A LEARNING COMMUNITY?

The term *learning community* is currently applied in different ways across diverse contexts. In higher education, it may be used to describe individual classrooms, curricular learning communities, living-learning communities, on-line learning communities, or faculty learning communities. From an organizational development perspective, as in the work of Senge (1994) and other system theorists, the term is often used to describe organizations as "learning communities." "Learning communities" also describes community development: "Cities and towns with the capacity to learn from their own experience to become more healthy and sustainable places to live and work" (MacGregor, Smith, Matthews, & Gabelnick, 2001).

This chapter focuses on curricular learning communities as a model for promoting first-year student success. Curricular learning communities are defined as "a variety of approaches that link or cluster classes during a given term, often around an interdisciplinary theme, that enroll a common cohort of students. This represents an intentional restructuring of students' time, credit, and learning experiences to build community among students, among students and their teachers, and among disciplines" (Macgregor et al., 2001).

WHY LEARNING COMMUNITIES?

Learning communities are certainly not a new trend or best practice fad. They have strong roots in the work of John Dewey, Alexander Meiklejohn's Experimental College at the University of Wisconsin, Joseph Tussman's experience at Berkeley, the innovation of Patrick Hill at the State University of New York at Stony Brook, and the vision of the founding faculty of The Evergreen State College in Washington state (Shapiro & Levine, 1999). Dewey advocated for learning environments characterized by cooperative and collaborative approaches to learning, and he defined education as an ongoing process of reorganization, reconstruction, and transformation. Meiklejohn and Tussman's efforts are early examples of undergraduate learning communities that offered an alternative to the fragmented and incoherent curriculum students typically experienced.

In the past fifteen years, there has been a dramatic increase in the number of campuses installing learning communities. The scholarship of Alexander Astin (1993), Vincent Tinto (1993), Peter Ewell (1997), Ernest Pascarella and Patrick Terenzini (1991), and others teaches us a great deal about student success, student development, and good practice in higher education. The literature also helps explain how learning communities as a curricular structure can support students' intellectual, personal, and social growth while in college.

In his study of what matters in college, Astin (1993) discusses the types of teaching and academic behaviors that have a positive impact on student development: frequent student-faculty interaction, frequent student-student interaction, and time devoted to studying, tutoring, cooperative learning, and giving class presentations. Learning communities create the type of environment for success that Astin describes and by design promote deeper learning. Learners create their learning actively and uniquely; they are not empty vessels into which knowledge can be poured (Ewell, 1997). Learning is about making meaning, and students learn constantly—with us and without us. Direct experience has an impact on students' understanding, with students learning most effectively in the context of a compelling problem. Learning also requires reflection and is most likely to occur in a supportive environment characterized by personal support and interaction with others (p. 4). Learning communities are characterized by interpersonal collaboration, the application of concepts to real situations, rich and frequent feedback on performance, and a curriculum that emphasizes experience and cross-disciplinary learning—all, according to Ewell (1997), characteristics of effective approaches to learning.

HOW LEARNING COMMUNITIES AFFECT STUDENTS, FACULTY, AND INSTITUTIONS

Several studies indicate that participation in learning communities has a positive impact on student achievement and retention (Tinto, Goodsell Love, and Russo, 1993b). A Temple University study revealed that learning communities participants were retained to the second fall semester at rates 5 to 9 percent higher than comparison groups of nonparticipants (Temple University Retention Study, http://www.temple.edu/university_studies/reports.html). Researchers at the University of Missouri-Columbia studied students' academic records to determine if participation in freshman interest groups (FIGs) was associated with higher levels of academic achievement and persistence. Before and after controlling for entering ability, freshman students in the FIG cohort earned a higher mean grade point average than nonparticipants. A longitudinal retention study for the same group demonstrated a 12 percent higher retention rate for FIG members after three years (Student Life Studies Abstracts, 1996).

Participation in learning communities also has a positive effect on first-year students' intellectual and social development. Researchers working with the

QUANTA Interdisciplinary Learning Communities Program at Daytona Beach Community College measured students' cognitive development using the Measure of Intellectual Development (MID), an instrument that applies Perry's Scheme of Intellectual Development. Student essays were compared over the course of the academic year to determine if learning community participants showed movement along the Perry Scale. The majority of these first-year students showed at least a change of one-third position, and when the QUANTA results were compared to findings from a study of national norms, learning communities participants showed greater growth and development than students in traditional classes (Avens & Zelley, 1992).

Studies also reveal that learning communities help first-year students adapt more quickly to the college classroom environment. They are more likely to participate in class discussions, raise questions, and seek an instructor's assistance than nonparticipants. They report greater satisfaction with their classes and teachers and are also more likely to participate in a range of academic and social activities (Tinto, Goodsell Love, and Russo, 1993b; Reumann-Moore, El-Haj, & Gold, 1997). An end-of-year survey conducted by the Russell Scholar's Program at the University of Southern Maine revealed that program participants spent more time participating in organized activities and talking informally with other students than nonparticipants did (Johnson & King, 1996). At the University of Wisconsin, first-year students in the Bradley Learning Community reported greater satisfaction with the first year and greater participation in the university's opening of the school year activities than nonparticipants. Learning communities participants were also more likely to become orientation leaders (Brower, 1997).

Research (Avens & Zelley, 1992; Reumann-Moore et al., 1997) on student perceptions of the learning communities experience shows that first-year students value the interdisciplinary nature of learning communities courses, the emphasis on the development of certain academic and interpersonal skills, and the interactions between teachers and students. According to one student, "My learning community experiences helped me to adjust to college and meet other people in my major. This way if I had a question or problem, I could always count on someone in my class for help."

For faculty, participation in learning communities typically leads to greater attention to pedagogy and enhanced collegiality across disciplines. Many faculty report that as part of a learning community, they change their teaching practices or philosophy toward teaching and learning in some manner (Reumann-Moore et al., 1997). Learning communities faculty report greater use of group work or collaborative learning strategies in their classrooms. Faculty also report more out-of-class contact with students and an increased awareness of students' academic and personal needs. According to one learning community teacher, the learning community experience helped her become more aware of students' out-of-classroom commitments and pressures, such as jobs and financial concerns. "I am more understanding of students as I teach them, not that I let them turn in papers late, but I've gained more of a student perspective" (Reumann-Moore et al., 1997, p. 31).

Faculty do raise some concerns about teaching in learning communities. Some caution that the learning communities atmosphere can resemble that of high school, with faculty often investing time in helping students with the socialization process of becoming a college student. Faculty development workshops are a good setting to discuss this "grade 13 dynamic" and to introduce strategies that can help faculty support students in the transition to college learning without compromising curriculum or content teaching time. Another barrier that faculty face is the time required to prepare integrated or interdisciplinary learning experiences for students. Where possible, learning communities program leadership should provide support for faculty teaching teams to meet prior to and during the semester in which they are teaching in a community. Most important, the faculty reward structure should reflect the time and commitment necessary to teach successfully in a learning community environment.

The impact of learning communities reaches beyond first-year students and faculty and leads to institutional transformation as well. For a campus, the implementation of learning communities leads to increased opportunities for cross-department collaboration and for partnerships between units, such as academic affairs and student affairs. In addition, the process of implementing and sustaining learning communities typically leads to increased attention to—and resources for—teaching, learning, assessment, and student support.

CURRICULAR LEARNING COMMUNITIES

Learning communities aim to promote community, curricular connections, collaboration, and reflective practice and synthesis (MacGregor et al., 2001). Although definitions may vary, learning communities programs share several basic characteristics. First, they organize students and faculty into groups that tend to be smaller than other campus units (MacGregor, Smith, Matthews, & Gabelnick, 1997). This is accomplished through coenrollment in a defined set of curricular offerings, an essential characteristic of learning communities. Second, learning communities encourage integration of the curriculum. They effectively address fragmentation in the curriculum, particularly within general education (Goodsell Love, 1999), and they allow faculty to teach and students to learn in more interdisciplinary, intellectually stimulating, and challenging ways. Third, learning communities bring small groups of students together in the classroom, making it easier for students to establish academic and social support networks inside and outside the classroom. This is particularly important for first-year students.

Learning communities help first-year students become socialized to what it means to be college students, particularly when the pairing or cluster includes a first-year seminar or small group discussion session. Learning communities located within first-year experience programs often link academic, discipline-based courses to new or existing first-year experience courses or first-year seminars. This provides an ideal setting in which to introduce students to the expectations of the college classroom, while student interaction with peers reinforces the attitudes, values, and behaviors necessary to succeed as a member of the peer group. Students recognize the need for this type of support: "I made a very good choice to enroll in a learning community. It helped ease my transition from high school to college."

One approach to structuring a learning community experience that introduces students to the campus experience in and beyond the classroom is the use of instructional teams. Indiana University Purdue University Indianapolis (IUPUI) relies on an instructional team approach in the teaching of its learning communities. "An Instructional Team is a collaborative effort led by a member of the teaching faculty with a librarian, a technologist, a counselor, and a student mentor (and any other pedagogical and/or evaluation specialist as needs may dictate)" (http.//uc.iupui.edu/LC/). Team members work together on course design, implementation, and assessment.

Learning communities focus faculty and students on learning outcomes (Tinto et al., 1993b). As curricular structures, they move campuses from an emphasis on teaching to an emphasis on teaching and learning. Within teaching teams, learning communities faculty discuss their goals for the community and for student success, including plans for assessing student learning. Learning communities provide a setting for community-based delivery of student support services such as academic advising, career mentoring, or tutoring. Academic advising and career planning can be a focus of a linked seminar, and Supplemental Instruction or tutoring can be made available to students in the community. By making such resources readily available, learning communities help first-year students become accustomed to regularly using such supports (Reumann-Moore et al., 1997).

The University of Oregon involves academic advisers in the instructional delivery of its FIG program. An academic adviser or faculty member teaches the one-credit College Experience course included in the community. When faculty members teach the courses, advisers work with them to design and facilitate the academic planning unit (Bennett, 1999). This introduces first-year students in learning communities to academic advising and other support services and helps them recognize the value of such services to their success.

Finally, learning communities become a critical lens for examining the first year. While implementing learning communities, campuses often learn a great deal about how students move through the curriculum, use academic support resources, or perceive programs and services such as orientation, placement testing, residence hall programming, academic advising, and student activities.

DIMENSIONS OF LEARNING COMMUNITIES

Learning communities can be described as having five dimensions: (1) student collaboration, (2) faculty collaboration, (3) curricular coordination, (4) shared setting, and (5) interactive pedagogy (Goodsell Love & Tokuno, 1999). The first, student collaboration, describes how students are organized and the various opportunities they use to get to know each other and collaborate around learning tasks. Learning communities students can connect in the classroom through collaborative learning and group projects, and outside the class through field trips or electronic means such as e-mail, listservs, and discussion boards.

Faculty collaboration is the extent to which faculty interact around issues of teaching and learning. Learning communities faculty who meet regularly to discuss curriculum planning or student progress would rank high on this dimension. Regularly scheduled faculty development activities—opportunities for those teaching in learning communities to come together to discuss pedagogy, student learning, and classroom assessment—is essential to achieving faculty collaboration in and across learning communities. Curricular coordination describes level of curricular integration. While courses that are individually taught with virtually no integration demonstrate low levels of coordination, learning communities in which academic content is taught from interdisciplinary and cross-disciplinary perspectives rank high on this scale.

The fourth dimension, shared setting, describes the physical space in which teaching and learning occurs—classrooms, student lounges, computer labs, and other places on campus. The final dimension, interactive pedagogy, describes how the curriculum is delivered and shared across the community. A lecture format represents lower levels of interaction, while classrooms characterized by more active pedagogies—collaborative learning, problem-based learning, and experiential learning—are considered highly interactive.

Programs vary according to their approach to learning communities, location of the program in the undergraduate curriculum, and size of the initiative. Learning communities are found in first-year experience programs, general education, writing-across-the-curriculum initiatives, and the major or minor. Campuses are creating learning communities for different student populations from developmental studies to honors programs to students in math, science, and engineering programs. Most recently, many campuses are placing learning communities at the center of the first-year experience.

LEARNING COMMUNITY MODELS

Learning communities take different shapes as they are installed in undergraduate programs across different institutional types. Four common approaches are discussed here: paired or clustered courses, cohorts in large courses or FIGs, team-taught programs, and residence-based learning communities, models that intentionally link the classroom-based learning community with a residential life component.

Paired or Clustered Courses

Paired- or clustered-course learning communities link individually taught courses through cohort and often block scheduling (scheduling of courses in back-to-back time slots). The paired-course model links two courses and is considered the simplest of learning communities models in terms of curricular strategy. A paired-course learning community typically enrolls a group of twenty to thirty students in two courses. Offerings tend to be existing courses that traditionally enroll significant numbers of first-year students. One of the two courses in the pairing is usually a basic composition or communications course. These courses tend to be more interdisciplinary in nature and promote a classroom environment in which students and faculty get to know each other.

In paired-course learning communities, classes are often linked based on logical curricular connections and skill areas. A pairing of calculus with general chemistry promotes scientific discovery and quantitative reasoning skills. Other courses commonly used in pairs are college math, introductory courses across the social sciences, literature, philosophy, and first-term courses in science.

At Temple University, students can enroll in a linked course learning community that satisfies either general education requirements or an introductory requirement in the major. Students interested in communications might enroll in a community linking Introduction to Mass Media and College Composition. Faculty teaching in this community create a theme, such as Understanding Mass Media Through Literacy, around which they build class discussion, lectures, writing assignments, and activities. As the semester progresses, students begin to see connections between the courses: "We discuss the role of media in Introduction to Mass Media [Journalism]. Then we look at the media's hidden, encoded agenda in English [class]."

A pair might also include a first-year seminar course, a for-credit offering designed to assist students in the transition to college. A learning community commonly offered at Temple University pairs the first-year seminar course, Learning for the New Century, with the precollege composition course, Introduction to Academic Discourse. Skill development is an important goal in this community.

The cluster approach typically expands the paired-course model by linking three or four individually taught courses around a theme. Clusters are often small and usually enroll cohorts of twenty to thirty students. One course tends to be a writing course, and the cluster usually includes a weekly seminar. The weekly seminar plays an important role in helping students and faculty build curricular connections between the courses. These seminars offer ideal settings for synthesis and community-building activities.

All daytime students in the Liberal Arts and Sciences program at LaGuardia Community College are required to take an introductory cluster in their first semester. Students placed into remedial courses enroll in clusters in their second semester. Clusters include the LIB 110 (Liberal Arts) hour, a course that meets one hour a week and is usually team-taught by two or three faculty teaching in the cluster. This hour is typically reserved for activities that promote reflection and curricular integration of the disciplines represented in the community. To meet the LIB 110 requirement for the Drama, Culture and Communication cluster, students write a research paper on a theatrical production using sources from the Lincoln Center for the Performing Arts Library. They also participate in field trips to see and critique plays.

Cohorts in Large Courses

These learning communities are often referred to as FIGs—freshman interest groups. A less commonly used approach is the federated learning community: student cohorts enrolled in larger courses guided by a teacher who serves as a master learner. The federated learning community integrates courses around a theme. The master learner "enrolls" in the courses with the students and facilitates a weekly seminar to help students synthesize what they are learning. The master learner usually has no teaching responsibilities beyond the federated learning community (Gabelnick, MacGregor, Matthews, & Smith, 1990).

FIGs are the simplest model in terms of organization and cost (Gabelnick et al., 1990). This approach works well at large universities or at other institutions where first-year students are typically enrolled in at least one or two large lecture courses a semester. In this model, learning communities students represent a subset of the total enrollment. When a large lecture course also involves smaller recitation or discussion sessions, FIG students are typically enrolled in a designated learning community section. In addition to one or two large courses, FIGs typically include a smaller writing course and a weekly seminar. Enrollments in these sections are usually limited to FIG students. An undergraduate often facilitates the weekly seminar.

At the University of Washington, FIGs typically consist of two larger-sized lecture courses, a smaller English, humanities, or arts course, and a one-credit course, University Resources, Information, and Technology. Each FIG has a theme, typically coordinated around a general area of study such as business, liberal arts, sciences, or engineering. The Performing Arts: Drama FIG includes Greek and Roman Classics, Acting, and Survey of Music paired with the one-credit seminar.

Team-Taught Programs

Team-taught learning communities, also called coordinated studies programs, enroll varying numbers of students in two or more courses organized around an interdisciplinary theme. Team-taught programs are the most extensive in terms of curricular integration and faculty role. Some require full-time faculty and student involvement. Participation can also be part-time, involving two to five courses. In most but not all instances, the learning community constitutes students' entire schedule for at least a term and sometimes an entire academic year.

Themes are faculty generated and interdisciplinary. They can be broad and liberal arts based, or emphasize skill development in related disciplines such as math and science. Small group discussion sections, sometimes called book seminars, are an important part of the community. Students and a faculty member break off into smaller groups to discuss an assigned text and build on what students are learning in the other courses.

Total community enrollment varies, but can range from forty to seventy-five students. In larger team-taught programs, the cohort is often subdivided into smaller seminar groups to achieve a faculty-to-student ratio of one faculty member to twenty or twenty-five students (Gabelnick et al., 1990). Due to increasing fiscal pressures, typical enrollment in these programs is now more likely to be closer to seventy-five students and three teachers, with a teacher-to-student ratio of twenty-five to one.

Ecology of Hope is a year-long coordinated study program designed for first-year students at Evergreen State College. The curriculum focuses on global warming, rain forest devastation, industrial pollution, and other environmental concerns. Students and teachers explore many questions, including, "What can we do?" and "How can we have sustainable, meaningful lives that enable us to create appropriate and effective action for positive change over the long haul?" Upon completion of the program, students are awarded credit in several areas: writing, quantitative reasoning, environmental studies, art, cultural studies, scientific methods, history, and political economy.

Residence-Based Programs

A fourth approach to learning communities, residence-based programs, involves the adaptation of a particular curricular model to include a residential component. A primary goal of residence-based education is the integration of students' living and academic environments. Educational programming in residence halls centers around the belief that not all learning occurs in the classroom. A significant amount of what students learn during college comes from their experiences of daily living, and there is natural overlap between students' academic and social learning activities.

According to Schroeder (1994), "Learning communities are fostered by commonality and consistency of purpose, shared values, and transcendent themes" (p. 171). In residence-based learning communities, the role of residence life is to create conditions that promote these values. Residence-based learning communities involve more than assigning students with similar majors to the same floor of a residence hall. Rather, intentionally organized student cohorts enroll in specified curricular offerings and reside in dedicated living space.

Residence-based learning communities integrate diverse curricular and cocurricular experiences. For this reason, residence-based learning communities may be the most radical of the four learning communities approaches described in this chapter because they challenge and require change within multiple campus systems: curriculum, teaching, and housing (Shapiro & Levine, 1999). The curricular component of residence-based programs typically resembles one of the three learning communities approaches described previously in this chapter: clusters, FIGs, or team-taught programs. Academic and cocurricular community activities are scheduled in residence halls, and in many instances classes actually meet in classrooms located in residential spaces.

FIGs at the University of Missouri-Columbia evolved out of the collaborative efforts of academic and student affairs. Missouri's FIGs are residential learning communities, located in more than three-quarters of the university's residence halls, that involve courses from across the first-year curricula. Small cohorts of fifteen to twenty first-year students enroll in three sections of the same general education courses, share living space, and complete a one-credit seminar designed to integrate material from the general education courses and introduce students to support resources. The Family Studies FIG is designed for students interested in working with children and families through the agencies and organizations that serve them. Students enroll in three courses—Introduction to the Study of Families, General Psychology, and General Biology for Non-Majors—and are housed in a particular residence hall.

The Michigan Community Scholars Program at the University of Michigan creates a collaborative, supportive community of students, faculty, and staff who share an interest in and are committed to understanding their roles in various communities and in exploring service-learning opportunities. This residential community features introductory math and English courses, first-year seminars, and community service courses. There are leadership opportunities, programming, and academic support resources for students in the community.

Learning Communities for Specific Populations

Learning communities also represent an effective curricular strategy for supporting students in historically difficult courses, student populations with unique college transition and academic needs, or students with specific career objectives. There are also successful learning communities programs at institutions where all or most students live off-campus.

Learning communities bring students together in the classroom, where they can establish academic and social networks that are of tremendous benefit to the commuter student. Another benefit of learning communities for off-campus students is that they provide a setting for community-based delivery of support services such as tutoring, mentoring, or career counseling. Information technology can be used to help students and teachers in learning communities remain connected to each other outside the classroom. For off-campus students, learning communities provide a home base on campus and a sense of interpersonal and intellectual connectedness that is often lacking in the commuter experience (Levine & Shapiro, 2000).

The New Student House Program at LaGuardia Community College is a learning community for students with basic skills needs. Curriculum and instruction in reading, writing, and speech are coordinated and often organized around a theme, activities and assignments in the three courses are linked, and classes are sometimes team-taught. LaGuardia also offers a new student house community for students for whom English is a second language. New Student-ESL House features six credit hours of English as a Second language, four hours of basic reading with an additional reading lab, and a three-credit college-level speech communications course. The cluster also includes a first-year seminar that focuses on study skills and orientation to college.

The ASCENT program at the University of Northern Colorado annually enrolls approximately seventy-five students in a premedicine and prehealth learning community linking composition, biology, and chemistry courses. The community also features a team-taught seminar that covers prehealth issues and reviews information on professional school requirements. Supplemental Instruction for the biology and chemistry classes is offered as well.

IMPLEMENTING LEARNING COMMUNITIES

Implementing learning communities involves (1) recognizing opportunities for change, (2) creating structures to accommodate learning communities, (3) identifying resources, (4) making the program visible, and (5) assessing program effectiveness. The leadership for learning communities may come from faculty, academic administration, student affairs, or a combination of each. It is important that the implementation effort is broad and inclusive, recognizing the many individuals and resources that support student success. Early planning for learning communities should bring key players together in frequent conversations. A campuswide committee where participants can share ideas, explore assumptions, and build relationships should be formed. This type of collaborative planning is consistent with the goals and values of learning communities that campuses seek to create for their students (Shapiro & Levine, 1999).

Those designing learning communities on their campuses need to be sensitive to their particular student, faculty, and institutional cultures. The most successful programs are those fully integrated within the institution. How learning communities are organized, their location within the academic program, and how they will evolve and grow depend in large part on the broad goals for the program and where the initial inquiry and idea began. Common reasons a campus considers learning communities include a need to increase student involvement and engagement, a desire to create community among commuting students, or a mandate to improve retention.

Recognizing Opportunities for Change

Often the first step toward creating learning communities is motivated by the recognition that something needs to be fixed or improved. Perhaps the institution suffers from the perception that it is unfriendly or impersonal to undergraduates. Some campuses are driven by a desire to attract more and better-quality first-year students, and others implement learning communities to better educate and retain all students. Linking learning communities to a broader campus goal of improving undergraduate recruitment and retention can be another powerful motive for change. Look to the institutional mission statement, strategic plans or annual reports, department or program reviews, existing examples of collaboration between departments, programs and units, and external reviews or reports on trends in higher education for language and opportunities to intro-duce the concept of learning communities to the campus community (Shapiro & Levine, 1999).

It is also important to address sources of resistance such as faculty auton-omy, disciplinary boundaries, lack of resources, and inappropriate reward sys-tems. Avoid associating the idea and effort with one individual or office. Be aware of the various levels of approval and governance to which any new pro-gram is subjected. Involve decision makers with a voice in approval processes early in the planning.

Creating Structures to Support Learning Communities

Creating learning communities requires working within the existing structure and working outside existing structures (Shapiro & Levine, 1999). Whether the impe-tus for learning communities comes from faculty or administration, from academic affairs or student affairs, the same organizational principles apply. On most cam-puses, change happens through the work of committees with ongoing consulta-tion, and the first question that must be addressed is, Who should be involved?

Learning communities faculty can be broadly defined to include those not typically involved in the teaching enterprise. Others who can be members of learning communities teaching teams in addition to faculty members are learn-ing support specialists, academic advisers, residence life staff, librarians, and computer technology specialists (MacGregor et al., 2001). Students—both under-graduate and graduate—can serve as teachers, peer advisers, tutors, mentors, and resident assistants in learning communities.

Collaborative relationships develop through personal contacts, so it makes sense that early planning for learning communities should bring key players together in frequent, informal discussions. Identify priorities and then establish goals and intended outcomes for the learning communities program. It is very important to develop a planning calendar consistent with regularly scheduled events, procedures, and deadlines for the campus planning process.

Identifying Resources

Be realistic about cost and resource needs. When starting learning communities, consider the costs to departments and colleges in faculty time. Work with units to reach compromises on sharing resources and costs. Promote departmental col-laboration by offering incentives from release time to money for faculty devel-opment. Because cross-disciplinary learning communities are more interesting and more viable in the long run, it is worth the extra effort and time it takes to work out the details between departments. According to Elliot and Decker (1999), campuswide support for learning communities comes from four sources:

- People (faculty administrators, academic support staff, and student affairs professionals)
- Organizational culture (the administrative home for the program and connections that placement entails)

- Context (the role and purpose of the learning community on a campus)
- Financial support (redirected funding and new money)

As a campus begins projecting the cost of learning communities, it is useful to have an inventory of additional resources needed. There are typically three categories of costs for learning communities: (1) one-time start-up costs for which a campus might seek outside grant or gift support; (2) logistical and operating expense support that allows the learning community to become part of the sustainable infrastructure of the institution; and (3) faculty development and reward structure costs that should be considered long-term investments in teaching and learning (Shapiro & Levine, 1999). Any requests for resources should be consistent with program goals, expected outcomes, size and scope of the program, and model of learning communities.

Many campuses start small, gradually scaling up in terms of the numbers of communities offered, students enrolled, and faculty involved. Decisions to expand must be explored in the context of program goals, available resources, sources of support, and evidence of the impact that learning communities are having on the institution. One effective way to increase the size of a learning communities program, particularly at a larger institution, is to network with other programs. Temple University expanded its learning communities initiative by partnering with its undergraduate school of business to provide learning clusters for all entering business students. After learning of the value of learning communities for students in other programs, a committee of business faculty and administration decided to revise its undergraduate curriculum to require a community experience for all of its full-time students. Students enroll in a cluster that includes business, law, first-year writing, computer applications, and a two-credit introduction to business seminar. The School of Business and the Learning Communities program share responsibility for scheduling the course in the community. The Learning Communities program coordinates faculty development, and academic advisers from the business school register students and teach the seminar. This collaborative effort enrolls an additional 350 to 400 students in communities each fall.

Making the Program Visible

Provide learning communities updates at department, faculty senate, and curriculum committee meetings. It is also important that the program have representation on various campus committees, including those charged with reviewing academic advising or admissions policies. Keeping the campus community informed of the learning communities work creates shared ownership. Consider giving interviews to the student and faculty newspapers. Invite others on campus not already involved with the program to visit classes and talk to learning communities faculty and students.

Use print and on-line resources to market the program to prospective and current students. Develop a program brochure as well as promotional literature describing the individual communities. Ask faculty teaching in the communities to provide descriptions that can be given to students during orientation or registration. Create a learning communities Web site that contains basic program information, a list of offerings, and answers to frequently asked questions.

ASSESSING LEARNING COMMUNITIES

Decisions about assessment and evaluation should be part of the ongoing planning and implementation process, and assessment plans should be made alongside decisions about the intended outcomes of learning communities. Using the comprehensive model of assessing first-year programs suggested by Upcraft in Chapter Twenty-Seven, learning communities administrators and faculty should know a lot about the backgrounds and characteristics of first-year student participants, assess their needs, measure their satisfaction with the learning community experience, and, perhaps most important, assess whether participation in a learning community is associated with desired outcomes such as grades, retention, and other program-specific outcomes.

For example, if an intended outcome of participation in learning communities is greater student involvement with faculty, this should be a focus of the research. Assessment plans can and will be amended with program development and as the institution learns more about what students and faculty experience as members of learning communities. There will be many questions that need to be answered. Start small, and consider addressing research questions that yield important and usable information and can be easily answered within a reasonable time frame using available methods or researchers (Ketcheson & Levine, 1999).

An assessment plan should be developed in the context of other evaluation activities taking place. Consider uses of data already collected. Many institutions collect new student data as part of the admissions, placement testing, or orientation process. This information can be useful in describing participants, as well as nonparticipants, in learning communities. If an institution already collects information on the reading and writing skills of entering students, consider ways of linking those data to a learning communities study on the performance of learning communities participants and nonparticipants in first-year writing courses. In selecting research methods, consider an integrated research approach that relies on both quantitative and qualitative research methods. Using multiple methods available to educational researchers allows you to address a variety of research questions in rich contexts and from different perspectives (Shulman, 1988).

There is still a great deal to learn about what first-year students and faculty experience in learning communities. Quantitative research shows that learning communities students typically get higher grades and stay in school longer than their non–learning communities peers. Qualitative research shows that learning communities students are more likely to feel connected to the institution than non–learning community students. Several national surveys, including the National Survey of Student Engagement and College Student Experiences Questionnaire, are available to help campuses measure if learning communities students are more engaged and involved in the campus community than their peers. Even with a growth in available research on learning communities, questions remain. Are students learning in deeper, more meaningful ways? Do faculty change their teaching practices, and does this change extend to other areas of the curriculum?

RECOMMENDATIONS

Learning communities are a curricular model for enhancing student learning and deepening their engagement with the institution. They support first-year students in their academic and social transition to college. When learning communities for students are created, cross-campus partnerships take root, and communities of faculty, administrators, and staff are created and nurtured. Consider the following when developing and maintaining learning communities:

- *Monitor learning communities from their onset, and make changes as they grow and develop.* It is possible that the structures put in place at the start (collaborative committees, faculty liaisons between colleges, and policy committees) may not be the structures that emerge once learning communities begin to operate. An institution that starts out designing a coordinated studies program may instead install linked courses in the curriculum, while a campus beginning with links in a first-year experience program may grow to clusters. Institutions need to be open to the same change in practice we hope students and faculty in our communities will experience.
- *Be collaborative, take risks, and experiment.* Meet often with all involved to review the opportunities, challenges, and resources that affect learning communities work.
- *Obtain commitments from senior leadership and others in positions to offer support and provide resources for learning communities programs.* Maintaining the support of senior leadership is critical to the success of learning communities.
- *Form partnerships with other programs engaged in similar work.* Explore ways to share resources and expertise. If your campus has an established center for teaching and learning, seek advice there on faculty development. Meet regularly with institutional researchers to plan and conduct assessment.
- *Create structures to encourage and support faculty involvement.* Regularly scheduled workshops, retreats, and brown-bag lunch sessions are some approaches for bringing faculty together to form teaching teams and plan their learning community designs. Workshop topics might focus on pedagogy, assessment, or student development. Faculty development is also an important opportunity to recognize dedicated teachers for the hard work of teaching in learning communities.

- *Carefully consider policies that impede change or present barriers for faculty teaching in learning communities.* Do faculty tenure and promotion policies and practices recognize and reward the interdisciplinary and collaborative teaching that takes place in learning communities? How can we develop a cost-effective system for providing faculty with sufficient preterm planning time?

- *Regularly gather and disseminate credible evidence that the program works and is meeting its goals.* Such information can influence policy change.

- *Learn from the experiences of others.* The considerable growth in the development of learning communities has led to more writing on the subject from a variety of perspectives: impact on students and faculty, connections with first-year experience programs, partnerships between academic and student affairs, and good practice for teaching, learning, and assessment. Attend sessions on learning communities at national and regional conferences. Subscribe to list-servs that offer frequent discussions on learning communities or related topics.

CONCLUSION

While learning communities are not something new, they continue to be something different. Participation in a learning community requires campuses, sometimes in very radical ways, to rethink and restructure how they organize and deliver their curriculum. First-year students are challenged to learn with and from each other, and faculty are challenged to approach subjects in new and more interdisciplinary ways. When implemented effectively, learning communities provide a powerful source of challenge and support in helping first-year students make a successful transition to college and fulfill their educational goals.

CHALLENGING AND SUPPORTING FIRST-YEAR STUDENTS OUTSIDE THE CLASSROOM

What We Know About Today's First-Year Students and Institutional Efforts to Help Them Succeed

In Part Four, we explored the many ways in which institutions can directly challenge and support first-year students to achieve academically. But academic success is not simply a matter of first-year students going to class, studying hard, and using academic support services. As Pascarella, Terenzini, and Blimling (1996) demonstrated in their extensive study of first-year student academic success, student achievement in the classroom is very much affected, both positively and negatively, by students' engagement outside the classroom. And Astin (1976) found that student involvement in the life of the institution plays an important role in persistence. Thus, if we are to provide a maximum opportunity for first-year students to learn, grow, and succeed, institutions must challenge and support them outside the classroom as well.

More specifically, Terenzini and others (1996), after reviewing this body of literature, concluded that academic and cognitive learning are positively shaped by a wide variety of out-of-class experiences, such as living in residence halls, particularly ones in which the various dimensions of students' academic and nonacademic lives are purposefully integrated; working part-time on campus; socializing with others of different racial or ethnic groups; having an internship; spending a term studying abroad; and interacting with other students and faculty members, particularly when the topics of discussion are academically or intellectually related. However, they also found that some out-of-classroom activities exert a negative influence on student learning, including belonging to a fraternity, participating in men's intercollegiate basketball or football, working full time, spending more hours socializing with friends, or having fewer academically related out-of-class encounters with faculty members and other students. They also conclude that the most powerful source of influence on student learning appears to be students' interpersonal interactions, whether with peers or faculty.

What does all this mean for first-year student success? First, it means that if we are committed to first-year student success, we must pay attention not only to what goes on inside the classroom but outside the classroom as well. Second, it means that student services, programs, and activities must be targeted to first-year students and their needs, and oriented (in some cases *reoriented*) toward enhancing their success, both academically and developmentally. And finally, as Schroeder pointed out in Chapter Twelve, it means that student affairs must work in collaboration with academic affairs to help first-year students succeed.

Student affairs and academic affairs have not always worked together to serve the best interests of first-year students. In fact, in some cases, just the opposite is true: student affairs worked exclusively outside the classroom, and academic affairs worked inside the classroom. Moreover, students' academic development was considered the exclusive domain of faculty, while social development was the exclusive domain of student affairs professionals. Yet the evidence suggests that student learning is a more seamless endeavor that ignores the artificial boundaries established by institutional organizational structures.

Thus, the chapters in this part are devoted to the many ways in which students may be challenged and supported outside the classroom to make a successful transition to college to achieve their educational goals and progress in their personal development. In Chapter Twenty-Three, Richard Mullendore and Leslie Banahan review the components of a comprehensive challenging and supportive orientation program that includes not only students but their families as well. Such programs begin before first-year students enroll and continue through their first year of college.

Because many studies (Astin, 1976; Chickering, 1974) have shown that when first-year students live in residence halls, they are more likely to earn higher grades, persist to graduation, and be more involved in their collegiate experience, in Chapter Twenty-Four, William J. Zeller looks at how residential environments, both on and off campus, can be structured to challenge and support first-year students.

Other student services are also influential in first-year student success. Thus, in Chapter Twenty-Five, John H. Schuh reviews the importance to first-year students of career services, counseling services, health services, student activities, campus recreation facilities, and services designed to meet the needs of special first-year populations such as adult learners, women, disabled students, international students, gay/lesbian/bisexual/transgendered students, honors students, and athletes.

Finally, there is extensive research to show that alcohol and other drug use and abuse among students is related to just about everything that contributes to their lack of success in college, including academic difficulties, sexual assault, mental and physical health problems, and dysfunctional interpersonal relations. There is also evidence that many campus problems, such as crime, safety, and destruction of property, are also related to alcohol and other drug abuse. In Chapter Twenty-Six, Philip Meilman and Cheryl Presley discuss this difficult problem and ways in which institutions can deal with them from the moment first-year students are admitted and enrolled.

CHAPTER TWENTY-THREE

Designing Orientation Programs

Richard H. Mullendore
Leslie A. Banahan

*Orientation, number one, helped me meet people. My friends, the ones
I hang with now, I met at orientation. We've been together since then!
Number two, I wasn't too sure about coming here. I thought I wanted
to go to another school, but after orientation, I was very, very excited
about coming here. Orientation made all the difference.*
—First-year student

Orientation is about new beginnings for first-year students, their families, and the institution. It can be the defining moment in the transition to college for the student (and family)—a time in which basic habits are formed that influence students' academic success and personal growth—and marks the beginning of the new educational experience. Orientation is the college's best opportunity to introduce a strong learning environment, build the foundations for academic success, welcome students and families to the campus community, promote student interactions with faculty and staff, and convey the values and traditions of the new institution. All of this is not accomplished in a one- or two-day orientation event, but it can and should be done through a comprehensive, multifaceted orientation process beginning at the time of admission and continuing throughout the entire first year.

Designing successful orientation programs is a complex and challenging process, but it is clear that effective orientation programs are essential to a quality first-year experience. This chapter will discuss the importance of orientation as an ongoing process rather than a single event; the value of CAS standards (Miller, 1999) for implementing and improving orientation programs; an overview of the organization and administration of orientation programs; a sample of typical program components; the importance of parent/family orientation programs; the difference between two-year commuter and four-year residential orientation experiences; program ideas for transfer students, adult learners, and other special populations; methods for determining program effectiveness; uses for technology; an exploration of current trends; and recommendations for improving campus-based orientation programs. In summary, orientation is the first opportunity for institutions to challenge first-year students to excel educationally and introduce them to the many ways in which the institution provides support for their success.

TRENDS IN ORIENTATION

Orientation has experienced its own transition over the past decade, due in large part to the research and training activities sponsored by the National Orientation Directors Association (NODA), and both the content and administration of orientation programs have been influenced by a number of changes. First, orientation has become more academic in nature. The total amount of time spent in testing, advising, scheduling, and learning how to negotiate the academic environment has increased. Faculty involvement in orientation is more prevalent as student affairs and academic affairs collaborate to enhance the learning environment (Strumpf & Wawrynski, 2000). For example, at many institutions, faculty and student orientation leaders jointly present important academic information such as core curriculum requirements, the academic vocabulary, and effective study skills for the college learning environment.

Second, technological advances have not only dramatically altered the administrative functions associated with orientation program implementation, but also have required institutions to find balance with the ease and efficiency technology offers and the need for orientation to provide the human connection between students and their institutions.

Third, the college population has changed. Today, we provide orientation for an increasing number of nontraditional students. Their needs, interests, and time constraints require flexible, purposeful, innovative, and efficient orientation programs. According to Newman and Miller (2002), this population's needs are met with programs of a "serious and vocational purposive nature. This means that for many non-traditional students, on-campus programming and friendship development is secondary to the business of attending classes and working toward a degree" (p. 3).

Fourth, increased family attendance and involvement in orientation have provided opportunities for college staff and faculty to develop specific programs for this important constituency (Hatch, 2000). The depth and breadth of literature regarding student and family orientation programs have improved over the past decade. For example, in 1993, the National Resource Center for The First-Year Experience and Students in Transition (FYE) and NODA collaborated on a major monograph. *Designing Successful Transitions: A Guide for Orienting Students to College* (Upcraft, Mullendore, Barefoot, & Fidler, 1993). In 2000, a second collaboration resulted in the publication of *Helping Your First-Year College Student Succeed: A Guide for Parents* (Mullendore & Hatch, 2000).

Finally, the increasing diversity of students has challenged professionals "to develop orientation services and programs that focus on what students have in common, while at the same time recognizing and legitimizing their differences" (Upcraft, 1993, p. 7).

DEFINITION AND GOALS OF ORIENTATION

Building on previous definitions (Dannells & Kuh, 1977; Upcraft & Farnsworth, 1984; Perigo & Upcraft, 1989), orientation can be defined as a collaborative institutional effort to enhance student success by assisting students and their families in the transition to the new college environment. Orientation programs generally provide information and guidance regarding academic programs, administrative processes, campus services, facilities, and cocurricular programs. They are designed to meet the needs of first-year, transfer, nontraditional, and graduate students, as well as parents and family members. The initial components of the orientation process are frequently offered during the summer or immediately prior to the beginning of the term.

Perigo and Upcraft (1989) outlined four goals for orientation programs. With minimal modification, those goals are valid today. First and foremost, orientation should help new students succeed academically. Students need to know academic requirements, course offerings, and registration procedures. They should also be informed about the breadth of academic support and resources available to assist with advising, study skills, time management, and tutoring.

A second goal of orientation is to assist students in their adjustment to and involvement with the college. A student's comfort level with a college is often established during orientation. The orientation program provides the college with a great vehicle to educate new students about campus resources, social programs, and leadership opportunities. Orientation is the time for students to become familiar with campus facilities and the area in which the college is located. Because of the critical importance of interaction between students and faculty, an orientation program can facilitate the development of those connections as well.

Third, orientation programs should be designed to assist parents and other family members in understanding the complexity, demands, and services of the collegiate environment. Family members know their student better than do professors, peers, and college staff; therefore, they are often in the best position to encourage and support behaviors that may lead to academic and personal success (Mullendore & Hatch, 2000).

Finally, orientation should provide the college an opportunity to learn more about incoming students through formal and informal means. Orientation is an excellent time to conduct research about incoming students to provide baseline data that can be helpful to faculty and staff. These data can be used to assist faculty in understanding the nature of today's students, their academic preparation, and the life experiences they bring to the classroom. For staff, these data provide important information for the development or enhancement of institutional retention efforts.

At the end of a successful orientation program, a student will possess more than a schedule of classes for the upcoming term. "If successful, the orientation process can lead to earlier and more enduring involvement in the academic and social systems of an institution. It is also reasonable to expect that student involvement will be greatest if new students can be immediately linked with people who are already invested in the institution, whether faculty members or other students" (Pascarella & Terenzini, 1991, p. 650). Successful orientation programs also have been linked to student retention. "The research on orientation clearly indicates that successful orientation programs have a powerful influence on first-year social and academic integration and, furthermore, that social and academic integration have a significant effect on student persistence and educational attainment" (Rode, 2000, p. 3).

To accomplish orientation goals and to have a positive impact on retention, it is imperative that orientation be considered a comprehensive process rather than a single event. Such a process should also include implementing a first-year seminar program, frontloading of financial resources for social programs and other involvement opportunities, developing a student-friendly environment, and incorporating ongoing assessment activities.

For orientation to be successful, it should comply with the standards established by the Council for the Advancement of Standards in Higher Education (CAS), balance academic and social components, and provide ample opportunities for informal interaction between and among students and faculty. Furthermore, staff should be aware that students often attend more than one institution's orientation program and that "determination for fit is still taking place" (Perigo & Upcraft, 1989, p. 87). Organizing and implementing a program that adequately accomplishes its mission is a difficult balancing act for the director, given that orientation programs are often packed with tests, academic advisement, class registration, social activities, and information sessions.

PROGRAM STANDARDS

Development of a successful, retention-based orientation program can be greatly simplified by implementing the standards for orientation developed by CAS, a consortium of thirty-four professional organizations that is responsible for the development, promulgation, and promotion of professional standards. Currently, standards exist for twenty-eight functional areas in higher education, including orientation, academic advising, admissions, commuter programs, counseling services, learning assistance programs, and disability services. "The CAS materials represent an excellent set of tools to develop, expand, explain and defend important campus services" (Smith, 1998, p. 9). Using the CAS standards can assist in identifying key ingredients for a mission statement, creating comprehensive program goals, staffing an office, developing a cohesive set of program components, educating the campus community, defending budgetary requests, assessing program effectiveness, preparing for institutional reaccreditation, and increasing program credibility. An example of a CAS standards-based orientation mission statement is the one that guides the University of Virginia program: "Orientation is designed to welcome and introduce all entering students and their families to the University. It helps new students make the transition from their previous environment to the diverse academic, intellectual, and social culture of the University" (Most & Miller, 1998, p. 2). The program has these goals:

- To introduce entering undergraduate students to the opportunities and responsibilities of academic life at the University
- To integrate entering students into life at the University
- To help students maintain their personal health and wellness
- To familiarize the families of new students with the University experience
- To introduce students to the wealth of University resources [Most & Miller, 1998, p. 2]

Mullendore speaks to the importance of standards:

Why should orientation professionals be concerned with operationalizing standards? More than almost anyone on campus, orientation directors work across division lines to communicate with and involve the entire institution in the implementation of their programs. Often these programs are developed by student affairs staff who do not feel as though they are equal partners in the institutional political structure. As a result, program credibility must be achieved so that all constituencies within the institution understand, accept, and embrace the value of the orientation function [Mullendore, 1992, p. 43].

A credible program is one that facilitates the transition of new students, prepares them for their new learning environment, and integrates them into the academic and social fabric of their new institution (Miller, 1999).

ORGANIZATION AND ADMINISTRATION OF ORIENTATION

"Quality orientation programs do not just happen; they are complex endeavors that require strong organizational skills and considerable human and financial resources" (Mullendore & Abraham, 1993, p. 61). Current emphasis on student retention has heightened the visibility and importance of issues such as the locus of orientation within the administrative hierarchy, staffing, funding, and timing.

According to *NODA Data Bank* (Strumpf & Wawrynski, 2000), the orientation function reports through the division of student affairs in at least 68 percent of NODA member colleges. The reporting line through academic affairs occurs in 10 percent of the institutions. In small institutions (fewer than five thousand students), orientation is even more likely to report to student affairs (76 percent), while in large institutions (over fifteen thousand students), the percentage of programs reporting through academic affairs increases to 20 percent. Reporting lines for orientation programs appear to have remained stable over the past ten years. While orientation is housed primarily in a stand-alone orientation office or within student activities, the function is also found in counseling centers, dean of students' offices, student development, admissions, advising, enrollment management, and other areas.

According to Mullendore and Abraham (1993), while orientation may report to many different parts of an institution's organization, orientation typically reports to student affairs for the following reasons:

Student affairs professionals constantly work within and beyond division lines. They are trained to understand how an institution functions, what services are available and provided, and they possess significant knowledge of student development theory and practice that is extremely important in deciding what an orientation program should do. They are often in the best position to recruit, select, train, and evaluate student orientation leaders. In addition, student affairs professionals often have an appropriate conceptualization of the value of both academic and social integration into the college or university [p. 65].

Many of the skills necessary to be an effective orientation professional are taught in student affairs preparation programs, including student development theory, organizational development, management, marketing, and supervision. A combination of classroom preparation and campus-based experience is critical to the development of a competent orientation professional. This person must understand the needs of first-year students, the needs of their families, as well as the institution and how it functions. The staff member who is responsible for orientation must be able to interact effectively with all institutional constituencies in order to secure facilities, speakers, programs, and amenities. Positive working relationships must be developed with academic departments and advising offices, physical plant, residence life, food services, business services, campus security, and others. "This person must be able to recruit, select, and train student staff; manage a budget; and plan and implement a complex series of programs. It seems unreasonable to expect a new professional to possess the skills to direct a successful, comprehensive orientation program" (Mullendore & Abraham, 1993, p. 64).

Too often, colleges hire or assign entry-level professionals to administer and lead orientation. In a workshop on designing orientation programs, we are surprised each year to find a large number of participants who have minimal higher education experience yet have been given this important responsibility. It is even more surprising that a significant percentage of orientation professionals (16 percent) have only a bachelor's degree (Strumpf & Wawrynski, 2000), which may pose issues for program credibility and effectiveness. Moreover, when orientation is buried deep in the organizational structure of the institution, it is easier to justify hiring entry-level professionals and paying them low salaries. Institutions that engage in this practice communicate the relative unimportance of helping their first-year students make a successful transition to college and achieve their educational goals.

A comprehensive orientation program requires staffing appropriate to the size and mission of the institution. Obviously there is no way that a program director can individually meet, connect with, and be responsive to the hundreds or thousands of people who come to orientation programs during the year; therefore, student orientation leaders are a critical component of an orientation program. In many institutions, the orientation leader position is one of the most prestigious leadership opportunities available to students. Elaborate selection and training programs exist in order for the college to put its best foot forward during orientation. Faculty nominations of potential student orientation leaders are often solicited in order to recruit successful students from a variety of majors.

For their effort, student orientation leaders may be paid a salary and receive free housing, food, and orientation program clothing. In some institutions, orientation leaders receive their training through a credit-bearing class (Pierson & Timmerman, 2000). Orientation leaders get to know many faculty and administrators on an informal basis and are frequently worthy of valuable letters of recommendation for graduate or professional school applications or job searches. Orientation leaders must know and understand the standards and values expected of the orientation program. They must have excellent communication skills and knowledge about how the campus functions and what programs and services exist. They should be informed and committed ambassadors for the institution and should reflect the diversity of their institution's student population.

Quality support staff are also extremely important for a successful orientation program. As the staff who set the tone for the program, they are often the voice on the telephone that determines the first impression for the new student or parent. The staff should enjoy students, be knowledgeable about the college, possess good communication and organizational skills, and have an eye for details, along with tremendous amounts of patience. Depending on the size of the institution and the scope and complexity of the orientation program, support staff may be dedicated solely to the orientation program or have other responsibilities throughout the year.

Effective orientation programs require adequate resources as they often include publications, technology, leader training programs, facility rentals, course instruction, meals, and the requisite T-shirts. "In addition to institutional funding through general funds, other funding sources may be considered, including state appropriations, student fees, user fees, donations, contributions, fines, concession and store sales, rentals, and dues" (Miller, 1999, p. 139). Implicit within this standards statement is the belief that some form of institutional commitment should exist to establish a base level of program operation. In private colleges, there is often a reticence to charge extra fees; therefore, institutional funds may provide total support for the orientation function as the cost is included in tuition.

Public institutions, in contrast, typically rely on user fees for the bulk of program support (Strumpf & Wawrynski, 2000). Developing a fee-based program eliminates the need to compete with other institutional units for scarce state dollars and provides a secure and permanent funding base. Advocates of fee-based programs often cite budget flexibility and protection from institutional budget reductions as valid reasons to continue to charge user fees. Yet fee-based orientation programs may place a hardship on first-year students from economically disadvantaged backgrounds, so a fee waiver procedure may be needed to help these students.

One of the benefits of directing an orientation program is the opportunity to interact with a multitude of internal and external constituencies. Within those interactions are excellent opportunities to supplement traditional orientation program funding sources. While institutional funding, user fees, and mandatory student fees are the most frequent sources of funding, it is not uncommon for orientation staff to seek external donations or advertising revenue from local businesses. Many businesses specifically target and depend on the revenue generated by the student population, and they are eager to get early exposure to new students. Orientation staff often capitalize on this phenomenon for the benefit of both commercial enterprises and orientation funding.

PROGRAM COMPONENTS

Any discussion of program components must relate to the mission and goals of the orientation function within the specific college setting. The orientation program must

> assist new students in understanding their responsibilities within the educational setting. . . . Provide new students with information about academic policies, procedures, requirements, and programs sufficient to make well-reasoned and well-informed choices. . . . Inform new students about the availability of services and programs. . . . Assist new students in becoming familiar with the campus and local environment. . . . Provide intentional opportunities for new students to interact with faculty, staff, and continuing students [Miller, 1999, pp. 137–138].

Typical student orientation program components can be divided into four categories: academic activities, student services, cocurricular and recreational events, and sessions for special populations. Academic activities might include academic structure and requirements, grading, academic advising, registration, academic assistance resources, meals and receptions with faculty, the library, class lectures and demonstrations, academic department displays and open houses, summer book reading discussions, and more formal rituals such as convocations and president's receptions.

Student services activities might include residence life and housing, food services, financial aid, vehicle registration, career services, counseling services, health services, services for special student groups, campus computer and technology resources, campus safety, wellness programs, diversity appreciation, alcohol and other drug programs, service-learning, learning communities, and identification cards.

Cocurricular activities might include getting-acquainted activities, recreational opportunities, social events, and exposure to student organization and leadership opportunities. Programs for special first-year student populations such as commuters, racial/ethnic minorities, and international students, as well as programs that focus on interactions among various student groups, might also be implemented.

Recognizing the breadth and volume of information that new students need, it is easy to see why the orientation program director must play the role of gatekeeper, deciding which offices, programs, and functions get access to students and parents within the brief time span of the initial orientation event. Priorities for program components should be established based on timeliness, quality, and participant readiness. What do students need to know immediately? Is the program material appropriate for new students at the time of the initial orientation event, or might it be better provided to them at a later date? Do the presenters represent the best the institution has to offer? The director should give careful consideration to the selection of all orientation speakers. Personable, high-energy, articulate speakers have the ability to connect with their audiences and create a comfortable and trusting environment for all orientation participants.

Successfully orchestrating the logistics involved in a program that encompasses the components listed above is an enormous task for the orientation director. Often the placement testing function alone consumes over three hours of valuable time while doing little to increase a new student's comfort level with the college. Anecdotal reports indicate the percentage of colleges administering placement tests at orientation is declining as a number of institutions are administering tests on-line, using national standardized test results, or scheduling testing on weekends prior to orientation. Institutions must regularly examine and assess the orientation program to determine appropriate components.

Parent and Family Orientation

There is substantial evidence (Pascarella & Terenzini, 1991) that family support is critical to first-year student success. For traditional-age students, that means support from parents; for adult learners, that means support from significant others, including spouses, children, other relatives, and friends. Families enter the orientation process with a lot of questions about how their son, daughter, wife, husband, or sister will succeed in college and how they might help.

Many of the parents of traditional-age students have created an enormous amount of structure in their student's life. Often, activities have been carefully selected and scheduled, with virtually every hour of every day programmed. These parents have been strong, vocal, involved advocates for their students in school, athletics, music, and other activities. Often, they have carefully managed every aspect of their student's incredibly busy life. When there was a bump in the road, parents rushed to the rescue to fix the problem. Now these same parents are sending their students to college, and their desire to be an active part of their student's college experience is strong. The orientation program is key to helping parents redefine their role within the life of their student.

Orientation programs for parents can be designed to help parents renegotiate the relationship based on the student's new status as a college student and as an adult. One resource that may be useful in setting an appropriate tone for parents is *Helping Your First-Year College Student Succeed: A Guide for Parents* (Mullendore & Hatch, 2000). This twenty-eight-page booklet helps parents focus on the events and feelings their student will likely experience during the first college year and how they can assist their student throughout this critical time and is available from the National Resource Center for The First-Year Experience and Students in Transition at the University of South Carolina.

The families and friends of adult learners face somewhat different challenges. They may have to adjust their lives in response to the increased demands put on their newly enrolled first-year student. Changes in relationships and time demands can create tensions that must be handled, and issues such as child care, transportation, and finances must be addressed. These families and friends also need help in adjusting to the new realities of their lives and learning how to be supportive of their first-year students' educational ambitions.

Another consideration is the families of first-generation first-year students. What are their needs, and how can the institution increase their understanding of and comfort level with the college environment? Parents and families want to learn as much as they can about the institution and its services and programs. They want to know how they can stay connected to their student and the college, and they need accurate and clear contact information (including names of appropriate faculty and staff) for questions or concerns they may have in the future. "A well-organized, upbeat, informative parent/family program will pay rich dividends throughout the student's college career. Parents who understand how the institution functions, who meet and interact with resource people, and who are committed to developing effective communication patterns with their students can become institutional advocates and positive retention agents" (Mullendore, 1998, p. 58).

In developing a program for parents and other family members, it is important to be sensitive to their time schedule as well as their anxieties and concerns. For parents and families, it may be helpful to think in terms of Maslow's hierarchy of needs and begin with the basics. Early in the program, speakers and panels can address issues such as housing, food services, transportation, billing procedures, child care, and financial aid. These topics can be followed by speakers on campus safety, health services, and alcohol, drugs, and other wellness issues. Other important topics are academic advising, academic support services, career services, counseling services, student unions, counseling services, student religious organizations, adult learner services, recreational facilities, and opportunities for student involvement and leadership in clubs and organizations.

Activities for parent and family orientation programs should include meal and social functions, as these activities allow family members to meet faculty and staff informally as well as spend time with others who are sending a student to college. It is also helpful for the institution and the families to discuss how they can stay connected in the months and years to come. Newsletters (paper or electronic) specifically designed for students' parents and families are an effective and economical means for ongoing communication. Many institutions have developed parent and family associations to channel parents' involvement and to raise funds to support specific student-centered initiatives. Parent and family weekends provide another involvement opportunity; dates and schedules of events can be provided at orientation.

At some point during a parent and family orientation program, preferably as the final session, a speaker should address the issues of student and parent and family transitions. For traditional-age first-year students, the primary transition issues are freedom and responsibility (developing self-discipline, managing time and money, overcoming homesickness, and so on). For parents, the transition issues are less obvious but equally challenging and important. Parents must let go of their children and negotiate a new adult-to-adult relationship with their son or daughter. Family dynamics change when someone attends college, and this change may bring about a closer examination of all aspects of the parents' lives (career, family, marriage, and so on).

It is helpful to point out to parents of traditional-age students that sending a student to college may be emotionally difficult. Program speakers should encourage parents to embrace this new phase of life, envision the relationship they want to have with their adult children, and understand there will be a new set of parenting challenges during the next few years. A staff member who is also the parent of a college student can be particularly effective in delivering this message.

Another aspect for orientation planners to consider is that students' siblings may attend an orientation program. Providing free college souvenirs and snacks or meals to brothers and sisters increases their comfort level and helps them enjoy their on-campus experience. It is also important to remember that on some residential campuses, not all students will be living in residence halls; therefore, attention should be paid to the issues of parenting a commuter student. Community college orientation programs should also address the issues relative to parents and family members of students who live at home while attending college. Planning and implementing a comprehensive parent and family orientation requires considerable expertise and effort; however, it can be an incredibly rewarding experience for those staff and faculty who participate.

For the families of adult learners, other transition issues emerge. Spouses, children, and significant others must, at a minimum, accept the fact that their student will have less time for them as academic demands take precedence. Perhaps even more important, they must come to understand that their support, as well as their acceptance, may be critical to their student's transition to college and academic success. Moreover, employers must also be supportive by adjusting work schedules to the academic schedules of the adult learner and otherwise being supportive of the return to school.

Family finances may become strained as a result of tuition and other college-related costs. Families must be given an opportunity during orientation to become aware of these issues and learn strategies for coping with them.

Orientation at Two-Year Colleges

"Two-year community colleges have had a significant impact on American higher education. With increased enrollments, two-year colleges have played a large role in expanding access to higher education and making it a reality for many that had never thought of higher education as a possibility" (Cook, 2000, p. 19). These institutions attract a diverse student population (adult learners; traditional-age students; and students seeking occupational, vocational, technical, enrichment, or transfer opportunities). Courses are offered not only during the weekday, but also in evenings and on weekends, to respond to the needs of these students.

Orientation programs at two-year institutions tend to reflect the nature of the students they serve. While programs may vary from college to college, most are a half-day in length and are offered at various times of the day. A large percentage of community college students work full time and have significant family responsibilities; therefore, orientation programs rely on core elements in order to be sensitive to students' time commitments. Cook (2000) outlines three central components to two-year-college orientation programs.

The first element is preenrollment assessment. Most two-year institutions have open enrollment, and students arrive with differing levels of skill in reading comprehension, writing, mathematics, and other areas. In order to place students appropriately, skill levels need to be determined. Second, two-year college staff often engage in developmental academic advising, a process that goes well beyond class scheduling. This type of advising assists students in goal clarification, exploration of future potential, and understanding available institutional resources. Scheduling appropriate courses becomes a natural outgrowth of this type of advising process.

The third orientation component is class registration. Like the four-year colleges, the opportunity to register is often the hook that entices students to attend these programs. Many two-year colleges also offer sessions on financial aid; time management; alcohol, drug, and wellness education; money management; involvement opportunities; study skills; and others. Hearing this information during an orientation program is helpful, but if it is to be truly effective, students need an ongoing orientation experience. A recent study found that approximately 80 percent of four-year institutions and 60 percent of two-year institutions provide first-year-seminar programs (Policy Center on the First Year of College, 2002). Given the students' range of academic preparation and skills, these seminars can be especially helpful for those enrolling in two-year colleges. Results from another study found higher grade point averages and increased retention rates among two-year college students who enrolled in a first-year seminar compared with those who did not take the course (Green & Miller, 1998). Finally, as at four-year institutions, orientation programs at two-year community colleges must develop orientation programs for the families and friends of first-year students, along the lines suggested in the previous section.

Two-year colleges are often ahead of their four-year counterparts in the use of technology for student services delivery. Richland College, a fourteen-thousand-student community college in Texas, created an orientation CD-ROM that students may watch at their leisure. To maintain a personal touch, Richland has put its resources into advising individual students prior to registration. At Richland, the average age of students is thirty-two, and 80 percent of them hold outside jobs, so the efficient use of student time is important (Lords, 2000).

Orienting Transfer Students

Transfer students arrive on both two-year and four-year campuses from a variety of paths and with a range of experiences. Most transfers are from two-year to four-year institutions; however, a large number are four-year to four-year transfers, or "reverse transfer" students who already hold a baccalaureate degree but have returned to two-year colleges for further undergraduate study in a different field. Knowing the demographics of the transfer population is critical to the design of a successful orientation program for these students. What is most important to transfers, however, is that they do not wish to be treated as first-year students. They desire acknowledgment of their previous experience in higher education regardless of the success or failure of that experience. Many erroneously believe that orientation programs are for first-time enrollees and do not want to "waste" their time in extensive programs and sessions. They may also believe that because they made a successful transition to college the first time, they do not need any help the second time. A daunting challenge may be getting transfer students to attend any orientation programs at all.

In designing a program for transfer students, it is important to give careful consideration to the timely and accurate evaluation and transfer of their academic credits. The credit evaluation process can occur prior to or during orientation and will provide the basis for the rest of the program. Academic advising is also critical to transfers; these students want to gain the maximum credit from their previous educational experiences and develop a plan to help them meet their future goals. Because many transfer students may be somewhat resentful of having to attend an orientation program, it is important that they be treated in a straightforward manner and that the program be designed to meet their specific needs.

Typical transfer student orientation programs are abbreviated versions of first-year student programs. Transfers are familiar with the general college environment and many of its resources, so they are less willing to sit through sessions on residential life and housing, food services, and student activities. Orientation directors should be sensitive to the concerns of transfer students and design programs appropriate to their needs in content and length. Transfer student program timing is also important to the student. Most transfer orientation programs occur just before the start of a term, although some institutions provide late spring and summer sessions for students entering in the fall. A program that is well designed can set a tone for transfer student satisfaction that may lead to increased retention to graduation.

Orientation for Adult Learners

"The emergence of non-traditional students as a major constituency has been one of the most profound changes in higher education during the past 25 years" (Hatch, 2002, p. 1). These students may be found in two-year colleges, four-year colleges, distance learning programs, and research universities. Many work full time, have family responsibilities, and attend college on a part-time basis. Some of these students are returning to college, and others are just beginning. Providing an institutional environment that fosters success for adult learners is a challenge that must be recognized.

Orientation programs should be designed with sensitivity to the many demands on time that may already exist for these students. Abbreviated programs and written or on-line orientation materials should be available. The orientation program should strive to provide adult learners with opportunities to develop connections with the college and other adult learners. Where possible, attention should be given to family members who attend orientation with an adult learner so that they may gain an understanding and appreciation of the demands of the college experience.

The timing of orientation for adult learners is as important as the content. Evening and weekend programs where food is served can be particularly effective. It may be helpful to provide child care during the orientation program. The program director and other staff and faculty involved with adult learner orientation should consider appropriate ways to assess prior learning experiences, provide major and career guidance, recommend courses, and ensure a smooth transition to the institution. Adult learners are an exciting and challenging population, and they bring a wealth of experience to the college classroom that can be beneficial to traditional-age students as well as faculty.

Orienting Other Special Populations

The increasing diversity of students entering higher education is reflected in the orientation programs currently being offered. Conference-style breakout sessions, extended programs, and even separate programs exist to meet the perceived needs of these students. According to *NODA Data Bank* (Strumpf & Wawrynski, 2000), special programming is provided for honors students as well as those who are academically disadvantaged, disabled, international, minority, athletes, veterans, and others.

The scope, length, and timing of orientation programs for special populations are dependent on several factors: institutional mission, size, resources, and participant interest. Separate and distinct programs are most commonly offered for international students, graduate students, and nontraditional students. To increase student comfort level and enhance institutional fit, some institutions have had success with pre- or postorientation sessions for special populations such as minority students. Orientation professionals know that the combination of successful academic and social integration results in improved retention rates. Understanding the specific factors that may influence the persistence rate for minority students has tremendous implications for orientation programs. For example, Brown (2000) argues that colleges must find ways to increase African American student satisfaction and social support in order to increase retention rates. Currently, 47 percent of reporting institutions provide special orientation programs for students of color (Strumpf & Wawrynski, 2000). Research is needed to determine if these programs have an impact on satisfaction and social support and whether there is a difference in meeting these goals through separate programs or breakout sessions within the orientation program. A challenge for orientation professionals is to seek a balance between meeting the needs of special populations while appreciating the diversity and benefits of having the student body together.

Increasing the satisfaction and retention of the many special populations should be viewed as an institutional priority rather than an orientation program mandate. Extended orientation programs, first-year seminars, developmental programs, time management seminars, and intentional social programming can all contribute to college satisfaction and increased retention. Placing the responsibility for increasing minority satisfaction and retention solely on the one- or two-day orientation event is unreasonable and in all likelihood will not yield the desired results.

Using Technology to Augment Orientation

As Junco suggested in Chapter Thirteen, technology is having an impact on just about every aspect of today's first-year students' lives. Any discussion of technology should be framed with the understanding that whatever is written may be obsolete or at least archaic within a relatively short time. In addition, it is important that administrators and faculty be aware of the computer skills of today's first-year students and the ease with which they negotiate the technological environment. It is equally important to understand that orientation professionals consider the human touch to be critical to the success of their programs. How, then, can an appropriate balance of high tech and high touch be achieved?

Orientation planners, in collaboration with other academic and service departments within the college, have a great opportunity to showcase institutional technology capabilities, reduce administrative cost and time, and provide quality service to new students. Prior to orientation, students and families can register for the program and pay appropriate fees (if applicable) electronically. College Web sites can offer virtual tours of the campus and information about services provided. CD-ROMs can be created to provide focused information on a range of issues and services to new students. E-mail accounts can be established and tested, thereby becoming a means for official correspondence. Academic placement testing (such as English, mathematics, foreign language, and science) can be developed for on-line administration, thus reducing or eliminating a very time-consuming on-site function.

During orientation, presenters should use technology where appropriate, recognizing that today's students are less than enthusiastic about lengthy "talking-heads" presentations. Computers greatly enhance the advising process as students and advisers explore course options based on college core and degree requirements and student interest. Degree audit software programs can be especially helpful to advisers, transfers, and students who are returning to higher education, and class scheduling is now done on the Web at most institutions. Tuition and fee payment may be expected at the time of registration and can be handled on-line as well. A library orientation is an important component of a comprehensive orientation program, and college libraries are rapidly moving toward total electronic access. At the end of orientation, program evaluations can be submitted electronically, providing immediate feedback to orientation staff.

These ideas are only a starting point. The technological evolution is so dramatic that we can only imagine what will transpire over the next decade. The challenge for orientation staff is to seek balance between the efficiencies of technology and the basic human need to belong within the social framework of the institution.

ASSESSMENT OF ORIENTATION

"The student orientation program must regularly conduct systematic qualitative and quantitative evaluations of program quality to determine whether and to what degree the stated mission and goals are being met. . . . Results of these evaluations must be considered when revising and improving the student orientation program and in recognizing staff performance" (Miller, 1999, p. 140). Assessing orientation as an event is a fairly straightforward task. The challenge lies in the assessment of orientation as a process. A review of the literature indicates an indirect positive effect between orientation and student persistence (Rode, 2000), but there is a dearth of research in this area.

Because there is considerable pressure on the orientation director to provide a comprehensive retention-based program, there must be a corresponding comprehensive assessment program as well. It is imperative that every component, activity, and process be assessed. Adapting the comprehensive assessment model suggested in Chapter Twenty-Seven, we suggest the following model for assessing orientation programs:

- Use existing institutional databases to learn and disseminate information about entering first-year classes, such as demographics, characteristics, academic preparation, and fields of study. When possible, compare current first-year students with previous cohorts.

- Assess first-year student needs. This is best done by conducting focus groups or surveys of students after they have completed their first term or at the time they leave the institution.

- Assess the satisfaction of first-year students with orientation programs and services. Immediate feedback may be gathered at the time of the program and Web-based surveys administered at a later date. (For a sample satisfaction instrument, see Chapter Twenty-Eight.)

- Assess orientation outcomes. It may be very important to assess the relationship, if any, between participation in orientation and some desired outcome, such as learning, academic achievement, or persistence into the second year of college. These studies are difficult to conduct, but may be the most important of all efforts to assess the impact of orientation.

- Assess orientation using national standards. The CAS standards may be used as a yardstick for assessing individual institutional efforts in orientation. These standards include assessment guides that provide valuable tools for program staff and advisory committees.

Mullendore and Biller (1998) recommend follow-up assessment efforts during and beyond the first semester to determine program effectiveness. Telephone interviews and focus groups are excellent methods to gain appropriate evaluative feedback. Another resource is materials provided to members of

NODA, including sample program evaluation instruments in the *Orientation Planning Manual.*

TRENDS IN ORIENTATION PRACTICE

We recognize that specific program examples would be helpful to explain how certain quality orientation programs function; however, orientation program staff and components change frequently, thus increasing the potential for dated information. To find current best practices, readers are encouraged to access the Web sites and listservs for NODA and the National Resource Center for The First-Year Experience and Students in Transition.

A number of trends have emerged over the past several years that appear likely to continue to influence the direction of college orientation programs:

• *Faculty involvement in orientation programs.* Between 1993 and 1996, 48 percent of the institutions surveyed indicated that faculty involvement had increased during that period (Strumpf & Sharer, 1997). Between 1996 and 2000, 41 percent of the institutions surveyed again indicated increased faculty involvement (Strumpf & Wawrynski, 2000). This increased involvement is tied directly to the second trend, academic program emphasis.

• *Academic program emphasis.* Between 1993 and 2000, time devoted to academic matters increased at approximately the same percentage of colleges as faculty involvement (Strumpf & Wawrynski, 2000; Strumpf & Sharer, 1997). Orientation staff, seeking balance between social and academic integration, have increased the number of sessions and amount of time devoted to helping new students understand and negotiate the complex academic environment.

• *Parent and family attendance.* Parent and family attendance at orientation has increased dramatically (Strumpf & Wawrynski, 2000; Strumpf & Sharer, 1997). Today's families are a source of encouragement and support for first-year students, so their participation in orientation and desire for ongoing involvement in their student's college experience should come as no surprise.

• *Student attendance.* As colleges have placed greater expectations on orientation to be an experience that promotes first-year student success, efforts to increase student attendance at these programs have been successful. Responding institutions indicated that 86 percent of incoming first-year students and 62 percent of new transfers attended orientation (Strumpf & Wawrynski, 2000). Still, it is a concern that 14 percent of first-year students do not attend an orientation program. Institutions should carefully consider barriers to attendance such as cost, travel, distance, timing, and length of program in trying to improve program attendance.

• *Technology.* At the 1995 NODA National Conference, a presentation depicted a Web-based orientation program that included welcomes from the president and an orientation leader; a virtual campus tour; on-line testing, advising, and registration; tuition and fee payment; chatroom; and more. The audience was outraged! Today, threads of technology run through almost all aspects of orientation programs, and this trend will certainly continue. Web-based programs provide efficiency, convenience, and economy with many administrative tasks, including placement testing and class scheduling, and can provide up-to-the-minute accurate and in-depth orientation information.

• *Summer reading programs.* As a way to increase academic integration, many colleges provide a book for required summer reading by some or all first-year students. This practice is especially prevalent at small colleges (23 percent; Strumpf & Wawrynski, 2000). Some of these institutions invite the author to speak at an opening convocation ceremony, although convocations are common at colleges that do not have required readings as well. However, summer reading programs are not without controversy. At the University of North Carolina, three students unsuccessfully sued the university over a book about the Koran that was part of a required summer reading program (Morgan, 2002).

• *Orientation-related experiences.* Many colleges offer opportunities that serve as expanded orientations at off-campus sites. These programs may be wilderness experiences, camping trips, or leadership workshops, all designed to increase the bond between new student and college. An excellent example of this type of program is Fish Camp at Texas A&M University. Fish Camp (freshman camp) began in 1954 and has grown to be what is generally regarded as one of the most unique and intensive orientation activities in higher education. Run by students, Fish Camp accommodates more than half of the first-year class in six four-day sessions designed to ease the transition from high school to college. It is an optional, off-site program where new students establish friendships, learn about campus services and organizations, meet student leaders, and become familiar with the university's traditions.

RECOMMENDATIONS

Based on the authors' professional experiences with orientation at a variety of institutions, as well as a review of current literature and practices, the following recommendations are offered for consideration:

• *Develop and support an orientation process that continues at least throughout the first semester.* Move beyond orientation as a single event.

• *Develop orientation programs that introduce and reflect the mission and goals of the institution.* The CAS standards provide an excellent framework of nationally endorsed criteria to assist institutions in the development of such programs.

• *Seek an appropriate balance between the efficiency of technology and the need for effective person-to-person interaction.* Just as all components of orientation must be evaluated, so too should new uses of technology be carefully assessed for program enhancement.

• *Select orientation program directors who possess appropriate academic credentials,* including a graduate degree, and have at least three years of full-time work experience in higher education administration.

- *Explore options to on-site testing during orientation.* Many colleges continue to spend an inordinate amount of orientation time in placement testing for students.
- *Use resources available from several national entities,* including the National Orientation Directors Association, the National Resource Center for The First-Year Experience and Students in Transition, and the Policy Center on the First Year of College.
- *Encourage the participation of parents and other family members in the orientation process.* They can be both a solid support system and effective institutional advocates.
- *Build support of senior institutional officials for orientation programs.* Orientation provides an excellent forum for introducing new students to senior administrators.
- *Encourage collaboration between student affairs and academic affairs in orientation.* Orientation must be viewed as the greatest opportunity for a collaborative partnership between these two entities.
- *Assess orientation programs.* Orientation must integrate assessment into every aspect of its programs, with a particular emphasis on showing the relationship between orientation participation and desired outcomes such as academic achievement, retention, and learning.
- *Continue to include student orientation leaders in the development and implementation of orientation programs.* Well-trained peers provide an effective delivery system for information in ways that faculty and staff cannot.

CONCLUSION

Orientation presents the first opportunity to challenge and support students to make a successful transition to college and fulfill their educational goals. It should be an ongoing process rather than a single event and be related to first-year students' transition to college, learning outcomes, academic achievement, and retention. What may be missing from this chapter is the sense of excitement, enthusiasm, fun, overwhelming satisfaction, and exhaustion that is so much a part of orientation for both students and orientation staff. All students should have the opportunity to be challenged and supported by a quality, comprehensive orientation program as they begin their collegiate experience.

CHAPTER TWENTY-FOUR

First-Year Student Living Environments

William J. Zeller

This is a big, unfamiliar place for incoming freshmen. Resident hall communities are thus crucial in making the University feel like home. These resident halls are the prime locations for making new friends and learning to deal with people of differing opinions, cultures, and religions. They create endless situations for questioning one's comfort zones and taking risks to test one's limits.
—First-year student

Where first-year students live matters. Residential environments, and the experiences and support systems within these environments, influence first-year students' learning and academic success (Astin, 1993; Pascarella & Terenzini, 1991). Many first-year students live in on-campus residence halls, but a majority live off campus with family or friends. Obviously, there are significant differences between these living environments, yet more and more campuses are recognizing the need to provide similar out-of-class educational program and service offerings to all first-year students, no matter where they live.

Furthermore, where first-year students live can significantly influence the overall quality of their collegiate experience. It will affect the likelihood of their making an easy transition into the campus environment, succeeding academically, matriculating through to graduation, and having a fulfilling educational experience. Some first-year students have no choice about where they live: the institutions they attend require them to live on campus. Most, however, have a choice, and that choice may well affect their success in the first year.

This chapter will provide an overview of current trends and future directions for the modern first-year residential experience, both on and off campus. Particular focus will be given to the development of learning-centered residential communities, including residence hall design trends, campus master planning initiatives, the lifestyle needs of the modern student, new first-year residential program initiatives, and the off-campus housing experience for first-year students.

THE ON-CAMPUS RESIDENTIAL FIRST YEAR

Like other aspects of the reform movement that have shaped new directions for the first-year experience, the residential first year has undergone significant transformation over the past fifteen years. Since 1987, when Ernest Boyer and others reported on the "separation, sometimes to the point of isolation between academic and social life on campus" (p. 5), national and institutional leaders have worked diligently to strengthen the linkages between the curricular and cocurricular aspects of undergraduate life. In many new and exciting ways, academically supportive campus residence hall environments are being viewed as critical to the attainment of institutional missions and goals. At the time of his study, Boyer (1987) reported finding residence hall environments that were often disconnected from and even antithetical to the educational mission of their institutions. Today, they are an integral setting on many campuses for linking the curriculum and cocurriculum and for achieving pedagogical and curricular innovation.

IMPORTANT POLICY QUESTIONS FOR HOUSING FIRST-YEAR STUDENTS

Before reviewing the many ways in which on-campus residential environments can promote first-year student success, three policy questions must be addressed: whether to require first-year students to live on campus, whether to cluster first-year students in exclusive living environments, and whether to assign men and women to the same floor or building. On the first policy question, many institutions require first-year students to live in on-campus residence halls for one or two terms. This requirement is often justified as a way of ensuring that first-year students develop a sense of the mission of the institution, make a successful transition into the institution, and receive the developmental and educational benefits provided in the residence halls, including increased academic achievement and persistence, compared to students living elsewhere. Although seldom officially stated and legally suspect, some institutions have first-year residency requirements to guarantee minimum occupancy levels that ensure the fiscal stability of their residential operations.

Opponents of first-year residency requirements argue that they are seldom, if ever, enforced on all first-year students, since adult learners, married students, and commuters are typically exempt from such requirements, and many campuses do not have sufficient on-campus housing facilities to accommodate all first-year students. At their worst, residency requirements can backfire if resentment toward them is so great that they create disruptive residential environments in the first year and mass migrations of students off campus in the sophomore year.

Because of the increase in interest over the past decade in living on campus, some institutions have reconsidered the necessity of these requirements. Nonetheless, if institutions choose to maintain a first-year residency requirement, they should develop and articulate an educational rationale that serves as the foundation for what staff and faculty should provide and achieve for their first-year students and develop evidence that supports this goal. Furthermore, these institutions should work to develop programs and services that are designed to promote the success of first-year students who are exempt from residence requirements and living elsewhere.

The second policy question is whether to cluster first-year students together in exclusive living arrangements or assign them with upperclass students. Proponents of clustering argue that courses, programs, and services that meet the unique needs of first-year students are more easily developed and more effective if first-year students are housed together. Certainly the positive impact of freshman interest groups (FIGs) on grades, satisfaction, and persistence make a strong case for clustering. Furthermore, proponents would argue that on the whole, upperclass students have a negative influence on first-year students, particularly on such issues as alcohol abuse, multicultural awareness, and engagement in academic activities.

Opponents of clustering argue that while upperclass students may exert some negative influence, they can also serve as valuable sources for curricular and cocurricular information and opportunities and serve as positive role models for first-year students. Opponents would also argue that mixed living arrangements can provide first-year students with greater diversity of ideas, lifestyles, and social interactions. In a review of the limited research on this issue, Pascarella, Terenzini, and Blimling (1994) and Ballou (1996) reached the tentative conclusion that only a slight advantage in academic performance may be gained from clustering first-year students.

The third policy question, whether to assign men and women to the same floor or building, was studied in the 1970s when these living arrangements were introduced. In a review of the research on this issue, Pascarella et al. (1994) concluded that living in coeducational residences does not appear to have an appreciable impact on academic achievement or participation in extracurricular activities. Some evidence suggests that students living in coeducational arrangements have more informal and friendship-type social involvement than in single-sex halls, thus having the potential for reducing stereotypical gender role perceptions, but the evidence on this point is mixed. Of course, if coeducational living is inconsistent with the mission and values of an institution (as is the case with many church-related institutions), this type of living arrangement would be prohibited.

CREATING LEARNING-CENTERED RESIDENTIAL ENVIRONMENTS

Residence hall environments can support and facilitate student learning. In fact, these settings are being viewed on many campuses as providing unique learning environments that are not being duplicated anywhere else in the institution.

Research being conducted on these new educational offerings indicates that student learning, academic achievement, and retention are being significantly enhanced by these environments (Pascarella & Terenzini, 1991; Kuh, Schuh, Whitt et al., 1991; Inkelas, 1999). The baseline standard of quality for modern residence hall environments now demands that student learning and academic support be at the center of their mission.

Astin (1993) argued that if modern residence halls are to become true learning environments, they should manifest the following characteristics:

- Quality student-to-student interactions
- Quality faculty-to-student interactions
- Quality study environments and significant hours devoted to studying
- Opportunities for altruism and social activism
- Quality social engagement opportunities between students
- Promotion of diversity and discussion of racial/ethnic issues with other students
- Promotion of mentoring and tutoring connections between students

In order to achieve these goals, all elements of the hall should be designed and structured to create a learning-centered environment. Facilities must be designed to allow these types of interactions and activities to occur. Dining programs should support quality interactions between students and other campus community members. Program models and staffing patterns must be configured to support academic success, multicultural understanding, and personal skill development. Mentoring and peer facilitation must be part of the residence hall culture. Quality study spaces must be provided. Perhaps most important, faculty must have a presence within the student residential community.

DESIGNING RESIDENCE HALLS FOR FIRST-YEAR STUDENTS

Many institutions have undertaken long-term master planning projects that have allowed them to explore opportunities for configuring the physical elements of the campus to better support the achievement of the institution's missions and goals. As new halls are being constructed and existing buildings are being renovated, traditional planning concepts are being challenged with the hope of breaking down existing boundaries between students, between students and faculty, and between academic and nonacademic spaces. Although some campuses are approaching first-year student residential models through comprehensive residence hall master planning initiatives, an even larger number of campuses have embarked on major initiatives to construct new residence halls or renovate existing halls with the expressed goal of better addressing the lifestyle and educational needs of new students.

Fundamental to these master planning initiatives is the changing lifestyle needs of today's students, who arrive on campus with backgrounds and needs that are much different from those of students of past decades (Brooks, 2001; Newton, 2000). As students move into residence halls today, instead of just a trunk and suitcase, we see vans and trailers bringing a full array of furniture, technological devices, clothing, and other "necessities" that often overwhelm the available room space and the electrical systems of residence halls that were built for an earlier generation. Many of today's students come from homes where they had their own bedrooms, did not have to share their space with others, and often had access to their own televisions, CD players, computers, and other resources. They have become accustomed to having certain levels of privacy, yet still seek a closely knit community and the support that a roommate can provide.

The driving dilemma that is shaping new student residence hall design is the increased desire today's students have for privacy and for additional room for their personal belongings, versus the institution's need for creating quality interactions with peers, faculty and staff, and the larger campus community. The question being asked by those designing residence halls for first-year students is how to balance these two needs. Although certainly a challenge, these issues are not necessarily at odds with one another. The following design elements are being introduced into new residence halls and facility renovation projects.

New Room Configurations

An important design element is the issue of the single room versus the traditional double room configurations. Market studies and other analyses of first-year student preferences would quickly lead designers to believe that new students today want single rooms and private bathrooms. However, upon further analysis, studies are showing that these students still favor the connections and support they obtain through a roommate (Biddison & Hier, 2000). Therefore, in order to achieve quality student-to-student interactions, most campuses should still design first-year student rooms as double occupancy rooms, with sufficient space and furniture configurations to facilitate some level of privacy. If a mix of upper-level students is desired within first-year student residence halls, room configurations specifically designed for these students should be added in the building. Upper-level students often want single rooms, semiprivate bathrooms, and other spaces designed to address their needs. Therefore, a residence hall environment designed to have a mix of first-year student and upper-level students should have a mix of appropriate room configurations.

Educationally Purposeful Designs

Some campuses are constructing and renovating first-year student residence halls as living-learning centers, designed to support specific themes (for example, substance-free halls, discipline-specific halls, halls related to areas of student interest), while others are being designed to support more general learning initiatives for first-year students. Common design elements within these facilities include classrooms, faculty offices or apartments, and spaces for academic support services such as advising, tutoring, and technology utilization.

Public Spaces for Socializing and Interacting with Peers

Students want to interact with their peers in spaces outside their personal rooms. Quality social space for groups of all sizes should be incorporated into the design of the facility. The design of these spaces should be educationally purposeful to allow students to make connections between their academic and social lives.

Quality Study Space

When designed effectively, residence halls can provide quality study spaces that address the learning styles and study needs of first-year students. Whatever their particular approach to studying, first-year students prefer spaces in their residence hall that support their own study patterns. Some students need quiet spaces where they can study alone, without noise or commotion. Others prefer studying in informal or formal study groups, often assigned through class or structured within the residence hall environment. Furthermore, many faculty are requiring formal group-based class work. Residence hall spaces should be configured to allow groups to study together, do group class assignments together, and receive group advising and tutoring assistance.

Flexible Dining Spaces

Dining centers are being recognized for their value in contributing to quality interactions between students and between students and faculty. These spaces are clearly a hub of community where campus environmental outcomes can be achieved. In addition, the space of the dining center can and should be used as a community focal point and should be flexible enough to be adapted to other uses when not used for dining purposes.

Classrooms

Today's residence halls offer a primary setting for connecting student's academic and social lives. Increasingly, the desire to make residence halls more academically purposeful has created the need for incorporating classroom space within first-year student residence halls. The design and function of these classrooms should support the unique curricular and pedagogical goals of residentially based instruction.

Academic Support Spaces

Placing academic advising, tutoring, and other academic support functions in the residence halls provides first-year students with convenient and comfortable access to services that are critical to first-year success. These offices and other spaces should be centrally located and of high quality.

Safety and Security

Over the past decade, parental and student expectations have increased significantly regarding the provision of safe and secure first-year student residential environments. In addition, federal and state regulations regarding safety standards in college and university residence halls have made campuses more responsible and accountable for safety issues in first-year student residential communities. Court decisions and federal legislation have also influenced heightened approaches to safety issues. For example, when students elect to live in campus housing, they yield control of their own protection, and thus institutions have a legal duty to protect them from foreseeable violence (Gehring, 2000). Furthermore, the Student Right-to-Know and Campus Security Act as amended by the Higher Education Amendments of 1998 requires the publication of campus crime statistics and a variety of other information that must be given to prospective students (Gehring, 2000).

As a result of these requirements, a wide range of safety issues has been addressed:

• *Enhanced publicity and communication of safety-related issues on campus.* Parents and students are being informed of safety issues prior to attendance and continuing during the entire first year. New student orientation programs often introduce students to personal safety issues and the importance of taking responsibility for one's own safety. A greater emphasis is being placed on reporting crimes that have occurred and keeping campus community members apprised of safety concerns.

• *Enhanced door access systems for exterior doors, corridor doorways, and room doorways.* New electronic card readers are taking the place of traditional key systems. Exterior doors are locked for longer periods of time, with many doors being locked twenty-four hours per day.

• *Enhanced fire and life safety systems, including sprinklers.* Many state and federal regulatory agencies are increasing standards for fire and life safety systems in college and university residence halls. In some states, sprinklers are being required.

• *Additional security staff in first-year residence halls.* Many campuses are adding staff and enhanced security systems in first-year halls. More comprehensive training is also being provided to residence staff members regarding first-year student safety issues.

Luxury Amenities

Over the past decade, many campuses have initiated the construction or major renovation of first-year student residence halls as a means of recruiting and retaining first-year students. These initiatives have not only focused on the configuration of rooms and traditional public spaces, but also on what other types of amenities should be incorporated into the facility, bringing a new complexity and even controversy to the design of modern residence halls. The result in many cases has been the introduction of more and more luxury amenities into residence halls than ever before. State of-the-art recreation facilities and health spas, movie theaters, food courts, coffee shops, and swimming pools are being incorporated into new residence hall design concepts.

Many institutions have felt compelled to change the way they think about designing residence halls in order to meet the changing expectations of students. These luxury facilities have been viewed as necessary for the institution and the housing program to remain competitive for top students. Once one institution goes in this direction, other peer institutions feel the need to follow (Winter, 2003). A similar competition is developing among off-campus housing providers.

Some higher education leaders are beginning to believe that this issue is spinning out of control. Clare Cotton, the president of the Association of Independent Colleges and Universities in Massachusetts, states, "This issue is exactly the psychology of an arms race. From the outside, it seems totally crazy, but from the inside it feels necessary and compelling. . . . Critics call them multimillion dollar luxuries that are driving up institutional debts and inflating the cost of education. Colleges defend them as compulsory attractions in the scramble for top students and faculty" (Winter, 2003, p. 1). As budget cutbacks are producing program cuts and faculty and staff cutbacks, the debate around this issue has grown even more intense (Simon & Silverstein, 2003). Ultimately, campuses must design residential facilities that will shape the student experience and not be shaped by perceptions of student expectations. When well conceived, these types of communities are the most powerful and the most educationally beneficial.

FIRST-YEAR ON-CAMPUS RESIDENTIAL PROGRAM INITIATIVES

Over the past decade, significant change has occurred in the programmatic offerings being provided to residential first-year students. Prior to these changes, first-year student halls were often viewed as the most difficult and unhealthy environments to manage. However, as the first-year experience movement took hold, campus leaders began to recognize the potential that residence halls provide for achieving the ambitious outcomes of their first-year experience programs. Once disconnected from the educational mission, these programs have become centerpieces of many campus programmatic offerings for first-year students. Through collaboration between academic and student affairs staff, these first-year student residential initiatives have become the settings that support new student success and connect in-class and out-of-class experiences. Three programmatic models stand out as being among the most successful and prevalent in this movement: living-learning programs, residential freshman interest group models (FIGs), and residential first-year experience programs.

Living-Learning Programs

Over the past ten years, many campuses have pursued the development of academically based residential programs or living-learning programs as a means of fulfilling their goals for first-year students. These programs are designed to bring an academic theme or purpose to a particular residence hall environment. These programs have been found to greatly enhance new student learning by strengthening student interactions with peers, faculty, and the institution itself. The themes of these programs vary from campus to campus, and the most successful have often been those that uniquely fit the needs, resources, and interests of a particular campus. On larger campuses, they are often viewed as a way of providing a small campus experience at a large institution. The other great benefit that has been achieved on many campuses is the strengthening of collaborations between academic and student affairs staff, which often did not previously exist. (Examples of living-learning programs can be obtained by visiting www.bgsu.edu/colleges/clc/rlcch/submissions/.)

Residential Freshman Interest Groups

This model originated at the University of Oregon in the mid-1980s as a means of helping students find coherence between their courses and build connections with their peers and with faculty. Although simple in design, it has been highly effective in enhancing student learning. The FIG model assigns students to small groups that take one or more classes together, often with a discussion or seminar component attached. Students get to interact with one another around an academic theme, have built-in study partners, and provide support to one another as they make a transition into colleges and universities.

Carrying this model one step further, residential FIGs have been developed to provide the same benefits while strengthening the residential experience. These models assign students who live together in a common residential community to one or more common classes. Some models have been developed for campus living-learning programs, while others are connected to nonthematic first-year student halls. Living-learning program models assign students to course clusters, which support the themes of the program. These models not only facilitate healthier interactions between students, but also make faculty visits to the halls more inviting and purposeful. The University of Missouri–Columbia (www.missouri.edu/ ~ figwww) and Washington State University (www.wsu.edu/hdrl/ResLife/Programs/atc.html) are two examples of residential FIGs programs.

First-Year-Experience Programs

These programs are specifically designed to help students successfully make the transition from high school to college by providing a highly supportive residence hall environment that particularly focuses on their needs. In many ways, these programs provide a year-long continuing orientation focus and prepare students to enter their sophomore year and beyond. Included within them is the provision of conveniently located academic support services such as academic advising, tutoring, technology assistance, and counseling. In addition, program and workshop offerings on such topics as choosing a major, career planning, study skills, and test preparation are offered in a more comprehensive fashion.

Program Examples

There are many excellent examples of first-year residential programs in the country.

Freshman Connections Program, Ball State University. In this program, the first-year class is split into groups of about five hundred students who live near one another in the same residence complex. The student groups are served by a Freshman Connections Complex. The complex is composed of one or more learning teams and a convener who serves as a coordinator. Each learning team is composed of a small group of faculty from different disciplines, an academic adviser, a residence hall assistant director, supplemental instructors, and mentors. Each student in the complex has two classes with other students in the complex.

Making Connections Program, Clarion University. The two primary goals of this program are to help students (and faculty) synthesize academic skills and knowledge across disciplines and facilitate first-year students' transition from high school to the university. A cohort of twenty-five students is coenrolled in linked courses. Faculty work together to establish a central theme that ties the courses together.

FOCUS Interdisciplinary Program, Duke University. The goals of FOCUS are to introduce entering undergraduates to small group, interdisciplinary, and shared learning during the first semester. The structure of FOCUS is a set of thematic programs in which thirty students may enroll. Participants explore their program's theme from different disciplinary perspectives through two seminars, a weekly evening discussion course, and a university writing course associated with each program. Programs sponsor guest speakers, retreats, and field trips as part of their educational enhancement. Students in each program live in the same residential unit.

Residential Learning Communities, Iowa State University. Iowa State has fourteen academic-residence learning communities located in the residence halls. Each program is a unique collaboration with an academic unit on campus. General program goals are to increase retention, improve academic achievement, increase awareness and use of university resources, increase collaborative interactions with other students and faculty and staff, and give students a better understanding of career options as well as differences and similarities among people and cultures.

ARC to Success Program, University of Wisconsin, Stevens Point. An ARC (academic resource coordinator) is a student staff member who resides in the residence halls. The ARC to Success program is the incoming student program that assists with their transition and study skills. During summer orientation, incoming first-year students sign up to participate in the program. In the fall, each ARC is assigned approximately ten participants whom they will meet on an individual basis every other week and cover topics of transition and study skills. The goal of this semester-long program is to build a positive academic atmosphere within the residence hall community at the peer level. The program focuses on encouraging a successful transition to the university environment by promoting and using existing academic support services.

STAFFING OF ON-CAMPUS RESIDENTIAL PROGRAMS

As the transformation of first-year student residence halls has taken place over the past decade, residence hall staffing patterns have become more specialized and focused toward fulfilling the educational outcomes of a particular program. Previously, a hall director and staff of undergraduate resident advisers was the standard model for staffing a campus residence hall. Today, expectations for these traditional staff are changing, and a wide array of new staff have been added to the residence hall environment in order to address the educational and community development needs of first-year students more effectively. Included in the new complement of residence hall staff are the following:

- *Living-learning administrative staff and faculty.* On campuses that have chosen to develop living-learning programs for first-year students, academic faculty and staff are becoming a significant component of the residence hall staff. Often the administrative directors of these programs are faculty members who either have reduced teaching loads or are on leave from their teaching assignments. In addition, faculty teaching in the programs and holding office hours in the building are providing a great addition to the residence hall staff. Campuses with faculty directors include the University of Pennsylvania, the University of Wisconsin, the University of Michigan, Bowling Green State University, and the University of South Carolina.
- *Academic advising staff.* These staff members are either peer advisers who have been trained through the campus academic advising area or professional advisers with offices in the residence halls. Some campuses have a combination of the two. The University of Michigan and Washington State University are examples of campuses that have residential academic advising programs.
- *Tutors.* Upper-level undergraduates and graduate students are being introduced into the first-year student residence halls to provide convenient access to tutoring services. Some tutors are able to work with individuals and with groups of students.
- *Technology support staff.* Many campuses have introduced student or professional technology staff into the residence halls. These staff members provide specific assistance to first-year students in their introduction to the campus technology system, train them in basic technology skill areas, and assist them with questions or problems they may have.

Although these positions are being added on many campuses and are quite prevalent, other campuses are introducing highly specialized residence hall staff in order to address specific goals or needs. These have included diversity educators, health educators and nutrition experts, librarians, and service-learning program coordinators.

DIVERSITY EDUCATION

Another high priority being placed on first-year residence halls is the important contribution they make to the achievement of campus diversity and multicultural educational outcomes. Many of today's students arrive on campuses from nondiverse high school experiences. They have come from town and neighborhood settings that have offered few opportunities to interact with people different from themselves. Living in an on-campus residential setting, which provides students with an intensive opportunity for interacting with a highly diverse population, provides the potential for multicultural learning and skill development that cannot be duplicated anywhere else on campus. Studies have shown that education is enhanced when a diverse student body is brought together in and out of the classroom (Gurin, 1999; Inkelas, 1999). The residence hall experience, when structured appropriately, can greatly complement the academic benefits that accrue from a diverse student body.

TECHNOLOGY

A significant number of new technologies have been introduced into the residential environment over the past decade. In-room connectivity, computer labs, technological support services, and television and cable systems have become expected and commonplace on most campuses. Although campuses have often spent millions of dollars to achieve this goal, realizing the full educational potential of these resources has not been achieved, particularly for first-year students. These residential technologies should be the gateway for introducing first-year students to the technology resources that an institution offers. On many campuses, the variances in technological competence and skill level are often a major gap in the academic preparation within the first-year student class. Residential technology program structures could be shaped to ensure that all new students are brought to a minimal level of competency by the time they begin their sophomore year.

Residential technologies can also be used to enhance community. Floor and hall e-mail groupings can quickly communicate issues and news. Hall Web sites can be the center of information for the community. Hall electronic newsletters and daily program briefings can be used to articulate current information and programs. Hall virtual yearbooks can record events. Hall chatrooms allow students to have virtual discussions and "bull sessions" within their residence hall communities. Hall television stations can be used for a variety of educational and academic purposes. Electronic surveys can provide a means for assessing hall interests and needs on a regular basis.

As the use of residential technologies increases, it will be important that the quality of student-student and student-faculty interactions not be diminished. Some fear that these technologies will minimize interpersonal connections on campus and students will be able to avoid each other by conversing and interacting on-line. In addition, students may have a tendency to spend more time in their rooms or in computer labs as opposed to seeking each other out in public spaces and social gatherings. This concern is an important one. Certainly the nature of interaction and the understanding of community will be shaped and influenced by these new technologies. It is important to assess how the undergraduate experience is being affected by technology, and ensure that institutional goals are being enhanced, and not diminished, by these resources.

THE OFF-CAMPUS RESIDENTIAL FIRST YEAR

Students living off campus during their first year of college are often at a disadvantage from their peers who are living in on-campus residences. The educational benefits of living on campus during the first year of college are well documented (Astin, 1977; Chickering, 1974; Inkelas, 1999, Pascarella, 1985). Astin's findings showed that students who live on campus were more likely to persist in college and achieve higher grade point averages. On-campus residents were more likely to interact with faculty, achieve in extracurricular activities, aspire to graduate or pursue professional degrees, and plan future careers more effectively. Overall, students living on campus expressed much more satisfaction with their undergraduate experience than commuters, particularly in the areas of friendships, faculty-student relations, institutional reputation, and social life.

Students residing in settings away from campus often have family and work responsibilities while attending school and do not have the luxury of living on campus and attending school full time. "The differences in personal development outcomes exhibited by residents and commuting students have been attributed in part to the limited number of opportunities commuting students have to interact with new acquaintances who have different attitudes and values" (Kuh, Schuh, Whitt et al., 1991, p. 13). Peer groups of precollege acquaintances or new friends who resist adapting to challenges inherent in the college environment can inhibit a student's academic and social integration into the college community. This is often associated with dissatisfaction, poor academic performance, and departure from the institution (Tinto, 1987).

Off-Campus Living Options

First-year students living off campus and commuting to colleges and universities live in a variety of housing arrangements for a variety of reasons.

Regardless of the living circumstances, off-campus students need to create space that separates home life from schoolwork. Personal study space within the living environment and a commitment from family and friends to respect this space can go a long way toward the creation of a supportive off-campus living environment for the student. An area in the living environment with an identity to the student's institution can help the student build an identity and stay connected to the academic environment while in that living environment. Hosting study groups in these facilities can also help family and friends connect with the student's academic life. It is important for orientation leaders and faculty members to discuss these issues with nonresidential first-year students.

At Home with Their Parents. In this arrangement, students generally continue to have many of the same social and support networks that they had from high school. For some students, this may be a positive situation if they are not fully prepared to make the full transition away from their familial situation; for others, this may be an inhibiting factor in their transition to college.

There is another group of traditional aged first-year students living at home: those who are still in high school but taking advanced placement (AP) courses that allow them to receive college credit while still in high school. These high-achieving "pre-first-year" students are often obtaining enough credit to have sophomore status or higher when they matriculate at the colleges and universities of their choice. They take courses through a variety of sources, including local community colleges, local colleges and universities, and, increasingly, online opportunities. Parents are often involved in selecting these educational pursuits. These new nontraditional first-year students are achieving at high academic levels while still living in a traditional high school home environment with substantial involvement and decision making on the part of the parent. How this shapes and influences students' experiences as they enroll at their college of choice is a question that must be asked.

At Home with Family. Adult learners typically work full or part time and have other family obligations to balance while being a student. Single, nontraditional students may live by themselves and have a full array of adult responsibilities. Students with families have more complexities to balance while being students. Whether the student has a spouse, significant other, or is a single parent, the balancing act can be a challenge. Adult learners often work full time or are obtaining higher education with the support of a spouse or partner.

With High School Acquaintances or Others in an Apartment or House. Although this arrangement provides some of the autonomy of moving away to college, it does inhibit the development of new peer groups with students who have different backgrounds and perspectives and may disconnect the student from the support services and academic resources of the campus.

In an Off-Campus Greek Chapter. Allowing students to move into a Greek chapter during their first year can have significant effects on their entire undergraduate career. Depending on the quality of the experience, first-year students can find strong support and mentoring from a positive Greek chapter community (Kuh, Schuh, Whitt et al., 1991, p. 193). A more negative Greek chapter environment can greatly diminish quality and breadth of an undergraduate career, especially in the areas of cognitive development and critical thinking (Pascarella, Whitt, Nora, Edison, Hagedorn, & Terenzini, 1996). At the very least, it is important to be aware that students who affiliate with Greek chapters early in their first-year experience run the risk of not being exposed to the wide array of social and educational opportunities that most campuses provide. It is often quite difficult for new first-year students to make informed decisions about whether to join a Greek organization, as they are not aware of other alternatives on campus.

Probably the most suitable Greek chapter environments for first-year students are on campuses where the chapter houses are owned and operated by the institution. Within these chapters, consistent staffing and supervision is provided that often parallels other first-year residence halls on campus. At campuses where Greek chapters are not owned by the institution, great care and consideration needs to be given to the experiences and support systems provided to new first-year students in those chapters. If first-year students are allowed to live in Greek chapters, close institutional oversight is essential. Incidents of binge drinking are more prevalent in off-campus Greek chapters, and allowing first-year students to live in these chapters increases the likelihood that they will binge-drink at greater levels and more often than their peers who live on campus.

New Initiatives for Off-Campus First-Year Students

Although the educational value of living on campus has been substantiated in several studies, many institutions over the past decade have developed a wide range of innovative and effective strategies for helping off-campus first-year students obtain similar benefits and opportunities to those their residential peers enjoy. The primary goal of these initiatives has been to shape a campus environment for these students that will allow them to benefit from the experiences that Astin (1993) has found to be so beneficial.

Thus, campuses are working to help off-campus first-year students achieve quality student-to-student and student-to-faculty interactions, develop relationships with diverse peer groups, and have quality study environments, social environments, and opportunities for tutoring and peer mentoring. One of the major challenges to achieving equitable experiences for these students is time. Because they typically have more time restrictions and often budget time only to attend class, the offering of specialized services and programs for them must be done strategically and efficiently. Through the work of countless faculty and academic administrators, campuses of all types are helping off-campus first-year students obtain many of the same benefits of their residential peers through a wide range of initiatives.

Freshman Interest Groups. These programs allow interested first-year students to join a group of peers who take several common courses together. The groups are often identified with a common theme (for example, prelaw, social issues, the environment). The groups may have a common faculty and courses that help build curricular coherence in the courses being taken, as well as solidify group interpersonal connections.

Other Learning Community Models. Numerous other learning community models help build connections and support systems for first-year students (Shapiro & Levine, 1999; Lenning & Ebbers, 1999). Among them are linked course models, course clusters, federated learning communities, and coordinated studies.

Study Group Formation. A simple initiative for connecting nonresidential students is to facilitate the development of study groups. It is often difficult for commuter students to develop relationships with classmates that would allow them to form study groups on their own. Faculty and staff can work to provide easy ways for students to form groups. Study groups can meet within the campus environment, or others can be created so students host them in their own homes. This greatly helps students connect with peers, have interactions pertaining to academic subject matter, and have a support network of peers. The institution should provide space to allow commuter students to study together, and tutor-assisted study opportunities can be even more beneficial.

Opportunities for Engagement with Residential Students. Campuses that have an on-campus residential program for first-year students can work to build connections between commuter students and the on-campus residential community. For example, Murray State University assigns all first-year students to a residential college, whether they live on campus or not. Thus, every first-year student has a significant connection to peers, faculty, and academic resources. Other campuses, such as the University of Maryland, have worked to ensure that commuting first-year students can participate in residential learning communities. There may be some complications (Shapiro & Levine, 1999), but the benefits can be substantial for these students. The Office of Commuter Affairs and Community Service at the University of Maryland coordinates these types of program offerings to first-year students.

Virtual Support Networks. Campus leaders are increasingly recognizing the potential of new technological advances for helping students connect with each other, with faculty, and with academic support systems. Commuting students who visit campus only to attend class can maintain these connections asynchronously from their homes. Faculty can arrange for office hours, group projects, study groups, and homework assignments to be completed through technological resources. Tutoring and advising can also occur through these offerings. As these opportunities become more sophisticated, they will become a primary means of building quality campus connections for commuting students.

ASSESSING FIRST-YEAR STUDENT LIVING ENVIRONMENTS

Throughout this chapter, I have presented much evidence regarding student living environments. However, the question remains: What must an individual institution do to assess these living environments? Based on the assessment model presented in Chapter Twenty-Seven, living environment policymakers and practitioners should know the backgrounds and characteristics of the resident population both on and off campus, assess the living environment of residents both on and off campus, conduct studies of residents' satisfaction with their living environments, assess the residential climates of first-year students, compare institutional living environments with similar institutions, and ensure that residential environments are consistent with national standards.

Two other assessment approaches bear discussion. First, institutions should be conducting studies to explore the relationship, if any, between various living environments and desirable outcomes such as academic achievement, persistence, student learning, and transition to college. While many national studies that support these relationships were cited earlier in this chapter, assessing those relationships at a specific institution can go a long way toward building support for educationally sound residential living environments.

Second, institutions should be conducting cost-effectiveness studies to determine if first-year students are getting a fair return for their investment. For example, on-campus room and board rates must compare favorably with other comparable institutions that compete for the same applicant pool. Furthermore, on-campus residence costs must compare favorably with the costs of living off campus, particularly if institutions have first-year on-campus residency requirements.

RECOMMENDATIONS

Whether students live on campus or commute from an off-campus location, their place of residence will have a significant impact on the quality of their educational experience in the first year of college and beyond. In recognition of the important link between living and learning, the following recommendations are offered for campus leaders and residence life professionals:

• *Provide common and consistent educational opportunities for on-campus and off-campus first-year students*. Students should not be at an educational or social disadvantage because of their living circumstances.

• *Design first-year residential communities that complement and support the educational and curricular goals* of the institution, student learning, and the successful transition of first-year students into the campus community. Residential communities can be an integral part of institutional efforts to promote first-year student success.

• *Provide convenient, high-quality academic support services within on-campus residence halls.* Such services will be far more accessible when they are located near first-year students' living environments.

• *Ensure that residential environments promote quality student-student and student-faculty interactions.* Peer and faculty interactions are critical to first-year student success and more easily facilitated in residential environments.

• *Use campus residential communities as opportunities for creating and maintaining interactions between diverse groups of students.* Residential communities provide a unique environment for developing multicultural awareness and teaching diverse students how to relate to one another.

• *Design residential facilities that support first-year student success.* That means designing and supervising residential facilities so that first-year students may achieve well academically, have a safe and orderly environment, live in a situation that meets their lifestyle preferences, and have access to campus technologies and resources.

• *Assess residential living environments, both on and off campus.* A comprehensive assessment effort will help institutions determine policies and practices in residential environments that promote first-year student success.

• *Train residential staff to support the specific needs of first-year students.* Residence staff should know the unique needs of first-year students, and develop programs and services to meet those needs.

CONCLUSION

The residential first-year experience has changed dramatically over the past twenty years. What was once a common on-campus experience for new eighteen-year-old students has now become highly complex and multifaceted. First-year students reside in many different settings for many different reasons. Adult learners and commuters, long neglected in the residential initiatives of many institutions, are now the focus of new and innovative ways to include them in residential learning environments. These settings have implications for supporting or impairing student learning and academic success. If campuses continue to expect their students to have quality connections with each other, with faculty and staff, and with campus resources, they will need to be more creative and comprehensive in their approaches to challenging and supporting first-year students, no matter where they live.

CHAPTER TWENTY-FIVE

Student Support Services

John H. Schuh

I didn't know anything about the learning center until I visited the learning center as part of a freshman seminar assignment. At first I thought the assignment was stupid, but when I failed my first math test, I went to the learning center and got some terrific help. The efforts I am making to seek out help have made me feel more comfortable at this institution.
—First-year student

Contemporary practice indicates that student affairs programs, services, and activities have recast their thinking about their functions and purposes (see, for example, Blimling, Whitt, & Associates, 1999; Schuh & Whitt, 1999; Engstrom & Tinto, 2000). Whereas student affairs at one time primarily was devoted to providing quality services, programs, facilities, and out-of-class activities for students, more current thinking has framed the role of student affairs as providing experiences that enhance student learning and success. As Schroeder aptly argues in Chapter Twelve, student affairs leaders have sought partnerships with academic administrators and faculty in order to design a holistic learning experience for students.

The challenge for institutions is to provide high-quality student support services that help first-year students succeed and make sure that they are aware of and use these services when appropriate. The challenge for first-year students is to see these services as important to their success, and not think that using them is some kind of weakness on their part. This chapter reviews a conceptual framework for student affairs and discusses how student services and programs may be transformed into organizations that promote first-year student success.

A CONCEPTUAL FRAMEWORK FOR STUDENT AFFAIRS

If student affairs is to become a partner with academic affairs in enhancing student learning and success, then it must redefine itself more appropriately to this task. One such effort was the Student Learning Imperative (SLI) (American College Personnel Association, 1996). Originally released in 1994, this document makes the case that the "philosophical tenets that guide the professional practice of student affairs" need to be reexamined to "help students attain high levels of learning and personal development" (p. 118). According to the SLI, those who are responsible for student affairs are urged to make sure that their "programs and services are designed and managed with specific student learning and personal development outcomes in mind" (p. 119). Partnerships with academic affairs are recommended, and designing educationally purposeful experiences is encouraged. In short, the student affairs division should be recast, according to this document, as a learning-oriented organization.

Several documents built on the SLI and provided suggestions for practice. One of these is the joint report of the American Association for Higher Education (AAHE), the American College Personnel Association (ACPA), and the National Association of Student Personnel Administrators (NASPA), *Powerful Partnerships: A Shared Responsibility for Learning* (1998). Among the principles of this report are that learning is developmental, focuses on the whole person, and attempts to integrate the old with the new. This principle suggests that faculty and student affairs administrators take several steps to create a learning experience for students that integrates all aspects of their lives. Specifically, the report recommends that educational programs build progressively on one another, that student development is tracked through portfolios, that mechanisms are established to encourage student-faculty interaction, and that opportunities are presented for discussion and reflection on the meaning of all collegiate experiences.

This principle, one of ten published in the report with attendant specific recommendations, maps out a clear relationship for student and academic affairs and makes it obvious that student affairs has an important role to play in developing learning experiences for students. Also included in the report are recommendations for establishing powerful learning environments and connecting student affairs professionals and other staff connect with academic units. It is important that student affairs staff initiate connections with faculty since it is unlikely that faculty will initiate such relationships or possibly even see students holistically. In fact, faculty may see student affairs as ancillary, supplementary, or complementary to the academic mission of the institution (Schroeder, 1999b). Some faculty may go so far as to see student affairs as irrelevant or even frivolous.

Blimling, Whitt, and Associates (1999) added to this discussion by cochairing a group that developed Principles of Good Practice for Student Affairs. The recommendations of this effort complemented "Powerful Partnerships." Among the principles of good practice was a recommendation that "good practice in student affairs forges educational partnerships that advance student learning." This includes the formation of partnerships with faculty and others inside and outside the institution. Most recently, ACPA and NASPA have added to this body of literature with *Learning Reconsidered: A Campus-Wide Focus on Student Experience* (2004). So the context for good student affairs practice has been established in the past several years, with a focus on promoting learning in concert with faculty. The next obvious issue deals with the extent to which various student affairs programs, services, and experiences make a difference in students' lives.

STUDENT AFFAIRS PROGRAMS AND SERVICES FOR FIRST-YEAR STUDENTS

Although there are chapters in this book on student services and programs that are most relevant to first-year student success (including residential life, orientation, and academic advising), many other such programs and services also have a role in promoting first-year student success, including financial aid, student employment, counseling services, health services, campus recreation, college unions, career services, adult learner services, services and programs for women, services for student athletes, services and programs for gay, lesbian, bisexual, and transgender students, services for students with disabilities, international student services, and religious and faith-based services.

Financial Aid and Student Employment

For prospective first-year students, financing their education is a critical issue in determining whether they attend college, and if they do, what college they attend (Coomes, 2004). Furthermore, once they are in college, problems with financing their education may well be related to their persistence (St. John, 1989). Thus, helping first-year students develop the wherewithal to finance their education is central to their initial and continuing enrollment. Schuh and Upcraft (2001) point out that financial aid typically can be divided into three distinct areas of support: grants, loans, and work-study. That aid comes from a variety of sources, including the institution, state and federal governments, and private sources.

The ever-increasing cost of attending college is a subject that has been discussed frequently in contemporary literature (Mortenson, 1998; Zusman, 1999). Financial aid policy for the past two decades has been oriented toward loans rather than work or grants, and over half the student aid in recent years has taken the form of loans rather than grants or work (Hearn, 1998). As a consequence, students are incurring increasing debt (Scherschel, 1998). For example, 87 percent of low-income undergraduates who enroll on a full-time basis have unmet financial need (National Center for Education Statistics, 2000).

Since federal policy has moved to the issuance of loans as the most common form of aid, institutions may be well advised to encourage first-year students to work on campus as well as provide awards that do not have to be repaid, be they need based or merit based. Astin (1993, p. 388) concluded that student part-time work on campus "is positively associated with attainment of a bachelor's degree and with all areas of self-reported cognitive and affective growth." Off-campus work full time is seen as having a wide range of negative consequences for students. Astin also concluded that "about the only form of financial aid that seems to have measurable direct effects on student development is a grant from the college" (1993, p. 368). He observes that these grants "may be perceived as a form of special recognition" (p. 369), and as a consequence students may feel a greater sense of responsibility to live up to the expectation and promise implied by the award.

There are many implications for first-year students. First, institutions should provide prospective first-year students with accurate financial aid information and advice that is tailored to their needs. Second, institutions should, as best they can, rely on aid that does not have to be repaid. Third, when student loans are necessary, institutions have a clear responsibility to make sure that first-year students and their families understand the realities of immediate debt repayment, should the student drop out, as well as the amount and timetable of repayment should the student graduate. Fourth, institutions should stand ready to provide alternative forms of aid if students' financial situations change during their enrollment. Fifth, institutions should take an active role in helping students find jobs, preferably on campus, with the caveat that full-time jobs are often detrimental to their success.

Student Counseling Services

As Crissman Ishler and Upcraft point out in Chapter One, today's first-year students arrive on campus with more problems than ever before (Archer & Cooper, 1998). As a result, more students are seeking help, causing an increase in demand for counseling services on college campuses. They also note that use of medications to treat psychological problems such as depression, anxiety, eating disorders, and other problems is on the increase. Moreover, there is some evidence that students who experience personal and psychological problems are more likely than other students to drop out of college. There is also some evidence (Wilson, Mason, & Ewing, 1997) that students who obtain personal counseling are more likely to remain in college than those who did not seek such services. Thus, student counseling services are critical to the success of first-year students.

According to Yarris (1996), the three fundamental purposes of student counseling services are to help students address problems that already exist (remedial), assist students in preventing problems from occurring (preventive), and help students deal with developmental problems, including roommate problems and interpersonal relationship issues. This approach to counseling services is built on the model developed by Morrill, Hurst, and Oetting, and others (1980). Providing recommendations for modifying the campus environment also may be a potential target for intervention by counseling services, as are consultative services to the campus community (Council for the Advancement of Standards, 1997).

Individuals who are prepared as counseling psychologists or social workers or other mental health workers provide services in campus counseling centers. Other institutional staff on campus also provide counseling assistance, such as academic advisers and career counselors (Winston, 1996). All of these individuals are interested in providing assistance to students so that they can achieve their educational objectives.

Contemporary counseling centers tend to provide short-term psychological and developmental assistance to students through a fairly short number of visits (say, three to five) or through group work. Counseling center staff also consult with faculty on such issues as classroom management strategies. In addition, they work with student affairs staff on behavioral issues in the residence halls or developmental problems that student affairs staff encounter in working with students. These services provide an opportunity for students to address their psychological problems with a trained, professional representative of the institution who can help them deal with their presenting problems. Usually that means just a few sessions, so that the student can continue to make progress toward his or her academic objective.

There are many implications for first-year students. First, students are often reluctant to seek counseling services because they are embarrassed, afraid, do not recognize that they need help, or, perhaps most common, think that counseling services are only for severely disturbed students. Thus, counseling services must be very active in making students aware of the services available, stressing the confidentiality of the counseling relationships and that most students seeking counseling are "normal students" with "normal problems." Second, counseling centers should be prepared to deal with the problems that may be typical of first-year students: homesickness, parent and family problems, academic difficulties, roommate relationships, work-school conflicts, sexual assault, sexual identity, and others. Third, because first-year students are often reluctant to go to counseling centers for fear that what they disclose may get back to parents, friends, or the administration, counseling services must make sure that they understand the parameters and limits of confidentiality policies and practices. Fourth, counseling services must make a special effort to let first-year students know of their services and programs by participating actively in orientation, first-year seminars, and other efforts to promote student success.

Student Health Services

Student health services play similar roles on campus to those of student counseling services. According to Spear (2001), the current reality of health services in higher education is one of great variance. Options range from no services at all (about 20 percent of higher education institutions) to limited services (a nurse who provides basic first aid and personal health advice), to comprehensive primary care services delivered by health care professionals, and a full complement of ancillary services (such as x-ray, pharmacy, and labs). But increasingly these comprehensive health services have given way to more limited services that treat fairly routine health problems, referring students requiring more intensive care to community health resources.

Student health services are much broader than simply treating students who are ill. Staff provide guidance for the institutional community on a wide range of issues, including substance abuse prevention policies, immunization policies, the needs of special populations of students, accidents and other emergencies, and occasionally will work with staff and other members on the campus community as the need arises (Kaplan, Whipple, & Wright, 1996). While traditional-age college students essentially are a population of healthy individuals, problems can arise that can have tremendous implications for the entire campus community such as an outbreak of meningitis or measles (Schuh, 1983). On a campus where the mean student age is over twenty-five, provision of health care for students is more complex and more difficult to evaluate (Spear, 2001).

Campus wellness programs are also part of most health services offerings (although sometimes jointly sponsored with other institutional programs, such as recreation services or academic departments) that provide a variety of education and prevention programs and services. Among the dimensions of a wellness program are physical fitness, diet and nutrition, and education about the harmful effects of the use of controlled substances, and they may include spiritual and social development (Leafgren, 1989). The specific organizational structure as to where wellness programs are found in a college or university is less important than the educational services that are provided, since they contribute to first-year student growth and development in a variety of ways.

An important issue for first-year students and their families is the cost of health care. Spear (2001) states that in previous times, health services were funded from general funds, prepaid student health fees, or student health insurance. But health services have been forced to look at a myriad of other funding models to respond to the increasing demands of financially strapped students and families, including fees for services and health insurance. However, many students may not be able to afford additional fees or have no or inadequate health insurance. Of those with insurance, more are enrolled in managed care organizations.

What does all this mean for first-year students? First and foremost, health services units must make clear to students and their families what services are offered (and those that are not), how they are paid for, and the community health resources that are available for treating more serious health problems. Of particular importance is helping them understand the complex issues associated with coordinating health services with managed care providers. Second, health services must ensure continuing care for first-year students who are being treated for chronic health problems such as asthma, diabetes, or mental health problems that require medication or other medical treatment. Third, health services must be actively involved in orientation programs, particularly educational programs focused on health education and wellness issues. Fourth, if there are no health services offered, institutions must help first-year students and their families learn about community resources that will meet their health care needs. And finally, health services and health promotion and education programs must take the leadership in dealing with alcohol use and abuse. (For a more detailed discussion of alcohol use, see Chapter Twenty-Six.)

Campus Recreation Programs

A variety of programs and activities comprise campus recreation programs and services. Among these are individual fitness programs, intramural and club sports, and outdoor recreation (Sandeen, 1996). The Council for the Advancement of Standards (CAS) (1997, p. 145) also point out that recreation programs include "structured contests, meets, tournaments and leagues limited to individuals within the institution." Recreation services staff have responsibilities that include managing diverse facilities in addition to organizing recreational activities.

There are many implications for first-year students. First, recreation services and programs provide an excellent opportunity for first-year students to connect with each other socially. Whether they are a member of a team, or engage in individual recreational activities, campus recreation "programs promote good health, teach physical skills and encourage positive social interaction" (Sandeen, 1996, p. 445), which speaks directly to the social connections that were part of Tinto's (1993) retention model. Second, recreation programs provide other benefits, such as the increased self-confidence and teamwork skills developed by intramural officiators (Schuh, 1999). Third, first-year students should be encouraged to participate in recreational activities on campus since they promote a sense of connection with the institution and with each other.

College Unions

College unions are a complex mix of programs and facilities designed to provide services and activities for students and other members of the campus community. According to Yates (1992), some or all of union functions include food facilities (cafeterias, private dining rooms, food and beverage machines), leisure-time facilities (bowling alleys, craft centers, exercise rooms), revenue-generating areas (banks, bookstores, travel agencies), social and cultural facilities (art galleries, auditoriums, ballrooms), general lounges (commuter facilities, day care rooms, study lounges), service facilities (computer labs, postal services, meeting and conference rooms), and office areas (student government, campus newspaper, student organizations).

Sandeen (1996, p. 440) points out that on some campuses, "there may be efforts to coordinate parts of the student activities program with the curriculum, especially the general education core curriculum." The CAS Standards for college unions (1997) point out that "the union also educates the students involved in its governance and program boards and those it employs." A good summary statement about student unions is offered by Whipple (1996), who asserts that both social and academic activities should be promoted with a goal of contributing to the overall campus community.

The implications for first-year students of activities and services of student unions are much like campus recreation programs. First, various union activities and experiences are offered to first-year students so that their out-of-class experiences are complementary to what they learn in the classroom. Second, the college union provides a good opportunity for first-year students to make social connections with each other through activities planning, volunteering for various organizations, or assisting in the governance of the campus union. In short, the union can be "the center of student, campus and community life" at many colleges and universities (Schuh, Upcraft, and Associates, 2001, p. 327).

Career Services

Historically, career service units have been thought of as placement agencies that would help students find jobs upon graduation (Kroll & Rentz, 1996). However, the contemporary career services office, according to Rayman (1993), consists of several functions, including career planning and counseling (individual and group career counseling, computer-assisted career counseling, courses for credit), job placement (on-campus recruiting, job listing services, placement skills development workshops), career programming (outreach programming and seminars, programs for special populations), information support (placement library, career information, Web-based information on employers), communications (brochures, Web pages, placement manuals), professional development and training (training programs for professionals, graduate and undergraduate students, employers), and assessment (postgraduation follow-up studies, employer satisfaction studies, evaluation of career services).

First-year students probably do not need the placement functions of career services, but they certainly will find many of the services and programs useful as they begin their academic careers. For example, career counseling is important in helping first-year students process information "in a way that is useful for making career decisions and developing plans of action" (Winston, 1996, p. 352). While majors in some disciplines lead nearly automatically to a certain occupation, such as a major in elementary education leads to a teaching career, majors in other disciplines, say philosophy or history, provide a less clear path to certain occupations. Career services can be helpful in working with first-year students who are unclear as to how a major in a certain discipline will result in a specific career.

Student participation in such experiences as internships or service-learning can be tied directly to student satisfaction and persistence. Astin and Sax (1998, p. 257), for example, found that participation in service-learning "enhances the student's college grade point average (GPA), general knowledge, knowledge of a field or discipline, and is also associated with increased time devoted to homework and studying and increased contact with faculty."

There are many ways that career services can contribute to first-year student success. First, career services should be active in orientation programs and first-year seminars that inform students about the many functions of career services. This is especially important because there is some reason to believe that first-year students rarely use career services. Second, career services should target its services and programs specifically to first-year students, who often experience career and major indecision or confusion. Third, career services professional staff can help first-year students strengthen their bond with the institution. This relationship can emphasize that the institution is interested in student success, that learning and competence are tied to career opportunities, and that the institution is willing to invest its time and resources for students.

Adult Learner Services and Programs

Nearly one-third of today's undergraduate students are over the age of twenty-four (Phillips, 2000). According to the National Center for Education Statistics (2000), adult students often have delayed enrollment into postsecondary education, attend part time, are financially independent of their parents, work full time while enrolled, have dependents other than a spouse, are a single parent, and lack a standard high school diploma. "Most literature assumes . . . that older-adult students have life circumstances and needs that differ substantially from younger students" (Breese & O'Toole, 1994, p. 183).

Unfortunately, these differences are sometimes not taken into account in institutional efforts to help first-year students succeed, particularly at institutions where adult first-year students are a minority. Copland (1989) suggests that environmental variables such as finances, hours of employment, family responsibilities, transportation, and peer and family support systems are very important to adult student success. Thus, orientation programs geared to these needs become critical to helping adult students make a successful transition to college.

Adult learner services can do much to help first-year adult learners. First, orientation programs and services must specifically target these learners to help them with their unique transition to college. Unfortunately, some orientation efforts include adult students only as an afterthought in traditional orientation programs or ignore them altogether. Nothing is more irrelevant (or even offensive) to adult students than orientation activities focused on eighteen-year-old issues such as homesickness, getting along with your roommate, joining a fraternity or sorority, and institutional-based correspondence addressed "To the parents of . . .". The world of the adult student often consists of full-time work, family responsibilities, day care, financial crises, academic adjustments after years away from formal education, and little or no contact with the institution other than going to classes. Second, adult learner services need to be available to first-year students at times convenient to adult students, such as early mornings, evenings, and weekends. Third, adult learner services can provide connections among adult students, building peer support systems that can be critical to their success. Fourth, adult services can help adult students feel as though they belong and that the institution cares about them as full members of the institution's community.

Services and Programs for Women

As pointed out in Chapter Two, women students consistently earn higher grades and graduate from college at higher rates than men. This does not mean, however, that women students do not have unique barriers to overcome in making a successful transition to college and achieving their educational goals. Often, as a consequence of cultural stereotypes, first-year women students "face difficulties in attaining and succeeding in campus leadership positions that were different than those faced by men students" (Torre, 1992, p. 555). Women have "limited personal, academic and professional choices" (Chapman, 1989, p. 288). To deal with inequalities on campus, institutions of higher education have established women student services and programs. The CAS Standards (1997, p. 164) refer to these as "personal and career counseling, developmental workshops and classes, small weekly programs and large campus events." These activities are designed to "help women students achieve success in their chosen careers and better understand the changing roles of women in society" (p. 164). Women student programs and services "promote unrestricted access and full involvement of women students in all aspects of the college or university experience" (p. 165).

In general, the functions of women's centers include advocacy for women and women's issues, information about gender issues, educational programming (classroom and campus climate for women, sexual harassment, violence against women, women of color issues, lesbian and bisexual women's issues, and campus safety issues), counseling and advising services, sexual assault crisis intervention, the resource library, facilities for student activities focused on women's issues, coordination with campus and community organizations concerned with women, and referrals to other services for women.

There are many ways in which women's centers can help in the success of first-year women and men students. First, women's centers must overcome typical but inaccurate stereotypes. For example, women's centers are often incorrectly thought of as offering services only to women, or as dominated by lesbians or radical feminists, or as pursuing a politically correct agenda for women. Participation in first-year student orientation programs and services can help overcome these stereotypes. Second, women's centers can sponsor orientation programs that can begin raising the consciousness of both men and women on the important gender issues, but especially issues important to first-year students such as campus safety, sexual assault, sexual harassment, and gender roles in social relationships. Third, women's centers can help first-year women feel as though they are a part of the institutional community. Chapman (1989, p. 300), for example, asserts that "every opportunity must be taken to encourage first-year women students to further educate themselves about women's issues and to commit themselves to becoming social change agents, whenever and wherever possible, within their sphere of influence related to persistence."

Services for Student Athletes

Of increasing concern in contemporary American higher education is how student athletes can be integrated into the life of their institution and ultimately graduate. Howard-Hamilton and Watt (2001, p. 1) describe the situation this way: "We find more and more student services and athletic administrators seeking ways to integrate athletes in the mainstream of college student experiences and provide them with a successful transition from high school to college." From this point of view, interventions, programs, and services offered by colleges and universities to first-year student athletes have roughly the same objectives as those offered to other groups of students who potentially are at risk of not persisting to graduation. As a consequence, a variety of athlete services have been developed in the past decade or so designed to encourage the persistence of student athletes.

It is important to draw distinctions between the various sports in which athletes compete and the various levels with which their institutions are affiliated. For example, "The general understanding is the athletes who compete at (NCAA) Division II and III colleges and universities do so for the love of the sport rather than for external rewards" (Watt & Moore, 2001, p. 12). These athletes presumably are less likely to pursue careers as professional athletes and more likely to compete before smaller crowds and play less demanding schedules than athletes who compete at the Division I level.

At the Division I level, athletes also can be disaggregated into two groups. One of these groups includes those athletes who compete in sports that generate substantial revenue and compete for space on the sports page with professional athletes. Among them are football players, men's and women's basketball players, and perhaps athletes in other sports that generate intense regional interest, such as ice hockey in the Northeast and baseball in the Southwest. Others are athletes in the so-called Olympic sports who are unlikely to pursue professional careers and compete before smaller crowds and achieve less public scrutiny and notoriety.

There are many ways in which institutions can help first-year student athletes make a successful transition to college and succeed academically. First, a program sponsored by the National College Athletic Association (NCAA), the CHAMPS/Life Skills program (NCAA, 2001), is available to institutions in all NCAA divisions. This program is designed to "provide services and support to the membership, public and media to develop and enhance the life of the student-athlete through education programs and resources focusing on gender equity, student-athlete welfare, and life skills." Among the elements of the program is a commitment to help athletes in their career development, serving their communities, and the development of a well-balanced lifestyle.

Second, there are other programs available for first-year student athletes, including specialized counseling (Broughton & Neyer, 2001) and programs for female athletes and athletes of color (Person, Benson-Quaziena, & Rogers, 2001). Programs that help athletes succeed in the classroom must also be a significant part of helping student athletes succeed, including study halls, basic skills tutoring, and time management.

Third, some institutions require first-year student athletes to enroll in first-year seminars specifically targeted to their needs. Many of the issues described above are typically an important part of these seminars.

Services for Lesbian, Gay, Bisexual, and Transgender Students

First-year students who are openly lesbian, gay, bisexual, or transgender (LGBT), or who are "closeted" or confused about their sexual identity, present unique challenges to institutions committed to first-year student success, for two reasons. First, unlike all other minorities, sexual minorities may not be protected against discrimination by institutional policies or state legislation. Second, unlike other minorities, there is a moral dimension to their identities. That is, no one argues that it is wrong to be a woman, Hispanic, disabled, or older, but there are some who would argue that being lesbian, gay, bisexual, or transgendered is morally wrong. These two realities may, in some cases, influence the way in which the needs of this student population are met, or not met as the case may be.

Nevertheless, institutions must recognize that LGBT students are a significant presence on most campuses, and their needs must be addressed. Estimates of the percentage of these students vary, and this information is very difficult to gather, but studies that do gather such information typically find that the percentage of students who identify themselves as lesbian, gay, bisexual, or transgender is around 4 percent or less. The percentage of students identifying as attracted to someone of the same sex was around 7 percent (Eyermann & Sanlo, 2002), and one must assume that these percentages are low, because there are some students who would not reveal their sexual orientation or attraction under any circumstances. Of course, these percentages vary by institution, but one can safely assume that in any first-year student population, there will be some sexual minorities.

Developing programs and services for first-year LGBT students is problematic because of the varying degrees of openness about their sexual orientation. While openly lesbian, gay, bisexual, and transgender first-year students may have no qualms about attending an orientation program on how sexual minorities can make a successful transition to college, closeted LBGT students or those with sexual identity confusion would be unlikely to attend, for obvious reasons. Nevertheless, institutions can meet the needs of these students if they present these programs and services in ways that respect their confidentiality and dignity. These programs and services should include heterosexuals as well, since their attitudes and behaviors may well affect the success of LGBT first-year students.

First and foremost, institutions must create campus climates that ensure the physical and psychological safety of LGBT students. Unfortunately, in a review of the research in this regard, Sullivan (1998) found continuing evidence of homophobic prejudice, harassment, and violence against LGBT students. First-year LGBT students must know that their institution will not tolerate such behavior and that those who perpetrate harassment and violence will be severely sanctioned.

Second, when recruiting first-year students, institutions should be inclusive of sexual minorities in their presentations and literature, if those institutions do, in fact, have a commitment to creating a safe, tolerant, and affirmative climate for LGBT students. A critical factor in recruiting these students may well be the inclusion of sexual orientation in an institution's nondiscrimination policies.

Third, institutions should establish safe zones where first-year students may go when they need to talk or require assistance. According to Sanlo, Rankin, and Schoenberg (2002), "Typically, a safe zone marker, such as a sticker, magnet, or mug, identifies people who are knowledgeable about LGBT issues. On some campuses safe zone participants must attend one or more group or individual training sessions before receiving a safe zone marker" (p. 95).

Fourth, programs designed to increase awareness of LGBT issues among heterosexual first-year students must be a part of orientation. These students are the dominant culture of colleges and universities; thus, their attitudes and behaviors are critical to developing a safe and tolerant climate for LGBT students.

Fifth, institutions must develop safe and confidential opportunities for first-year students who are confused about their sexual identity to discuss their concerns. Typically, this is done by counseling and psychological services, so they must present themselves as being willing to help such students in a non-judgmental way. Other resources may include residence hall professional staff, health services personnel, and LGBT centers.

Finally, LGBT student organizations can be an important part of helping LGBT first-year students make a successful transition to college through their participation in orientation programs, assistance to individual students, and advocacy of LGBT issues in the institution and the community.

Of course, institutions whose history and mission do not tolerate the presence of sexual minorities among their student bodies will undoubtedly want to develop alternative strategies for dealing with LGBT issues.

Services for First-Year Students with Disabilities

Primarily because of federal legislation such as Section 504 of the Rehabilitation Act of 1973 and the Americans with Disabilities Act (ADA) of 1990, persons with disabilities who heretofore had little access to or full participation in college were able to pursue their education (Schuh, 2000). As a result, the participation of students with disabilities in higher education has increased dramatically, and they now account for approximately 9 percent of all first-year students entering college, a substantial increase from 3 percent in 1978 (Henderson, 1999). Furthermore, the range of disabilities among students has expanded to include learning disabilities, hearing impairment, sight impairment, speech impairment, mobility impairment, physical impairment, health-related disabilities, attention deficit hyperactivity disorders, and disabilities that may not be as obvious as those. Thus, students with disabilities present a legal and educational challenge to colleges and universities.

According to Simon (1999), the legal challenge is how to comply fully with Section 504 and the ADA. Section 504 not only imposes a prohibition against discrimination but also an obligation to make reasonable accommodations. Section 504 provides that institutions shall make such modifications to their academic requirements as are necessary to ensure that such requirements do not discriminate or have the effect of discriminating on the basis of disability. The Supreme Court in *Alexander* v. *Choate* (1985) ruled that otherwise qualified students with disabilities are entitled to meaningful access and reasonable accommodation. Thus, institutions must modify their programs and services to provide accommodations to students with disabilities.

The educational challenge is to create collegiate environments for first-year students that meet not only the letter but also the spirit of these legal requirements. According to Palombi (2000), such efforts must begin with the recruitment and admission of students with disabilities. Institutions must ensure that prospective disabled students have sufficient information about the efforts made to accommodate them. Furthermore, according to Kavale and Forness (1996), the type and extent of special services that are available to disabled students are important determiners of their college selection. The admissions process must also be disabled student friendly, such as accommodations in SAT and ACT test administrations, and flexibility in qualifications. All of this, however, assumes that prospective students will disclose their disability early in the admissions process, and that is frequently a very difficult decision for students to make.

When first-year students with disabilities arrive on campus, they must be provided with the reasonable accommodations they will need in order to become successful students. That means helping them with their housing arrangements, making them familiar with the campus physical plant and facilities and overcoming the barriers they may encounter, encouraging them to participate in campus life activities, and helping them to take advantage of the many student support services available, such as academic advising, career services, counseling services, and especially health services, where they may need maintenance and treatment for their disability. Furthermore, orientation programs must be sensitive to the needs and inclusive of students with disabilities and make sure that their issues are addressed and necessary accommodations for their participation in orientation are in place.

The classroom provides significant challenges for disabled students. Special assistance such as tutoring may be required. Other accommodations may also be necessary. For example, sight-impaired students may need print-enlarged tests, hearing-impaired students may need signers and note takers, mobility-impaired students may need special access to classrooms, and so on. Perhaps even more important are the attitudes of faculty. In a study of first-year disabled students at the University of Maryland, Mitchell and Sedlacek (1995) found that students with learning disabilities were concerned that faculty were unknowledgeable about learning disabilities, and therefore less sympathetic, less understanding, and less likely to provide reasonable accommodations. Thus, it is incumbent on institutions committed to reasonable accommodation of first-year students with disabilities to initiate faculty development programs that increase faculty awareness of the needs of these students.

Finally, and perhaps most important, first-year students with disabilities must have someone or some office that can advocate for their concerns and meet their unique needs. When they encounter difficulties, they must believe that they are not alone and that the institution will meet the spirit and the letter of its commitment to promoting their success.

International Student Services

First-year international students present unique challenges to institutions committed to first-year student success. For example, according to Gregory (1997), foreign-born students are more likely than native-born students to need financial aid and to come from academic backgrounds where they lacked access to computers and scientific equipment. The may also be unfamiliar with the teaching and learning styles of American higher education. They need, among other things, specifically designed orientation programs that meet their unique needs.

While in some ways first-year international students share the same transition concerns as other students, they do present some unique problems that must be addressed in orientation programs specifically designed to meet their needs. This process starts with helping them get admitted. That is not necessarily an easy task, because of language barriers, immigration procedures and paperwork, financing, admissions procedures, transportation, and other issues associated with gaining admission. Furthermore, since the terrorist attacks of September 11, 2001, many prospective international students, especially those from Middle Eastern countries, have been subjected to more careful scrutiny than in the past by the Bureau of Citizenship and Immigration Services (Jacobson, 2003). Typically, an international programs office handles most of these concerns and is the primary source of communication and contact with the institution prior to enrollment.

Once international students arrive, there are a myriad of issues to be revolved. According to T. Wortman (personal communication to the author, 2002), an international student orientation program starts with making sure that first-year international students have correctly completed all the paperwork necessary to comply with U.S. immigration laws. Second, there may be health-related issues that need to be addressed, including medical treatment options and health insurance. Third, housing must be arranged if those arrangements were not made prior to their immigration. Fourth, "culture shock" programs can educate first-year international students to American culture and how their cultures may differ in areas such as gender relationships, community relations, and personal hygiene. Fifth, because the typical way of determining language competence is through the use of a written examination, first-year international students may need help in improving their English verbal skills. Sixth, first-year international students should become acquainted with nationality student organizations that can provide peer support and community-based hospitality groups that can help them integrate successfully into the community. Finally, they must become familiar with the requirements of their academic department and their academic adviser.

Religious and Faith-Based Services

Recently, there has been a renewed interest in students' spiritual experiences and needs (Love & Talbot, 1999; Jablonski, 2001). Most of the student development theory and research that occurred in the last four decades of the twentieth century ignored the spiritual and faith dimensions of the student experience. Except for church-related institutions, most colleges and universities have assumed that students' spiritual development is their own responsibility and taken a hands-off stance on this aspect of development. Typically this aspect of the student experience was left to on-campus faith-based student organizations or community-based religious denominations. That situation appears to be changing. According to Watanabe (2000), this long-standing bias against religion has blinded many scholars to religion's powerful role in shaping the lives of students.

While institutions are now cautiously and carefully giving attention to the spiritual side of students' development, there is little research yet on this issue. Lee (2002) did find that while students tended to experience changes in religious beliefs, contrary to popular stereotypes, more students experienced a strengthening rather than a weakening of religious convictions. She also found that attending religious services strengthened religious beliefs, as well as identifying with other students who share similar religious orientations.

What does all this mean for helping first-year students deal with the religious and faith-based aspect of their transition to college? First, opportunities to explore the spiritual aspect of their development should be included in orientation programs. Faculty, students, and persons with religious backgrounds and training should be involved in programs that both challenge and support first-year students' spiritual development. Second, institutions must make sure that first-year students know of the opportunities available to them from student religious organizations. Third, there must be a campus environment that legitimizes and confirms faith-based discussions and participation without a built-in prejudice either for or against such activities. Fourth, while religious student organizations and denominations must be given full access to first-year students, they should do so on the condition that they tolerate and show respect for each others' religious beliefs and commitments. Fifth, first-year students must know of the opportunities for participation in the religious life of the surrounding communities. Sixth, orientation programs that discuss topics such as sexual orientation, abortion, war, genetic engineering, and gender roles should include the many religious perspectives on these issues. Finally, orientation programs should include discussions of religious participation and practices that may be potentially harmful, such as involvement in religious cults.

RECOMMENDATIONS

It is important to target student support services to first-year students. It is not enough to offer services and programs for all students on the assumption that there is no need to adapt services to this special population.

- *Market student support services aggressively and directly to first-year students,* from the point of admission through orientation, first-year seminars, and aggressive marketing efforts on the part of individual units. When appropriate, student services and programs should partner with faculty and academic services to promote student success.
- *Establish making a successful transition to college and student success as the primary goals of student support services,* so that first-year students see these services as having educational value.

CONCLUSION

This chapter has focused on how specific student services and programs can contribute to first-year student success, guided by the contemporary emphasis on student learning that shapes student affairs practice. These programs and services both challenge and support first-year students to succeed. The challenge for first-year students is to overcome their reluctance to use these services and recognize the support they offer to help them succeed. Student support services can provide a connection between first-year students and their institution if the institution offers them and students use them. However, these support services are more powerful when they are the product of collaboration between student affairs and academic affairs.

CHAPTER TWENTY-SIX

The First-Year Experience
and Alcohol Use

Philip W. Meilman
Cheryl A. Presley

Like ev'ry honest fellow I like my whiskey clear,
For I'm a student of old Dartmouth and a son of a gun for beer.
And if I had a son, sir, I'll tell what he'd do.
He would yell "To Hell with Harvard" like his daddy used to do.
—College drinking song (Rivinus, 1988)

Drinking on campus is not a new problem, and alcohol use accompanied the founding of and earliest experiences in many of our great collegiate institutions. Mory's, Yale's legendary drinking establishment established nearly 150 years ago, was immortalized in song by that well-known group, the Wiffenpoofs (Branch, 1999). In similar fashion, almost every college has its share of drinking songs and traditions and venues.

Although these traditions may sound like fun, there is substantial downside risk to excessive alcohol consumption. As just one example, a small group of students at a midwestern university were drinking off campus during the mid-day to celebrate the completion of midterms. After consuming alcohol for three to four hours, they returned to their residence hall to get more money in order to fund a return trip to the neighborhood bars. One student, her behavior and emotions severely affected by drinking, went into her room and slit her wrist while her friends waited. The other students all experienced varied degrees of trauma at seeing this and as a result were adversely affected in terms of their ability to function academically for the remainder of that year. The mobilization of university resources needed to respond to this incident was considerable. Stories like this, and worse, are repeated at institutions all over the country, year in and year out.

Alcohol use and abuse threatens first-year students as well as their more senior counterparts. Because first-year students are new to campus and do not fully know what to expect, and in many cases do not know their drinking limits, they are especially vulnerable. The daunting problem of alcohol use and abuse on college campuses has challenged researchers and programmers to respond. Understanding what is happening to students generally and to first-year students in particular is critical so that college administrators and staff can respond appropriately. This understanding can be maximized by simultaneously examining current experiences regarding alcohol use on college campuses, studying past and present use patterns, and keeping abreast of new developments in the field.

In this chapter we will first take a look at the collegiate environment in which student drinking occurs, and then review the research related to student alcohol use and abuse. Next is a review of first-year students' drinking behaviors as described in the Core Alcohol and Drug Survey national database, followed by some of the reasons first-year students consume alcohol. Various strategies for preventing excessive drinking are then presented, along with examples of outreach programs targeted to first-year students. Finally, we discuss how to assess the effectiveness of efforts to reduce alcohol use and abuse, and offer some recommendations and conclusions.

THE COLLEGIATE ENVIRONMENT

The relationship between the college environment and individual behavior is complex. Collegiate environments can no longer be typified as a single culture, and students are not as homogeneous as in the past (Upcraft, 2000). There are more international students, women, students from diverse racial/ethnic backgrounds, and nontraditional students than a few decades ago. As Crissman Ishler and Upcraft reminded us in Chapter One, "Joe College doesn't live here anymore." There is growing recognition that what constitutes a campus environment is changing with distance learning, courses taken electronically, service-learning, international programs, campuses in multiple locations, and fieldwork placements.

The very boundaries of "campus" have become increasingly difficult to describe. So-called off-campus housing options located nearby and the local business environment both on and just outside the campus boundaries make it hard to describe what is truly "off" campus and what is "on" campus. We can expect the lines to grow increasingly blurry in the years ahead with new developments in technology. All of this affects the nature of the educational experience, and that in turn affects the culture around campus and the culture surrounding alcohol use.

Our experience is that traditional-aged first-year students enter college excited but also nervous, worried if they will "make it," often experiencing an underlying loss of structure and familiar surroundings. For these students, alcohol may be particularly attractive because they believe it provides instant camaraderie and connection at a time when they are feeling vulnerable and need to establish themselves in a world of new relationships and structures. They may not yet know their drinking limits, something that can occur only with experience. Thus, first-year college students are at particularly high risk for overdosing. A 1986 study found that the majority of alcohol-related admissions to medical facilities for emergency care at a private, liberal arts New England college occurred among first-year students (Meilman, Yanofsky, Gaylor, & Turco, 1989).

RESEARCH ON ALCOHOL USE AMONG COLLEGE STUDENTS

There is much we already know about alcohol use among college students, based on extensive research that has been done over the past few decades. For example, among the many research findings, we know that:

- Drinking is inversely proportional to grade point average. This robust finding has been demonstrated repeatedly (Presley, Meilman, & Lyerla, 1993, 1995; Presley, Meilman, Cashin, & Lyerla, 1996; Presley, Meilman, & Cashin, 1996).

- Alcohol use is greater among Greek members than nonmembers (Cashin, Presley, & Meilman, 1998).

- Alcohol use is greater among athletes than nonathletes (Leichliter, Meilman, Presley, & Cashin, 1995).

- Alcohol use is greater among white students than black students (Meilman, Presley, & Lyerla, 1994).

- There have been slight reductions in lifetime, annual, and thirty-day prevalence rates of college student drinking over the past two decades (Johnston, O'Malley, & Bachman, 2001). (Thirty-day prevalence refers to any use in the past month.)

- There is less binge drinking among women at women's colleges than at coeducational colleges (Wechsler, Dowdall, Davenport, & Costillo, 1995).

- There is less drinking among students at historically black colleges and universities than at predominantly white colleges and universities (Meilman, Presley, & Cashin, 1995).

However, research about student alcohol use and abuse is not without its problems. For example, there has been a great deal of discussion in recent years regarding students engaging in binge-drinking practices, but use of the term *binge drinking* has been controversial. Technically, the term is meant to be an operational definition that many researchers use to indicate consumption of five or more drinks at one sitting. (However, findings from the College Alcohol Study have used a five-drink standard for men and a four-drink standard for women; Wechsler, Davenport, Dowdall, Moeykens, & Castillo, 1994.)

The controversy over the use of the term *binge drinking* has two parts. One part revolves around the fact that the term *binge* implies a "bender" in the alcoholism treatment community, that is, a period of drinking to excess that typically lasts for several days. Thus, the treatment community does not consider five drinks a binge. The other part of the concern comes from students themselves and college alcohol abuse prevention workers. Some students argue that consuming five drinks in a row is so commonplace that to call it a binge is to overstate the behavior. And some prevention workers and students argue that five drinks consumed over five hours might actually be viewed as responsible drinking.

With regard to the operational research definition, the terms *heavy episodic drinking* and *high-risk drinking* have drawn favor in the recent past. For example, the *Journal of Studies on Alcohol,* one of the premier journals in the field of alcohol research, typically asks authors to use one of these alternate phrases rather than the term *binge drinking* when the operational definition is intended. This keeps the definitions clear.

Whatever the term one uses, though, the reported percentages of students engaging in risky drinking patterns (according to the operational definition) in the two weeks prior to survey administration have generally hovered in the high 30s to low 40s over the past ten years in the Monitoring the Future study from the Institute for Social Research at the University of Michigan (Johnston, O'Malley, & Bachman, 2001), the College Alcohol Study from the Harvard School of Public Health (Wechsler et al., 1994), and the Core Institute studies from Southern Illinois University at Carbondale (Presley et al., 1993, 1995; Presley, Meilman, Cashin, & Lyerla, 1996; Presley, Meilman, & Cashin, 1996).

A second problem related to research on student alcohol use and abuse is that some studies are challenged because of the variations in the units of analyses that different methodologies employ. With regard to alcohol consumption, is it most appropriate to use quantity or frequency, or some combination based on quantity *and* frequency? Is the term *binge drinking* gender specific? Are we interested in heavy episodic drinking during the past two weeks or the past thirty days?

In spite of these problems and limitations and methodological inconsistencies and variations in the reported studies, there is a common thread in what is known. The evidence is overwhelming that some students drink often, and some drink to harmful levels. Yet many do not. There is no question that the negative consequences of drinking are antithetical to the academic mission of the university and college environment.

For example, approximately 30 percent of all first-year students leave their colleges before their second year (National Center for Education Statistics, 1998), whether it is in the form of "stopping out" or dropping out, and although there are no good statistical accountings of the phenomenon, experience and anecdotal reports clearly indicate that student persistence to graduation is severely challenged by the heavy consumption of alcohol. In fact, some of the major causes of withdrawal identified by major researchers—academic difficulty, adjustment difficulties, weak commitment, financial inadequacies, isolation, and poor fit (see Tinto, 1987)—are all potentially exacerbated when students use alcohol excessively. The connection between student difficulties and alcohol has been increasingly recognized in recent years. Surprisingly, for example, the indexing to the 1966 book, *The College Dropout and the Utiliza-*

tion of Talent (Pervin, Reik, & Dalrymple, 1966), and even the 1991 classic, *How College Affects Students* (Pascarella & Terenzini, 1991), contain no entry for alcohol. However, a chapter in the later, 1993 standard, *The Handbook of Student Affairs,* identifies substance abuse as the second leading health risk for college students (Bridwell & Kinder, 1993), and any major health risk certainly affects retention and is recognized as an impediment to academic success.

FINDINGS ON FIRST-YEAR STUDENTS FROM THE CORE ALCOHOL AND DRUG SURVEY

Let us look specifically at what is happening with first-year students. For this analysis, we examined Core Alcohol and Drug Survey data collected from 60,098 first-year students in calendar years 1999, 2000, and 2001 from 438 institutions of higher education: 373 four-year colleges and universities and 65 two-year colleges.

Instrument

The Core Alcohol and Drug Survey was developed in the late 1980s by a committee of grantees from the U.S. Department of Education's Drug Prevention Program in Higher Education, funded by the Fund for Improvement of Postsecondary Education (FIPSE). The committee was originally intended to serve as an instrument selection committee, and its task was to identify a single survey tool that all institutions could use to measure alcohol and other drug use before and after the implementation of their FIPSE-funded prevention programs. The idea was to ensure uniformity of data, allow for cross-institutional comparisons and national data aggregation, and prevent wasteful duplication of efforts. Little time elapsed before it became obvious that there was no single survey instrument then in existence that would adequately meet the needs of public and private, two-year and four-year, and large and small institutions. At that point, the committee set out to develop a new survey questionnaire that would meet these needs and would also be easy to administer, cost-effective, reliable, and valid, and provide institutions with a quick turnaround with respect to data analysis.

The result was the Core Alcohol and Drug Survey. The term *core survey* was used with the idea that the questionnaire would form a basic, or core, set of questions around which institutions could formulate more specific or additional research inquiries. The original instrument was a two-page, optically scanned self-report questionnaire that looked at demographics, use, and consequences of use. Several years later, in response to grantee requests, the Core Survey was expanded by another two pages to include questions on campus climate issues, violence, and sexuality as related to alcohol and other drug use, perceived risks of use, and secondary effects of alcohol use.

In order to obtain the most accurate results, institutions that use the Core Alcohol and Drug Survey are asked to survey their students in a random and representative fashion. The completed survey forms are sent to Southern Illinois

University at Carbondale for optical scanning and machine scoring, and a summary report of the institution's data is sent back to the reporting institution within about two weeks. The staff at Southern Illinois University employ a quality control check to make sure that the sample at each institution is random and representative. Samples that meet these criteria are aggregated for further analysis. Samples that are not random and representative are excluded.

Demographics

The present sample of 60,098 first-year students is 40.4 percent male and 59.6 percent female, of whom 79.7 percent are white, 9.0 percent black, 4.0 percent Hispanic, 3.5 percent Asian/Pacific Islander, 0.8 percent American Indian or Alaskan Native, and 3.0 percent other. Almost all of the students are single (96.4 percent), and 72.3 percent live on campus. Another 16.7 percent report that they live with parents. The percentage of full-time students is 96.4, with a modal age of eighteen, although there is considerable variability in age. These demographics are not necessarily representative of all first-year students (see Chapter Two), but this does give a picture in broad brushstrokes of what is happening nationally with traditional-aged, full-time first-year students, most of whom are living on campus.

Results

The results of this survey reveal several important findings about the use and abuse of alcohol among first-year students:

- Overall, there is an average weekly consumption rate of 3.9 drinks for women and 8.6 drinks for men (overall total is 5.8 drinks per student per week). These figures include the 41.7 percent of students who report consuming zero alcoholic beverages per week on average.

- One of four first-year students report that they consumed ten or more drinks per week on average.

- With regard to heavy episodic drinking, 45.6 percent of the first-year students report having consumed five or more drinks in a row in the previous two-week period. Thus, it appears that nearly half are consuming in excess, in spite of the fact that most cannot legally purchase or consume alcohol.

A conundrum that exists relative to these figures, even if one can overlook illegal under-age drinking, is that the operational definition of *heavy episodic drinking* and the reporting of the averages actually mask some of the real problems that are associated with drinking for first-year students. Those who are having personal difficulties with alcohol and whose difficulties with alcohol are challenging their academic careers (and perhaps their safety) are hidden in these averages and definitions. Actually, if a student chooses to drink five drinks in one sitting and that sitting is five hours long, could we not consider him or her a responsible drinker, legal or not? When one looks at the percentage of students who are drinking ten or more drinks per week, the differences begin to become more apparent. Core Institute personnel are currently examining a profile of students who have high frequency, high quantity, and a high number of negative consequences. We suggest that in the future, this may be a more accurate way to identify the first-year students who are most at risk for alcohol-related challenges in the college setting.

Let us return to the data at hand and further examine what is happening with first-year students. As an indicator of the social acceptability of alcohol, 69.5 percent of the first-year students in our large sample reported that they would support the availability of alcohol on their campuses if there were a choice as to whether their colleges should or should not allow alcohol to be used on campus (presumably, legally). However, there is a silent minority (30.5 percent) of students who said they did not wish to have it available on or around campus. These figures were essentially reversed when students were asked about other drugs; that is, the vast majority of students (76.8 percent) do not support the availability of drugs at their colleges.

First-year students come to college with an established drinking history in many cases. With regard to the age of their first use of alcohol, 16.7 percent of the first-year students reported that they had never used alcohol, 5.5 percent said that they initially consumed alcohol when they were under twelve years of age, 36.9 percent first consumed between the ages of twelve and fifteen, and 28.2 percent first consumed between the ages of sixteen and seventeen.

The family histories of our first-year students with respect to alcohol and other drug use are noteworthy: 5.3 percent of students report that their mothers have had alcohol and drug problems, and the figure almost triples with regard to fathers. Brothers and sisters come in at 9.2 percent. By the time one adds in the percentages of students reporting alcohol and other drug problems in step-parents, grandparents, and aunts and uncles, a picture emerges showing that half of first-year students come from backgrounds where alcohol and drug use is problematic in the family constellation. Students bring these family experiences with them to college. Thus, colleges inherit some of the problems that have had their roots in past adolescent and even preadolescent experience.

In terms of present consumption, the first-year students reported various frequencies in response to the question, "Within the last year about how often have you used alcohol (beer, wine, liquor)?" We also asked them, "How often do you think the average student on your campus uses alcohol (beer, wine, liquor)?" Table 26.1 provides their responses,

In these data, several things become evident. More than a fifth of the first-year students are drinking with significant regularity (three times a week or more often), yet the majority of students are drinking less than once a week. At the same time, first-year students overestimate the amount of frequent drinking on campus and underestimate the percentage of students who drink rarely or not at all. This is certainly peer pressure, or at least perceived peer pressure, and is a point emphasized by the social norms researchers.

Table 26.1. Frequency of Alcohol Use by First-Year Students
and Their Perceptions of Other First-Year Students' Use

Frequency	Self	Perceived Use by Others
Never	20.3%	2.2%
Once a year	7.6	0.6
Six times a year	10.9	0.9
Once a month	7.2	1.7
Twice a month	12.8	4.5
Once a week	20.9	28.8
Three times a week	16.3	39.3
Five times a week	3.3	12.4
Every day	0.7	9.7

In terms of their drinking venues, we obtained the information shown in Table 26.2 from the first-year students in response to the question, "Where have you used alcohol?"

Thus, there is no single location that can be identified where drinking either does or does not take place for these first-year students, the vast majority of whom are not legal drinkers. Depending on the degree of enforcement (colleges vary on this due to staffing levels, policies regarding enforcement of alcohol regulations, and the capacity of staff to address alcohol issues), campus authorities such as the judicial administration, campus safety and security, and residence hall staff have significant challenges facing them. Local authorities, such as the town or city police, face similar challenges in managing what occurs at off-campus bars and parties.

Of great significance are the consequences of substance use. The Core Survey asks, "Please indicate how often you have experienced the following due to your drinking or drug use during the last year." While the figures noted in Table 26.3 include the effects of drugs other than alcohol, alcohol is the primary

Table 26.2. Location of Drinking

Location	Percentage of students
Never used	17.5
On-campus events	14.8
Residence hall	35.3
Fraternity or sorority	27.1
Bar or restaurant	35.0
Where you live	45.4
In a car	20.2
Private parties	62.4
Other	22.7

Table 26.3. Frequency of Consequences of Alcohol and Other Drug Use in the Past Year

Consequence	None	Once	Twice	3 to 5	6 to 9	10 or more
Had a hangover	43.4	14.4	10.4	12.8	6.3	12.7
Performed poorly on a test or important project	77.0	9.1	5.8	5.1	1.6	1.5
Been in trouble with police, residence hall, or other campus authorities	84.1	10.1	3.2	1.9	0.3	0.4
Damaged property, pulled fire alarm	91.7	3.5	1.9	1.6	0.5	0.9
Got into an argument or fight	70.6	11.4	7.7	6.2	1.8	2.2
Got nauseated or vomited	49.7	18.2	12.2	11.7	4.1	4.2
Driven a car while under the influence	73.8	8.8	4.9	5.1	2.2	5.3
Been arrested for driving while intoxicated	98.5	0.9	0.2	0.1	0.1	0.2
Missed a class	71.4	7.9	6.9	7.3	2.9	3.6
Been criticized by someone I know	68.1	11.4	8.0	6.7	2.0	3.8
Thought I might have a drinking or other drug problem	90.3	3.8	2.0	1.5	0.6	1.7
Had a memory loss	69.2	10.4	7.7	6.3	2.4	4.1
Done something I later regretted	62.5	15.0	9.3	7.6	2.5	3.1
Tried unsuccessfully to stop using	93.6	2.6	1.6	1.1	0.3	0.8
Been hurt or injured	84.1	7.5	4.2	2.4	0.7	1.1
Have been taken advantage of sexually	87.0	7.6	2.7	1.4	0.3	1.0
Have taken advantage of another sexually	95.1	2.4	1.0	0.7	0.2	0.6
Seriously tried to commit suicide	98.2	1.0	0.4	0.2	0.1	0.2
Seriously thought about suicide	94.8	2.3	1.2	0.7	0.3	0.7

drug of choice in this cohort by a wide margin, and so these percentages can largely be attributed to alcohol consumption.

These results are troubling for many reasons. First, from an academic standpoint, about a quarter of the first-year students are reporting that they have performed poorly on a test or important academic project on account of their use. Second, almost 29 percent have missed a class, and a slightly larger number are reporting blackouts, meaning that brain function is so impaired that memory functions are temporarily lost. Third, over half are reporting hangovers, and half have experienced nausea or vomiting, compromising the ability to function academically.

Finally, from a community standpoint, we are seeing significant percentages of first-year students engaging in risky driving, fights and arguments, and regretted actions. The quality of the academic experience and the broader collegiate experience is compromised when such things happen.

The Core Survey also asks about personal experiences of violence and harassment in and around campus within the past year and whether any such events happened while the respondent was under the influence. Table 26.4 presents the findings among first-year students from calendar years 1999–2001.

Although episodes of violence and harassment were relatively low, the percentages of first-year student victims who were under the influence of alcohol or other drugs at the time of these events is substantially higher. Such an analysis is not meant to blame the victim but instead is intended to demonstrate that first-year students are significantly more vulnerable as a result of alcohol and other drug use. This is particularly true in the area of sexual conduct.

Attitudes toward alcohol and its anticipated effects (sometimes known as "expectancies") have a significant impact on whether students choose to drink. In our first-year cohort, we examined whether students believed alcohol had various effects. Our findings are reported in Table 26.5.

These data provide an understanding of some of the challenges in the collegiate alcohol abuse prevention field. One of the primary issues for traditional-aged first-year students is to fit in and adjust to the social setting of college.

Table 26.4. Experiences of Violence or Harassment and the Percentage of Victims Who Were Under the Influence of Alcohol or Other Drugs

Violent or Harassing Acts	Respondents Who Experienced These Events	Percentage of the Victims Who Were Under the Influence at the Time
Ethnic or racial harassment	5.2%	10.9%
Threats of physical violence	9.9	37.7
Actual physical violence	4.9	33.8
Theft involving force or threat of force	1.9	18.0
Forced sexual touching or fondling	6.2	45.8
Unwanted sexual intercourse	3.5	37.2

Table 26.5. Attitudes Toward Alcohol and Its Anticipated Effects

Belief About Alcohol	Percentage Saying Yes
Enhances social activity	70.2%
Breaks the ice	69.8
Gives people something to do	69.0
Gives people something to talk about	62.9
Allows people to have more fun	57.8
Facilitates a connection with peers	55.0
Facilitates male bonding	54.5
Facilitates sexual opportunities	50.9
Facilitates female bonding	42.9
Makes it easier to deal with stress	38.2
Makes women sexier	25.9
Makes men sexier	15.4
Makes me sexier	15.4
Makes food taste better	14.5

With a clear majority of students saying that alcohol breaks the ice and enhances social activity, they would have substantial reason to include alcohol in their activities. And although some first-year students felt that it makes people sexier, about half believe that alcohol facilitates sexual opportunities. Alcohol and sex are a potentially troublesome combination, given the increased risk of sexual assault and the spread of HIV and other sexually transmitted diseases that can occur with alcohol use.

Other data from the Core Survey indicate that of the 58.4 percent of first-year students who reported that they had had sexual intercourse within the previous year, 20.4 percent reported that they had been drinking during the last occasion when they had sexual intercourse. One only has to consider the one-in-500 college students who are HIV positive (Gayle et al., 1990) to begin to contemplate the potential public health problem.

When we asked if the social atmosphere on their campus promotes alcohol use, 51.9 percent of the first-year students said yes. This contrasts with the 22.6 percent of first-year students who said that the social atmosphere on campus promotes other drug use. There is good news in that 53.3 percent of the sample reported that they lived in a designated alcohol-free, drug-free residence hall. Of those who did not, 29.1 percent said they would like to live in such a residence hall if it were available.

Another area of concern is not only how drinking affects the drinker, but also how other students' drinking affects the environment. This is sometimes referred to as "second-hand effects of drinking," modeled after the concept of "second-hand effects of smoking." To get at such experiences, the Core Survey asks, "In which of the following ways does other students' drinking interfere with your life on or around campus?" The findings from the 1999–2001 first-year student cohort are set out in Table 26.6.

Table 26.6. Second-Hand Effects of Drinking

Reported Experience	Percentage Saying Yes
Makes you feel unsafe	16.3%
Messes up your physical living space (cleanliness, neatness, organization)	25.2
Adversely affects your involvement on an athletic team or in other organized groups	12.1
Prevents you from enjoying events (concerts, sports, social activities)	16.2
Interferes in other way(s)	30.8
Doesn't interfere with my life	45.8

It is evident from these data that a majority of first-year students believe that alcohol has had an adverse effect on the quality of their college experiences.

WHY FIRST-YEAR STUDENTS DRINK

The results from the Core Survey clearly indicate that alcohol is a frequent and often negative part of first-year students' collegiate experience. There are many reasons that first-year, traditional-age students drink. The search for connectedness is a special need of first-year students. Drinking can provide instant camaraderie and thus is seen as desirable. In fraternity pledging, where being accepted, affirmed, and joining a group are relevant issues, similar pressure with respect to alcohol use also occurs. (Fortunately, on many, but not all, campuses, pledging is not allowed during the first year.)

Second, drinking provides excitement. It gives students something to do and something to talk about. It is fun to talk about who did what last night ("Can you believe it!") and who will be doing what tonight and with whom (now *that* can be *really* interesting). Drunk people provide great entertainment.

Third, alcohol structures time. It gives students a way to spend five or six hours they otherwise might not know what to do with, particularly the hours from 10:00 P.M. to 3:00 A.M., when undergraduates are often not yet asleep. At the same time, some might say that alcohol unstructures time and gives students a way to blow off steam resulting from stresses in the academic setting. Probably both principles are at work.

Fourth, alcohol promotes sexuality. Sex seems to be a psychosocial demand in the college setting in addition to being a human need and biological urge. In undergraduate parlance, we hear about students wearing "beer goggles" (translation: everyone looks good through the bottom of a beer bottle; that is, if one is intoxicated enough) and "hooking up," which can mean anything from getting acquainted to engaging in sexual activities. Never mind that when drinking, students may fail to take precautions against pregnancy or sexually transmitted diseases, or will wake up with someone they do not know, or will sleep unprotected with someone who is infected with HIV, or will commit or be the victim of date rape. The risks are significant, but the peer pressure and environmental demands to be sexually active in college are powerful forces, and alcohol promotes sexual activity. Thus, students have considerable motivation to drink on this account.

Fifth, alcohol facilitates male bonding, a concept frequently referenced when discussing alcohol, men, and fraternities. It is an important issue. Like all of us, college men have attachment needs, though these are frequently suppressed for fear of appearing unmanly. With the slap-on-the-back, throw-care-to-the-wind camaraderie provided by alcohol, college males can feel connected with one another in a brotherly or paternal or best-friend-pal kind of way. The last time some of our students un-self-consciously had such an experience (while sober) was during childhood, and so drinking helps fill an important need. (Gender roles allow women to be less constrained in their emotional expression in this regard, at least in our experience, and so alcohol takes on less importance in meeting affiliative needs. However, women are still at risk because biologically they can become more intoxicated at the same body weight and consumption levels as men.)

Sixth, alcohol is the world's oldest and most popular tranquilizer and anesthetic. It reduces fears and anesthetizes feelings. It works well, it is fast, and it is inexpensive (and often free). These attributes of alcohol are not lost on students.

Seventh, society is ambivalent about alcohol, though not about other drugs, and we communicate this attitude to students. What other psychoactive drug is legal for people over twenty-one? A dean we know asked on several occasions if we really cared if an under-age student has a single beer while watching a ballgame with a roommate, a reasonable question. At the same time, the law is clear. So we do indeed give students mixed messages, and they have learned to read between the lines.

Eighth, alcohol is portrayed by the advertising and alcohol beverage industries as sexy. Television and magazine advertisements suggest that drinking will make one more attractive and socially successful. These advertisements often contain overt, covert, or subliminal sexual imagery. This strategy is not specific to alcohol, of course—sex has been used to sell everything from cars to cigarettes to athletic equipment. The reason is that it works. But these commercial messages perpetuate the image of sexual opportunity, and the linkage between alcohol and sex clearly encourages excessive drinking.

Ninth, alcohol is associated with college students' sense of autonomy, and its use comes to represent an assertion of their rights. Having escaped the restrictions and structure of home and parents, students want to taste the freedom that college and drinking seem to represent, and they strongly defend their right to drink.

Finally, students generally do not think of challenging another student's abusive drinking as acceptable. No student wants to be an alcoholic, and no one wants to think that his or her friend or classmate is one. We can add to this the fear of treading on another student's autonomy or of offending a peer. So the otherwise corrective feedback loop that students can sometimes use to address each other's bothersome behaviors becomes inoperative when it comes to abusive drinking. This void leaves drinking problems unaddressed and contributes to their continuation. Another term for this is *enabling*.

Some of these issues facing traditional-age students may also affect nontraditional students, such as the worry about fitting in and surviving academically. Furthermore, adult learners may come to college feeling awkward because of their age and may feel out of place. However, many come with work experiences in the past or present, many are married and have children, and developmentally there may be less need for bonding, sexual experimentation, and assertion of independence. They may not reside in residence halls, fraternities, and sororities. There is greater life experience and greater maturity. It is not surprising, therefore, that older students typically demonstrate somewhat less heavy episodic drinking and somewhat fewer adverse consequences than younger students (Presley et al., 1995). Even so, the research shows that older students are still subject to risk due to the misuse of alcohol, and they may have had more years to engage in problematic drinking behaviors or to solidify their drinking patterns. Thus, we need to pay attention to nontraditional students as well when we consider the issue of collegiate alcohol use.

Each of the items identified in this section is worthy of a much lengthier discussion. Mentioned briefly and together, however, they provide an overview of some important collegiate drinking dynamics that affect students, and first-year students in particular. Clearly, we have a lot of work to do to understand and better address student drinking in our midst. By doing so, we will help first-year students and all students reach their maximum potential to grow and develop in healthy ways.

STRATEGIES DESIGNED TO PREVENT ABUSIVE DRINKING

What must colleges and universities do to respond to the overwhelming influence of alcohol use and abuse on the first-year collegiate experience? The reality is that drinking on campuses has persisted and represents a considerable ongoing problem, although there have been slight reductions in annual prevalence and binge drinking rates over the past twenty years (Johnston et al., 2001). During this time, several philosophies regarding alcohol use and alcohol abuse prevention have been espoused, including "maturing out," individual change, parental notification, social norms, and motivation and feedback.

Maturing Out

An early philosophy that characterized much of higher education until the 1970s was to consider excessive drinking as a rite of passage, a developmental stage, that students would stop as they progressed toward their chosen professions

(Jessor & Jessor, 1975). This sometimes is discussed under the rubric of "maturing out." In reality, some students do and some students do not mature out. A dean of students at a small private college shared with us that all three of his senior-year roommates, who were heavy drinkers, are now, some twenty years later, confirmed alcoholics. So the strategy of waiting for students to outgrow their abusive drinking did little to prevent excessive drinking, and sometimes resulted in alcohol problems beyond college.

Individual Change

Recognizing that some students were more vulnerable to the negative effects of prolonged excessive alcohol use, an intervention strategy used in the 1980s and early 1990s focused on changing the "individual" within the academic environment. The idea was that those who experienced problems with alcohol did so because of some characterological deficit or genetic predisposition (Wallack & DeJong, 1995). The prevention programming response to this view included education outreach programs and advertising about the legal and personal consequences of use and misuse.

Though useful in selected individual cases, this strategy did not stem the tide of campuswide alcohol abuse. With this approach, the line between education and treatment was not always clear, but perhaps that was unavoidable, because education and treatment have much in common. But perhaps the last word on this type of approach came from Herbert Kleber, former assistant director for demand reduction of the Office of National Drug Control Policy, who made the wry and astute observation, "Education is the cure to the extent that ignorance is the disease" (personal communication, 1989). By this he meant that students have the information but do not necessarily change their behavior. In spite of the limitations of this strategy, prevention programming is still a well-accepted component of college student health and student affairs efforts to deal with alcohol use and abuse throughout the United States.

Parental Notification

Since the passage of the Higher Education Reauthorization Act of 1998, parental notification for alcohol infractions is another strategy that has been used as part of the prevention and disciplinary process at a number of institutions. This legislation has allowed colleges to notify parents of underage drinkers who violate campus alcohol regulations. Preliminary reports describe some degree of efficacy in reducing the number of alcohol violations occurring at these institutions (Palmer, Lohman, Gehring, Carlson, & Garrett, 2001), although more studies are needed to fully assess efficacy.

Social Norms Initiatives

A more recent strategy used in prevention programming has been the "social norms" initiative. According to this view, the environment is the focus of attention rather than the individual student. This strategy is based on the notion that if the environmental norms and expectations around drinking can be changed in a constructive direction (meaning downward), then individual students' drinking patterns will follow suit. It is based on the finding that students consistently overestimate the amount of drinking (and drug use and sexual activities, for that matter) that other students engage in and then try to live up to what they believe is the norm, not realizing that the situation is far more conservative than they had perceived (Perkins, 2002). Although one recent study did not find evidence to support the efficacy of this approach (Wechsler et al., 2003), a larger body of evidence suggests that when the norms are correctly perceived (which means adjusted downward), drinking declines as well (Perkins, 2002, 2003; Haines & Spear, 1996).

Motivation and Feedback Strategies

Brief motivation and feedback strategies are yet another type of research-based intervention that has received attention. Incorporating information about the properties of alcohol, drinking-reduction techniques, and personalized feedback, "motivational interviewing" has shown some promise in large-scale demonstration projects involving fraternity members, first-year students, and other groups (Larimer & Cronce, 2002). Motivational interviewing entails presenting students with nonjudgmental conversations regarding drinking, expectations, and consequences, and it capitalizes on students' ability to rethink their behavior. It does not necessarily espouse abstinence, but rather takes a "harm-reduction" approach by taking students where they are and helping them rethink their behavior to make informed choices. It often goes by the name of BASICS (Brief Alcohol Screening and Intervention for College Students) (Dimeff, Baer, Kivlahan, & Marlatt, 1999).

As an example of this approach, a harm-reduction conversation might entail the question, "How can you keep yourself from getting into disciplinary trouble again?" with the answer coming back, "I'll cut back to eight drinks rather than twelve." This would be seen as a positive step forward on the part of a student and is reinforced. Ideally, it would be followed up with further conversation as to what happened when the student actually consumed eight drinks.

What these approaches have in common is excitement, energy, and commitment on the part of their proponents, and frequently substantial penetration into the campus environment. These factors may be as important as any actual approach that is undertaken, whether it is social norms, motivational interviewing, advertising, education, outreach, or peer counseling programs. And indeed, it is likely that market penetration, energy, enthusiasm, and consistency of message are all important factors in achieving success, no matter what the approach.

Furthermore, there is some research-based evidence to show that student participation in programming efforts is important. Ziemelis, Bucknam, and Elfessi (2002) conducted a meta-analysis looking at outcomes of ninety-four FIPSE-funded prevention programs and found that three factors—student participation and involvement, educational and informational processes that encouraged communication between students and professionals, and policy implementation that incorporated significant student input—were most closely associated with demonstrable reductions in binge drinking practices. The thread that weaves through all three factors is student involvement. This is a particularly helpful piece of information, and one of the few that has been demonstrated through research.

Although we do not have the final word on what strategies work, there have been modest decreases in both annual prevalence and binge drinking rates in the past two decades (Johnston et al., 2001). It would appear that although the problem of alcohol on the college campus is significant, continued attention to programming efforts appears to be having some desirable effects, albeit in a slow, incremental fashion. However, none of these strategies has had a dramatic effect on reducing alcohol use and abuse among college students.

ALCOHOL OUTREACH PROGRAMS FOR FIRST-YEAR STUDENTS

The results of the Core Survey clearly indicate that first-year students use and abuse alcohol, even though most are not legally entitled to drink. So what specifically must be done to help first-year students deal with this issue? There are many different approaches to alcohol use and abuse, and they may be separated into programs that educate and those that attempt to change behaviors. Certainly there is a place for alcohol education programs focused on information, and there are many examples of such programs, including alcohol information sessions during orientation and various media approaches, including student newspaper ads, posters, and handouts. The content of these efforts typically addresses basic information about how alcohol affects the body, the negative consequences of drinking, under-age drinking, and related topics.

Another outreach opportunity occurs when a faculty member is unable to meet his or her class, and alcohol educators provide a "Don't Cancel That Class" program offering alcohol education in lieu of canceling the class. More sophisticated efforts include the concept of curriculum infusion, where alcohol issues are touched on in the course content of various classes, such as biology, nutrition, health education, psychology, and a wide variety of other disciplines. First-year seminars offer an especially effective way to reach first-year students.

Also, if there are sufficient resources, peer counseling and peer educational programs can be used. Peer educators can be helpful in offering outreach programs, provided that they are sufficiently trained and supervised. They can also serve as resources for other students on an individual basis if the program is properly marketed and respected by first-year students. However, peer programs tend to take considerable staff time to manage and supervise, and the conventional wisdom is that such programs tend to benefit the peer counselors at least as much as the students they serve. Even so, these programs may be beneficial if there are sufficient staffing, training, and resources.

As pointed out earlier in this chapter, education is the cure to the extent that ignorance is the disease. Information-only approaches rarely, if ever, produce desired changes in alcohol consumption, so other approaches that are designed to effect behavioral change must be part of any first-year alcohol programming.

Two approaches discussed in greater detail earlier in this chapter seem to have some merit. Social norms initiatives, which focus on the campus drinking environment rather than the student, appear to result in declines in drinking behaviors. Brief motivational feedback approaches involving motivational interviewing techniques also have shown promise. But we would be the first to admit that no one approach has been proved to be completely effective in reducing alcohol consumption and negative alcohol-related behavior.

Alcohol outreach programs have the advantage of providing large numbers of first-year students with exposure to the topic and contact with those who are doing the alcohol prevention work. In all these activities, credibility on the part of outreach programmers is essential; otherwise, students will not hear the message. Put more succinctly, these programmers need to be seen—in student parlance—as "cool" or "okay." In addition, educational programs should steer clear of abstinence messages, as these will lose many in the audience. A focus on health and informed decision making has a much greater chance of success.

Another approach is to create alcohol-free and drug-free residence halls. Some first-year students prefer to live in a residence hall where alcohol and other drugs are prohibited, on the assumption that the problems associated with use of these substances would be reduced or eliminated. Since this approach is relatively new, there is little evidence one way or the other to demonstrate that these residential environments actually reduce alcohol-related problems. However, it is probably prudent for colleges and universities to provide such living options because some first-year students prefer them.

Finally, substantial efforts need to be made to reach out to Greek organizations because they can heavily affect the campus culture, and this influences how first-year students drink (or how they think they need to drink). Moreover, while alcohol outreach programs can be put in place as stand-alone programs, they will be much more effective if they are integrated into other institutional efforts to promote first-year student success, such as orientation, learning-centered residential programs, and especially first-year seminars.

The reality is, however, that all these efforts have yet to fully and completely deal with the problem of alcohol use and abuse among first-year students, even though modest gains have been made. We must continue to refine current strategies, develop new and innovative approaches to reduce the negative effects of alcohol use and abuse among first-year students, and assess the effectiveness of these efforts.

ASSESSMENT OF ALCOHOL INITIATIVES

Assessment of alcohol prevention initiatives is important to this work, and the question naturally arises as to how to measure the impact of campus-based alcohol interventions. As Upcraft points out in Chapter Twenty-Seven, there are essentially three ways to assess: quantitative, qualitative, or a combination of both. With respect to quantitative measures, there are both invasive and non-invasive methods of collecting data.

Nonintrusive quantitative approaches entail counting or looking for information that is already available in the collegiate community, such as the number of parties registered with the campus police or Greek Life office, the number of alcohol-related admissions to the local or campus emergency room, the number of health service visits for alcohol-related injuries, the dollar value of alcohol-related residence hall damage, and even the number of beer cans and plastic cups on fraternity grounds the morning after a party. From health services and other sources, the number of alcohol-related unwanted pregnancies, sexually transmitted infections, sexual assaults, and alcohol poisonings may be instructive. We can also note the number of alcohol education outreach programs offered to residence halls, athletic teams, and Greek chapters, as well as the number of attendees. The number of students seen at college mental health services for alcohol-related problems is yet another nonintrusive measure of alcohol use and abuse.

Invasive approaches are those where a specific activity is undertaken to gather data from the subjects of the investigation, such as use of a questionnaire or an individual or group interview. As noted earlier, the Core Alcohol and Drug Survey is one such survey instrument (Presley, Meilman, & Cashin, 1996). This instrument reports demographics, use patterns, age of first use, direct consequences, second-hand effects of drinking, violence, campus climate, and beliefs about alcohol. This information is useful on an institutional level to assess the impact of alcohol education outreach and prevention programs and was designed specifically for that purpose. The College Alcohol Study (Wechsler et al., 1994) is another useful survey instrument, although to date this questionnaire has been used primarily as a research tool in national aggregate studies. National surveys can be useful not only in assessing the effectiveness of alcohol education initiatives, but also in tracking alcohol-related issues over time and comparing results from similar institutions. Individual and group interviews could theoretically also be used but are not very efficient in assessing large numbers of students.

Qualitative approaches (individual interviews and focus groups) can provide an important context and better understanding for the data collected through qualitative methods. Qualitative approaches can be far more useful, however, in looking at issues such as why first-year students drink and the role of peer pressure in alcohol consumption. Focus groups of a cross-section of all first-year students and interviews with selected groups of students such as athletes, Greek organization officers and members, residence hall staff and students, judicial administrators and judicial board members, women, men, racial and ethnic minorities, adult students, and others can provide greater insight into the problems of alcohol use and abuse among first-year students. Qualitative approaches can help provide an understanding of alcohol issues in terms of institutional culture—that unique corporate personality that every institution of higher education possesses and which has a profound impact on students, staff, and faculty.

Finally, the Council for the Advancement of Standards in Higher Education (1997) has published professional standards and guidelines for alcohol and other drug programs that can provide guidance to institutions that wish to initiate or assess their alcohol and other drug prevention initiatives.

RECOMMENDATIONS

Based on our work and that in the field over the past twenty-five years, it is clear that alcohol is a problem that is not going to go away. It is woven into the fabric of the collegiate experience as well as society as a whole. Prohibition was tried, and it failed. We need to work with the reality of campus alcohol use and abuse, and we need to help campuses find effective approaches to the problem. There is no magic cure, and there is no single answer. Nevertheless, there are some activities and initiatives that will help address and mitigate the difficulties caused by alcohol:

- *Create a dialogue and agreement among institutional administrators as to what time, effort, and resources can be dedicated to addressing alcohol issues.* Without a common understanding, a shared philosophy, and agreement as to resources, it is difficult, if not impossible, to work on campus alcohol issues in a comprehensive or effective way.
- *Initiate an alcohol and substance abuse task force to serve as a coordinating body or review team* to look at issues of policy, enforcement, outreach programming, education, and treatment. Representatives of the faculty, residence life, campus safety and security, the mental health service, the health service, the dean of students office, the judicial affairs office, and the president's office should all be included. Ideally, such a task force should include the highest levels of administration possible to maximize its impact.
- *Offer alcohol outreach programs with extensive market penetration* because they are important in reaching students who would not otherwise seek help or be exposed to education about alcohol issues. As noted earlier, though, "education is the cure to the extent that ignorance is the disease." Education alone will not solve the problem, so programs designed to reduce alcohol use and abuse such as social norms initiatives or brief motivational interviewing and feedback approaches should also be implemented, along with treatment offered by the counseling and health services.
- *Establish an alcohol programming and treatment coordinator position,* and supplement this position with additional personnel as needed to ensure appropriate staffing and coverage.
- *Develop policies that encourage students and organizations to seek medical help when there are health emergencies related to alcohol abuse,* because saving lives is paramount. "Good Samaritan" policies, which eliminate or minimize disciplinary consequences where help is sought, are useful in this regard

(Meilman, 1992). Such policies help to lower barriers for students seeking emergency care for themselves and others in cases of alcohol poisoning. Nevertheless, Good Samaritan policies are not meant to absolve students of alcohol-related misconduct such as vandalism or sexual assault, nor are they meant to absolve students or organizations of flagrant or repeated violations.

- *Train residence hall staff to know how to intervene with and address students whose drinking has become problematic* for themselves or to the other residents whose health or educational experience has been compromised on account of alcohol consumption and related behavior.

- *Provide counseling and mental health staff on campus with needed training* to be able to competently assess substance abuse issues, as well as provide ongoing treatment where it is feasible. Effective working relationships with off-campus treatment facilities as well as local Alcoholics Anonymous groups are useful when students require more or different types of service than the counseling center can provide.

- *Train health services personnel to inquire about alcohol use as part of a health history and to respond with appropriate interventions.* They also need to ask about alcohol use in relation to accidents, injuries, unprotected sex, unwanted pregnancies, and sexually transmitted diseases and to provide non-judgmental guidance as to what students can do to protect their health better.

- *Establish policies ensuring coordination of care with the local hospital's emergency room,* so that students can get follow-up health and counseling care on campus after they are seen at the emergency room for alcohol-related difficulties.

- *Develop campus judicial system procedures for dealing with students who commit alcohol-related infractions of the campus code of conduct.* These will no doubt involve coordination with the counseling service, the dean of students office, and other campus agencies.

- *Provide a substantial amount of alcohol-free activity programming in the evenings and on weekends,* particularly late at night, in order to provide alternatives to local bars and parties.

- *Establish a town-gown task force for dealing with alcohol issues of mutual concern.* Such a group should include representatives from the institution that meet on a regular basis with community representatives such as the local police, the local hospital, the public school system, social service agencies with alcohol-related missions, town council members, town executives, local bar owners, and alcohol distributors.

- *Reconsider policies of parental notification for alcohol-related disciplinary infractions.* Some campuses have begun to notify parents of alcohol-related infractions of the campus code of conduct. Whether parental notification makes sense for a given institution and fits with the institution's culture is a decision that only an individual institution can make. However, preliminary informal reports suggest that there may be some utility to such notification as a way to minimize or eliminate further drinking problems.

CONCLUSION

No one approach by itself will fully address campus alcohol problems or save all students from alcohol-related difficulties. Time and experience have demonstrated that that is an unrealistic goal. Rather, we should work toward mitigating the ill effects of alcohol abuse and achieving campus social environments that are less tolerant of alcohol-related misbehavior and drunkenness. In so doing, we will protect first-year students from pressure to consume alcohol to excess and perhaps spare them years of pain during the course of their college careers, as well as later in life.

PART SIX

ASSESSING THE FIRST COLLEGE YEAR

Irst-year students' participation in first-year student courses, programs, and services have some intended and desired outcomes, such as academic achievement and persistence to graduation, as well as the many others defined in the introduction to this book: developing intellectual and academic competence, establishing and maintaining interpersonal relationships, exploring identity development, deciding on a career, maintaining health and wellness, considering the faith and spiritual dimensions of life, developing multicultural awareness, developing civic responsibility, and other institution-specific desired outcomes.

Of course, there are many questions related to assessment—for example: Do courses, programs, and services meet the needs of first-year students, faculty, the institution, and other stakeholders? Are first-year students satisfied with these offerings? Do these courses, programs, and services meet nationally accepted standards? Do they compare favorably with other comparable institutions? Are they cost-effective? These questions must be answered because it is the only certain way to ensure the quality and accountability of first-year initiatives. Moreover, the only certain way to answer them is by implementing a continuous, systematic, and comprehensive assessment effort.

In Chapter Twenty-Seven, M. Lee Upcraft discusses the many reasons that assessment is important to first-year courses, programs, and services and offers a comprehensive model for assessing all aspects of these efforts. In Chapter Twenty-Eight, M. Lee Upcraft, Jennifer L. Crissman Ishler, and Randy L. Swing offer advice to those who want to begin an assessment program, and describe a step-by-step process for assessing first-year efforts. In Chapter Twenty-Nine, Randy L. Swing and M. Lee Upcraft describe and discuss the many quantitative and qualitative instruments that can be used to assess first-year student success.

CHAPTER TWENTY-SEVEN

Assessing the First Year of College

M. Lee Upcraft

Perhaps no other area in higher education has been more subjected to assessment than efforts to promote first-year student success. For example, first-year seminars seem to be held to a higher standard of assessment than almost all other academic courses, subjected to questions about learning outcomes, academic respectability, and their possible relationship to academic achievement and retention that are seldom, if ever, asked about other courses. Also, orientation programs are frequently under fire for their supposed "fun and games" emphasis. And the most burning question is, In an era of declining resources, can we really afford all these "nonessential" (in the minds of some) courses, programs, and services for first-year students?

The cold reality is that the effectiveness of efforts to promote first-year student success is not self-evident, nor should it be. There should be evidence of their effectiveness, evidence that is gathered as a result of a comprehensive assessment program based on well-designed and controlled assessment studies, systematically and continuously conducted. Put another way, Peter Ewell (2001) suggests that assessment must answer two basic questions: "What happened?" and "What mattered?" In practitioners' terms, how do we know if what we did to enhance first-year student success actually worked?

This chapter introduces some of the basic definitions surrounding the issue of assessment, provides some reasons to assess, offers a comprehensive model for assessing the first year of college, explores the ethics of assessment, and

---

This chapter is a summary of issues discussed in greater detail in J. H. Schuh and M. L. Upcraft, *Assessment Practice in Student Affairs: An Applications Manual* (San Francisco: Jossey-Bass, 2001), and in M. L. Upcraft and J. H. Schuh, *Assessment in Student Affairs, A Guide for Practitioners* (San Francisco: Jossey-Bass, 1996).

offers some advice to practitioners. Assessment perhaps represents the greatest challenge of all in creating climates that promote first-year student success, and institutions must support assessment if they expect to achieve this goal.

SOME BASIC DEFINITIONS

One of the first problems encountered when discussing assessment is definitional. Too often, assessment is thought of as simply doing a survey or running a focus group. Some terms are used interchangeably (*assessment* and *evaluation*), some phrases are used incorrectly ("statistics show . . . "), and some terms are so vague as to strip them of any commonly accepted meaning (*quality* or *excellence*).

We start with the term *assessment.* There are many definitions in the assessment and evaluation literature, with no conclusive consensus among the so-called experts. For the purposes of this chapter, *assessment* is any effort to gather, analyze, and interpret evidence that describes institutional, divisional, or agency effectiveness (Upcraft & Schuh, 1996).

Effectiveness includes not only assessing student learning outcomes, but also assessing other important indicators, such as cost-effectiveness, clientele satisfaction, clientele needs, professional standards, benchmarking, policies and practices, and outcomes such as student learning, academic achievement, and persistence. Assessment of the first year of college is not restricted to students, but may include other constituents within the institution, such as the faculty, administration, and governing boards, and outside the institution, such as alumni, legislators, funding sources, and accreditation agencies.

One further clarification when using the term *assessment* is that it does not include assessing individual student or other individual clientele outcomes except in the aggregate. For example, while an institution may not want any information about why an individual student may persist to graduation, it may want to know why, in the aggregate, students drop out or graduate.

Assessment must be contrasted with but also linked to *evaluation.* Here there is less agreement among the experts. Again, for the purposes of this chapter, *evaluation* is any effort to use assessment evidence to improve institutional, departmental, divisional, or institutional effectiveness (Upcraft & Schuh, 1996). While assessment describes effectiveness, evaluation uses these descriptions in order to improve effectiveness, however that might be defined by an institution. For example, determining why adult students have difficulty in making a successful transition to college is assessment. Using that assessment to make changes in policy and practice to ease adult students' transition to college is evaluation.

Another term also must be defined: *measurement. Measurement* refers to the methods used to gather information for the purposes of assessment. Typically, measurement methods are divided roughly into two not very discrete categories: quantitative and qualitative. Quantitative methodologies assign numbers to objects, events, or observations according to some rule (Rossman & El-Khawas, 1987). Instruments with established psychometric properties are used to collect data, and statistical methods are used to analyze data and draw conclusions. For example, the ability to predict college success might involve gathering all the quantifiable data about those variables thought to predict persistence and degree completion, such as high school grades, scores on standardized tests, involvement in high school activities, and parents' education and income. These data might then be correlated with subsequent student behavior (dropping out or persisting) to determine which ones and in which combination best predict college success.

Qualitative methodologies are the detailed descriptions of situations, events, people, interactions, and observed behaviors; the use of direct quotations from people about their experiences, attitudes, beliefs, and thoughts; and the analysis of excerpts or entire passages from documents, correspondence, records, and case histories (Patton, 1990). For example, an assessment of first-year student needs might include individual interviews and focus groups of first-year students, asking them to recall what, if anything, the institution did to help or hinder them in their transition to college.

The selection of an assessment methodology may not be an either-or decision; in fact, there are many instances when the use of both methodologies is not only appropriate but also more powerful. These two methodologies also tend to feed each other because the results from each can suggest promising work for the other.

Another definition worth mentioning, although it will not be the focus of this chapter, is *research.* In the 1960s and 1970s, it was fashionable to use the term *research* to refer also to assessment and evaluation efforts. This term proved to be confusing, particularly to faculty, who had a much narrower definition of research. When comparing *research* and *assessment,* Erwin (1991) argues that although they share many processes in common, they differ in at least two respects. First, assessment, informed by theory, guides good practice, while research guides and tests theory and conceptual foundations. Second, assessment typically has implications for a single institution, while research typically has broader implications for higher education. I would add a third: assessment studies often cannot meet traditional social science research criteria in determining their rigor, viability, and worth. According to Cronbach (1982), while assessments use research methods, the central purpose of assessment differs from that of basic social science research because assessment is designed to fit different institutional and political contexts. He argued that many methods of social science research are ill suited to assessment studies designs.

Upcraft and Schuh (2002) offer a series of modifications necessary to conduct viable and useful assessment studies:

- Resource limitations: Assessment studies are often modified because of limited money, as well as staff who lack the time and sufficient assessment expertise.

- Time limitations: Assessment studies often must meet much shorter time deadlines than research studies. Often the window of opportunity to influence policy and practice may be as little as a month, and rarely is it more than a year.

- Organizational contexts: Different organizational contexts may dictate different assessment approaches, even if the problems are the same. Furthermore, the same organizations may vary over time, forcing modifications in an original assessment design.

- Design limitations: While assessment studies are conceived using the best possible designs, problems can arise as the project proceeds. Low response rates, useable samples that do not reflect the characteristics of the population, or poor attendance at focus groups may dictate modifications in the original design.

- Political contexts: As Schuh and Upcraft (2000) suggested, assessments almost always occur in political contexts that must be taken into account in assessment designs. A study may never be done, be discontinued in progress, or suppressed on completion because the results may be politically or ideologically unacceptable to institutional leadership.

The question then becomes, When does an assessment design become so modified that it should never be done, or discarded even if conducted? Rossi and Freeman (1996) argued that the assessment investigator must choose the best possible design, having taken into account the potential importance of the program, the practicality and feasibility of each design, and the probability that the design chosen will produce useful and credible results. Schuh and Upcraft (2000) add the caveat that all modifications must be clearly identified when an assessment study is published, cautioning all prospective audiences to take into account the study's various limitations as they decide what credence to give the study. My colleague Pat Terenzini probably said it best: "In assessment, you start with the perfect design (recognizing that there really isn't any such animal) and then keep making modifications and compromising until you have a doable study." The failure to understand the differences between research and assessment has enormous consequences for the credibility of assessment studies, particularly with faculty well schooled in the tenets of social science research.

THE BASIC QUESTION:
WHY ARE WE DOING THIS ASSESSMENT?

The pressure to demonstrate the worth of efforts to promote first-year student success continues to be high, and we cannot afford to ignore the tough questions surrounding their effectiveness. Questions range from quality and efficiency to the ultimate question: Do we really need this first-year course, program, or service? So the first answer to the question, "Why are we doing this assessment?" may be the very survival of efforts to promote first-year student success. A comprehensive assessment program can help answer these questions in systematic and credible ways.

One might easily respond, "Isn't there a substantial body of research demonstrating that many, if not most, efforts to promote first-year student success contribute to first-year students' learning, personal development, academic achievement, persistence, transition to college, and other desirable outcomes?" The answer is yes (see Pascarella & Terenzini, 2005; Kuh, Branch Douglas, Lund, & Ramin-Gyurnek, 1994), but this fact often does not help for three reasons. First, some of this research is poorly done and thus lacks credibility. Second, even if done well, this research is not well known among administrators and faculty and not often taken into account in developing and implementing courses, programs, and services. And even if it is well known, the question of local applicability always arises. "Okay, so the research evidence shows that first-year students who enroll in first-year seminars are more likely to earn higher grades and persist to graduation than students who do not, but is that true at our institution?" National studies may be more elegant in design, sophisticated in research techniques, and more lucid in the presentation and results, but locally produced studies, if well done, often will have more impact on a particular campus. In this sense, all assessment is local.

In general, I believe assessment can and will demonstrate the effectiveness and worth of efforts to promote first-year student success and show positive relationships between student participation in these efforts and curricular goals (such as content mastery, higher-order cognitive skills development, academic achievement, persistence), as well as cocurricular goals (such as identity development, diversity awareness, social development, and spiritual development). However, one should be prepared to deal with local results that may not be consistent with the findings of national studies, since students make their own environments based on interactions with their institutions (Baird, 1996). Furthermore, even if there are local studies that are consistent with national findings, policymakers and decision makers may choose to ignore this evidence for other reasons. Thus, all assessment is a potential risk: we can never be certain that local assessment studies will have the desired impact of demonstrating the worth of what we are doing to promote first-year student success.

While survival may be a primary motivator for assessing the first year of college, there are other reasons. Even if it is demonstrated that efforts to promote first-year student success are essential and needed, a second answer to why we are doing a study may be to assess quality. Assessment can be a powerful tool in linking goals to outcomes, helping define quality, and determining if efforts to promote first-year student success are of the highest quality.

A third reason for assessment is to gauge affordability and cost-effectiveness. The questions often go something like this: "Sure, this course or that program or that service is needed, and there is evidence of their quality, but in an era of declining resources, can we afford them? Can we continue to fund them at current levels? Can we afford them at all?" Decisions to eliminate first-year initiatives based on their affordability may have to be made, but other affordability questions abound. Might it be less expensive to outsource this service or program? Can the goals of a first-year seminar be met in other courses? Can this service or program generate income from fees? Can this service do more with less, or less with less? And how do we know? Unfortunately, these decisions are often made without adequate assessment, in part because there are few, if any, cost-effectiveness models used in higher education.

Another reason for assessing the first year of college is strategic planning. Strategic planning, according to Baldridge (1983), examines the big issues of an organization: its mission, purpose, long-range goals, relationship to its environment, share of the market, interactions with other organizations. Since many higher education institutions are seriously involved with strategic planning, it is important that first-year faculty and administrators be active and effective participants in this process. Assessment contributes to strategic planning by helping define goals and objectives and pointing to critical issues or problems that must be resolved successfully if the organization is to achieve its goals. Assessment is especially important in the early phases of strategic planning to identify strengths, weaknesses, and opportunities for the future. It is also critical in the later stages of planning, when evaluation of policies and programs occurs.

A fifth answer to the question, "Why are we doing this study?" is to gain more information and insight into policy development and decision making. What evidence do we have to help us make a decision or develop or revise a policy? Assessment can provide systematic information, which can be critical in developing policy, and decision makers make valid judgments about policy, decide on important issues, and make decisions about resource allocations for efforts to promote first-year student success. Making these kind of judgments based on systematic information is not only important within an institution, but also with stakeholders outside the institution, such as boards of control, legislatures, alumni, and the general public.

Assessing the first year of college may also be done for political reasons. Sometimes we must do assessment because a stakeholder of importance wants some information, which makes it politically important to produce. It may be the president of the institution, a faculty governing group, an influential governing board member, an outspoken legislator, or a concerned alumnus or alumna. We must also be concerned about the political impact of our assessment findings. All assessment is political; thus, assessment investigators must be attuned to the impact of their studies from the moment an assessment idea emerges. If one of the purposes of assessment is to influence policy and practice, then the political context within which decisions are made must be accounted for in the assessment process.

The last answer to the question, "Why are we doing this assessment?" is that it may be required for accreditation. According to the Commission on Higher Education's *Characteristics of Excellence in Higher Education* (1994), one of the criteria for accreditation is outcomes or institutional effectiveness. "The deciding factor in assessing the effectiveness of any institution is evidence of the extent to which it achieves its goals and objectives. The necessity of seeking such evidence continually is inescapable; one of the primary hallmarks of faculty, administration, and governing boards is the skill with which they raise questions about institutional effectiveness, seek answers and significantly improve procedures in the light of their findings" (pp. 17–18). This moves assessment from the "nice to have if you can afford it" category to the "you better have it if you want to stay accredited" category.

All of these reasons are important because the first step in the assessment process is to determine why a particular study needs to be done, and there may be one or several answers. Different assessment designs will be developed depending on the reasons the study is conducted. Too often, however, an assessment study is started without a clear idea of why it is being done, thus often yielding results that are not useful to policymakers in addressing the problem that precipitated the study in the first place.

A COMPREHENSIVE MODEL FOR ASSESSING THE FIRST COLLEGE YEAR

Assuming that the "why" question has been answered, the next question is, "What should we do?" Too often, an assessment study is planned without any real understanding of the options available. Crissman and Upcraft (2001) developed a comprehensive model for assessing the first year of college, adapted from Upcraft and Schuh (1996), that describes eight components of a comprehensive assessment program.

Know the Backgrounds and Characteristics of First-Year Students

Efforts to promote student success, both inside and outside the classroom, should be based on what is known about the first-year cohort. For example, how is this group represented by gender, race/ethnicity, age, marital status, disability, and other defining characteristics? It is also important to know, particularly from the point of view of faculty, first-year students' overall level of academic preparation and their possible need for improvement in their academic skills. Although such information is almost always a part of institutional databases, often these data are not presented in concise, readable reports that are useful to faculty in their courses.

Outside the classroom, it is important to keep track of who participates in the institutional initiatives designed to promote first-year student success. How many and what type of first-year students use the services, programs, and facilities designed for this purpose? This component is very important, because if first-year students do not use the available services, programs, or facilities, then the institution's intended purposes cannot be achieved. However, sheer numbers do not tell the whole story, especially if users are not representative of entering students in general. The quantity and distribution of users have important implications for policy and practice and must be assessed.

Finally, there are some commercially available instruments that provide information about entering students. The most frequently used and best known of these instruments is the *Annual Survey of American College Freshmen,* administered by the Higher Education Research Institute at UCLA. Others include the *Entering-Student Questionnaire* published by the National Center for Higher Education Management Systems, and the *Entering Student Survey* by the American College Testing Program.

Assess First-Year Students' Needs

Assessing the needs of entering students is a crucial activity in the overall assessment process. This is especially critical for first-year students because efforts to promote first-year student success must in part be based on these needs. In the classroom, faculty should be aware of the motivations, career objectives, possible needs for academic remediation, and others. Outside the classroom, what kinds of services, programs, and facilities do entering students (and often their families) need, based on student and staff perceptions, institutional expectations, and research on student needs? How do we distinguish between wants and needs? How do we know if what we offer fits with our entering students?

The problem is how to identify these needs. One important source for identifying first-year student needs is the existing research on student needs. For example, in the Introduction to this book, Upcraft, Gardner, and Barefoot offer a framework for considering first-year student needs, including their intellectual and academic, interpersonal, identity, career, health and wellness, spiritual, diversity, and civic responsibility needs.

A second source for identifying first-year student needs is to ask students themselves. Although this is an effective way of determining needs, it is best done after they have been enrolled for a while rather than at the start of their enrollment. For example, entering students can be asked, either individually or in focus groups, to reflect on their experiences during the first few weeks of college and discuss what the institution did or might have done to help them during this time. A few commercially available general needs assessment instruments might be helpful, such as the *College Student Needs Assessment Survey* (American College Testing Program) or the *Community College Goals Inventory* (Educational Testing Service).

Assess Entering Students' Satisfaction with Their Collegiate Experiences

Even if efforts to promote first-year student success are grounded in first-year students' needs, these needs will not be met if those efforts do not meet their needs. There must be systematic studies of student satisfaction with their curricular and cocurricular experiences, focusing on what was done well and what might be done to improve them. Clearly, student satisfaction is important because if entering students are not satisfied, they are less likely to participate in the curricular and cocurricular activities designed to help them succeed.

We are also interested in first-year student satisfaction because it gives valuable information about how to improve our efforts to help them succeed. In the classroom, faculty should seek student feedback on their learning experience on a frequent basis, even after every class session. Outside the classroom, first-year students who participate in services and programs should also be asked for their level of satisfaction. (For examples of orientation program satisfaction assessments, see Chapter Twenty-Eight.) At a more global level, several test publishers have a wide variety of student satisfaction instruments, including the American College Testing Program, the Educational Testing Service, the National Center for Higher Education Management Systems, the Noel Levitz Centers, and the Clearinghouse for Higher Education Assessment.

Assess the Climate for First-Year Students

While assessing individual characteristics, needs, and satisfaction is important, it is also critical to take a look at first-year students' collective perceptions of the campus climate within which they conduct their day-to-day lives. This component of the assessment model can help answer a number of questions—for example: What is the climate for first-year women on this campus? What is the academic environment for first-year students, both inside and outside the classroom? What is the overall quality of life in residence halls? Does this campus provide a safe, welcoming, and inclusive environment for students of color? What is the campus climate for first-year adult learners?

There are two primary ways to assess campus climates using both quantitative and qualitative methods. For example, individual interviews and focus groups might be conducted with first-year students in general, or with selected subgroups such as men, women, students of color, adult students, disabled students, and students of various sexual orientations. The focus groups should ask very broad, open-ended questions such as, "How would you describe the classroom climate for first-year students at this institution?" Or "What is it like to be a first-year African American student on this campus?" Or "What might our institution do to make the climate for adult learners more welcoming and inclusive?"

A second way is to administer any one of several commercially available instruments that measure overall campus climates. The advantage of these instruments is that test publishers typically provide psychometrically sound instruments, scoring and reporting services, and national norms that allow comparisons of results with peer institutions. For example, the *National Survey of Student Engagement* (Center for Postsecondary Research at Indiana State University), provides an excellent profile of several environmental variables, such as student perceptions of their in-class and out-of-class climates, as well as self-reported learning outcomes. Other climate instruments include the *University Residence Environment Scale* (Consulting Psychologist Press), *Your First College Year* (Higher Education Research Institute at UCLA), and the *Residence Satisfaction Survey* (Education Benchmarking).

Assess Outcomes

These assessments get at the basic questions raised by Peter Ewell (2001) earlier in this chapter: "What happened?" and "What mattered?" Put another way, is there any relationship between first-year student participation in various curricular and cocurricular activities and intended outcomes, such as learning, development, transition to college, academic success, and persistence? Can these activities be isolated from other variables that may influence outcomes, such as background, characteristics, and other noncollegiate experiences? These kinds of studies are not often done and they are very difficult to design, implement, and interpret, but in some ways they attempt to answer the most fundamental question of all: Is what we are doing having any effect, and is that effect the intended one? (Chapter Twenty-Eight provides a more detailed discussion of outcomes assessments.)

Benchmark with Comparable Institutions

How does the quality of the first year of college compare with best-in-class comparable institutions? An important way of assessing quality, often described as benchmarking, is to compare oneself to other institutions that appear to be doing a better job with promoting first-year student success. One purpose would be to discover how others achieve their results and then to translate their processes to one's own environment. The key to this assessment component is to select comparable institutions that have good assessment programs rather than relying on anecdotal or reputational information. Criteria that should be used in selecting comparable institutions include size, selectivity, type, location, and mission, as well as entering student characteristics such as gender, marital status, race/ethnicity, age, and percentage of students living on campus (if any).

Benchmarking assessment is often a single-point-in-time data collection rather than a pre/posttest effort. The most common form provides aggregated data from a single institution and data aggregated from a number of similar institutions, using the criteria suggested above. While such gross benchmarking can be helpful, the aggregation of scores can mask actual variation, especially when comparison groups are too broadly drawn.

There are two ways of benchmarking. The first is to use an instrument (such as the National Survey of Student Engagement [NSSE]) that creates benchmarks based on groups of institutions similar in size and type and provides an average score for each grouping. However, the average, a measure of central tendency, does not show the range of scores within the original group. The second way is to use an instrument (such as the First-Year Seminar Benchmarking Survey, developed by the National Policy Center on The First Year of College and Education Benchmarking, Inc.) that allows each participating institution to select six peer institutions for comparison. Institutions might select aspirational peers (institutions with first-year seminar formats they would like to be like) or contextual peers (those that have similarly designed first-year seminars). Both averaged data as a gross measure and individual-level data are presented so that variations within the peer group can be seen.

Assess Using Nationally Accepted Standards

How does our first year of college match with national standards? In the curricular arena, professional associations of various academic fields and disciplines offer standards for assessing the effectiveness of curricular offerings. Some even extend accreditation to those academic programs that meet these standards, such as those developed by the Accreditation Board for Engineering and Technology, the National Council for Accreditation of Teacher Education, and others.

Outside the classroom, the Council for the Advancement of Standards (CAS) for Student Services/Development Programs (1997) has promulgated standards for selected student services and programs. For example, the CAS standards for student orientation include guidelines for mission, program, leadership, organization and management, human resources, financial resources, facilities, technology and equipment, equal opportunity, access, affirmative action, campus and community relations, diversity, ethics, and assessment and evaluation. Various national and regional accrediting agencies and professional organizations may also promulgate relevant standards. These standards are particularly useful in establishing first-year programs and services, as well as offering a template for selected assessment studies.

Assess Cost-Effectiveness

Are the benefits students derive from their first year of college worth the cost, and how do we know? There is very little guidance offered by the existing higher education literature except at the crudest level of analysis: divide the cost of various institutional interventions by the number of students. Such an "analysis" is often fraught with so many methodological problems that its conclusions may be meaningless. Cost-benefit analysis is difficult and somewhat imprecise in a nonprofit, service-oriented organization, for two reasons. First, as surprising as it might seem, as Kennedy, Moran, and Upcraft (2001) point out, establishing the actual cost of a program or service is very difficult. For example, some costs are direct, easily traced to and associated with an operational budget, while others are indirect (program costs that are funded by the institution, such as utilities, staff benefits, and building maintenance).

A second problem is establishing the benefits of a program or service, since they are often not easily identified or measured. Kennedy, Moran, and Upcraft (2001) suggested a framework for considering benefits, including:

- Benefits to students: What are these benefits, how are they determined, and how would these benefits change if costs were reduced or expanded?

- Benefits to staff: What, if any, are staff benefits, how are they determined, and how would these benefits change if costs were reduced or expanded?

- Benefits to the institution: What are the benefits to the institution from efforts to promote first-year student success? For example, an institution may gain tuition and other revenue when these efforts can be associated with first-year student persistence.

- Benefits to the public and graduates: What are these benefits, and how are they determined? For example, good retention rates often contribute to the reputation of an institution and encourage applicants. Thus, a first-year seminar that has been shown to enhance first-year student retention may improve the reputation of the institution as well. Similarly, graduates who found some value participating in efforts to promote their success during the first year of college may lean toward continuing involvement in and donating money to their institution.

These difficulties in conducting cost-benefit analyses should not be used as an excuse for avoiding this type of assessment. When done at all, even crudely, these studies can be of enormous benefit in justifying institutional efforts to promote first-year student success.

OVERCOMING BARRIERS TO ASSESSMENT

Even if there is a good-faith effort to develop a comprehensive approach to assessment, there may be institutionally based barriers that can make assessment difficult. As Schuh, Upcraft, and Associates (2001) pointed out, assessment does not get done for many reasons.

Lack of Commitment and Support from Leadership

Sometimes educators involved in first-year programs, including some faculty, feel like "lone wolves" in their institutions, wanting desperately to do assessment but finding no support whatsoever from senior leadership. The starting place for convincing senior leadership of the importance of assessment is to refer to the reasons for assessment identified earlier in this chapter. One or more of these reasons may be particularly appealing to senior leadership. Another strategy is to assess a first-year initiative that is especially important to the external reputation of the institution, such as a program designed to increase student persistence or enhance the academic skills of at-risk students. A third, and perhaps most convincing, argument to senior leadership is that regional accrediting bodies are demanding more evidence of the quality, worth, and effectiveness of all institutional programs and services.

Lack of Assessment Expertise

Often those in charge of first-year student initiatives lack the technical expertise to conduct high-quality assessment studies. But that is no excuse, for three reasons. First, with some training and supervision by assessment experts, most first-year student educators can conduct many types of viable assessment studies on their own. Second, if that is not possible, most campuses abound with faculty, professional staff, and even students who have the expertise to conduct studies, some of whom may be in search of opportunities to use or develop their skills or sites to conduct their research. Third, outside assessment consultants may be hired to plan and direct assessment efforts (see Schuh, Upcraft, and Associates, 2001, for guidance in using an outside consultant).

Lack of Money

This is an especially effective excuse, because there always seem to be "more important" priorities than assessment. However, the reality is that assessment does not have to be expensive. The major expense of most assessment is staff time to conduct studies. Staff time can be reallocated without additional resources, although some staff functions may have to be temporarily postponed or covered in other ways. There may be campus resources that can be tapped if the study is of mutual interest to faculty or other professional staff. Student volunteers with proper training can also be helpful in data collection. To be sure, other elements in a study, such as printing, secretarial support, and data analysis, may require additional funding, but usually such costs are manageable within existing budgets. In addition, sampling can be effectively used to reduce the costs of assessment. There is often little to be gained from testing everyone in a large population rather than testing a well-formulated sample of the population.

Lack of Professional Staff Support

In many instances, asking busy and overworked professional staff to take on assessment responsibilities is a real problem. The irony is that often it is the best and most hard-working staff who are the most resistant, because they are the most reluctant to take time away from their jobs to conduct assessments. These staff must come to understand that assessment is a high priority and they must devote the necessary time to conduct assessment studies. Put another way, there are always things they must do (such as assessment) in order to continue to do the things they were hired to do. Senior leadership must be willing to tolerate temporary disruptions of services to students or instruction as a way of building staff support for assessment efforts.

Fear of Results

Perhaps the most significant barrier to assessment is the fear of results, because all assessment is a risk. There is no guarantee that assessment will necessarily make us look good or yield positive results. For example, we know that in general, living on campus is associated with persistence to graduation, even when other variables that contribute to that outcome are taken into account. What if an institution does a study that shows that there is no relationship or, worse yet, a negative relationship between participating in service-learning and retention? In this instance, isn't this fear legitimate? It all depends on the reasons the study was done in the first place. If it was to improve the course, service, or program, then there is less risk than if it was to determine whether the institution should continue to offer them. The risk must be considered in the light of potential consequences. Put another way, can we live with all the possible results of an assessment study?

These barriers, of course, are very real, but nevertheless must be overcome if credible assessment studies are to be conducted.

THE ETHICS OF ASSESSMENT

A major concern in any assessment study is that the highest ethical standards guide the activity. While I have suggested that an assessment study may have to be modified in order to meet certain realities, one should never make compromises, engage in shortcuts, or in any other way fail to uphold the highest ethical standards. Such standards are built on commonly accepted statements of ethical principles, such as those promulgated by the American College Personnel Association, the American Psychological Association, various ethical statements promulgated by academic disciplines, and other professional organizations.

However, as Schuh, Upcraft, and Associates (2001) have argued, the heart of conducting assessment studies in ethical ways has to do with working with subjects. This is not only an ethical requirement but a legal one as well. There are federal regulations governing the protection of human subjects that require an institution, through its Institutional Review Board (IRB), often referred to as the "human subjects" committee, to review assessment studies. Before anyone is permitted to collect data from subjects, an institution-based IRB, consisting of faculty members and administrators, must certify that the rights of subjects are protected. IRBs will require a written consent form from study participants that outlines the purpose of the study, the procedures, the sponsors, any potential benefits and risks, confidentiality parameters, compensation conditions (if any), a statement that expresses that the individual is participating willingly, and other issues. Individual campuses may vary in their approach to protecting the rights of participants, so it is essential that before conducting a study, assessment investigators consult with the chair of their local IRB to determine how federal and institutional regulations are applied.

RECOMMENDATIONS

The first step in the assessment process is to determine why a particular assessment is needed. This assumes, however, that the assessment must be developed within the context of institutional vision, mission, and goals. Given this context, the following recommendations for practice are put forth:

• *Understand and overcome barriers to assessment.* Unfortunately, understanding the importance of assessment and how to do assessment does not necessarily result in getting it done. Strategies must be developed to overcome the barriers.

• *Select qualified professionals to conduct studies.* In the eyes of many intended assessment audiences, the qualifications and skill of the persons conducting the study may determine the study's credibility. On the one hand, some may argue that many studies can and should be done by faculty and staff whose training and background include assessment expertise. On the other hand, some would argue that a study is credible only if it is done exclusively by social science researchers or institutional research personnel, based on the questionable assumption that most, if not all, first-year practitioners and faculty lack the necessary skills to conduct rigorous and unbiased studies. Schuh and Upcraft (2001) take the middle ground that some studies may in fact be conducted by faculty and first-year practitioners if they have the appropriate education and training and if those studies meet acceptable standards. Other studies, in which designs and analyses may be more complex, require investigators with more assessment expertise. Either way, someone with assessment design and analysis expertise should review all assessment studies to ensure that these studies are rigorous, unbiased, and defensible.

• *Develop strategies for ensuring maximum participation in assessment studies.* A frequent complaint of assessment investigators is the failure to generate acceptable response rates for quantitative studies. There are several strategies to improve response rates:

Consider data collection procedures. Response rates may vary by the type of data collection procedures used. For example, telephone surveys and on-line data collection procedures may yield higher response rates than mailed surveys.

Consider incentives. While monetary incentives often yield increased response rates, there are very few institutions that can afford such a strategy. Other incentives include gift certificates to campus food services or bookstores (thus keeping the money within the institution and encouraging students to become customers), lotteries (where legal), food at focus groups, and personal follow-up contacts.

Collect data in classes. Response rates are often increased when assessment investigators cooperate with faculty to collect data in classes. But this typically requires taking class time (which, understandably, faculty guard jealously), and the resulting sample may not be representative of the student population.

Two caveats: First, a low response rate may not necessarily doom a study. Statistical strategies may be used to deal with small samples. Second, a high response rate does not necessarily guarantee that the sample is representative of the population. Weighting responses by selected demographic characteristics (such as gender, age, and race/ethnicity) may help overcome an unrepresentative sample.

• *Make special efforts to ensure that participation in assessment studies is accessible to all students.* Too often, certain student groups are left behind in the assessment process. For example, racial/ethnic minorities are often underrepresented in higher education in general, and thus assessment studies in particular. The same is often true of males, adult students, part-time students, commuters, and off-campus students. Special efforts must be made to ensure that these groups are represented in assessment studies, including sampling adjustments, special incentives to participate, collaboration with student organizations that represent these groups, and, perhaps most important, making sure that instruments and interview protocols are sensitive to their perceptions and needs.

• *Understand that all assessment is political.* As Schuh and Upcraft (2000) pointed out, too often assessment studies are given initial attention and then forgotten, or roundly criticized as hopeless flawed and dismissed, or suffer the ultimate ignominy: being ignored completely. Of course, there are many reasons for these unintended results, but almost always the reason that studies end up gathering dust on some policymaker's shelf is the failure of the assessment investigator to account for the institutional political context within which all assessment studies are conducted. Put another way, the challenge of the assessment investigator is to plan and conduct a study and report the results in ways that build support for its recommendations:

Do not do a study nobody wants. This may mean that some needed studies will never be started or completed because influential leaders fear the consequences of the findings.

Identify important constituents before the study is conducted. This includes persons whose support will be needed to conduct and implement the study, as well as those who are likely to oppose the study or dispute the results.

Involve key constituents before the study is conducted. If key constituents know about and have the opportunity to have input into the study, they are more likely to take the findings seriously.

Build support from senior leadership. Because support from senior leadership is especially critical in implementing assessment results, their involvement is essential. Often this involves making leaders aware of the benefits of the study from a policy or public relations standpoint and the increasing role of assessment in accreditation.

Build support among faculty and staff. Sometimes assessment studies are torpedoed by faculty and staff themselves, for whatever reasons, so it is important to involve them from the beginning in any assessment studies that may affect their jobs or careers.

Conduct a good study. This advice may seem too obvious to mention, but as Upcraft and Schuh (1996) point out, the quality of a study may determine if it will be used by decision makers or have credibility with intended audiences. The best way to determine the quality of a study is to pose the question, "If I were an unfriendly critic of this study, what would I attack?" Then, point by point, deal with the criticisms by acknowledging limitations or strengthening the study based on anticipated criticisms. A poorly done study may do more harm than good and will allow critics to marginalize the results by focusing on its flaws.

Write a good report. Report formats are critical to the success of assessment studies in influencing policy and practice.

- *Market assessment reports in ways that intended audiences are reached and influenced.* More than one well-done, credible assessment study has failed to have the intended influence because of the ineffective ways in which the results were reported and distributed. Upcraft and Schuh (1996) argue that the most common mistake assessment investigators make is to send a complete and comprehensive report (most often modeled after the format of a dissertation) to all intended audiences. Suskie (1992) suggests the following to ensure that assessment reports will have their intended impact:

Determine which audience or audiences should read and use the findings. Depending on the study, potential audiences may include students, student affairs professional staff, faculty, the chief student affairs officer, other senior leadership, alumni, the local community, state legislatures, and the general public.

Write multiple reports for multiple audiences. Briefer reports should be tailored to the needs and interests of the intended audiences. Reports to busy decision makers should be short, to the point, and no more than one page.

Write reports that are well organized, succinct, and attractive. Reports should be written in ways that are clear, organized, and keep the reader's interest, while at the same time ensuring the integrity of the work.

Format the report properly. Include a meaningful title, an executive summary, a statement of purpose, summary of the design, a summary of results, and, most important, recommendations for practice.

Write reports that are persuasive. The likelihood that a report will be taken seriously is enhanced if there are hard-hitting, succinct recommendations based on the findings. There are some researchers who believe their responsibility ends with reporting the findings of a study, leaving the implications of the study to decision makers. While that may be appropriate for research, it is a near-fatal mistake for assessment. Decision makers should be guided by the recommendations of an assessment study with the caveat that decision makers have the ultimate responsibility for deciding how assessment results will be used.

CONCLUSION

Assessment is not just another educational fad that will disappear when newer fads emerge. For the many reasons discussed in this chapter, assessment will continue for the foreseeable future. The pressure to assess is particularly high with first-year programs and services. But even without these pressures, assessment must be done because it is the best way to ensure commitment to accountability and high quality of first-year courses, programs, and services. In the end, whatever assessments are done, they must be able to answer Peter Ewell's (2001) questions: "What happened?" and "What mattered?"

CHAPTER TWENTY-EIGHT

A Beginner's Guide for Assessing the First College Year

M. Lee Upcraft
Jennifer L. Crissman Ishler
Randy L. Swing

Starting a comprehensive assessment program may seem to be an overwhelming task because on many campuses, not much has been done and it is difficult to know where to start. This chapter provides a beginner's guide to help institutions get started on the very important task of developing comprehensive assessment programs discussed in the previous chapter.

Three premises undergird the concept of assessment presented in this chapter. First, the success of an assessment effort is best judged by the use of the results; in other words, assessment is a means to an end and not an end in itself. Successful assessment efforts either create change (hopefully improvement) or confirm current practice; either way, assessment done right shapes future policies, programs, and practice. In contrast, efforts that result in unused reports and reams of undigested statistics fall far short of our definition of assessment.

Second, successful assessment efforts depend on the goodwill of students, faculty, and other stakeholders. Assessment designs that judiciously use the time of all involved are more likely to produce appropriate participation and thus trustworthy results. In contrast, bombarding students with surveys and tests is likely to discourage participation, reduce the level of effort given, and spoil reliability of measures. Building a foundation of support at the start of an assessment effort requires identifying the parties involved and understanding the motivations and hesitations likely to be encountered.

Third, assessment plans must be consistent with local institutional mission and climate and developed to take advantage of unique institutional characteristics and opportunities. The best assessment plans evaluate specific objectives at the institutional, program, or course level that grow out of the core unit mission. In other words, assess first what matters most in a manner consistent with local conditions.

UNIQUE CHALLENGES AND OPPORTUNITIES OF FIRST-YEAR ASSESSMENT

While our three core premises are broadly applicable to higher education assessment, there are unique opportunities and challenges associated with assessing first-year programs and students. The best way to describe the unique challenges of first-year assessment is to compare "easy" assessment situations to the organization and structures that are most common across the first year in American higher education.

It is easiest to design assessment when there are well-defined and common goals for learning outcomes, similar educational treatment, and a narrow range of student entry-level characteristics. These conditions are seldom descriptive of the first year of college, but when they are present, they provide useful assessment opportunities. Understanding the unique nature of the first college year allows educators to minimize restrictions that are inherent in assessing first-year programs and maximize available opportunities.

The first year of college is the best opportunity to establish baseline data by recording entry-level skills, attitudes, expectations, and other information consistent with the first dimension of the comprehensive assessment model presented in the previous chapter. Such data serve three critical roles: they are a pretest that can be used to calculate change when compared with later posttests, they provide control variables for advanced statistical treatment of data, and they are useful to faculty and program administrators in planning effective educational interventions. If entry-level data are not collected at the start of the first year, it is usually impossible to develop this important information retrospectively.

Some first-year structures such as orientation, registration, required academic advising, introductory courses such as English and mathematics, and first-year seminars provide a central location to embed assessment that will capture data from all or most new students. These structures, while seldom designed specially for assessment activities, afford unique opportunities to assess an entire cohort of new students. Unfortunately, time spent on assessment activities may reduce or conflict with the original goals of these efforts; for example, tests and surveys may be contradictory to best structures for welcoming new students through an orientation program.

First-year students are generally compliant, especially in the first weeks of college, and so are willing to take part in assessment activities when told or asked to do so. High school graduates of the past decade have considerable experience with K–12 assessment and generally understand that assessment is part of the normal experience of education. Nontraditional students may be motivated to participate in something that is new and piques their curiosity.

Because first-year students receive the benefits of the many courses, programs, and services designed to help them succeed, they may be overwhelmed by a proliferation of satisfaction and effectiveness surveys created independently by each of the campus units serving first-year students. "Too many assessments" is a common complaint among first-year students who are asked to evaluate everything from campus parking and residence halls to advising and teaching.

Some first-year students may exhibit immature behaviors that can be detrimental to assessment efforts or produce erroneous results. Immature behaviors such as purposefully marking all the wrong answers on a survey, making belligerent comments, participating in assessment while under the influence of intoxicating substances, or giving inadequate effort because of sleep deprivation are likely to be observed in a small percentage of first-year students. Assessments of first-year populations should include a review of outliers (data points that are considerably outside of the normal range of responses), and appropriate cleaning of data to remove or control for these unusual data points.

The variation of skills and experiences among first-year students, especially at open admission or less selective institutions, makes it particularly difficult to develop assessment instruments and methods capable of identifying both high- and low-performing students. Assessments that are too narrowly defined risk failing to differentiate true variance among students by being either too difficult (few students can perform at the tested level) or too easy (everyone can perform most tasks presented). It is difficult to develop first-year assessment instruments with adequate room at the top of the scale to accommodate future measures of change and adequate depth at the bottom of the scale to capture the level of skills for the lowest performing students.

First-year courses, programs, and services often have unclear or unrealistically broad goals. The first step in assessing the first year of college often requires formation of defined outcome objectives, a time-consuming process built on consensual agreement across stakeholders. First-year initiatives also often lack defined leadership and cross several organizational units. The process of gathering unit-level records and scheduling assessment data collection may be complicated by the loosely coupled structure of these interventions. On campuses where "nobody" is in charge of the first college year, it is difficult to create a home base for assessments capable of looking holistically at the first year.

Furthermore, the goals of many first-year efforts are unlikely to be realized in the short term, meaning that assessment should be conducted at some distance after completion of these programs. The longer the time before follow-up measures, the greater the challenge becomes to isolate the impact of the original interventions from the variety of additional experiences students gather over time.

First-year students may also transfer, drop out of college, or matriculate part time so that follow-up studies are complicated by variations in experience and incomplete data sets. Pretests and posttests that span more than one term frequently result in analysis containing many missing data points from the original population, creating a limitation to generalizability of the findings.

Some first-year courses, programs, and services are mandatory for all students, meaning that no control group (students who were not part of the treatment) exists for comparison. In the absence of a comparative group, it can be difficult to estimate the impact of these efforts. Other interventions are voluntary and provide opportunities for control groups but introduce volunteer effect issues—the need to disaggregate the impact of naturally occurring differences between students who choose to participate and those who do not. Especially on large campuses, it may be difficult to locate common experiences for first-year students. Variations in the first-year experience provide opportunities to compare outcomes across unique courses, programs, and services but also increase the challenge to control for the other variables that affect the first college year. Only the very rare assessment of first-year interventions can approach proving cause and effect; more commonly, first-year assessments are limited to finding correlations between interventions and outcomes.

On most campuses, first-year students pass through a common admissions process that produces a restricted range of entering student characteristics. For example, admissions criteria often create a skewed bell shape curve of admissions scores where the bulk of students have scores just over a set admissions cut-off level. Homogeneity of entering student characteristics can be helpful in some statistical analyses but is detrimental to generalizability to other populations of students and can affect statistical treatments such as regression analyses. Most first-year assessment studies must acknowledge that they do not begin with a random population representing all of American higher education.

Many existing baseline data, such as high school grades, may not be stored electronically or consistently reported. It is usually difficult to use assessment results from secondary education, even though college outcomes are often linked to prior learning experiences.

Although the processes of admissions, financial aid, registration, and orientation produce a great deal of information on each new student, those data often remain in disparate campus offices and are not linked or shared for cross-unit assessment. Much information collected on first-year students is used narrowly and discarded without acknowledgment of the value of the data.

STEPS IN THE ASSESSMENT PROCESS

In the preceding chapter and in this one, we have provided general guidance for assessing first-year student programs and services. The next step is to translate these generalities into specific examples. (The following steps in the assessment process were adapted from Upcraft and Schuh, 1996.)

Step 1: Define the Problem

All assessment flows from an attempt to solve some problem, so establishing a clear and concise definition of the problem facing the institution is the first step in the assessment process. Quite often, the "problem" is simply lack of information needed to initiate or improve courses, services, programs, policies, or practices. Another way of framing this step is to refer to the previous discussion of why an assessment is being done. Everything else flows from this question, for the "why" determines what we do, how we do it, and how we use the results. Other questions might help define the problem:

- *What specific circumstances or situations are driving assessment efforts?* Examples might include low enrollments, consideration of a policy to protect students from being discriminated against on the basis of their race or sexual orientation, pressures to reduce budgets, commitment to improving services and programs, or impending accreditation review.
- *What external pressures are driving assessment efforts?* Pressures external to the institution might include the general public ("costs are rising more quickly than inflation"), institutional boards of control ("we need to increase minority enrollments"), institutional leadership ("there are too many problems arising from students abusing alcohol"), alumni ("the sinking feeling that student life just isn't what it used to be"), and in state-supported institutions, legislatures and governors ("we need to cut state allocations by X percent") and accrediting agencies (assessment is required for reaccreditation).
- *What internal circumstances are driving assessment?* There is always a need to improve institutional interventions designed to help first-year students succeed, regardless of their quality; thus, improvement is a primary internal circumstance that drives assessment efforts. Other internally driven variables may include a concern that services and programs might not be meeting student needs or might not be equally accessible and used by all types of students. We may need to know more about whether interventions are achieving their intended outcomes, and if so, if they are being administered in cost-effective ways.

Step 2: Determine the Purpose of the Study

Assessment is the process of gathering, analyzing, and interpreting evidence (information). Given the particular problem identified in step 1, what information do we need to help solve it? What information will be critical to responding to external and internal pressure to do assessment? The answers to these questions frame the purpose statement of a study.

Step 3: Determine Where to Get the Information Needed

Information can be retrieved from a wide variety of sources. The most obvious source is students or other clientele, but there are many other sources. Institutional or functional unit records may well contain valuable information needed to solve a problem. There may be others who might have insight into the problem, including staff, faculty, administrators, community leaders, or even the general public. Other sources of information might be institutional documents, student newspaper articles, and field observations.

Step 4: Determine the Best Assessment Methods

Another way of framing this step is to answer the question, "What is the best way to get the information I need?" Of course, the best assessment method depends on the purposes of the study. Basically there are three choices: quantitative methods, which include gathering data from a survey or other instrument; qualitative methods, which include gathering information from interviews, observations, and documents; and combinations of quantitative and qualitative methods.

Generally, if we need information about what is occurring, quantitative methods are more appropriate. If we need information on why something is going on, qualitative methods are more appropriate. If we need both, then a mixed methodology study is most useful. For example, if we were studying the development of critical thinking in first-year students, a pre- and posttest measure of critical thinking would reveal if such a development did occur. Focus groups might best indicate why or why not. Most often, qualitative methods require much smaller samples than quantitative methods, but the results are less generalizable to the study population. Quantitative measures require much larger samples but are more generalizable to the population under study.

Step 5: Determine Whom to Study

Having decided on the population to be studied, as Upcraft and Schuh (1996) point out, it is desirable to collect data from the entire population under study, and often feasible to do so, particularly if the population is narrowly defined. But more often, a sample of the population is more feasible if that sample is chosen in ways that ensure that those selected are representative of that population according to some criteria. For quantitative studies, the most typical criteria are the demographics of the population, such as gender, age, race/ethnicity, and disability. In the collegiate setting, factors such as class standing, grades, place of residence, full-time or part-time enrollment, major field, and others may also be important. If the sample is representative, then one can generalize with much more confidence to the whole population. In qualitative studies, however, although strict adherence to the representativeness is not required, it is still nonetheless important within general parameters.

There are many different ways of sampling, depending on the methodology chosen for a study. The object of quantitative studies is to select a sample that is representative of the population. For quantitative studies, Borg and Gall (1989) suggest four possible sampling options:

- Simple random sampling: A procedure in which all the individuals in a defined population have an equal and independent chance of being selected.

- Systematic sampling: A procedure in which the total population is placed on a list, and, for example, every fourth person is selected until the sample size has been reached.

- Stratified sampling: A procedure that selects the sample in a way that ensures that certain subgroups in the population will be represented in the sample in proportion to their numbers in the population itself.

- Cluster sampling: A procedure that is used when the sample unit is not an individual but rather a naturally occurring group of individuals and is used when it is more feasible or convenient to select groups of individuals than it is to select individuals from a defined population.

The question of sample size is frequently raised. In quantitative studies, it is important to have a sample big enough for the statistical analyses used in the study. But it is equally important to have a sample big enough to create credibility among the intended audiences of the study. The minimum number of useable responses to meet these criteria is approximately three hundred, which means that the initial sample would have to be much larger to take into account projected return rates. But from an assessment point of view, the representativeness of the sample is probably more important than the size of the sample. A small, useable sample, if it is representative of the population, is probably more credible than a large sample that is not representative. It should be noted that sample size is a very complex issue that may well determine the credibility of the study; thus, a statistical consultant should be used in helping to determine a sample size consistent with the purposes of the study.

Qualitative sampling methods, according to Patton (1990), typically focus in depth on a relatively small sample, and sometimes even single cases, selected purposefully. Patton (1990) suggested fifteen sampling approaches for qualitative studies, the most typical of which include:

- Stratified purposeful sampling: Consists of taking a sample of the above-average, average, and below-average cases.

- Purposeful random sampling: Selects cases in advance of the knowledge of how outcomes would appear, aimed at reducing suspicion about why certain cases were selected.

- Intensity sampling: Consists of information-rich cases that manifest the phenomenon of interest, but not unusual cases.

- Typical case sampling: Provides a profile of one or more typical cases selected with the cooperation of key informants who have knowledge of potential subjects.

- Snowball or chain sampling: Allows the researcher to locate information-rich key informants or critical cases by asking participants, "Who else knows a lot about . . . ?"

- Convenience sampling: Aims for sampling that is fast, cost-effective, and convenient but is neither purposeful nor strategic. It should be the last resort in any assessment study.

Unfortunately, many intended audiences, steeped in quantitative methodology criteria, often scoff at a qualitative study that has few subjects or is not representative of the population. Thus, reports of qualitative studies should contain thorough explanations of sampling procedures and the credibility of their usefulness.

Step 6: Determine How Data Will Be Collected

Data can be collected in a wide variety of ways, including mailed questionnaires, telephone surveys, individual interviews, focus groups, Web-based surveys, and other data collection procedures. Each procedure has strengths and limitations, but all are intended to get the desired number of participants in the study. For example, mailed questionnaires typically yield the fewest number of participants and are often more costly, but more thorough information will be collected. Telephone surveys yield a higher percentage of return, but will be limited in the amount of information collected. Web-based data collection shows great promise, because, as pointed out in Chapter Thirteen, today's students are much more at ease with computer use and thus are more likely to respond to Web-based surveys.

Individual interviews and focus groups require a more personal touch, and incentives such as food or token monetary compensation may be helpful. Whatever data collection procedures are chosen, they should be consistent with the purpose of the study and yield the optimum number of participants needed.

Step 7: Determine What Instruments Will Be Used

The instruments used to collect data depend on several factors, including which methodologies are chosen. For qualitative methodologies, an interview protocol must be developed consisting of standardized, open-ended questions that retrieve the information needed for the study. According to Patton (1990), an item is standardized when it is written out in advance *exactly* the way it is to be asked during the interview. Clarifications or elaborations should be included, as well as any probing questions. Variations among interviewers can be minimized, and comparisons across interviews can be made if the interview protocol is standardized. Open-ended means there are no prescribed answers (such as yes/no); respondents are free to provide any answer they choose. Although this may seem obvious, there should be a direct connection between the questions asked and the information needed to help solve the problem. For example, if we wanted to know more about students who dropped out of college at a particular institution, the following interview protocols (developed by Schuh, Upcraft, and Associates, 2001) might be helpful:

Interview Protocol for Students Who Dropped Out

1. Why did you decide to leave this college?

2. What, if anything, did you like about this college?

3. How might this college be improved?

4. What, if anything, might this college have done better to help you attain your educational goals here?

5. What, if any, educational plans do you have?

6. How, if at all, might this college be helpful to you in the future?

7. Any other comments?

For quantitative methodologies, an instrument must be chosen that yields results that can be statistically analyzed. Beyond that, we need to decide whether to use an already constructed instrument with appropriate psychometric properties and standardized norms or a locally constructed instrument that may be more appropriate to this particular study, but lacks validity, reliability, and other psychometric properties. Generally, instruments available from any one of several national test publishers are preferable if there is an opportunity to add locally developed items. But if the problem under study is unique to a particular campus, then test construction experts should be consulted when developing local instruments. (See Chapter Twenty-Nine for further information about quantitative instruments.) For example, if the goal was to get feedback about orientation programs, the locally developed instrument in Exhibit 28.1 (Crissman, 2001) may be helpful.

Step 8: Determine Who Should Collect the Data

At first glance, this question may not seem to matter much. Obviously, data should be collected by people who are competent to do so. But often the most qualified people are also those who have a vested interest in the outcome. This is less of a problem with quantitative methodologies, where bias is more likely to have occurred in the selection or development of the instrument. In qualitative methodologies, however, where the data are collected and filtered by those who conduct the study and record the data, bias becomes a much larger issue.

There is also the lingering problem of the face credibility of the study. Can we trust a study that was done entirely by those with a vested interest in the outcome? Or can we really trust a study that was done entirely by outside experts who know little or nothing about the context and nuances of the study? In general, if the study and the people who are doing it have integrity, there is usually no problem with involving those who have a vested interest in the outcome in the data collection process.

Step 9: Determine How the Data Will Be Analyzed

Analysis of quantitative data depends on the purpose of the study. Probably the most important first step is to determine if the respondents are in fact representative of the population to be studied. Then appropriate descriptive and infer-

Exhibit 28.1. Instrument for Collecting Feedback About Orientation Programs

Title of Program _____   Date _____   Presenter _____

5. Strongly Agree   4. Agree   3. Neutral   2. Disagree   1. Strongly Disagree

ITEM

1. I now know much more about the   5   4   3   2   1
   topic of this program.

2. I learned more about the skills I need to   5   4   3   2   1
   make a successful transition to college

3. I am now more confident about making   5   4   3   2   1
   a successful transition to college.

4. I now know more about where to get   5   4   3   2   1
   help on the topic of this program.

5. The presenters were well prepared.   5   4   3   2   1

6. The presenters communicated effectively   5   4   3   2   1

What did you learn from this program/activity?

How could this program/activity be improved?

Please share other comments you have about this program.

Do you have suggestions for other programs/activities? Please indicate on back.

ential statistical analyses can be applied. In order to determine which statistical analyses are most appropriate and how to interpret statistically generated results, we recommend using statistical consultants familiar with social science research methodologies for both data analysis and interpretation.

Analysis of qualitative data should be done in systematic ways by persons who are skillful in listening to and searching for meaning in interview and focus group audiotapes or transcripts, looking for themes, trends, variations, and generalizations. This process should be an inclusive one, with data gatherers collaborating with colleagues, students, and even subjects in the interpretation of the data.

Step 10: Determine the Implications of the Study for Policy and Practice

Too often, investigators are content with reporting the findings and conclusions of a study, leaving its implications for policy and practice to various audiences. We believe that in reporting assessment results, the implications of the study should be spelled out. Here we are clearly crossing over from assessment to evaluation. Remember that assessment is the gathering and analysis of information, and evaluation is using assessment information to solve the problem that precipitated the study. What approaches to solving the problem should be considered in the light of the findings? What policies or practices need to be revised, eliminated, or created because of the findings? There should be clear calls for action in assessment reports that motivate the reader to do something about the precipitating problem.

Step 11: Report the Results Effectively

Once the findings have been reported and analyzed and the implications for policy and practice identified, how do we report the results? In what form do we report the results? To whom should the study be reported? Should every stakeholder get the whole report? More studies end up filed under "I" for "Interesting" or gathering dust on someone's shelf because we fail to package results in ways that move decision makers to make changes based on the study. In fact, how a study is formatted and distributed may be more important than the results of the study. Probably the biggest mistake is to send the full report to all audiences and hope for the best.

There are several ways to overcome this problem. Providing multiple reports for multiple audiences is one way, highlighting the results most applicable to a particular audience. Executive summaries that summarize the study, its findings, and recommendations for policy and practice are effective. Getting results to the right people who can do something about the problem studied is very important. Offering to discuss the results in greater detail in person may be appropriate. Even going so far as to suggest how decision makers may make best use of the study is not out of the question. Clearly, if the purpose of the study is to solve a problem, the report must not only set out the results but specify how the results can be used to solve the problem.

Another useful and effective strategy is to use Web-based methods to present and market assessment results. As Baughman and Swing (2001) reported, a sortable database and Web interface can easily be constructed so that large data sets are sorted on key variables to produce focused reports of greatest interest to the viewer. A second Web-based method is to present data using a standard Web interface to show PowerPoint slides combined with voice narration. The resulting presentation provides auditory and visual elements to produce an engaging dissemination of findings.

OUTCOMES ASSESSMENT

As pointed out in Chapter Twenty-Seven, outcomes assessments are probably the cornerstone of any assessment effort, yet undoubtedly the most difficult to do. These assessments get at the basic question raised by Peter Ewell (2001): "What happened?" and "What mattered?" Put another way, is there any relationship between first-year student participation in various curricular and cocurricular activities, programs, and services and the expected outcomes of these efforts, such as student learning, academic achievement, persistence, or some other desired outcome?

These kinds of studies are rarely done, rarely done well, and very difficult to design and implement, for several reasons. First, whatever intervention is being assessed (participation in first-year efforts to promote first-year student success, such as a first-year seminar, Supplemental Instruction, academic advising, learning communities, service-learning, or orientation) must be isolated from other variables that may influence outcomes, such as the backgrounds and characteristics of the students (high school grades, admissions test scores, gender, race/ethnicity, age, marital status), and both collegiate (major, place of residence, full- or part-time enrollment, student engagement, peer relations, use of services and programs, and others) and noncollegiate (working off campus, family responsibilities, and others) experiences. Furthermore, the desired outcomes must be identified and measured in valid and reliable ways. Finally, the results must be carefully analyzed and interpreted, including a full exposure of design limitations. Probably the most poorly done, and hence misleading, outcome studies are those that compare persisters and dropouts without taking into account the many factors described that influence persistence. This is particularly true at institutions where students are more diverse and have a greater variety of educational goals and enrollment patterns.

Alexander Astin (1977) was the first researcher to postulate the Input-Environment-Outcome (I-E-O) conceptual guide to outcome studies. He started with the basic commonsense notion that student success is a function of who students were before they entered college and what happened to them after they enrolled. According to Terenzini and Upcraft (1996), the primary purpose of the IEO model is to identify and estimate institutional effects on desired educational outcomes. In particular, this model is a useful tool for identifying and estimating the effects of those college experiences over which institutions have some programmatic or policy control, such as student experiences, which can be shaped into educational advantage through an institution's programmatic or policy concerns.

Thus, the most appropriate assessment method for an outcomes study is one that takes into account both inputs and environmental influences on selected outcomes. While outcomes studies can be done using both qualitative and quantitative methods, quantitative methods are most often used, particularly when the study involves student persistence. If qualitative methods are used, input and environmental influences must still be identified as data are collected, analyzed, and interpreted.

STEPS IN THE OUTCOMES ASSESSMENT PROCESS

Essentially, the steps in the outcomes assessment process are the same as those elaborated in the previous section. The first three steps are the same: the reasons that the study is being done must be elaborated, the purpose of the study must be identified, and the best assessment approach must be selected. But for outcomes studies, three additional steps must be inserted.

Step A: Determine and Define Outcomes

Although outcome is the third component of Astin's IEO model, it should be the first one specified because the selection of the input and environment variables is determined by possible or demonstrated relationships between the outcomes and these other variables. The next question to be asked is, "What are the outcomes that are most important to the problems identified and the purposes of the study?"

Defining outcomes and determining how they are measured, however, is often a difficult task. Something as simple as persistence may not be easy to define, even though its measurement is obvious. Do we mean persistence to the end of the first term, or reenrollment into the second term, or reenrollment into the sophomore year, or persistence to graduation in four years, or persistence to graduation no matter how long it takes? Learning outcomes are even more problematic because we need crisp definitions of concepts such as critical thinking, content mastery, reflective judgment, civic responsibility, multicultural awareness, and many others that are not only difficult to define but often even more difficult to measure. Nevertheless, an outcomes study will be doomed from the outset unless outcomes are defined and measurable.

Step B: Identify the Input or Control Variables

As pointed out by Terenzini and Upcraft (1996), identifying appropriate input variables is easy, but retrieving and managing data on them in an outcomes study are another matter. Astin (1993) identified 146 possible input variables; most institutions have neither the time nor the ability to gather data on all these. At a minimum, however, most outcomes studies should include input variables that previous research has shown can influence outcomes and in most cases can be easily retrieved from institutional databases:

- Gender
- Race/ethnicity
- Admissions test scores: combined SAT scores
- High school achievement (high school adjusted grade point average)
- Parents' education
- Age
- Marital status
- Dependent children

In addition, if one is interested in assessing change or development over time (such as changes in the development of student critical thinking over the first year), then some measure of that variable must be included and collected at the point of initial enrollment. The problem with this input variable is that such data are not typically included in institutional databases and must be gathered through a separate data collection procedure prior to enrollment.

Step C: Identify Environmental Variables

Defining the many environmental variables that affect persistence is easy (Astin, 1993, discussed 192 of them), but in reality, most outcome studies restrict these variables to a few that are easily retrieved from institutional records or first-year students themselves. The environmental variables that could be retrieved from institutional records include these:

- Academic major, clustered by science, nonscience, or undecided
- Enrollment status (full-time or part-time)
- Place of residence (on-campus, off-campus apartment, off-campus with family)
- First- and second-semester grade point averages, when appropriate
- Participation in the first-year seminar
- Grade earned in the first-year seminar
- Degree sought (certificate, associate, or nondegree)

The environmental variables retrieved directly from students at the time of withdrawal or during the second term of enrollment include:

- Number of hours worked per week
- Number of hours spent on academic work per week
- Contacts with faculty outside the classroom
- Contacts with academic adviser
- Use of basic skills tutoring center
- Use of career advising center

The next several steps are essentially the same as described earlier in this chapter: determine where to get the information needed, determine the best assessment method, determine whom to study, determine how the data will be collected, determine what instruments will be used, and determine who should collect the data.

Step 9 (determine how the data will be analyzed) presents a special problem if a quantitative study is conducted. In order to conduct an outcomes study that is credible, a multivariate statistical analysis (such as stepwise regression, setwise regression, or path analysis) should be used. A multivariate analysis can allow a study of a relationship of several variables to an outcome. For example, if one is studying first-year student persistence, a multivariate statistical analysis will determine to what extent, if any, persistence is influenced by various environmental variables, taking into account the influence of input variables. It is recommended that a statistical expert be consulted when determining and interpreting statistical analyses, including multivariate analyses.

The remaining steps (determine the implications of the study for policy and practice and report the results effectively) are the same as described earlier in this chapter.

RECOMMENDATIONS

In order to conduct assessment studies that have an impact on first-year programs, services, policies, and practices, we recommend the following:

- *Remember that assessment is a means to an end, not an end in itself.* Assessment is a tool that is used to improve quality and accountability and should be thought of in that way.
- *Recognize that assessment depends largely on the goodwill and cooperation of those studied.* Without their cooperation, assessment studies will be seriously flawed or not possible at all.
- *Build support for assessment efforts from those in the institution whose cooperation and collaboration may be critical,* including those at the highest leadership positions in the institution, those affected by the results, and those whose support is needed to conduct the study.
- *Recognize that assessment is not an easy task* because of the complexity of first-year student services and programs.
- *Outline all the steps in the assessment process before the study is begun,* and follow all the steps as the assessment is conducted and completed.
- *Assessment efforts are not complete until the results are used.* How results are compiled and disseminated may well be as important as the results themselves.

CONCLUSION

As we asserted at the beginning of this chapter, getting started in assessing first-year programs can be a daunting but not impossible task if it is approached systematically. There are problems to be addressed and barriers to be overcome, but if assessment studies are conducted properly, they will have an enormous impact in improving the quality of first-year courses, programs, and services; providing guidance for promoting the success of first-year students; and defending institutional efforts to help first-year students make a successful transition to college.

CHAPTER TWENTY-NINE

Choosing and Using
Assessment Instruments

Randy L. Swing
M. Lee Upcraft

Selecting assessment instruments can be perhaps the most important decision made in designing and developing an assessment study, and often the most perplexing. A poorly designed instrument can ruin an otherwise credible assessment design, and a perfectly designed instrument that does not fit the purposes of the study can be equally destructive. This chapter discusses some of the issues in choosing and using assessment instruments, both qualitative and quantitative, and reviews in some detail the quantitative instruments and qualitative tools that directly or indirectly focus on the first college year.

A basic assumption of this chapter is that selecting an assessment instrument includes both a review of the content of the instrument and the technical aspects of the instrument. A collaboration between skilled partners can be helpful. For example a helpful partnership might be formed by a first-year program staff member as content expert, capable of knowing how fine nuances of terms might be understood or misunderstood by first-year students, and an assessment or institutional research officer as an expert on evaluating scales, instrument reliability statistics, and survey layout.

ISSUES IN CHOOSING ASSESSMENT INSTRUMENTS

There are many issues to be considered in choosing an appropriate assessment instrument.

Design the Study, Then Select the Instrument

The most common mistake is to choose the instrument and then design the study. An instrument should be chosen on the basis of its compatibility with

501

the purposes of the study and the design of the study. As noted in Chapter Twenty-Eight, instrument selection is step 7, after defining the problem, determining the purpose, determining where to get the information needed, determining the best assessment method(s), determining whom to study, and determining how the data will be collected. It is important to select an instrument that is appropriate for the level of motivation of the desired respondents and fits the time and other constraints of the collection process. Generally, response rates decline as data collection methods increase in length and complexity. Survey subjects receiving an instrument in class or in another captured audience setting may tolerate longer survey instruments than participants approached through a mailed survey design. First-year assessment studies often take advantage of group meetings, such as new student orientation, academic advising, or residence hall meetings, and required courses, such as first-year seminars or first-year English courses, to administer surveys. Administering instruments in naturally occurring settings is an advantage in assessment of first-year students and programs, which influence the instrument selection process.

Select an Instrument Consistent with the Purposes of the Study

An important decision in the design of the study is to determine the best assessment methods, choosing from among qualitative and quantitative methods or a combination of both. If a quantitative study is chosen, a good instrument must be selected or developed; if a qualitative study is chosen, a good interview protocol must be developed.

The ultimate use of the data is a critical consideration in instrument selection. If the results carry consequences for individuals (such as a placement test or qualifying exam), then the instrument must be carefully tested for validity and reliability. When results will be restricted to group analyses, however, some degree of uncontrolled variability will have little effect on the aggregated data. In other words, a more sophisticated instrument is needed to measure individual characteristics than is needed to measure an average across a group of individuals.

Choose Good Instruments

For quantitative studies, an instrument must be chosen that is psychometrically sound (meets accepted standards of validity, reliability and other criteria), easily scored, yields results that can be statistically analyzed, and offers nationally established norms against which local results may be compared (Upcraft & Schuh, 1996). For qualitative studies, interview protocols must be developed that consist of questions that are clearly worded, open-ended, and properly sequenced (Schuh, Upcraft, and Associates, 2001).

Avoid Locally Developed Quantitative Instruments

Institutionally based assessment designers are often tempted to develop their own quantitative instruments, for reasons including costs, convenience, and tailoring the instrument to the specific needs of the study. In general, this is a bad idea. Institutionally based assessment designers often lack the skills to develop psychometrically sound instruments. Such instruments are very difficult to develop and almost always lack face credibility with intended audiences. Moreover, there is a wide variety of commercially developed instruments that in most cases can be consistent with the purposes of an assessment study. However, if no commercially developed instrument fits the purposes of the study, Schuh, Upcraft, and Associates (2001) offer several suggestions for developing a quantitative instrument, including issues such as the format of questions, measurement scales, wording of questions, sequencing of questions, instrument format, and psychometric analyses.

TYPES OF QUANTITATIVE INSTRUMENTS

In the past five years, a number of new instruments, developed with focus on first-year assessment, joined the small number of classic instruments in the field. The following typology provides an overview of the types of instruments readily available for first-year assessment initiatives.

Preenrollment/Baseline Data

These surveys are typically administered at the end of high school, during the admissions process, or during new student orientation. Survey participants report their expectations, impressions, goals, and hopes for the college experience or they report their preenrollment behaviors and experiences. In addition to surveys, both the SAT and ACT admissions tests collect data about student characteristics, aspirations, and family demographics. The key point is that students complete these surveys before having any significant interaction with higher education. These surveys provide baseline data (students at the point of entry), are useful in calculating changes in first-year students when matched with posttest data, and provide useful information in later analyses by providing a way to statistically control for entering characteristics.

The oldest and most frequently used preenrollment/baseline instrument is the *Annual Survey of American College Freshmen,* developed and conducted by the Cooperative Institute Research Program (CIRP) of the Higher Education Research Institute (HERI) at the University of California Los Angeles (UCLA). Since 1966, this annual survey of entering first-year students, commonly known as the CIRP, has surveyed entering students' attitudes and values at the beginning of their first year of college. These data provide a snapshot of students entering higher education. Each participating institution receives tabulated local results, national results, and comparative data (based on admissions selectivity level and other institutional characteristics).

Other examples of preenrollment surveys include the *College Student Inventory* (CSI; Noel-Levitz), the *Entering Student Survey* (ESS; American College Testing Program), the *National Center on Postsecondary Teaching, Learning, and Assessment Pre-College Survey* (Center for the Study of Higher Education at Penn State University), and the *College Student Expectations Questionnaire* (CSXQ; Center for Postsecondary Research at Indiana University).

End-of-First-Year Surveys

Until recently, there were no survey instruments especially designed for administration at the end of the first college year. There are now several instruments in this category. These instruments record what a student did during the first year and how he or she has changed in terms of attitudes, behaviors, knowledge, and skills as a result of collegiate enrollment. The common link is that these surveys are administered near the end of the first year.

Two instruments measure student engagement with college. The most frequently used end-of-first-year survey is the *National Survey of Student Engagement* (NSSE; Center for Postsecondary Research at Indiana University) for use at four-year campuses. This instrument gathers information on an annual basis about student participation in programs and activities that institutions provide for their learning and personal development, as well as students' estimate of gains and demographic information. (For a more detailed discussion of the NSSE, see Chapter Five.) The *Community College Survey of Student Engagement* (CCSSE; Community College Leadership Program at the University of Texas at Austin) is similarly designed for use in community college settings. Both NSSE and CCSSE are administered to random samples of first-year students, making them best examples of an instrument using a strictly controlled randomized sampling procedure that provides unique opportunities for generalizing the results across institutions. The estimation-of-gains section may be especially helpful in identifying self-reported educational outcomes.

The *Your First College Year* (YFCY) survey, also designed for use at the end of the first year of college, was developed as a result of a partnership between the Policy Center on the First Year of College and the Higher Education Research Institute at UCLA, with funding from The Pew Charitable Trusts and The Atlantic Philanthropies. The survey provides information about students as they enter their sophomore year and, when used in conjunction with the CIRP, provides measurements of change (pre- and posttest measures) in selected student attitudes, values, experiences, and learning outcomes.

Two instruments, the *College Student Experiences Questionnaire* (CSEQ; Center for Postsecondary Research at Indiana University) and the *Community College Student Experiences Questionnaire* (CCSEQ; Center for the Study of Higher Education at the University of Memphis), specifically measure how students invest their time and effort in educationally purposeful activities inside and outside the classroom, as well as students' perceptions of the institutional environment and self-reported estimates of gains in student learning and personal development. Both instruments can be administered at any point after students have had adequate time to experience college: the end of one term, several terms, or at the completion of the college experience. The CSEQ, when merged with data from its companion "expectations" instrument (CSXQ), provides opportunities to compare the degree to which student expectations were or were not fulfilled by their college experiences.

Another post-first-term student instrument is the *First-Year Initiative* Survey (FYI), which assesses student learning gains produced by first-year seminars.

FYI was developed by Educational Benchmarking, Inc. and the Policy Center on the First Year of College with support from The Atlantic Philanthropies and The Pew Charitable Trusts. Using a benchmarking approach, FYI is designed to provide comparative data for seminars with similar goals and institutional context. The *Student Adaptation to College Questionnaire* (SACQ; Western Psychological Services) measures students' reactions to college, including instruction, program planning, administrative affairs, and out-of-class activities. And the *Student Development Task and Lifestyle Inventory* (Student Development Associates) measures Arthur Chickering's first three vectors of student development that are considered typical of first-year student development.

Student Needs Assessment Instruments

While Schuh and Upcraft (2001) recommend using qualitative assessment methods to assess student needs, there are a few quantitative instruments available, including the *College Student Needs Assessment Survey* (American College Testing Program), which assesses the educational and personal needs of college students, such as career and life goals and educational and personal needs.

Student Satisfaction Instruments

There are many general student satisfaction instruments, only one of which is specifically designed for first-year students, but all the others can be used to assess first-year student satisfaction. One of the most frequently used is the *Student Satisfaction Inventory* (SSI; Noel-Levitz), which measures student satisfaction with a variety of institutional programs at two- and four-year institutions. Unique to the SSI is a dual measurement scale that records ratings of both "importance" and "satisfaction." Resulting analyses highlight areas of highest importance and lowest satisfaction, where change is most needed. Another is the *Student Opinion Survey* (SOS; American College Testing Program), which measures student satisfaction with college services and the overall collegiate environment. Finally, *Student Satisfaction: The Freshman Experience* (Clearinghouse for Higher Education Assessment) measures first-year student satisfaction with all aspects of collegiate life.

Surveys of Specific Services, Units, and Programs

These surveys investigate a particular slice of the college experience with a series of narrowly drawn and specific questions about the full range of a given service, unit, or program. Instruments may include demographic and self-report questions so that opinions can be disaggregated by student characteristics. Here are some examples of available instruments:

- Academic advising: Instruments include *Survey of Academic Advising* (ACT), the *Academic Advising Inventory* (Student Development Associates), and the *Developmental Advising Inventory* (Developmental Advising Inventories).
- Residence life: Educational Benchmarking, Inc. (EBI) and the Association of College and University Housing Officers-International (ACUHO-I) have jointly

developed the following instruments: *Apartment Survey; Resident Satisfaction Survey;* and the *Resident Assistant Survey.* The *University Residence Environment Scale* (Consulting Psychologists Press) assesses the social climates of student living groups and has two versions: an expected social climate for entering students and a form for current residents.

- Campus unions: Educational Benchmarking, Inc. and the Association of College Unions International have jointly developed the *ACUI/EBI Student Survey* to assess user satisfaction with union facilities, services, and programs.

- Health services: Instruments designed to assess health services include the *Health Services Student Survey* (University Health Services at Penn State University) and the *Student Health Services Student Survey* (Office of Planning and Assessment at the University of Kentucky).

Surveys of Specific Student Populations

These instruments primarily provide information to evaluate the needs, experiences, satisfaction, and learning of specific group of students. Examples of instruments include:

- Adult learners: The *Adult Learner Needs Assessment Survey* (American College Testing) assesses perceived needs in life-skill and career development, educational planning, and relationships with others at the point of entry into higher education. The *Adult Student Priorities Survey* (Noel-Levitz) asks students over the age of twenty-five to rate their satisfaction with a wide range of college services and also to rate how important they consider each service to be.

- Greek life members: Examples include the *Fraternity and Sorority Survey* (Educational Benchmarking, Inc.), which includes topics such as self-reported gains from Greek life involvement, satisfaction with institutional services, and behaviors such as alcohol use patterns.

- Alumni: Although at first glance, surveys of alumni may appear to have little to do with assessing the first-year experience, alumni recollections of their collegiate experience may provide valuable insights for those designing and implementing first-year programs and services. ACT's *Alumni Outcomes Survey* is one example of a survey of recent graduates.

Too often, first-year assessment efforts include only successful first-year students, that is, those who stay enrolled, and ignore those who drop out, thus providing a very skewed view of the first-year experience. However, those who leave college during or at the end of their first year of college can provide extremely valuable insights into the effectiveness of first-year efforts, although these students are often hard to find after they leave, and if found, may not want to participate in an assessment of their experiences. Schuh and Upcraft (2001) recommend qualitative telephone surveys or quantitative on-line surveys instead of mailed surveys, but if a mailed survey is desired, the *Withdrawing/Non-returning Student Survey* (ACT), which includes reasons for leaving college, college services satisfaction, and background information is one possibility.

The instruments mentioned earlier for use at the end of the first college year may prove to be the most useful for understanding students who complete the first year but do not return for the sophomore year. Because the NSSE, CCSSE, CIRP, and YFCY are administered before the end of the first year and collect a student identification number, it is possible to later code the survey responses for those students who drop out by merging the survey data with official student records. These data, collected before the student departs, are likely to produce the largest collection of information for studying students after they stop out, drop out, or transfer out.

A new source of information about dropouts is the National Student Clearinghouse. Originally the database tracked only financial aid recipients, but now it includes enrollment data from nearly 80 percent of all students who have attended college in recent years. This multiyear data source allows institutions to track withdrawn students over time to determine if they stopped out and later returned to college, stopped attending postsecondary education anywhere, or transferred to another institution.

Academic Knowledge and Skills Instruments

These instruments are designed to test academic knowledge and skills. Unlike opinion and satisfaction surveys, these instruments usually have a right or wrong answer, and the student is judged on his or her ability to select the best (right) answer. Some instruments contain a mix of subjects, but it is more common for tests to be designed to measure one specific knowledge domain. These instruments are generally used in three ways: (1) to place students into the appropriate level of college courses based on knowledge at the point of admissions, to screen first- or second-year students for admission into majors, and to assess academic programs by measuring gain in knowledge accrued by students who are completing a particular curriculum or academic intervention.

Probably the most frequently used academic knowledge tests are the *Collegiate Assessment of Academic Proficiency* (CAAP; ACT) and the *SAT II* (College Board). Both the SAT II and CAAP tests can be used at the point of entry into college to establish precollege skill levels. The CAAP tests are also used with rising juniors or graduating seniors as a posttest of general education knowledge and skills. CAAP tests are a collection of individual instruments measuring reading, writing, mathematics, science reasoning, and critical thinking. For assessing factual knowledge and the application of knowledge, the *SAT II Subject Achievement Tests* (College Board) include tests in English, history and social studies, mathematics, science, and languages. The *Academic Profile* (long and short forms; ETS) and *CollegeBASE* (Assessment Resource Center at the University of Missouri-Columbia) also provide measures of general education subjects. *Accuplacer* (computer version) and *Companion* (paper version), published by ETS, are specifically designed to measure writing skills at the point of entry into college.

Also included in this category are instruments that measure critical thinking, often favored by faculty teaching first-year students because these faculty place a high value on this skill as an outcome of their teaching. These instruments include the *Watson-Glaser Critical Thinking Appraisal* (Psychological Corporation), the *California Critical Thinking Skills Test* and the *California Critical Thinking Dispositions Inventory* (California Academic Press), and the *Cornell Critical Thinking Test* (Critical Thinking Press and Software).

HOW TO SELECT QUANTITATIVE ASSESSMENT INSTRUMENTS

Often the array of quantitative instruments available can be confusing, if not overwhelming. We suggest several ways in which this task can become less daunting:

• *Find out more about an instrument's purpose and the ways in which the instrument has been used.* From a wide variety of sources (including publishers' Web sites, annotated reviews of instruments, and instrument manuals), determine if, from an overall perspective, the instrument fits your intended purpose. Has it been used for studies with similar purposes? Has it been used at comparable institutions with comparable student populations? If it has been used at other institutions, what do they think about it?

• *Evaluate the psychometric properties of the instrument.* High-quality assessment instruments will have data about the various psychometric properties such as validity (Does the instrument measure what it purports to measure?), reliability (Does the instrument elicit consistent responses?), and other factors. Someone with expertise in this area should review the instrument to determine if it meets accepted psychometric criteria.

• *Find out about the scoring and analyses services of the publisher.* Most instrument publishers offer scoring and analysis services that can provide the user with more sophisticated and timely results than local scoring and analyses. Sometimes publishers provide these services in the cost of the instrument, while others assess an additional charge.

• *Determine if national norms are available.* Most instrument publishers provide norms based on previous administrations of the instruments that can become minimum passing scores or the basis for judging individual student performance, if that is the purpose of the study. But if one of the purposes of the study is to compare one institution's results with those of other institutions, then instruments with national norms or a purposeful benchmarking process must be selected. It is important to know if published norms were established as user norms (uncontrolled collection of scores) or created by a controlled sampling methodology.

• *Consider the cost of the instrument.* Instruments vary greatly in their costs, so some judgment must be made about the affordability of an instrument. Typically, publishers charge by the number of instruments ordered, so the size of the sample or population may determine whether an instrument is affordable. Expensive instruments may be efficiently used for aggregate-level studies by randomly or purposefully selecting a sample set of students to receive the instrument.

• *Identify the factors measured by the instrument.* Typically, instrument items are clustered together in order to explain larger or more complex behaviors.

These factors may result from logical or intuitive clusters of questions or from more sophisticated statistical analyses. Either way, it must be determined if these factors are logically consistent with the purposes of the study, easily understood, and useful in interpreting results.

- *Read through the instrument for a broad overview of the instrument's content,* to get an overall sense of whether it fits the purposes of the study. Seldom does one commercially developed instrument fit exactly, but those with the option to add locally developed items can help customize the instrument for the purposes of the study.

- *Complete a sample copy.* One key step in evaluating an instrument is to complete a sample copy (not just read over it) as the fine nuances often become apparent only when attempting to answer each survey question. When selecting an instrument's content, know that off-the-shelf instruments frequently contain some irrelevant data. It is not unusual for assessment officers to ignore a segment of survey data that is not appropriate for the local campus conditions. For example, one question about residence halls may not spoil an instrument's usefulness for a commuter campus or community college without residence halls. At some point, however, students may not take seriously an instrument with numerous questions that are not appropriate for their own campus experience.

- *Pilot the instrument.* Select a small group of participants (maybe a dozen) who are roughly representative of the population under study, and administer the instrument. Inform the participants of the purpose of the study and how the instrument will be used. After the participants complete the instrument, score the instrument for each participant, and ask for their feedback. For example, the feedback might include questions such as, "Overall, what did you think of this instrument?" "Are the items clear?" "Is your score indicative of how you think and feel about this subject?" "Is this an instrument that would work with participants like yourselves?" "Does this instrument measure what it says it measures?" "What are the downsides of using this instrument, given the purposes of the study?" Information gained from piloting the instrument can help considerably in deciding how the instrument should be used or if the instrument should be discarded in favor of another.

Of course, no one instrument will satisfy all of these considerations, so most instruments are selected with some downsides. In general, commercially available instruments should be used instead of locally developed ones. However, if a locally developed instrument is the only alternative, it should be constructed using accepted standards of instrument construction.

QUALITATIVE ASSESSMENT TOOLS

There are many equally credible ways of assessing first-year initiatives other than quantitative approaches. The use of qualitative methods, including focus groups, one-minute papers, portfolios, "mystery shoppers," field observations, and other tools can provide important information about services, programs, and individual student progress.

Focus Groups

The traditional focus group (Morris, 2001; Krueger, 1988) and the technology-enhanced focus group (Swing, 2001) are capable of producing rich data for stand-alone study or for merging with instrument-based data sets. Focus groups must be planned and designed very carefully to ensure that information is collected in a way that is consistent with the purposes of the study. (An example of the use of focus groups in assessing orientation programs was discussed in Chapter Twenty-Three.)

One-Minute Papers

Virginia Commonwealth University (Hodges & Yerian, 2001) adapted the concept of the one-minute paper (Angelo & Cross, 1993) to collect brief, impromptu written statements from students in first-year English classes. Each week students were given a prompt and asked to write for five minutes on the topic. Topics covered subjects such as feelings and experiences in large classes, the registration process, and orientation. Papers were read by teams of faculty who identified common themes and created summaries with direct quotes from students. The resulting reports, powerful statements about the structures of the first college year, led to changes in parking for commuter students and a reduction in the number of large classes offered in the first college year. Systematically capturing the student voice and involving faculty directly in the assessment process proved particularly effective in this assessment effort.

Portfolios

Portfolios are usually associated with summative assessment, but a number of institutions of higher education are requiring students to begin developing an academic portfolio during the first year of college. The process of developing a portfolio requires each student to archive examples of academic work, select the most meaningful pieces, and reflect on the relative merits of the works presented. Some portfolio collections allow students to add new work over time but do not allow students to remove prior work, so that the portfolio develops a picture of the student's progress over time. Other portfolio assessments use randomly selected examples of student work to form a course or curricular assessment process, which is transparent to the student. In the first example, the focus of the assessment is on the individual student, and in the second example the focus is on the educational intervention.

Mystery Shoppers

Charles Schroeder (2001) suggests a "mystery shopper" program as an assessment strategy for campus auxiliary services. A service unit (such as the bookstore or cafeteria) establishes goals for customer service with defined levels of acceptable performance for each goal, and students are trained to recognize the acceptable level of performance and goals of the service unit. The trained student then uses the service, records the actual level of service provided, and provides an anonymous report to the service unit showing the degree to which unit goals were met during the student's use of the unit's services. Mystery shopper programs are intended to provide formative evaluation for continuous improvement, not to discipline individual employees.

Field Observations

Sometimes the best data collection instrument is simply observing and counting actual students as they participate in an activity or use a particular service. In planning for remodeling of an existing library, one institution performed hourly counts of students in the library over a two-week period. This field observation established the times associated with highest use of library facilities and recorded the distribution of students in the library facilities (small group meeting rooms, audiovisual room, individual study carrels, computer stations, or somewhere else). A more sophisticated field observation was conducted by Karen Schilling and Karl Schilling (1999) as a study of how first-year students spend their time. Students were given electronic beepers that could be activated by the research team and told to record the activity they were engaged in anytime they were "beeped." Students were randomly assigned to one of several time schedules so that each student was beeped a few times each day, forming a sampling pattern across the whole group of students. The collected records provided a picture of how students use their time.

ASSESSMENT USING EXISTING DATA

Not all assessment requires collecting new data from an instrument or qualitative assessment tool. Some assessment is built completely on existing data. It is good practice to conduct a data audit to discover the sources of existing data and develop a plan to link those data so they can be used in assessment work. An excellent guide for conducting a first-year data audit is available from the National Center for Higher Education Management Systems in Boulder, Colorado.

For example, using existing data, Stephen R. Porter and Paul D. Umbach (2002) investigated a concern that many University of Maryland students were arriving late to class. The disruption of class was annoying to teachers and believed to be harmful to the learning environment. Porter and Umbach incorporated campus mapping data to determine the travel time between campus buildings and merged those data with student class schedules. The finding that 28.8 percent of students had back-to-back classes with walking times between classes that exceeded ten minutes, the scheduled time between classes, explained a significant proportion of late class arrivals. Because first-year students enroll in a wide range of courses, more of them (35 percent) had schedules containing long travel times than the schedules of upperclassmen (24 percent) who, after declaring a major, tended to have courses in fewer and more tightly grouped buildings requiring shorter travel times. This study showed that compacting class schedules using back-to-back classes is an unnecessary disruption that could be addressed by advisers in schedule planning to create an improved first college year.

RECOMMENDATIONS

Choosing and using assessment instruments is never an easy task. We offer the following advice in instrument selection, use, and interpretation:

- *Design the study first; then select the instrument.* Resist the temptation to select an instrument and then determine how it will be used. Instrument selection is a part of the assessment process, not the starting point.
- *Select an instrument consistent with the purposes of the study.* Make sure that the instrument selected (either qualitative or quantitative) actually gathers the information needed to fulfill the purposes of the study.
- *For a quantitative study, follow these guidelines:*

  1. Select an instrument with acceptable psychometric properties.
  2. Select a publisher that provides scoring and analysis services, as well as standardized national norms.
  3. Select an instrument that is affordable and cost-effective.
  4. Inspect the instrument, and complete a sample copy.
  5. Pilot the instrument with a group of potential participants in the study.

- *For a qualitative study, develop interview protocols for a focus group that consist of clearly worded, open-ended, and properly sequenced questions.* Consider other qualitative tools such as one-minute essays, portfolios, field observations, and mystery shoppers.
- *Consider using existing data to assess first-year programs and services.* Sometimes studies can be designed that do not involve gathering new data.

CONCLUSION

The quality of an assessment is directly influenced by the quality of the data collection process. No amount of statistical analyses can mitigate problems created by a poorly constructed instrument or one improperly matched to the assessment plan. Selection should be consistent with the purposes of an assessment study. Fortunately, there is an array of high-quality instruments available for assessing first-year students as well as their courses and programs. Choosing the most appropriate assessment instrument, quantitative or qualitative, requires knowledge of first-year structures and assessment design, levels of knowledge that are usually available on college campuses. Consultation and advice should be sought from those who are qualified to evaluate how an instrument will fit appropriate statistical analyses, if response scales properly match questions, and other technical aspects of survey design beyond the scope of this chapter. Educators who work directly with first-year students and programs should also be included in the selection process because of their expert knowledge of these students and support structures. The ultimate measure of a successful assessment instrument selection is not how it was chosen or how it was developed, but whether the resulting data are useful for improving first-year structures and learning outcomes.

CONCLUSION

Principles of Good Practice for the First College Year and Summary of Recommendations

John N. Gardner
M. Lee Upcraft
Betsy O. Barefoot

We began this book by asking, "Why another look at the first year of college?" We hope we have answered that question by updating readers on the many accomplishments and improvements in efforts to help first-year students succeed and offering possible solutions to many of the challenges that remain. We framed this task within Sanford's (1962) concept of challenge and support.

We hope we have provided readers with a basis for a continuing dialogue on the first year of college, recognizing that time and space prevented us from looking at all the ways in which first-year student success is enhanced.

PRINCIPLES OF GOOD PRACTICE FOR THE FIRST COLLEGE YEAR

While this book contains a myriad of issues, topics, and initiatives relative to challenging and supporting first-year student success, we believe that certain defined principles constitute a framework for good practice in the first year. The following principles are based on our experience in teaching, counseling, and advising first-year students; our knowledge of the literature and research on the first college year; our involvement in this research; our vast and various experiences in administering first-year courses, services, and programs; observations of hundreds of campus-based first-year initiatives; and our educational values that place student learning as our highest priority:

- The foundation of first-year student success is an institutional commitment by its leadership, faculty, staff, and governing boards to support the first year of college. This means developing policies and practices, courses, programs and services, and resources necessary to fulfill this commitment. It also means that each institution must clearly state its objectives for first-year students and make a commitment to first-year student success that pervades all of its educational initiatives, both inside and outside the classroom, and involves all its faculty and staff.

• Efforts to promote first-year student success begin with a focus on student learning, both inside and outside the classroom. Institutions that recognize that student learning is their highest priority will provide classroom environments that focus on teaching and learning and develop out-of-class environments that are linked to learning goals. While first-year students' engagement in their classrooms and related activities contributes directly to their success, what they do outside the classroom also affects their cognitive development and academic achievement.

• Partnerships between student affairs and academic affairs are essential in integrating first-year students' in-class and out-of class learning experiences. Institutions can no longer afford to treat student affairs and academic affairs as separate entities operating as if the other did not exist. This may have implications for alignments of organizational structures. First-year students have a better chance of success if these two units work closely together and implement jointly sponsored programs such as first-year seminars, service-learning, and learning communities.

• A delicate balance of both challenge and support is necessary to foster first-year student success. There must be a judicious mixture of challenging students to achieve their educational goals while at the same time providing support for that task. Furthermore, colleges and universities must create learning environments that both challenge and support students and avoid creating an imbalance between the two, both inside and outside the classroom.

• First-year student success is most likely when institutions hold students to high standards of academic performance and personal conduct by establishing and communicating high expectations. First-year students need to know that their institution maintains academic standards that challenge them to perform to the best of their abilities and also establishes standards of conduct necessary for an orderly and educational campus climate. They must also be held accountable for their academic performance and their personal conduct.

• Campus climates that are inclusive and supportive of all first-year students are more likely to produce higher levels of student learning and success. Campus climates should be built on the basis of the actual backgrounds and characteristics of students, not some stereotypical notion of what students are presumed to be. That means building climates that treat students with equity and dignity regardless of their age, gender, race/ethnicity, nationality, religion, sexual orientation, disability, or other defining characteristics.

• Systematic assessments are essential in order to improve student and institutional performance and demonstrate the effectiveness of first-year initiatives. Assessment is a necessary and integral component of all first-year initiatives and should be conducted within accepted professional standards. Assessment results can be used to measure first-year student needs, their satisfaction with first-year initiatives, the effectiveness of these initiatives given desired outcomes, campus climates, and cost-effectiveness of first-year initiatives. Assessment is also an integral part of regional accreditation criteria.

• Students are more likely to succeed in an atmosphere where they are treated with dignity and respect. While some progress has been made, too often first-year students are still seen as objects to be "weeded out," and in rare cases "hazed," rather than persons who need help in pursuing their educational goals. Perhaps the most devastating show of disrespect is the failure to provide first-year initiatives that help them succeed, or to provide piecemeal, ineffective services and programs. Treating first-year students with respect also means admitting only those who have a reasonable chance of succeeding, and providing them with the support they need to meet their educational goals.

• First-year students can be taught the strategies and skills they need to fulfill their educational goals. Institutions must promote first-year student success by teaching them what and how to learn, providing them with opportunities to grow and develop, and teaching them the skills necessary to become responsible citizens.

• Faculty are an important key to first-year student success. It is their skill in challenging and supporting student learning inside the classroom and engaging students outside the classroom that makes a difference in first-year student success. Failure to get faculty involved in first-year student success will seriously undermine institutional efforts to promote that success.

• Ultimately, first-year students themselves must assume responsibility for their own success. To be sure, institutions have a responsibility to create educational environments that both challenge and support first-year students and promote their success. However, first-year students must assume the ultimate responsibility to engage themselves in the learning process, work hard to achieve their educational goals, take advantage of institutional efforts to help them succeed, and assume responsibility for their own success.

SUMMARY OF RECOMMENDATIONS

Within these principles of good practice, the following summary of recommendations provides ways in which institutions can develop an integrated, comprehensive approach to challenging and supporting students as they attempt to achieve their educational goals.

Organizing for First-Year Student Success

• Include a strong commitment to promoting first-year student success in the institution's mission statement. All efforts to promote first-year student success flow from an institutional mission statement that includes a strong commitment to the first year of college. Intentional efforts inside and outside the classroom to help students make a successful transition to college and achieve their educational goals, resource allocation to make these interventions happen, and assessment to demonstrate their worth all must flow from a mission statement. An institution cannot be too intentional about the design and promulgation of its mission and its connection to first-year initiatives. Moreover, an institution should have a philosophy and mission statement for its first college year.

- Develop a strong commitment of the administrative leadership of the institution, including the chief executive officer, the chief academic officer, the chief fiscal officer, and the chief student affairs officer to provide the leadership and resources necessary to promote first-year student success. While middle management, faculty, and staff affect change in focusing on first-year student success, a strong commitment from the leadership of an institution is absolutely necessary to help students make a successful transition to college and achieve their educational goals. The executive leadership of an institution can make a real difference in the quality and effectiveness of first-year initiatives, from the "bully pulpit" of the president's or chancellor's office to institutional resource allocation to setting a tone that determines the real values of the organization.

- Engage deans and department heads in initiatives that promote first-year student success inside and outside the classroom. All the executive leadership in the world will have little impact if the academic leadership of the institution (such as academic deans and department and program heads) are not committed to first-year student success and willing to devote needed time and resources to meet this goal.

- Create a permanent advisory board to assist policymakers and decision makers in matters pertaining to first-year student success. An advisory board with access to the highest levels of institutional policy development and decision making will keep first-year student success high on the list of priorities for institutional leaders, as well as provide valuable advice in creating and maintaining high-quality and effective first-year student initiatives. Advisory boards can also help coordinate the many first-year initiatives.

- Focus the institution's enrollment management function not only on recruitment and admission of qualified students, but in subsequent student success initiatives. Enrollment managers must constantly improve their ability to predict first-year student success, coordinate their efforts with other first-year initiatives such as academic advising, financial aid, and orientation, and become an integral part of an institution's retention efforts.

Promoting First-Year Student Success in the Classroom

- Place faculty at the center of initiatives designed to promote first-year student success, and reward them for their efforts in ways consistent with the institution's promotion and tenure policies. Faculty will have more influence on first-year student success than anyone else, or any particular program or service, so they must be encouraged to become actively engaged in first-year student success. That encouragement will be considerably enhanced if the institution's promotion and tenure policies reflect engagement in first-year student success.

- Provide professional development opportunities for full-time faculty, part-time faculty, and teaching assistants that improve their ability to teach first-year students. They must be given professional development opportunities to learn ways in which to help first-year students succeed, including curricular and teaching reforms, as well as involvement outside the classroom in initiatives such as learning communities.

• Develop first-year seminars that have academic integrity, and address issues that are related to first-year student success. They must include elements commensurate with the norm of academic credibility on campus, reflect the needs of entering students, include significant academic content, and be assessed to determine their relationship to first-year student academic success.

• Reform classroom practices so that they reflect an emphasis on student learning and include teaching strategies consistent with the needs of today's first-year students. Classroom activities must be focused on student learning, help students understand why they are learning what they are being taught, provide sufficient structure and practice, reflect a variety of instructional strategies, and include technology as a learning tool.

• Create developmental education programs that promote the intellectual, social, and emotional growth of all students. These programs must be based in the reality that there are some students who are better prepared to achieve than others and build on first-year students' strengths rather than their deficiencies. These programs must stress the transferability of skills to other learning settings, engage students actively in the learning process, and provide academic support services to enhance achievement among all students.

• Create Supplemental Instruction programs that assist first-year students in courses that are challenging to them. First-year students in traditionally difficult courses are invited to participate in regularly scheduled, small group collaborative learning sessions led by instructor-approved, properly trained upperclass students who previously achieved high grades in these courses.

• Develop academic advising that is tailored to the specific needs of an institution and its students, and focused on helping students succeed academically. There are many different advising models, and an institution must decide which model best suits its mission and the needs of its first-year students, but all models must focus on helping these students succeed academically.

• Focus the library services on the unique needs of first-year students by teaching them how to become more information literate. Libraries are no longer just places to look for information and study. They are comprehensive information delivery systems in which extensive resources are available to all students, regardless of their location. Therefore, libraries have an obligation to teach first-year students how to access, verify, and use information relevant to their classroom and curricular demands. Furthermore, librarians must be more involved in campuswide efforts to promote first-year student success.

Promoting First-Year Student Success Outside the Classroom

• Develop orientation programs that help first-year students make a successful transition to college, both inside and outside the classroom. Such programs must focus on helping first-year students succeed academically, helping them in their adjustment to and involvement in their college experience, involving parents and family in helping them make a successful transition to college, and fully integrating first-year students into the collegiate environment. Orientation must be a continuous process that is sensitive to the needs of an increasingly diverse first-year population, incorporates technology into its delivery systems, involves faculty in its programs, includes transfer students, and, above all, has academic substance.

• Create learning environments, both on campus and off campus, that are consistent with the educational and curricular goals of an institution. On campus, this means residence halls must be orderly, safe, and secure; provide programs that help first-year students integrate their in-class and out-of-class learning experiences; create environments that promote and affirm diversity; and offer programs that help first-year students make a successful transition to college. Off campus, this means encouraging first-year students to become actively engaged in student-to-student and student-to-faculty relationships and participate in freshman interest groups, and providing opportunities for engagement with residential students and programs.

• Target all student support services to first-year student success. These services include financial aid; student counseling and health services; campus recreation programs; college unions; career services; adult student services; women's centers; student athlete support services; gay, lesbian, bisexual, and transgendered student services; disabled student services; services for international students; honors students programs; and services for racial/ethnic minorities.

• Develop alcohol and other drug educational and prevention initiatives that combat the negative influence of alcohol and drugs on first-year student success. These efforts must include coordinated outreach programs designed to communicate accurate information and reduce alcohol use and abuse, emergency and counseling services to treat students with alcohol-related problems, judicial systems that hold students accountable for their behavior as well as encouraging alcohol-related behavior change, and readily available alcohol-free programming activities.

Promoting Collaboration and Partnerships Between Student Affairs and Academic Affairs

• Involve the chief student affairs officer and the chief academic officer in intentional initiatives that help first-year students integrate their in-class and out-of-class learning experiences. These initiatives must have the common purpose of helping first-year students succeed and be well coordinated and jointly supported, and systematically link and align a variety of resources. Partnerships must be ongoing journeys rather than discrete events and must involve all stakeholders in their implementation.

• Develop service-learning initiatives that help first-year students develop a sense of civic responsibility. Credit-bearing educational experiences in which first-year students participate in an organized activity that meets community needs and results in an enhanced sense of civic responsibility must be an essential part of first-year student initiatives. Service-learning projects must be supported by faculty and the community, designed to challenge the capabilities of first-year students, and fully integrated into other institutional efforts designed to help first-year students succeed.

• Develop learning communities that help first-year students better integrate their in-class and out-of-class learning experiences. Clusters of courses organized around a curricular theme that students take as a group strengthen and enrich students' connections to each other, their faculty, and the subject matter they are studying, as well as promoting academic achievement and retention; they must be an integral part of an institution's first-year student initiatives. They depend on the collaboration of student affairs and academic affairs at all levels, and often, although not exclusively, are residence based.

Making Assessment an Essential Part of Promoting First-Year Student Success

• Develop a comprehensive assessment program that provides information necessary to evaluate initiatives that promote first-year student success. Assessment approaches must include tracking first-year students' backgrounds and characteristics, assessing their needs, and assessing their satisfaction with first-year initiatives. Assessments must also provide evidence of any relationships between first-year initiatives and desired first-year outcomes, such as academic achievement, retention into the sophomore year, and selected developmental outcomes. Assessments can provide useful comparisons to other comparable institutions, assess cost-effectiveness, and measure campus climates.

• Disseminate assessment results in ways that establish and revise institutional policies and practices as well as maintain accountability of first-year student initiatives. Assessment results must be used to demonstrate the worth of first-year initiatives and improve their quality. But they must also play an important role in institutional strategic planning, policy development, decision making, accreditation, and other institutional processes. Moreover, new partnerships must be established between institutional research offices and policymakers and practitioners in which information is shared and used.

Helping Students Make Constructive Use of Technology

• Use technology in ways that promote, not detract from, first-year student success. The reality is that technology pervades almost every aspect of first-year students' lives and must be recognized as a powerful influence, for good or for ill, on first-year student success. Therefore, institutions must develop and manage technology in their classrooms, residence halls, student support services, and administrative systems in ways that take full advantage of the learning potential of technology while limiting its negative effects.

Other Recommendations

• Develop school-college partnerships that are designed to involve secondary schools in first-year student success efforts. As traditional-aged first-year students enter college, institutions are hardly working with a tabula rasa. Because there is a powerful connection between the first year of college and first-year students' educational experiences prior to college, we must all be more invested in improving the K–12 experience. Such partnerships must be the responsibility of the whole institution, not just teacher-education academic programs.

• Look beyond the first year of college to subsequent transitions. Institutions must not abandon students as they successfully complete their first year of college. For example, there are important challenges to be met and support to be provided during the sophomore year, when students must make career and major decisions. The senior year also presents unique challenges to students, including securing employment or gaining admission to graduate or professional schools. So first-year initiatives must be concerned not only with immediate challenges, but longer-term ones as well.

LOOKING TOWARD THE FUTURE

Although those of us who are dedicated to improving the first year of college can take pride in all that we have accomplished, there remain many challenges. We have cited numerous examples of best practices in campus-specific efforts in this book, yet many of these practices have yet to be empirically validated. One approach to solving this problem is to go beyond the microlevel of best practices at the individual institutional level and concentrate instead on the macrolevel—that is, look at what selected campuses are doing in a coherent, intentional, and integrated manner to achieve excellence in the first year of college.

In 2002, the Policy Center on the First Year of College located in Brevard, North Carolina (funded by The Atlantic Philanthropies and Lumina Foundation for Education), undertook two projects designed to examine first-year initiatives at the macrolevel. The first was a study entitled "Institutions of Excellence in the First Year of College." The Policy Center developed a set of criteria for excellence in the first year of college and then invited chief academic officers in the United States to measure their institutions against these criteria. Some 130 institutions responded to this invitation to be evaluated for excellence in the first year. These institutions represented the full spectrum of higher education institutions, including community colleges, regional comprehensive public universities, research universities, private institutions, and military service academies. The thirteen finalists in this project present a compelling portrait of excellence revealed in a number of unique and common themes that will be published in a forthcoming book by Jossey-Bass.

The second initiative undertaken by the Policy Center on the First Year of College is designed to develop standards of excellence that can be validated through a vigorous research effort. This two-year research project, entitled "Foundations of Excellence in the First College Year™," is being implemented by the Policy Center in partnership with the American Association of Colleges and Universities and the Council for Independent Colleges. Of the 219 members of these organizations that expressed interest in participating in this research, 24 were selected to work with the Policy Center to develop and validate sector-specific standards (referred to as Foundational Dimensions™) for the first college year. Each participating institution will undergo a performance audit involving internal assessment and external validation to determine their level of achievement of the Foundational Dimensions.

The ultimate goals of this project are to develop a research-based, comprehensive model of the first college year that has the potential of increasing first-year student success and develop a method for participating campuses to assess their own level of achievement. This research will use both the National Survey of Student Engagement and surveys developed by the Center for the Study of Higher Education at Penn State University under the leadership of Patrick Terenzini. Following the completion of the pilot study, the project will be expanded (resources permitting) to other types of institutions, including research universities and community colleges. We believe that this project has the potential to offer a research-validated blueprint for policy and action, recognize institutions that are truly exemplary, and move efforts to promote first-year student success beyond the individual institutional level to a more comprehensive view of what an exemplary first college year should entail.

In the short run, perhaps the greatest challenge facing higher education is to encourage institutions to implement their commitment to the first year of college by providing the resources to promote first-year student success. This is not an easy task and will happen only if higher education makes the first year of college a high priority and develops proven strategies to make institutions "walk the walk" as well as "talk the talk." This will more likely happen if a culture of assessment develops in each institution that can validate efforts to promote first-year student success.

CONCLUSION

This concludes our book. But as good liberal arts graduates of many years ago, we realize that the conclusions that matter the most are yours. And you, our readers and colleagues, are the ones who have the ability to write the next chapters of the first-year reform movement on your campus. This is an ongoing process that must remain forever dynamic as our country, campuses, and students continue to change and evolve. So in a sense, there is really no concluding chapter to this important national conversation, only the next chapter.

If you were not already with us as an active partner in this huge national and international community of higher educators and external policymakers interested in increasing the success of beginning college students, we hope this work has encouraged you to join us in some appropriate manner. Drawing on our own professional and personal lives, we can bear personal testimony that there is enormous professional and personal gratification to be derived by us and the students when we increase their success by such means as those explored in this book. We have experienced, and thus believe, that first-year students can and will do better when placed in intentional intellectual and social campus environments that challenge and support their efforts to succeed.

We invite and look forward to your reactions to this book, and we also invite you to assist us in improving the assessment of this entire body of work, the first year of college as a unit of analysis, all as a means to the end of increasing first-year student learning, success, and retention. Given the demographic profile of this author team, it may well be that some of you readers will be writing a future Jossey-Bass book revisiting this book as the scholarly basis of departure for your newer thinking and experiences. We believe you are out there. Our country and our students need you.

REFERENCES

Abbey, A., Ross, L. T., McDuffie, D., & McAuslan, P. (1996). Alcohol and dating risk factors for sexual assault among college women. *Psychology of Women Quarterly, 20,* 147–169.

Abbey, A., Zawacki, T., Buck, P., Clinton, M., & McAuslan, P. (2001). Alcohol and sexual assault. *Alcohol Research and Health, 25,* 43–51.

Abbott, J. (1996). The search for next-century learning. *AAHE Bulletin, 48*(7), 3–6.

Abraham, A. A. (1987). *Report on college-level remedial/developmental programs in SREB states.* Atlanta, GA: Southern Regional Education Board.

Access and Excellence. (2001). Minneapolis: Campaign Minnesota, General College, University of Minnesota.

Adan, A., & Felner, R. D. (1995). Ecological congruence and adaptation of minority youth during the transition to college. *Journal of Community Psychology, 23,* 256–269.

Adelman, C. (1999). *Answers in the tool box: Academic intensity, attendance patterns, and bachelor's degree attainment.* Washington, DC: U.S. Department of Education. Available at: http://www.ed.gov/pubs/Toolbox/toolbox.html.

Albrecht, R., & Baron, S. (2002). The politics of pedagogy: Expectations and reality for information literacy in librarianship. *Journal of Library Administration. 36*(1, 2), 71–95.

Alexander v. Choate, 469 U.S. 287 (1985).

Allen, D. (1999). Desire to finish college: An empirical link between motivation and persistence. *Research in Higher Education, 40,* 461–480.

Allen, G. J., Giat, L., & Cherney, R. (1974). Locus of control, test anxiety, and student performance in a personalized instruction course. *Journal of Educational Psychology, 66,* 968–973.

Allen, W. R. (1992). The color of success: African American college student outcomes at predominately white and historically black public colleges and universities. *Harvard Educational Review, 62,* 45–65.

Allport, G. W. (1954). *The nature of prejudice.* New York: Doubleday.

Alpert, R., & Haber, R. N. (1960). Anxiety in academic achievement situations. *Journal of Abnormal and Social Psychology, 61,* 207–215.

Alvidrez, J., & Weinstein, R. S. (1999). Early teacher perceptions and later student academic achievement. *Journal of Educational Psychology, 91*(4), 731–746.

American Association for Higher Education, American College Personnel Association, & National Association of Student Personnel Administrators. (1998). *Powerful partnerships: A shared responsibility for learning.* Washington, DC: Authors. Available at: http://www.acpa.nche.edu/pubs/powpart.html.

American College Personnel Association. (1994). *The student learning imperative: Implications for student affairs.* Alexandria, VA: Author.

American College Personnel Association. (1996). The student learning imperative. *Journal of College Student Development, 37,* 118–122.

American College Personnel Association (ACPA) & National Association of Student Personnel Administrators (NASPA). (2004). *Learning reconsidered: A campus-wide focus on the student experience.* Washington, DC: Author.

American College Personnel Association & National Association of Student Personnel Administrators. (1997). *Principles of good practice for student affairs.* Washington DC: Authors.

American College Testing. (1997). ACT Institutional Data File. Iowa City: Author.

American College Testing (2000). *National college dropout and graduation rates, 1999.* Iowa City: ACT, Inc.

American College Testing (2002). *National collegiate dropout and graduation rates, 2001.* Iowa City: ACT, Inc.

Angelo, T. A. (1993, April). A "teacher's dozen": Fourteen general, research-based principles for improving higher learning in our classrooms. *AAHE Bulletin,* 3–7, 13.

Angelo, T. A. (2000). Doing faculty development as if we value learning most: Transformative guidelines from research to practice. In D. Lieberman (Ed.), *To improve the academy: Resources for faculty, instructional, and organizational development,* Vol. 19 (pp. 97–112). Fort Collins, CO: The POD Network.

Angelo, T. A. (2003). Doing faculty development as if we value learning most: Transformative guidelines from research to practice. *To Improve the Academy, 22,* 97–112.

Angelo, T. A., & Cross, K. P. (1993). *Classroom assessment techniques: A handbook for college teachers* (2nd ed.). San Francisco: Jossey-Bass.

Anselmo, A. (1997). Is there life after the freshman seminar? The case for the freshman seminar class reunion. *Journal of The Freshman Year Experience and Students in Transition, 9,* 105–130.

Anttonen, R., & Chaskes, J. (2002) Advocating for first-year students: A study of the micropolitics of leadership and organizational change. *Journal of The First-Year Experience and Students in Transition, 14*(1) 81–96.

Archer, J. (1986). Stress management: Evaluating a preventive approach for college students. *Journal of American College Health, 34,* 157–160.

Archer, J., & Cooper, S. (1998). *Counseling and mental health services on campus.* San Francisco: Jossey-Bass.

Archer, J., Jr., & Lamnin, A. (1985). An investigation of personal and academic stressors on college campuses. *Journal of College Student Personnel, 26,* 210–215.

Arendale, D. R. (1997a). Leading the paradigm shift from teaching to learning. *National Association for Developmental Education Newsletter, 20*(3), 1.

Arendale, D. R. (1997b). Learning centers for the 21st century. *Journal of Developmental Education, 20*(3), 16.

Arendale, D. R., & Martin, D. (1997). *Review of research concerning the effectiveness of Supplemental Instruction from the University of Missouri–Kansas City and other institutions.* Kansas City, MO: University of Missouri-Kansas City. (ERIC Document Reproduction Services No. ED 370 502)

Arenson, K. W. (2000, September 19). Remedial program refuses to die. *New York Times,* p. B1.

Arkin, R. M., Detchon, C. S., & Maruyama, G. M. (1982). Roles of attribution, affect, and cognitive interference in test anxiety. *Journal of Personality and Social Psychology, 43,* 1111–1124.

Arkin, R. M., & Maruyama, G. M. (1979). Attribution, affect, and college exam performance. *Journal of Educational Psychology, 71,* 85–93.

Association of American Colleges and Universities. (2002). *Greater expectations: The commitment to quality as a nation goes to college.* Washington, DC: Author.

Association of College and Research Librarians. (2002). *Information literacy competency standards for higher education.* Chicago: Author.

Astin, A. W. (1975). *Preventing students from dropping out.* San Francisco: Jossey-Bass.

Astin, A. W. (1977). *Four critical years: Effects of college on beliefs, attitudes, and knowledge.* San Francisco: Jossey-Bass.

Astin, A. W. (1985). *Achieving educational excellence.* San Francisco: Jossey-Bass.

Astin, A. W. (1991). *Assessment for excellence.* Old Tappan, NJ: Macmillan.

Astin, A. W. (1993). *What matters in college? Four critical years revisited.* San Francisco: Jossey-Bass.

Astin, A. W., & Oseguera, L. (2002). *Degree attainment rates at American colleges and universities.* Los Angeles: University of California, Higher Education Research Institute.

Astin, A. W., Parrott, S. A., Korn, W. S., & Sax, L. J. (1997). *The American freshman: Thirty-year trends, 1966–1996.* Los Angeles: University of California, Higher Education Research Institute.

Astin, A. W., & Sax, L. J. (1998). How undergraduates are affected by service participation. *Journal of College Student Development, 39,* 3, 251–263.

Astin, A. W., Tsui, L., & Avaolos, J. (1996). *Degree attainment rates at American colleges and universities: Effects of race, gender, and institutional types.* Los Angeles: University of California, Higher Education Research Institute. (ERIC Document Reproduction Service No. ED 400 749)

Atkinson, R. C. (2001, February). *Standardized tests and access to American universities.* Atwell Lecture at American Council on Education, Washington, DC. Available at: http://www.ucop.edu/ucophome/pres/comments/satspch.html.

Attanasi, L. C., Jr. (1989). Getting in: Mexican Americans' perceptions of university attendance and the implications for freshman year persistence. *Journal of Higher Education, 60,* 247–277.

Avens, C., & Zelley, R. (1992). *QUANTA: An interdisciplinary learning community.* Daytona Beach, FL: Daytona Beach Community College. (ERIC Document Reproduction Service No. ED 349 073)

Bader, C. H., & Hardin, C. (2002). History of developmental studies in Tennessee. In D. B. Lundell & J. L. Higbee (Eds.), *Histories of developmental education.* Minneapolis, MN: Center for Research on Developmental Education and Urban Literacy, General College, University of Minnesota. Available at: http://www.gen.umn.edu/research/crdeul.

Bader, C. H., & Higbee, J. L. (2002). Community partnerships, collaboration, and civic engagement. In D. B. Lundell & J. L. Higbee (Eds.), *Proceedings of the Second Meeting on Future Directions for Developmental Education.* Minneapolis: Center for Research on Developmental Education and Urban Literacy, General College, University of Minnesota.

Baird, L. L. (1996). Learning from research on student outcomes. In S. R. Komives & D. B. Woodard, Jr. (Eds.), *Student services: A handbook for the profession* (3rd ed., pp. 515–535). San Francisco: Jossey-Bass.

Baker, R. W., McNeil, O. V., & Siryk, B. (1985). Expectations and reality in freshmen adjustment to college. *Journal of Counseling Psychology, 32,* 94–103.

Baldridge, J. V. (1983). Strategic planning in higher education: Does the emperor have any clothes? In J. V. Baldridge (Ed.), *Dynamics of organizational change in education.* Berkeley, CA: McCutchen.

Baldridge, J. V., Curtis, D., Ecker, G., & Riley, G. (1978). *Policy making and effective leadership.* San Francisco: Jossey-Bass.

Baldridge, J. V., & Riley, G. (Eds.). (1977). *Governing academic organizations.* Berkeley, CA: McCutchen.

Ballou, R. (1996). Assigning first-year students to college residence halls. In W. J. Zeller, D. S. Fidler, & B. O. Barefoot (Eds.), *Residence life programs and the first-year experience* (2nd ed., pp. 19–26). Columbia: University of South Carolina, National Resource Center for The Freshman Year Experience and Students in Transition.

Bandura, A. (1977). Self efficacy: Toward a unifying theory of behavior change. *Psychological Review, 84,* 191–215.

Bandura, A. (1982). Self-efficacy mechanism in human agency. *American Psychologist, 37,* 122–147.

Banks, J. A. (1993). The canon debate, knowledge construction, and multicultural education. *Educational Researcher, 22*(5), 4–14.

Banks, J. A. (Ed.). (1996). *Multicultural education, transformative knowledge, and action.* New York: Teachers College Press.

Banks, J. A. (1997a). *Teaching strategies for ethnic studies* (6th ed.). Boston, MA: Allyn & Bacon.

Banks, J. A. (1997b). *Educating citizens in a multicultural society.* New York: Teachers College Press.

Barajas, H. L. (2001). Is developmental education a racial project? Considering race relationships in developmental education spaces. In D. B. Lundell & J. L. Higbee (Eds.), *Theoretical perspectives for developmental education* (pp. 65–74). Minneapolis, MN: Center for Research on Developmental Education and Urban Literacy, General College, University of Minnesota. Available at: http://www.gen.umn.edu/research/crdeul.

Barber, B. (1984). *Strong democracy: Participatory politics for the modern age.* Berkeley, CA: University of California Press.

Barefoot, B. O. (1993). *Exploring the evidence: Reporting outcomes of freshman seminars.* Columbia: University of South Carolina, National Resource Center for The Freshman Year Experience.

Barefoot, B. O. (2000). The first-year experience: Are we making it any better? *About Campus, 4*(6) 12–18.

Barefoot, B. O., & Fidler, P. P. (1992). *1991 national survey of freshman seminar programming: Helping first-year college students climb the academic ladder.* Columbia: University of South Carolina, National Resource Center for the Freshman Year Experience.

Barefoot, B. O., & Fidler, P. P. (1996). *The 1994 National Survey of Freshman Seminar Programs: Continuing innovations in the collegiate curriculum.* Columbia: University of South Carolina, National Resource Center for The First-Year Experience and Students in Transition.

Barefoot, B. O., & Gardner, J. N. (1998). Introduction. In B. O. Barefoot, C. L. Warnock, M. T. Dickinson, S. E. Richardson, & M. R. Roberts (Eds.), *Exploring the evidence, Volume 2: Reporting outcomes of first-year seminars.* Columbia: University of South Carolina, National Resource Center for The First-Year Experience and Students in Transition.

Barefoot, B. O., Warnock, C. L., Dickinson, M. T., Richardson, S. E., & Roberts, M. R. (Eds.). (1999). *Exploring the evidence, Volume 2: Reporting outcomes of first-year seminars.* Columbia: University of South Carolina, National Resource Center for The First-Year Experience and Students in Transition.

Barovick, H. (2001, Sept. 3). Indiana University: A web of friendly interest groups makes this big research university feel less intimidating. *Time.* Available at: http://www.time.com/time/2001/coy/university.html.

Barr, R., & Tagg, J. (1995). From teaching to learning—A new paradigm for undergraduate education. *Change, 27*(6), 12–26.

Barrett, B. N., & Simmons, J. L. (1998). Violence comes to college. *National Association of Student Affairs Professionals Journal, 1,* 93–101.

Bassarear, T. (1991). An examination of the relationship between attitudes and beliefs on achievement in a college developmental mathematics course. *Research and Teaching in Developmental Education, 7*(2), 43–56.

Baughman, K., & Swing, R. L. (2001). Closing the loop: Assessment data for decision makers. In R. L. Swing (Ed.), *Proving and improving: Strategies for assessing the first college year* (pp. 87–94). Columbia: University of South Carolina, National Resource Center for The First-Year Experience and Students in Transition.

Baum, S. (1998). Balancing act: Can colleges achieve equal access and survive in a competitive market? *The College Board Review, 186,* 12–17.

Baxter Magolda, M. B. (2002). Epistemological reflection: The evolution of epistemological assumptions from age 18 to 30. In B. K. Hofer & P. R. Pintrich (Eds.), *Personal epistemology: The psychology of beliefs about knowledge and knowing* (pp. 89–102). Mahwah, NJ: Erlbaum.

Beal, P. E., & Noel, L. (1980). *What works in student retention?* Iowa City: American College Testing Program and National Center for Higher Education Management Systems.

Bean, J. C. (1996). *Engaging ideas: The professor's guide to integrating writing, critical thinking, and active learning in the classroom.* San Francisco: Jossey-Bass.

Bean, J. P. (1986). *Assessing and reducing attrition.* San Francisco: Jossey-Bass.

Bean, J. P., & Metzner, B. (1985). A conceptual model of nontraditional student attrition. *Review of Educational Research, 55,* 485–540.

Bean, J. P., & Vesper, N. (1992, October). *Student dependency theory: An explanation of student retention in college.* Paper presented at the annual meeting of the Association for Higher Education, Minneapolis.

Beckwith, H. (1997). *Selling the invisible.* New York: Warner Books.

Belch, H. A., Gebel, M., & Maas, G. M. (2001). Relationship between student recreation complex use, academic performance, and persistence of first-time freshmen. *Journal of the National Association of Student Personnel Administrators, 38,* 254–268.

Belcheir, M. J. (1997). *An evaluation of the early impacts of the cluster program and first year experience seminar on new freshmen.* Boise, ID: Boise State University. (ERIC Documentation Reproduction Services, No. ED 409 769)

Belenky, M. F., Clinchy, B. M., Goldberger, N. R., & Tarule, J. M. (1986). *Women's ways of knowing: The development of self, voice, and mind.* New York: Basic Books.

Bell, C., et al. (1999). A longitudinal study of the effects of academic and social integration and commitment on retention. *Journal of the National Association of Student Personnel Administrators, 37*(Fall), 376–385.

Bennett, J. (1999). Learning communities, academic advising, and other support programs. In J. H. Levine (Ed.), *Learning communities: New structures, new partnerships for learning* (pp. 71–75). Columbia: University of South Carolina, National Resource Center for the First-Year Experience and Students in Transition.

Berdie, R. F. (1966). College expectations, experiences, and perceptions. *Journal of College Student Personnel, 7,* 336–344.

Berdie, R. F. (1968). Changes in university perceptions during the first two college years. *Journal of College Student Personnel, 9,* 85–89.

Berkner, L. K., Cucarro-Alamin, S., & McCormick, A. C. (1996). *Descriptive summary of 1989–90 beginning postsecondary students: Five years later.* Washington, DC: U.S. Government Printing Office.

Best, L., & Lees, B. (2000). A vision for skills development: The general education program at Kean University. *Research and Teaching in Developmental Education, 16*(2), 119–122.

Biddison, G., & Hier, T. (2000, October). The myth of the "dorm"—Getting more mileage from what you've got. *ACUHO-I Talking Stick,* 10–11.

Birnbaum, R. (1988). *How college works.* San Francisco: Jossey-Bass.

Bitner, J., Austin, S., & Waddington, E. (1994). A comparison of math anxiety in traditional and non-traditional developmental college students. *Research and Teaching in Developmental Education, 10*(2), 34–44.

Blake, E. S. (1979). Classroom and context: An educational dialectic. *Academe, 65,* 280–292.

Blake, E. S. (1996). The yin and yang of student learning in college. *About Campus, 1*(4), 4–9.

Blanc, R. A., DeBuhr, L., & Martin, D. C. (1983). Breaking the attrition cycle: The effects of Supplemental Instruction on undergraduate performance and attrition. *Journal of Higher Education, 54*(1), 80–89.

Blimling, G. S. (2001). Uniting scholarship and communities of practice in student affairs. *Journal of College Student Development, 42*(4), 381–396.

Blimling, G. S., Whitt, E. J., & Associates. (1999). *Good practice in student affairs.* San Francisco: Jossey-Bass.

Blinn, J., & Sisco, O. (1996). "Linking" developmental reading and biology. *National Association for Developmental Education Selected Conference Papers, 2,* 8–9. Available at: http://www.nade.net.

Bloland, P. A., Stamatakos, L. C., & Rogers, R. R. (1996). Redirecting the role of student affairs to focus on student learning. *Journal of College Student Development, 37*(2), 217–226.

Bloom, A. (1987). *The closing of the American mind.* New York: Simon & Schuster.

Bloom, H. (1994). *The Western canon: The books and schools of the ages.* New York: Harcourt Brace.

Bloomsburg University tests its FYE Program's effectiveness. (2000, Spring). *FYE: Newsletter of the National Resource Center for the First-Year Experience and Students in Transition,* pp. 4–5.

Bohr, L. (1996). College and precollege reading instruction: What are the real differences? *Learning Assistance Review, 1*(1), 14–28.

Borg, W. R., & Gall, M. D. (1989). *Educational research: An introduction.* (5th ed.). White Plains, NY: Longman.

Borland, K. W., Orazem, V., & Donnelly, D. (1999). Freshman seminar service-learning: For academic and intellectual community integration. *Academic Exchange Quarterly, 3*(4), 42–53.

Boyer, E. L. (1987). *College: The undergraduate experience in America.* New York: Harper & Row.

Boyer, E. L. (1990). *Scholarship reconsidered: Priorities of the professoriate.* Princeton, NJ: Carnegie Foundation for the Advancement of Teaching.

Boyer, E. L. (1996). From scholarship reconsidered to scholarship assessed. *Quest, 48*(2), 129–139.

Boyer, E. L. (1997). *Ernest L. Boyer: Selected speeches 1979–1997.* San Francisco: Jossey-Bass.

Boyer Commission on Educating Undergraduates in the Research University. (1998). *Reinventing undergraduate education: A blueprint for America's research universities.* Available at: http://naples.cc.sunysb.edu/Pres/boyer.nsf/.

Boylan, H. R., Bliss, L. B., & Bonham, B. S. (1997). Program components and their relationship to student performance. *Journal of Developmental Education, 20*(3), 2–8.

Boylan, H. R., & Bonham, B. S. (1994). Seven myths about developmental education. *Research and Teaching in Developmental Education, 10*(2), 5–12.

Boylan, H. R., Bonham, B. S., & Bliss, L. B. (1992). *National study of developmental education: Students, programs, and institutions of higher education. Summary report.* Boone, NC: National Center for Developmental Education, Appalachian State University.

Boylan, H. R., Bonham, B. S., & Bliss, L. B. (1994). Who are the developmental students? *Research in Developmental Education, 11*(2), 1–4.

Boylan, H. R., Bonham, B. S., & Rodriguez, L. M. (2000). What are remedial courses and do they work? Results of national and local studies. *Learning Assistance Review, 5*(1), 5–14.

Boylan, H. R., & Saxon, D. P. (1998). The origin, scope, and outcomes of developmental education in the twentieth century. In J. L. Higbee & P. L. Dwinell (Eds.), *Developmental education: Preparing successful college students.* Columbia: University of South Carolina, National Resource Center for The First-Year Experience and Students in Transition.

Bradbury, S. (1991). Self-esteem and learning. National Association for Developmental Education Selected Conference Abstracts, 21–22.

Bradford, C. & Farris, E. (1991). *Survey on retention at higher education institutions: Higher Education Surveys Report.* Rockville, MD: Westat.

Branch, M. A. (1999, April). A very special saloon. *Yale Alumni Magazine,* 36–41.

Braunstein, A., McGrath, M., & Pescatrice, D. (2000–2001). Measuring the impact of financial factors on college persistence. *Journal of College Student Retention, 2*(3), 191–203.

Braxton, J. M. (2000). *Reworking the student departure puzzle.* Nashville, TN: Vanderbilt University Press.

Braxton, J. M., Vesper, N., & Hossler, D. (1995). Expectations for college and student persistence. *Research in Higher Education, 36,* 595–612.

Bray, D. (1987). The assessment and placement of developmental and high risk students. In K. M. Ahrendt (Ed.), *Teaching the developmental education student.* San Francisco: Jossey-Bass.

Breese, J. R., & O'Toole, R. (1994). Adult women students: Development of a transitional status. *Journal of College Student Development, 35,* 183–189.

Breivik, P. S. (1998) *Student learning in the information age.* Phoenix: Oryx Press.

Breland, H., Maxey, J., McClure, G. T., Valiga, M. J., Boatwright, M. A., Ganley, V. L., & Jenkins, L. M. (1995). *Challenges in college admissions: A report of a survey of undergraduate admissions policies, practices, and procedures.* Washington, DC: American Association of Collegiate Registrars and Admissions Officers, American

College Testing, College Board, Educational Testing Service, and National Association for College Admissions Counselors.

Bridwell, M. W., & Kinder, S. P. (1993). Confronting health issues. In M. J. Barr (Ed.), *The handbook of student affairs administration* (pp. 481–492). San Francisco: Jossey-Bass.

Bringle, R. G., & Hatcher, J. A. (1996). Implementing service learning in higher education. *Journal of Higher Education, 67,* 221–239.

Brookfield, S. D. (1995). *Becoming a critically reflective teacher.* San Francisco: Jossey-Bass.

Brookfield, S. D., & Preskill, S. (1999). *Discussion as a way of teaching: Tools and techniques for democratic classrooms.* San Francisco: Jossey-Bass.

Brooks, D. (2001, April). The organization kid. *Atlantic Monthly,* 40–54.

Brooks, S. H. (1996). Econometric modeling of enrollment behavior. *Journal of Student Aid, 3,* 3–17.

Brothen, T., & Wambach, C. (2000). A research-based approach to developing a computer-assisted course for developmental education students. In J. L. Higbee & P. L. Dwinell (Eds.), *The many faces of developmental education* (pp. 59–72). Warrensburg, MO: National Association for Developmental Education. Available at: http://www.nade.net.

Brothen, T., & Wambach, C. (2001). A selectionist approach to developmental education. In D. B. Lundell & J. L. Higbee (Eds.), *Theoretical perspectives for developmental education.* Minneapolis, MN: Center for Research on Developmental Education and Urban Literacy, General College, University of Minnesota. Available at: http://www.gen.umn.edu/research/crdeul.

Broughton, E., & Neyer, M. (2001). Advising and counseling student athletes. In M. F. Howard-Hamilton & S. K. Watt (Eds.), *Student services for athletes* (pp. 47–53). San Francisco: Jossey-Bass.

Brower, A. (1997). *End-of-year evaluation on the Bradley Learning Community.* Unpublished report, Madison: University of Wisconsin-Madison,.

Brown, M., Higgins, K., & Hartley, K. (2001). Teachers and technology equity. *Teaching Exceptional Children, 33*(4), 32–39.

Brown, T. C. (2000). Gender differences in African American students' satisfaction with college. *Journal of College Student Development, 41*(5), 279–287.

Bruch, P. (2001). Democratic theory and developmental education. In D. B. Lundell & J. L. Higbee (Eds.), *Theoretical perspectives for developmental education* (pp. 37–48). Minneapolis, MN: Center for Research on Developmental Education and Urban Literacy, General College, University of Minnesota. Available at: http://www.gen.umn.edu/research/crdeul.

Bruch, P. L., & Higbee, J. L. (2002). Reflections on multiculturalism in developmental education. *Journal of College Reading and Learning, 33*(1), 77–90.

Bruch, P. L., Higbee, J. L., & Lundell, D. B. (2003). Multicultural legacies for the 21st century: A conversation with Dr. James A. Banks. In J. L. Higbee, D. B. Lundell, & I. M. Duranczyk (Eds.), *Multiculturalism in developmental education* (pp. 35–42). Minneapolis, MN: Center for Research on Developmental Education and Urban Literacy, General College, University of Minnesota.

Bruch, P. L., Higbee, J. L., & Lundell, D. B. (2004). Multicultural education and developmental education: A conversation about principles and connections with Dr. James A. Banks. In P. L. Bruch, J. L. Higbee, & D. B. Lundell (Eds.), *Research and Teaching in Developmental Education, 20*(2), 77–90.

Bullock, T., Madden, D., & Harter, J. (1987). Paired developmental reading and psychology courses. *Research and Teaching in Developmental Education, 3*(2), 22–29.

Burd, S. (1996, April 12). Colleges fear lawmakers will cut funds for remedial students. *Chronicle of Higher Education.* Available at: http://www.chronicle.com/index.htm.

Burrell, K. B., & Kim, D. J. (1998). International students and academic assistance: Meeting the needs of another college population. In P. L. Dwinell & J. L. Higbee (Eds.), *Developmental education: Meeting diverse student needs* (pp. 81–96). Morrow, GA: National Association for Developmental Education.

Cabrera, A. F. (1998). *Estimated student aid by source, 1996–1997.* University Park, PA: Unpublished paper, The Pennsylvania State University.

Cabrera, A. F., Nora, A., Terenzini, P. T., Pascarella, E., & Hagedorn, L. S. (1999). Campus racial climate and the adjustment of students to college: A comparison between white students and African-American students. *Journal of Higher Education, 70,* 134–160.

Cabrera, A. F., Stampen, J. O., & Hansen, W. L. (1990). Exploring the effects of ability to pay on persistence in college. *Review in Higher Education, 13,* 303–336.

Callan, P. M., & Finney, J. E. (2003). *Multiple pathways and state policy: Toward education and training beyond high school.* San Jose, CA: National Center for Public Policy in Higher Education.

Cantor, N., & Mischel, W. (1977). Traits as prototypes: Effects on recognition memory. *Journal of Personality and Social Psychology, 35,* 38–48.

Carbone, E., & Greenberg, J. (1998). Teaching large classes: Unpacking the problem and responding creatively. In M. Kaplan (Ed.), *To improve the academy,* vol. 17, Stillwater, OK: New Forums Press and Professional and Organizational Development Network in Higher Education.

Carey, A., & Fabiano, P. M. (1997). Welcome to Western: A community's approach to convocation. *About Campus, 3*(6), 23–24.

Carskadon, T. G. (1994). Student personality factors: Psychological type and the Myers-Briggs Type Indicator. In K. W. Prichard & R. M. Sawyer (Eds.), *Handbook of college teaching: Theory and applications.* Westport, CT: Greenwood Press.

Carter, D. T. (1995). *The politics of rage: George Wallace, the origins of the new conservatism, and the transformation of American politics.* New York: Simon & Schuster.

Casazza, M. E. (1999). Who are we and where did we come from? *Journal of Developmental Education, 23*(1), 2–4, 6–7.

Casazza, M. E. (2000). A case study from South Africa. *Learning Assistance Review, 5*(1), 29–40.

Cashin, J. R., Presley, C. A., & Meilman, P. W. (1998). Alcohol use in the Greek system: Follow the leader? *Journal of Studies on Alcohol, 59*(1), 63–70.

Cass, V. C. (1979). Homosexual identity formation: A theoretical model. *Journal of Homosexuality, 4,* 219–235.

Caverly, D. C., & Peterson, C. L. (1996). Foundations for a constructivist, whole language approach to developmental college reading. In J. L. Higbee & P. L. Dwinell (Eds.),

Developmental education: Theory, research, and pedagogy. Carol Stream, IL: National Association for Developmental Education. Available at: http://www. nade.net.

Center for Supplemental Instruction. (1998). *Supplemental Instruction (SI): Review of research concerning the effectiveness of SI from the University of Missouri-Kansas City and other institutions from across the United States.* Kansas City, MO: Center for Academic Development Publishers.

Centers for Disease Control, Division of STD Prevention. (1998). *Sexually transmitted disease surveillance, 1997.* Atlanta, GA: U.S. Department of Health and Human Services, Public Health Service.

Chaffee, J. (1992). Critical thinking skills: The cornerstone of developmental education. *Journal of Developmental Education, 15*(3), 2–17.

Chaffee, J. (1997). *Thinking critically* (5th ed.). Boston: Houghton Mifflin.

Chang, M. J. (1999). Does racial diversity matter? The educational impact of a racially diverse undergraduate population. *Journal of College Student Development, 40,* 377–395.

Chang, M. J. (2001). The positive educational effects of racial diversity on campus. In G. Orfield & M. Kurlaender (Eds.), *Diversity challenged: Evidence on the impact of affirmative action* (pp. 175–186). Cambridge, MA: The Civil Rights Project, Harvard University.

Chapman, S. C. (1989). Women students. In M. L. Upcraft, J. N. Gardner, & Associates (Eds.), *The freshman year experience: Helping students survive and succeed in college,* (pp. 287–302). San Francisco: Jossey-Bass.

Chaskes, J. (1996) The first-year student as immigrant. *Journal of The Freshman Year Experience and Students in Transition. 8*(1), 79–91.

Cheatham, H. E., & Associates. (1991). *Cultural pluralism on campus.* Alexandria, VA: American College Personnel Association.

Checkoway, B. (1997). Reinventing the research university for public service: Comments and observations. *Journal of Planning Literature, 11,* 308–319.

Chickering, A. W. (1969). *Education and identity.* San Francisco: Jossey-Bass.

Chickering, A. W. (1974). *Commuting versus resident students: Overcoming the educational inequities of living off campus.* San Francisco: Jossey-Bass.

Chickering, A. W., & Gamson, Z. (1987). Seven principles for good practice in undergraduate education. *AAHE Bulletin, 39,* 3–7.

Chickering, A. W., & O'Connor, J. (1996). The university learning center: A driving force for collaboration. *About Campus, 1*(4), 16–21.

Chickering, A. W., & Reisser, L. (1993). *Education and identity* (2nd ed.). San Francisco: Jossey-Bass.

Chism, N., Lees, N. D., & Evenbeck, S. E. (2002). Faculty development for teaching innovation. *Liberal Education, 88*(3), 34–41.

Choy, S. P. (2002). *Access and persistence: Findings from ten years of longitudinal research on students.* Washington, DC: American Council on Education.

Christensen, P. M. (1990). *A comparison of adult baccalaureate graduates and nonpersisters.* Unpublished doctoral dissertation, University of Minnesota. *Dissertation Abstracts International, 51,* 0130A.

Chronicle of Higher Education. (1998, August 29). *Chronicle of Higher Education Almanac Issue, 45*(1) [Whole Issue].

Chronicle of Higher Education. (2000, September 1). *Chronicle of Higher Education Almanac Issue, 47*(1) [Whole Issue].

Chronicle of Higher Education. (2001, August 31). *Chronicle of Higher Education Almanac Issue, 48*(1) [Whole Issue].

Chronicle of Higher Education, (2002). *Chronicle of Higher Education Almanac Issue, 49,* 1.

Chronicle of Higher Education. (2003). *Chronicle of Higher Education Almanac Issue, 50*(1).

Chung, C. J. (2001). Approaching theory in developmental education. In D. B. Lundell & J. L. Higbee (Eds.), *Theoretical perspectives for developmental education* (pp. 19–25). Minneapolis: Center for Research on Developmental Education and Urban Literacy, General College, University of Minnesota. Available at: http://www.gen.umn.edu/research/crdeul.

Chung, C. J., & Brothen, T. (2002). Some final thoughts on theoretical perspectives—Over lunch. In D. B. Lundell & J. L. Higbee (Eds.), *Proceedings of the Second Meeting on Future Directions in Developmental Education* (pp. 39–43). Minneapolis: Center for Research on Developmental Education and Urban Literacy, General College, University of Minnesota.

Claxton, C. S., & Murrell, P. H. (1987). *Learning styles: Implications for improving educational practices.* Washington, DC: Association for the Study of Higher Education.

Clinchy, B. M. (2002). Revisiting "Women's ways of knowing." In B. K. Hofer & P. R. Pintrich (Eds.), *Personal epistemology: The psychology of beliefs about knowledge and knowing* (pp. 63–87). Mahwah, NJ: Erlbaum.

Coate, L. E. (1990). TQM on campus: Implementing total quality management in a university setting. *NACUBO Business Officer, 26,* 26–35.

Cofer, J., & Summers, P. (2000). Within-year persistence of students at two-year colleges. *Community College Journal of Research and Practice, 24,* 785–807.

Colby, A., & Ehrlich, T. (2000). Introduction. In T. Ehrlich (Ed.), *Civic responsibility and higher education* (pp. xxi–xliii). Phoenix, AZ: Oryx Press.

College Board. (2001, August 28). *2001 college-bound seniors are the largest, most diverse group in history: More than a third are minority but gap remains.* New York: Author. Available at: http://www.collegeboard.com/press/senior01/082801.html.

Collins, T., & Bruch, P. (2000). Theoretical frameworks that span disciplines. In D. B. Lundell & J. L. Higbee (Eds.), *Proceedings of the first intentional meeting on future directions in developmental education* (pp. 19–22). Minneapolis, MN: Center for Research on Developmental Education and Urban Literacy, General College, University of Minnesota. Available at: http://www.gen.umn.edu/research/crdeul.

Collins, W. (1982). Some correlates of achievement among students in a Supplemental Instruction Program. *Journal of Learning Skills, 1,* 19–28.

Colton, G. M., Connor, U. J., Schultz, E. L., & Easter, L. M. (1999). Fighting attrition: One freshman year program that targets academic progress and retention for at-risk students. *Journal of College Student Retention, 1*(2), 147–162.

Commander, N. E., & Smith, B. D. (1995). Developing adjunct reading and learning courses that work. *Journal of Reading, 38*(5), 352–360.

Commander, N. E., Stratton, C. B., Callahan, C. A., & Smith, B. D. (1996). A learning assistance model for expanding academic support. *Journal of Developmental Education, 20*(2), 8–16.

Commission on Higher Education. (1994). *Characteristics of excellence in higher education: Standards for accreditation.* Philadelphia: Middle State Association of Colleges and Schools.

Confessore, N. (2003, November). What makes a college good? *Atlantic Monthly,* 118–126.

Congos, D. (2001–2002). How Supplemental Instruction generates revenue for colleges and universities. *Journal of College Student Retention, 3,* 301–309.

Conley, D. T. (Ed.). (2003). *Understanding university success: A report from Standards for Success.* Eugene, OR: Center for Educational Policy Research, University of Oregon.

Cook, L. P. (2000). Constructing comprehensive programs on the two-year campus. In M. J. Fabich (Ed.), *Orientation planning manual 2000.* Pullman, WA: National Orientation Directors Association.

Coomes, M. D. (2004). Student financial aid. In F. D. MacKinnon & Associates, *Rentz's student affairs practice in higher education* (3rd ed.) (pp. 336–368). Springfield, IL: Thomas.

Cooper, J., & Mueck, R. (1990). Student involvement in learning: Cooperative learning and college instruction. *Journal on Excellence in College Teaching, 1,* 68–76.

Copland, B. A. (1989). Adult learners. In M. L. Upcraft & J. N. Gardner, & Associates (Eds.), *The freshman year experience: Helping students survive and succeed in college* (pp. 303–315). San Francisco: Jossey-Bass.

Cortés, C. E. (2000). *The children are watching: How the media teach about diversity.* New York: Teachers College Press.

Cotter, M. (1996). Systems-thinking in a knowledge-creating organization. *Journal of Innovative Management, 2*(1), 15–30.

Council for the Advancement of Standards. (1997). *The book of professional standards for higher education.* Washington, DC: Author.

Creamer, D. G. (2000). Use of theory in academic advising. In V. N. Gordon & W. R. Habley (Eds.), *Academic advising: A comprehensive handbook* (pp. 18–34). San Francisco: Jossey-Bass.

Creeden, J. E. (1988). Student affairs biases as a barrier to collaboration: A point of view. *NASPA Journal, 26*(1), 2–7.

Crisco, V. (2002). Conflicting expectations: The politics of developmental education in California. In J. L. Higbee, D. B. Lundell, & I. M. Duranczyk (Eds.), *Developmental education: Policy and practice* (pp. 45–54). Auburn, CA: National Association for Developmental Education.

Crissman, J. L. (2001). Clustered and nonclustered first-year seminars: New students' first-semester experiences. *Journal of The First-Year Experience and Students in Transition, 13,* 69–88.

Crissman, J. L., & Upcraft, M. L. (2001). Assessing first year programs. In J. H. Schuh, M. L. Upcraft, & Associates (Eds.), *Assessment practice in student affairs* (pp. 261–274). San Francisco: Jossey-Bass.

Crissman Ishler, J. L., & Schreiber, S. (2002). First-year female students: Perceptions of friendsickness. *Journal of The First-Year Experience and Students in Transition, 14,* 89–104.

Crockett, D. S. (1984). *Advising skills, techniques, and resources.* Iowa City: American College Testing.

Cronbach, L. J. (1982). *Designing and evaluating social programs.* San Francisco: Jossey-Bass.

Crookston, B. (1972). A developmental view of academic advising as teaching. *Journal of College Student Personnel, 13,* 12–17.

Crookston, B. (1994). A developmental view of academic advising as teaching. *NACADA Journal, 14*(2), 5–9.

Cross, K. P. (1981). *Adults as learners.* San Francisco: Jossey-Bass.

Cross, W., Parham, T., & Helms, J. (1991). The stages of Black identity development: Nigrescence models. In R. Jones (Ed.), *Black psychology* (pp. 319–338). Berkeley, CA: Cobb & Henry.

Cuccaro-Alamin, S., & Choy, S. (1998). *Postsecondary financing strategies: How under-graduates combine work, borrowing, and attendance* (NCES 98-088). Washington, DC: U. S. Department of Education, National Center for Education Statistics, U. S. Government Printing Office.

Cuseo, J. B. (1999). Instructor training: Rationale, results, and content basics. In M. S. Hunter & T. L. Skipper (Eds.), *Solid foundations: Building success for first-year seminars through instructor training and development.* Columbia: University of South Carolina, National Resource Center for The First-Year Experience and Students in Transition.

Cuseo, J. B. (2000, February). *The empirical case for first-year seminars: Well-documented effects on student retention and academic achievement.* Supplementary handout for concurrent session presented at the Nineteenth Annual National Conference on The First-Year Experience, Columbia, SC.

Cutright, M. (Ed.). (2002). *Strengthening first-year student learning at doctoral/research extensive universities: Examples of current practice.* Brevard, NC: Policy Center on the First Year of College.

Cyberatlas. (2002, January). *Men still dominate worldwide Internet usage.* Available at: http://www.cyberatlas.internet.com/big_picture/demographics/article/0,,5901_959421,00.html.

Dahl, R. (1998). *On democracy.* New Haven, CT: Yale University Press.

Dannells, M., & Kuh, G. D. (1977). Orientation. In W. T. Packwood (Ed.), *College student personnel services.* Springfield, IL: Thomas.

Davis, B. G. (1993). *Tools for teaching.* San Francisco: Jossey-Bass.

Davis, B. O., Jr. (1992). Freshman seminar: A broad spectrum of effectiveness. *Journal of The Freshman Year Experience, 4*(1), 79–94.

Davis, T. M. (Ed.). (1999). *Open doors: Report on international educational exchange.* New York: Institute of International Education.

Deardorff, P. A., Kendall, P. C., Finch, A. J., & Sitarz, A. M. (1977). Empathy, locus of control and anxiety in college students. *Psychological Reports, 40,* 1236–1238.

Decker, T. W., & Russell, R. K. (1981). Comparison of cue-controlled relaxation and cognitive restructuring versus study skills counseling in treatment of test-anxious college underachievers. *Psychological Reports, 49,* 459–469.

D'Emilio, J. (2000). The campus environment for gay and lesbian life. In V. Cyrus (Ed.), *Experiencing race, class, and gender in the United States* (pp. 434–438). Mountain View, CA: Mayfield Publishing Company.

Dendato, K. M., & Diener, D. (1986). Effectiveness of cognitive/relaxation therapy and study skills training in reducing self-reported anxiety and improving the academic performance of test-anxious students. *Journal of Counseling Psychology, 33,* 131–135.

Dervaries, C. (2001). Report finds modest increase in minority enrollment, graduation rates. *Black Issues in Higher Education, 18,* 9–13.

Dewey, J. (1938/1997). Experience and education. In S. M. Cahn (Ed.), *Classic and contemporary readings in the philosophy of education* (pp. 325–363). New York: McGraw-Hill.

Dimeff, L. A., Baer, J. S., Kivlahan, D. R., & Marlatt, G. A. (1999) *Brief alcohol screening and intervention for college students: A harm reduction approach.* New York: Guilford Press.

Dimon, M. (1981). Why adjunct courses work. *Journal of College Reading and Learning, 21,* 33–40.

Dockser, M. A. (1999, August 31). New weights can alter SAT scores: Family is factor in determining who's a striver. *Wall Street Journal,* pp. B1, B8.

Douglas, K. A., Collins, J. L., Warren, C., Kann, L., Gold, R., Clayton, S., Ross, J. G., & Kolbe, L. J. (1997). Results from the 1995 National College Health Risk Behavior Survey. *Journal of American College Health, 46,* 55–66.

Drinking is biggest campus drug problem. (1999, August 26). *USA Today.* Available at: http://usatoday.com/life/health/addiction/lhadd015.htm.

D'Souza, D. (1991). *Illiberal education: The politics of race and sex on campus.* New York: Vintage.

Duch, B. J., Groh, S. E., & Allen, D. E. (2001). *The power of problem-based learning.* Sterling, VA: Stylus Publishing.

Duckenfield, M. (2002). Look who's coming to college: The impact of high school service-learning on new college students. In E. Zlotkowski (Ed.), *Service-learning and the first-year experience: Preparing students for personal success and civic responsibility* (pp. 39–50). Columbia: University of South Carolina, National Resource Center for The First-Year Experience and Students in Transition.

Duckitt, J. (1992). *The social psychology of prejudice.* New York: Praeger.

Dweck, C. A., & Leggett, E. L. (1988). A social-cognitive approach to motivation and personality. *Psychological Review, 95*(2), 256–273.

Dwinell, P. L., & Higbee, J. L. (1990). The role of assessment in predicting achievement among high risk freshmen: A bibliographic essay. *Journal of Educational Opportunity, 5*(1), 29–34.

Dwinell, P. L., & Higbee, J. L. (1991). Affective variables related to mathematics achievement among high risk college freshmen. *Psychological Reports, 69,* 399–403.

Edgerton, R. (1999). *Education white paper.* Available on-line: http://www.pewtrusts.com.

Education Commission of the States (2001). Meeting needs and making profits: The rise of for-profit degree-granting institutions. Denver, CO: Author.

Edwards, J., & Waters, L. K. (1981). Moderating effect of achievement motivation and locus of control on the relationship between academic ability and academic performance. *Educational and Psychological Measurement, 41,* 585–597.

Eisenberg, M. (2001). Differences in sexual risk behaviors between college students with same-sex and opposite-sex experience: Results from a national survey. *Archives of Sexual Behavior, 30,* 575–582.

El Khawas, E. (1987, 1995). *Campus trends.* Washington, DC: American Council on Education.

Elliot, J. L., & Decker, E. (1999). Garnering the fundamental resources for learning communities. In J. H. Levine (Ed.), *Learning communities: New structures, new partnerships for learning* (pp. 19–28). Columbia: University of South Carolina, National Resource Center for The First-Year Experience and Students in Transition.

Ellis, D. B., & Gardner, J. N. (1997). *A meeting of the minds: Two perspectives on new student seminars* [Teleconference video]. (Available from the National Resource Center for The First-Year Experience and Students in Transition, University of South Carolina, Columbia, SC)

Engstrom, C. M., & Tinto, V. (2000). Developing partnerships with academic affairs to enhance student learning. In M. J. Barr, M. K. Desler, & Associates (Eds.), *The handbook of student affairs administration* (pp. 425–452). San Francisco: Jossey-Bass.

Erickson, B. L., & Strommer, D. W. (1991). *Teaching college freshmen.* San Francisco: Jossey-Bass.

Erikson, E. H. (1963). *Childhood and society* (2nd ed.) New York: Norton.

Erwin, T. D. (1991). *Assessing student learning and development: A guide to principles, goals, and methods of determining college outcomes.* San Francisco: Jossey-Bass.

Evans, N. J. (2003). Psychosocial, cognitive, and typological perspectives on student development. In S. R. Komives, D. B. Woodard Jr. & Associates (Eds.), *Student services: A handbook for the profession* (4th ed., pp. 179–202). San Francisco: Jossey-Bass.

Evans, Z. (2001). Maintaining an open pipeline to higher education: Strategies that work. *Black Issues in Higher Education, 18,* 136–142.

Evenbeck, S. E., Jackson, B., & McGrew, J. (1999). Faculty development in learning communities: The role of reflection and reframing. In J. H. Levine (Ed.), *Learning communities: New structures, new partnerships for learning.* Columbia: University of South Carolina, National Resource Center for The First-Year Experience and Students in Transition.

Ewell, P. T. (1997). Organizing for learning: A new imperative. *AAHE Bulletin, 50*(4), 3–6.

Ewell, P. T. (2001). Observations on assessing the first-year experience. In R. L. Swing (Ed.), *Proving and improving: Strategies for assessing the first college year.* Columbia: University of South Carolina, National Resource Center for The First-Year Experience and Students in Transition.

Eyermann, T., & Sanlo, R. (2002). Documenting their existence: Lesbian, gay, bisexual and transgender students on campus. In R. Sanlo, S. Rankin, & R. Schoenberg (Eds.), *Our place on campus: Lesbian, gay, bisexual and transgender services and programs in higher education.* Westport, CT: Greenwood Press.

Eyler, J., Root, S., & Giles, D. E., Jr. (1998). Service-learning and the development of expert citizens: Service-learning and cognitive science. In D. K. Duffy & R. G. Bringle (Eds.), *With service in mind: Concepts and models for service-learning in psychology.* Washington, DC: American Association for Higher Education.

Faculty Inventory: Principles for Good Practice in Undergraduate Education (1989). Winona, MN: The Seven Principles Resource Center, Winona State University.

Fairtest. (2001). SAT scores not needed for fair, valid admissions: Focus on annual score variations obscures real problems of SAT's inaccuracy, biases, and coachability. http://www.fairtest.org/pr/2001%20SAT%20Scores.html.

Farrell, F. F. (2003, October 31). Public-college tuition rise is largest in 3 decades. *Chronicle of Higher Education,* p. A1.

Feather, N. T. (1966). Effects of prior success and failure on expectations for success and subsequent performance. *Journal of Personality and Social Psychology, 3,* 287–298.

Felder, R. M. (1996). Matters of style. *ASEE Prism, 6*(4), 18–23.

Feldman, D. C. (1981). The multiple socialization of organization members. *Academy of First-Year Experience, 14*(1), 81–96.

Feldman, K. A., & Newcomb, T. M. (1969). *The impact of college on students.* San Francisco: Jossey-Bass.

Fennema, E., & Sherman, J. A. (1976). Fennema-Sherman Mathematics Attitudes Scales. *Catalog of Selected Documents in Psychology, 6,* 31–32.

Fidler, D. S. (1997). Getting students involved from the get-go: Summer reading programs across the country. *About Campus, 2*(5), 32.

Fidler, P. P., & Fidler, D. S. (1991). *First National Survey on Freshman Seminar Programs: Findings, conclusions, and recommendations.* Columbia: University of South Carolina, National Resource Center for The Freshman Year Experience.

Fidler, P. P., & Moore, P. S. (1996). A comparison of effects of campus residence and freshman seminar attendance of freshman dropout rates. *Journal of The Freshman Year Experience, 8*(2), 7–16.

Fidler, P. P., Neururer-Rotholz, J., & Richardson, S. (1999). Teaching the freshman seminar: Its effectiveness in promoting faculty development. *Journal of The First-Year Experience and Students in Transition, 11*(2), 59–74.

Fine, M., & Asch, A. (2000). Disability beyond stigma: Social interaction, discrimination and activism. In M. Adams, W. J. Blumenfeld, R. Castaneda, H. W. Hackman, M. L. Peters, & X. Zuniga (Eds.), *Readings for diversity and social justice.* Rockville, MD: Maryland Leadership Workshop.

Fitts, C. T., & Swift, F. H. (1928). The construction of orientation courses for college freshmen. *University of California Publications in Education, 1897–1929, 2*(3), 145–250.

Flint, T. (2000). *Serving adult learners in higher education: Principles of effectiveness.* Chicago: Council for Adult and Experiential Learning.

Follow-up study of college drinking released. (1998). News and notices of the Harvard School of Public Health. http://www.hsph.harvard.edu/ats/Sep18/.

Foreign-student enrollment stagnates. (2003, November 7). *Chronicle of Higher Education,* p. A1.

Forrest, A. (1985). Creating conditions for student and institutional success. In L. Noel, R. Levitz, D. Saluri, & Associates, *Increasing student retention.* San Francisco: Jossey-Bass.

Forrest, A. (1987). Managing the flow of students through higher education. *National Forum: Phi Kappa Phi Journal, 68,* 39–42.

Foundation donates $1 million for service projects. (1995, Fall). *FYE Newsletter, 8*(2), 11.

Freire, P. (1985). *The politics of education: Culture, power, and liberation.* New York: Bergin & Garvey.

Fried, J. (1999). Two steps to creative campus collaboration. *AAHE Bulletin, 52*(2), 10–12.

Friedman, P., Rodriguez, F., & McComb, J. (2001). Why students do and do not attend classes: Myths and realities. *College Teaching 49*(4), 124–133. Available at: http://www.cyberatlas.internet.com/big_picture/demographics/article/0,,590.

Frost, S. H. (1991). *Academic advising for student success: A system of shared responsibility.* Washington, DC: Association for the Study of Higher Education.

Fulkerson, K. F., Galassi, J. P., & Galassi, M. D. (1984). Relation between cognition and performance in math anxious students: A failure of cognitive theory? *Journal of Counseling Psychology, 31,* 376–382.

Fuller, A. G. (1983). A strategy to improve retention. *NACADA Journal, 3*(1), 65–72.

Full-Lopez, J. (1991). Self-esteem and academic success in the writing class. *National Association for Developmental Education Selected Conference Abstracts,* 22–23.

Furco, A. (2002). High school service-learning and the preparation of students for college: An overview of research. In E. Zlotkowski (Ed.), *Service-learning and the first-year experience: Preparing students for personal success and civic responsibility* (pp. 3–14). Columbia: University of South Carolina, National Resource Center for the First-Year Experience and Students in Transition.

Gabelnick, F., MacGregor, J., Matthews, B. S., & Smith, B. L. (1990). *Learning communities: Creating connections among students, faculty, and disciplines.* San Francisco: Jossey-Bass.

Gandara, P., & Maxwell-Jolly, J. (1999). *Priming the pump: A review of programs that aim to increase the achievement of underrepresented minority undergraduates.* New York: College Board.

Gardner, H. (1983). *Frames of mind: The theory of multiple intelligences.* New York: Basic Books.

Gardner, J. N. (1986). The freshman year experience. *Journal of the American Association of Collegiate Registrars and Admissions Officers, 61,* 261–274.

Gardner, J. N. (1999, Jan.). *Current trends in improving the first college year experience.* Invited presentation to Indiana University faculty and staff, Bloomington, IN.

Gardner, J. N. (2001, June). *Session materials.* Asheville, NC: Chief Executive and Chief Academic Officers Summer Institute, Sponsored by the Policy Center on the First Year of College and the National Resource Center for the First-Year Experience and Students in Transition.

Gardner, J. N. (2003, Feb. 24). Remarks at the Annual National Conference on the First-Year Experience, Atlanta, GA.

Gardner, J. N., Barefoot, B. O., & Swing, R. L. (2001). *Guidelines for evaluating the first-year experience (four-year college version)* (2nd ed.). Columbia, SC: University of South Carolina, National Resource Center for The First-Year Experience and Students in Transition.

Garrison, H. H. (1987). Undergraduate science and engineering education for blacks and Native Americans. In L. S. Dix (Ed.), *Minorities: Their underrepresentation and career differentials in science and engineering.* Proceedings of a workshop. Washington, DC: National Academy Press.

Garvin, D. A. (1993). Building a learning organization. *Harvard Business Review, 71*(4), 78–91.

Gayle, H. D., Keeling, R. P., Garcia-Tunon, M., Kilbourne, B. W., Narkunas, J. P., Ingram, F. R., Rogers, M. F., & Curran, J. W. (1990). Prevalence of HIV among college and university students. *New England Journal of Medicine, 323,* 1538–1541.

Gehring, D. D. (2000). Understanding the legal implications of student affairs practice. In M. J. Barr, M. K. Desler, & Associates (Eds.), *The handbook of student affairs administration* (2nd ed., pp. 347–376). San Francisco: Jossey-Bass.

Gehring, J. (2001a, April 18). Corporate leaders decry emphasis on SATs. *Education Week on the Web.*

Gehring, J. (2001b, May 9). SAT said to be reliable predictor of college success. *Education Week on the Web.*

Gelmon, S. B., Holland, B. A., Driscoll, A., Spring, A., & Kerrigan, S. (2001). *Assessing service-learning and civic engagement: Principles and techniques.* Providence, R.I.: Campus Compact.

Gess, J. K., & Klindworth, M. M. (2002). The new center for multidisciplinary studies: No longer an experiment. In J. L. Higbee, D. B. Lundell, & I. M. Duranczyk (Eds.), *Developmental education: Policy and practice* (pp. 77–84). Auburn, CA: National Association for Developmental Education.

Ghere, D. L. (2000). Teaching American history in a developmental education context. In J. L. Higbee & P. L. Dwinell (Eds.), *The many faces of developmental education* (pp. 39–46). Warrensburg, MO: National Association for Developmental Education. Available at: http://www.nade.net.

Ghere, D. L. (2001). Constructivist perspective and simulations in developmental education. In D. B. Lundell & J. L. Higbee (Eds.), *Theoretical perspectives for developmental education* (pp. 101–108). Minneapolis, MN: Center for Research on Developmental Education and Urban Literacy, General College, University of Minnesota. Available at: http://www.gen.umn.edu/research/crdeul.

Gilligan, C. (1977). In a different voice: Women's conceptions of the self and of morality. *Harvard Educational Review, 47,* 481–517.

Giroux, H. (1997). *Pedagogy and the politics of hope: Theory, culture, schooling.* Boulder, CO: Westview.

Gladieux, L., & Swail, W. (1998). Postsecondary education: Student success, not just access. In S. Halperin (Ed.), *The forgotten half revisited.* Washington, DC: American Youth Policy Forum. http://www.collegeboard.com/policy/html/tfh.html.

Glover, J. W. (2002). Developing online mathematics: Using policy, theory, and research to create a course. In J. L. Higbee, D. B. Lundell, & I. M. Duranczyk (Eds.), *Developmental education: Policy and practice* (pp. 101–112). Auburn, CA: National Association for Developmental Education.

Goggin, W. J. (1999, May). A "merit aware" model for college admissions and affirmative action. *Postsecondary Education Opportunity Newsletter, 6–12.*

Gonyea, R., Kish, K., & Kuh, G. D. (2001, May). *Estimating and interpreting student expectations for college.* Paper presented at the Annual Meeting of the Association for Institutional Research, Long Beach, CA.

Goodsell Love, A. (1999). What are learning communities? In J. H. Levine (Ed.), *Learning communities: New structures, new partnerships for learning* (pp. 1–8). Columbia: University of South Carolina, National Resource Center for The First-Year Experience and Students in Transition.

Goodsell Love, A., & Tokuno, K. A. (1999). Learning communities models. In J. H. Levine (Ed.), *Learning communities: New structures, new partnerships for learning.* (pp. 9–17). Columbia: University of South Carolina, National Resource Center for The First-Year Experience and Students in Transition.

Gordon, V. N. (1989). Origins and purposes of the freshman seminar. In M. L. Upcraft, J. N. Gardner, & Associates (Eds.), *The freshman year experience: Helping students survive and succeed in college* (pp. 183–197). San Francisco: Jossey-Bass.

Gordon, V. N., Habley, W. R., & Associates. (2000). *Academic advising: A comprehensive handbook.* San Francisco: Jossey-Bass.

Gratz v. Bollinger, 122 F. Supp.2nd 811 (E.D. Mich. Dec. 13, 2000.)

Gray, M. J., Ondaatje, E. H., Fricher, R. D., & Geschwind, S. A. (2000). Assessing service learning: Results from a survey of *Learn and Serve America, Higher Education. Change, 32*(2), 30–39.

Green, J. T., & Miller, M. T. (1998). A comparison study of enrollees and non-enrollees in an orientation course at a two-year college. *Journal of College Orientation and Transition, 5*(2), 14–20.

Greenleaf, R. (1970). Essentials of servant leadership. In M. Lawrence & L. C. Spears (Eds.). *Focus on leadership: Servant leadership for the 21st Century* (pp. 19–25). New York: Wiley.

Gregory, S. (1997). Planning for the increase in foreign-born students. *Planning for Higher Education, 26,* 23–28.

Grites, T., & Gordon, V. (2000). Developmental academic advising revisited. *NACADA Journal, 20*(1), 12–15.

Grunder, P. G., & Hellmich, D. (1996, Fall). Academic persistence and achievement of remedial students in a community college's college success program. *Community College Review, 24,* 21–33.

Grutter v. Bollinger, 288 F.3rd 732 (6th Cir. 2002)

Guerrero, D. (1998). Targeting diversity. In C. C. Swann & S. E. Henderson (Eds.), *Handbook for the college admissions profession.* Westport, CT: Greenwood Press.

Gurin, P. (1999). *Evidence for the educational benefits of diversity in higher education: Response to the critique by the National Association of Scholars of the expert Patricia Gurin.* University of Michigan. Available at: http://www.umich.edu/~urel/admissions/new/gurin.html.

Habley, W. R. (1983). Organizational structures for academic advising: Models and implications. *Journal of College Student Personnel, 26*(6), 535–540.

Habley, W. R. (1995). Adviser training in the contest of a teaching enhancement center. In R. E. Glennen & F. N. Vowell (Eds.), *Academic advising as a comprehensive campus process.* Manhattan, KS: National Academic Advising Association.

Habley, W. R., & McCauley, M. E. (1987). The relationship between institutional characteristics and the organization of advising services. *NACADA Journal, 7*(1), 27–39.

Habley, W. R., & Morales, R. H. (1998). *Current practices in academic advising: Final report on ACT's Fifth National Survey of Academic Advising.* Manhattan, KS: National Academic Advising Association.

Haines, M. P., & Spear, S. F. (1996). Changing the perception of the norm: A strategy to decrease binge drinking among college students. *Journal of American College Health, 45,* 134–140.

Hall, L. M., & Belch, H. A. (2000). Setting the context: Reconsidering the principles of full participation and meaningful access for students with disabilities. In H. A. Belch (Ed.), *Serving students with disabilities* (pp. 5–18). San Francisco: Jossey-Bass.

Hamilton, S. J. (2004). A principle-based approach to assessing general education in the major. *Journal of General Education, 52*(4) 283–303.

Hamrick, F. A., Schuh, J. H., & Shelley, M. C. (2002). *Institutional characteristics and resource allocation: Predictors of graduation rates.* Ames, IA: Iowa State University, Unpublished paper.

Hansen, E. J. (1998). Essential demographics of today's college students. *AAHE Bulletin, 51*(3), 3–5.

Hardin, C. J. (1988). Access to higher education: Who belongs? *Journal of Developmental Education, 12*(1), 2–6.

Hardin, C. J. (1998). Who belongs in college: A second look. In J. L. Higbee & P. L. Dwinell (Eds.), *Developmental education: Preparing successful college students* (pp. 15–24). Columbia: University of South Carolina, National Resource Center for The First-Year Experience and Students in Transition.

Hart, D., & Keller, M. J. (1980). Self-reported reasons for poor academic performance of first-term freshmen. *Journal of College Student Personnel, 21,* 529–534.

Hasenfeld, Y. (1992). The nature of human service organizations. In Y. Hasenfeld (Ed.), *Human services as complex organizations* (pp. 3–21). Newbury Park, CA: Sage.

Hashway, R. M., Jackson Hammond, C., & Hawkins Rogers, P. (1990). Academic locus of control and the collegiate experience. *Research and Teaching in Developmental Education, 7*(1), 45–54.

Hatch, C. (2000). Parent and family orientation—programs supporting student success. In M. J. Fabich (Ed.), *Orientation planning manual 2000.* Pullman, WA: National Orientation Directors Association.

Hatch, C. (2002, Winter–Spring). Welcome to the adult learner network. *Adult Learner Newsletter.* Flint, MI: National Orientation Directors Association.

Hatcher, J. A., Bringle, R. G., & Muthiah, R. (2002). Institutional strategies to involve first-year students in service. In E. Zlotkowski (Ed.), *Service-learning and the first-year experience: Preparing students for personal success and civic responsibility* (pp. 79–90). Columbia: University of South Carolina, National Resource Center for The First-Year Experience and Students in Transition.

Haycock, K. (1999, Fall). Ticket to nowhere: The gap between leaving high school and entering college and high-performance jobs. *Thinking K–16*, pp. 1–2.

Hearn, J. C. (1998). The growing loan orientation in federal financial aid policy. In R. Fossey & M. Bateman (Eds.), *Condemning students to debt* (pp. 47–75). New York: Teachers College Press.

Hebel, S. (2002, Oct. 25). Skyrocketing public-college tuition renews calls for better policy. *Chronicle of Higher Education.*

Heitzmann, D., & Nafziger, K. L. (2001). Assessing counseling services. In J. H. Schuh & M. L. Upcraft (Eds.), *Assessment practice in student affairs* (pp. 390–412). San Francisco: Jossey-Bass.

Heller, D. (2001). *The states and public higher education policy: Affordability, access, and accountability.* Baltimore, MD: Johns Hopkins University Press.

Henderson, C. (1999). *College freshmen with disabilities: A biennial statistical profile.* Washington, DC: American Council on Education.

Herndon, S. (1984). Recent findings concerning the relative importance of housing to student retention. *Journal of College and University Student Housing, 14,* 27–31.

Herrnstein, R., & Murray, C. (1994). *The bell curve: Intelligence and class structure in American life.* New York: Free Press.

Higbee, J. L. (1988). Student development theory: A foundation for the individualized instruction of high-risk freshmen. *Journal of Educational Opportunity, 3*(1), 42–47.

Higbee, J. L. (1995). Misplaced priorities or alternative developmental opportunities: A case study. *Research and Teaching in Developmental Education, 11*(2), 79–84.

Higbee, J. L. (1996). Ability, preparation, or motivation? *Research and Teaching in Developmental Education, 13*(1), 93–96.

Higbee, J. L. (2000a). Bridging the gap: High school to college matriculation. In D. B. Lundell & J. L. Higbee (Eds.), *Proceedings of the First Intentional Meeting on Future Directions in Developmental Education* (pp. 37–39). Minneapolis, MN: Center for Research on Developmental Education and Urban Literacy, General College, University of Minnesota. Available: http://www. gen.umn.edu/research/crdeul.

Higbee, J. L. (2000b). Commentary: Who is the developmental student? *Learning Assistance Review, 5*(1), 41–50.

Higbee, J. L. (2001). Promoting multiculturalism in developmental education. *Research and Teaching in Developmental Education, 18*(1), 51–57.

Higbee, J. L. (2002). The application of Chickering's theory of student development to student success in the sixties and beyond. *Research and Teaching in Developmental Education, 18*(2), 24–36.

Higbee, J. L. (Ed.). (2003). *Curriculum transformation and disability: Implementing Universal Design in higher education.* Minneapolis, MN: Center for Research on Developmental Education and Urban Literacy, General College, University of Minnesota.

Higbee, J. L., Bruch, P. L., Jehangir, R. R., Lundell, D. B., & Miksch, K. L. (2003). The multicultural mission of developmental education: A starting point. *Research and Teaching in Developmental Education, 19*(2), 47–51.

Higbee, J. L., & Dwinell, P. L. (1990a). Factors related to the academic success of high risk freshmen: Three case studies. *College Student Journal, 24,* 380–386.

Higbee, J. L., & Dwinell, P. L. (1990b). The high risk student profile. *Research and Teaching in Developmental Education, 7*(1), 55–64.

Higbee, J. L., & Dwinell, P. L. (1992a). The developmental inventory of sources of stress. *Research and Teaching in Developmental Education, 8*(2), 27–40.

Higbee, J. L., & Dwinell, P. L. (1992b). The development of underprepared freshmen enrolled in a self-awareness course. *Journal of College Student Development, 33,* 26–33.

Higbee, J. L., & Dwinell, P. L. (1995). Affect: How important is it? *Research and Teaching in Developmental Education, 12*(1), 71–74.

Higbee, J. L., & Dwinell, P. L. (1996). Correlates of self-esteem among high risk students. *Research and Teaching in Developmental Education, 12*(2), 41–50.

Higbee, J. L., & Dwinell, P. L. (1997). Do developmental education programs really enhance retention? A commentary. In P. L. Dwinell & J. L. Higbee, J. L. (Eds.), *Developmental education: Enhancing student retention* (pp. 55–60). Carol Stream, IL: National Association for Developmental Education. Available at: http://www.nade.net.

Higbee, J .L., & Dwinell, P. L. (1998). Transitions in developmental education at the University of Georgia. In J. L. Higbee & P. L. Dwinell (Eds.), *Developmental Education: Preparing successful college students.* Columbia: University of South Carolina, National Resource Center for The First-Year Experience and Students in Transition.

Higbee, J. L., Dwinell, P. L., & Thomas, P. V. (2002). Beyond University 101: Elective courses to enhance retention. *Journal of College Student Retention: Research, Theory, and Practice, 3,* 311–318.

Higbee, J. L., Ginter, E. J., & Taylor, W. D. (1991). Enhancing academic performance: Seven perceptual styles of learning. *Research and Teaching in Developmental Education, 7*(2), 5–9.

Higbee, J. L., & Thomas, P. V. (1999). Affective and cognitive factors related to mathematics achievement. *Journal of Developmental Education, 23*(1), 8–10, 12, 14, 16, 32.

Higbee, J. L., & Thomas, P. V. (2000). Creating assessment tools to determine student needs. *Research and Teaching in Developmental Education, 16*(2), 83–87.

Hill, K. T. (1984). Debilitating motivation and testing: A major educational problem—Possible solutions and policy applications. In R. E. Ames & C. Ames (Eds.), *Research on motivation in education, Volume 1: Student motivation* (pp. 245–274). Orlando, FL: Academic Press.

Hills, S., Gay, B., & Topping, K. (1998). Peer-assisted learning beyond school. In K. Topping & S. Ehly (Eds.), *Peer-assisted learning* (pp. 291–331). Mahwah, NJ: Erlbaum.

Himelein, M. J., Vogel, R. W., & Wachowiak D. G. (1994). Non-consensual sexual experiences in pre-college women: Prevalence and risk factors. *Journal of Counseling and Development, 72,* 411–415.

Hirsch, B. J. (1980). Natural support systems and coping with major life changes. *American Journal of Community Psychology, 8,* 159–172.

Hodges, E., & Yerian, J. (2001, November 19). *The first-year Prompts Project: A qualitative research study revisited.* Available at: http://www.brevard.edu/listserv/remarks/hodges.htm.

Hodges, R. B., Corkran, G. M., & Dochen, C. W. (1997). A state-mandated basic skills program: An interview with Kenneth H. Ashworth. *Journal of Developmental Education, 21*(2), 20–22.

Hodges, R. B., Dochen, C. W., & Sellers, D. C. (2001). Implementing a learning framework course. In J. L. Higbee (Ed.), *2001: A developmental odyssey* (pp. 3–13). Warrensburg, MO: National Association for Developmental Education. Available at: http://www.nade.net.

Horn, L. (1998). *Stopouts or stayouts? Undergraduates who leave college in their first year.* Washington, DC: U.S. Department of Education, National Center for Education Statistics.

Horn, L. J., & Berktold, J. (1998). *Profile of undergraduates in U.S. postsecondary education institutions, 1995–96 with an essay on undergraduates who work.* Washington, DC: U.S. Government Printing Office.

Hossler, D. (1984). *Enrollment management: An integrated approach.* New York: College Board.

Hossler, D. (1999). Using the Internet in college admission: Strategic choices. *Journal of College Admission, 162,* 12–18.

Hossler, D. (2001). *Enrollment Management Review, 17*(3), 1–8.

Hossler, D., Bean, J. P., & Associates. (1990). *The strategic management of college enrollments.* San Francisco: Jossey-Bass.

Hossler, D., Braxton, J., & Coppersmith, G. (1989). Understanding student college choice. In J. Smart (Ed.), *Higher education: Handbook of theory and research, IV.* New York: Agathon Press.

Hossler, D., & Foley, E. M. (1996). Reducing the noise in the college choice process: The use of college guidebooks and ratings. In D. Walleri & Marsha Moss (Eds.), *Assessing the impact of college guide and rating books* (pp. 21–31). San Francisco: Jossey-Bass.

Hossler, D., Kuh, G. D., & Olsen, D. (2001). Finding fruit on the vines: Using higher education research and institutional research to guide institutional policies and strategies (Part II). *Research in Higher Education, 42,* 223–235.

Hossler, D. & Litten, L. H. (1993). *Mapping the higher education landscape.* New York: College Board.

Hossler, D., Schmit, J., & Vesper, N. (1998). *Going to college: Family, social and educational influences on postsecondary decision making.* Baltimore: The Johns Hopkins University Press. http://www.acenet.edu/washington/college_costs/1998/07july/straight_talk.html.

House, J. D. (1995). Noncognitive predictors of achievement in introductory college mathematics. *Journal of College Student Development, 36,* 171–181.

House, J. D., & Kuchynka, S. J. (1997). The effects of a freshman orientation course on the achievement of health sciences students. *Journal of College Student Development, 38*(5), 540–541.

Howard-Hamilton, M. F., & Watt, S. K. (2001). Editors' notes. In M. F. Howard-Hamilton & S. K. Watt (Eds.), *Student services for athletes* (pp. 1–6). San Francisco: Jossey-Bass.

Hu, S., & Kuh, G. D. (2001a). Computing experience and good practices in undergraduate education: Does the degree of campus "wiredness" matter? *Education Policy Analysis Archives, 9*(49). Available at: http://epaa.asu.edu/epaa/v9n49.hmtl.

Hu, S., & Kuh, G. D. (2001b, November). *The effects of interactional diversity on selected self-reported learning and personal development outcomes.* Paper presented at the annual meeting of the Association for the Study of Higher Education, Richmond.

Hulme, T., & Barlow, A. R. (1998). A fair chance for all. *NADE Selected Conference Papers, 1,* 13–15.

Hunter, M. S., & Gardner, J. N. (1999). Outcomes and future directions of instructor training programs. In M. S. Hunter & T. L. Skipper (Eds.), *Solid foundations: Building success for first-year seminars through instructor training and development.* Columbia: University of South Carolina, National Resource Center for The First-Year Experience and Students in Transition.

Hunter, M. S., & Linder, C. W. (2003). College seminars for first-year students. In J. W. Guthrie (Ed.), *Encyclopedia of education.* (2nd ed.) New York: Macmillan.

Hurtado, S., Carter, D. F., & Spuler, A. (1996). Latino transition to college: Assessing difficulties and factors in successful college adjustment. *Research in Higher Education, 37,* 135–157.

Hurtado, S., Milem, J., Clayton-Pedersen, A., & Allen, W. (1999). *Enacting diverse learning environments: Improving the climate for racial/ethnic diversity in higher education.* Washington, DC: The George Washington University.

Hutchings, P., & Shulman, L. (1999, September/October). The scholarship of teaching: New elaborations, new developments. *Change,* 10–15.

Hutchinson, G. (2000). Service-learning: Vygotsky, Dewey, and teaching writing. *Academic Exchange Quarterly, 4*(4), 73–79.

Hyers, A. D., & Joslin, M. N. (1998). The first-year seminar as a predictor of academic achievement and persistence. *Journal of The Freshman Year Experience and Students in Transition, 10*(1), 7–30.

Immersion Key to DePaul FYE Program. (2000, Fall). *FYE: Newsletter of the National Resource Center for The First-Year Experience and Students in Transition,* pp. 1–2.

Inkelas, K. K. (1999, September). *A tide on which all boats rise: The effects of living-learning program participation on undergraduate outcomes at the University of Michigan.* Ann Arbor: University of Michigan, University Housing.

Internet is now pervasive and powerful element in college choice. (2000). *Student Poll, 4*(1). Art and Science Group, LLC. Available at http://www.artsci.com/admin/pdf/ACF3038.pdf.

Ishitani, T. T., & DesJardins, S. L. (2002–2003). A longitudinal investigation of dropout from college in the United States. *Journal of College Student Retention, 4*(2), 173–201.

Jablonski, M. A. (Ed.). (2001). *The implications of student spirituality for student affairs practice.* San Francisco: Jossey-Bass.

Jacobson, J. (2003, Nov. 7). Foreign student enrollment stagnates. *Chronicle of Higher Education.* Available at http://chronicle.com/prm/weekly/v50/i11/11a00101.htm.

Jacoby, B. (1996). Service-learning in today's higher education. In B. Jacoby (Ed.), *Service-learning in higher education: Concepts and practices* (pp. 3–25). San Francisco: Jossey-Bass.

James, J. P., & Haselbeck, B. (1998). The arts as a bridge to understanding identity and diversity. In P. L. Dwinell & J. L. Higbee (Eds.), *Developmental education: Meeting diverse student needs* (pp. 3–19). Morrow, GA: National Association for Developmental Education. Available at: http://www. nade.net.

Jehangir, R. R. (2001). Cooperative learning in the multicultural classroom. In D. B. Lundell & J. L. Higbee (Eds.), *Theoretical perspectives for developmental education* (pp. 91–99). Minneapolis, MN: Center for Research on Developmental Education and Urban Literacy, General College, University of Minnesota. Available at: http://www. gen.umn.edu/research/crdeul.

Jehangir, R. R. (2002). Higher education for whom? The debate about developmental education and public higher education. In J. L. Higbee, I. M. Duranczyk, & D. B. Lundell (Eds.), *Developmental education: Policy and practice.* Auburn, CA: National Association for Developmental Education.

Jensen, M., & Rush, B. (2000). Teaching a human anatomy and physiology course within the context of developmental education. In J. L. Higbee & P. L. Dwinell (Eds.), *The many faces of developmental education* (pp. 47–57). Warrensburg, MO: National Association for Developmental Education. Available at: http://www.nade.net.

Jessor, R., & Jessor, S. L. (1975). Adolescent development and the onset of drinking. *Journal of Studies on Alcohol, 36,* 27–51.

Jewler, A. J. (1989). Elements of an effective seminar: The University 101 Program. In M. L. Upcraft, J. N. Gardner, & Associates (Eds.), *The freshman year experience: Helping students survive and succeed in college* (pp. 198–215). San Francisco: Jossey-Bass, 1989.

Johnson, A. B. (2001). Theoretical views and practices supporting in-context developmental strategies in the physical sciences. In D. B. Lundell & J. L. Higbee (Eds.), *Theoretical perspectives for developmental education* (pp. 153–161). Minneapolis, MN: Center for Research on Developmental Education and Urban Literacy, General College, University of Minnesota. Available at: http://www.gen.umn.edu/research/crdeul.

Johnson, D. W., Johnson, R. T., & Smith, K. A. (1991). *Cooperative learning: Increasing college faculty instructional productivity.* Washington, D.C.: George Washington University, School of Education and Human Development.

Johnson, D. W., Johnson, R. T., & Smith, K. A. (1998). Cooperative learning returns to college: What evidence is there that it works? *Change, 30*(4), 26–35.

Johnson, J. L. (2000–2001). Learning communities and special efforts in retention of university students: What works, what doesn't, and is the return worth the investment? *Journal of College Student Retention, 2*(3), 219–238.

Johnson, J. L., & King, S. G. (1996). *Russell Scholars Program: Evaluation of the inaugural year.* Unpublished report. Gorham: University of Southern Maine.

Johnston, L. D., O'Malley, P. M., & Bachman, J. G. (2001). *Monitoring the Future: National Survey Results on Drug Use, 1975–2000. Volume 2: College Students and Young Adults Ages 19–40.* Washington, DC: National Institute on Drug Abuse, U.S. Department of Health and Human Services.

Jones, B. W. (1998). Rediscovering our heritage: Community service and the historically black university. In E. Zlotkowski (ed.), *Successful service-learning programs: New models of excellence in higher education.* Bolton, MA: Anker.

Jones, W. T. (1987). Enhancing minority-white peer interactions. In D. J. Wright (Ed.), *Responding to the needs of today's minority students* (pp. 81–94). San Francisco: Jossey-Bass.

Junco, R., & Salter, D. W. (2004). Improving the campus climate for students with disabilities through the use of online training. *Journal of the National Association of Student Personnel Administrators 41,* 2. Retrieved from: http://publications.naspa.org.naspajournal/vol41/art4.

Kamens, D. (1971). The college "charter" and college size: Effects on occupational choice and college attrition. *Sociology of Education, 44,* 270–296.

Kanoy, K. W., & Bruhn, J. W. (1996). Effect of a first-year living-learning residence hall on retention and academic performance. *Journal of The Freshman Year of Experience and Students in Transition, 8,* 7–24.

Kaplan, J., Whipple, E. G., & Wright, J. (1996). Student health. In A. L. Rentz & Associates (Eds.), *Student affairs practice in higher education* (2nd ed., pp. 365–379). Springfield, IL: Thomas.

Katzenbach, J. R., & Smith, D. K. (1993, March–April). The discipline of teams. *Harvard Business Review,* 111–120.

Kaufman, M., & Creamer, D. (1991). Influences of student goals for college on freshman year quality of effect and growth. *Journal of College Student Development, 32,* 197–206.

Kavale, K. A., & Forness, S. R. (1996, Jan.–Mar.). Learning disability grow up: Rehabilitation issues for individuals with learning disabilities. *Journal of Rehabilitation,* 34–41.

Keller, G. (2001). The new demographics of higher education. *Review of Higher Education, 24,* 219–236.

Kellogg Commission on the Future of State and Land Grant Universities. (1998). *Returning to our roots: The student experience.* Washington, DC: National Association of State Universities and Land-Grant Colleges.

Kemerer, F. R., Baldridge, J. V., & Green, K. C. (1992). *Strategies for effective enrollment management.* Washington, DC: American Association of State Colleges and Universities.

Kendall, J. C. (Ed.). (1990). *Combining service and learning: A resource book for community and public service.* Raleigh, NC: National Society for Experiential Education.

Kennedy, K., Moran, L., & Upcraft, M. L. (2001). Assessing cost effectiveness. In J. H. Schuh, M. L. Upcraft, & Associates. *Assessment practice in student affairs* (pp. 175–195). San Francisco: Jossey-Bass.

Kerr, C. (1991). *The great transformation in higher education, 1960–1980.* Albany: State University of New York Press.

Kerr, T. J. (2000). Recognition and reward for excellence in advising. In V. N. Gordon, W. R. Habley, & Associates (Eds.), *Academic advising: A comprehensive campus handbook* (pp. 349–364). San Francisco: Jossey-Bass.

Ketcheson, K. A., & Levine, J. H. (1999). Evaluating and assessing learning communities. In J. H. Levine (Ed.), *Learning communities: New structures, new partnerships for learning* (pp. 97–108). Columbia: University of South Carolina, National Resource Center for The First-Year Experience and Students in Transition.

Kiernon, K. (1992). The impact of family disruption in childhood on transitions made in young adult life. *Population Studies, 46,* 213–234.

Kimball, B. A. (1995). Toward pragmatic liberal education. In R. Orrill (Ed.), *The condition of American liberal education: Pragmatism and a changing tradition* (pp. 3–122). New York: College Entrance Examination Board.

King, H., & Walsh, W. B. (1972). Change in environmental expectations and perceptions. *Journal of College Student Personnel, 13,* 331–337.

King, J. E. (1998, May 1). Too many students are holding jobs for too many hours. *Chronicle of Higher Education,* p. A72.

King, M. C. (1988). Advising delivery systems. In W. R. Habley (Ed.), *The status and future of academic advising.* Iowa City: American College Testing Program.

King, P. M., & Kitchener, K. S. (1994). *Developing reflective judgment: Understanding and promoting intellectual growth and critical thinking in adolescents and adults.* San Francisco: Jossey-Bass.

Knox, D. (1997). Why college students end relationships. *College Student Journal, 31,* 449–452.

Kochenour, E. O., Jolley, D. S., Kaup, J. G., Patrick, D. L., Roach, K. D., & Wenzler, L. A. (1997). Supplemental instruction: An effective component of student affairs programming. *Journal of College Student Development, 38*(6), 577–586.

Koehler, A. G. (2000). Teaching on television. *Research and Teaching in Developmental Education, 16*(2), 97–108.

Kohlberg, L. (1976). Moral stages and moralization: The cognitive development approach. Stages of moral development. In T. Lickona (Ed.), *Moral development and behavior: Theory, research, and social issues* (pp. 31–53). New York: Holt.

Kolins, C. A. (2000). An appraisal of collaboration: Assessing perceptions of chief academic and student affairs officers at public two-year colleges. *Student Development in the Two-Year Colleges, 14,* 9–12.

Kozol, J. (1991). *Savage inequalities: Children in America's schools.* New York: Crown.

Kozol, J. (1995). *Amazing grace: The lives of children and the conscience of a nation.* New York: Crown.

Kramer, G. L., & Childs, M. W. (2000). *The "e" factor in delivering advising and student services.* Manhattan, KS: National Academic Advising Association.

Kramer, G. L., & Peterson, E. D. (1999). Project 2000: A Web based student planning system. In M. Beede & D. Burnett (Eds.), *Planning for student services: Best practices for the 21st century.* Ann Arbor, MI: Society for College and University Planning.

Kramer, G. L., & White, M. T. (1982). Developing a faculty mentoring program: An experiment. *NACADA Journal, 2*(2), 47–58.

Krauth, B. (1999). Trends in support services for distance learners. In M. Beede & D. Burnett (Eds.), *Planning for student services: Best practices for the 21st century.* Ann Arbor, MI: Society for College and University Planning.

Kroll, J., & Rentz, A. L. (1996). Career services. In A. L. Rentz & Associates (Eds.), *Student affairs practice in higher education* (2nd ed., pp. 108–142). Springfield, IL: Thomas.

Krueger, R. A. (1988). *Focus groups: A practical guide for applied research.* Thousand Oaks, CA: Sage.

Kubey, R. W., Lavin, M. J., & Barrows, J. R. (2001). Internet use and collegiate academic performance decrements: Early findings. *Journal of Communication, 51,* 366–382.

Kuh, G. D. (1981). *Indices of quality in the undergraduate experience.* AAHE ERIC/ Higher Education Research Report No. 4. Washington, DC: American Association for Higher Education.

Kuh, G. D. (1993). Ethos: Its influence on student learning. *Liberal Education, 79*(4), 22–31.

Kuh, G. D. (1994). Creating campus climates that foster student learning. In C. Schroeder, P. Mable, & Associates (Eds.), *Realizing the educational potential of residence halls,* (pp. 109–132). San Francisco: Jossey-Bass.

Kuh, G. D. (1996). Guiding principles for creating seamless learning environments for undergraduates. *Journal of College Student Development, 37*(2), 135–148.

Kuh, G. D. (1997, June). *Working together to enhance student learning inside and outside the classroom.* Paper presented at the annual AAHE Assessment and Quality Conference, Miami, FL.

Kuh, G. D. (1999). Setting the bar high to promote student learning. In G. S. Blimling, E. J. Whitt, & Associates (Eds.), *Good practice in student affairs: Principles to foster student learning.* San Francisco: Jossey-Bass.

Kuh, G. D. (2001). College students today: Why we can't leave serendipity to chance. In P. Altbach, P. Gumport, & B. Johnstone (Eds.), *In defense of American higher education* (pp. 277–303). Baltimore: Johns Hopkins University Press.

Kuh, G. D. (2003). What we're learning about student engagement from NSSE. *Change, 35*(2), 24–32.

Kuh, G. D., & Banta, T. W. (2000). Faculty-student affairs collaboration on assessment—lessons from the field. *About Campus, 4*(6), 4–11.

Kuh, G. D., Branch Douglas, K., Lund, J. P., & Ramin-Gyurnek, J. (1994). *Student learning outside the classroom: Transcending artificial boundaries.* Washington, DC: George Washington University Press.

Kuh, G. D., Hayek, J. C., Carini, R. M., Ouimet, J. A., Gonyea, R. M., & Kennedy, J. (2001). *NSSE technical and norms report.* Bloomington: Indiana University Center for Postsecondary Research and Planning.

Kuh, G. D., & Pace, C. R. (1998). *College Student Expectations Questionnaire.* Bloomington, IN: Center for Postsecondary Research and Planning, School of Education, Indiana University.

Kuh, G. D., Schuh, J. H., Whitt, E. J., Andreas, R. E., Lyons, J. W., Strange, C. C., Krehbiel, L. E., & MacKay, K. A. (1991). *Involving colleges: Successful approaches to fostering student learning and personal development outside the classroom.* San Francisco: Jossey-Bass.

Kuh, G. D., & Vesper, N. (2001). Do computers enhance or detract from student learning? *Research in Higher Education, 42*(1), 87–102.

Kuh, G. D., Vesper, N., Connolly, M. R., & Pace, C. R. (1997). *College Student Experiences Questionnaire: Revised norms for the third edition.* Bloomington: Center for Postsecondary Research, School of Education, Indiana University.

Kuhlthau, C. C. (1993). Implementing a process approach to information skills: A study identifying indicators of success in library media programs. *School Library Media Quarterly, 22*(1), 11–18.

Kulik, C., Kulik, J., & Schwab, B. (1983). College programs for high-risk and disadvantaged students: A meta-analysis of findings. *Review of Educational Research, 53,* 397–414.

Kurfiss, J. G. (1988). *Critical thinking: Theory, research, practice, and possibilities.* Washington, DC: Association for the Study of Higher Education.

Lamb, C. H., Lee, J. B., Swinth, R. L., & Vinton, K. L. (2000). Learning well by doing good: Service-learning in management education. In P. C. Godfrey & E. T. Grasso (Eds.), *Working for the common good: Concepts and models for service-learning in management* (pp. 167–178). Washington, DC: American Association for Higher Education.

Lang, D. C., & Nora, A. (2001, June). *Pre-college psychosocial factors related to persistence.* Paper presented at the Association for Institutional Research, Long Beach, CA.

Lao, R. C. (1970). Internal-external locus of control and competent and innovative behavior among Negro college students. *Journal of Personality and Social Psychology, 14,* 263–270.

Larimer, M. E., & Cronce, J. M. (2000). Identification, prevention and treatment: A review of individual-focused strategies to reduce problematic alcohol consumption by college students. *Journal of Studies on Alcohol,* Supplement 14, 148–163.

Larson, E. (1997, March 17). Why colleges cost too much. *Time, 149*(11) pp. 46–53.

Larson, R., & Csikszentmihalyi, M. (1983). The experience sampling method. In H. T. Reis (Ed.), *Naturalistic approaches to studying social interaction.* San Francisco: Jossey-Bass.

Laufgraben, J. L. (2003). Faculty development: Growing, reflecting, learning, and changing. In J. O'Connor and others (Eds.), *Learning communities in research universities* (pp. 33–37). Olympia, WA: Evergreen State College, Washington Center for Improving the Quality of Undergraduate Education, in cooperation with the American Association for Higher Education.

Leafgren, F. A. (1989). Health and wellness programs. In M. L. Upcraft, J. N. Gardner, & Associates (Eds.), *The freshman year experience: Helping students survive and succeed in college* (pp. 156–167). San Francisco: Jossey-Bass.

Leamnson, R. (1999). *Thinking about teaching and learning: Developing habits of learning with first year college and university students.* Sterling, VA: Stylus Publishing.

Lee, J. J. (2002). Religion and college attendance: Change among students. *Review of Higher Education, 25*(4), 369–384.

Leichliter, J. S., Meilman, P. W., Presley, C. A., & Cashin, J. R. (1998). Alcohol use and related consequences among students with varying levels of involvement in college athletics. *Journal of American College Health, 46*(6), 257–262.

Lemelin, R. (1998). Barriers to higher education and strategies to remove them: An international perspective. In P. L. Dwinell & J. L. Higbee (Eds.), *Developmental education: Meeting diverse student needs* (pp. 97–100). Morrow, GA: National Association for Developmental Education. Available at: http://www.nade.net.

Lemelin, R. E. (1992). The European dimension of developmental education: An interview with Maggie Woodrow. *Journal of Developmental Education, 15*(3), 24–26, 28–29, 35.

Lemire, D. S. (1998). Three learning styles models: Research and recommendations for developmental education. *Learning Assistance Review, 3*(2), 26–40.

Lenning, O. T., & Ebbers, L. H. (1999). *The powerful potential of learning communities: Improving education for the future.* Washington, DC: The George Washington University, School of Education and Human Development.

Lent, R. W., & Russell, R. K. (1978). Treatment of test anxiety by cue-controlled desensitization and study skills training. *Journal of Counseling Psychology, 25,* 217–224.

Levine, A. (1989). Who are today's freshmen? In M. L. Upcraft & J. N. Gardner (Eds.), *The freshman year experience: Helping students survive and succeed in college* (pp. 15–24). San Francisco: Jossey-Bass.

Levine, A., & Cureton, J. S. (1998a). What we know about today's college students. *About Campus, 3*(1), 4–9.

Levine, A., & Cureton, J. S. (1998b, May–June). Collegiate life: An obituary. *Change, 30*(3), 12–17, 51.

Levine, A., & Cureton, J. S., (1998c). *When hope and fear collide: A portrait of today's college student.* San Francisco: Jossey-Bass.

Levine, J. H., & Shapiro, N. S. (2000). Curricular learning communities. In B. Jacoby (Ed.), *Involving commuter students in learning.* New Directions for Higher Education, no. 109. San Francisco: Jossey-Bass.

Lewallen, W. (1993). The impact of being "undecided" on college-student persistence. *Journal of College Student Development, 34,* 103–112.

Lewis, J. E., Malow, R. M., & Ireland, S. J. (1997). HIV/AIDS risk in heterosexual college students: A review of a decade of literature. *Journal of College Health, 45,* 147–158.

Light, R. J. (2001). *Making the most of college: Students speak their minds.* Cambridge, MA: Harvard University Press.

Litten, L. H. (1984). Extending the applications of portfolio analysis in higher education: The student body portfolio and enrollment management. *Liberal Education, 79*(2), 167–181.

Llabre, M. M., & Suarez, E. (1985). Predicting math anxiety and course performance in college men and women. *Journal of Counseling Psychology, 32,* 283–287.

Longman, D., Atkinson, R., Miholic, V., & Simpson, P. (1999). Building long-range workplace literacy projects: The ABC reading apprenticeship and task analysis. In J. L. Higbee & P. L. Dwinell (Eds.), *The expanding role of developmental education* (pp. 31–41). Morrow, GA: National Association for Developmental Education. Available at: http://www.nade.net.

Loomis-Hubble, L. (1991). *Tuition discounting: The impact of institutionally funded financial aid.* Washington, DC: National Association of College and University Business Officers.

Lords, E. (2000, September 22). A revolution in academic advising at a Texas community college. *Chronicle of Higher Education,* p. A47.

Love, P., & Talbot, D. (1999). Defining spiritual development: A missing consideration for student affairs. *Journal of the National Association of Student Personnel Administrators, 37,* 361–375.

Love, P. G., Jacobs, B. A., Poschini, V. J., Hardy, C. M., & Kuh, G. D. (1993). Student culture. In G. D. Kuh (Ed.), *Cultural perspectives in student affairs work.* Washington, DC: American College Personnel Association.

Lundell, D. B. (2000a). Collaboration and partnerships: Within and between disciplines, programs, and institutions. In D. B. Lundell & J. L. Higbee (Eds.), *Proceedings of the First Intentional Meeting on Future Directions in Developmental Education* (pp. 43–45). Minneapolis, MN: Center for Research on Developmental Education and Urban Literacy, University of Minnesota. Available at: http://www.gen.umn.edu/research/crdeul.

Lundell, D. B. (2000b). Enhancing credibility, gaining recognition, and eliminating any stigma associated with developmental education. In D. B. Lundell & J. L. Higbee (Eds.), *Proceedings of the First Intentional Meeting on Future Directions in Developmental Education* (pp. 57–59). Minneapolis, MN: Center for Research on Developmental Education and Urban Literacy, General College, University of Minnesota. Available at: http://www. gen.umn.edu/research/crdeul.

Lundell, D. B. (2000c). Institutional fit: Mission and structure of programs within different types of institutions. In D. B. Lundell & J. L. Higbee (Eds.), *Proceedings of the First Intentional Meeting on Future Directions in Developmental Education* (pp. 51–53). Minneapolis, MN: Center for Research on Developmental Education and Urban Literacy, General College, University of Minnesota. Available at: http://www. gen.umn.edu/research/crdeul.

Lundell, D. B., & Collins, T. C. (1999). Toward a theory of developmental education: The centrality of "Discourse." In J. L. Higbee & P. L. Dwinell (Eds.), *The expanding role of developmental education* (pp. 3–20). Morrow, GA: National Association for Developmental Education. Available at: http://www.nade.net.

Lundquist, C., Spalding, R. J., & Landrum, R. E. (2002–2003). College student's thoughts about leaving the university: The impact of faculty attitudes and behaviors. *Journal of College Student Retention, 4*(2), 123–134.

MacGregor, J., Smith, B. L., Matthews, R., & Gabelnick, F. (1997). Learning Community Models. Paper presented at National Conference on Higher Education, American Association of Higher Education, Washington, DC, March 1997.

MacGregor, J., Smith, B. L., Matthews, R., & Gabelnick, F. (2001, May). *Learning community models.* Available at: http://www.evergreen.edu/user/washcntr/resnconv.shtm.

Maehr, M. L. (1984). Meaning and motivation: Toward a theory of personal investment. In R. E. Ames & C. Ames (Eds.), *Research on motivation in education, Volume 1: Student motivation* (pp. 115–144). Orlando, FL: Academic Press.

Magolda, P. M. (2001). Border crossings: Collaboration struggles in education. *Journal of Educational Research, 94*(6), 346–358.

Maguire, J. (1976). To the organized go the students. *Bridge Magazine, 39*(i). Boston: Boston College.

Mahoney, C. A., Thombs, D. L., & Ford, O. J. (1995). Health belief and self-efficacy models: Their utility in explaining college student condom use. *AIDS Education Preview, 7,* 32–49.

Malone, D., Jones, B. D., & Stallings, D. T. (2001, April). Transforming perspectives through service learning: Inspiring growth and mindfulness in undergraduates. Paper presented at the American Educational Research Association Annual Meeting, Seattle, WA.

Mangold, W. D., Bean, L. G., Adams, D. J., Schwab, W. A., & Lynch, S. M. (2002–2003). Who goes who stays: An assessment of the effect of a freshman mentoring and unit registration program on college persistence. *Journal of College Student Retention, 4*(2), 95–122.

Manuel, K. (2002). Teaching information literacy to generation Y. *Journal of Library Administration. 36*(1–2), 195–217.

Marchese, T. (1996). Resetting expectations. *Change, 28*(6), 4.

Marchese, T. (1998). Disengaged students II. *Change, 30*(3), 4.

Marchese, T. J. (1997). The new conversations about learning: Insights from neuroscience and anthropology, cognitive science and work-place studies. In *Assessing impact: Evidence and action* (pp. 79–95). Washington, DC: American Association for Higher Education.

Martin, D. C., & Arendale, D. (1993). Foundation and theoretical framework for supplemental instruction. In D. C. Martin & D. Arendale (Eds.), *Supplemental instruction: Improving first-year student success in high-risk courses* (2nd ed., pp. 41–50). Columbia, SC: National Resource Center for The Freshman Year Experience and Students in Transition.

Martin, D. C., & Blanc, R. A. (1994). Video-based Supplemental Instruction: A pathway to mastery and persistence. In D. C. Martin & D. R. Arendale (Eds.), *Supplemental Instruction: Increasing achievement and retention* (pp. 83–92). San Francisco: Jossey-Bass.

Martin, D. C., & Blanc, R. A. (2001). Video-based Supplemental Instruction (VSI). *Journal of Developmental Education, 24*(3).

Martin, D. C., Lorton, M., Blanc, R. A., & Evans, C. (1977). *The learning center: A comprehensive model for colleges and universities.* Grand Rapids: Aquinas College. (ERIC Document Reproduction Service No. ED 162 294)

Martin, W. B. (1982). *A college of character.* San Francisco: Jossey-Bass.

Maslow, A. H. (1970). *Motivation and personality.* New York: HarperCollins.

Maton, K. I., Hrabowski, F. A., & Schmitt, C. L. (2000). African American college students excelling in the sciences: College and post-college outcomes in the Meyerhoff Scholars program. *Journal of Research in Science Teaching, 37*(7), 629–654.

Matthews, R. (1994). Enriching teaching and learning through learning communities. In O'Banion, T. (Ed.), *Teaching and learning in the community college.* Washington, DC: American Association of Community Colleges

Maxwell, M. (1987). Improving student learning skills: An update. *Journal of Educational Opportunity, 3*(1), 1–9.

Maxwell, M. (1998). A commentary on the current state of college developmental reading programs. In J. L. Higbee & P. L. Dwinell (Eds.), *Developmental education:*

Preparing successful college students (pp. 153–167). Columbia: University of South Carolina, National Resource Center for The First-Year Experience and Students in Transition.

Mayo, M. W., & Christenfeld, N. (1999, April). Gender, race, and performance expectations of college students. *Journal of Multicultural Counseling, 27*(2), 93–105.

McCabe, R. H. (2000). *No one to waste.* Washington, DC: Community College Press.

McClenney, B. N. (2000). Remediation is everyone's responsibility. *Community College Week, 13*(3), 4–6.

McCormick, A. C., & Horn, L. J. (1996). *A descriptive summary of 1992–1993 bachelor's degree recipients one year later, with an essay on time to degree.* Washington, DC: U.S. Department of Education, National Center for Educational Statistics, US Government Printing Office.

McCormick, J. (2001). *Beyond surviving to thriving.* Kansas City: University of Missouri, Kansas City.

McDade, C. E. (2002). Success breeds success: Jacksonville State University's learning services. In J. L. Higbee, D. B. Lundell, & I. M. Duranczyk (Eds.), *Developmental education: Policy and practice* (pp. 91–100). Auburn, CA: National Association for Developmental Education.

McDaniel, N., James, J. B., & Davis, G. (2000). The student success center at Auburn University. *About Campus, 5*(1), 25–28.

McEwen, M. K. (2003). New perspectives on identity development. In S. R. Komives, D. B. Woodard Jr., & Associates (Eds.), *Student services: A handbook for the profession* (pp. 147–163). San Francisco: Jossey-Bass.

McGrath, D. (1996). Teaching new students at the community college: A unique time in a unique setting. In J. N. Hankin (Ed.), *The community college: Opportunity and access for today's first-year students* (pp. 105–113). Columbia, SC: University of South Carolina, National Resource Center for The Freshman Year Experience and Students in Transition.

McKeachie, W. J. (1999). *Teaching tips.* Boston: Houghton Mifflin.

McKeachie, W. J., Pintrich, P., Lin, Y., Smith, D., & Sharma, R. (1990). *Teaching and learning in the college classroom: A review of the research literature.* Ann Arbor, MI: National Center for Research to Improve Post Secondary Teaching and Learning.

McLanahan, S., & Sandefur, G. (1994). *Growing up with a single parent: What hurts, what helps.* Cambridge, MA: Harvard University Press.

Meilman, P. W. (1992). College health services should promote good samaritan rules as part of university alcohol policies. *Journal of American College Health, 40*(6), 299–301.

Meilman, P. W., Presley, C. A., & Cashin, J. R. (1995). The sober social life at the historically black colleges. *Journal of Blacks in Higher Education, 9,* 98–100.

Meilman, P. W., Presley, C. A., & Lyerla, R. (1994). Black college students and binge drinking. *Journal of Blacks in Higher Education, 4,* 70–71.

Meilman, P. W., Yanofsky, N. N., Gaylor, M. S., & Turco, J. H. (1989). Visits to the college health service for alcohol-related injuries. *Journal of American College Health, 37*(5), 205–210.

Menges, R. J., Weimer, M., & Associates. (1996). *Teaching on solid ground.* San Francisco: Jossey-Bass.

Metzner, B. (1989). Perceived quality of academic advising: The effect on freshman attrition. *American Educational Research Journal, 26,* 422–442.

Meyers, C., & Jones, T. B. (1993). *Promoting active learning.* San Francisco: Jossey-Bass.

Miksch, K. L. (2002). Education law and student access: Why isn't education a fundamental right? In J. L. Higbee, D. B. Lundell, & I. M. Duranczyk (Eds.), *Developmental education: Policy and practice* (pp. 65–76). Auburn, CA: National Association for Developmental Education.

Miksch, K. L., Bruch, P. L., Higbee, J. L., Jehangir, R. R., & Lundell, D. B. (2003). The centrality of multiculturalism in developmental education: Piloting the Multicultural Awareness Project for Institutional Transformation (MAP IT). In J. L. Higbee, D. B. Lundell, & I. M. Duranczyk (Eds.), *Multiculturalism in developmental education* (pp. 5–13). Minneapolis: Center for Research on Developmental Education and Urban Literacy, General College, University of Minnesota.

Miller, T. K. (Ed.). (1999). *CAS: The book of professional standards for higher education 1999.* Washington, DC: Council for the Advancement of Standards in Higher Education.

Milone, M. N., & Salpeter, J. (1996). Technology and equity issues. *Technology and Learning, 16*(4), 38–47.

Mitchell, A. A., & Sedlacek, W. E. (1995). Freshmen with learning disabilities: A profile of needs and concerns. *Journal of The Freshman Year Experience, 7*(2), 27–42.

Mooney, S. P., Sherman, M. F., & LoPresto, C. T. (1991). Academic locus of control, self-esteem, and perceived distance from home as predictors of college adjustment. *Journal of Counseling and Development, 69,* 445–448.

Moore, J., Lovell, C. D., McGann, T., & Wyrick, J. (1998). Why involvement matters: A review of the research on student involvement in the collegiate setting. *College Student Affairs Journal, 17,* 4–17.

Moore, R. (2002). The fates of developmental education students at two-year and four-year colleges. In J. L. Higbee, D. B. Lundell, & I. M. Duranczyk (Eds.), *Developmental education: Policy and practice* (pp. 55–64). Auburn, CA: National Association for Developmental Education.

Morelon, C., Patton, L., Whitehead, D., & Hossler, D. (2003). *Campus based retention initiatives: Does the emperor have clothes?* Indianapolis: Lumina Foundation for Education.

Morgan, C., & Cotten, S. R. (2003a). The relationship between Internet activities and learning. *Research in Higher Education, 42*(1), 87–102.

Morgan, C., & Cotten, S. R. (2003b). The relationship between Internet activities and depressive symptoms in a sample of college freshmen. *Cyberpsychology and Behavior, 6*(2), 133–142.

Morgan, R. (2002, August 2). Three students sue the University of North Carolina over assigned reading about Koran. *Chronicle of Higher Education,* p. A9.

Morrill, W. H., Hurst, J. C., Oetting, E. R., & others. (1980). *Dimensions of intervention for student development.* New York: Wiley.

Morris, L. V. (2001, October 10). *The basics of focus groups.* Available at: http://www.brevard.edu/listserv/remarks/morris.htm.

Morrison, T. L., & Morrison, R. L. (1978). Self-esteem, need for approval, and self-estimates of academic performance. *Psychological Reports, 43,* 503–507.

Morrison, T. L., Thomas, M. D., & Weaver, S. J. (1973). Self-esteem and self-estimates of academic performance. *Journal of Consulting and Clinical Psychology, 41,* 412–415.

Mortenson, T. G. (1998). How will we do more with less? The public policy dilemma of financing postsecondary education opportunity. In R. Fossey & M. Bateman (Eds.), *Condemning students to debt* (pp. 37–46). New York: Teachers College Press.

Most, R., & Miller, S. (1998). Re-orienting: New student orientation at the University of Virginia. Charlottesville, VA: unpublished internal document.

Moxley, D., Dumbrigue, C., & Najor-Durack, A. (2001). *Keeping students in higher education: Successful strategies and practices for retention.* London: Kogan.

Mullendore, R. H. (1992). Standards-based programming in orientation. In D. P. Nadler (Ed.), *Orientation director's manual.* Statesboro, GA: National Orientation Directors Association.

Mullendore, R. H. (1998). Including parents and families in the orientation process. In R. H. Mullendore (Ed.), *Orientation planning manual.* Bloomington, IN: National Orientation Directors Association.

Mullendore, R. H., & Abraham, J. (1993). Organization and administration of orientation programs. In M. L. Upcraft, R. H. Mullendore, B. O. Barefoot, & D. S. Fidler (Eds.), *Designing successful transitions: A guide for orienting students to college* (pp. 61–78). Columbia, SC: National Resource Center for The Freshman Year Experience.

Mullendore, R. H., & Biller, G. M. (1998). Assessment and evaluation of orientation programs. In R. H. Mullendore (Ed.), *Orientation planning manual.* Bloomington, IN: National Orientation Directors Association.

Mullendore, R. H., & Hatch, C. (2000). *Helping your first-year college student succeed: A guide for parents.* Columbia, SC: National Orientation Directors Association and National Resource Center for The First-Year Experience and Students in Transition.

Murie, R., & Thomson, R. (2001). When ESL is developmental: A model program for the freshman year. In J. L. Higbee (Ed.), *2001: A developmental odyssey* (pp. 15–28). Warrensburg, MO: National Association for Developmental Education.

Murtaugh, P. A., Burns, L. D., & Schuster, J. (1999). Predicting the retention of university students. *Research in Higher Education, 40,* 355–371.

National Association for Developmental Education. (1995). *Definition and goals statement.* Carol Stream, IL: Author.

National Association for Developmental Education. (2000). *NADE fact sheet 2000: Responses to frequently asked questions about the National Association for Developmental Education.* Warrensburg, MO: Author.

National Center for Education Statistics. (1999). *Students with disabilities in postsecondary education.* Washington, DC: U.S. Department of Education.

National Center for Education Statistics. (2000). *Low income students: Who they are and how they pay for their education.* Washington, DC: U.S. Department of Education.

National Center for Education Statistics. (2001a). *Digest of education statistics, 2000.* (NCES 2001–034). Washington, DC: U.S. Department of Education.

National Center for Education Statistics. (2001b). *The condition of education, 2001.* Available at: http://nces.ed.gov/pubsearch/pubsinfo.asp?pubid = 200172.

National Collegiate Athletic Association. (2001). *NCAA CHAMPS/Life Skills.* Available at: http://www.ncaa.org/edout/champs_lifeskills.

National Commission on the Cost of Higher Education. (1998). *Straight talk about college costs and prices.* Washington, DC: American Institutes for Research.

National Commission on Excellence in Education. (1984). *A nation at risk: The imperative for educational reform.* Washington, DC: National Endowment for the Humanities.

National Institute of Education. (1984). *Involvement in learning: Realizing the potential of American higher education.* Washington, DC: U.S. Department of Education.

National On-Campus Report. (1992, September 15). p. 5.

National Resource Center for The First-Year Experience and Students in Transition. (1997). *National survey of first-year seminar programming.* Unpublished data. Columbia, SC: University of South Carolina.

National Resource Center for The First-Year Experience and Students in Transition. (2002). *The 2000 national survey of first-year seminars programs: Continuing innovations in the collegiate curriculum.* Columbia, SC: University of South Carolina, Author.

National Survey of Student Engagement: The College Student Report. (2000). Excerpts: *The NSSE 2000 report: National benchmarks of effective educational practice.* Bloomington, IN: Indiana University, Center for Postsecondary Research and Planning.

National Survey of Student Engagement. (2001). *Improving the college experience: National benchmarks of effective educational practice.* Bloomington: Indiana University Center for Postsecondary Research.

National Survey of Student Engagement. (2003). *From promise to progress: How colleges and universities are using student engagement results to improve collegiate quality.* Bloomington, IN: Indiana University Center for Postsecondary Research.

Nelson, C. B. (2002, February). Why you won't find St. John's College Ranked in *U.S. News & World Report. University Business,* p. 56.

Nettles, M. T. (Ed.). (1988). *Toward black undergraduate student equality in American higher education.* Westport, CT: Greenwood Press.

Newman, R., & Miller, M. (2002, Winter–Spring). Developing institutional trust for non-traditional students in orientation. *Adult Learner Newsletter,* pp. 3–4.

Newton, F. B. (2000, November-December). The new student. *About Campus, 5*(5), 8–15.

Nielsen & Cyberatlas. (2002, January). *Men still dominate worldwide Internet usage.* Available at: http://www.cyberatlas.internet.com/big_picture/demographics/article/0,,5901_959421,00.html.

Nisbet, J., Ruble, V. E., & Schurr, K. T. (1982). Predictors of academic success with high risk college students. *Journal of College Student Personnel, 23,* 227–235.

Noel, L. (1985). Increasing student retention: New challenges and potential. In L. R. Noel-Levitz, D. Saluri, & Associates (Eds.), *Increasing student retention* (pp. 1–27). San Francisco: Jossey-Bass.

Noel-Levitz, L. R. (2000). *2000 report on national enrollment management survey: Findings for fall 1999 for four-year institutions.* Iowa City, IA: Author.

Nora, A. (2001–2002). The depiction of significant others in Tinto's "rights of passage": A reconceptualization of the influence of family and community in the persistence process. *Journal of College Student Retention, 3*(1), 41–56.

Nora, A., & Cabrera, A. F. (1996). The role of perceptions of prejudice and discrimination on the adjustment of minority students to college. *Journal of Higher Education, 67,* 119–148.

Novak, G. M., Patterson, E. T., Gavrin, A., & Christian, W. (1999). *Just-in-time teaching: Blending active learning with Web technology.* Upper Saddle River, NJ: Prentice Hall.

Nowicki, S. (1978). Reported stressful events during developmental periods and their relation to locus of control orientation in college students. *Journal of Consulting and Clinical Psychology, 46,* 1552–1553.

Nugent, C., and Myers, R. (2000). Learning by doing: The freshman-year curriculum and library instruction. *Research Strategies, 17,* 147–155.

Nunez, A. M., & Cuccaro-Alamin, S. (1998). *First-generation students: Undergraduates whose parents never enrolled in postsecondary education.* Washington, DC: U.S. Department of Education, National Center for Education Statistics.

O'Connell, T. (2002). A matter of experience: Service-learning and the adult student. In E. Zlotkowski (Ed.), *Service-learning and the first-year experience: Preparing students for personal success and civic responsibility* (pp. 51–61). Columbia: University of South Carolina, National Resource Center for The First-Year Experience and Students in Transition.

O'Hear, M. (2002). Assessment and outcomes. In D. B. Lundell & J. L. Higbee (Eds.), *Proceedings of the First Intentional Meeting on Future Directions in Developmental Education* (pp. 49–50). Minneapolis, MN: Center for Research on Developmental Education and Urban Literacy, General College, University of Minnesota.

Olsen, D., Kuh, G., Shilling, K. M., Shilling, K., Connolly, M., Simmons, A., & Vesper, N. (1998, November). *Great expectations: What students expect from college and what they get.* Paper presented at the annual meeting of the Association for the Study of Higher Education, Miami, FL.

Olson, L. (2001). A quiet crisis: Unprepared for high stakes. *Education Week, 20,* A1, A12, A13, A16.

Orfield, G. (2001). Introduction. In G. Orfield (Ed.), *Diversity challenged: Evidence on the impact of affirmative action.* Cambridge, MA: Harvard Education Publishing Group.

Orfield, G., & Yun, J. T. (1999). *Resegregation in American schools.* Cambridge, MA: Civil Rights Project, Harvard University.

Ory, J. C., & Braskamp, L. A. (1988). Involvement and growth of students in three academic programs. *Research in Higher Education, 28,* 116–129.

Oskamp, S. (2000). Multiple paths to reducing prejudice and discrimination. In S. Oskamp (Ed.), *Reducing prejudice and discrimination.* London: Erlbaum.

Pace, C. R. (1984). *Measuring the quality of college student experiences.* Los Angeles: University of California Higher Education Research Institute.

Pace, C. R. (1990). *The undergraduates: A report of their activities and progress in college in the 1980s.* Los Angeles: Center for the Study of Evaluation, Graduate School of Education.

Pace, R. H., Jr. (1970). Student expectations and later expectations of a university enrollment. *Journal of College Student Personnel, 11,* 458–462.

Pace, R. H. (1979). *Measuring outcomes of college: Fifty years of findings and recommendations for the future.* San Francisco: Jossey-Bass.

Palmer, C. J., Lohman, G., Gehring, D. D., Carlson, S., & Garrett, O. (2001). Parental notification: A new strategy to reduce alcohol abuse on campus. *NASPA Journal, 38*(3), 372–385.

Palmer, P. J. (1998). *The courage to teach: Exploring the inner landscape of a teacher's life.* San Francisco: Jossey-Bass.

Palombi, B. J. (2000). Recruitment and admission of students with disabilities. In H. A. Belch (Ed.), *Serving students with disabilities* (pp. 31–40). San Francisco: Jossey-Bass.

Parang, E., Raine, M., and Stevenson, T. (2000). Redesigning freshman seminar library instruction based on information competencies. *Research Strategies, 17,* 269–280.

Parker, W. C. (1982, February). *Black culture: Implications for educational change.* Address delivered for Black History Week, Saint Louis University.

Parker, W. M., Archer, J. Jr., & Scott, J. (1992). *Multicultural relations on campus: A personal growth approach.* Muncie, IN: Accelerated Development Inc.

Parsad, B., Lewis, L., & Greene, B. (2003). *Remedial education at degree-granting postsecondary institutions in Fall 2000.* Washington, DC: U.S. Department of Education. Available at: http://nces.ed.gov/pubs2004/2004010.pdf.

Pascarella, E. T. (1985). College environmental influences on learning and cognitive development. In J. C. Smart (Ed.), *Higher education: Handbook of theory and research.* New York: Agathon.

Pascarella, E. T. (1993). Cognitive impacts of living on campus versus commuting to college. *Journal of College Student Development, 34,* 216–220.

Pascarella, E. T. (2001, May/June). Identifying excellence in undergraduate education: Are we even close? *Change, 33,* 18–23.

Pascarella, E. T., Palmer, B., Moye, M., & Pierson, C. (2001). Do diversity experiences influence the development of critical thinking? *Journal of College Student Development, 42*(3), 257–271.

Pascarella, E. T., & Terenzini, P. T. (1991). *How college affects students: Findings and insights from twenty years of research.* San Francisco: Jossey-Bass.

Pascarella, E. T. & Terenzini, P. T. (2005). *How college affects students: A third decade of research* (2nd ed.). San Francisco: Jossey-Bass.

Pascarella, E. T., Terenzini, P. T., & Blimling, G. S. (1996). The impact of residential life on students. In C. Schroeder, P. Mable, & Associates (Eds.), *Realizing the educational potential of residence halls* (pp. 22–52). San Francisco: Jossey-Bass.

Pascarella, E. T., Terenzini, P. T., & Wolfle, L. (1986). Orientation to college and freshman year persistence/withdrawal decisions. *Journal of Higher Education, 57,* 155–175.

Pascarella, E. T., Whitt, E. J., Nora, A., Edison, M., Hagedorn, L. S., & Terenzini, P. T. (1996). What have we learned from the first year of the National Study of Student Learning? *Journal of College Student Development, 37,* 182–192.

Patton, M. Q. (1990). *Qualitative evaluation and research methods* (2nd ed.). Thousand Oaks, CA: Sage.

Paul, E. L., & Brier, S. (2001). Friendsickness in the transition to college: Precollege predictors and college adjustment correlates. *Journal of Counseling and Development, 79,* 77–89.

Paul, E. L., & Kelleher, M. (1995). Precollege concerns about losing and making friends in college: Implications for friendship satisfaction and self-esteem during the college transition. *Journal of College Student Development, 36,* 513–521.

Paul, E. L., Poole, A., & Jakubowyc, N. (1998). Intimacy development and romantic status: Implications for adjustment to the college transition. *Journal of College Student Development, 39,* 75–86.

Paul, E. L., & White, K. M. (1990). The development of intimate relationships in late adolescence. *Adolescence, 25,* 375–397.

Paulsen, M. B. (1990). *College choice: Understanding student enrollment behavior.* Washington, DC: ERIC Clearinghouse on Higher Education and George Washington University.

Paulsen, M. B., & Feldman, K. A. (1999). Student motivation and epistemological beliefs. In M. Theall (Ed.), *Motivation from within: Approaches for encouraging faculty and students to excel.* San Francisco: Jossey-Bass.

Payne, E. M., & Lyman, B. G. (1996). Issues affecting the definition of developmental education. In J. L. Higbee & P. L. Dwinell (Eds.), *Developmental education: Theory, research, and pedagogy.* Carol Stream, IL: National Association for Developmental Education. Available at: http://www.nade.net.

Pedelty, M. (2001). Stigma. In J. L. Higbee (Ed.), *2001: A developmental odyssey* (pp. 53–70). Warrensburg, MO: National Association for Developmental Education. Available at: http://www. nade.net.

Pedelty, M. H., & Jacobs, W. R. (2001). The place of "culture" in developmental education's social sciences. In D. B. Lundell & J. L. Higbee (Eds.), *Theoretical perspectives for developmental education* (pp. 75–90). Minneapolis, MN: Center for Research on Developmental Education and Urban Literacy, General College, University of Minnesota. Available at: http://www.gen.umn.edu/research/crdeul.

Pedersen, P. (1994). *A handbook for developing multicultural awareness* (2nd ed.). Alexandria, VA: American Counseling Association.

Peltier, G. L., Laden, R., & Matranga, M. (1999). Student persistence in college: A review of research. *Journal of College Student Retention, 1*(4), 357–376.

Perigo, D. J., & Upcraft, M. L. (1989). Orientation programs. In M. L. Upcraft, J. N. Gardner, & Associates (Eds.), *The freshman year experience: Helping students survive and succeed in college.* San Francisco: Jossey-Bass.

Perkins, H. W. (2002). Social norms and the prevention of alcohol misuse in collegiate contexts. *Journal of Studies on Alcohol,* Supplement No. 14, 164–172.

Perkins, H. W. (Ed.). (2003). *The social norms approach to preventing school and college age substance abuse: A handbook for educators, counselors, and clinicians.* San Francisco: Jossey-Bass.

Perry, W. G. (1970). *Forms of intellectual and ethical development in the college years: A scheme.* Troy, MO: Holt.

Person, D. R., Benson-Quaziena, M., & Rogers, A. M. (2001). Female student athletes and student athletes of color. In M. F. Howard-Hamilton & S. K. Watt (Eds.), *Student services for athletes* (pp. 55–64). San Francisco: Jossey-Bass.

Pervin, L. A. (1967). Aptitude, anxiety and academic performance: A moderator variable analysis. *Psychological Reports, 20,* 215–221.

Pervin, L. A., Reik, L. E., & Dalrymple, W. (1966). *The college dropout and the utilization of talent.* Princeton, NJ: Princeton University Press.

Pew Internet and American Life Project. (2002). *The Internet goes to college: How students are living in the future with today's technology.* Available at: http://www.perinternet.org/reports/pdfs/PIP_College_Report.pdf.

Pew Internet and American Life Project. (2003). *Tracking online life: How women use the Internet to cultivate relationships with family and friends.* Available at: http://www.perinternet.org/reports/pdfs/Report1.pdf.

Phillippe, K. (1997). *National profile of community colleges: Trends and statistics, 1997–1998.* Washington, DC: American Association of Community Colleges.

Phillips, V. (2000). *Never too late to learn: The adult student's guide to college.* New York: Random House.

Piaget, J. (1970). Piaget's theory. In P. Mussen (Ed.), *Carmichael's manual of child psychology* (pp. 703–732). New York: Wiley.

Pierson, G. C., & Timmerman, C. M. (2000). Training orientation leaders. In M. J. Fabich (Ed.), *Orientation planning manual 2000.* Pullman, WA: National Orientation Directors Association.

Pisapia, J. (1994). *Technology: The equity issue. Research Brief #14.* Richmond, VA: Metropolitan Educational Research Consortium.

Polanco, R., Calderon, P., & Delgado, F. (2001, April). *Effects of a problem-based learning program on engineering students' academic achievement skills development and attitudes in a Mexican university.* Paper read at American Educational Research Association, Seattle, WA.

Policy Center on the First Year of College. (2001). *National survey of first-year curricular practices.* Brevard, NC: Author. Available at: http://www.brevard.edu/fyc/survey/Curricular/survey.htm.

Policy Center on the First Year of College. (2003). *Institutions of excellence in the first college year.* Brevard, NC: Author. Available at: http://www.brevard.edu/fyc/instofexcellence/data.htm.

Pollard, K. D., Benson, S. E., & Hinz, K. (1983). The assessment of developmental tasks of students in remedial and regular programs. *Journal of College Student Personnel, 24,* 20–23.

Ponterotto, J. G., & Pedersen, P. (1993). *Preventing prejudice: A guide for counselors and educators.* Thousand Oaks, CA: Sage.

Porter, S. R., & Umbach, P. D. (2002). We can't get there in time: Assessing the time between classes and classroom disruptions. *Planning in Higher Education, 32*(2), 35–40.

Potter, W. (2003, Oct. 31). Breaking a promise. *Chronicle of Higher Education.*

Presley, C. A., Meilman, P. W., & Cashin, J. R. (1996). *Alcohol and drugs on American college campuses: Use, consequences, and perceptions of the campus environment. Vol. 4, 1992–94.* Carbondale: Southern Illinois University.

Presley, C. A., Meilman, P. W., Cashin, J. R., & Lyerla, R. (1996). *Alcohol and drugs on American college campuses: Use, consequences, and perceptions of the campus environment. Vol. 3: 1991–93.* Carbondale: Southern Illinois University.

Presley, C. A., Meilman, P. W., & Lyerla, R. (1993). *Alcohol and drugs on American college campuses: Use, consequences, and perceptions of the campus environment. Vol. 1: 1989–91.* Carbondale: Southern Illinois University.

Presley, C. A., Meilman, P. W., & Lyerla, R. (1995). *Alcohol and drugs on American college campuses: Use, consequences, and perceptions of the campus environment. Vol. 2: 1990–92.* Carbondale: Southern Illinois University.

Price, M., & Rust, C. (1995). Laying firm foundations: The long-term benefits of Supplemental Instruction for students on large introductory courses. *Innovations in Education and Training International, 32,* 2, 8–22.

Princeton official ousted for snooping on Yale files. (2002, Aug. 14). *Chicago Tribune,* p. 11.

Rahn, W. M. (1998, May 8–9). *Generations and American national identity: A data essay.* Presented at the Communication in the Future of Democracy Workshop, Annenberg Center, Washington, DC.

Rajasekhara, K., & Hirsch, T. (2000, May). *Retention and its impact on institutional effectiveness at a large urban community college.* Paper presented to the Association for Institutional Research, Cincinnati, OH.

Ramaley, J. (2001). Why do we engage in engagement? *Metropolitan Universities, 12*(3), 13–19.

Ramirez, G. (1997). Supplemental Instruction: The long-term impact. *Journal of Developmental Education, 21,* 2–28.

Ratcliff, J. L. (1992). What they took and what they learned: Learning from assessment and transcript analysis. In M. Moseley (Ed.), *Proceedings from the Asheville Institute on General Education.* Washington, DC: Association of American Colleges.

Rayman, J. R. (Ed.). (1993). *The changing role of career services.* San Francisco: Jossey-Bass.

Raymond, L., & Napoli, A. R. (1998). An examination of the impact of a freshman seminar course on student academic outcomes. *Journal of Applied Research in the Community College, 6,* 27–34.

Redd, K. E. (2000a). Tuition discounting: A view from the financial aid office. *NASFAA Journal of Student Financial Aid, 30,* 27–37.

Redd, K. E. (2000b). *Discounting toward disaster: Tuition discounting, college finances, and enrollments of low-income undergraduates.* Indianapolis, IN: USAGroup Foundation.

Resnick, J. (1993). A paired reading and sociology course. In P. Malinowski (Ed.), *Perspectives in practice in developmental education* (pp. 62–64). Canandaigua, NY: New York College Learning Association.

Reumann-Moore, R., El-Haj, A., & Gold, E. (1997). *Friends for school purposes: Learning communities and their role in building community at a large urban university.* Philadelphia: Temple University. Available at: http://www.temple.edu/university_studies/reports.html.

Rhem, J. (1995). Deep/surface approaches to learning: An introduction. *National Teaching and Learning Forum, 1,* 1–5.

Richmond, J. (2002). The University of Rhode Island's new culture for learning. In E. Zlotkowski (Ed.), *Service-learning and the first-year experience: Preparing students for personal success and civic responsibility* (pp. 15–26). Columbia: University of South Carolina, National Resource Center for The First-Year Experience and Students in Transition.

Rivinus, T. (1988). Introduction. In T. Rivinus, *Alcoholism/chemical dependency and the college student* (pp. 1–18). New York: Haworth Press.

Roach, R. (2000). Mastering technology's tools and techniques. *Black Issues in Higher Education, 17*(20), 28–31.

Roach, R. (2001). Is higher education ready for minority America? *Black Issues in Higher Education, 18,* 29–31.

Roberts, G. H. (1989). Personal and academic stressors affecting developmental education students. *Research and Teaching in Developmental Education, 5*(2), 39–53.

Robinson, R. (1993). *Protecting your constitutional rights: The conservative guide to campus activism.* Herndon, VA: Young America's Foundation.

Rode, D. (2000). The role of orientation in institutional retention. In M. J. Fabich (Ed.), *Orientation planning manual 2000.* Pullman, WA: National Orientation Directors Association.

Rokeach, M. (1979). *Understanding human values: Individual and societal.* New York: Free Press.

Rossi, P. H., & Freeman, H. E. (1996). *Evaluation: A systematic approach* (5th ed.). Thousand Oaks, CA: Sage.

Rossman, J. E., & El-Khawas, E. (1987). *Thinking about assessment: Perspectives for presidents and chief academic officers.* Washington, DC: American Council on Education & American Association for Higher Education.

Rost, J. (1993) *Leadership for the twenty-first century.* London: Pager.

Rotter, J. (1966). Generalized expectations for the internal versus external control of reinforcement. *Psychological Monographs, 80* (1, Whole No. 169).

R. Sharpe's parent's fury at MIT: A study of mental illness on campus. (2002, January 25). *USA Today,* p. A1.

St. John, E. P. (1989). The influence of student aid on persistence. *Journal of Student Financial Aid, 19,* 3, 52–67.

St. John, E. P. (1990). Price response in persistence decisions: An analysis of the high school and beyond cohort. *Research in Higher Education, 31,* 387–403.

St. John, E. P. (1991). The impact of student financial aid: A review of recent research. *Journal of Student Financial Aid, 21*(1), 18–32.

St. John, E. P. (2003). *Refinancing the college dream.* Baltimore, MD: Johns Hopkins University Press.

St. John, E. P., Cabrera, A. F., Nora, A., & Asker, E. H. (2000). Economic influences on persistence reconsidered. In J. M. Braxton, (Ed.), *Reworking the student departure puzzle* (pp. 29–47). Nashville, TN: Vanderbilt University Press.

St. John, E. P., Kirshstein, R., & Noell, J. (1991). The effects of student aid on persistence: A sequential analysis of the High School and Beyond senior cohort. *Review of Higher Education, 14*(3), 383–406.

St. John, E. P., Paulsen, M. B., & Starkey, J. B. (1996). The nexus between college choice and persistence. *Research in Higher Education, 37*(2), 455–480.

St. John, E. P., Simmons, A. B., & Musoba, G. D. (1999). *Merit-aware admissions in public universities: Increasing diversity.* Bloomington: Indiana Education Policy Center.

Sandeen, A. (1996). Organization, functions, and standards of practice. In *Student services: A handbook for the profession* (3rd ed., pp. 435–457). San Francisco: Jossey-Bass.

Sanders, L., & Burton, J. (1996, Oct.). From retention to satisfaction: New outcomes for assessing the freshman experience. *Research in Higher Education, 37,* 555–567.

Sanford, N. (Ed.). (1962). *The American college.* New York: Wiley.

Sanford, N. (1967). *Where colleges fail: A study of the student as a person.* San Francisco: Jossey-Bass.

Sanlo, R., Rankin, S., & Schoenberg, R. (2002). *Our place on campus: Lesbian, gay, bisexual and transgender services and programs in higher education.* Westport, CT: Greenwood Press.

Sax, L. J., Astin, A. W., Korn, W. S., & Mahoney, K. M. (1997). *The American freshman.* Los Angeles: University of California, Los Angeles, Higher Education Research Institute.

Sax, L. J., Astin, A. W., Korn, W. S., & Mahoney, K. M. (1999). *The American freshman: National norms for fall 1999.* Los Angeles: University of California, Los Angeles, Higher Education Research Institute.

Sax, L. J., Lindholm, J. A., Astin, A. W., Korn, W. S., & Mahoney, K. M. (2001a). *The American freshman: National norms for fall 2002.* Available at: http://www.gseis.ucla.edu/heri/findings.html.

Sax, L. J., Astin, A. W., Lindholm, J. A., Korn, W. S., Saenz, V. B., & Mahoney, K. M. (2003). *The American freshman: National norms for fall 2003.* Los Angeles: University of California, Los Angeles, Higher Education Research Institute.

Sax, L. J., Ceja, M., & Teranishi, R. T. (2001). Technological preparedness among entering freshmen: The role of race, class, and gender. *Journal of Educational Computing Research, 24*(4), 363–383.

Sax, L. J., Astin, A. W., Lindholm, J. A., Korn, W. S., & Mahoney, K. M. (2001b). *The American freshman: National norms for fall 2000.* Los Angeles: Higher Education Research Institute, University of California, Los Angeles.

Scherer, M. M. (1999). Perspectives. *Educational Leadership, 57*(3), 5.

Scherschel, P. M. (1998). Reality bites: How much do students owe? In *Student loan debt: Problems and prospects* (pp. 15–37). Institute for Higher Education Policy, Sallie Mae Education Institute, & Education Resources Institutes.

Schilling, K. L. (2001). Spurring our professional curiosity about the first-year experience. In R. Swing (Ed.), *Proving and improving: Strategies for assessing the first college year* (pp. 15–20). Columbia, SC: University of South Carolina, National Resource Center for The First-Year Experience and Students in Transition.

Schilling, K. M., & Schilling, K. L. (1999). Increasing expectations for student effort. *About Campus, 4*(2), 4–10.

Schlesinger, A. (1991). *The disuniting of America: Reflections on a multicultural society.* New York: Norton.

Schmickle, S. (2002, January 29). "U" Nobel laureate wins science foundation medal. *Minneapolis Star Tribune,* p. B4.

Schoch, R. (1980). As Cal enters the 80s, there'll be some changes made. *California Monthly, 90*(3), 1–3.

Schoenecker, C., Bollman, L., & Evens, J. (1998, Summer). Developmental education outcomes at Minnesota community colleges. *Association of Institutional Research Professional File, 68,* 1–14.

Schön, D. A. (1983). *The reflective practitioner: How professionals think in action.* New York: Basic Books.

Schön, D. A. (1995). The new scholarship requires a new epistemology: Knowing-in-action. *Change, 27*(6), 27–34.

Schroeder, C. C. (1993). New students—new learning styles. *Change, 25*(5), 21–26.

Schroeder, C. C. (1994). Developing learning communities. In C. C. Schroeder, P. Mable, & Associates (Eds.), *Realizing the educational potential of residence halls* (pp. 165–189). San Francisco: Jossey-Bass.

Schroeder, C. C. (1999a). Partnerships: An imperative for enhancing student learning and institutional effectiveness. In J. H. Schuh & E. J. Whitt (Eds.), *Creating successful partnerships between academic and student affairs* (pp. 5–18). San Francisco: Jossey-Bass.

Schroeder, C. C. (1999b). Forging educational partnerships that advance student learning. In G. S. Blimling & E. J. Whitt, *Good practice in student affairs: Principles to foster student learning* (pp. 133–157). San Francisco: Jossey-Bass.

Schroeder, C. C. (2000, Fall). Understanding today's students in a changed world. In *Priorities* (pp. 1–16). Washington DC: Association of Governing Boards of Universities and Colleges.

Schroeder, C. C. (2001). The Mystery Shopper Program: An innovative tool for assessing performance. In R. L. Swing (Ed.), *Proving and improving: Strategies for assessing the first college year* (pp. 75–78). Columbia: University of South Carolina, National Resource Center for The First-Year Experience and Students in Transition.

Schroeder, C. C., Minor, F. D., & Tarkow, T. A. (1999). Learning communities: Partnerships between academic and student affairs. In J. H. Levine (Ed.), *Learning communities: New structures, new partnerships for learning.* Columbia, SC: University of South Carolina, National Resource Center for The First-Year Experience and Students in Transition.

Schuh, J. H. (1983). When the measles come to college: Implications for student affairs administrators. *College Student Affairs Journal, 5*(2), 32–36.

Schuh, J. H. (1999). Student learning and growth resulting from service as an intramural official. *NIRSA Journal, 23*(2), 51–61.

Schuh, J. H. (2000). Fiscal pressures on higher education and student affairs. In M. J. Barr, M. K. Dressler, & Associates (Eds.), *The handbook of student affairs administration* (2nd ed., pp. 73–96). San Francisco: Jossey-Bass.

Schuh, J. H., & Upcraft, M. L. (2000). Assessment politics. *About Campus, 5*(4), 14–21.

Schuh, J. H., Upcraft, M. L., & Associates. (2001). *Assessment practice in student affairs: An applications manual.* San Francisco: Jossey-Bass.

Schuh, J. H., & Whitt, E. J. (Eds.). (1999). *Creating successful partnerships between academic and student affairs.* San Francisco: Jossey-Bass.

Schwartz, R. A., & Washington, C. M. (1999). Predicting academic success and retention for African-American women in college. *Journal of College Student Retention, 1*(2), 177–191.

Scouller, K. (1988). The influence of assessment method on students' learning approaches: Multiple choice question examination versus assignment essay. *Higher Education, 35,* 453–472.

Sehr, D. (1997). *Education for public democracy.* Albany: State University of New York.

Senge, P. M. (1994). *The fifth discipline: The art and practice of the learning organization.* New York: Doubleday.

Seymour, E., & Hewitt, N. M. (1997). *Talking about leaving: Why undergraduates leave the sciences.* Boulder, CO: Westview Press.

Shapiro, N. S., & Levine, J. H. (1999). *Creating learning communities: A practical guide to winning support, organizing for change, and implementing programs.* San Francisco: Jossey-Bass.

Shaw, M. E. (2002). Recovering the vision of John Dewey for developmental education. In D. B. Lundell & J. L. Higbee (Eds.), *Histories of developmental education* (pp. 29–33). Minneapolis, MN: Center for Research on Developmental Education and Urban Literacy, General College, University of Minnesota. Available at: http://www.gen.umn.edu/research/crdeul.

Shuell, T. J., & Farber, S. L. (2001). Students' perceptions of technology use in college courses. *Journal of Educational Computing Research, 24*(2), 119–138.

Shulman, L. (1999). *Visions of the possible: Models for campus support of the scholarship of teaching and learning.* Princeton, NJ: Carnegie Foundation for the Advancement of Teaching. http://carnegiefoundation.org/elibrary/docs?Visions.htm.

Shulman, L. S. (1988). Disciplines of inquiry in education: An overview. In R. M. Jaeger (Ed.), *Complementary methods for research in education.* Washington, DC: American Education Research Association.

Siegel, R. G., Galassi, J. P., & Ware, W. B. (1985). A comparison of two models for predicting math performance: Social learning versus math aptitude anxiety. *Journal of Counseling Psychology, 32,* 531–538.

Silverman, S. L., & Casazza, M. E. (2000). *Learning and development: Making connections to enhance teaching.* San Francisco: Jossey-Bass.

Simon, J. A. (1999). Legal issues in serving students with disabilities in postsecondary education. In H. A. Belch (Ed.), *Serving students with disabilities* (pp. 69–82). New Directions for Student Services Sourcebook No. 91. San Francisco: Jossey-Bass.

Simon, S., & Silverstein, S. (2003, October 12). Colleges rethink goals as they cut. *Los Angeles Times*, p. A1.

Simpson, M. L., Hynd, C. R., Nist, S. L., & Burrell, K. I. (1997). College academic assistance programs and practices. *Educational Psychology Review, 9*(1), 39–87.

Singer, M. (2002). Toward a comprehensive learning center. In D. B. Lundell & J. L. Higbee (Eds.), *Histories of developmental education* (pp. 65–71). Minneapolis, MN: Center for Research on Developmental Education and Urban Literacy, General College, University of Minnesota. Available at: http://www.gen.umn.edu/research/crdeul.

Smedley, B. D., Myers, H. F., & Harrell, S. P. (1993). Minority-status stresses and the college adjustment of ethnic minority freshmen. *Journal of Higher Education, 64,* 434–452.

Smith, B. F. (1998). Planning standards-based orientation programs. In R. H. Mullendore (Ed.), *Orientation planning manual.* Bloomington, IN: National Orientation Directors Association.

Smith, D. G. (1999). Strategic evaluation: An imperative for the future of campus diversity. In M. Cross, N. Cloete, E. Beckham, A. Harper, J. Indiresan, & C. Musil (Eds.), *Diversity and unity: The role of higher education in building democracy.* Cape Town: Maskew Miller Longman.

Smith, D. M., & Kolb, D. A. (1986). *The user's guide for the learning style inventory: A manual for teachers and trainers.* Boston: McBer & Company.

Soldner, L., Lee, Y., & Duby, P. (1999). Welcome to the block: Developing freshman learning communities that work. *Journal of College Student Retention, 1*(2), 115–129.

Somers, P. (1995). First to second semester persistence: A case study. *Journal of The Freshman Year Experience, 7*(2), 43–62.

Somers, P. (1996). The freshman year: How financial aid influences enrollment and persistence at a regional comprehensive university. *College Student Affairs Journal, 16,* Fall, 27–38.

Somers, P. A. (1993). The influence of price on year-to-year persistence of college students. *NASPA Journal, 33,* 94–104.

Sorcinelli, M. D., & Elbow, P. (Eds.). (1997). *Writing to learn: Strategies for assigning and responding to writing across the disciplines.* San Francisco: Jossey-Bass.

Sotto, R. (2000). Technological delivery systems. In V. N. Gordon, W. R. Habley, & Associates (Eds.), *Academic advising: A comprehensive handbook* (pp. 249–257). San Francisco: Jossey-Bass.

Spady, W. (1970). Dropouts from higher education: An interdisciplinary review and synthesis. *Interchange, 1,* 64–85.

Spann, M. G., Jr., & McCrimmon, S. (1998). Remedial/developmental education: Past, present, and future. In J. L. Higbee & P. L. Dwinell (Eds.), *Developmental education: Preparing successful college students* (pp. 37–47). Columbia: University of South Carolina, National Resource Center for The First-Year Experience and Students in Transition.

Spear, M. E. (2001). Assessing health services. In J. H. Schuh, M. L. Upcraft, & Associates (Eds.), *Assessment practice in student affairs* (pp. 341–364). San Francisco: Jossey-Bass.

Spence, S. D., Autin, G., & Clausen, S. (2000). Reducing the cost of remediation: A partnership with high schools. *Research and Teaching in Developmental Education, 16*(2), 5–23.

Spicuzza, F. J. (1992, Fall). A customer service approach to advertising: Theory and application. *NACADA Journal,* 49–58.

Spitzberg, B. H. (1999). An analysis of empirical estimates of sexual aggression victimization and perpetration. *Violence and Victims, 14,* 241–260.

Spriggs, L., & Gandy, C. (1997). The changing nature of learner support in English universities. *NADE Selected Conference Papers, 3,* 44–46.

Stage, F. K., & Hossler, D. (2000). Where is the student? Linking student behaviors, college choice, and college persistence. In J. Braxton (Ed.), *Reworking the student departure puzzle* (pp. 170–195). Nashville, TN: Vanderbilt University Press.

Stahl, N. A., Simpson, M. L., & Hayes, C. G. (1992). Ten recommendations from research for teaching high-risk college students. *Journal of Developmental Education, 16*(1), 2–8.

State of New Jersey. (2003). New Jersey School Report Card. Secondary 2001–2002. Available at: http://compschools.evalsoft.com/nj.

Steele, C. M. (1997). A threat in the air: How stereotypes shape intellectual identity and performance. *American Psychologist, 52,* 613–629.

Steele, C. M. (2000). Thin ice: "Stereotype threat" and black college students. *About Campus, 5*(2), 2–5.

Steele, C. M., & Aronson, J. (1995). Stereotype threat and the intellectual test performance of African Americans. *Journal of Personality and Social Psychology, 69,* 797–811.

Steele, S. (1990). *The content of our character: A new vision of race in America.* New York: St. Martin's Press.

Stein, R. B., & Short, P. M. (2001). Collaboration in delivering higher education programs: Barriers and challenges. *Review of Higher Education, 24*(4), 417–436.

Stepfamily Association of America. (1998). http://stepfam.org.

Stern, G. G. (1970). *People in context.* New York: Wiley.

Stone, N. R. (1994). Self-evaluation and self-motivation for college developmental readers. *Research and Teaching in Developmental Education, 10*(2), 53–62.

Stones, E. (1970). Students' attitudes toward the size of teaching groups. *Educational Review, 21*(2), 98–108.

Strage, A. A. (2000, April). *Service-learning as a tool for enhancing student outcomes in a college level lecture course.* Paper presented at the American Educational Research Association, New Orleans, LA.

Stratton, C. B. (1998a). Bridge: Summer retention program for pre-college African American students. In P. L. Dwinell & J. L. Higbee (Eds.), *Developmental education: Meeting diverse student needs* (pp. 45–62). Morrow, GA: National Association for Developmental Education. Available at: http://www. nade.net.

Stratton, C. B. (1998b). Transitions in developmental education: Interviews with Hunter Boylan and David Arendale. In J. L. Higbee & P. L. Dwinell (Eds.), *Developmental education: Preparing successful college students* (pp. 25–36). Columbia: University of South Carolina, National Resource Center for The First-Year Experience and Students in Transition.

Strumpf, G., & Sharer, G. (Eds.). (1997). *NODA databank 1995–97.* College Park: University of Maryland, National Orientation Directors Association.

Strumpf, G., & Wawrynski, M. (Eds.). (2000). *NODA databank 2000.* College Park: University of Maryland, National Orientation Directors Association.

Student Life Studies Abstracts. (1996). *A student success story: Freshman interest groups at the University of Missouri-Columbia.* Columbia: University of Missouri.

Study Group on the Conditions of Excellence in American Higher Education. (1984). *Involvement in learning: Realizing the potential of American higher education.* Washington, DC: National Institute of Education.

Sullivan, P. (1998). Sexual identity development: The importance of target or dominant group membership. In R. L. Sanlo (Ed.), *Working with lesbian, gay, and transgender college students: A Handbook for faculty and administrators.* Westport, CT: Greenwood Press.

Suskie, L. A. (1992). *Questionnaire survey research: What works.* Tallahassee, FL: Association for Institutional Research.

Svinicki, M. D., & Dixon, N. M. (1987). Kolb Model modified for classroom activities. *College Teaching, 35*(4), 141–146.

Swing, R. L. (1998). Unpublished research, Appalachian State University, Office of Institutional Research, Assessment, and Planning.

Swing, R. L. (2001). Technology-supported assessment. In R. L. Swing (Ed.), *Proving and improving: Strategies for assessing the first college year* (pp. 75–78). Columbia: University of South Carolina, National Resource Center for The First-Year Experience and Students in Transition.

Swing, R. L. (2002, March). *A national study of first-year seminar learning outcomes: The First-Year Initiative (FYI), a benchmarking survey.* Handout for session presented at the AAHE Annual Conference, Chicago.

Swing, R. L., & Barefoot, B. O. (2002, April 5). *What matters in first-year seminars: Results of a national survey.* Handout for session presented at the AAC&U Conference on Learning Communities, Atlanta, GA.

Tatum, B. D. (1997). *Why are all the black kids sitting together in the cafeteria? and other conversations about race.* New York: Basic Books.

Taylor, D., Schelske, B., Hatfield, J., & Lundell, D. B. (2002). African American men from Hennepin County at the University of Minnesota, 1994–1998: Who applies, who is accepted, who attends? In D. B. Lundell & J. L. Higbee (Eds.), *Exploring urban literacy and developmental education* (pp. 109–125). Minneapolis, MN: Center for Research on Developmental Education and Urban Literacy, General College, University of Minnesota.

Teitelbaum, H. (2000). Anticipating, implementing and adapting to changes in academic advising. In V. N. Gordon, W. R. Habley, & Associates (Eds.), *Academic advising: A comprehensive handbook* (pp. 393–408). San Francisco: Jossey-Bass.

Terenzini, P. T., & Pascarella, E. T. (1994). Living with myths: Undergraduate education in America. *Change, 26*(1), 28–32.

Terenzini, P. T., Pascarella, E. T., & Blimling, G. S. (1996). Students' out-of-class experiences and their influence on learning and cognitive development: A literature review. *Journal of College Student Development, 37*(2), 149–162.

Terenzini, P. T., & Upcraft, M. L. (1996). Assessing program and service outcomes. In M. L. Upcraft & J. H. Schuh, *Assessment in student affairs.* San Francisco: Jossey-Bass.

Thomas, G., & Gordon, S. (1983). *Evaluating the payoffs of college investments for black, white, and hispanic students.* Baltimore: Johns Hopkins University, Center for Social Organization of Schools.

Thomas, N. (2000). The college and university as citizen. In T. Ehrlich (Ed.), *Civic responsibility and higher education* (pp. 63–97). Phoenix, AZ: Oryx Press.

Thomas, P. V., & Higbee, J. L. (1996). Enhancing mathematics achievement through collaborative problem solving. *Learning Assistance Review, 1*(1), 38–46.

Thomas, P. V., & Higbee, J. L. (1998). Teaching mathematics on television: Perks and pitfalls. *Academic Exchange Quarterly, 2*(2), 29–33.

Thomas, P. V., & Higbee, J. L. (2000). The relationship between involvement and success in developmental algebra. *Journal of College Reading and Learning, 30*(2), 222–232.

Thomas, R. O. (1990). Programs and activities for improved retention. In D. Hossler & J. P. Bean (Eds.), *The strategic management of college enrollments.* San Francisco: Jossey-Bass.

Thompson, J. (1993). The effects of on-campus residence on first-time college students. *NASPA Journal, 31,* 41–47.

Tierney, W. G. (1992). An anthropological analysis of student participation in college. *Journal of Higher Education, 63,* 603–618.

Ting, S. R., & Robinson, T. L. (1998). First-year academic success: A prediction combining cognitive and psycho-social variables for Caucasian and African American students. *Journal of College Student Development, 39*(6), 599–610.

Tinto, V. (1975). Dropouts from higher education: A theoretical synthesis of recent research. *Review of Educational Research, 45,* 89–125.

Tinto, V. (1982). Defining dropout: A matter of perspective. In E. T. Pascarella (Ed.), *Student attrition.* San Francisco: Jossey-Bass.

Tinto, V. (1987). *Leaving college: Rethinking the causes and cures of student attrition.* Chicago: University of Chicago Press.

Tinto, V. (1993). Principles of effective retention. *Journal of The Freshman Year Experience, 2*(1), 35–48.

Tinto, V. (1993). *Leaving college: Rethinking the causes and cures of student attrition* (2nd ed.). Chicago: University of Chicago Press.

Tinto, V. (1996). Reconstructing the first year of college. *Planning for Higher Education, 25,* 1–6.

Tinto, V., & Goodsell, A. (1993). *A longitudinal study of freshman interest groups at the University of Washington.* University Park, PA: Pennsylvania State University, National Center on Postsecondary Teaching, Learning and Assessment.

Tinto, V., & Goodsell Love, A. (1995). *A longitudinal study of learning communities at LaGuardia Community College.* University Park, PA: Pennsylvania State University, National Center on Postsecondary Teaching, Learning and Assessment.

Tinto, V., Goodsell Love, A., & Russo, P. (1993a). Building community. *Liberal Education, 79*(4), 16–21.

Tinto, V., Goodsell Love, A., & Russo, P. (1993b). *Building learning communities for new college students: A summary of research findings of the Collaborative Learning Project.* University Park, PA: National Center on Postsecondary Teaching, Learning, and Assessment.

Tobias, S. (1978). *Overcoming math anxiety.* Boston: Houghton Mifflin.

Torre, E. L. (1992). Exploring gender related concerns. *Journal of College Student Development, 33,* 555–556.

Tracey, T. J., & Sedlacek, W. E. (1985). The relationship of noncognitive variables to academic success: A longitudinal comparison by race. *Journal of College Student Personnel, 26,* 405–410.

Tripp, R. (1997). Greek organizations and student development: A review of the literature. *College Student Affairs Journal, 16,* 31–39.

Turnbull, C. (1962). *The forest people.* New York: Simon & Schuster.

Turner, R. C. (1998). *Teaching English to another generation of students.* Unpublished manuscript.

Turner, V., & Sotello, C. (2002). *Diversifying the faculty: A guidebook for search committees.* Washington, DC: Association of American Colleges and Universities.

Umbach, P., & Kuh, G. D. (2003, May). *Student experiences with diversity at liberal arts colleges: Another claim for distinctiveness.* Paper presented at the annual meeting of the Association for Institutional Research, Tampa, FL.

UMKC Center for Academic Development. (2000). *SI awareness.* (Conversation on the video – Champ Cudahy, SI leader and student). University Park, PA: Author.

UMKC Center for Academic Development/National Center for Supplemental Instruction. (2000). *Review of the research concerning the effectiveness of SI from the University of Missouri-Kansas City and other institutions from across the United States.* Kansas City, MO: Author.

U.S. Census Bureau (2001). Hispanic population in the United States, Figure 7, March 2000, and Black population in the United States, Table 7, March 2000. *Black Issues in Higher Education, 18*(16).

U.S. Department of Commerce, National Telecommunications and Information Administration. (2000). *Falling through the net: Toward digital inclusion.* Available at: http://www.ntia.doc.gov/ntiahome/fttn00/contents00.html.

U.S. Department of Education (1996). *Eighteenth annual report to Congress on the implementation of the Individuals with Disabilities Education Act.* Office of Special Education and Rehabilitation Services. Washington, DC: U.S. Department of Education.

U.S. Department of Education (1997). *Youth indicators 1996/Indicator 26.* Available at: http://nces01.ed.gov./NCES/pubs/yi/9626a.html.

University of Utah. (1998). Educating the good citizen: Service-learning in higher education. In E. Zlotkowski (Ed.), *Successful service-learning programs: New models of excellence in higher education* (pp. J-1–13). Bolton, MA: Anker.

The university's online program attracts students, profits, and praise. (2002, November 1). *Chronicle of Higher Education,* p. A1.

Upcraft, M. L. (1993). Orienting today's students. In M. L. Upcraft, R. H. Mullendore, B. O. Barefoot, & D. S. Fidler (Eds.), *Designing successful transitions: A guide for orienting students to college* (pp. 1–8). Columbia: National Resource Center for The Freshman Year Experience.

Upcraft, M. L. (1995). Insights from theory: Understanding first-year student development. In M. L. Upcraft & G. L. Kramer (Eds.), *First-year academic advising: Patterns in the present, pathways to the future* (pp. 15–24). Columbia, SC: National Resource Center for The Freshman Year Experience and Students in Transition.

Upcraft, M. L. (2000). *Today's first-year students and alcohol.* Paper prepared for the Task Force on College Drinking, National Advisory Council on Alcohol Abuse and Alcoholism, Bethesda, MD.

Upcraft, M. L., & Farnsworth, W. M. (1984). Orientation programs and activities. In M. L. Upcraft (Ed.), *Orienting students to college* (pp. 27–38). San Francisco: Jossey-Bass.

Upcraft, M. L., & Gardner, J. N. (1989). A comprehensive approach to enhancing freshman success. In M. L. Upcraft, J. N. Gardner, & Associates (Eds.), *The freshman year experience: Helping students survive and succeed in college* (pp. 1–12). San Francisco: Jossey Bass.

Upcraft, M. L., Gardner, J. N., & Associates. (1989). *The freshman year experience: Helping students survive and succeed in college.* San Francisco: Jossey-Bass.

Upcraft, M. L., Mullendore, R. H., Barefoot, B. O., & Fidler, D. S. (Eds.), *Designing successful transitions: A guide for orienting students to college* (Monograph No. 13). Columbia, SC: National Resource Center for The Freshman Year Experience.

Upcraft, M. L., & Schuh, J. H. (1996). *Assessment in student affairs: A guide for practitioners.* San Francisco: Jossey-Bass.

Upcraft, M. L., & Schuh, J.H. (2002). Assessment vs. research: Why we should care about the difference. *About Campus, 7*(1), 16–20.

Upcraft, M. L., Srebnik, D. S., & Stevenson, J. (1995). Assessment of academic advising. In M. L. Upcraft & G. L. Kramer (Eds.), *First-year academic advising: Patterns in the present, pathways to the future* (pp. 141–146). Columbia: University of South Carolina, National Resource Center for The First-Year Experience and Students in Transition.

Upcraft, M. L., & Stephens, P. S. (2000). Academic advising and today's changing students. In V. N. Gordon, W. R. Habley, & Associates (Eds.), *Academic advising: A comprehensive handbook* (pp. 73–83). San Francisco: Jossey-Bass.

Van Lanen, R. J., & Lockie, N. M. (1997). Using Supplemental Instruction to assist nursing students in chemistry: A mentoring program's support network protects high-risk students at St. Xavier University. *Journal of College Science Teaching, 26*(6), 419–423.

Vogelgesang, L. J., Ikeda, E. K., Gilmartin, S. K., & Keup, J. R. (2002). Service-learning and the first-year experience: Learning from the research. In E. Zlotkowski (Ed.), *Service-learning and the first-year experience: Preparing students for personal success and civic responsibility* (pp. 15–26). Columbia: University of South Carolina, National Resource Center for The First-Year Experience and Students in Transition.

Vygotsky, L. (1962). *Thought and language.* Cambridge, MA: MIT Press.

Vygotsky, L. S. (1978). *Mind in society: The development of higher psychological processes.* Cambridge, MA: Harvard University Press.

Walker, C. J. (2002). Faculty well-being review: An alternative to post–tenure review? In C. M. Licata & J. C. Morreale (Eds.), *Post-tenure faculty review and renewal* (pp. 229–241). Washington, DC: American Association of Higher Education.

Wallack, L., & DeJong, W. (1995). *Mass media and public health: Moving the focus of change from the individual to the environment.* Rockville, MD: U.S. Department of Health and Human Services, National Institute on Alcohol Abuse and Alcoholism.

Wambach, C., & Brothen, T. (2002). The General College base curriculum: Description, historical antecedents, theoretical structure, and education outcomes. In D. B. Lundell & J. L. Higbee (Eds.), *Histories of developmental education* (pp. 73–81).

Minneapolis, MN: Center for Research on Developmental Education and Urban Literacy, General College, University of Minnesota. Available at: http://www.gen. umn.edu/research/crdeul.

Wambach, C., Brothen, T., & Dikel, T. N. (2000). Toward a developmental theory for developmental educators. *Journal of Developmental Education, 24*(1), 2, 6, 8, 10, 29.

Wambach, C., & delMas, R. (1998). Developmental education at a public research university. In J. L. Higbee & P. L. Dwinell (Eds.), *Developmental education: Preparing successful college students* (pp. 63–72). Columbia: University of South Carolina, National Resource Center for The First-Year Experience and Students in Transition.

Warburton, E. C., Chen, X., & Bradburn, E. M. (2002). *Teaching with technology: Use of telecommunications technology by postsecondary instructional faculty and staff in Fall 1998.* Available at: http://nces.ed.gov/pubs2002/2002161.pdf.

Watanabe, T. (2000, October 18). The new gospel of academia. *Los Angeles Times,* p. A-1.

Waterman, R. H., Jr. (1990). *Adhocracy.* New York: Norton.

Watt, S. K., & Moore, III, J. L. (2001). Who are student athletes? In M. F. Howard-Hamilton & S. K. Watt (Eds.), *Student services for athletes* (pp. 7–18). San Francisco: Jossey-Bass.

Weaver, R. A., Kowalski, T. J., & Pfaller, J. E. (1994). Case-method teaching. In K. W. Prichard & R. M. Sawyer (Eds.), *Handbook of college teaching: Theory and applications.* Westport, CT: Greenwood Press.

Webopedia. (2003, November). *Online dictionary for computer and internet technology.* Available at: http://www.webopedia.com/.

Wechsler, H. (1996). Alcohol and the American college campus: A report from the Harvard School of Public Health. *Change, 28,* 20–27.

Wechsler, H., Davenport, A., Dowdall, G., Moeykens, B., & Castillo, S. (1994). Health and behavioral consequences of binge drinking in college: A national survey of students at 140 campuses. *Journal of the American Medical Association, 272,* 1672–1677.

Wechsler, H., Dowdall, G. W., Davenport, A. & Costillo, S. (1995). Correlates of college student binge drinking. *American Journal of Public Health, 85,* 921–926.

Wechsler, H., Nelson, T. F., Lee, J. E., Seibring, M., Lewis, C., & Keeling, R. P. (2003). Perception and reality: A national evaluation of social norms marketing interventions to reduce college students' heavy alcohol use. *Journal of Studies on Alcohol, 64*(4), 484–494.

Weiner, B. (1984). Principles for a theory of student motivation and their application within an attributional framework. In R. E. Ames & C. Ames (Eds.), *Research on motivation in education, Vol. 1: Student motivation* (pp. 15–38). Orlando, FL: Academic Press.

Weiner, B. (1986). *An attributional theory of motivation and emotion.* New York: Springer-Verlag.

Weinstein, C. E. (1987). Fostering learning autonomy through the use of learning strategies. *Journal of Reading, 30,* 590–595.

Weinstein, C. E., Dierking, D., Husman, J., Roska, L., & Powdrill, L. (1998). The impact of a course in strategic learning on the long-term retention of college students. In J. L. Higbee & P. L. Dwinell (Eds.), *Developmental education: Preparing successful college students* (pp. 85–96). Columbia: University of South Carolina, National Resource Center for The First-Year Experience and Students in Transition.

Weinstein, C. E., Palmer, D. R., & Hanson, G. R. (1995). *Perceptions, expectations, emotions and knowledge about college.* Clearwater, FL: H & H Publishing.

Weinstein, R. S., & McKown, C. (1998). Expectancy effects in "context": Listening to the voices of students and teachers. In J. Brophy (Ed.), *Advances in research on teaching. Vol. 7: Expectations in the classroom.* Greenwich, CT: JAI Press.

Wenger, E. (1998). *Communities of practice: Learning, meaning, and identity.* Cambridge: Cambridge University Press.

Wenger, E., McDermott, R., & Snyder, W. N. (2002). *Cultivating communities of practice.* Boston: Harvard Business School Press.

Wergin, J. F. (1993). Departmental awards. *Change, 25*(3), 32–36.

Western Cooperative for Educational Telecommunications. (2003). *Guidelines for creating student services online.* Available at: http://www.wcet.info/projects/laap/ guidelines/.

Whipple, E. G. (1996). Student activities. In A. L. Rentz & Associates, *Student affairs practice in higher education* (2nd ed., pp. 298–333). Springfield, IL: Thomas.

White, E. R. (2000). Developing mission, goals and objectives for the advising program. In V. N. Gordon, W. R. Habley, & Associates (Eds.), *Academic advising: A comprehensive handbook* (pp. 180–191). San Francisco: Jossey-Bass.

Whiteley, J. H. (1982). Effects on the freshman year. In J. M. Whiteley, B. D. Bertin, J. S. Jennings, L. Lee, H. A. Magana, & A. Resnikoff (Eds.), *Character development in college students: Vol. 1. The freshman year* (pp. 129–172). Schenectady, NY: Character Research Press.

Whitt, E. J. (1996). Some propositions worth debating. *About Campus, 1*(4), 31–32.

Whitt, E. J. (Ed.). (1999). *Student learning as student affairs work: Responding to our imperative.* Washington, DC: National Association of Student Personnel Administrators.

Whitt, E. J., Edison, M. I., Pascarella, E. T., Terenzini, P. T., & Nora, A. (2001). Influences on students' openness to diversity and challenge in the second and third years of college. *Journal of Higher Education, 72,* 172–204.

Widmar, G. E. (1994). Supplemental instruction: From small beginnings to a national program. In D. C. Martin & D. R. Arendale (Eds.), *Supplemental Instruction: Increasing achievement and retention* (pp. 3–10). San Francisco: Jossey-Bass.

Wilcox, K. J., & Jensen, M. S. (2000). Writing to learn in anatomy and physiology, *Research and Teaching in Developmental Education, 16*(2), 55–71.

Wilds, D. J., & Wilson, R. (1998). *Minorities in higher education 1997–98: Sixteenth Annual Status Report.* Washington, DC: American Council on Education.

Wilkerson, L., & Gijselaers, W. H. (1996). *Bringing problem-based learning to higher education: Theory and practice.* San Francisco: Jossey-Bass.

Wilkie, C., & Jones, M. (1994). Academic benefits of on-campus employment to first-year developmental education students. *Journal of The Freshman Year Experience, 6*(2), 37–56.

Wilkie, C., & Kuckuck, S. (1989). A longitudinal study of the effects of a freshman seminar. *Journal of The Freshman Year Experience, 1,* 7–16.

Williams, J. M., Decker, T. W., & Libassi, A. (1983). The impact of stress management training on the academic performance of low-achieving college students. *Journal of College Student Personnel, 24,* 491–494.

Williford, A. M., Cross Chapman, L. C., & Kahrig, T. (2000–2001). The university experience course: A longitudinal study of student performance, retention, and graduation. *Journal of College Student Retention, 2*(4), 327–340.

Wilson, S. B., Mason, T. W., & Ewing, M.J.M. (1997). Evaluating the impact of receiving university-based counseling services on student retention. *Journal of Counseling Psychology, 44*(3), 316–320.

Wingspread Group on Higher Education. (1993). *An American imperative: Higher expectations for higher education.* Racine, WI: Johnson Foundation.

Winston, Jr., R. B. (1996). Counseling and advising. In S. R. Komives, D. B. Woodard, Jr., & Associates (Eds.), *Student services: A handbook for the profession* (3rd ed., pp. 335–360). San Francisco: Jossey-Bass.

Winston, R. B., Miller, T. R., Erder, S. C., & Grites, T. G. (1984). *Developmental academic advising.* San Francisco: Jossey-Bass.

Winston, R. B., & Sandor, J. A. (1994). Developmental academic advising: What do students want? *NACADA Journal, 4,* 5–13.

Winter, G. (2003, October 5). Jacuzzi U? A battle of perks lure students. *New York Times,* p. 1.

Wlodkowski, R. J. (1999). Motivation and diversity. In M. Theall (Ed.), *Motivation from within: Approaches for encouraging faculty and students to excel.* San Francisco: Jossey-Bass.

Wolf-Wendel, L. E., Toma, J. D., & Morphew, C. C. (2000). "There's no 'eye' in 'team'": Lessons from athletes on community building. *Review of Higher Education, 24*(4), 369–396.

Woodard, B. S., and Hinchliffe, L. J. (2002). Technology and innovation in library instruction management. *Journal of Library Administration, 36*(1,2), 39–55.

Woodard, D. B., Love, P., & Komives, S. R. (2000). *Leadership and management issues for a new century.* San Francisco: Jossey-Bass.

Wulff, D. H., Nyquist, J. D., & Abbott, R. D. (1987). Students' perceptions of large classes. In M. Weimer (Ed.), *Teaching large classes well.* San Francisco: Jossey-Bass.

Wuthrick, M. A. (1991). Getting students involved: A commentary on developmental education. *Research and Teaching in Developmental Education, 7*(2), 111–114.

Xiao, B. (1999, May). *The impact of freshman year academic success on student persistence and bachelor's degree completion.* Paper presented at the Association for Institutional Research, Seattle, WA.

Yarris, E. (1996). Counseling. In A. L. Rentz & Associates, *Student affairs practice in higher education* (2nd ed., pp. 143–174). Springfield, IL: Thomas.

Yates, M. C. (1992). The college union facility of the future. In T. E. Milani & J. W. Johnson (Eds.), *The college union in the year 2000* (pp. 49–60). San Francisco: Jossey-Bass.

Yockey, F. A., & George, A. A. (1998). The effects of a freshman seminar paired with Supplemental Instruction. *Journal of The First-Year Experience and Students in Transition, 10*(2), 57–76.

York, C. M., Bollar, S., & Schoob, C. (1993, August). *Causes of college retention: A systems perspective.* Paper presented to the American Psychological Association, Toronto, Canada.

Young, I. M. (1990). *Justice and the politics of difference.* Princeton, NJ: Princeton University.

Young, R. B. (1999). Reexamining our rituals. *About Campus, 4*(4), 10–16.

Young, V., Adams, T., Davis, D., Haase, K., & Shaffer, T. (1996). New perspectives on learning and writing centers: Applying Vygotsky. *NADE Selected Conference Papers, 2,* 51–53.

Zajonc, R. B., & Brickman, P. (1969). Expectancy and feedback as independent factors in task performance. *Journal of Personality and Social Psychology, 11,* 148–156.

Ziemelis, A., Bucknam, R. B., & Elfessi, A. M. (2002). Prevention efforts underlying decreases in binge drinking at institutions of higher education. *Journal of American College Health, 50*(5), 238–252.

Zlotkowski, E. (Ed.). (1998). *Successful service-learning programs: New models of excellence in higher education.* Bolton, MA: Anker.

Zusman, A. (1999). Issues facing higher education in the twenty-first century. In P. G. Altbach, R. O. Berdahl, & P. J. Gumport (Eds.), *American higher education in the twenty-first century* (pp. 109–148). Baltimore, MD: Johns Hopkins University Press.

NAME INDEX

A

Abbey, A., 23–24
Abbott, J., 362
Abbott, R. D., 61
Abraham, A. A., 294
Abraham, J., 395, 396
Adams, D. J., 44
Adams, T., 296, 303
Adan, A., 133
Adelman, C., 71, 80, 243
Albrecht, R., 343
Allen, D., 33
Allen, D. E., 254
Allen, G. J., 305
Allen, W., 97, 106
Allen, W. R., 126
Allport, G. W., 150
Alpert, R., 305
Alvidrez, J., 127
Anderson, D. K., 67
Andreas, R. E., 60, 94, 100, 110, 413, 422, 424
Angelo, T. A., 247, 262, 269, 305, 510
Anselmo, A., 42
Anttonen, R., 191, 192, 193, 197, 198, 199, 201, 202
Archer, J., 23, 150, 305, 431
Arendale, D. R., 44, 265, 267, 296, 303
Arenson, K. W., 135
Arkin, R. M., 305
Aronson, J., 126, 127
Asch, A., 295
Asker, E. H., 40

B

Astin, A. W., 3, 30, 33, 36, 38, 40, 42, 54, 58, 60, 61, 74, 87, 90, 94, 100, 107n.1, 198, 200, 223, 226, 234, 243, 276, 305, 312, 373, 389, 390, 410, 413, 422, 424, 430, 435, 497, 498, 499
Atkinson, R., 304
Atkinson, R. C., 78
Attanasi, L. C., 72
Austin, S., 305
Autin, G., 304
Avaolos, J., 33
Avens, C., 374

Bachman, J. G., 447, 448, 458, 461
Bader, C., 299, 301, 304, 305
Baer, J. S., 460
Baird, L. L., 473
Baker, R. W., 114
Baldridge, J. V., 75, 193, 194, 195, 474
Ballou, R., 412
Banahan, L., 391
Bandura, A., 88, 114, 296
Banks, J. A., 150, 296
Banta, T. W., 211
Barajas, H. L., 296
Barber, B., 296
Barefoot, B. O., 42, 47, 63, 106, 178, 181, 197, 204, 277, 281, 286, 287, 288, 392, 515
Barlow, A. R., 293
Baron, S., 343
Barr, R., 4, 110, 257, 296

SUBJECT INDEX

A

Academic achievement: assessment instruments for, 507–508; impact of technology on, 229; of minority students, 19, 126; of off-campus students, 422; and orientation goals, 393; overview of, 320–321; as predictor of persistence, 33; survey results regarding, 55

Academic advising: assessment of, 332–333, 505; communities of practice for, 264; of commuting students, 171; components of, 328–331; delivery of, 331; director of, 329; and diversity, 335–336; effects of, 332; expectations-experience gap for, 92, 105; future of, 336, 337; importance of, 320; for minority students, 133–134; models for, 321–328; as predictor of persistence, 43; recommendations for, 336–338; for residence halls, 420; standards for, 329; students' need for, 311; and technology, 331, 333–335; in traditional developmental education, 300; for two-year institutions, 327; at urban universities, 171

Academic Advising Inventory (Student Development Associates), 505

Academic advisors: expertise of, 336, 337; rewards for, 330–331; role of, 320; training for, 329–330; types of, 322–323

Academic affairs department, 209, 210–211. *See also* Student-academic affairs partnership

Academic challenge, 5

Academic competence, 8, 27–28

Academic expectations, 112–113, 199

Academic major. *See* Major

Academic preparation, 242–244, 258–259, 310–311

The Academic Profile (Educational Testing Service), 507

Academic seminars, 279–280

Academic-student affairs partnership. *See* Student-academic affairs partnership

Access: for minority students, 151; at urban public universities, 160

Accommodations, 440–441

Accommodator, 245

Accreditation, 474–475

ACE. *See* American Council on Education (ACE)

ACRL. *See* Association of College and Research Librarians (ACRL)

ACT test, 79

ACUI/EBS Student Survey (Association of College Unions International), 506

Ad hoc groups, 250, 251

ADA. *See* Americans With Disabilities Act (ADA)

Addiction, to technology, 236–237

Administrators: in coalition building, 201; collaboration tips for, 208; and diversity problems, 146–147; in enrollment management structure, 76–78; responsibilities to minority students, 137–138, 139; and service-learning, 186; at urban universities, 169–170, 173–174; values of, 195. *See also* Leadership; Presidents

National Center for Education Statistics, 17, 18, 20, 21, 233, 242, 243, 430, 448

National Center for Higher Education Management Systems, 476

National Center for the First-Year Experience and Students in Transition, 3

National Collegiate Athletic Association (NCAA), 20, 438

National Commission on Excellence in Education, 2

National Commission on the Cost of Higher Education, 25

National Institute of Education, 2, 110

National norms, 508

National Orientation Directors' Association, 52, 277, 392

National Resource Center for The First-Year Experience and Students in Transition, 3, 84, 198, 264, 270, 276, 277, 278, 279, 281, 282, 283, 284, 286, 288, 392

National Science Foundation, 4, 160

National Survey of First-Year Practices, 48–50, 50–59, 371

National Survey of First-Year Seminar Programming, 278, 279, 282, 284, 286

National Survey of Student Engagement, 4, 81–82, 92, 243, 278, 345, 477, 504

National Telecommunications and Information Administration, 227

Native American students: SAT scores of, 24; types of colleges selected by, 18; within-group diversity of, 19

NCAA. See National Collegiate Athletic Association (NCAA)

New Jersey, 223

NODA Data Bank, 52

Noel-Levitz, 83, 84, 506

Noncredit developmental courses, 301

Nontraditional students: characteristics of, 18; retention of, 34. See also Older students

North Carolina State University, 169

Northern Kentucky University, 270

O

Oberlin College, 278

Observations, 511

Off-campus living environments, 422–425

Older students: alcohol consumption of, 458; assessment instruments for, 506; characteristics of, 34; expectations-experience gap for, 89; interpersonal relationships of, 8; number of, 17–18; orientations for, 403–404; support services for, 435–436. See also Nontraditional students

One-minute papers, 510

On-line learning: definition of, 232; for developmental education, 303; survey results regarding, 57

Orientation: administration of, 395–398; assessment of, 406–407; attendance at, 407; benefits of, 393–394; and closure of expectations-experience gap, 105; components of, 398–405; definition of, 393; diversity recommendations for, 152; and enrollment management, 72–73; and faculty, 407; for families, 52, 392, 399–401; funding of, 53, 397; goals of, 393–394; for international students, 442; to libraries, 340; for minority students, 132–133, 152, 404–405; organization of, 395–396; overview of, 391; as predictor of persistence, 42; standards for, 394–395; survey results regarding, 52–53; technology for, 235–236, 392, 405, 407–408; trends in, 392, 407–408; at two-year colleges, 401–402

Outcomes, 30

Outcomes assessment. See Assessment, outcomes

Oxford Brookes University, 313

P

Paired-course learning communities, 377–379

Paraphrasing, 251

Parents: living with, 423; notification of, about alcohol consumption, 459, 465; as predictor of persistence, 34–35. See also Family

Participants in the Preparing Future Faculty Program, 154

Partnerships. See Collaboration; Student-academic affairs partnership

Part-time faculty, 262

Part-time students, 19–20, 37

Pathfinders Program, 75

PBL. See Problem-based learning (PBL)

PDAs. See Personal digital assistants (PDAs)

Peer advisors, 327–328

Peer counseling, 461

Peer instructors, 54

Pennsylvania State University, 329, 330, 335

Pepperdine University, 347

Perceptions, Expectations, Emotions, and Knowledge About College (PEEK), 112

Persistence: institutional concern with, 28; and institutional variables, 35–44; models of, 29–31; overview of, 27–28; and student inputs, 30, 32–35; trends in, 28–29. See also Retention

Personal digital assistants (PDAs), 225

Personal expectations, 112–113

Pew Charitable Trust, 4, 48, 278, 304, 504

Pew Internet and American Life Project, 226, 227, 228, 230

Physical space, 197, 354–355, 414

Piloting instruments, 509

Pima Community College, 335

Pine Manor College, 280

Plagiarism, 232–233, 236, 347